BY JULIA CHILD, SIMONE BECK, AND LOUISETTE BERTHOLLE

Mastering the Art of French Cooking (1961)

VOLUME ONE

———————————

BY JULIA CHILD

The French Chef Cookbook (1968)

From Julia Child's Kitchen (1975)

Julia Child & Company (1978)

Julia Child & More Company (1979)

The Way to Cook (1989)

Cooking with Master Chefs (1993)

In Julia's Kitchen with Master Chefs (1995)

Julia's Kitchen Wisdom (2000)

My Life in France, with Alex Prud'homme (2006)

———————————

BY JULIA CHILD AND JACQUES PÉPIN

Julia and Jacques Cooking at Home (1999)

———————————

BY SIMONE BECK

Simca's Cuisine (1972)

———————————

These are Borzoi Books, published in New York by Alfred A. Knopf

Mastering the Art of French Cooking

VOLUME TWO

Illustrations by
SIDONIE CORYN
BASED ON PHOTOGRAPHS BY PAUL CHILD
WHO ALSO CONTRIBUTED 36 DRAWINGS TO THE TEXT

Mastering the Art of
FRENCH COOKING

Volume Two

NEW REVISED EDITION

BY JULIA CHILD
AND
SIMONE BECK

NEW YORK

Alfred · A · Knopf

2009

VOL. II

PUBLISHED OCTOBER 22, 1970
HARDCOVER EDITION REPRINTED TWENTY-NINE TIMES
THIRTY-SECOND PRINTING, SEPTEMBER 2009
PAPERBACK EDITION REPRINTED TWENTY-NINE TIMES
THIRTY-SECOND PRINTING, SEPTEMBER 2009

THIS IS A BORZOI BOOK
PUBLISHED BY ALFRED A. KNOPF, INC.

Library of Congress Cataloging in Publication Data

Child, Julia.
Mastering the art of French cooking.

Rev. ed. of: Mastering the art of French cooking
by Simone Beck, Louisette Bertholle, Julia Child.
Vol. 2 by Julia Child and Simone Beck.
Includes index.
1. Cookery, French.   I. Bertholle, Louisette.
II. Beck, Simone.   III. Beck, Simone.
Mastering the art of French cooking.   IV. Title.
TX719.C454 1983   641.5944   83-48113
ISBN 0-394-53628-2 (set)
ISBN 0-394-72114-4 (pbk.: set)
ISBN 0-394-53399-2 (v. 1)
ISBN 0-394-72178-0 (pbk.: v. 1)
ISBN 0-394-40152-2 (v. 2)
ISBN 0-394-72177-2 (pbk.: v. 2)

To

Alfred Knopf

who is as much an appreciator of good writing, type faces, layout, and paper as he is of fresh *foie gras, truite au bleu,* and Meursault Les Perrières. In short, he is the ideal publisher for this kind of book, just as he is the ideal dinner guest for those who have mastered the art of French cooking.

Foreword

MASTERING ANY ART is a continuing process, and that explains *Mastering the Art of French Cooking,* Volume II, which came about in the following way. When the idea of our first book was forming in the early 1950's, we were so naïve as to propose not only to ourselves but also to an indulgent publisher, who invested two hundred and fifty dollars in the project, a complete one-volume treatise covering the whole of *la cuisine française.* After laboring for six years it was clear that our detailed method of approach called for a multi-volume study; we therefore sent our publisher eight hundred pages of manuscript on French sauces and French poultry. This early outpouring was quickly rejected as unpublishable, although it covered every conceivable sauce and every imaginable poultry detail, including such marginal esoterica as advice on what to do if you have a bloodless *canard* for the duck press—we shall not reveal the solution other than to say it involved a quick trip to the slaughterhouse. That first publishing rebuff, cruel as it was, shook us into a more rational and realistic approach. Meanwhile, we had opened our cooking school in Paris, L'Ecole des Trois Gourmandes, first located in a rooftop kitchen on the rue de l'Université and later in the comfortable apartment of Louisette, the third member of our team. Now married to Henri de Nalèche, and living in the beautiful hunting country near Bourges, La Sologne, Louisette did not collaborate with us on Volume II. It was through her inspiration, however, that we three started both the first book and the school together.

The cooking school catapulted us into almost all areas of French cooking, because you cannot teach the subject and not include the standard dishes that everyone has heard about—*quiche lorraine,* onion soup, *boeuf bourguignon, coq au vin, sole bonne femme, mousse au chocolat,* and *soufflé Grand Marnier* —to name a very familiar handful. Thus Volume I in its final form was the natural result of our teaching. It also goes into the fundamental techniques of *la cuisine bourgeoise,* meaning expert French home-style cooking—how to make the flour and butter *roux* for the sauce *velouté,* how to beat egg whites and fold them into the soufflé to get the maximum puff, how to sauté the meat so that it will brown, and the mushrooms so they will not exude their juice, how to peel and seed the tomato, boil the beans, peel the asparagus, and fold the omelette. Volume I is, in fact, a long introduction to French cooking, and anyone who has mastered it has covered most of the primary methods and recipes.

Volume II is a continuation. But rather than continuing on every front, we have selected seven subjects, and having so long ago rejected complete treatises, we have pursued each only in the directions that we felt were most useful or interesting. We wanted to add to the repertoire of informal vegetable soups, for example, and these take up a large part of the first chapter. We felt the need for a fine lobster bisque; this gave rise to a study of lobster cutting, and in turn led us to crabs, which are not adequately explored in most recipes (the whole matter of crab tomalley is almost never mentioned, yet it is every bit as precious as lobster tomalley). Then, although we adore *bouillabaisse* (which is in Volume I), there are other French fish stews that make marvelous one-dish meals, so we have added a *marmite,* a *matelote,* and a *bourride.* Thus the soup chapter is an enlargement in breadth.

Meat, poultry, and vegetables we have attacked in depth, following the same system of theme and variations used in Volume I, but taking it perhaps even further. *Poulet poché au vin blanc,* starting on page 253, is a prime example. Ordinary pieces of frying chicken are poached in white wine and aromatic vegetables, making a deliciously non-fattening dish that you can serve informally as is, with boiled rice and a green vegetable. Nothing could be simpler, yet you can take this same chicken out of the peasant kitchen, as it were, and serve it at the château. You can transform it into an elegant aspic or *chaud-froid,* or turn its poaching liquid into a creamy *velouté* and create a *gratin* of chicken Mornay, a splendid dish for a buffet supper. With egg yolks and cream the original chicken dish becomes a Belgian *waterzooi,* with garlic mayonnaise it is a chicken *bourride,* and with slightly different vegetable flavors but the same cooking methods it is a *bouillabaisse* of chicken. Thus, starting with one master technique, you are putting your cooking vocabulary to use the way it should be used, and if you are just beginning to cook, this is an exercise in recognition. You will begin to relate the sauce you used for the casserole of chicken to the *velouté* you made for the *coquilles Saint-Jacques* in another recipe, as well as to the *velouté* base you made for a cream of crab soup; the flavors are different, the proportions are not identical, especially for the soup, but the basic method is the same. You will recognize that sauce when you run into it again in some other guise. Again, if you are new to it, and have finally conquered your fear of scrambling the egg yolks as you stir them over the burner for that lovely custard sauce, *crème anglaise,* you will be nonchalant about heating egg yolks in the sauce for a *bourride*—or vice versa: you know what to expect, you have been there before, and, in effect, you are beginning to feel like a cook. For the experienced, we hope these ideas will start you off on further ventures in other categories.

Beef stews, veal chops and steaks, and veal stews take the same type of tour, our object being to show what you can do with reasonably priced meats for family meals as well as for entertaining. On the other hand, the luxurious tenderloin of beef also has its series of transformations. It is roasted whole, baked in a cloak of mushrooms *duxelles* and wine, as well as being, in another recipe, cut into slices and stuffed before roasting. Finally, in an original version of Beef Wellington, it is sliced, stuffed, and baked in a special type of *brioche* crust. An expensive roast of veal undergoes a group of variations, as does a whole roasting chicken, which finally appears with a boned breast and a corseting of pastry.

We hope you will enjoy the vegetable chapter as much as we do, because we have had fun with these recipes. Although there are a few of the classics, like *pommes Anna* and *pommes duchesse,* most of the recipes are originals that we have been working on for a number of years until we felt they were ripe for you and this volume. The chapter starts with broccoli, which we have treated freely *à la française* although it is almost unknown in France; we love its color, its flavor, and its year-round availability. We also love eggplant, not only for its beauty as a vegetable object, but also for its adaptability and versatility; we have broiled it, sautéed it in *persillade,* creamed it, souffléed it, served it hot, cold, stuffed, and wished we had room to do more. A lovely recipe for pumpkin-in-pumpkin introduces a group of unusual zucchini dishes stemming from sautéed chunks of it to an original clutch of grated zucchini treatments. Spinach, chard, and turnips all have representation, as do several versions of sautéed potatoes. There are stuffed onions, stuffed cabbage, stuffed zucchini, and cold stuffed artichoke hearts. Again, most of the vegetable chapter is built on themes and variations, and is designed to engender the flow of your creative juices.

Two entirely new categories are the chapters on breads and pastry doughs and on *charcuterie.* One is not really dining *à la française* without proper French bread to mop up the sauce on one's plate, without a fine *terrine* or *pâté* to start the meal, without *boudins blancs* for New Year's Eve or for the turkey stuffing. One needs also a symmetrically baked, beautifully textured sandwich bread for hors d'oeuvre, and *brioches* and croissants for breakfast. These everyday staples in France were once considered luxury items here and, in fact, when you buy them now in gourmet shops they *are* luxuries. But you can make them yourself with pride and pleasure and at a fraction of the cost.

Until our editor, in her gentle but compelling way, suggested that we really owed it to our readers to include a recipe for French bread, we had no plans at all to tackle it. Two years and some 284 pounds of flour later, we had tried out all the home-style recipes for French bread we could find, we had two professional French textbooks on baking, we had learned many things about yeasts and doughs, yet our best effort, which was a type of peasant sourdough loaf, still had little to do with real French bread. Then we met Professor Calvel of the Ecole Française de Meunerie in Paris, and it was like the sun in all his glory suddenly breaking through the shades of gloom. Fortunately those two years on the wrong road had been useful, because as soon as Professor Calvel started in, we knew what he was talking about, even though every step in the bread-making process was entirely different from anything we had heard of, read of, or seen. His dough was soft and sticky; he let it rise slowly twice, to triple its original volume—the dough must ripen to develop its natural flavor and proper texture. Forming the dough into its long-loaf or round-loaf shapes was a fascinating process, and so logical; slashing the top of the risen loaves before sliding them into the oven was another special procedure.

This was a tremendously exciting day for us, as you can imagine. We now knew we could succeed, because we had seen and felt with our own hands so clearly where we had failed. We rushed home and went to work again while Professor Calvel's teaching was vividly with us. There remained the problem of working out the formula with American all-purpose bleached flour instead of the softer French unbleached flour. There was also the matter of adapting the home oven by some simple means into a simulated baker's oven, with a hot surface for the bread to bake on, and some kind of effective steam contraption. Although you can produce a presentable loaf without these two professional oven requirements, you will not get quite the high rise or quite the crust. Paul Child and his usual Yankee ingenuity solved the hot baking surface by lining the oven rack with red quarry tiles, which he heated up with the oven; he created a great burst of steam by placing a pan of water in the bottom of the oven, and dropping a red-hot brick into it. The flour problem solved itself; although our maître loathes bleached flours, we found, thank heaven, that the familiar brands of all-purpose bleached flour work remarkably well. We are thus delighted to report that you can make marvelous French bread in your own kitchen with ordinary American ingredients and equipment.

Pastry doughs, pâte brisée and pâte feuilletée, also go hand in hand with cooking and eating traditions in France. While packaged dough mixes and frozen adaptations can certainly serve in emergencies, it is part of your training as a cook that you be able to turn out at least the dough for a pastry shell as a matter of course. It is actually, we think, when you have made the dough for your first quiche or tart, and have been complimented enthusiastically and specifically on the crust, that you begin to feel you are stepping out of the kindergarten and into a more advanced class of cooking. If you have had troubles or qualms, therefore, about handmade dough, try the recipe on page 104; the electric mixer or food processor works quickly and beautifully. And if you have hesitated to tackle the traditional flan ring lined with dough and weighted down with foil and beans, try the upside-down cake-pan method illustrated on pages 106–7, which is an easy way to make pastry shells. Furthermore, the egg formula in the recipe makes a deliciously crisp, tender, buttery crust.

As soon as you feel confident with pie-crust dough, we urge you to take on the larger and more fascinating challenge of *pâte feuilletée*. This is the French puffing dough, which consists of hundreds of very thin layers of flour paste separated by hundreds of layers of butter; it rises in the oven to several times its original height, to form *vol-au-vent* and patty shells, puffed entrées like the cheese tart on page 140, as well as the cookies on pages 476–80, and the tarts and desserts starting on page 453. Properly made, it is flakily tender, and a delight to both tongue and palate. Although few French home cooks make puff pastry, since they can buy freshly baked *feuilletées* at their local *pâtisseries*, it is something that you, as a cook, will find tremendously useful all the rest of your kitchen life. We have spent years on puff pastry ourselves, wanting to make sure that the recipe in this book would be as good with American flour as it is with French flour—the trouble with American all-purpose flour being that it has a higher gluten content than French flour, and that makes differences all along the line. We worked out combinations of unbleached pastry flour and all-purpose flour, we have tried instant-blending flour, and we have finally settled on a mixture of regular all-purpose flour and cake flour as being the most sensible. Although it takes a little longer to work with, it produces a beautifully tender, high-rising dough that is even more impressive, we think, than its French counterpart. The illustrated recipe for simple puff pastry starting on page 113 is easy to follow, and we suggest your first creation be a handsome puff pastry tart, the cheese, page 140, or the jam, page 145. Both of them are quick to form, yet give a very handsome effect to start you off in a whirl of success.

Our forefathers did the kind of cooking in Chapter V, *Charcuterie,* if they lived on a farm and made their own sausages and cured their own pork. Few French householders, again, attempt any of this today, because they can buy all kinds of sausages *chez le charcutier,* as well as salted pork, preserved goose, sausage in *brioche,* molds of parslied ham, fresh liver *pâté, terrines,* and all the other marvelous concoctions that embellish French gastronomical life. The particularly wonderful taste of these creations is derived from the fact that they are freshly made, on the premises. We, who want to partake of the same pleasures, must make our own. And for anyone who enjoys cooking, producing *charcuterie,* like making bread and pastry, is a deeply satisfying occupation. You will be amazed, if you have never tried your own before, how rewarding just a homemade sausage patty can be; it is only freshly ground pork mixed with salt and spices, but it tastes the way one dreams sausage meat should taste. The large *saucissons à cuire,* starting on page 292, will make you think of France, as will the *jambon persillé.* When you want a real *cassoulet,* you can make the real *confit d'oie,* and have enough preserved goose left in the crock for many more meals. The difficult Christmas present or the gifts to hostesses need bother you no more—bring along one of your own *pâtés en croûte.*

The final chapter contains favorite desserts and cakes that we have been testing out on our guinea pigs—our students and families—for a number of years. The frozen desserts, so useful for all of us who need attractive finales that we may complete well in advance, are made without benefit of the ice-cream freezer; they vary in complexity from quickly made fruit sherbets to an elegant chocolate mousse dressed in meringues, and a flaming French baked Alaska, *la surprise du Vésuve.* We also give you a group of original fruit desserts, custards, and a liqueur-soaked French shortcake, a number of hand-some desserts made with puff pastry, and a selection of *petits fours.* Among the eight cakes at the end of the chapter are a fine French honey bread, *pain d'épices,* a walnut cake, a beautiful meringue-nut layer cake called variously *Le Succès, Le Progrès,* or *La Dacquoise,* and two chocolate cakes. It will be for you to judge whether we have achieved the ultimate in chocolate with *La Charlotte Africaine* or with *Le Glorieux,* or whether that perennial cake winner made of chocolate and almonds, *La Reine de Saba,* in Volume I, still retains the title.

In all of our recipes, and especially in those for desserts and cakes, we have taken full advantage of modern mechanical aids wherever we have found them effective. While Volume I reflects France in the 1950's and the old traditions of French cooking, Volume II, like France herself, has stepped into contemporary life. We must admit, in Volume I, to a rather holy and Victorian feeling about the virtues of sweat and elbow grease—that only paths of thorns lead to glory, *il faut souffrir pour être belle* and all that. However, we are teachers; we want people to learn. And if we make it hard to cook through snobbish insistence on always beating egg whites by hand in a copper bowl, for instance, or always mixing pastries by hand (*il faut mettre la main dans la pâte*), when it is the hot hand that makes all the trouble, we know we have already lost a great part of our audience. We have therefore developed our own methods for machine-beaten egg whites, page 539, for machine-made cakes, pages 481–504, and there are directions for doing all the pastries and doughs by machine as well as by hand. Because machines make cooking so much easier, and because recipes that take tedious effort by hand—like *quenelles,* mousses, and meringues—can be done in minutes by machine, we urge you to provide yourself with the best you can afford, and refer you to the illustrated suggestions on pages 539–41.

We have so far said hardly a word about the illustrations, which are, to our mind, the glory of Volume II. We can speak of them without a hint of modesty because they are the result of a remarkable feat of teamwork between Paul Child, our action photographer, and Sidonie Coryn, our illustrator. Because of their tireless expertise we have been able to picture step-by-step operations that to our knowledge have never been adequately illustrated before; we now feel confident that this combined visual and verbal presentation makes absolutely clear the most complicated sounding process. For French bread alone there are 34 drawings, showing the procedure from the start: mixing the dough, kneading it, how it looks when risen, how to deflate it, and the intricacies of forming the dough into various loaf shapes. Tenderloin of beef is pictured in such detail that you can buy a whole one and trim it yourself. With an illustrated guide before you, you can bone out the breast of a chicken, trim and tie a saddle of lamb, or cut up a lobster. Puff pastry and croissants are illustrated every step of the way, as are *brioches* and *bouchées.* You can see how to form upside-down pastry shells, how to stuff a whole cabbage leaf by leaf, and if you have never done or even seen a *pâté en croûte* in your life, you can be assured of success, because you have 12 drawings to show you every necessary move.

Without the team of Child and Coryn such coverage would have been impossible. Paul Child, ready at a moment's notice, was there to make careful, detailed, perfect photographs of any step of any recipe at any time during the day or night. Occasionally, when on-the-spot drawings served better than photographs, he contributed his talents to such techniques as the art of cutting up lobsters and crabs, carving a saddle of lamb, or depicting the bone structure of a breast of veal, and he was happy to draw the tricky arrangement of an eggplant dish that our words alone had confused. The major load of illustrating fell, of course, to Sidonie Coryn—her 458 drawings for this book are an incredible achievement. From grapefruit knives and cake pans to the step-by-step illustrations for a *Pithiviers* and *Dacquoise,* from electric mixers and garlic presses to the intricacies of a *poularde en soutien-gorge,* she has skillfully and stylishly drawn the essence of Paul Child's photographs, eliminating nonessentials and putting the right emphasis on the points of crucial interest.

Words and pictures must be arranged carefully on a page if they are to communicate all that they intend. Again we authors may speak with gratitude of the loving attention that has gone into the layout and typography of this book. Now, when you have a long sequence of illustrated events to follow, like cutting and forming croissants or stuffing sausages, the whole operation of one particular step will be open before you, and you will not have to stop to turn the pages with a sticky finger nearly so often. This is a tighter setup than that for Volume I; although the type is the same size, the illustrations are more closely integrated with the text so that words and pictures can be absorbed more easily, and once you have mastered a technique, a glance at the illustrations will serve as sufficient reminder. The art work and production in this book contribute greatly to the understanding of cookery, we think, and we are pleased that our publisher has been willing to take the time and space, as well as the expense, to present recipes with such intelligent elegance.

We have little else to add to this leisurely meander. Words of advice, such as "Do read the recipe before you start in to cook," "Be sure your oven thermostat is accurate," and other sage admonitions are in the foreword to Volume I. We shall therefore only repeat the hope that you will keep your knives sharp and that, above all, you will have a good time.

Best wishes and *bon appetit!*

S. B. and J. C.

Paris and Cambridge
June 1971

FOREWORD TO THE SECOND EDITION

Volume II has needed only a few changes in this new edition. We've brought in the food processor for dough making, added a little more butter to the croissants, a little more sugar on top of the puff pastry cookies, and changed the weight of a leg of lamb to conform with the modern mode. Otherwise it is as before, the classic cuisine of France, continued.

S. B. and J. C.

Bramafam and Santa Barbara
February 1983

Acknowledgments

OUR FRIENDS, students, families, and husbands have continued to act graciously and courageously as guinea pigs throughout the accumulation of years since Volume I began and Volume II came to its fruition; we owe them very special thanks. Again the U.S. Department of Agriculture has been a wonderful source of assistance, as has the U.S. Bureau of Fisheries, especially its Boston Branch. We are also grateful to the National Livestock and Meat Board for technical advice on many occasions, and we are deeply indebted to R. A. Seelig of the United Fresh Fruit and Vegetable Association, whose bulletins and letters have taught us so many things we never knew before. Gladys Christopherson has been our faithful and cheerful manuscript typer, putting neatly onto paper the scrawls and spots of working copy; we thank her every finger. Avis DeVoto, still acting as foster mother, wet nurse, guide, and mentor, has also taken on the copy editing for our side, as well as the position of indexer-in-chief; our admiration and gratitude can only be expressed by her weight in fresh truffles. Paul Child, tireless photographer at a moment's notice, pinch-hitting illustrator, clever turner of phrases when the well is dry—we can only continue to love him and to feed him well. We have also our peerless editor, Judith Jones, to thank most sincerely and affectionately; her conception of the book has produced what you now hold in your hands.

Contents

Illustrations

Illustrations by Sidonie Coryn

Technical Drawings by Paul Child

Mastering the Art of French Cooking

VOLUME TWO

✳ This symbol preceding a recipe title indicates that variations follow.

(✳) Wherever you see this symbol in the body of recipe texts you may prepare the dish ahead of time up to that point, then complete the recipe later.

CHAPTER ONE

Soups from the Garden—
Bisques and
Chowders from the Sea

THERE IS HARDLY A MAN ALIVE who does not adore soup, particularly when it is homemade. Hot soup on a cold day, cold soup on a hot day, and the smell of soup simmering in the kitchen are fundamental, undoubtedly even atavistic, pleasures and solaces that give a special kind of satisfaction.

Although many of us think immediately of French onion soup when we put France and soups together in our minds, informal vegetable combinations are far more typical of that best of all cuisines—the cooking one finds in French homes and small family-style restaurants. Leek and Potato Soup, the *potage Parmentier,* and its numerous variations in Volume I, pages 37–40, is the most typical of all, but there are many other vegetable combinations, including spinach, cucumbers, green peppers, celery, peas and pea pods, even eggplant, that are interesting, unusual, easy to make, and delicious to serve. In many of these soups the vegetables are simmered in water rather than meat or poultry stock because water does not disguise the natural taste of a subtle vegetable like asparagus, for example. We shall begin with a group of these, follow with an opulent series of bisques and other shellfish soups, and end with three hearty fish stews, each one a meal in itself.

A NOTE ON PURÉEING

Most soups need puréeing at some point in the cooking, and we think the best puréeing instrument is the imported vegetable mill that has interchangeable disks illustrated in the appendix, page 535. It is very efficient even with somewhat tough items like asparagus stems; it also performs the important function of holding back stringy fibers that you would otherwise have to sieve out. To use the vegetable mill, set it over a large bowl and pour the soup from saucepan through the mill, to strain liquid from solids; pour the liquid back into the saucepan. Purée the solid ingredients, adding some of the liquid now and then to ease their passage; scrape any adhering purée off the bottom of the machine and into the bowl, then pour contents of bowl into saucepan. (Some electric mixers come with puréeing attachments that work very well.)

If you prefer an electric blender or processor, pour liquid off solids and into a bowl; ladle a cup or so of the solids and a cup of the liquid into the container. Purée by turning the machine on and off every second or two to avoid that too-smooth effect of baby food, since you will usually want the soup to have some texture. Then, if you are doing a fibrous vegetable like asparagus butts or pea pods, strain all of the soup through a sieve just fine enough to hold back the fibers. A little experimentation and always an analytical sampling of the soup yourself will tell you what you need to do.

SOUP THICKENERS—LIAISONS

Puréed soups need a binder or liaison, which thickens the soup liquid enough so that the puréed ingredients remain in suspension rather than sinking to the bottom of the bowl. The simplest liaison is a starch of some sort, like grated potatoes, puréed rice, farina, or tapioca. Other soups, usually called *veloutés,* are thickened with a flour-and-butter *roux*. A more elegant liaison is raw egg yolks, which, when beaten into and heated with the soup, thicken it lightly. All of these liaisons are more or less interchangeable, and which one to use depends on what effect and taste you want to achieve.

ENRICHMENTS

Butter, cream, and, again, egg yolks, alone or in combination, are stirred into many soups just before serving. They give a final smoothness and delicacy of taste. You can omit them if you wish, or use just a small amount.

Sour cream, if you prefer less butter fat, may often be substituted for heavy cream. But *crème fraîche* is the perfect soup enrichment: mix 2 parts heavy cream with 1 part sour cream, let thicken at room temperature (5–6 hours), and refrigerate (keeps 10 days).

LEFTOVERS, CANNED SOUPS, AND IMPROVISATIONS

When you are the cook in the family, plan your vegetables ahead so that you will have leftovers for soup; it will save you a great deal of time, and make you feel remarkably clever besides. Extra rice, pasta, and creamed or mashed potatoes are always needed as thickeners, while onions and mushrooms can always be added for flavor. Leftover cauliflower, for instance, can be combined with watercress to make the delicious soup on page 13; spinach is the main ingredient for the *velouté Florentine* on page 9; white beans or eggplant go into the *soupe à la Victorine* on page 22. Save also any extra bits of sauce or meat juices; these often provide that extra depth of taste and personality you are searching for. For example, a few tablespoons of leftover sauce from a chicken fricassee would be delicious in the Cream of Celery Soup on page 15; you could certainly stir hollandaise instead of butter into the *potage aux champignons* on page 12; and some juices saved from the roast would enhance any onion soup. Finally, save any leftover soup; you can add it to a new one, or use it to give a homemade touch to canned soups.

GREEN SOUPS FROM GREEN VEGETABLES

POTAGE, CRÈME D'ASPERGES VERTES
[Cream of Fresh Green Asparagus Soup]

At the peak of the asparagus season, when you can bear not to eat it whole, here is a marvelous soup to catch all the essence of that beautiful vegetable.

For 7 to 8 cups, serving 4 to 6

---

1) *The onion flavoring*

⅔ to ¾ cup sliced onions
4 Tb butter
A 3-quart heavy-bottomed stainless saucepan with cover

While you are preparing the asparagus, cook the onions slowly in the butter for 8 to 10 minutes, until tender but not browned. Set aside.

---

2) *Preparing the asparagus*

About 2 lbs. fresh green asparagus (24 to 28 spears 8 by ¾ inches)

Slice ¼ inch off the butt of each asparagus. Peel the skin from the butt ends up to where the green begins, and remove scales. Wash thoroughly in warm water. Cut the tops 3 inches long and set aside. Cut the lower part of the asparagus stalks into ¾-inch crosswise pieces.

---

3) *Blanching the asparagus*

6 cups water
2 tsp salt

Bring the water and salt to a rapid boil, add the asparagus stalks and boil slowly, uncovered, for 5

A 3-quart saucepan
A salad or vegetable basket
 or 2 slotted spoons

minutes. Remove and drain, reserving the water, and stir the stalks into the cooked onions; cover and cook slowly for 5 minutes. Meanwhile bring the water back to the boil, add the reserved asparagus tops and boil slowly, uncovered, for 6 to 8 minutes or until just tender. Remove immediately and drain. Set aside, reserving water for the soup base.

---

4) *The soup base*

4 Tb flour
The asparagus blanching
 water
1 cup or so of milk if
 needed

After the stalks and onions have stewed together for 5 minutes, uncover the pan, stir in the flour to mix thoroughly, and cook slowly, stirring, for 1 minute. Remove from heat and blend in half a cup of the hot blanching water; gradually stir in the rest, being sure not to add any sand that may be at the bottom of the pan. Simmer slowly, partially covered, for about 25 minutes or until the stalks are very tender. If soup seems too thick, thin out with milk.

---

5) *Finishing the soup*

The blanched asparagus
 tops
A food mill with medium
 disk (or an electric
 blender and sieve)
A 3-quart bowl
½ to ⅔ cup heavy cream
2 to 3 egg yolks
A wire whip
Salt and white pepper to
 taste

Line up the blanched asparagus tops and cut the tip ends into ¼-inch crosswise slices; reserve as a garnish. Purée the rest of the tops and the soup base into a bowl. (Pass soup through sieve to remove any fibers, if you have used a blender.) Pour the cream into the saucepan, blend in the egg yolks with a wire whip; by driblets, beat in 2 cups of the hot soup. Pour in the rest of the soup, and the sliced tip ends.

(*) May be cooked ahead to this point; set aside uncovered until cool, then cover and refrigerate.

---

2 to 4 Tb soft butter

Shortly before serving, set over moderate heat and stir slowly with a wooden spoon, reaching all over the bottom of the pan until soup comes almost to the simmer. Remove from heat, carefully correct seasoning, and stir in the enrichment butter half a tablespoon at a time. Serve immediately.

Cold Asparagus Soup

Omit the final butter enrichment and oversalt slightly. Stir several times as the soup cools, then cover and chill. Blend in more cream, if you wish, just before serving.

Using frozen asparagus

Frozen asparagus can never achieve the magic of fresh asparagus, but you can still turn out an excellent soup. Follow the Master Recipe, making the changes in each step as indicated.

1) **Increase the sliced onions to 2¼ cups in this step, or use a combination of onions and leeks.**

2) **A 10-ounce package frozen cut green asparagus**
A 10-ounce package whole frozen green asparagus spears

Use the cut asparagus to replace the stalks and the whole spears to replace the tops.

3) **2 cups chicken stock**
Optional: big pinch of monosodium glutamate

Substitute 2 cups of chicken stock for 2 cups of the water called for in this step, and a little MSG will probably be useful. Drop the cut asparagus into the boiling liquid for a minute or two, merely to defrost them, then add to the onions. Boil the whole spears until just tender.

4 and 5) Follow Master Recipe

Fresh white European asparagus

European asparagus is either all white or tinged with mauve or green near the tip, depending on the variety. Since the peel is often slightly bitter as well as being much tougher than that of all-green asparagus, peeling is essential. Peel each spear ¹⁄₁₆ of an inch deep up to the tender part near the tip. After boiling the stalks, taste the cooking liquid; if it is bitter, discard it and use fresh boiling water for cooking the tops. Although the soup would normally be a pale cream color, you may turn it green by puréeing into it a cup of blanched chard or spinach leaves.

SOUPE BELLE POTAGÈRE
[Pea-pod Soup]

You can make an excellent green pea soup using both pods and peas. Next time you are shelling them, and have crackling fresh pods, keep out the greenest and best of the lot, wrap them in a plastic bag, and refrigerate for a soup the next day. A cup of shelled peas would be nice, too, but frozen ones will do for the garnish.

For 7 to 8 cups, serving 4 to 6

---

1) *The onion flavoring*

1 cup sliced leeks and
  onions or onions only
3 Tb butter
A heavy-bottomed, 3-quart
  stainless or enameled
  saucepan with cover

Cook the leeks or onions slowly in the butter for 8 to
10 minutes, until tender but not browned. Set aside.

---

2) *The pea-pod soup base*

1 lb. fresh green peas with
  very crisp pods

Pulling off and discarding stems and tips from the pea
pods, shell the peas and set aside—you should have
about 1 cup. Wash pods and chop roughly into 1-inch
pieces, making about 4 cups. Stir the chopped pods
into the leeks and onions, cover and cook slowly for
10 minutes.

---

3 Tb flour
4 cups hot water
1½ tsp salt
1 large potato, peeled and
  sliced (about 1 cup)

Blend the flour into the pea pods and cook, stirring,
for 1 minute. Remove from heat, gradually blend in
1 cup of the hot water, then stir in the rest along with
the salt and sliced potatoes. Simmer, partially covered,
for about 20 minutes or until vegetables are tender.

---

3) *The peas*

1 cup fresh peas (or
  a 10-ounce package of
  frozen peas)
A heavy-bottomed 6- to
  8-cup saucepan with
  cover
1½ cups water for fresh
  peas; ½ cup for frozen
  peas
1 large sliced scallion or
  shallot
6 to 8 large outside leaves
  of Boston lettuce,
  chopped
1 Tb butter
¼ tsp salt

For fresh peas: Boil them in the covered saucepan
with the water, scallion, lettuce, and other ingredients
for 10 to 15 minutes or until peas are just tender,
adding 2 to 3 tablespoons more water if liquid evaporates entirely before peas are done; uncover and set
aside.
For frozen peas: Cook the same way but with only ½
cup water, and boil only long enough for the peas to
be tender.

---

4) *Finishing the soup*

A food mill set over a bowl (or an electric blender and sieve)

A cup or so of milk if needed

Salt, white pepper, and sugar to taste

¼ cup or more of heavy cream or sour cream

Purée the peas, then the soup base. If you are using a blender, sieve the soup base after puréeing to remove pea-pod fibers. Return to saucepan, bring to simmer, and thin out with milk if soup seems too thick. Taste carefully for seasoning, and add pinches of sugar to taste, which will help bring out the flavor. Stir in the cream.

(*) Set aside uncovered until cool, then cover and refrigerate.

1 to 4 Tb soft butter

Reheat to simmer just before serving. Check seasoning again, remove from heat, and stir in the butter a half tablespoon at a time. Serve immediately.

Cold Pea-pod Soup

Omit the final butter enrichment, and oversalt slightly. Stir several times as the soup cools, then cover and chill. Blend in more cream, if you wish, just before serving.

∗ POTAGE À LA FLORENTINE
[Cream of Spinach Soup]

Fresh and frozen spinach do almost equally well in this elegant soup of spinach simmered with rice and enriched with cream and egg yolks. Since it is good hot or cold, you may use the same system for a soup of green herbs, as you will see in the variations following.

For 7 to 8 cups, serving 4 to 6

1) *The soup base*

½ cup sliced onions

2 Tb butter

A heavy-bottomed stainless or enameled pan with cover

Cook the onions slowly in the butter for 8 to 10 minutes, until tender but not browned.

1½ to 2 lbs. fresh spinach (or a 10 ounce package frozen spinach)

For fresh spinach, trim, wash thoroughly, and chop roughly. For frozen spinach, thaw in a large bowl of cold water, drain and squeeze dry. Stir spinach into onions; cover and cook over low heat for 5 minutes, stirring occasionally to prevent spinach from scorching.

5 cups liquid (light chicken
    stock, or canned chicken
    broth and water)
⅓ cup plain raw white
    rice
Pinch nutmeg
Salt and pepper to taste
A food mill or electric
    blender
Chicken stock or milk
    if needed

Add the liquid to the spinach, bring to the boil, and stir in the rice. Season with the nutmeg, salt, and pepper. Simmer partially covered for 20 minutes or until rice is tender. Purée, bring again to the simmer and thin out, if too thick, with more liquid. Remove from heat.

2) *Finishing the soup*

A 2-quart bowl
A wire whip
½ cup heavy cream
2 egg yolks

Blend the cream and egg yolks in the bowl with the wire whip; by driblets, beat in 2 cups of the hot soup. Pour back into the saucepan.

(*) May be cooked ahead to this point. Set aside uncovered until cool, then cover and refrigerate.

Salt, pepper, and lemon
    juice
2 to 4 Tb soft butter

Shortly before serving, set over moderate heat and stir slowly with a wooden spoon, reaching all over the bottom of the pan until soup comes almost to the simmer. Remove from heat, carefully correct seasoning, adding lemon juice if you wish; stir in the enrichment butter a teaspoon at a time. Serve immediately.

Cold Spinach Soup

Omit the final butter enrichment, and oversalt slightly. Stir several times as the soup cools, then cover and chill. Blend in more cream if you wish, just before serving, or top each serving with a spoonful of sour cream.

VARIATION

Potage aux Herbes Panachées
[Green Herb Soup]

For those green-thumbed wonders who grow their own herbs, here is a way to show off your tarragon, chervil, flat-leaved, pungent Italian parsley, shallots, spring onions or scallions, and chives. For those of us who wish to simulate the possession of an herb garden, the supermarket combination is leeks or onions, watercress, parsley, and dried tarragon.

1) *The soup base*

About 1½ cups onion
 flavoring (chopped shal-
 lots, scallions, onions and/
 or leeks)
3 Tb butter

for herb gardeners:

1 packed cup parsley in-
 cluding tender stems; a
 handful of chervil;
 a branch of tarragon
 leaves; chives

for supermarket shoppers:

1½ packed cups of a com-
 bination of parsley and
 watercress, including
 tender stems, and ½ tsp
 dried tarragon
1 Tb flour
3 cups hot water
⅓ cup plain raw white rice
1 tsp salt

Following the system for the preceding Spinach Soup, cook the onion flavoring in butter until tender. Chop greens roughly, stir into onion flavoring and cook 1 to 2 minutes or until wilted. Then add the flour and cook 1 minute, stirring. Remove from heat, beat in the hot water, and bring to the boil. Sprinkle in the rice and the salt. Simmer 25 minutes, then purée.

2) *Finishing the soup*

2 to 3 cups milk
More salt and tarragon
 if needed
White pepper to taste
A small saucepan
1 packed cup minced
 fresh greens (same com-
 bination as in Step 1)
1 Tb butter
½ cup heavy cream
2 egg yolks
2 to 4 Tb soft butter

Bring soup base to the simmer; thin out to desired consistency with milk. Season carefully. In a separate saucepan, stir the minced greens and butter over moderate heat for several minutes until herbs are wilted. Remove from heat and let cool a moment, then stir in the cream; blend in the egg yolks with a wire whip, and gradually dribble in 2 cups of the hot soup base. Pour back into the saucepan. Just before serving, stir over moderate heat until soup comes almost to the simmer, correct seasoning again, remove from heat and stir in the butter.

Cold Green Herb Soup

See directions for the preceding Spinach Soup.

VEGETABLE VELOUTÉS

* *POTAGE AUX CHAMPIGNONS, ÎLE DE FRANCE*
[Cream of Mushroom Soup II]

Cream of Mushroom Soup appeals to almost everyone, even to those who claim they hate mushrooms. This is a very simple version compared with the full-dress recipe in Volume I, page 40. Here puréed raw mushrooms simmer in an onion-flavored soup base, and if you have only a handful of stems rather than the 2 to 4 cups of fresh mushrooms specified, you will still have a delicious soup.

For 6 to 7 cups, serving 4 to 6

1) *The velouté soup base*

½ cup finely minced onions
4 Tb butter
A 2½- to 3-quart heavy-bottomed stainless or enameled saucepan with cover
A wooden spoon
3 Tb flour
2 cups hot water
A wire whip
4 cups milk
2 tsp salt
Pinch white pepper
Big pinch tarragon

Cook the onions slowly in the butter for 8 to 10 minutes, until tender but not browned. Add the flour and cook, stirring, for 1 minute. Remove from heat, and blend in ½ cup of the hot water with a wire whip. Gradually beat in the rest of the hot water, then the milk, seasonings, and tarragon. Bring to the simmer, stirring with wire whip; simmer very slowly for several minutes while preparing the mushrooms.

2) *The mushrooms*

2 to 4 cups (5 to 12 ounces) fresh whole mushrooms or just the mushroom stems
A food mill with grating disk (large holes), an electric blender, or a large knife

Trim and wash the mushrooms. If you are using a food mill with grating disk, chop the mushrooms roughly and grate directly into the soup base. If using a blender, chop roughly, and blend ½ cup at a time with an equal amount of soup base, flicking switch on and off rapidly to avoid too fine a purée. Otherwise chop the mushrooms into ⅛-inch pieces with a knife, and add to soup.

3) *Finishing the soup*

More milk if needed, or light chicken stock

Simmer the soup, partially covered, for 25 minutes. Add more liquid if soup seems too thick, then stir in

⅓ to ½ cup or more
  heavy cream
Salt, white pepper, and
  drops of lemon juice

the cream. Carefully correct seasoning, adding drops of lemon juice if you feel they are needed.

(*) May be completed to this point. Set aside uncovered until cool, then cover and refrigerate.

---

2 to 4 Tb soft butter
2 to 3 Tb minced fresh
  tarragon and/or parsley

Bring soup to simmer again just before serving. Remove from heat and stir in first the butter, a half tablespoon at a time, then the herbs. Serve immediately.

A more elaborate garnish

Omit all or most of the cream and butter enrichments if you wish. Ladle the hot soup into bowls, drop a spoonful of sour cream in each and top with minced herbs, or with sliced or fluted mushroom caps previously simmered in water, butter, and lemon juice (Volume I, page 510).

Cold Mushroom Soup

Omit the final butter enrichment, and oversalt slightly. Stir several times as the soup cools, then cover and chill. Blend in more cream, if you wish, just before serving.

VARIATIONS

The following recipes are all for 6 to 7 cups of soup, serving 4 to 6. All may be served either hot or cold, as for the mushroom soup.

Potage de la Fontaine Dureau

[Cream of Cauliflower and Watercress Soup]

This is a delicious and unusual, as well as a pretty, soup.

---

1) The velouté base

1 cup sliced leeks and/or
  onions
4 Tb butter
3 Tb flour
6 cups liquid (hot water,
  or part hot water and
  part milk)
2 tsp salt
Pinch white pepper

Following the Master Recipe for mushroom soup, cook the onions in the butter until tender, stir in the flour and cook 1 minute, blend in the liquid, then simmer slowly while preparing the vegetables.

---

2) *The vegetables—finishing the soup*

A 6- to 7-inch head of
cauliflower (1¼ to
1½ lbs.)
A large pan of boiling
salted water
1 bunch watercress (about
2 packed cups)
⅓ to ½ cup or more
heavy cream
2 to 4 Tb soft butter

Break cauliflower into flowerettes and peel central
stem; retain any tender leaves. Drop flowerettes and
stem (not leaves) into the boiling water, bring rapidly
back to the boil; boil uncovered for 2 minutes. Drain,
add to soup base, and simmer 15 minutes. Meanwhile,
discard any wilted leaves and stems from watercress,
wash cress and chop roughly. After cauliflower has
simmered 15 minutes, add the cress and reserved
cauliflower leaves. Simmer 10 minutes more; purée.
Add the cream, and correct seasoning. Reheat only
just before serving, to preserve the watercress green,
then remove from heat and stir in the butter enrichment.

Potage Crème aux Oignons, Soubise
[Cream of Onion Soup]

This is a soup for onion lovers, and a pleasant change from the usual
brown onion soup. The little touch of curry and a bit of wine give it special
flavor, while the addition of rice turns it into a *soubise*.

1) *The onion-velouté soup base*

3 to 4 cups sliced onions
4 Tb butter
1 tsp curry powder
2 Tb flour
2 cups hot water
2 cups chicken stock or
canned chicken broth
½ cup dry white wine or
⅓ cup dry white French
vermouth
⅓ cup plain white rice
1 bay leaf
Salt and white pepper
to taste

Following the Master Recipe for mushroom soup,
cook the onions in the butter until tender but not
browned. Add curry and cook 1 minute more, then
add flour and cook 2 minutes without browning. Remove from heat, beat in the hot water, then the
chicken stock and the wine. Bring to simmer and
sprinkle in the rice; add bay leaf, and season to taste.
Simmer 30 minutes. Purée.

2) *Finishing the soup*

2 to 3 cups milk
⅓ to ½ cup or more
heavy cream

Bring soup to the simmer. Thin out to desired consistency with milk, stir in the cream, and carefully
correct seasoning. Reheat again to simmer just before

2 to 4 Tb soft butter
2 to 3 Tb fresh minced
  chervil or parsley

serving; remove from heat and stir in the butter, then the herbs.

A POTATO-BASED SOUP

POTAGE CÉLESTINE
[Celery Soup with Potatoes, Leeks, and Rice]

This is leek and potato soup with a celery twist, and is equally good hot or cold.

For about 8 cups, serving 6 people

---

1) *The leeks and celery*

The white part of 2
  medium leeks, sliced; or
  1¼ cups sliced onions
3 cups sliced celery stalks
¼ tsp salt
3 Tb butter
A heavy-bottomed 3-quart
  stainless or enameled
  saucepan with cover
4 cups light chicken stock,
  or canned chicken
  broth and water
⅓ cup plain white rice

Cook the vegetables slowly with the salt and butter in the covered saucepan until tender but not browned—about 10 minutes. Add the liquid, bring to the boil, stir in the rice, and simmer uncovered for 25 minutes.

---

2) *The potatoes*

3 or 4 medium baking
  potatoes, peeled and
  chopped (about 3 cups)
2 cups water
½ tsp salt
Another heavy 3-quart
  saucepan
A food mill with medium
  disk, a potato ricer, or
  an electric blender
2 cups milk heated in a
  small pan
A wire whip and a wooden
  spoon

Meanwhile, boil the potatoes with the water and salt. When tender, drain their cooking water into the leeks and celery. If you are using a food mill or ricer, purée the potatoes, return to saucepan, and beat in the milk to make a smooth, white cream. If you are using a blender, purée the potatoes with a cup of the milk, pour into saucepan, and beat in the rest of the milk.

3) *Finishing the soup—herb-butter and croûton garnish*

⅛ teaspoon sugar (to
  bring out the flavor)
Salt and white pepper

Purée the leek and celery mixture with its liquid into the potato cream. Blend well with wire whip and bring to the simmer; beat in sugar and seasonings to taste.

(*) Set aside uncovered until shortly before serving.

A heated soup tureen, or
  a bowl and soup cups
4 to 6 Tb soft butter
3 Tb minced fresh chervil
  or tarragon;
  or minced fresh parsley
  and ¼ tsp crumbled
  dried tarragon
½ to ¾ cup croûtons
  (see directions following
  Cold Soup)

Bring the soup to the simmer. Mash the butter and herbs in the soup tureen (or in the bowl, and divide among your soup cups). Blend the hot soup into the herb butter, sprinkle the croûtons on top, and serve immediately.

Cold Celery Soup

Omit the butter enrichment and the croûtons; oversalt soup slightly. Mash the herbs with ¼ cup heavy cream or sour cream, stir into the soup, and chill. Stir in more chilled cream, if you wish, before serving, and decorate with fresh minced herbs or parsley.

Croûtons

[Small Cubes of Bread Sautéed in Butter]

Stale, homemade-type
  white bread
A baking sheet
Clarified butter (butter
  melted, skimmed, and
  poured off milky residue
  in bottom of pan)
A frying pan, preferably
  the no-stick kind

Preheat oven to 325 degrees. Remove crusts and, if unsliced, cut bread into ¼-inch slices. Then cut into ¼-inch strips; cut strips crosswise to make ¼-inch cubes. Spread cubes on baking sheet and dry out in middle level of oven for 10 to 15 minutes, until outside is dry but not browning; this will prevent bread from absorbing too much butter when sautéed. Film pan with a ⅛-inch layer of clarified butter, set over moderate heat until it bubbles; add just enough bread cubes to make 1 layer. Sauté, shaking and tossing pan by handle, until cubes are a light golden brown, adding a little more butter if necessary to keep bread from burning. Let cool on paper towels.

(*) May be cooked in advance. May also be frozen, then thawed and crisped for a few minutes in a 375-degree oven.

SOUPS WITH A FARINA THICKENING

Rather than thickening soups with flour, rice, or potatoes, you may use *semoule de blé,* semolina, also known as farina or cream of wheat. This makes a pleasant change and also imparts its own subtle taste and texture.

* *POTAGE AUX CONCOMBRES*

[Cream of Cucumber Soup]

The only thing to say about this soup is that it is perfectly delicious; it is especially good cold, but then it is also especially good hot.

For 6 to 7 cups, serving 4 to 6

1) *The cucumbers*

1½ lbs. cucumbers (3, about 8 inches long)

Peel the cucumbers. Cut 18 to 24 paper-thin slices and reserve in a bowl for later. Cut the rest of the cucumbers into half-inch chunks: you will have about 4½ cups.

2) *The soup*

½ cup minced shallots, or a combination of shallots, scallions, and/or onions
3 Tb butter
A heavy-bottomed stainless or enameled saucepan with cover
6 cups liquid: light chicken stock, or canned broth and water
1½ tsp wine vinegar
¾ tsp dried dill weed or tarragon
4 Tb quick-cooking farina (cream of wheat) breakfast cereal
A food mill with medium disk, or an electric blender
More liquid if necessary
Salt and white pepper

Cook the shallots, scallions, or onions slowly in the butter for several minutes until tender but not browned. Add the cucumber chunks, chicken broth, vinegar, and herbs. Bring to the boil, then stir in the farina. Simmer, partially covered, for 20 to 25 minutes. Purée, and return the soup to the pan. Thin out with more liquid if necessary; season carefully with salt and pepper.

(*) May be prepared in advance to this point.

Soup bowls
1 cup sour cream
1 to 2 Tb minced fresh
   dill, tarragon, or
   parsley

Bring to simmer just before serving, and beat in ½ cup sour cream. Ladle into soup bowls, place a dollop of sour cream in each bowl, float slices of cucumber on top of cream, and decorate with a sprinkling of herbs.

Cold Cucumber Soup

After stirring in the ½ cup sour cream, oversalt slightly and let cool uncovered, stirring occasionally. Then cover and chill. Ladle into chilled soup cups, adding a big spoonful of sour cream to each cup; float cucumber slices on top of the cream and decorate with herbs.

VARIATION

Potage aux Courgettes
[Cream of Zucchini Soup]

You may substitute zucchini for cucumbers in the preceding soup, but do not peel them. Cut off stem and tip, scrub with a vegetable brush, and proceed exactly as for the cucumber soup. Decorate with herbs, however, rather than with zucchini slices.

POTAGE UNTEL
[Green Turnip Soup]

This is one of those soups with a marvelous and unusual flavor that is difficult to decipher unless you are told the combination. Then the tastes of turnip and greens disclose themselves. You may not find any green leaves attached to your turnips unless they grow nearby and it is turnip season, which is winter or early spring. Spinach leaves do nicely, however.

1) The turnips

1½ lbs. fresh white turnips,
   peeled and quartered
   (about 5 cups)
3 Tb butter
1 tsp salt
1 tsp sugar
1½ cups water

Boil the turnips slowly with the seasonings, butter, and water in a covered saucepan for 15 to 20 minutes, or until tender when pierced with a knife. Uncover, raise heat, and boil to evaporate liquid; toss turnips in the butter, which remains, for 2 minutes.

A heavy-bottomed 3-quart
stainless or enameled
saucepan with cover

2) *The greens*

Either 4 packed cups tender
fresh turnip greens and
fresh spinach;
Or a 10-ounce package of
fresh spinach;
Or ½ package frozen
spinach thawed in cold
water and squeezed dry
2 Tb butter
A 10-inch stainless or
enameled skillet
2 wooden spoons
½ tsp salt
¼ tsp sugar

Meanwhile, discard any wilted leaves from fresh
greens and spinach, wash thoroughly and drain well.
Heat butter in a skillet to bubbling over moderately
high heat. Add greens and spinach, turn and toss with
the 2 wooden spoons; sprinkle with salt and sugar
and continue tossing for 2 to 3 minutes until greens
are limp and fairly tender.

3) *The soup*

A food mill with medium
disk, or an electric
blender
4 cups liquid: light chicken
stock, or canned broth
and water
3 Tb quick-cooking farina
(cream of wheat)
breakfast cereal
1 to 2 cups milk
Salt and pepper
1 to 2 Tb lemon juice

Purée the 2 vegetables together and bring to simmer
in turnip-cooking pan with the broth. Sprinkle in the
farina and simmer 5 to 6 minutes until farina is tender.
Thin out to desired consistency with milk; season
carefully with salt, pepper, and lemon juice.

(*) May be prepared in advance to this point.

2 to 4 Tb soft butter

Bring again to simmer just before serving; remove
from heat and stir in the butter a teaspoon at a time.

Alternate enrichments, cold soup

You may wish to enrich the soup with sour cream instead of butter, as for the
preceding Cucumber Soup, or with cream and egg yolks as in the Spinach Soup on
page 9. In any case, you may also serve it cold as suggested in both recipes.

THREE PEASANT SOUPS

POTAGE MAGALI

[Mediterranean Tomato Soup with Rice]

Typically Mediterranean, with its onions, tomatoes, garlic, saffron, and native herbs, this fragrant soup is even named after the Provençal heroine of many an operetta. It is best when tomatoes are at the season's peak, but the hothouse type can be pepped up with a bit of tomato paste.

For 7 to 8 cups, serving 4 to 6

1) *The soup base*

¾ cup combination of
  thinly sliced leeks and
  onions, or onions only
3 Tb olive oil
A heavy-bottomed 3-quart
  stainless or enameled
  saucepan with cover
1½ lbs. fresh, ripe,
  red tomatoes
4 large cloves garlic,
  minced or mashed
4 to 5 cups liquid: light
  chicken stock, or
  canned broth and water
¼ cup plain, raw, white rice
The following tied in
  washed cheesecloth:
  6 parsley sprigs, 1 bay
  leaf, ¼ tsp thyme, 4
  fennel seeds, and, if
  available, 6 large fresh
  basil leaves
A large pinch of saffron
  threads
Salt and pepper

Cook the leeks and onions slowly in the oil until tender but not browned. Meanwhile, peel and halve the tomatoes, squeeze out seeds and reserve juice. Chop tomato pulp roughly and stir into the cooked leeks and onions. Add the garlic and stir over moderate heat for 3 minutes. Then add the tomato juice and liquid, bring to the boil, and sprinkle in the rice. Add the herbs and saffron; season to taste with salt and pepper. Simmer, partially covered, for 30 minutes.

2) *Finishing the soup*

If necessary:
  pinches of sugar
1 tsp or more tomato
  paste
Salt and pepper

Carefully taste for seasoning, adding pinches of sugar to bring out flavor and counteract acidity, and small amounts of tomato paste if needed for color and taste. Remove herb bouquet.

(*) May be prepared ahead to this point.

2 or more Tb minced fresh   Serve either hot or chilled, sprinkled with fresh herbs.
  basil, chervil, or
  parsley

SOUPE CATALANE AUX POIVRONS
[Catalonian Pepper and Leek Soup]

Another Mediterranean soup uses the same principles as the preceding
potage Magali, and the same general ingredients. Here the character comes
from sweet peppers rather than tomatoes, a touch of ham or salt pork, and a
typically regional final liaison of egg yolks and olive oil.

For 7 to 8 cups, serving 4 to 6

1) *The soup base*

2½ to 3 ounces lightly
  smoked ham or lean salt
  pork, cut into ¼-inch
  dice (⅔ cup)
2 Tb olive oil
A heavy-bottomed 3-quart
  stainless or enameled
  saucepan with cover
2 cups diced onions
2 cups thinly sliced leeks
  (or more onions)
1½ cups diced bell peppers,
  red or green
4 large cloves garlic,
  minced or mashed
1 Tb flour
1 quart hot water
3 to 4 cups light beef
  stock, or canned
  chicken broth
¼ cup pasta (rice- or
  pepper-corn shaped, or
  broken vermicelli), or
  plain white rice
A large pinch of saffron
  threads
¼ tsp savory
Salt and pepper

Sauté the ham or salt pork in the oil over moderate
heat until it barely begins to brown, then stir in the
onions and leeks. Cook slowly several minutes until
fairly tender but not browned; stir in the peppers and
garlic, and cook again for 3 to 4 minutes without
browning. Finally sprinkle in the flour, stirring for 1
minute, and remove from heat. Blend in the hot water
gradually, stir in the stock or broth, and bring to the
simmer; skim off any surface scum for a minute or
two, then stir in the pasta or rice. Add the saffron and
savory, season to taste, and simmer partially covered
for 20 minutes. Carefully correct seasoning.

(*)May be prepared ahead to this point; let cool
uncovered. Bring again to the simmer just before
serving. You may also make the egg-yolk and oil enrichment in advance and store it in a covered jar.

2) *Finishing the soup*

2 egg yolks	Beat the egg yolks in the bottom of the tureen or bowl
A wire whip	until thick and sticky; by droplets, beat in the olive
A soup tureen or large	oil exactly as though you were making a thick may-
mixing bowl	onnaise. Stirring it, dribble in the hot soup until you
¼ cup olive oil	have added 2 cups; gradually stir in the rest. Serve
A ladle	immediately.

---

* SOUPE À LA VICTORINE
[Purée of White Bean Soup, Eggplant and Tomato Garnish]

This meal-in-itself will fill up the family on a cold day, especially if you include pork or sausage with the beans. The eggplant and tomato garnish makes a lively and unusual touch to an otherwise traditional bean purée.

For about 8 cups, serving 4 to 6

1) *Soaking the beans—1 hour*

1 quart of water	Bring the water to a rapid boil, drop in the beans, and
A 3-quart saucepan with	bring water rapidly back to the boil again; boil un-
cover	covered for exactly 2 minutes. Remove from heat,
⅓ cup dry white beans,	cover pan, and let soak for exactly 1 hour. Meanwhile,
such as Great Northern	you may prepare all the rest of the ingredients for the
or Small White	soup.

2) *The soup base—1½ hours of simmering*

2 cups combination of	Cook the leeks and onions slowly in the oil or butter
sliced leeks and onions,	until tender and translucent; raise heat slightly and
or onions only	cook for a few minutes more until very lightly
3 Tb olive oil or butter	browned. As soon as the beans have had their 1-hour
An 8-inch enameled, stain-	soak, scrape the vegetables into them, and add the rest
less, or no-stick	of the ingredients for the soup base (if using sausage
frying pan	rather than pork, add only for last 30–40 minutes of
2 bay leaves	cooking). Bring to the simmer, partially cover the
½ teaspoon thyme	pan, and cook slowly for about 1½ hours or until
½ teaspoon sage	beans are tender. Set pork or sausage aside for final
Optional:	step, purée the soup, and return to the pan.
½ lb. lean side pork	(*) May be prepared ahead; set aside uncovered until
(fresh unsmoked bacon),	cool.

or fresh fat-and-lean pork
butt (shoulder), or
Italian or Polish sausage
1½ tsp salt
⅛ tsp peppercorns
A food mill or an electric
blender

---

3) *The eggplant and tomato garnish*

A firm, shiny, 1-lb. eggplant
(about 8 inches long
and 3½ inches at widest
diameter)
A 2-quart glazed or stainless mixing bowl
1½ tsp salt
1 lb. fresh, firm, ripe, red
tomatoes (3 medium),
peeled, seeded, and
juiced
2–3 Tb olive oil
The 8-inch frying pan again
4 large cloves garlic,
minced or mashed
A cover for the frying pan

Peel the eggplant and cut into ½-inch dice. Toss in the bowl with the salt and let stand at least 20 minutes. Meanwhile, prepare the tomatoes and cut pulp into ½-inch squares; strain and reserve juice. When eggplant has stood its 20 minutes, drain and dry on paper towels. Heat the oil in the pan and sauté the eggplant, tossing it, to brown very lightly. Then toss with the tomato pulp and garlic, add the juice from the tomatoes, and cover the pan. Simmer slowly for 10 to 15 minutes until eggplant is tender but still holds its shape. Set aside.

(*) May be prepared ahead; let cool uncovered.

---

4) *Finishing the soup*

2 to 3 cups chicken stock
or canned broth
3 Tb minced fresh green
herbs: basil, parsley,
and chives (or parsley
only and dried basil
or oregano to taste)

About 15 minutes before serving, bring the soup base to the simmer and thin out to desired consistency with chicken stock or broth. Cut the pork or sausage into slices ⅜ inch thick and add to the soup along with the eggplant and tomato. Simmer 3 to 4 minutes to blend flavors. Carefully correct seasoning, stir in the herbs, and serve.

VARIATION

Fennel and Tomato Garnish

Sliced fresh fennel cooked until just tender and then simmered for a moment with diced tomatoes and herbs makes an attractive alternate to the

eggplant. Soak the beans and simmer the soup base as described in the preceding recipe; prepare the garnish as follows.

---

2 cups thinly sliced fresh
    fennel bulbs
2 Tb olive oil or butter
¼ cup minced shallots or
    scallions
2 large cloves garlic,
    minced or mashed
1 lb. tomatoes, peeled,
    seeded, juiced, and diced
Salt and pepper

Cook the fennel slowly in the oil or butter in a covered
skillet for 8 to 10 minutes, or until just tender but not
browned. Add the shallots or scallions, garlic, and
tomatoes; toss with fennel, cover skillet and cook for
a few minutes until tomatoes have rendered the rest
of their juice. Uncover, raise heat slightly and cook
for a few minutes more to evaporate the juice. Season
to taste. Set aside until you are ready to serve, then
add to the soup as directed in the Master Recipe,
Step 4.

LE POTIRON TOUT ROND
[Pumpkin Soup Baked in a Pumpkin]

This amusing presentation may be prepared either as a soup or a vegetable;
the recipe for it is on page 361, among the squashes in the Vegetables Chapter.

SHELLFISH SOUPS
Bisques

A bisque is a rich, thick, highly seasoned soup of puréed shellfish. Undoubtedly the bisque came into being because it is an easy as well as elegant
way to eat small crustaceans with complicated constructions like crayfish and
crabs, and it is a wonderful solution for the chests and legs of lobsters.

This is the kind of recipe to pick for a group of friends who enjoy cooking together, since a bisque is not tricky to make—it just takes a long time. To
get the true flavor, the raw shellfish are cut up and sautéed in their shells before
being simmered with wine and aromatic ingredients. The meat is then removed from the shells; some of it is saved for a garnish while the rest is puréed.
Finally, to extract every remaining bit of flavor and color from the shells, they
are puréed with butter, and everything is combined into a splendid soup.

We shall begin with illustrated directions on how to cut up lobsters and
crabs, and follow with lobster bisque and its other shellfish variations.

LOBSTERS

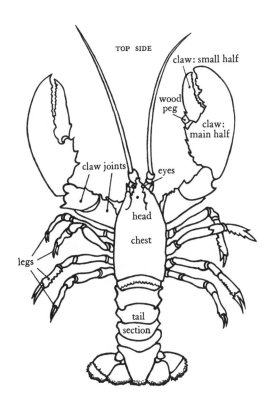

TOP SIDE

claw: small half

wood peg

claw: main half

claw joints

eyes

head

chest

legs

tail section

BUYING LOBSTERS

A live lobster should be lively: it spreads its claws, arches its back, and flaps its tail noisily against the underside of its chest when you pick it up. To do so you must grab it with your thumb and index finger at its shoulder just behind the claw joints. You can keep live lobsters in the refrigerator at around 37 degrees for a day or two in a heavy paper bag pierced with air holes, but you should cook them as soon as possible.

When you are picking store-bought boiled lobsters, look closely at their tails, which should curl up against the underside of the chests and spring back into place when straightened. A limp tail indicates that the lobster was moribund before cooking. Be sure also, in buying boiled lobster, that it smells absolutely sweet and fresh. Freshly boiled, cooled, and wrapped lobsters will keep for 2 to 3 days in the refrigerator at around 37 degrees. You may even wrap airtight and freeze a boiled lobster in its shell for several weeks.

*To tell the sex of a lobster, look at
the last pair of swimmerets on the
underside, where chest meets tail. If
they are soft and hairy, the lobster
is female; if they are hard, pointed,
and hairless, the lobster is male.*

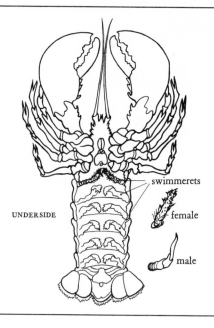

UNDERSIDE

swimmerets

female

male

ON DEALING WITH LIVE LOBSTERS

A number of the best French lobster recipes, including *homard à
l'américaine* and *bisque de homard,* call for the sautéing of cut-up raw lobster.
This means you must buy live lobster and either have it cut up for you and cook
it immediately, or do the cutting yourself. The serious cook really must face
up to the task personally. While professionals simply cut up the lobsters with
never a qualm nor a preliminary, you may find this difficult. If so, we suggest that you plunge them two at a time, head first and upside down, into
boiling water; leave for about a minute, until lobsters are limp, and immediately remove them. Because the nervous and circulatory systems of the lobster
center in the head area, a head-first plunge into boiling liquid not only kills
the lobster almost instantly, but also eliminates muscle spasms. There is a
misguided notion that lobsters suffer less if set to boil in cold water; far from
being a humane procedure, this is slow death by drowning!

HOW TO CUT UP RAW LOBSTER

Furnish yourself with sharp-pointed lobster scissors or kitchen scissors, a large
knife, a cutting board with groove to catch juices or a board set on a tray, a bowl
to pour juices into, and another bowl for the lobster tomalley. You now want to
split the lobster in two, lengthwise, as follows. Turn the lobster top side up. With
scissors, cut through center of shell from end of tail up to but not through eyes in
center of head. Turn lobster over and again with scissors cut through shell from
end of tail to within ½ inch of tip of head. Then with your knife cut completely
through the under side of the lobster lengthwise, following scissor cuts, from ½ inch
below tip of head down through tail, thus splitting lobster neatly in two except at

the head. Finally grasp lobster in both hands where claw joints meet chest, and break the shell apart at the head to open it up.

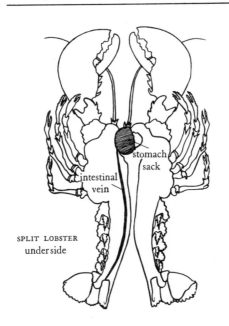

SPLIT LOBSTER
underside

Nestled in the head on one side of the lobster or the other is a pouch an inch long and ¾ inch in diameter which is the stomach sack. Locate the sack with your fingers, twist it out, and discard it. (If you have cut sack in two while splitting the lobster, no harm is done; remove the 2 halves.) Pull out and discard the intestinal vein, a thin, flexible translucent or blackish tube that runs from the area of the stomach sack down through the tail meat. The greenish, and sometimes almost blackish, soft matter lying in the chest cavity is the tomalley; scoop it out into a small bowl. If your lobster is female, there will usually be some orange-red roe as well; add this to the tomalley.

With a knife or scissors, separate the two tail sections from the chests. Cut the legs and the claw joints from the chests, and cut claws from end of joints. Crack claws in one or two places with a sharp whack of the knife. Drain juices into a bowl and reserve them, along with the tomalley. The lobster is now ready for sautéing.

HOW TO REMOVE THE MEAT FROM COOKED LOBSTERS

Split and open boiled lobster exactly as described in the preceding directions for raw lobster. Discard stomach sack and intestinal vein. Scoop tomalley from inside the chest sections into a bowl. After lifting meat out of tail sections, you want to remove meat from claws, claw joints, chest sections, and legs. With scissors, cut the claw joints from the chests, and separate each claw from its joint. Cut through shell on each side of joints, lift off shell, and remove meat.

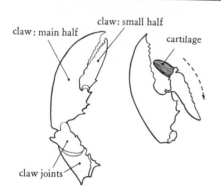

The first step in removing the meat from the claws is to *bend the small, hinged half rather slowly but firmly back on itself, toward the bottom of the claw;* this will withdraw its cartilage from inside the meat of the main half of the claw. Dig the point of meat out of this small shell with a nut pick or the point of your scissors.

Again with scissors, *cut a window out of the main claw shell* and remove the whole piece of claw meat with your fingers.

Pull chest section from its outside shell. Note that there are spongy, hairy strips attached to outside side of chest at leg joints; these are gills. Pull off and discard them. Scrape out and add to the tomalley any coagulated white matter clinging to the inside of the shell.

CHEST HALVES
underside

Cut or twist off legs where they join the chest. *Dig out meat from inside side of chest, going in between cartilaginous interstices with the point of a knife.* This is never a fast operation, but the small amount of meat you extract is the sweetest and tenderest of all.

cut

cut

shell

meat

To remove the meat from the legs, sever them at each of their joints. *Place on a board and squeeze the meat out of each piece by rolling a pin (pestle or broom handle) over it.* You will not get much, but again the meat is sweet, tender, and worth the time spent on extraction.

CRABS

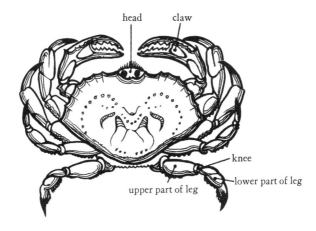

head   claw

knee

lower part of leg

upper part of leg

HOW TO CLEAN AND CUT UP RAW CRABS FOR CRAB BISQUE

Stone crabs, rock crabs, sand crabs, blue crabs, and their ilk and size are especially good for bisques because they are otherwise somewhat complicated to eat. If you are at the seashore you can gather them yourself, or ask lobster-men please not to throw them out, as they often do, but to save all crabs for you. However you obtain them, they must be alive. Just before you are ready to clean and cut them, place them upside down in a large bowl or stoppered sink and cover with very hot water. As soon as air bubbles cease to rise, in a minute or two, the crabs will be limp and ready to work on. Your object in cleaning and cutting is to remove the main body, or chest-leg-claw portions of each crab, from the hard shell, called the carapace, and to collect the tomalley, which is the creamy substance in the chest cavity and carapace.

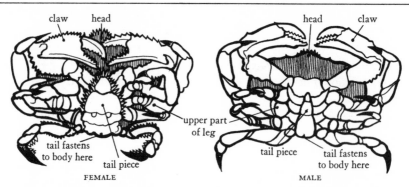

Turn crabs upside down. Note that female crabs have a wider tail flap than male crabs and the female's is usually edged with hair.

Lift point of flap away from chest, then grasp flap close to the body of the crab and with a rather slow twisting movement, pull it horizontally free from the end of the crab. The intestinal vein should draw out of the body at the same time.

point of flap lifted away from chest

Break off claw-joint sections where they join the body. *To remove the leg-chest section, hold carapace firmly in your left hand and grasp all the legs close to the body in your right hand.* Rock leg-chest portion back and forth and it will come loose from the carapace; pull it free. Both chest and interior of carapace should smell fresh and appetizing; your nose is the best judge.

On either side of the chest, where it
fitted into the shell, are feathery,
spongy strips, which are the gills;
pull off and discard them. Scrape
the creamy tomalley out of the chest
with your fingers and a spoon handle;
place in a sieve set over a bowl.

With a vegetable brush, scrub shell on underside of chest and around the legs under
a stream of cold water; scrub the claw-joint pieces also. *Finally cut the chest in half
lengthwise as shown.* (Trim off any mossy bits of shell with a knife or scissors.)

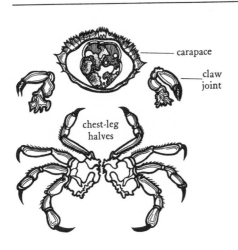

You now have prepared for
cooking the chest-leg sections, which
are cut in two, and the claw-joint
sections. The other edible portion
of the crab is the rest of the
tomalley, which is in the carapace.

Crab tomalley

The greenish, brownish, and sometimes orange creamy matter left in the carapace is also called tomalley. It, along with the juices in the shell, constitutes some of
the best parts of the crab.* Pour the juices through the sieve containing the chest
tomalley; scoop soft matter out of the shell with your fingers, and into the sieve.
When all the crabs are done, pour accumulated liquid into a separate container and
reserve. Rub the tomalley through the sieve with a wooden spoon, scrape it off bottom of sieve into a bowl; reserve for Step 7, where it will simmer with the crab-meat
garnish. (After puréeing, the raw tomalley will become a rather dark green, which
then becomes dark red when cooked.)

HOW TO REMOVE THE MEAT FROM COOKED CRABS

Provide yourself with a board and wooden mallet or wooden object of some
sort for cracking the shells, and a grapefruit knife for extracting the meat. For a
bisque made from small crabs, do not bother to delve too thoroughly because it will
take all day; remove only what meat you easily can, and the shell debris will be sim-

---

* When a whole crab is boiled, the tomalley turns greenish and orange while the liquid
usually becomes white.

mered again anyway to extract all remaining flavor. Begin by twisting the legs from the chest sections, then break each leg off at the knee by bending it back upon itself at the joint, thus drawing the cartilage out of the upper leg meat. For a bisque, chop lower legs into quarter-inch pieces, and reserve for shellfish butter; otherwise discard them. To remove meat from upper legs, as well as from claws and joints, crack shell sharply but lightly with mallet, being careful not to shatter the shell into the meat. Then dig out what meat you easily can with the point of your grapefruit knife. To remove meat from chests, dig out what you can from the holes left by the legs, then from the other side, being careful not to include bits of shell or cartilage. You will get about 1 solid cup of meat from 6 to 8 crabs measuring 3 to 4 inches across the back of the shell.

---

* *BISQUE DE HOMARD À L'AMÉRICAINE*
[Lobster Bisque]

Considering the price of lobsters and the puréed nature of a bisque, we think it is a waste to use whole lobster here. We therefore suggest only the chests and the legs for the bisque, and the tails, claws, and tomalley for a splendid main dish, such as the *homard à l'Américaine* described in Volume I on page 223. In fact, you could well combine the two, starting them out together, since both follow much the same pattern. Serve the main dish one night, and the bisque a day or two later. That is up to you, however, and we shall content ourselves with the chests and legs from 3 or 4 lobsters for the following recipe. As in most dishes of this type, you can expand or contract the ingredients to a certain extent without upsetting the balance of tastes, and you need not be disturbed if you have a little more or a little less of anything that is called for.

A NOTE ON TECHNIQUES AND EQUIPMENT

In the old days you would have needed an 8-quart marble mortar, a large wooden pestle, a 12-inch tamis sieve, a tortoise-shell scraper, and either a flock of kitchen minions or the strength of a Japanese wrestler to produce a proper bisque. Today's electric blender eliminates these colorful requirements, but there are still multiple simmerings, strainings, and puréeings, as well as numerous bowls, sieves, and spoons that you will need. Do not wash anything off until the soup is done because you will be using the same utensils repeatedly and you don't want any marvelous tidbits of flavor losing themselves down the drain.

For about 2 quarts, serving 6 to 8

1) *Preliminaries*

1 cup *mirepoix* (equal
  parts finely diced onions,
  carrots, and celery)
1½ Tb butter
A heavy, 3-quart stainless
  or enameled saucepan
  with cover
1½ cups chopped, fresh
  tomato pulp (3 to 4
  medium tomatoes peeled,
  seeded, and juiced)
The chest parts with the
  shells and the legs from
  3 or 4 fresh, raw, 1¼-
  to 1½-lb. lobsters

Cook the *mirepoix* slowly in the butter, in the saucepan, for 6 to 8 minutes, or until vegetables are tender
but not browned. Meanwhile, prepare the tomatoes.
Cut lobster chests in half lengthwise. (Illustrated directions for cutting lobster are on pages 26–7.)

2) *Sautéing the lobster*

2 or more Tb olive oil or
  cooking oil
A heavy, 10- to 12-inch
  no-stick or enameled
  casserole (or chicken
  fryer or deep frying pan)
Cooking tongs

Film the bottom of the casserole with ⅟₁₆ inch of
oil; set over moderately high heat until oil is very
hot but not smoking. Add the lobster chests cut side
down and the legs. Do not crowd pan: sauté in 2
batches if all will not fit easily in one layer. Toss and
turn frequently until shells are a deep red (4 to 5
minutes in all). Color is important here, as it is the
shells that tint the soup.

3) *Simmering the lobster and removing the meat*

Salt and pepper
⅓ cup Cognac
Either 1½ cups dry white
  wine;
Or 1 cup dry white
  vermouth
2 Tb fresh tarragon or
  1 Tb dried tarragon
1 bay leaf
The *mirepoix* and toma-
  toes from Step 1
1 clove mashed garlic
Large pinch of cayenne
  pepper
A cover for the casserole

When the lobster is sautéed, lower heat slightly, salt
and pepper the lobster, and pour on the Cognac. Ignite
by shaking pan vigorously or tilting it into heat source,
or use a lighted match. When flames have died down,
pour on the wine, mix in the tarragon, and add the
bay leaf and other ingredients. Cover casserole, and
simmer slowly for 20 minutes.

(*) AHEAD-OF-TIME NOTE: May be simmered a day in
advance; let cool uncovered, then cover and refrigerate
(or freeze).

2 medium-sized bowls
A food mill with medium
    disk, or a sieve and
    a wooden spoon
An electric blender

(Before proceeding, you may wish to start the rice in the next step, so that it will be done by the time you are through here.) Remove the pieces of lobster from their cooking sauce and extract the meat from the shells following illustrated directions, pages 28–9. You will have about 1 cup; place in one of the bowls. Purée the cooking sauce through food mill or sieve into the other bowl, and scrape into jar of blender; reserve for Step 5. Chop shells into ½-inch pieces and reserve in a bowl for Step 6.

4) *Simmering the rice*

3 cups fish stock or
    canned clam juice
2 cups beef stock or canned
    beef bouillon
The saucepan from Step 1,
    in which the *mirepoix*
    cooked
¼ cup plain, raw, white
    rice

Bring the fish stock or clam juice and the beef stock or bouillon to a boil in the saucepan; sprinkle in the rice. Stir up once, and simmer for 20 minutes. Set aside for Step 5.

5) *Puréeing rice and lobster meat*

The saucepan of boiled
    rice
A large, fine-meshed sieve
    set over a 2½- to
    3-quart bowl
A rubber spatula
The blender jar containing
    the puréed lobster-
    cooking sauce
Half the lobster meat

Drain rice through sieve, reserving its cooking liquid in the bowl. Scrape rice and the half portion of lobster meat into the blender. Purée, adding a little of the rice-cooking liquid if mixture is too thick for easy blending in the machine. Scrape the purée out of the blender and into the rice-cooking saucepan.

6) *Shellfish butter for final enrichment—lobster butter*

6 Tb butter
The casserole in which the
    lobster cooked
The bowl of chopped
    lobster shells
The electric blender
The sieve from Step 5

Heat butter to bubbling in casserole, stir in the chest and leg shells, and sauté for 2 to 3 minutes, tossing and turning, to heat thoroughly. Immediately scrape into blender and purée, flicking switch on and off and scraping shells down into blades as necessary. Scrape purée into sieve, and mash vigorously with spoon to extract as much butter as possible. Scrape all butter off

A wooden spoon
A rubber spatula
A small bowl to hold the
butter

bottom of sieve with rubber spatula and pack into
bowl. Set aside for Steps 7 and 8.

The bowl of rice-cooking
liquid from Step 5
The saucepan containing
the puréed rice and
lobster from Step 5

To extract all remaining flavor from blender jar,
shells, and sieve, pour rice-cooking liquid into the
casserole in which you just sautéed the shells. Heat to
the simmer and pour liquid into blender to rinse it,
then pour liquid back into casserole. Scrape shell
debris from sieve into casserole, and swish sieve about
in the hot rice-cooking liquid to dislodge all debris.
Simmer 3 to 4 minutes; strain liquid through the sieve
and into the saucepan of puréed rice and lobster.

7) *The lobster garnish*

2 Tb of the lobster butter
from Step 6
A small frying pan
The remaining lobster
meat from Step 3
Salt and pepper
2 Tb Cognac or dry white
vermouth

Heat the butter to bubbling in the frying pan; stir in
the lobster meat, and sprinkle with salt and pepper.
Sauté over moderate heat for 2 minutes, tossing and
turning. Pour on the Cognac or vermouth, and cook
for a moment until liquid has evaporated. Scrape the
lobster into the saucepan containing the rest of the
soup mixture from Step 6, and you are finally almost
ready to serve.

(*) AHEAD-OF-TIME NOTE: Recipe may be completed to
this point; let cool uncovered, then cover and refrigerate or freeze.

8) *Final flavoring and serving*

If needed: more fish stock,
clam juice, or bouillon
Salt, pepper, cayenne, and
tarragon
½ to 1 cup heavy cream
The lobster butter from
Step 6
2 to 3 Tb minced fresh
chervil, tarragon, or
parsley
Croûtons (diced bread
sautéed in butter, page
16); or Melba toast,
page 82; or your own
French bread, page 57

Shortly before serving, bring the bisque to the simmer.
It should be quite thick, but if it needs thinning, stir
in a little stock or bouillon. Carefully correct seasoning. Just before serving, stir in the cream, then remove
from heat and stir in the lobster butter by tablespoons-
ful. Pour the bisque into a hot tureen or soup cups,
and decorate with the fresh herbs. Pass the croûtons,
Melba toast, or bread separately.

VARIATIONS

Because all of the other shellfish bisques follow almost the same pattern as lobster bisque, you can really substitute shrimp, crab, or crayfish for lobster in the Master Recipe every time you see the word "lobster." To account for the very slight differences in method, here is a paragraph of special instructions for each.

Bisque de Crevettes
[Shrimp Bisque]

You must have shrimp in the shell for this recipe because the shells give the bisque its characteristic color and flavor. It is of prime importance, therefore, that you use only the freshest smelling and finest quality of shrimp, whether they are live and whole or frozen, raw, and headless. If the shrimp are whole, meaning with head and shell, simply wash and drain before sautéing them; if frozen, thaw in cold water until you can separate them, then sauté. Since they need only 5 minutes of simmering, cook the tomatoes and other ingredients called for in Step 3 for 10 minutes before adding the shrimp; after their simmer, let them cool 10 minutes in the cooking sauce before draining and peeling them. Use the shells and several whole, cooked shrimp for the shellfish butter in Step 6, and if the shrimp are very large, slice in half lengthwise those you are reserving for the garnish in Step 7. You will need 1¼ to 1½ pounds of raw shrimp for 2 quarts of bisque.

Bisque de Crabes
[Crab Bisque]

Crab bisque is even more one of love's labors than lobster bisque, but it is so marvelously rich and deeply flavored that if you pick the right guests your reward will be in watching their pleasure, as well as relishing your own. Clean and cut the crabs as illustrated on pages 30–1, then substitute crab for lobster in the Master Recipe, starting on page 32, with the following slight modifications. Because crab pieces will bulk larger than lobster chests, you will need 2 big casseroles for the sautéing in Step 2, but may combine all together for the simmering in Step 3. You will not have enough liquid to cover all of the crab pieces in this step, and should toss the pieces several times during the 20 minutes of cooking; do not forget to add the liquid from the carapaces and the tomalley to simmer here, along with everything else. Note that it is only the chopped-up lower legs that go into the shellfish butter in Step 6, but add as well all the debris from the chests, claws, and upper legs to simmer at the end of the step, allowing a good 10 minutes of cooking to extract every bit of flavor. For 2 quarts of wonderful soup, you will need 6 to 8 live crabs measuring 3 to 4 inches across the top of the shell.

Bisque d'Écrevisses
[Crayfish Bisque]

Fresh-water crayfish, crawfish, or *écrevisses,* as they are variously called, are miniature lobsterlike crustaceans 4 to 5 inches long. They are considered a supreme delicacy in Europe as well as in the southern Atlantic, the Pacific, and the Midwestern states where they are gathered. With the few minor differences noted here, substitute the word "crayfish" for the word "lobster" in the Master Recipe starting on page 32. To clean live crayfish, drop them headfirst in a basin of very hot water and leave for 2 to 3 minutes or until bubbles cease to rise. After draining them, pull out the central flap at the base of the tail to draw out along with it the intestinal tube. (This action of removing the intestine is called *châtrer* in French recipes.) Sauté and simmer the crayfish whole, as directed in the Master Recipe, but they need only 10 minutes of cooking in Step 3. To shell them, remove the tail meat only, and use all of it for the garnish in Step 7; the chests and shell debris go into the butter, Step 6. If you wish to be very *haute cuisine,* have a dozen extra crayfish and make a small amount of a simple fish mousse, using the raw tail meat. Then remove chest-leg sections (but not claws and feelers) from covering shell, and fill the shells with the mousse. Poach 5 minutes in stock or bouillon before floating them in the bisque at serving time. You should have 24 to 30 live crayfish for 2 quarts of soup, plus 12 or so extra if you are doing the mousse.

TWO SCALLOP SOUPS WITH A CRAB
OR LOBSTER VARIATION

Scallops are so easy to come by, fresh or frozen, that we feel they should have their place in the soup repertoire. Although scallops are rarely so used in France, they are delicious as the unique fish in a *bouillabaisse* or *bourride,* and they make a marvelous *velouté* or cream soup.

LES SAINT-JACQUES EN BOUILLABAISSE
[Bouillabaisse of Scallops]

This heady Mediterranean brew of leeks, onions, garlic, tomatoes, and herbs plus scallops can be a complete meal when served with plenty of fresh French bread and followed by fruit and cheese.

Serving 4 as a main course, 6 as a soup course

1) *The soup base*

1½ cups combination
  finely sliced leeks and
  onions, or onions only
¼ cup olive oil
A heavy-bottomed stainless
  or enameled 3-quart
  saucepan with cover
2 large cloves minced or
  mashed garlic
1¼ to 1½ cups chopped
  fresh tomato pulp (4
  medium tomatoes peeled,
  seeded, and juiced)
4 cups liquid: white-wine
  fish stock, or equal parts
  clam juice, water, and
  white wine or vermouth
The juice from the
  tomatoes
2 large pinches saffron
  threads
The following tied in
  washed cheesecloth: 6
  parsley sprigs, 1 bay leaf,
  ¼ tsp thyme, ½ tsp
  basil, 4 fennel seeds, and
  a 2-inch piece of dried
  orange peel or ¼ tsp
  bottled dried peel
Salt and pepper

Cook the leeks and onions slowly with the oil in the covered saucepan for 5 to 6 minutes until tender but not browned. Add garlic and tomatoes, raise heat slightly, and cook 3 to 4 minutes more. Add the rest of the ingredients, bring to the boil, and simmer partially covered for 30 minutes. Carefully taste for seasoning, adding salt and pepper as needed.

2) *Preparing the scallops*

1 lb. (2 cups) bay or sea
  scallops, fresh or frozen
A large bowl and sieve

Soak the scallops in cold water for 2 or 3 minutes if fresh, until completely defrosted if frozen. Lift out and drain, looking over each for sand; wash again if necessary. Leave bay scallops whole. Cut sea scallops into ⅜-inch chunks.

3) *Finishing the soup*

The soup base
The scallops
2 to 3 Tb coarsely chopped
  fresh parsley

Bring the soup base to a rapid boil, add the scallops, bring to the boil again and boil slowly uncovered for 3 minutes. Check seasoning again. Serve either from a warm tureen or in soup cups or plates, and decorate

French bread
Optional: a bowl of freshly
grated Parmesan cheese

with parsley. Pass the bread and optional cheese separately.

(*) Soup may be cooked several hours before serving. Let cool uncovered, then cover and refrigerate. Bring to a full boil for 2 or 3 seconds before serving. Note that a full boil is necessary to redistribute the olive oil into the liquid.

Other ideas

For a more nourishing soup, you can add 2 cups of diced "boiling" potatoes or a handful of pasta to the soup base 10 minutes before the end of its simmering. You could enrich the soup with an egg yolk and oil liaison, as for the *soupe aux poivrons* on page 21, or with a *rouille,* as for the *bouillabaisse* in Volume I, page 52. See also the recipe for *bourride* with its *aïoli* enrichment on page 50.

* ## VELOUTÉ DE SAINT-JACQUES

[Cream of Scallop Soup—hot or cold]

This deliciously creamy soup is a cousin of the Breton *mouclades,* mussel soup, and you may serve it either hot or cold.

For 6 to 7 cups, serving 4 to 6

1) The court bouillon

4 cups liquid: 2 cups dry
white wine or 1½ cups
dry white vermouth
plus water
1 cup thinly sliced onions
¼ cup thinly sliced carrots
¼ tsp each: fennel seeds,
thyme, and curry powder
4 peppercorns
1 clove mashed garlic
½ bay leaf
6 parsley sprigs
1½ tsp salt
A heavy-bottomed stain-
less or enameled sauce-
pan with cover
A sieve set over a bowl

Simmer the ingredients for the *court bouillon* in the partially covered saucepan for 20 minutes. Strain, pressing liquid out of ingredients, and return the *court bouillon* liquid to the pan.

2) *Cooking the scallops*

1 lb. (2 cups) scallops, fresh or frozen	Soak the scallops in cold water for 2 or 3 minutes if fresh, until completely defrosted if frozen. Lift out and drain, looking over each for sand; wash again if necessary. Cut into ¼-inch dice. Bring the *court bouillon* to a boil, add scallops, bring again to just under the boiling point, and simmer uncovered for 3 minutes. Drain the liquid into the bowl, leaving scallops in sieve. Rinse and dry the saucepan.

3) *The velouté soup base*

3 Tb butter **4 Tb flour** **A wooden spatula or spoon** **The *court bouillon*** **A wire whip** **1½ to 2 cups milk** **½ to ¾ cup heavy cream** **2 egg yolks** **The scallops** **Salt and white pepper**	Melt the butter in the saucepan, stir in the flour, and cook slowly for 2 minutes without browning. Remove from heat and let cool a moment, then pour in all the warm *court bouillon* at once, beating vigorously with a wire whip to blend thoroughly. Bring to the boil for 2 to 3 minutes, stirring to reach all over bottom of pan. Thin with milk as necessary; soup should not be too thick, since the egg yolks to come will also thicken it. Remove from heat. Pour ½ cup of the cream into the bowl, blend in the egg yolks with a wire whip, and gradually dribble in about 2 cups of the hot soup, beating. Return mixture to the pan and stir in the scallops. Carefully correct seasoning. (*) Soup may be prepared to this point several hours in advance. Clean off sides of pan with a rubber spatula and float a spoonful of cream on the surface to prevent a skin from forming. When cool, cover and refrigerate.

4) *Finishing the soup, and serving*

3 to 4 Tb soft butter **2 to 3 Tb minced fresh parsley, chervil, or chives**	Shortly before serving, set soup over moderate heat and stir continually with a wooden spoon until soup comes to just below the simmer. Remove from heat and stir in the butter, a tablespoon at a time. Serve in a warm tureen or soup cups, and decorate with the minced herbs.

To serve cold

Omit the final butter enrichment, and oversalt slightly. Clean off sides of pan with a rubber spatula and float a spoonful of cream on the surface. When cool, cover and refrigerate. Blend in more cream, if you wish, just before serving.

CREAM OF SHELLFISH SOUP

VARIATION

Velouté de Crustacés

[Cream of Shellfish Soup—for canned crab, and
cooked or frozen crab or lobster meat]

Although the best shellfish soups are made, like the bisques, from fresh, raw shellfish in the shell, because every bit of the flavor goes into the soup, you can produce an excellent result with the cooked meat alone, plus either a fish stock or clam juice. This is a useful type of recipe for those times when you want something special on the spur of the moment. The technique here is almost the same as for the preceding scallop soup, but there is no *court bouillon*. (NOTE: this recipe works especially well with freshly cooked crab or lobster meat, as well as with the frozen meat or with canned crab. We have not found canned lobster to be at all successful.)

For about 6 cups, serving 4 people

1) Preparing and flavoring the shellfish meat

7 to 8 ounces (1 packed cup) canned crab meat, or cooked or frozen crab or lobster meat
A large sieve and bowl
2 Tb butter
An 8-inch enameled or stainless frying pan
1 Tb minced shallots or scallions
⅛ tsp tarragon
Salt and pepper
Either **¾ cup dry white wine;**
Or **½ cup dry white French vermouth**

Commercially canned or frozen shellfish meat is usually packed with a preservative, which should be washed off. Therefore soak the meat in cold water for several minutes (or until completely thawed). Pick it over carefully to remove all bits of tendon, particularly if you are using crab meat. Drain thoroughly. Melt butter in pan, stir in shallots or scallions, then the shellfish meat. Season with the tarragon, salt, and pepper and sauté over moderate heat for 2 to 3 minutes so that butter and flavorings will penetrate meat. Add wine or vermouth, boil rapidly to reduce liquid by half, and set aside.

2) The velouté soup base

½ cup very finely minced onion
4 Tb butter
A 2½- to 3-quart heavy bottomed stainless or enameled saucepan with cover

Cook the onions slowly in the butter until tender but not browned. Stir in the flour and cook for 2 minutes. Remove from heat, and beat in the hot liquid. Simmer partially covered for 20 minutes, thinning out as necessary with milk. Add the shellfish meat, simmer 2 to 3 minutes to blend flavors, thinning out again with milk if necessary. Correct seasoning. Pour ½ cup

3 Tb flour
3 cups fish stock or clam
   juice brought to the simmer in a small saucepan
2 to 3 cups milk
Salt and pepper to taste
The shellfish meat
½ to ¾ cup heavy cream
2 egg yolks

cream into shellfish pan, blend in the egg yolks, then about 2 cups of hot soup added by driblets. Pour back into the soup.

(*) May be prepared ahead to this point, as directed in preceding recipe.

3) *Finishing the soup and serving*

Follow directions in preceding recipe.

FRENCH FISH STEWS AND CHOWDERS

Bouillabaisse is not the only French fish chowder. From that same Mediterranean coast comes the *bourride*—thick, rich, and reeking of garlic, while from the opposite corner of France comes the *marmite dieppoise,* with its mussels, sole, cream, and eggs. Inland France has its own special chowders too, called *matelotes, meurettes,* and *pauchouses,* made from fresh-water fish. These are all hearty dishes with big chunks of fish, and easily suffice as the main course of an informal lunch or supper.

FISH TO USE

For this type of recipe the fish should be fairly firm-fleshed so that it will keep its shape while it cooks. Whether fresh or frozen, it must smell as fresh as a breeze from the open sea or the primeval forest. You cannot, of course, duplicate a fresh-water chowder from Burgundy with ocean fish from the New Jersey or Oregon coast, but we do not think the fish itself is all that important: it is the rest of the ingredients and the general method that give each dish its special character. Here are some suggestions for both ocean fish and fresh-water fish with their French translations or equivalents.

Ocean fish

Cod (*cabillaud, morue fraîche*)
Conger eel (*congre, fiélas*)
Cusk (*brosme,* rare in France)
Goosefish, monkfish (*lotte de mer, baudroie*)
Haddock (*églefin*)
Halibut (*flétan,* rare in France)

Ocean whitefish, wolf fish, catfish (*loup anarrhique,* rare in France)

Pollack, green cod, coalfish (*lieu jaune* is a near equivalent)

Sea bass (*bar, loup*)

Whiting, silver hake (*merlu* or *colin* is the European cousin; *merlan* is no relation but a good choice)

Various rockfish, if you are a fisherman (the American sculpin is a cousin of the Mediterranean *rascasse*)

Fresh-water fish

Bass and perch (*perche*)

Carp (*carpe*)

Catfish (*lotte de rivière*)

Eel (*anguille*)

Pike (*brochet*)

Trout (*truite*)

Small carplike fishes (*tanche, barbeau, barbillon* are typical, and frequently mentioned in French recipes)

Scallops

Though rarely used for soups and chowders in France, scallops are delicious used in any of the following recipes, alone or in combination with other fish.

PREPARING FISH FOR COOKING

Small fish (6 to 8 inches) for stews and chowders are cleaned and scaled, and left whole. Larger fish, after cleaning and scaling, are cut into slices ¾ to 1 inch thick. Very large fish are cut into thick fillets or steaks, and then into serving pieces about 3 by 4 inches in diameter. Bones and skin are usually not removed, but you may do so if you wish. As soon as you have prepared the fish, wrap and refrigerate it until you are ready to cook. Make fish stock out of scraps, heads, skin, and so forth (Volume I, page 114).

MATELOTES, MEURETTES, PAUCHOUSES

[Burgundy Fish Stew with Wine, Onions, *Lardons,* and Mushrooms]

You might call this dish the fisherman's *coq au vin,* fish simmered in wine with onions, pork bits, and mushrooms, and the wine becomes the sauce. Even those who are not enthusiastic fish eaters usually love this recipe, and although it is supposed to be made with fresh-water fish or eels alone, we have used ocean fish like halibut, haddock, or scallops with complete success. As usual with French regional recipes, you can have endless arguments as to whether a *matelote* is cooked with red wine or white, or if it is only the *pauchouse* (spelled *pôchouse* by some) that simmers in white wine, and only the *meurette* that has *lardons* of pork, or vice versa, including a garnish of poached eggs and truffles for some versions. We shall not enter into the argument at all except to say that either a fish-stock or clam-juice base to the sauce is essential, or your *matelote/meurette/pauchouse* will lack the savor and character it must have.

If this is a main course, you may wish to add a side dish of boiled potatoes to eat with the stew, as well as plenty of French bread. Serve either a strong dry white wine or a red, preferably Burgundy, to match whichever wine cooked with the fish. A green salad or cold vegetables vinaigrette could follow the stew, and then cheese and fruit or a dessert.

For 4 to 6 people

---

1) *The sauce base*

¼ lb. (½ cup) fresh fat-and-lean pork belly or butt, or a chunk of salt pork, or bacon
A 4- to 5-quart flameproof casserole or saucepan
1 Tb pork fat or cooking oil
Either 2 cups sliced onions;
Or ½ cup sliced onions and 24 to 30 braised onions to be added at end of cooking
2 Tb flour

Cut pork into *lardons* 1 inch long and ¼ inch thick. If you are using salt pork or bacon, drop into 2 quarts of water, simmer 10 minutes, drain, rinse, and dry in paper towels. Cook with the pork fat or oil over moderately low heat for 4 to 5 minutes, stirring frequently, until pork is very lightly browned. Then stir in the sliced onions, cover pan, and cook slowly for about 5 minutes until onions are tender. Raise heat and brown very lightly. Sprinkle on the flour and stir over moderately high heat to cook and brown the flour for 2 minutes. Remove from heat.

---

2 cups *either* red wine such as Côtes-du-Rhône or Mountain Red; *or* dry white wine such as Côtes-du-Rhône or Pinot Blanc; *or* 1½ cups dry white French vermouth
2 cups fish stock or clam juice

Gradually stir in the liquids to blend smoothly with the flour. Add the herbs and garlic and bring to the simmer. Salt lightly to taste. Simmer half an hour. Liquid should be lightly thickened; thin out with a little more wine or stock if necessary. Carefully correct seasoning.

(*) AHEAD-OF-TIME NOTE: May be cooked in advance; when cool, cover and refrigerate.

Big pinch pepper
1 imported bay leaf
2 allspice berries
½ tsp thyme
1 clove garlic, mashed
Salt (none if using clam
   juice)

---

2) *Optional additions—to be prepared in advance of final cooking*

1 lb. fresh mushrooms,
   quartered and sautéed
   in butter
8 to 12 canapés (triangles
   of crustless homemade-
   type white bread sautéed
   in clarified butter)

The mushrooms may be sautéed and set aside in a covered dish; they will simmer in the sauce just before serving. Reheat the canapés in the oven for several minutes before serving.

---

3) *Finishing the stew and serving*

Either 2 to 2½ lbs. fish
   from the list on page 42,
   one or several varieties
   prepared as described;
Or scallops only
More stock or clam juice
   if needed

Twenty minutes before you wish to serve, bring the sauce base to the boil and add the fish. Pour on more liquid if necessary, so fish is just covered. Rapidly bring back to the boil and boil slowly 8 to 10 minutes (3 to 4 minutes only for scallops) until fish is done; flesh comes easily from bone, or will just flake—do not overcook.

A hot serving dish
The optional braised onions
   and sautéed mushrooms
Parsley sprigs or minced
   fresh parsley
The optional canapés

Arrange fish on hot dish, cover, and keep warm. Skim off any surface fat and rapidly boil down sauce, if necessary, to concentrate its flavor or to thicken it. Add optional braised onions and/or mushrooms and simmer for a moment to blend flavors. Carefully correct seasoning. Spoon sauce and vegetables over fish, decorate with parsley and optional canapés, and serve immediately.

(*) AHEAD-OF-TIME NOTE: If you find you cannot serve immediately, return fish to pan after sauce has been finished and optional vegetables added. Remove from heat, and just before serving reheat to the simmer, basting fish with sauce until hot through.

MARMITE AUX FRUITS DE MER—MARMITE DIEPPOISE—CHAUDRÉE NORMANDE

[Normandy-style Fish Stew with Sole, Shellfish,
and White-wine Sauce]

When you order *marmite dieppoise* in Dieppe on the Normandy coast or at Prunier's in Paris, you are served an elegant combination of channel sole, turbot, red mullet, mussels, shrimps, scallops, and *langoustines,* those small, European, lobsterlike prawns, all steaming together in an abundant, deliciously winey-smelling, ivory-colored sauce. It will cost you quite a number of francs, since *marmite dieppoise* is definitely in the luxury category. This is another dish we cannot fully duplicate in America because channel soles, turbots, mullets, and *langoustines* do not live here, but other soles, halibuts, and lobsters do, as do shrimp, scallops, and mussels. The following recipe, therefore, is an overseas version of the original. You may serve the *marmite* as a first course, although we suggest it as the main attraction of the meal. You could start with a *pâté* or a *saucisson en brioche,* follow with asparagus or artichokes vinaigrette, and it would be fully in the Normandy tradition to end with an apple dessert such as the individual soufflés on page 437, or the *tarte aux pommes* on page 457. With the *marmite* itself, serve a fine white Burgundy, Graves, or Gewürtztraminer.

FISH TALK

Although you may use any of the choices listed on pages 42–3, you will have a combination more like the original with the equivalent of a fillet of sole, two 2-inch pieces of halibut, 4 to 6 shrimp, scallops, and/or mussels, and ⅓ of a lobster per person, for the first serving, and half the amount for seconds. Whatever you have chosen, be sure each piece of fish smells absolutely fresh; pay particular attention to the shrimp if frozen, because they can overpower everything else unless of unquestionable quality. A well-flavored fish stock is essential here; if you cannot get bones and trimmings from fresh sole, buy an extra pound or so of fish.

For 6 people as a main course, 10 to 12 as a soup course

1) *Preliminaries—may be done several hours in advance preparing the fish—see also preceding paragraph:*

1½ lbs. skinless and boneless sole or flounder fillets	Wash and drain all the fish. Trim sole or flounder fillets if necessary; cut in half crosswise. If scallops are

1 to 1½ lbs. scallops
1 to 1½ lbs. raw shrimp,
  medium size, and in the
  shell if possible
1 to 1½ lbs. halibut steaks
  1 inch thick
Waxed paper
A bowl large enough to
  hold all the fish

large, cut into ½-inch pieces. Peel and de-vein the shrimp, reserving peel and also heads if you have whole fresh shrimp. Remove skin and bones from halibut, cut meat into pieces roughly 2 inches in diameter, and reserve bones and trimmings. Place each type of fish on waxed paper and pack into bowl in the order listed; cover and refrigerate. Refrigerate trimmings and reserve for the fish stock.

DECORATION NOTE: You may wish to save out some whole cooked shrimp, lobster claws, or mussels to decorate each serving; we leave this up to you.

optional fresh mussels:

2 quarts fresh mussels
½ cup dry white wine or
  dry white French ver-
  mouth

Scrub and soak the mussels, and steam them open in the wine as described in Volume I, pages 226–7. Reserve 12 pairs of shells for garnish. Place meat in a small bowl and moisten with a little of the cooking liquid; decant rest of liquid into another bowl, being sure to include no sand.

the lobsters:

You may use 8 to 12 ounces of cooked lobster meat rather than fresh lobsters; thaw if frozen, then warm in butter, wine, and seasonings, page 41, before adding to the *marmite* in the next step.

2 live lobsters, 1¼ to 1½
  lbs. each
A sieve set over a 1-quart
  bowl or small saucepan
2 to 3 Tb olive oil or cooking oil
The *marmite* (a heavy-
  bottomed, 6- to 8-quart
  enameled or stainless
  casserole or kettle, with
  cover)
2 cups combined sliced
  white of leek and onions;
  or onions only
½ cup each of sliced carrots
  and celery
2 imported bay leaves
½ tsp thyme
8 to 10 parsley stems and/
  or roots (not the leaves)

Split the lobsters in half lengthwise, discard stomach sacks in head and intestinal veins, scoop green matter and roe into sieve, and chop lobster into pieces (illustrated on page 27). Film *marmite* with ⅛ inch of oil, heat to very hot but not smoking, and sauté lobster for 3 to 4 minutes, turning frequently until lobster shells are bright red. Remove to a side dish. Lower heat, stir vegetables and herbs into pan, and sauté 8 to 10 minutes until tender but not browned. Season lobster lightly with salt, return to *marmite,* add wine, cover, and simmer slowly for 20 minutes. Then lift out lobster pieces, remove the meat and reserve it in a bowl; chop shells and return to *marmite.* At some convenient time, add soft butter to lobster green matter and rub butter with green matter through sieve into bowl; beat in the egg yolks and cream, and set aside or refrigerate. (Rinse sieve in lobster-cooking liquid to get all the flavor possible.)

Salt (none if using mussel
  or clam juice)
2 cups dry white wine or
  1½ cups dry white French
  vermouth
4 Tb soft butter
3 egg yolks
⅔ cup heavy cream

---

the fish stock—for 6 to 8 cups:

Either 2 to 3 lbs. (2 or more
  quarts) bones, heads,
  trimmings, and shells
  from the fresh fish you are
  using;
Or an extra pound of fish;
Or 3 cups clam juice

Either 2 more cups dry
  white wine;
Or 1½ cups dry white
  French vermouth (half
  the amount of either if
  you are using mussel-
  cooking liquid)
The optional mussel-
  cooking liquid and/or
  necessary cold water
2 tsp salt (none if using
  mussel liquid or clam
  juice)

Add all ingredients to the lobster-cooking *marmite*,
bring to simmer, skim, and simmer partially covered
for 40 minutes. Strain liquid into a bowl and discard
residue. Wash out *marmite* and return liquid to it;
you should have 6 to 8 cups of deliciously flavored
brew. Boil down to concentrate flavor and volume if
necessary; carefully correct seasoning.

---

2) *Final cooking and serving—about 30 minutes*

cooking the fish:

The fish stock in its
  marmite
4 Tb butter
A heavy-bottomed 3-quart
  enameled or stainless
  saucepan
⅓ cup flour (scoop cup into
  flour and level off with
  a knife)

Bring the fish stock to the boil. During this time melt
the butter in the saucepan, blend in the flour, and cook
slowly, stirring, until butter and flour foam together
for 2 minutes without browning at all. Set this *roux*
aside: it is for the sauce, next step. When stock is boiling, add the halibut (or other firm-fleshed fish);
bring liquid rapidly to the simmer and simmer 5
minutes. Then add the sole, scallops, and shrimp,
pressing them down into the liquid. If really neces-

A wooden spoon, a wire whip, a perforated skimmer, and a ladle

The bowl of prepared and refrigerated fish

The cooked lobster meat and optional mussels

More fish stock, white wine, or boiling water if needed

A large soup tureen or bowl-shaped platter set over a pan of almost simmering water

sary, add a little more liquid: ingredients should be almost covered. Bring again rapidly to the simmer for 2 minutes, then add the cooked lobster meat and optional cooked mussels. Bring again to simmer for 1 minute and remove from heat. Lift fish out and arrange in tureen; cover loosely. (Some of the fish, like sole, may have flaked apart; lift only what you easily can into the tureen.)

---

the sauce:

The flour-and-butter *roux* and cooking liquid from preceding step

More stock or cream if needed

The lobster green-matter, cream, and yolk mixture

Salt, white pepper, Cayenne pepper, and lemon juice

Reheat *roux* if necessary, remove from heat, and whisking it with a wire whip, gradually ladle into it by driblets 2 cups of hot cooking stock. When perfectly smooth, set over moderately high heat and rapidly beat in 4 to 5 more cups of stock. Simmer, stirring, for 2 minutes: sauce should be a little thicker than a fairly heavy cream soup. Boil down rapidly, stirring, if too thin; beat in a little more stock if too thick. Then, and again by driblets, beat 2 cups of hot sauce into the lobster green-matter mixture, heating it gradually to prevent it from curdling. Gradually beat it back into the hot sauce, and set sauce over moderate heat. Stir slowly with a wooden spoon, reaching all over bottom of pan until sauce thickens and comes almost to the simmer. If sauce seems too thick, stir in a little more cream or stock. Taste very carefully for seasoning, adding salt, pepper, drops of lemon juice, and so forth if you feel them necessary. Proceed immediately to the next step.

---

serving:

The optional fish decorations, such as whole shrimp, lobster shells, mussels, etc.

2 to 3 Tb minced fresh parsley and or chervil

Gently fold the hot sauce into the warm fish in the tureen. Float optional fish decorations on top and sprinkle the herbs over all. Serve as soon as possible, ladling the stew into hot plates and adding a canapé or two to each portion. This is eaten with large soup spoon, knife, and fork.

12 to 18 canapés (triangles
  of crustless homemade-
  type white bread sautéed
  in clarified butter)
Warm soup plates

(*) AHEAD-OF-TIME NOTE: May be completed a day before, serving in the *marmite* instead of a tureen. When
cold, cover and refrigerate; heat slowly to below the
simmer before serving. Like a good New England
chowder or lobster stew, it gains in flavor when made
in advance.

BOURRIDE

[Provençal Fish Stew with *Aïoli*—Garlic Mayonnaise]

This marvelous fish dinner from Provence is for garlic lovers only, as the
big chunks of fish are cooked in a broth that is then enriched with egg yolks
and a mayonnaise into which at least 1 large clove of garlic per person has been
puréed. Like *bouillabaisse,* the fish is served on a platter and the enriched broth
in a tureen, but both are eaten together in soup plates. This is such a rich dish
we suggest you serve it for lunch, and you will want nothing else but perhaps
a bit of green salad and fresh fruit. You will need a strong, dry white wine,
such as a Côtes-du-Rhône or Pinot Blanc.

For 6 to 8 people as a main course

---

1) *Preliminaries—may be done several hours before final cooking*

the fish:

3 to 4 lbs. assorted lean,
  firm-fleshed white fish,
  such as those suggested on
  pages 42–3

Prepare the fish as described, cutting it into chunks or
steaks about 3 inches in diameter and 1 to 1½ inches
thick. Refrigerate until cooking time.

the cooking broth:

1 cup each of sliced onions,
  carrots, and white of leek
  (or additional onion)
3 to 4 Tb olive oil
A heavy-bottomed 7- to 8-
  quart flameproof casserole
  or kettle
2 medium tomatoes,
  chopped
2 to 3 quarts fish trimmings,
  bones, heads; *or* 2 to 3
  cups fish; *or* 1 quart
  clam juice

Cook the vegetables in oil over low heat for 8 to 10
minutes, until tender but not browned. Add the tomatoes and cook 2 minutes, then add all the rest of
the ingredients. Bring to the simmer, skimming occasionally, and simmer partially covered for 40 minutes. Strain into a bowl, wash out casserole, and return the stock to it. Correct seasoning, adding salt if
necessary.

(*) AHEAD-OF-TIME NOTE: If prepared in advance,
cover when cool and refrigerate.

3 quarts water (2 quarts if
  you use clam juice)
2 cups dry white wine or
  1½ cups dry white French
  vermouth
2 imported bay leaves
¼ tsp each of thyme, fennel,
  and dried orange peel
2 large cloves of garlic,
  unpeeled, halved
2 large pinches saffron
  flowers
1½ Tb salt (none if you use
  clam juice)

the aïoli mayonnaise:

⅓ cup stale crumbs from
  homemade-type
  unsweetened white bread
Wine vinegar
A heavy 2½-quart mixing
  bowl or a mortar
A wooden pestle, masher,
  or heavy ladle (for
  pounding)
6 to 8 cloves garlic and
  garlic press
½ tsp salt
6 egg yolks (2 now, the rest
  later)
1½ to 2 cups olive oil
A large wire whip
White or Cayenne pepper

Moisten crumbs with a tablespoon or two of vinegar
and pound to a paste in the bowl. Purée garlic through
press into the paste and continue pounding several
minutes until absolutely smooth. Add salt and 2 of
the egg yolks and pound until mixture is very thick
and sticky. Then begin pounding and stirring in oil
by droplets until sauce is thick and heavy. Thin out
with drops of vinegar and begin beating in teaspoons
of oil with whip. Sauce should be heavy enough to
hold its shape in a spoon. Season to taste. (Note that
a more detailed recipe on *aïoli* and on mayonnaise in
general is in Volume I, page 92.)

A 2-cup serving bowl
Plastic wrap
A covered jar if needed

Scrape half the sauce into serving bowl, cover airtight,
and set aside for dining room. Beat the 4 remaining
egg yolks into the rest of the sauce; cover airtight.
(If doing in advance, transfer to a smaller container
and cover.) This second half is to be combined with
the stew just before serving.

2) *Cooking and serving*

cooking the fish:

The cooking broth
The prepared fish

About 15 minutes before serving, bring cooking broth
to a rolling boil and add the fish, pushing it down into

A large perforated skimmer
A serving platter set over a
   pan of almost simmering
   water, and a cover
2 to 3 Tb coarsely chopped
   parsley

the broth, which should barely cover it. (Add a little boiling water if necessary.) Boil slowly, uncovered, for 6 to 10 minutes, depending on thickness of fish (2 to 3 minutes only for scallops); it is done when springy rather than squashy to the touch—do not overcook. As soon as fish is done, arrange on platter, moisten with a little of the cooking broth, decorate with parsley, and cover to keep it warm.

combining cooking broth and aïoli:

The egg-yolk enriched *aïoli*
   in a 3-quart bowl
A large wire whip, a ladle,
   and a wooden spoon
A 3-cup serving bowl
Salt and white pepper
A warm soup tureen

Whisking *aïoli* with wire whip, gradually dribble in several ladlesful of hot cooking broth until 2 to 3 cups have gone in. (Ladle a cup or so of broth also into serving bowl and keep warm.) Pour *aïoli* mixture back into casserole with rest of cooking stock and set over moderate heat. Stir continually and rather slowly with wooden spoon until broth slowly thickens enough to coat the spoon—4 to 5 minutes—being careful that liquid does not come to simmer and scramble the egg yolks. Carefully correct seasoning; broth will be a beautiful, smooth, richly aromatic yellow-ivory color. Pour it into the tureen and serve immediately.

serving:

12 or more slices of hot
   French bread, ¾ inch
   thick
Wide soup plates
The reserved plain broth
The hot fish on its platter,
   and the tureen
The reserved *aïoli*
   mayonnaise

For each serving, place 2 slices of bread in a soup plate and moisten with a spoonful of plain broth. Arrange chunks of fish over the bread and ladle over it the *aïoli* broth from the tureen. Each guest adds a spoonful of *aïoli* mayonnaise, and eats the *bourride* with soup spoon and fork.

CHAPTER TWO

Baking: Breads, Brioches, Croissants, and Pastries

YEAST DOUGHS
Les Pâtes Levées

THE AVERAGE FRENCH HOUSEHOLD does no yeast baking at all except for *babas, savarins,* and an occasional *brioche.* It certainly does no bread making, and there is no need to because every neighborhood has its own *boulangerie* serving freshly baked bread every day of the week but one, usually Monday, when the *boulanger* takes his day off. Thus you cannot even find a bread pan in a French household supply store, and there are no French recipes for home-made bread. All of the recipes here, therefore, are those used by professionals whose techniques we have worked out for the home baker, using standard ingredients and household equipment.

Whether you are a home or a professional baker, you will find that time is really the key to successful bread making. Just as it takes time for cheese to ripen and wine to age, it takes time for yeast to do its full work in a dough. The function of yeast is not only to push the dough up but, equally important, to develop its flavor and its texture. Yeast feeds and multiplies on the starch in the flour. Flour also contains gluten, and it is the gluten that allows the dough to rise and stay risen in the oven because gluten molecules become gluey when moistened and join together in an elastic web throughout the dough. Then, while the yeast cells are feeding and multiplying on the starch, their voracious activity forms tiny pockets of gas that push up the sur-rounding mesh of gluten, making the dough rise. At the same time the gluten itself, if given time, goes through a slow ripening process that gives the dough flavor, cohesion, and elasticity. These important developments in the gluten must take place if a very simple dough, such as that for plain French bread, is to turn into something splendidly satisfying to eat. Thus, rather than trying to speed things up by using lots of yeast and a warm rising temperature, you want to provide time for ripening by slowing everything down with a minimum of yeast, a tepid temperature, and several risings.

Many reasons are given for the doleful state of much contemporary bread both here and in France: it is not baked in wood-fired ovens; both the flour and water are full of chemicals; it is machine-kneaded; and so forth. The villain in the bread basket is speed: the yeast has not been given the time it needs to accomplish its triple function of developing flavor and texture as well as volume.

YEAST

Yeast is a living organism, but it is inactive or dormant when you buy it, either as a fresh cake wrapped in silver paper or as dry yeast in a sealed envelope. Fresh cake yeast must be a uniformly creamy gray with no spots of discoloration, and is perishable; it will keep only about a week under refrigeration but for several weeks when wrapped airtight and frozen. Dry-active yeast should be stored in a cool, dry place, or in the refrigerator or freezer; use it before the expiration date stamped on the envelope. Either type of yeast may be used, but both must be completely liquefied before the yeast is ready to become active. Although you can mix it, as is, into the dry ingredients and blend in warm water, we prefer the almost as rapid but visually positive method of liquefying it separately.

Proving yeast

When you know your yeast is fresh, you need have no doubts about its capacities. If you think it may be stale do not hesitate to make it prove itself by dissolving it in the warm water called for in your recipe; stir in also a tablespoon of flour and a pinch of sugar. It is active and ready to use if it begins to foam and to increase in volume in about 8 minutes: the yeast cells, spurred on by the sugar, are feeding on the flour.

DOUGH TEXTURE, VOLUME OF RISE, TEMPERATURE

Anyone used to American bread making will be surprised to find that the doughs for all of the following recipes are light, soft, and sticky when first made because the dough is to triple rather than double in volume during its first and usually its second rise: this is the period during which it develops its flavor and texture. Rather than rising in a warm place of around 85 degrees, which would cause it to ferment and acquire an unpleasant yeasty-sour taste, it must rise in the low 70's if you can possibly manage it, or at an even lower temperature if you wish to delay the process.

THE WEATHER

We therefore suggest that you do not attempt your first bread-making spree in a hot kitchen. When you are used to doughs and know how they should look, smell, and feel, you can adjust your procedures to the weather, letting the dough rise part of the time in the refrigerator, for instance, or deflating it when partially risen and letting it push itself up several times. Rainy or humid weather and steamy rooms also have their adverse affect, making dough unduly sticky, even sweaty; pick a dry day and a dry room, then, for your first venture. In other words, make everything as easy as possible for yourself.

TIMING AND DELAYED ACTION

Although it will take you a minimum of 7 hours from start to finish for most of these recipes, that does not mean that you are hovering over your dough for 7 straight hours. During almost all of this time the dough is sitting quietly by itself, rising in one form or another. Because you can slow down the rise by lowering the temperature, you may set it in the refrigerator or the freezer when you have to go out, and continue when you return. Thus, although you cannot successfully speed things up, you can otherwise fit bread making into almost any pattern that suits your schedule. Each of the recipes indicates various stopping points, and a delayed-action chart is on page 68, at the end of the French bread recipe.

MACHINE VERSUS HAND MIXING

A heavy-duty table-model electric beater with a dough hook works very well for mixing and kneading dough, and can be adapted nicely to the French processes. Notes are at the end of each Master Recipe.

PLAIN FRENCH BREAD

Pain Français

A fine loaf of plain French bread, the long crackly kind a Frenchman tucks under his arm as he hurries home to the family lunch, has a very special quality. Its inside is patterned with holes almost like Swiss cheese, and when you tear off a piece it wants to come sideways; it has body, chewability, and tastes and smells of the grain. Plain French bread contains only flour, water, salt, and yeast, because that is the law in France. The method, however, is up to each individual baker. Until the 1800's and before commercial yeast was known, all bread was made with a *levain,* meaning dough left over from the previous batch; the procedure involved numerous risings and mixings to develop sufficient yeast cells for the day's quota of bread. Later a brewer's-yeast-and-flour batter was developed that simplified the process, but it was not until the 1870's that the kind of yeast we use today was manufactured in France. Since then the making of French bread has undergone many changes, some of which, notably the accelerated mechanical kneading and fast rising systems used by some bakers, have had a disastrous affect on quality. Again, this is a question of trying to save time at the expense of taste and texture, because excellent bread may be made using modern ingredients, equipment, and methods.

We have had the great good fortune of being able to work with Professor R. Calvel, of the École Professionelle de Meunerie, a trade school established in Paris to teach the profession of milling and baking to students and bakers from all over France. The science of bread making and the teaching of its art are the life work of Professor Calvel, and thanks to his enthusiastic help, which set us on the right track, we think we have developed as professional a system for the home baker as anyone could hope for. You will be amazed at how very different the process is from anything you have done before, from the mixing and rising to the very special method of forming the dough into loaves.

FLOUR

French bakers make plain French bread out of unbleached flour that has a gluten strength of 8 to 9 per cent. Most American all-purpose flour is bleached and has a slightly higher gluten content as well as being slightly finer in texture. It is easier to make bread with French flour than with American all-purpose flour, and the taste and texture of the bread are naturally more authentic. (The so-called bread flour available in some mail-order houses usually has an even higher gluten content than all-purpose flour, so do not use it for plain French bread.) You will undoubtedly wish to experiment with flours if you become a serious bread maker, but because we find that any of the familiar brands of all-purpose flour works very well, we shall not complicate the recipe by suggesting an obscure or special brand. If you do experiment, however, simply substitute your other flour for the amount called for in the recipe; you may need a little bit more water or a little bit less, but the other ingredients and the method will not change.

BAKERS' OVENS VERSUS HOME OVENS

Bakers' ovens are so constructed that one slides the formed bread dough from a wooden paddle right onto the hot, fire-brick oven floor, and a steam-injection system humidifies the oven for the first few minutes of baking. Steam allows the yeast to work a little longer in the dough and this, combined with a hot baking surface, produces an extra push of volume. In addition, steam coagulating the starch on the surface of the dough gives the crust its characteristic brown color. Although you can produce a good loaf of French bread without steam or a hot baking surface, you will get a larger and handsomer loaf when you simulate professional conditions. We give both systems—the Master Recipe, which requires no special equipment, and the simulated baker's oven system, which is described and illustrated on pages 70–2.

SOUR DOUGH

Sour dough is an American invention, not French, and you will not find anything like American sour dough in France. But you can adapt your sour dough recipe to the method described here for plain French bread. We think you will find that our recipe will give you an excellent result.

EQUIPMENT NEEDED FOR MAKING FRENCH BREAD

Unless you plan to go into the more elaborate simulation of a baker's oven, you need no unusual equipment for the following recipe. Here are the requirements, some of which may sound odd but will explain themselves when you read the recipe.

A 4- to 5-quart mixing bowl with fairly vertical rather than outward-slanting sides

A kneading surface of some sort, 1½ to 2 square feet

A rubber spatula and either a metal scraper or a stiff wide metal spatula

1 or 2 unwrinkled canvas pastry cloths or stiff linen towels upon which the dough may rise

A stiff piece of cardboard or plywood 18 to 20 inches long and 6 to 8 inches wide, for unmolding dough from canvas to baking sheet

Finely ground cornmeal, or pasta pulverized in an electric blender, to sprinkle on unmolding board so as to prevent dough from sticking

The largest baking sheet that will fit into your oven

A razor blade for slashing the top of the dough

A soft pastry brush or fine-spray atomizer for moistening dough before and during baking

A room thermometer to verify rising-temperature

✳ PAIN FRANÇAIS
[Plain French Bread]

Count on a minimum of 6½ to 7 hours from the time you start the dough to the time it is ready for the oven, and half an hour for baking. While you cannot take less time, you may take as much more time as you wish by using the delayed-action techniques described at the end of the recipe.

For 1 pound of flour, making 3 cups of dough, producing:

*3 long loaves, **baguettes**, 24 by 2 inches, or **bâtards**, 16 by 3 inches*
*Or 6 short loaves, **ficelles**, 12 to 16 by 2 inches*
*Or 3 round loaves, **boules**, 7 to 8 inches in diameter*
*Or 12 round or oval rolls, **petits pains***
*Or 1 large round or oval loaf, **pain de ménage** or **miche; pain boulot***

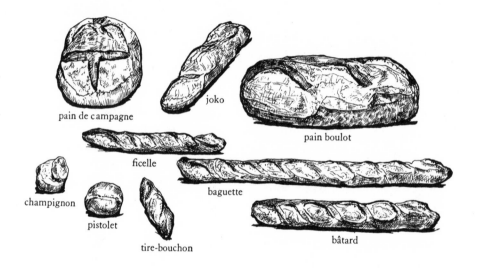

pain de campagne

joko

pain boulot

ficelle

champignon

pistolet

baguette

tire-bouchon

bâtard

---

1) *The dough mixture—le fraisage (or frasage)*

NOTE: List of equipment needed is in paragraph preceding this recipe.

---

1 cake (0.6 ounce) fresh yeast or 1 package dry-active yeast
⅓ cup warm water (not over 100 degrees) in a measure
3½ cups (about 1 lb.) all-purpose flour, measured by scooping dry-measure cups into flour and sweeping off excess
2¼ tsp salt
1¼ cups tepid water (70 to 74 degrees)

Stir the yeast in the warm water and let liquefy completely while measuring flour into mixing bowl. When yeast has liquefied, pour it into the flour along with the salt and the rest of the water.

NOTE: We do not find the food processor satisfactory here, since the dough is so soft the machine clogs; however, you can use a heavy-duty mixer with dough hook, and finish it up by hand as described on page 74.

*Stir and cut the liquids into the
flour with a rubber spatula,
pressing firmly to form a
dough, and making sure that all bits
of flour and unmassed pieces are
gathered in.* Turn dough out onto
kneading surface, scraping bowl
clean. Dough will be soft and sticky.
Let it rest for 2 to 3 minutes while
you wash and dry the bowl.

2) *Kneading—pétrissage*

The flour will have absorbed the liquid during this short rest, and the dough
will have a little more cohesion for the kneading that is about to begin. Use one hand
only for kneading and keep the other clean to hold a pastry scraper, to dip out extra
flour, to answer the telephone, and so forth. Your object in kneading is to render
the dough perfectly smooth and to work it sufficiently so that all the gluten molecules
are moistened and joined together into an interlocking web. You cannot see this
happen, of course, but you can feel it because the dough will become elastic and will
retract into shape when you push it out.

*Start kneading by lifting the near
edge of the dough, using a pastry
scraper or stiff wide spatula to
help you if necessary, and flipping
dough over onto itself.*
Scrape the dough off the surface
and slap it down; lift edge and flip
it over again, repeating the
movement rapidly.

In 2 to 3 minutes the dough
should have enough body so that
you can *give it a quick forward
push with the heel of your hand as
you flip it over.* Continue to knead
rapidly and vigorously in this way.
If it remains too sticky, knead
in a sprinkling of flour. (Whole
kneading process will take 5 to 10
minutes, depending on how
vigorous and expert you become.)

Shortly after this point, the dough should have developed enough elasticity so that it draws back into shape when pushed, indicating that the gluten molecules have united and are under tension like a thin web of rubber; the dough should also begin to clean itself off the kneading surface, although it will stick to your fingers if you hold a pinch for more than a second or two. Let it rest for 3 to 4 minutes. Knead again for a minute: the surface should now look smooth; the dough will be less sticky but it will still remain soft. It is now ready for its first rise.

3) *First rising—pointage premier temps (3 to 5 hours at around 70 degrees)*

You now have approximately 3 cups of dough that is to rise 3½ times its original volume, or to about 10½ cups. Fill the mixing bowl with 10½ cups of tepid water and make a mark to indicate that level on the outside of the bowl (note that the bowl should have fairly upright sides; if they are too outward slanting, the dough will have difficulty rising). Pour out the water, dry the bowl, and place the dough in it; slip bowl into a large plastic bag or cover with plastic, and top with a folded bath towel. Set on a wooden surface (marble or stone are too cold) or on a folded towel or pillow, and let rise free from drafts anyplace where the temperature is around 70 degrees; if the room is too hot, set bowl in water and keep renewing water to maintain it at around 70 degrees. Dough should take at least 3 hours to rise to 10½ cups; if the temperature is lower, it will simply take longer.

(*) DELAYED ACTION: See chart at end of recipe.

unrisen dough   risen dough

When fully risen, the dough will be humped into a slight dome, showing that the yeast is still active; it will be light and spongy when pressed. There will usually be some big bubbly blisters on the surface, and if you are using a glass bowl you will see bubbles through the glass.

4) *Deflating and second rising—rupture; pointage deuxième temps (1½ to 2 hours at around 70 degrees)*

The dough is now ready to be deflated, which will release the yeast-engendered gases and redistribute the yeast cells so that the dough will rise again and continue the fermentation process.

With a rubber spatula dislodge dough from inside of bowl and turn out onto a lightly floured surface, scraping the bowl clean. If dough seems damp and sweaty, sprinkle with a tablespoon of flour.

Lightly flour the palms of your hands and *flatten the dough firmly but not too roughly into a circle*, deflating any gas bubbles by pinching them.

Lift a corner of the near side and flip it down onto the far side. Do the same with the left side, then the right side. Finally lift the near side and tuck it just under the edge of the far side. The mass of dough will look like a rounded cushion.

Slip the sides of your hands under the dough and return it to the bowl. Cover and let rise again, this time to not quite triple, but again until it is dome-shaped and light and spongy when touched.

(*) DELAYED ACTION: See chart at end of recipe.

5) *Cutting and resting dough before forming loaves*

Loosen dough all around inside of bowl and turn out onto a lightly floured surface. Because of its two long rises, the dough will have much more body. If it seems damp and sweaty, sprinkle lightly with flour.

Making clean, sure cuts with a large knife or a scraper, divide dough into 3 equal pieces for long loaves, or whatever is specified for other shapes and sizes.

After you have cut each piece, lift one end and flip it over onto the opposite end to fold the dough in two; place dough at far side of kneading surface. Cover loosely with a sheet of plastic and let rest for 5 minutes before forming. This relaxes the gluten enough for shaping, but not long enough for the dough to begin rising again.

While the dough is resting, prepare the rising surface: smooth the canvas or linen toweling on a large tray or baking sheet, and rub flour thoroughly into the entire surface of the cloth to prevent the dough from sticking.

6) *Forming loaves—la tourne; la mise en forme des pâtons*

Because French bread stands free in the oven and is not baked in a pan, it has to be formed in such a way that the tension of the coagulated gluten cloak on the surface will hold the dough in shape. Following are illustrated directions for the familiar long loaf—the *bâtards* (baked size 16 by 3 inches); other shapes are described and illustrated at the end of the recipe. *Baguettes* are much too long for home ovens.

After the 3 pieces of dough have rested 5 minutes, form one piece at a time, keeping the remaining ones covered.

Working rapidly, turn the dough upside down on a lightly floured kneading surface and *pat it firmly but not too roughly into an 8- to 10-inch oval with the lightly floured palms of your hands.* Deflate any gas bubbles in the dough by pinching them.

Fold the dough in half lengthwise by bringing the far edge down over the near edge.

Being sure that the working surface is always very lightly floured so the dough will not stick and tear, which would break the lightly coagulated gluten cloak that is being formed, *seal the edges of the dough together, your hands extended, thumbs out at right angles and touching.*

Roll the dough a quarter turn forward so the seal is on top.

Flatten the dough again into an oval with the palms of your hands.

Press a trench along the central length of the oval with the side of one hand.

Fold in half again lengthwise.

This time seal the edges together with the heel of one hand, and roll the dough a quarter turn toward you so the seal is on the bottom.

Now, by rolling the dough back and forth with the palms of your hands, you will lengthen it into a sausage shape. *Start in the middle, placing your right palm on the dough, and your left palm on top of your right hand.*

Roll dough forward and backward rapidly, gradually sliding your hands toward the two ends as the dough lengthens.

Deflate any gas blisters on the surface by pinching them. Repeat the rolling movement rapidly several times until the dough is 16 inches long, or whatever length will fit on your baking sheet. During the extension rolls, keep circumference of dough as even as possible and try to start each roll with sealed side of dough down, twisting the rope of dough to straighten the line of seal as necessary. If seal disappears, as it sometimes does with all-purpose flour, do not worry.

Place the shaped piece of dough, sealed side up, at one side of the flour-rubbed canvas, leaving a free end of canvas 3 to 4 inches wide. (The top will crust slightly as the dough rises; it is turned over for baking so the soft, smooth underside will be uppermost.)

Pinch a ridge 2½ to 3 inches high in the canvas to make a trough, and a place for the next piece. Cover dough with plastic while you are forming the rest of the loaves.

long rolling pin

After all the pieces of dough are in place, brace the two sides of the canvas with long rolling pins, baking pans, or books, if the dough seems very soft and wants to spread out. Cover the dough loosely with a flour-rubbed dish towel or canvas, and a sheet of plastic. Proceed immediately to the final rising, next step.

7) *Final rise—l'apprêt—1½ to 2½ hours at around 70 degrees*

The covered dough is now to rise to almost triple in volume; look carefully at its pre-risen size so that you will be able to judge correctly. It will be light and swollen when risen, but will feel still a little springy when pressed.

It is important that the final rise take place where it is dry; if your kitchen is damp, hot, and steamy, let the bread rise in another room or dough will stick to canvas and you will have difficulty getting it off and onto the baking sheet. It will turn into bread in the oven whatever happens, but you will have an easier time and a better loaf if you aim for ideal conditions.

Preheat oven to 450 degrees 30 minutes before estimated baking time.

(*) DELAYED ACTION: See chart at end of recipe.

8) *Unmolding risen dough onto baking sheet—le démoulage*

The 3 pieces of risen dough are now to be unmolded from the canvas and arranged upside down on the baking sheet. The reason for this reversal is that the present top of the dough has crusted over during its rise; the smooth, soft underside should be uppermost in the oven so that the dough can expand and allow the loaf its final puff of volume. For the unmolding you will need a non-sticking intermediate surface such as a stiff piece of cardboard or plywood sprinkled with cornmeal or pulverized pasta.

Remove rolling pins or braces.
Place the long side of the board at
one side of the dough; pull the
edge of the canvas to flatten it; then
raise and flip the dough softly
upside down onto the board.

Dough is now lying along one edge of the unmolding board: rest this edge on the right side of a lightly buttered baking sheet. Gently dislodge dough onto baking sheet, keeping same side of dough uppermost: this is the soft smooth side, which was underneath while dough rose on canvas. If necessary, run sides of hands lightly down the length of the dough to straighten it. Unmold the next piece of dough the same way, placing it to the left of the first, leaving a 3-inch space. Unmold the final piece near the left side of the sheet.

9) *Slashing top of the dough—la coupe*

The top of each piece of dough is now to be slashed in several places. This opens the covering cloak of gluten and allows a bulge of dough underneath to swell up through the cuts during the first 10 minutes of baking, making decorative patterns in the crust. These are done with a blade that cuts almost horizontally into the dough to a depth of less than half an inch. Start the cut at the middle of the blade, drawing toward you in a swift, clean sweep. This is not quite as easy as it sounds, and you will probably make ragged cuts at first; never mind, you will improve with practice. Use an ordinary razor blade and slide one side of it into a cork for safety; or buy a barber's straight razor at a cutlery store.

For a 16- to 18-inch loaf make
3 slashes. Note that those at the 2
ends go straight down the loaf but
are slightly off center, while the
middle slash is at a slight angle
between the two. Make the first cut
at the far end, then the middle
cut, and finally the third.
Remember that the blade should
lie almost parallel to the surface
of the dough.

10) *Baking—about 25 minutes; oven preheated to 450 degrees*

As soon as the dough has been slashed, moisten the surface either by painting with a soft brush dipped in cold water, or with a fine-spray atomizer, and slide baking sheet onto rack in upper third of preheated oven. Rapidly paint or spray dough with cold water after 3 minutes, again in 3 minutes, and a final time 3 minutes later. Moistening the dough at this point helps the crust to brown and allows the yeast action to continue in the dough a little longer. The bread should be done in about 25 minutes; the crust will be crisp, and the bread will make a hollow sound when thumped.

If you want the crust to shine, paint lightly with a brush dipped in cold water as soon as you slide baking sheet out of oven.

11) *Cooling—2 to 3 hours*

Cool the bread on a rack or set it upright in a basket or large bowl so that air can circulate freely around each piece. Although bread is always exciting to eat fresh from the oven, it will have a much better taste when the inside is thoroughly cool and has composed itself.

12) *Storing French bread*

Because it contains no fats or preservatives of any kind, French bread is at its best when eaten the day it is baked. It will keep for a day or two longer, wrapped airtight and refrigerated, but it will keep best if you freeze it—let the loaves cool first, then wrap airtight. To thaw, unwrap and place on a baking sheet in a cold oven; heat the oven to 400 degrees. In about 20 minutes the crust will be hot and crisp, and the bread thawed. The French, of course, never heat French bread except possibly on Monday, the baker's holiday, when the bread is a day old.

13) *Canvas housekeeping*

After each bread session, if you have used canvas, brush it thoroughly to remove all traces of flour and hang it out to dry before putting away. Otherwise the canvas could become moldy and ruin your next batch of dough.

DELAYED ACTION

Starting and stopping the dough process

As noted in the Master Recipe, there are numerous points at which you can slow down the action or stop it altogether, by setting the dough in a colder place, or refrigerating or freezing it. Exact timings for any of these delaying procedures are impossible to give because so much depends on what has taken place during the slow-down, how cold the dough is when it starts to rise again, and so forth. All you need to remember is that you are in complete control: you can always push down a partially risen dough; you can slow the action with cold; you can speed it with warmth. You will work out your own systems and the following chart will help you:

TO DELAY THE FIRST RISING, SET DOUGH IN A COLDER PLACE

Approximate Hours of Rise   at Degrees F.

5–6	65
7–8	55
9–10	Refrigerator

TO STOP ACTION ALTOGETHER AFTER FIRST OR SECOND RISE

Deflate, wrap airtight, and freeze. *Limit:* A week to 10 days, probably more for plain French bread dough, and risky after 10 days for doughs with butter and eggs. (We shall not venture farther upon this uncertain limb.)

TO DELAY SECOND RISING

a) Set dough in a colder place.
b) Set a plate on top of dough and a 5-lb. weight; refrigerate.

TO DELAY OR FREEZE AFTER DOUGH IS FORMED

a) Set dough in a colder place.
b) Form dough on lightly oiled sheet; cover airtight and refrigerate or freeze, but note preceding time limit.

TO START ACTION AFTER THAWING

a) Thaw overnight in refrigerator; complete the rise at room temperature.
b) Set at 80 degrees until thawed; complete the rise at room temperature.

VARIATIONS

Other Forms for French Bread

Long thin loaves (*ficelles, baked size: 12 to 16 by 1½ inches*)

Cut the original dough, Step 5, page 61, into 5 or 6 pieces and form as illustrated in the recipe, but making thinner sausage shapes about ½ inch in diameter. When they have risen, slash as illustrated, Step 9.

Oval rolls (*petits pains, tire-bouchons*)

Cut the dough into 10 or 12 pieces and form like *bâtards,* but you will probably not have to lengthen them at all after the two foldings and sealings. When they have risen, make either 2 parallel slashes, or a single slash going from one end to the other.

Round loaves (*pain de ménage, miches, boules*)

When you want bread for big sandwiches or for toast, a big round loaf is attractive. The object here is to force the cloak of coagulated gluten to hold the ball of dough in shape: the first movement will make a cushion; the second will seal and round the ball, establishing surface tension. To begin the process, after the risen dough has been cut and has rested 5 minutes, Step 5, page 62, place it on a lightly floured surface.

Lift the left side of the dough with the side of your left hand and bring it down almost to the other side.

Scoop up that side and *push it back almost to the left side.* Revolve dough a quarter turn clockwise and repeat the movement eight to ten times. This movement gradually smooths the bottom of the dough and establishes the necessary surface tension; think of the surface of the dough as if it were a fine sheet of rubber you were stretching in every direction.

Then turn the dough smooth side up and *begin rotating it between the palms of your hands, tucking a bit of the dough under the ball as you rotate it.* In a dozen turns you should have a neatly shaped ball with a little pucker of dough, *la clé,* underneath where the edges have all joined together.

Place the dough pucker side up on flour-rubbed canvas; seal the pucker by pinching with your fingers. Flour lightly, cover loosely, and let rise to almost triple its size. After unmolding upside down on the baking sheet, slash it as follows:

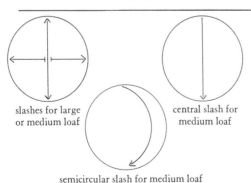

slashes for large or medium loaf

central slash for medium loaf

semicircular slash for medium loaf

Large loaves are usually slashed in a cross: make one vertical slash and complete the horizontal cuts as illustrated. Medium loaves may have a cross, a single central slash, or a semicircular slash around half the circumference.

Round rolls (*petits pains, champignons*)

Cut the original dough, Step 5, page 62, into 10 to 12 pieces. After they have rested 5 minutes, form them one at a time, leaving the rest of the dough covered. The principles are the same here as for the preceding round loaves, but make the preliminary cushion shape with your fingers rather than the palms of your hands.

For the second stage, during which the ball of dough is rotated smooth side up, *roll it under the palm of one hand, using your thumb and little finger to push the edges of the dough underneath and to form the pucker, where the edges join together.*

Place the formed ball of dough pucker side up on the flour-rubbed canvas and cover loosely while forming the rest. Space the balls 2 inches apart. When risen to almost triple its size, lift gently with lightly floured fingers and place pucker side down on baking sheet. Rolls are usually too small for a cross; make either one central slash or the semicircular cut.

THE SIMULATED BAKER'S OVEN

Baking in the ordinary way, as described in the preceding recipe, produces an acceptable loaf of bread, but does not nearly approach the glory you can achieve when you turn your home oven into a baker's oven. Merely providing yourself with the proper amount of steam, if you do nothing else, will vastly improve the crust, the color, the slash patterns, and the volume of your bread; steam is only a matter of plopping a heated brick or stone into a pan of water in the bottom of the oven. The second provision is a hot surface upon which the naked dough can bake; this gives that added push of volume that improves both the appearance and the slash patterns. When you have the hot baking surface, you will then also need a paddle or board upon which you can transfer dough from canvas to hot baking surface. For the complete setup, here is what you should have, and any building-supply store stocks these items.

For the hot baking surface

Metal will not do as a hot baking surface because it burns the bottom of the dough. The most practical and easily obtainable substance is ordinary red floor tiles $\frac{1}{4}$ inch thick. They come in various sizes such as 6 by 6 inches, 6 by 3 inches, and you need only enough to line the surface of an oven rack. Look them up under *Tiles* in your directory, and ask for "quarry tiles," their official name.

For unmolding the risen dough from its canvas

A piece of $\frac{3}{16}$-inch plywood about 20 inches long and 8 inches wide.

For sliding the dough onto the hot asbestos

When you are doing 3 long loaves, you must slide them together onto the hot asbestos; to do so you unmold them one at a time from the canvas with one board and arrange them side by side on the second board, which takes the place of the baker's wooden paddle, *la pelle.* Buy a piece of 3/16-inch plywood slightly longer but 2 inches narrower than your oven rack.

To prevent dough from sticking to unmolding and sliding boards

White cornmeal or small pasta pulverized in the electric blender until it is the consistency of table salt. This is called *fleurage.*

The steam contraption

Something that you can heat to sizzling hot on top of the stove and then slide into a pan of water in the oven to make a great burst of steam: a brick, a solid 10-lb. rock, piece of cast iron or other metal. A 9 x 12-inch roasting pan 2 inches deep to hold an inch of water and the hot brick.

Nonessential professional equipment

Instead of letting the formed dough rise on canvas, *sur couche,* many French bakers place each piece in a canvas-lined wicker or plastic form called a *banneton;* from this you turn the risen dough upside down directly onto a board and then slide it into the oven. Various sizes and shapes are available in French bakery-supply houses.

banneton—24 inches long

These are bakers's blades, *lames,* for slashing dough; they are about 4 inches long and 1/4 inch wide, with very sharp, curved ends.

USING THE SIMULATED BAKER'S OVEN

At least 30 to 40 minutes before the end of the final rise, Step 7 in the Master Recipe, line the rack of your oven with quarry tiles, slide onto upper-third level, and preheat oven to 450 degrees. At the same time set the brick or metal over very high heat on top of the stove so that it will get sizzling hot, the hotter the better.

Provide yourself with 2 stiff spoons or spatulas, or with fire tongs for lifting brick from stove top into pan of water in bottom of oven when the time comes, and test lifting the brick to be sure you have the instruments to do the job.
NOTE: You may use a spray bottle rather than a brick; it works reasonably well though less dramatically.

When the final rise is complete, sprinkle pulverized cornmeal or pasta on the long side of the unmolding board and on the surface of the sliding board. Your object now is to unmold the loaves one at a time from the canvas to the sliding board, then to slide the 3 of them together onto the hot tiles in the oven. Place the long side of board at one side of the dough, *then raise and flip the dough softly upside down onto board.*

Slip the dough, still upside down, from the unmolding board onto the right side of the sliding board. Line up the rest of the dough side by side in the same manner.

Slash the dough as described in Step 9, page 66.

Place pan of cold water on the lowest rack of an electric oven, or on the floor of a gas oven, add sizzling hot brick, and close oven door.

The 3 pieces of dough are now to be slid together off the sliding board onto the hot tiles in the oven: the movement is one quick, smooth jerk like that old magician's trick of pulling the cloth from under a tableful of dishes. Open the oven and, holding the sliding board at the two ends nearest you, rapidly extend your arms so the far end of the board rests on the far end of the asbestos at the back of the oven. Then with one quick jerk, pull the board toward you and the three loaves will slide off onto the tiles. This must be a fast and confident action because if you pause midway, the dough will rumple off the board and once it touches the hot tiles you cannot move or reshape it, although it will come loose after 5 to 6 minutes of baking. You may muff this every once in a while, and produce some queerly deformed shapes, but they will all bake into bread.

Remove the brick and pan of water after 5 to 8 minutes of baking; the crust will have started to brown lightly. The oven should be dry for the rest of the baking. Total baking time will be about 25 minutes for *bâtards;* the bread is done when it makes a hollow thump if tapped, and when the crust is crisp and, hopefully, nicely browned.

SELF-CRITICISM—OR HOW TO IMPROVE THE PRODUCT

Certainly one of the fascinating aspects of cooking is that you can almost endlessly improve upon what you have done, and when you realize that professional bakers have spent years learning their trade it would be surprising indeed if your first loaves were perfect in every respect. If they seem below standard in any of the following points, here are some possible explanations.

Crust did not brown

If you have not used the hot brick and pan of water steam-contraption, you will not get a very brown crust. Or if you have used the brick, perhaps it was not really sizzling hot; heat it 15 minutes longer the next time, or use 2 bricks. On the other hand, your oven thermostat might be inaccurate, and the oven was not really at the required 450 degrees. A third possibility is that your dough might have been under-salted; check your measurements carefully in Step 1 the next time.

Crust was too brown or too red

If you were using the brick system, you might have had too much steam in the oven; next time use a smaller brick, or heat it a little less, or take it out several minutes sooner. Another possibility is that the dough mixture in Step 1 got an overdose of salt, and salt affects color; next time be sure your teaspoons are level.

Crust was tough

A tough crust is usually due to humidity: the day was damp and sticky, or your kitchen was steamy, and the starch has coagulated and hardened on the surface of the dough.

Slashes did not bulge open in the crust

Go over the instructions in Step 9 to check on whether you cut them as directed. On the other hand, it might be that the bread had over-risen in Step 7, just before baking, and the yeast had no strength left for its final push in the oven. Conversely, you might not have let it rise enough in this step and the dough was too heavy to bulge out the way it should.

Bread seems heavy; no holes inside

This is always due to insufficient rising, particularly during the pre-bake rise in Step 7. Next time be sure it feels light and springy, and looks swollen, and that it has risen to almost triple its original size before it goes into the oven.

Flavor is uninteresting

Again, the only reason for this is insufficient time taken for rising: the yeast has not had an opportunity to produce the slow aging and maturing that develops flavor. For your next batch, follow the timing and temperature requirements particularly in Step 3, for the first rise.

Flavor is unpleasantly yeasty or sour

A yeasty over-fermented smell and taste are due more often to the dough having risen at too high a temperature than to its having over-risen. Next time, watch the room temperature at which it is rising, and if you are making bread in hot weather, you will have to take a longer time and let it rise in the refrigerator.

MACHINE MIXING AND KNEADING OF FRENCH BREAD DOUGH

French bread dough is too soft to work in the electric food processor, but the heavy-duty mixer with dough hook, illustrated in the equipment section at the end of the book, works perfectly. The dough-hook attachment that comes with some hand-held electric mixers and the hand-cranking bread pails are slower and less efficient, to our mind, than hand kneading. In any case, when you are using electricity, follow the steps in the recipe as outlined, including the rests; do not over-knead, and for the heavy-duty mixer, do not go over a moderate speed of number 3 or 4, or you risk breaking down the gluten in the dough. When the kneading is finished, take the dough out of the bowl and give it a minute or so of hand kneading, just to be sure it is smooth and elastic throughout. Then proceed with the recipe as usual, from Step 3 on.

---

* PAIN DE MIE

[White Sandwich Bread—for sandwiches, canapés, toast, and croûtons]

French covered pan

French cylindrical mold
with hinged cover

It is almost impossible in present-day America to find the firm, close-grained, evenly rectangular, unsliced type of white bread that is essential for professional-looking canapés, appetizers, and fancy sandwiches. In French this is *pain de mie,* meaning that the *mie,* the crumb or inside, is more important than the crust; in fact the crust exists merely as a thin and easily sliced covering. French *boulangeries* form and bake the bread in special covered molds; the bread rises during baking so that it fills the mold completely and emerges absolutely symmetrical. The form can be round or cylindrical, but it is usually rectangular. You can easily achieve the round or the rectangular shapes by baking in any straight-sided bread pan or baking dish, covering the pan with foil and a baking sheet, and topping that with some kind of weight to keep the bread from pushing up out of shape while it is in the oven.

For about 1 pound of flour, making 3 cups of dough, to fill one 8-cup covered pan or two 4-cup covered pans

---

1) *The preliminary dough mixture—le fraisage. Either by hand:*

1 cake (0.6 ounce) fresh yeast, or 1 package dry-active yeast

3 Tb warm water (not over 100 degrees) in a measure

2 tsp salt

1⅓ cups tepid milk in a measure

3½ cups unbleached all-purpose flour (scooped and leveled, page 544)

A 4- to 5-quart bowl with fairly straight sides

A rubber spatula, and a pastry scraper or stiff metal blade

Mix the yeast in the warm water and let it liquefy completely while measuring out the rest of the ingredients. Dissolve the salt in the tepid milk. Measure the flour into the mixing bowl. Then stir in the liquefied yeast and salted milk with a rubber spatula, cutting and pressing the dough firmly together into a mass, being sure all bits of flour and unblended pieces are gathered in. Turn dough out onto a flat kneading surface, scraping bowl clean. Dough will be quite soft and sticky; let it rest for 2 to 3 minutes while you wash and dry the bowl.

2) Kneading—pétrissage

Start kneading by lifting the near side of the dough, using a scraper or spatula to help you, and flipping it over onto the other side. Scrape dough off surface and slap down again; lift, flip over and slap down again, repeating the movement rapidly.

In 2 to 3 minutes dough should have enough body so that you can *give it a quick forward push with the heel of your hand as you flip it over.* If it remains too sticky for this, knead in a sprinkling of flour. When it begins to clean itself off the working surface and draw back into shape, it is ready for the next step—kneading in the butter.

3) Kneading in the butter

4 Tb (½ stick) chilled butter

When butter is incorporated into a dough in most French recipes, it is added after kneading.

Soften the butter by beating it with a rolling pin. Then smear it out with a scraper, spatula, or the heel of your hand until it is soft and malleable but still cold.

By tablespoon bits, start rapidly folding and smearing the butter into the dough with the heel (not the palm) of your hand, then gather the dough into a mass with your scraper and smear again. Keep working in more bits of butter as each previous addition is partially absorbed.

Dough will be ropy, very messy,
and even stickier until it begins to
absorb the butter. *Work fast to pre-*
vent the butter from turning oily,
always using the heel of your hand,
and also cutting the dough with
scraper or spatula. In a few minutes
dough will again become smooth
and elastic. Proceed to Step 4.

Or make the preliminary dough in the food processor (steel blade):

Using the same proportions as for hand-made dough, dissolve the yeast and add
it to the salted milk. Place the 3½ cups of flour in the container of the food processor
(unless you have a small machine, in which case divide all ingredients by half and
do it in two batches). Cut the butter into pieces, and add to the flour, along with
the salt. Process for several seconds until butter is broken into flour, then with the
processor going, pour in 1¼ cups of yeast-milk; continue pouring by driblets, watching carefully, until dough balls up on top of steel blade. Process, with dough riding
on blade, for 15 seconds—this constitutes the preliminary kneading. Turn the dough
out onto your work surface and proceed to Step 4, below.

NOTE: If you happen to add too much liquid and the machine clogs, sprinkle in
more flour and the machine will often start up again. If not, remove dough and
continue by hand.

4) Then let the dough rest 2 to 3 minutes. Knead again briefly with the heel of
your hand until dough begins to clean the butter off the kneading surface and off
your hand. It is now sufficiently kneaded, although it will remain quite soft and
somewhat sticky.

5) *First rising—pointage premier temps—3 to 4 hours*
   at around 70 degrees

The clean 4- to 5-quart
mixing bowl
A large plastic bag that
bowl will fit into, or
a large sheet of plastic
A bath towel

You will have about 3 cups of unrisen dough, and it
is to rise 3 ½ times in volume or to 10 ½ cups. Fill
the bowl with 10 ½ cups of tepid water and make a
mark on the outside to guide you; pour out the water,
dry the bowl, and place the dough in it. Slip bowl
into plastic bag or top with plastic and cover with the
towel. Set on a wooden or plastic surface or on a
folded towel or pillow and place at a temperature of
68 to 72 degrees.

Dough should take a minimum of 3 hours to rise for the yeast to do its best work. When dough has risen to the 10½-cup mark, or to 3½ times its original volume, it will feel light and springy when pressed, and is ready for its second rise.

(*) DELAYED ACTION: See chart on page 68.

6) *Deflating and second rising—rupture; pointage deuxième temps—1½ to 2 hours at around 70 degrees*

The dough is now to be thoroughly deflated and folded to expel accumulated gas, and to redistribute the yeast into an even finer network of gluten that will result in a close-grained texture when the bread is baked.

With a rubber spatula or the slightly cupped fingers of one hand, dislodge dough from inside of bowl and turn out onto a lightly floured surface, scraping the bowl clean. If dough seems damp and sweaty, sprinkle with a tablespoon of flour.

With the lightly floured palms of your hands, pat and push the dough out onto a roughly shaped rectangle 10 to 12 inches long.

With the help of a scraper or spatula, fold the right side over toward the center, then fold the left side over to cover it, as though folding a business letter. Pat the dough out again into a rectangle, fold again in three, and put the dough back in the bowl. Cover with plastic and towel and let rise a second time, to not quite triple in volume, or to slightly below the 10½-cup mark on the bowl.

(*) DELAYED ACTION: See chart on page 68. If you want to freeze the dough, however, you can do it after the next step.

6) *Molding and final rising—la mise en forme; l'apprêt—40 to 60 minutes at 75 to 80 degrees*

White vegetable shortening
An 8-cup rectangular
breadpan with vertical
or only slightly outward-
slanting sides (for
example, 9½ by 5½
inches, 2¾ inches deep),
or a round pan, or two
4-cup pans

Remember to preheat oven to 435 degrees in time for next step. Grease inside of bread pan (if pan is new, grease heavily then roll flour around inside and knock out excess). With a rubber spatula or the slightly cupped fingers of one hand, loosen dough from bowl and turn out onto a lightly floured surface. If you are making 2 loaves, cut dough cleanly in half with one chop of a long knife. Lift one end of dough and flip it over on to its opposite end. To relax the gluten and make dough easier to form, let rest 7 to 8 minutes covered with plastic.

Following are illustrated directions for forming rectangular loaves. For cylindrical and circular forms, use the French bread system, pages 68–9.

With the lightly floured palms of your hands, pat and push the dough out into a roughly shaped rectangle slightly longer than your bread pan.

Fold the dough in half lengthwise.

Seal edges of dough together with your thumbs as illustrated, or with the heel of one hand. Roll dough a quarter turn forward, so seal is on top.

*Flatten the dough again into
a rectangle.*

*Press a trench along the central
length of the dough with the
side of your hand.*

*Fold again in two lengthwise and
seal the edges together with the
heel of your hand.* Roll dough a
quarter turn toward you, so seal is
underneath.

*Place the dough smooth side up in
the prepared pan, pressing it down
snugly into the corners with your
knuckles.* Pan should be no more
than $\frac{1}{3}$ to $\frac{2}{3}$ full.

(*) You can freeze the dough at this point (see page 68), wrapping pan air-tight. To continue with the recipe, let thaw for several hours in the refrigerator or at room temperature.

For the final rising, set pan uncovered at a temperature of 75 to 80 degrees until dough has risen to slightly more than double, or to fill the pan by no more than ¾. It is important when you are to bake in a covered pan that you do not let the dough rise more than this, as it must have room to finish swelling and to fill the pan while it is in the oven. When dough has risen, bake at once.

(*) You can delay the rising action by setting the pan in the refrigerator, or even by weighting it down under refrigeration. In either case, the pan should be covered airtight, then set uncovered at room temperature for 20 to 30 minutes before baking. If dough has over-risen, bake it uncovered or deflate by pressing it down and letting it rise again to the correct height.

---

7) Baking, cooling, and storing—oven at 435 degrees; baking time 40 minutes

A perfectly smooth sheet of aluminum foil 1½ inches larger all around than bread pan, and greased on shiny side

A baking sheet or a pan large enough to cover entire top of bread pan

A 5-pound weight of some sort, such as a brick

A cake rack, for cooling bread after baking

Oven has been preheated to 435 degrees. Cover bread pan with aluminum foil, greased side down. Set pan on a rack in middle level of preheated oven, cover pan with baking sheet or second pan, and center the weight on top.

Bake undisturbed for 35 to 40 minutes (30 for small loaves), then slide rack to front of oven. Standing well enough aside in case bread should burst out of pan (which could occur only if you had let it over-rise before baking), see if bread is done. The bread should have shrunk slightly from sides of pan so it will unmold easily, and the crust should be lightly browned. When thumped, the loaf should make a hollow sound. If not quite done, return to pan, cover with foil and baking sheet, and bake 5 to 10 minutes more. Unmold and cool on a rack.

When thoroughly cool, in 1½ to 2 hours, wrap airtight and refrigerate. Flavor and texture improve after 12 to 24 hours, and you should probably wait 36 hours if you want very thin slices for sandwiches or Melba toast.

This bread freezes perfectly; thaw it in its wrapper either in the refrigerator or at room temperature.

VARIATIONS

Baking in an uncovered pan—the conventional loaf

If you want a loaf that swells up in the oven, bake the dough in an open pan, one that holds twice the volume of the unrisen dough, in this case a 6-cup pan. During its final rise, Step 6, let the dough come up almost to the edge of the pan. Just before baking, glaze the top of the dough by painting it with a tablespoon of milk in which you have dissolved ⅛ teaspoon of sugar. Oven temperature and timing are the same as in the preceding Master Recipe; if the top of the bread seems to be coloring too much, cover loosely with heavy brown paper or a sheet of aluminum foil.

Omitting the butter

You may omit the butter in the Master Recipe if you wish. This will give you a lighter and whiter loaf; you may prefer it this way for Melba toast.

Melba toast—to serve with consommé, foie gras, caviar

Use 2-day-old *pain de mie*. Cut off the crusts at the two ends. With a very sharp long knife, such as a ham slicer, cut the bread into even slices less than ⅟₁₆-inch thick. Arrange the slices, overlapping them by no more than a third of their length, on 1 or 2 large baking sheets and set in upper- and lower-middle levels of a 275-degree oven for about an hour, turning bread over once or twice and switching baking sheets from one rack to the other. Toast is done when bread is crisp, slightly curly, and a very pale brown. When cold and wrapped airtight, Melba toast freezes perfectly; thaw and re-crisp for a few minutes in a 350-degree oven.

Pain de Mie aux Raisins

[Raisin Bread—to serve with tea, or for toast. See also
Pain Brioché aux Raisins, page 84]

For 4 cups of risen dough, filling two 5-cup covered pans or
one 8-cup open pan

1 to 1½ cups (5 to 8 ounces) small currant raisins Ingredients for *pain de mie*, preceding Master Recipe	To soften the raisins, soak in 1 quart of very hot water for 10 to 15 minutes. Drain, twist hard in the corner of a towel to squeeze out as much accumulated water as possible. Pat thoroughly dry in paper towels; spread out on a dry towel until you are ready to use them. Knead the raisins into the dough near the end of Step 3, when the butter has been almost absorbed. Since the weight of the raisins will hold the dough

down, the first rise, Step 5, will be only to triple in
the allotted time. Baking time and oven temperature
are the same as for *pain de mie.*

Pain Brioché—Brioche Commune—Pain Louis XV

[Egg Bread—to serve with butter and jam, for fancy sandwiches
such as mousse of *foie gras,* for toast; an alternate to *brioche* dough for
Koulibiac, sausage in *brioche,* and their like]

This is a lovely light-textured yellow bread. With another egg and three
times the butter it would be a true *brioche.* Although you will find this dough
quite a bit stickier and softer to handle than *pain de mie,* the technique for
making it is the same.

*For about 1 pound of flour, making 4 cups of unrisen dough,
to fill two 6-cup covered pans, two 4-cup open pans, or for 2 dozen
individual rolls formed in small molds or muffin tins*

---

1) Mixing and kneading the dough—either by hand or machine

1 package (0.6 ounce) fresh
yeast or 1 package dry-
active yeast

¼ cup warm water in a
measure

1 Tb salt

2 Tb sugar

¼ cup tepid milk

3½ cups (about 1 lb.) all-
purpose flour (measure
by scooping dry-measure
cups into flour and
sweeping off excess)

A 4- to 5-quart mixing
bowl with fairly straight
rather than outward-
slanting sides

4 eggs (U.S. graded
"large"; if chilled, set
for 5 minutes in warm
water)

Sprinklings of flour as
needed

1 stick (4 ounces) chilled
butter

Sprinkle yeast in warm water and let liquefy completely. Then stir in the salt, sugar, and milk. Measure
the flour into the mixing bowl, make a well in the
center, add the eggs and the yeast mixture. Cut and
mix everything together with a rubber spatula to form
a dough. Turn out onto kneading surface and let
dough rest for 2 to 3 minutes. Following illustrated
directions for *pain de mie* pages 76–7, knead by lifting,
folding, slapping, and pushing with the heel of your
hand. Dough will be stickier than that for *pain de
mie;* if it remains unusually so, knead in a tablespoon
or so more flour. When dough begins to clean itself
off kneading surface, start working in the butter by
tablespoon bits. When butter is absorbed, let dough
rest for 2 to 3 minutes. Knead again briefly until
dough cleans butter off kneading surface and off your
hands.

*Or mix and knead the dough in a food processor, fol-
lowing directions for* pain de mie, *on page 77.*

2) *Completing the bread*

Follow Steps 5, 6, and 7 in the Master Recipe for the first and second risings in a covered bowl and the final rise in the bread pan. Follow Step 8 for baking, except preheated oven should be at 400 degrees and baking time will be about 35 minutes. The surrounding crust will be a little darker than for *pain de mie*. *Pain brioché* may be eaten warm or cold, although it will slice more easily after 24 hours. It freezes perfectly.

Pain Brioché aux Raisins
[Egg Bread with Raisins]

Pain brioché makes heavenly raisin bread, eaten plain with butter, or toasted. Follow directions for *pain de mie aux raisins,* page 82.

BRIOCHES

Although the wonderfully buttery, light, and thoroughly delectable texture of fresh *brioches* may persuade you they are manna from another planet, *brioche* dough differs from *pain de mie* dough only in that eggs are used rather than milk, and a very much larger proportion of butter is incorporated. Actually, you can use equal amounts of butter and flour, but we think the proportions of 3 parts butter to 4 parts flour make a much more manageable dough with a delicious texture and taste.

In France, *brioches* are served for breakfast with butter and jam, or for tea, or with the coffee break. Stale *brioche* may be sliced and toasted, or hollowed out and used as a container for sauced foods or appetizers.

NOTE: The following recipe is for the classic hand-made *brioche* dough. For making it in the electric food processor, follow the general directions for *pain de mie* on page 77, first dissolving the yeast, then mixing it with the eggs, before blending the butter and flour in the processor with the salt and sugar. Blend in ¾ of the liquid, then add the rest by dribbles until the dough balls up on the blade. Finish kneading briefly by hand, as described at the end of Step 4.

✳ *PÂTE À BRIOCHE FINE*

[*Brioche* Dough—for all sizes and shapes of *brioches*, and for *Koulibiac*, sausage in *brioche*, and their like]

large brioche   fluted tin   small brioche

You must allow a minimum 8½ hours from the time you start *brioche* dough to the time it is ready for the oven. Five hours are needed for the first rise, 2 for the second, half an hour for chilling, and 1 to 1½ hours for the final pre-bake rise. You may find it convenient to start the first rise in the late afternoon and complete the second one overnight in the refrigerator; you can then form and bake the *brioche* in the morning. However, as you will see from the delayed-action notes in the recipe, you can pretty well make it suit whatever schedule you wish.

For about ½ pound of flour, making 2⅔ cups of unrisen dough, enough to fill one 6-cup mold or nine to ten ½-cup molds

1) *The preliminary dough mixture—le fraisage*

3 eggs (U.S. graded "large"; if chilled, place in warm water for 5 minutes)
A 2-cup measure
A fork

Warm the eggs if chilled. Break them into the measure and blend with a fork. You should have ⅔ cup.

1 cake fresh yeast (0.6 ounce) or 1 package dry-active yeast
3 Tb warm water (not over 100 degrees) in a measure
1 tsp sugar

Mix the yeast in the warm water, add the sugar, and let yeast liquefy completely.

1¾ cups (about 8 ounces) all-purpose flour (measure by scooping dry-measure cups into flour and sweeping off excess)
A 3- to 4-quart mixing bowl
A rubber spatula
2 tsp sugar
1¼ tsp salt
A pastry scraper or stiff spatula

Measure the flour into the mixing bowl. Make a well in the center with the rubber spatula and pour in the eggs. Sprinkle on the additional sugar and the salt; scrape in the liquefied yeast mixture. Cut and stir liquids and flour together with a rubber spatula, then turn out onto kneading surface, scraping bowl clean. Dough will be very soft and sticky. Work it with scraper or stiff spatula for a moment to blend ingredients completely, then scrape to side of kneading surface and let dough rest while you prepare the butter, next step.

---

2) *Preparing the butter*

6 ounces (1½ sticks) chilled unsalted butter
A rolling pin

Soften the butter by beating it with a rolling pin.

Smear it out with a scraper, spatula, or the heel of your hand until it is soft and malleable but still cold. Place at one corner of kneading surface until you are ready to use it, Step 4 (refrigerate in hot weather).

3) Kneading—pétrissage

This will be a very soft and sticky dough that now contains the minimum amount of flour; you will probably knead in more if dough remains too soft. Knead with one hand, keeping the other clean for emergencies.

---

*Using scraper or spatula, start
flipping the near side of the dough
over onto the far side,* the right
side onto the left, and so forth,
rapidly and vigorously a dozen
times or more until dough begins
to have body and elasticity.

When dough has enough body,
*lift and slap it down roughly on the
kneading surface repeatedly,* using
scraper to help you. Sprinkle on
more flour by tablespoons (up to 3
or 4 in all if necessary) if dough
remains too soft and sticky.

It should be a soft dough that will stick to your fingers if you hold a pinch of it for more than 2 to 3 seconds. Knead until it has enough elasticity to draw back into shape when pushed out, probably 4 to 5 minutes, then let it rest for 2 to 3 minutes. Knead again for a moment and it is ready for the butter.

---

4) Kneading in the butter

*By 2-tablespoon bits, start
folding, kneading, and smearing
the butter into the dough with the
heel of your hand;* then gather
the dough into a mass, chopping it
into small pieces with your
scraper and smearing again. Keep
working in more bits of butter
as each previous addition is partially
absorbed.

Dough will be ropy, sticky, and very messy indeed until it begins to absorb the butter. Work rapidly, especially if the kitchen is warm, and be sure you are using the heel, not the palm, of your hand.

You may finish kneading with a scraper or spatula, which will prevent the butter from becoming too warm and turning oily. Do not hesitate to chill the dough for 20 minutes or so if this happens, and then continue.

When all the butter is absorbed, the dough will look rather fluffy. Let it rest for 2 to 3 minutes, and knead briefly again. Kneading is finished when dough draws back into shape after being pushed out.

5) *First rising—pointage premier temps—5 to 6 hours at around 70 degrees*

A clean 3- to 4-quart mixing bowl
A large plastic bag that bowl will fit into, or a large sheet of plastic
A bath towel

You have 2⅔ cups of dough that is to rise to almost triple in volume, or to about 7 cups. Fill bowl with 7 cups of tepid water, make a mark on the outside of the bowl to guide you, pour out water and dry the bowl. Place dough in bowl, slip into plastic bag or cover with plastic and arrange bath towel on top. Set on a wooden or plastic surface or on a towel or pillow. For best texture and flavor, dough should take 5 to 6 hours to rise to the 7-cup mark, at which point it will feel light and springy, though somewhat sticky because of the butter.

NOTE: In hot weather you will probably have to set bowl in refrigerator from time to time to prevent butter from melting and oozing out of dough.

(*) DELAYED ACTION: Set bowl in refrigerator for a short delay; for a longer one, cover with waxed paper, a plate, and a 10-lb. weight to slow or even prevent its rising.

6) *Deflating—rupture*

With a rubber spatula or the slightly cupped fingers of one hand, *dislodge dough from inside of bowl* and turn out onto a lightly floured surface, scraping bowl clean. Sprinkle surface of dough with a teaspoon or so of flour.

With the lightly floured palms of your hands, pat and push dough out into a roughly shaped rectangle about 10 inches long.

With the help of a scraper or spatula, flip the right side of the dough over toward the center, then flip the left side over to cover it, as though folding a business letter. Pat the dough out again into a rectangle, fold again in three, and replace the dough in the bowl. Cover again with plastic and a towel.

(*) If you want to freeze *brioche* dough, this is the best time to do so, but see notes on freezing on page 96.

7) Second rising—pointage deuxième temps—2 to 6 hours or more, depending on temperature

Brioche dough is usually chilled before it is formed so that it can be shaped easily; chilling may be done either during or after the second rise, whichever works out best for your cooking schedule.

room temperature method:

Let dough rise to 2 times its original volume, or to about 5½ cups, at a temperature of around 70 degrees. This should take 1½ to 2 hours. Then dislodge from bowl with a rubber spatula or the slightly cupped fingers of one hand, and refrigerate on a large plate or platter covered with waxed paper, another plate, and a weight. Dough should be ready to form in 30 to 40 minutes.

refrigerator method:

Let dough start to rise at around 70 degrees for an hour, then refrigerate. Dough will continue to rise for an hour or more until the butter congeals. If you wish to leave it overnight, cover with a plate and a weight when you refrigerate it.

Forming and baking brioches

Brioches are usually baked in fluted molds with slightly outward-slanting sides. However, you can use anything you have available, from a baking dish or ovenproof bowl for large brioches to pyrex cups or muffin tins for small ones.

Notes on final rise

The final rise before baking is to almost double in volume, until the dough feels light and softly springy when touched. The ideal rising temperature is around 75 degrees, and you have to watch the dough carefully on a hot day because higher temperatures melt the butter so that it oozes out of the dough. If this starts to happen, refrigerate the dough from time to time. It is difficult to predict how long the final rise will take; if the dough was thoroughly chilled before forming, it will take longer to rise. You must usually count on at least an hour, and it must really rise and soften or it will bake into a rather firm and dense *brioche*. Following are directions for forming and baking large, small, and ring *brioches*.

* GROSSE BRIOCHE À TÊTE
[Large *Brioche* with Ball-shaped Head]

1) Forming the brioche

1 tsp soft butter
A 6-cup circular fluted
  mold or a cylindrical
  baking dish
The preceding *brioche*
  dough, chilled

Butter the interior of the mold or dish. With lightly floured hands on a lightly floured board, form ¾ of the dough into a smooth ball by kneading it lightly and rolling it between the palms of your hands. Place the ball in the bottom of the mold.

Make a funnel-shaped hole in the center of the dough 2½ inches wide at the top diameter and about 2 inches deep, using your first 3 fingers. Roll the remaining dough between the lightly floured palms of your hands to make a ball, then a tear-drop shape. *Insert pointed end of tear drop into hole.*

2) *Final rising—1 to 2 hours at 75 degrees*

Set uncovered and free from drafts at a temperature of around 75 degrees until dough has almost doubled in volume, and feels light and softly springy when touched. Be sure your oven has been preheated to 475 degrees by the time the *brioche* is ready to bake.

(*) DELAYED ACTION: You can set mold in refrigerator, covering it with a bowl to prevent dough from crusting; you can cover the formed dough airtight and freeze, but see notes on page 96.

3) *Glazing and clipping*

1 egg beaten with 1 tsp water in a small bowl
A pastry brush
A pair of sharp-pointed scissors

Just before baking, paint surface with beaten egg, being sure not to glaze where the head joins the main body of the *brioche* as this could glue the two together and prevent the head from rising. In a moment, glaze with a second coat.

To help head in shaping up during baking, *make 4 to 5 scissor clips in the large ball close under the head and slanting inward about half the width of the head.*

4) *Baking, cooling, and storing—oven at 475 degrees, then 350; baking time: 40 to 50 minutes*

Place the mold with the risen, glazed, and clipped *brioche* on a baking sheet in the middle or lower-middle level of the preheated 475-degree oven. In 15 to 20 minutes, when the *brioche* has risen and started to brown lightly, turn thermostat down to 350 degrees. Total baking time will be 40 to 50 minutes; *brioche* is done when it has begun to show a very faint line of shrinkage from the mold, or when a knife or straw plunged down through the center comes out clean. If, during baking, *brioche* seems to be browning too much, cover loosely with heavy brown paper or foil.

Cool on a rack for 15 to 20 minutes before serving. *Brioches* may be eaten slightly warm or cool; cold *brioches* may be warmed for 10 to 15 minutes in a 350-degree oven.

(*) *Brioches* dry out and become stale almost within 12 hours of baking. To preserve their freshness, wrap airtight and freeze; large frozen *brioches* take about half an hour to thaw in a 350-degree oven.

VARIATIONS

Petites Brioches à Tête
[Small Individual *Brioches* with Ball-shaped Heads]

Choose either ½-cup, slant-sided fluted molds for small *brioches*, or baking cups or muffin tins. Form in the same way as large *brioches*, filling the molds half full and letting dough rise to almost double. Paint twice with egg glaze and clip under the heads in several places just before baking. Bake about 15 minutes at 475 degrees in middle level of oven.

Brioche en Couronne
[Ring-shaped *Brioche*]

The *brioche* dough, chilled A baking sheet Optional: an ovenproof bowl or cup	Knead the chilled dough into a ball and place on a lightly floured surface.

Make a hole in the center with your finger, twirling dough around your finger to enlarge the hole and inserting more fingers as the hole gets bigger.

When hole is large enough to do so, insert both hands and gently stretch dough while twirling it on floured surface. The object is to make a doughnut shape 10 to 12 inches in diameter.

Place shaped dough on a lightly buttered baking sheet and let rest 10 minutes to relax gluten, then widen the circle a little more.

To keep center of dough from closing in during rising and baking, *insert a lightly buttered ovenproof bowl or cup in hole.*

Let dough rise, uncovered, to almost double at a temperature of around 75 degrees, until dough is light and springy to the touch. Paint with a double coating of egg glaze (1 egg beaten with 1 tsp of water) just before baking.

Then clip top of dough at 1-inch intervals, making cuts about 1 inch deep, pointing scissors toward outside of ring at a 45-degree angle.

Bake 20 to 30 minutes in the middle level of a preheated 475-degree oven until nicely puffed and browned. A knife or straw plunged into the center of one side should come out clean. If *brioche* browns too much during baking, cover loosely with heavy brown paper or aluminum foil.

Kougloff
[*Brioche* with Raisins]

Whether or not this molded ring-shaped raisin *brioche* originated with Viennese bakers, it is usually considered by the French to be an Alsatian raisin

cake of uncertain orthography, as you will see it spelled also *Kugelhopf,
Kougelhof, Gougelhop,* and even *Gugelhupf.* Bakers frequently make *Kougloff* out of leftover *brioche* dough, softening it with a little milk or additional
butter as they knead in the raisins just before dropping the dough into its mold.

Kougloff mold

baked Kougloff

For a 6-cup Kougloff

Special requirements

¾ cup (4 ounces) small
  currant raisins
1 to 1½ tsp soft butter
A 6-cup *Kougloff* mold,
  or any fluted ring mold
  3½ to 4 inches deep
  and about 8½ inches at
  rim diameter that holds
  6 cups
¼ cup shaved blanched
  almonds (skinless
  almonds sliced paper
  thin, available in cans or
  plastic)

To soften raisins, soak 10 to 15 minutes in very hot
water; drain, twist hard in the corner of kitchen towel
to squeeze out accumulated water, and spread out on
a paper towel until needed. Butter the mold heavily,
then sprinkle a tablespoon of the almonds in the
bottom, reserving the rest until later.

1) Softening the dough

Brioche dough, Master
  Recipe, page 85
If needed, 3 to 4 Tb milk
  and/or butter

So that it will mold smoothly, dough for *Kougloffs*
must be soft and sticky. If you are making the dough
specifically for a *Kougloff,* knead in only 4 of the 6
ounces of butter called for in Steps 2 and 4 of the

Master Recipe and complete the recipe through Step 8. After the second rise, knead in the remaining 2 ounces of butter and the raisins. If you are using left-over *brioche* dough, soften it by kneading in milk and/or butter by half tablespoons, then knead in the raisins.

---

2) *Filling the mold and final rise*

A pastry scraper or stiff metal spatula
A rubber spatula
The remaining almonds
A tablespoon or so of flour

Gather a 2-tablespoon gob of the soft dough on the end of your scraper or metal spatula and use the rubber spatula to dislodge it and place it on the bottom of the prepared mold. Continue spreading it around the mold to make a layer. Sprinkle or press more almonds against inside of mold, and add another layer of dough; continue thus until all dough is used. Sprinkle lightly with flour and press dough gently against sides and cone of mold with floured fingers. Mold will be about ½ filled. Let rise uncovered at around 75 degrees for an hour or more, until mold is almost filled.

---

3) *Baking—oven at 475 degrees, then at 350; 30 to 40 minutes*

Bake at 475 degrees in middle or lower-middle level of preheated oven for about 15 minutes, or until dough has risen and started to color. Then lower thermostat to 350 degrees for rest of baking. *Kougloff* is done when it shows a faint line of shrinkage from sides of mold and when the sides are nicely browned. Serve slightly warm or cool, with butter.

The processor can work wonderfully with some doughs. The trick is to process the dry ingredients and butter first, then—with the machine running—to pour in ¾ of the liquid called for. Never stop the machine; add the rest of the liquid by dribbles until the dough masses on top of the blade and rolls around under the cover for 15 to 20 seconds, for the preliminary kneading. If dough is too damp, it will not mass; sprinkle in a little flour, which may help. If not, knead by hand. By experimenting, you will find the way that works best for you.

Freezing brioche dough

The best time to freeze *brioche* dough is after the second rise, but you may also do so after it has been formed and before the final rise. However, and probably because of the high butter and egg content, its life in the freezer is not long: a week to 10 days is all we would suggest.

CROISSANTS

The most delicious of French croissants, to our mind, are those called *croissants de boulanger,* which are made of risen yeast-milk-and-flour dough that is flattened out, slathered with butter, folded in three, and rolled and folded again three times as though you were making French puff pastry. There are other formulas for croissants, including some which are really puff pastry or *brioche* dough rolled into crescent shapes. And in some of the quick methods the yeast dough has only a short single rise, resulting in a semi–puff pastry. None of these, to our mind, produces the tenderly layered, puffy, deliciously buttery croissant one dreams of. The old classic method does just this—and why go to all the trouble of making croissants otherwise?

CROISSANTS

The minimum time required for making croissants is 11 to 12 hours. Included are 3 hours and 1½ hours for the rising of the initial dough, two rest periods of 1½ to 2 hours each, and a final pre-baking rise of about an hour. Therefore, if you want freshly baked croissants for breakfast you will have to stay up all night as the bakers do. However, they will taste just as fresh if you make them ahead and freeze them either fully baked or ready to bake, as indicated in the recipe.

For one dozen 5½-inch rolls

1) *The basic dough*

½ cake (0.3 ounce) fresh yeast or 1¼ tsp dry-active yeast

3 Tb warm water (not over 100 degrees) in a measure

1 tsp sugar

Mix the yeast in the warm water with the sugar and let liquefy completely while measuring out the rest of the ingredients.

1¾ cups (about ½ lb. all-purpose flour measured by scooping dry-measure cups into flour and leveling off with straight-edged knife)

A 3- to 4-quart mixing bowl

2 tsp sugar

1½ tsp salt

⅔ cup milk warmed to tepid in a small sauce-pan

2 Tb tasteless salad oil

A rubber spatula

A pastry scraper or stiff metal spatula

Measure the flour into the mixing bowl. Dissolve the additional sugar and the salt in the tepid milk. When yeast has liquefied, pour it along with the milk mixture and oil into the flour. Blend the elements into a dough by cutting and pressing with the rubber spatula, being sure all bits of flour are gathered in. Turn dough out onto kneading surface, scraping bowl clean. Let rest for 2 to 3 minutes while you wash and dry the bowl. The short rest allows flour to absorb liquid; dough will be quite soft and sticky.

Start kneading by lifting near edge, using scraper or spatula to help you, and flipping it over onto the other side. Rapidly repeat the movement from one side to the other and end over end 8 to 10 times until dough feels smooth and begins to draw back into shape when pushed out. This is all the kneading it should have; you want just enough body so dough will hold together when eventually rolled, but you do not want to over-activate the gluten and make dough difficult to handle.

2) *The two rises—first about 3 hours; second about 1½ hours—
at 70–72 degrees*

**The clean 3- to 4-quart
mixing bowl
A large plastic bag or
sheet of plastic
A bath towel**

You will have about 2 cups of dough that is to rise to
3 ½ times its original volume, or to 7 cups. Fill bowl
with 7 cups of tepid water, make a mark on the outside at the 7-cup mark to guide you. Pour out the
water, dry the bowl, and put the dough into it.

Cover with plastic and bath towel, and place at a temperature of between 70 and
72 degrees. In 3 or 4 hours dough should have risen to the 7-cup mark, and will be
light and springy when touched.

Deflate by loosening dough from edges of bowl with a rubber spatula or the
cupped fingers of one hand, and turn it out onto a lightly floured surface. With the
lightly floured palms of your hands, pat and push the dough out into a rectangle
about 8 by 12 inches. Fold in three as though folding a business letter. Return dough
to bowl; cover again with plastic and bath towel.

Let rise a second time, but only to double the original volume. Then loosen
dough from edges of bowl and turn out onto a lightly floured plate. Cover airtight
and refrigerate for 20 minutes, which will make the next step easier.

(*) DELAYED ACTION: Set dough in a colder place to rise, or let it rise the second
time overnight in the refrigerator. After second rise, when dough has been turned
out of bowl onto plate, you may freeze it for a week, but see page 96.

------

3) *Rolling in the butter; turns 1 and 2*

**4 to 7 ounces (1 to 1¾
sticks) chilled unsalted
butter
A rolling pin (see page 112
for illustrated comments)
Flour as needed
A pastry scraper
Waxed paper or plastic
A plastic bag**

Butter is now to be softened and rolled in layers with
the dough. If this is your first attempt, use the minimum quantity. During all the following operations,
roll rapidly and keep the dough well chilled—warm,
limp dough is impossible to work with!

Butter must now be worked into
a smooth but still cold paste that
can be spread evenly on the dough
and then rolled with it. *Beat
butter with rolling pin to soften it.*

Then smear it out with the heel of your hand or a scraper or spatula until it is of very easy spreading consistency but still cold; it must not become soft and oily—refrigerate if necessary.

Place chilled dough on a lightly floured pastry marble or board. *With the lightly floured palms of your hands push and pat it out into a rectangle about 14 by 8 inches.*

Spread butter as evenly as possible over the upper two thirds of the dough rectangle, leaving a ¼-inch unbuttered border all around.

Dough is now to be folded into three layers, just as though you were folding a business letter. *Fold the bottom (unbuttered) third up to the middle.*

Fold the top (buttered) third down to cover it, making three even layers of dough separated by 2 layers of butter. This is called Turn Number 1.

For Turn Number 2, lightly flour the top of the dough and your rolling surface, turn the dough so the edge of the top flap is to your right, as though it were a book you were going to open. *Roll the dough into a rectangle about 14 inches by 6 inches. Roll rapidly, starting an inch from the near end and going to within an inch of the far end.*

Fold again in three. You now have 7 layers of dough separated by 6 layers of butter; at the end of the fourth roll there will be 55 layers of dough.

Sprinkle dough lightly with flour, wrap in waxed paper or plastic, place in a plastic bag and refrigerate. Dough must now rest for 1 to 1½ hours to deactivate the gluten so that you can make the two final rolls without difficulty.

4) *Turns 3 and 4—after a rest of 1½ to 2 hours in the refrigerator*

Unwrap dough, sprinkle lightly with flour, and deflate by tapping lightly several times with rolling pin. Cover and let rest for 8 to 10 minutes, again to relax gluten. Being sure that the top and bottom of dough are always lightly floured, start rolling dough into a rectangle 14 by 6 inches. If you notice that butter has congealed into hard flakes, beat dough with light firm taps for a minute or so, going from one side to the other until butter has softened: it must be able to extend the length and width of the rectangle inside the dough as you roll it out. Fold rectangle in three, roll again into a rectangle, and fold in three to complete the final turn. Wrap and chill for 2 hours before forming dough into croissants, or leave overnight covered with a board and a 5-lb. weight.

5) *Forming croissants—after dough has rested 2 hours in refrigerator*

The dough is now ready to be rolled out into the usual rectangle and then cut into triangles that are rolled up and twisted into crescent shapes. Professionals use

either the ingenious triangle-cutting roller illustrated, or do all the cutting by hand.
To make everything as easy as possible for yourself, refrigerate all pieces of dough
you are not actually working on.

PRELIMINARIES

A large sheet of plastic
A large, lightly buttered
baking sheet (14 by 16
inches at least)

Unwrap chilled dough, place on a lightly floured
surface, and deflate by tapping several times gently
with rolling pin. Cover with plastic and let rest 10
minutes, to relax gluten.

FORMING TRIANGLES BY HAND	FORMING TRIANGLES WITH A CUTTER

Roll dough into a
rectangle 20 by 5
inches; *cut in half,*
crosswise (A and B)
and chill 1 half (B).

Roll chilled dough into
a rectangle 12 by 5
inches; *cut into 3,*
crosswise (A, B, and
C), *and chill 2 pieces.*

Roll piece of dough
(A) into a rectangle
15 by 5 inches; *cut*
into 3, crosswise,
and chill 2 of
the 3 pieces.

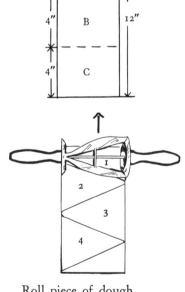

Roll piece of dough
(A-1) into a 5½-inch
square and *cut into 2*
triangles (x and y).

Roll piece of dough
into a rectangle 15 by 5
inches, *roll the cutter*
over it, and you will
have formed 4 triangles
(1, 2, 3, 4).

TURNING TRIANGLES INTO CRESCENTS OR CROISSANTS

Holding one of the triangles of dough by its large end, roll it out toward the point to make the triangle about 7 inches long.

Then, to extend the large end slightly, *stretch the 2 top angles of the triangle lightly between your thumbs and forefingers, enlarging end about an inch in all.*

Start rolling up the croissant first by folding the large end forward onto itself. Then, holding the point with the fingers of your left hand, finish the roll under the fingers and palm of your right hand.

Bend the 2 ends down to form a crescent shape and place on a lightly buttered baking sheet, with point resting inside curve and against surface of baking sheet. Form the rest of the triangles into croissants in the same manner.

(*) DELAYED ACTION: Formed croissants may be wrapped airtight and frozen for a week, if dough was not frozen before.

6) *Final rise—about 1½ hours at 75 degrees*

Cover croissants loosely with a large sheet of plastic and set at a temperature of around 75 degrees for their final pre-baking rise. Dough should almost triple in size and feel light and springy when touched; if it does not rise and feel light, the baked croissants will be heavy and hard rather than tender, puffy, and light. In hot weather you may have to set dough in refrigerator from time to time to prevent butter from softening and oozing out.

(*) DELAYED ACTION: For a slower rise, set dough in a colder place or refrigerate; if thoroughly chilled, leave at room temperature 20 to 30 minutes before baking. Risen croissants may be frozen for a few days and baked in their frozen state.

---

7) *Glazing, baking, and storing—oven preheated to 475 degrees*

A pastry brush	Just before baking, paint the croissants with egg glaze,
1 egg beaten with 1 tsp	then set in middle level of preheated oven for 12 to
water in a small bowl	15 minutes, until croissants are nicely puffed and
A cake rack	brown. Cool on a rack for 10 to 15 minutes before
	serving.

Croissants are at their best when freshly baked; even refrigerated in an airtight container, they are never as good the next day. Freezing is the best preservation: wrap airtight when croissants are thoroughly cool and freeze. To thaw and serve, set frozen croissants on a lightly buttered baking sheet and place in a preheated 400-degree oven for 5 minutes.

PASTRY DOUGHS

Pastry doughs, both tart and pie doughs and puff pastry, play an immensely important part in every phase of French cooking from little hot appetizers to *quiches,* and from *pâtés en croûte* to strawberry tarts, *mille feuilles,* and *Pithiviers.* If pie dough has always been your culinary bugaboo, remember that no one is born a pastry chef, everyone has had to learn, and that the first big step is to make the decision that you are now, today, going to learn to make a decent pie crust. Then make pie dough every day or two for a week or more; serve everything you can think of in pastry. You will be surprised how quickly you develop the technique, and you will then be in the masterful position of having an endless number of delicious concoctions at your fingertips. All the recipes here are for at least 1 pound of flour. Our feeling is that if you are going to make dough at all you might as well make a lot, because it keeps beautifully in the freezer.

TART AND PIE DOUGHS
Pâtes Brisées—Pâtes à Croustades

DOUGH TALK

French pastry dough is flour and butter worked together and then moistened with liquid. Liquid forces the gluten molecules in the flour to join into a continuous web so that the dough will keep its shape when rolled out; the dough must have its stated amount of liquid for this effect to take place. Butter gives the pastry its flavor and texture; as always, we suggest that about ¼ of the butter proportions be given over to vegetable shortening, which has a tenderizing effect that almost all American flours seem to need.

It is in the first step, working the butter and flour together, that many people have difficulty. Trying to do everything just right, they work too slowly and carefully, lingering over each squeeze of butter and flour until their hot fingers melt the butter; thus the liquid cannot mix in properly, and the dough is a wet, oily mess that, even after chilling, bakes into a miserable piece of cardboard. An electric food processor or mixer eliminates the problems.

ELECTRIC MIXER PIE DOUGH

PÂTE BRISÉE À L'OEUF—PÂTE À CROUSTADE

[Egg Pastry Dough for Free-standing Shells and Cases,
and for Turnovers]

The following dough formula is designed especially for pastry shells formed on upside-down tins, an informal and wonderfully easy way to make *quiche* and pie shells that is described and illustrated on pages 106–7. Whatever your dough formula, you can use exactly the same system outlined here.

For about 1 pound of flour, enough for three 10-inch shells

1) *Preliminaries*

¾ cup liquid (1 "large" egg plus necessary ice water); ¼ to ⅓ cup more ice water as needed
3½ cups (1 lb.) all-purpose flour (scooped and leveled, page 544)
8 ounces (2 sticks) chilled unsalted butter

Prepare the liquid and extra ice water. Measure the flour into the machine. Rapidly cut the butter into 4 lengthwise strips, then into ¼-inch pieces, and add to the flour along with the chilled shortening, and the salt and sugar. Plan to work rapidly so ingredients remain chilled—if you have to stop for any reason, place everything in the refrigerator until you can continue.

3 ounces (6 Tb) chilled
  vegetable shortening
2 tsp salt
¼ tsp sugar
Either an electric mixer
  or a food processor

―――――――――――――――

2a) *Making the dough in an electric mixer*

(If your electric mixer
  comes with a flat beater,
  so much the better; otherwise use the whisk-whip
  attachment)
A pastry scraper or rubber
  spatula
Plastic wrap
A little flour, as needed
A plastic bag

Run the machine at moderate speed, pushing fat and
flour into the blades with a rubber spatula (if you are
using a home-model whisk-type mixer). The object
here is to break the butter into pieces less than $\frac{1}{16}$
inch in size, each piece coated with flour. Then pour
¾ cup of liquid into the flour and beat a few seconds
at moderate speed, just until dough has absorbed
liquid and clogs in the blades—add up to ¼ cup more
ice water by dribbles if needed. Turn the massed
dough out onto the plastic; sprinkle droplets of ice
water on any unmassed bits in the bowl, and press
together as you add them to the rest of the dough.
With lightly floured hands, press the dough into a
roughly shaped cushion, wrap in plastic, and chill in
the plastic bag. Proceed to Step 3.

―――――――――――――――

2b) *Making the dough in an electric food processor*

A pastry scraper or rubber
  spatula
Plastic wrap
A plastic bag

(If you have a small—under 2-quart—container, divide ingredients in half and make the dough in 2
batches.) Flick the machine on and off 4 to 5 times
to blend dry ingredients and butter. Turn the machine
on and pour in the ¾ cup of liquid. Flick the machine on and off several times and the dough should
begin to mass on the blade. If not, dribble in a little
more water and repeat, repeating again if necessary.
Dough is done when it has begun to mass; do not
overmix it. Scrape the dough out onto your work
surface, and with the heel of your hand smear it out
by 2-tablespoon bits—making a 6-inch sweep (this is
the final blending). Gather it into a rough cushion
shape, wrap in plastic, and chill in a plastic bag. Proceed to Step 3.

―――――――――――――――

3) *Chilling the dough before forming—about 2 hours*

Once dough has been mixed, it must be well rested and chilled before you roll
it out. The rest relaxes the gluten in the flour, so the dough will roll easily; chilling

firms the butter, giving the dough enough body for rolling. In all of the following procedures, keep the dough chilled—it is impossible to work with otherwise; refrigerate it even in the midst of rolling.

(*) Dough may remain in refrigerator several days, or may be frozen for several months.

UPSIDE-DOWN PASTRY SHELLS AND CASES

The classic free-standing French pastry shell is formed by rolling out the dough and pressing it inside a flan ring or mold. The dough is then braced in place with another mold or with buttered foil and dried beans so that it will not collapse during baking. This method is illustrated in Volume I, pages 141–6, and produces the most professional result.

ring mold

oval baking dish

pastry shell from ringed mold

tartlet shells from muffin tins

pastry shell from oval mold

muffin tins

A more informal and simpler method is to bake the shell on an upside-down cake pan, or on any upside-down fireproof object whose shape appeals to you, such as a pie tin, bread pan, ring mold, saucepan, baking dish, or even muffin tin. For this type of shell you must have a pastry that is light and buttery but will hold its shape when molded and baked upside down. The preceding egg pastry dough was designed especially for upside-down shells.

UPSIDE-DOWN PASTRY SHELLS

*For a 10- by 1-inch round shell, or any shell formed
on any 6- to 8-cup mold*

---

1) *Forming shells*

1 tsp soft butter
**The mold: a round cake
pan or baking dish 9**

Butter the outside of the mold and set upside down. Rapidly roll out the dough into a circle ⅛ inch thick and at least 2½ to 3 inches wider in diameter than

to 10 inches bottom
diameter
½ the preceding egg pastry
dough, chilled

your mold. (Illustrated directions for rolling dough
are on pages 141–4 in Volume I.)

*Roll dough up on pin and unroll
over upturned bottom of mold,*
then run pin lightly over dough to
smooth it in place. With lightly
floured fingers, press dough
snugly against sides of mold, being
very careful not to pull or stretch
dough; it must retain its uniform
thickness of ⅛ inch.

*Even off the edges around the sides
of the mold with a ravioli wheel
or knife, making shell about
1 inch deep.*

*To prevent shell from puffing out
of shape during baking, prick all
over at ⅛-inch intervals with
a table fork.*

*To even the sides all around press
flat of fork against pastry, being
careful not to reduce thickness.* In
case any section of sides seems too
thin, paint lightly with cold
water and patch with raw dough.

So that dough will bake properly and not draw up or out of shape, it should now be refrigerated for at least an hour before it goes into the oven; this relaxes the gluten in the flour. Press raw leftover dough into a ball, wrap and refrigerate; you may need a little later on, after baking.

(*) Shell may be frozen at this point. Set as is in freezer for an hour or so until hardened, then wrap airtight. Bake shell while still frozen.

2) *Baking shells—after a rest of 1 hour*

Preheat oven to 425 degrees. You will need to weight down the top of the dough after it has baked for 4 to 5 minutes, otherwise the top will puff and draw the sides up: choose a saucepan or baking dish weighing about 2 pounds, or a pie plate filled with dried beans, and butter the bottom of the pan, dish, or plate.

Place chilled dough-covered mold, still upside down, on a baking sheet and set in middle level of oven. In 4 to 5 minutes, place the buttered weight on top, remove 2 to 3 minutes before shell is done.

A partially baked shell, the type used for *quiches* and oven-baked tarts and pies, needs 6 to 10 minutes in all depending on the thickness of the dough. It is sufficiently baked when it has started to color and can be raised gently from the mold. Fully baked shells usually need 10 to 15 minutes in all, until the shell is nicely browned and crisp. When done, remove from oven and let cool on mold for 8 to 10 minutes, then, being very careful not to crack shell, unmold on a rack.

First aid for cracked shells

If a partially baked shell develops a small split or crack, paint the area with beaten egg and patch with raw dough just before filling and baking. If sides seem thin or weak, you may paint with beaten egg and patch or strengthen them with a strip of raw dough, or you may fill the shell by no more than ⅓ so sides will not be under any strain during baking.

Freezing and leftovers

Baked shells may be wrapped airtight and frozen; it is wise to put them in a protective container of some sort. Leftover dough may be frozen and used again or combined with more of the same dough when you make another batch.

REFERENCE CHART FOR PASTRY DOUGH FORMULAS

Flour: Measure by scooping dry-measure cups into flour and sweeping off excess with straight edge of knife. Sift only *after* measuring.

Butter: Regular unsalted butter (not whipped butter) usually has a firmer texture and less water content than salted butter; we recommend it.

Liquid: Always start with the minimum amount of liquid called for, and add more by droplets as needed. The warmer and softer the butter, the less water the mixture will absorb. Hand-made dough, therefore, absorbs less liquid than machine-made.

DESCRIPTION	USES	FORMULA
ENTRÉE PASTRIES		
1) *Pâte Brisée Ordinaire*		
Regular pastry dough with less butter than the following, therefore easier to roll and form	For general pie crusts, plain *quiches,* turnovers, meat mixtures	3½ cups (1 lb.) flour 9 ounces (2¼ sticks) butter 2½ ounces (5 Tb) shortening 2 tsp salt ¼ tsp sugar ¾–1 cup iced water
2) *Pâte Brisée Fine*		
Finest pastry dough— delicate texture, fine flavor, fragile (Volume I, page 139)	For fancy appetizers and tartlets, rich *quiches,* and the best quality of pre-baked shells	3½ cups (1 lb.) flour 11 ounces (2¾ sticks) butter 3 ounces (6 Tb) shortening 2 tsp salt ¼ tsp sugar ¾–1 cup iced water
3) *Pâte Brisée à l'Oeuf*		
A light, crisp dough	Especially for shells and cases molded and baked on upside-down forms, and for turnovers	3½ cups (1 lb.) flour 9 ounces (2¼ sticks) butter 2½ ounces (5 Tb) shortening 2 tsp salt ¼ tsp sugar ¾–1 cup liquid (1 egg plus necessary iced water)
SWEET PASTRIES		
Pâtes Sucrées		
Any of the previous dough formulas	For the same uses	Same formulas except for salt and sugar proportions, which should be changed to: ⅛ tsp salt 5 Tb sugar

(continued on next page)

DESCRIPTION	USES	FORMULA

4) *Pâte Sucrée aux Jaunes d'Oeuf*

Less rich than #2, finer texture than #1 and #3	For baked tarts and tartlets, and pre-baked shells	3½ cups (1 lb.) flour 9 ounces (2¼ sticks) butter 2½ ounces (5 Tb) shortening ⅛ tsp salt 5 Tb sugar ¾–1 cup liquid (2 egg yolks plus necessary iced water)

5) *Pâte Sablée—Pâte Sèche*

Sweet cookie dough, crisp and buttery; the more sugar you add the more difficult the dough is to handle	For cookies, sweet tarts and tartlets, and especially for pre-baked shells	4⅓ cups (20 ounces) flour 9 ounces (2¼ sticks) butter 2½ ounces (5 Tb) shortening 8 to 18 Tb sugar ¼ tsp baking powder 3 eggs 1½ tsp vanilla extract ⅛ tsp salt

PÂTÉ DOUGHS

6) *Pâte à Croustade—Pâte à Pâté*

An excellent *pâté* dough that is also good to eat	For *pâtés* and meat pies that are molded in raw dough either in the spring-form *pâté* mold, or in a baking dish	3½ cups (1 lb.) flour 5½ ounces (11 Tb) butter 3 ounces (6 Tb) lard 2 tsp salt ¾–1 cup liquid (4 egg yolks plus necessary iced water)

7) *Pâte à Croustade à l'Envers*

A *pâté* dough that will hold its shape and is also good to eat	For *pâté* cases that are partially baked on upside-down forms before being filled with meat mixtures and baked; also for free-form *pâtés en croûte*	4⅓ cups (20 ounces) flour 7 ounces (1¾ sticks) butter 3½ ounces (7 Tb) lard 2½ tsp salt 1–1¼ cups liquid (2 eggs plus necessary iced water)

FRENCH PUFF PASTRY
Pâte Feuilletée

French puff pastry, *pâte feuilletée,* is literally what the French title implies: hundreds of leaves or layers of dough separated by hundreds of layers of butter. A piece half an inch thick puffs up 4 to 5 inches in the oven and is unbelievably light and tender to bite into. With almost as many uses as it has layers, puff pastry is the dough for *vol-au-vent* and Napoleons, for *coqs en pâte, gigots en croûte,* and all kinds of turnovers, tarts, pie toppings, first-course pastries, and luxurious cocktail tidbits. It dresses up the simplest store-bought cheese mixture, can add the final flourish to the grandest platter, and since it freezes perfectly for several months, puff pastry is tremendously useful to have available on those occasions when you need something fast to assemble that looks impressive.

If you enjoy working with your hands you will find it is the most fascinating of doughs to make, and if you want to acquire a facility in pastry, *pâte feuilletée* will teach you all the tricks. It most definitely takes practice to perfect, but when you have mastered puff pastry you will find it such a satisfying and splendid accomplishment you will bless yourself for every moment you spent learning its techniques.

THE TWO KINDS OF PUFF PASTRY

The classical, best-quality puff pastry, *pâte feuilletée fine,* contains equal parts of butter and flour, is made in a rigidly traditional manner, and you must count on 6 to 7 hours from the time you start it to the time you can form and bake it. This is what you use for *vol-au-vent,* patty shells, and fine desserts such as that most wonderful of almond tarts called the *Pithiviers.* However, it is not at all necessary to be so grand for cocktail appetizers, cheese-filled cases, leg of lamb baked in a crust, Beef Wellington, and a host of other delicious items. For these, and in fact for most of your puff pastry needs, simple puff pastry, *demi-feuilletée,* is very good indeed and can be made in half the time. Because it is so much easier to make, we suggest that you start your career on *demi-feuilletée,* and when you get around to the classic method it will then seem like only a variation on a familiar theme.

EQUIPMENT

Although you can mix pastry on a wooden table and roll it out with a broom handle, you will find it easier to make when you have a pastry marble and a good rolling pin. This is particularly true for puff pastry.

A pastry marble

The smooth, cool surface of marble is ideal to roll dough upon and scrapes clean easily while you work. A piece that can slide in and out of your refrigerator will be a miraculous help to pastry making in hot weather. You can usually find ready-cut polished marble in furniture stores; you can sometimes pick up an old marble table- or bureau-top in a junk shop; or look up marble suppliers in the telephone directory. The minimum size to consider is ¾ inch thick and the size of your refrigerator shelf, which is around 14 by 28 inches for the standard home-size model.

Rolling pins

A   Not this one

B   French rolling pin

C   Tutove pin

D   American ball-bearing pin

You should have a heavy pin with a rolling surface at least 14 inches long; 16 to 18 inches is preferable. You will probably have to try a restaurant supply house to find a decent pin, because a broom handle is certainly far more efficient than the ridiculous toy (A) that passes for a rolling pin in many household supply departments. The French pastry chef's pin (B) is of polished boxwood, 18 inches long and 2 inches in diameter; stores selling Italian cooking equipment often have a similar model of lighter wood.

The French Tutove pin (C) is sometimes available in import stores; its cannellated surface is designed especially for distributing the butter evenly throughout the dough when you roll puff pastry or croissants. The American-made pastry-chef's pin (D) is of polished hardwood and has ball-bearing handles; this fine, heavy pin is usually available only in restaurant supply houses.

FLOUR NOTE

The following recipes call for a mixture of all-purpose and cake flour, a combination always available and one that is used by many pastry chefs in this country. The nearest American approximation of French household pastry flour, "type 55," that we have discovered is a mixture of ⅔ unbleached pastry flour (not to be confused with cake flour) and ⅓ unbleached all-purpose flour. This combination has a lower gluten strength than the all-purpose and cake mixture, and it is easier and faster to handle because it needs shorter rest periods. However, unbleached flours, and especially unbleached pastry flour, are not to be found in most retail markets. Actually the cake and all-purpose combination, though slower to work with than either French flour or its American approximation, produces the lightest and puffiest pastry. (You may substitute French household flour or the ⅔–⅓ pastry flour and all-purpose flour combination in the following recipe.)

KEEPING COOL AND RELAXED

You will have very little trouble with puff pastry when you remember that you must keep the dough cold and that you must let it have the rest periods it needs.

Because of its high butter content, puff-pastry dough begins to soften as soon as you remove it from the refrigerator, just as butter softens. When you leave it too long at room temperature it becomes limp, sticky, and utterly impossible to work with until you refrigerate it again. Thus, if at any point your dough becomes limp and soft, stop where you are, refrigerate the dough for 30 minutes, then continue. Do the same if the dough retracts after rolling, or if it turns rubbery and refuses to extend itself; this means that the gluten in the dough is over-activated from having been rolled out, and the way to calm it down is to stop rolling and let the dough relax in the refrigerator for an hour or two. Most of the troubles most people have with puff pastry spring from unchilled dough and over-activated gluten.

✳ PÂTE DEMI-FEUILLETÉE

[Simple Puff Pastry—Flaky Pastry—Mock Puff Pastry]

For the many recipes like turnovers, toppings for meat pies, meats baked in a crust, appetizers, and so forth where you want a flaky, light dough, *demi-feuilletée* can be ready for baking in 3 to 4 hours. The pastry consists of an initial dough made of flour, water, salt, and a little oil, which acts as a tenderizer; this is pushed out into a 16-inch rectangle that is spread with softened butter. Then the rectangle is folded into 3, making a sandwich that has 3 dough layers and 2 butter layers. Rolled out and folded again 3 more times, as sketched in the recipe, the layers build up in geometric progression to make 72 layers of butter after the fourth fold. When the pastry finally goes into the oven, each of the many layers of dough puffs up between the layers of butter and the pastry bakes into a light, airy delight to both eye and tongue.

For about 1 pound of flour, making 2½ pounds of dough, enough for 2 of the 6- by 16-inch covered entrée pastries on page 140, or about 3 dozen of the cornets, or horns, described on pages 135-7.

---

1) *La détrempe—the dough mixture*

2¾ cups all-purpose flour and ¾ cup plain bleached cake flour, measured by scooping dry-measure cups into flour and leveling off with straight-edged knife

A 3- to 4-quart mixing bowl

A rubber spatula

A ½-cup measure to reserve flour for Step 2

¼ cup tasteless salad oil

2 tsp salt

1 cup iced water, plus a tablespoon or so more if needed

A 2-foot sheet of waxed paper

A plastic bag

Blend the 2 flours together in the mixing bowl with the rubber spatula. Remove ½ cup and reserve for Step 2.

Stir the oil into the flour and *mix thoroughly with rubber spatula*—you could use an electric mixer for this, but it hardly seems worthwhile. Then stir in the salt and the water, cutting and pressing ingredients firmly into a mass with spatula and then with the cupped fingers of one hand. Lift massed parts of dough out of bowl and place on pastry marble or board. Sprinkle unmassed bits of flour with drops of water in bowl; press together and add to dough.

Press dough firmly and rapidly into a cushion shape. Do not try to make a smooth surface; it will smooth out later. Consistency should be pliable, though not at all damp or sticky.

If you are in a terrible rush you can complete the next 2 steps now, but the dough will be easier to handle if you sprinkle it lightly with flour, *wrap in waxed paper,* slip it into a plastic bag, and refrigerate it for 40 minutes to an hour.

2) *Turn 1—adding the butter, and the first fold—1ᵉʳ tour*

12 ounces (3 sticks)
  chilled unsalted butter
A pastry scraper or stiff
  broad spatula
The ½ cup flour reserved
  from Step 1

When you are ready to roll out the
dough, *beat the butter with a
rolling pin to soften it.*

Smear out with scraper or *the
heel, not the palm, of your hand.*
When partially softened, work in
the flour and continue until
butter is perfectly smooth and of
easy spreading consistency but still
cold. If butter is not supple enough,
you cannot spread it over the dough;
if it is too soft it will ooze out as
the dough is rolled. Chill briefly
if you have softened it too much.

Lightly flour the dough and your
hands. *Push and pat the dough
out, in front of you, into a
rectangle 16 to 18 inches long and
about 8 inches wide.* Dough is
being pushed rather than rolled so
that you will activate the gluten
as little as possible for this first
operation. (Dough will be very soft
and sticky if you have not
chilled it.)

butter

dough

top view

butter

dough

side view

*Using a scraper or stiff spatula,
spread the softened butter over the
upper two thirds of the dough
leaving a ⅛-inch unbuttered border
all around.* The lower third is
unbuttered.

Fold the dough into three as follows: fold the bottom (unbuttered) third up to the middle.

Fold the top (buttered) third down to cover it, just as though you were folding a business letter. You have made 2 layers of butter and 3 of dough.

Rotate the dough a quarter turn counter-clockwise so the top flap of dough is to your right, as though it were a book you were about to open. Dough will still look rather rough and the spotty damp patches are oil; all will smooth out by the final turn.

3) *Turn 2—the four-layer fold—2ᵐᵉ tour*

In the second turn, you will roll out the dough and fold it so that it makes 4 layers. During the roll, be sure top and bottom of dough are always lightly floured and that your rolling surface is always scraped clean, to prevent dough from sticking; lift dough and slide it about between rolls to make sure.

Starting about an inch in from the near edge of the dough, roll your pin rapidly to within an inch of the far end, extending the dough as you roll. The rolling movement is a firm, even push away from you at a 45-degree angle. You are aiming for as even a rectangle of dough as possible; after several rolls you wish it to be 16 to 18 inches long and about 8 inches wide.

Even the sides of the rectangle with the side of your pin when necessary and occasionally roll across the rectangle to widen it. Sprinkle any breaks in the dough with flour. (If you did not chill the initial dough it will look messy and soft at this point; do not worry.)

*Fold the top and the bottom edges
of the rectangle so that they meet
at the center of the dough.*

butter dough

 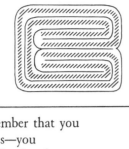

*Fold them together again, as
though you were closing a book.*
Now you have completed the
second turn, and have 8 layers of
butter sandwiched in between 9
layers of dough.

So that you will remember that you
have now made 2 turns—you
may decide to freeze the dough
at this point—*press 2 depressions in
the top of the dough with the
ball-ends, not the nails, of your*
fingers.

Wrap the dough in waxed paper, slip it into a plastic bag and refrigerate for 40
to 60 minutes (or overnight if you wish) until dough is much firmer and the gluten
has relaxed; it will then be easy to roll out for the final 2 turns.

4) *Finishing the dough: turns 3 and 4—after a 40- to 60-minute rest*

Unwrap the chilled dough and flour
it sparingly top and bottom.
If it is cold and hard, *beat it
evenly and firmly but not too
heavily with your rolling pin
to start it moving: beat crosswise
and lengthwise, and keep the
even rectangular shape.*

Then roll dough rapidly out into a rectangle 16 to 18 inches long. (Again, if
dough is very cold and you have not beaten it sufficiently to soften the butter, the
sides may split when you roll out the dough. Do not worry if this happens; remember
to beat it a little longer the next time.) Fold rectangle of dough into three, again as
though folding a business letter and as diagramed in Turn 1. Rotate dough so top flap
is to your right, book-opening fashion; roll again into a rectangle and fold into three.
You now have completed the fourth turn, and have 72 layers of butter. With the
ball-ends of your fingers, make 4 depression marks in the surface of the dough. Wrap
and chill for at least 2 hours to firm the butter and to relax the gluten. It is then
ready for forming and baking in any way your recipe directs. (You may, of course,

give the dough 2 more turns after it has chilled, tripling the layer count twice again to a total of 648; this is called for only rarely, however.)

Storage, ahead-of-time notes, and freezing

You may wrap and store puff pastry dough in the refrigerator at any step during its manufacture; however, remember that if you have not completed 4 turns the butter will be distributed in rather thick layers. Thus if the pastry is very cold, the congealed butter will break into lumps and flakes unless you give it a careful and thorough beating with your rolling pin before you attempt to roll it out. Puff-pastry dough may be frozen for as much as a year, when wrapped airtight and kept at zero degrees or less; thaw at room temperature or overnight in the refrigerator.

Forming and baking the dough—after a rest of 2 hours

A complete listing of recipes using puff pastry is in the index, page xl.

Use of leftover dough

See illustrated directions on page 134.

VARIATION

Pâte Feuilletée Fine

[Classic French Puff Pastry—for *vol-au-vent*, patty shells, fine desserts, and *petits fours*]

Classic French puff pastry has equal amounts of butter and flour, 6 rollings out and foldings, and develops 729 layers of butter sandwiched between 730 layers of dough. You may use it for any recipe requiring puff pastry, but its particular role lies in the realm of the patty shell, the fine dessert, and the elegant tea pastry. As you will see, the dough mixture contains butter rather than oil, and is made like pie dough; rather than being spread on, the main part of the butter is enclosed in the dough. Otherwise the technique for classic puff pastry does not differ too much from simple puff pastry. You must allow, however, a minimum of 6 to 7 hours from the time you start it to the time you can form and bake it. As usual, most of this time is taken up with rest periods; the actual work involved is probably not more than 30 minutes, and this can be spread over a period of several days.

For about 1 pound of flour, making 2½ pounds of dough, enough for one 8-inch vol-au-vent 5 inches high or 8 to 10 patty shells, plus leftovers which will make a 6- by 16-inch covered pastry such as the one on page 140, or 2 dozen of the cheese appetizers on page 135

1) *La détrempe—the dough mixture*

2¾ cups all-purpose flour and ¾ cup plain bleached cake flour, measured by scooping dry-measure cups into flour and leveling off with a straight-edged knife

A 4-quart mixing bowl, or the large bowl of an electric mixer

A rubber spatula

A ½-cup dry-measure cup (to reserve flour for Step 2)

3 ounces (¾ stick) chilled unsalted butter

A 2-foot length of waxed paper

Measure the 2 flours into the mixing bowl and stir thoroughly with rubber spatula to blend. Scoop out ½ cup and reserve for Step 2. Place chilled butter on waxed paper and cut into quarters lengthwise; rapidly cut quarters into ¼-inch pieces and add to the flour in the bowl. The butter is now to be cut into the flour and the liquid then added, just as though you were making pie dough. You may use an electric mixer as described in the *pâte brisée* recipe on page 104,

or *rub the flour and butter rapidly together between the tips of your fingers* until the butter is the size of small oatmeal flakes, or *chop with a pastry blender until the mixture resembles coarse meal.* OR make the entire *détrempe* in the food processor, including next step (page 105).

2 tsp salt

1⅛ cups iced water in a 2-cup measure, plus a few droplets more if needed

A plastic bag

Blend the salt into the iced water and pour into the flour and butter mixture. If you are using an electric mixer, mix for just a few seconds, stopping the machine as soon as dough clogs in the blades. Otherwise blend with a rubber spatula, pressing dough firmly into a mass with spatula and then with cupped fingers of one hand. Lift massed dough out onto marble or board; sprinkle unmassed bits in bowl with droplets of water, press together and add to main body of dough.

Press dough firmly and rapidly into a rough cushion shape; consistency should be pliable, though not at all damp and sticky. Sprinkle lightly with flour, wrap in waxed paper, and slide into a plastic bag. Refrigerate for 40 minutes to relax gluten and firm the dough.

2) *Preparing the butter—after dough has rested 40 minutes*

12 ounces (3 sticks) chilled
   unsalted butter
The ½ cup flour reserved
   from Step 1
A pastry scraper or stiff
   metal spatula

Beat the butter with a rolling pin to soften it, smear it out with the heel, not the palm, of your hand, or a pastry scraper or spatula. When partially softened, work in the flour. Butter must be absolutely smooth and supple, yet still cold. Form into a 5-inch square, place at the corner of your working surface, and proceed to the next step.

3) *The dough package*

Roll the chilled dough into a circle 12 to 13 inches in diameter; it will still look rough. *Place the butter in the center.*

Bring the edges of the dough over the butter to enclose it completely, being very careful not to stretch dough because you want it to have a uniform thickness at the sides of the square.

*Press dough well together on top
of package and seal edges with your
fingers.* Dough will still look
rough and uneven, which is
as it should be.

4) *Turns 1 and 2*

You now have a package with a layer of dough on the top and the bottom, and a layer of butter in between. Your object is to roll the package out into a rectangle, extending the butter the whole length and width of the rectangle between the 2 layers of dough: beat the package lightly but firmly its length and width with your rolling pin to get the butter moving, dust flour on the bottom and top of the dough, and rapidly roll it out into a rectangle 16 inches long and 8 inches wide. It is now to be folded in three, as though folding a business letter.

*Fold the bottom third up over the
center of the dough.*

*Fold the top third down to cover it,
making 3 even layers.* By folding
the dough in 3, you have made
3 layers of butter but only 4 of
dough, because the middle layers,
which touch, join to form a
single layer.

Place dough in front of you so that top flap is to your right, as though it were a book.

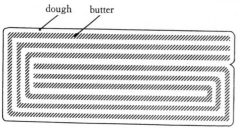

dough   butter

Roll again into a 16-inch rectangle and again fold in three, *making 9 layers of butter*. Press 2 depressions in the top of the dough with the ball-ends, not the nails, of your fingers so that you will remember you have made 2 turns.

Wrap dough in waxed paper and slip it into a plastic bag. Refrigerate for 40 to 60 minutes to relax the gluten and to firm butter for next turns, which it is best to complete within an hour if you can so that layers of butter do not become too firm and congealed.

5) *Turns 3 and 4—after a rest of 40 to 60 minutes*

If dough is hard and cold, beat with firm even strokes to soften butter. Complete Turns 3 and 4 in the same way as the previous turns. You may find during the rolling out that the bottom layer of dough does not stretch out to meet the top and middle layers at each end: turn dough over and roll upside down to even the layers. Make 4 depression marks in the dough to indicate the 4 turns; wrap and chill again for at least an hour before starting Turns 5 and 6.

(*) DELAYED-ACTION NOTE: This is the best point to refrigerate the dough for several days, or to freeze it for several months.

6) *Turns 5 and 6—after a rest of at least 1 hour, and 2 hours before you wish to form and bake the dough*

Complete Turns 5 and 6 in the same manner. (It is here that if you have given the dough only its minimum rest period you may find it hard to roll out and inclined to retract rather severely when extended. If this happens, stop immediately; forcing it will only make the gluten more tenacious and the dough more balky. Wrap and refrigerate the dough for an hour more before continuing.) Make 3 pairs of depression marks in the top of the dough to indicate the 6 turns. Wrap and refrigerate for 2 hours before forming and baking.

(*) DELAYED-ACTION NOTES: When you are making the dough for a *vol-au-vent*, you will usually get the highest rise when you form and bake the dough about 2 hours after the final turn. For all other purposes, dough may be refrigerated for several days, or frozen for several months.

Forming and baking the dough—after a rest of 2 hours

Except for the *vol-au-vent* and patty shells, which follow here, all other recipes using puff pastry will be found in their appropriate chapters, and there is a complete listing of recipes under puff pastry in the index, page xl.

Use of leftover dough

See illustrated directions on page 134.

Patty Shells
Bouchées et Vol-au-Vent

That beautifully sauced combination of sweetbreads, *quenelles,* truffles, mushrooms, and olives known as *ris de veau financière* has nowhere else to go but into a patty shell so light and airy it can fly with the wind, as the French title, *vol-au-vent,* suggests. Our litany ever seems to be "your own are so much better," and how true it is when your own puff pastry makes shells so light, buttery, and flaky you can hardly believe they are real even while the pastry is melting in your mouth. Whether you wish to serve individual shells or one dramatic large one for the whole table, small and large shells are constructed in similar fashion.

You are aiming for a hollow cylinder of pastry. To achieve it, you make 2 layers: a ring of dough that is set on a disk of dough. The ring forms the sides of the cylinder, and the disk, its bottom. Both ring and disk puff up in the oven, and when the pastry is done, you cut an opening in the top, as you will see, fork out the small amount of uncooked pastry inside, and you have a case ready for filling with creamed lobster, shrimp, mushrooms, or whatever delectable mixture you may have concocted. We shall start with individual pastry shells.

Both large and small shells require an extravagant amount of dough, and you will have as much left over as you have in the shells. However, the leftover dough is converted into puff pastry again as described and illustrated at the end of this section on page 134.

BOUCHÉES

[Patty Shells for Individual Servings]

For 9 shells 3½ inches in diameter

1) *Forming the dough*

The preceding recipe for 2½ lbs. chilled classic puff pastry

A pastry-cutting wheel or long knife

A 3½-inch plain, round cutter

A 2-inch plain, round cutter

A large baking sheet 12 by 16 inches at least

1 or 2 trays or baking sheets in the refrigerator for storing pieces of dough

A sharp, thin skewer (or large darning needle)

Because puff pastry softens so quickly out of the refrigerator, you will find it best to work on only part of the dough at a time, keeping the rest chilled. Each piece will make 3 patty shells. Roll the dough into a rectangle 18 inches long and 8 inches wide, cut into thirds crosswise using pastry wheel or long knife, and refrigerate 2 of the pieces of dough. Roll the remaining piece of dough into a 10- by 14-inch rectangle ¼ inch thick. Work rapidly from now on so that dough will not soften before you are through; if it does, stop immediately, refrigerate everything for 15 to 20 minutes and then continue. Soft, limp dough is impossible to work with.

With the 3½-inch round cutter, cut 6 disks in the pastry, spacing them half an inch from the edges of the pastry and from each other. *With the 2-inch cutter, cut circles from the center of three of the disks to make 3 rings.* (Carefully arrange all leftover dough in one layer and refrigerate; see page 134 for instructions.)

Rinse pastry sheet in cold water, shake off excess water, and place the 3 disks upside down on the sheet, spacing them ½ inch from edge of sheet and from each other. Paint tops of disks lightly with cold water and *press a ring of dough on each disk.*

Seal each ring to each disk by making slanting indentations ⅛ inch apart with the back of a knife, going all around the circumference, and pressing the 2 layers of dough together with the balls of your fingers as you go.

Prick all over exposed center of bottom disks with the tines of a table fork. Plunge a skewer down through the pastry at 3 points in the center of the pastry and 4 around the ring; this, hopefully, will ensure a vertical, even rise in the oven.

With a 2-inch round cutter or a knife, *press a circle outline ¹⁄₁₆ inch deep in each disk, where the inside edge of the ring meets it;* this will then be cut out after baking and serve as a cover.

Pastry will probably have softened; refrigerate baking sheet for 10 minutes, or at least while you are rolling out and cutting the next 2 pieces of dough. When all 9 *bouchées* are assembled on the sheet, cover with waxed paper and refrigerate for at least 40 minutes before baking, so that dough can relax and *bouchées* will not shrink or bake out of shape.

(*) DELAYED-ACTION NOTE: The formed pastry may be frozen at this point, and taken right from freezer to oven.

2) *Baking—20 to 25 minutes in a preheated 425-degree oven*

Just before baking, paint top surfaces of *bouchées,* not the sides, with a double coating of egg glaze (1 egg beaten with 1 tsp water), and decorate with cross-hatch knife or fork marks. (See *vol-au-vent,* step 2, page 129.) Bake in the middle level of preheated oven about 25 minutes. They are done when risen and brown, and when the sides are brown and crisp. Remove to a rack.

With a sharp small knife held vertically, cut out covers with an up-and-down sawing motion. Delicately scrape out any uncooked pastry from inside with the back of a teaspoon or the tines of a small table fork. Cool on a rack.

3) *Storing and serving*

The sooner you can fill and serve patty shells, the fresher, lighter, and more delicious they will be. If you are serving the same day, keep in a warming oven or the turned-off oven. Otherwise arrange in a covered pan and freeze them. To reheat and crisp shells, either frozen or not, preheat oven to 425 degrees, place shells on a lightly buttered baking sheet and set in middle level of oven. Turn oven off and shells will be crisp in 5 to 8 minutes.

VOL-AU-VENT

[*Large Patty Shell*]

A large patty shell is somewhat reminiscent of the oldtime *haute cuisine;* it is wonderfully dramatic to serve and always greatly enjoyed by your guests just because it is an unusual treat. The decorative cover, which is formed and baked separately, is optional and depends on how your table serving works out. If you have a cover, the filled *vol-au-vent* with cover poised on top of the food is presented for all to admire, then the cover must be removed to a separate dish for cutting and serving.

For an 8-inch shell about 5 inches deep, serving 6 people

1) *Forming the dough*

The preceding recipe for 2½ lbs. classic puff pastry, page 118

Place chilled puff pastry on a lightly floured marble or pastry board and roll rapidly into a rectangle ⅜ inch thick, 12 inches wide, and 20 inches long. (To insure

**An 8-inch and a 5-inch
round *vol-au-vent*
cutter, pan cover, plate,
or saucer for cutting
circles of dough
A heavy rolling pin with
rolling surface at least
14 inches long
A baking sheet or round
pizza tray rinsed in cold
water and not dried
1 or 2 baking sheets or
trays in the refrigerator
for leftover dough**

that stresses and strains are equalized for even baking,
be sure to roll dough crosswise as well as lengthwise.)

Work as rapidly as possible from now on so that dough will not soften and become difficult to handle; if it does soften, immediately stop whatever you are doing
and refrigerate everything for 15 to 20 minutes, then continue.

*Cut two 8-inch disks out of pastry, spacing them at least ½ inch from edges
of dough and from each other.* Lift surrounding dough off the disks and arrange
in one layer on baking sheet or tray and refrigerate; directions for re-forming it
into puff pastry are on page 134.

Roll one of the disks up on the
pin and *unroll upside down on
damp baking sheet.* (Damp surface
makes pastry stick to sheet, giving
it a grip so it can rise in the oven.)
Paint a 1½-inch border around
the top of the circle with cold water.

*Using a round cutter or guide 5
inches in diameter, center it in the
second disk of dough and cut
around it to make the 8-inch ring
for the second layer of the
vol-au-vent.*

So that you will not stretch the ring
of dough as you remove it from
the circle, brush lightly with flour
and fold it in half, then in quarters.
*Unfold it on the dampened
circumference of the first disk,*
pressing it in place with the balls
of your fingers. (Refrigerate disk of
leftover dough.)

*Seal the 2 layers of dough with the
back of a small knife, by pressing
slanting lines ⅛ inch deep and about
¾ inch apart all around the
circumference,* also pressing top of
circle with the balls of your fingers
as you go. (It is now wise to cover
and refrigerate *vol-au-vent* for an
hour before baking; this will relax
dough so that it will bake evenly.)

(*) AHEAD-OF-TIME NOTE: Unbaked *vol-au-vent* may be refrigerated for a day or
so, or frozen, but you will usually get a higher rise if you bake it within an hour of
forming.

2) *Final decoration and baking—about 1 hour;
oven preheated to 425 degrees*

Egg glaze (1 egg beaten
  with 1 tsp water in a
  bowl or cup)
A pastry brush
A small knife
A thin, sharp skewer or
  large darning needle

When oven has been preheated, paint top of ring and
exposed top of disk with egg glaze. (Do not paint
sides, because egg could prevent them from rising.)

With a small knife, cut lines ⅛ inch deep and 1½ inches apart (at outside edge) in top of ring, pointing knife always to center of vol-au-vent *so the marks will be evenly spaced, like the spokes of a wheel.*

Cut a line ¼ inch deep in the bottom disk, where inner edge of circle meets it; this marks the cover, which is removed after baking so that interior of *vol-au-vent* may be cleaned out.

Make decorative, shallow cross-hatch marks in the top of the dough through the glaze with the point of a knife or the tines of a table fork.

Finally, *plunge skewer or needle down through the top of the pastry sheet at 4 to 5 places around the circumference and 3 places in the center.* The purpose of this operation is presumably to hold the puff pastry layers in place and help the *vol-au-vent* rise evenly.

Immediately place *vol-au-vent* in lower middle level of preheated oven and bake at 425 degrees for about 20 minutes, until the pastry has tripled in height and is beginning to brown. Lower thermostat to 350 degrees and bake 30 to 40 minutes longer, until sides are brown and crisp. If pastry is coloring too much, lay a sheet of aluminum foil or heavy brown paper loosely over the top.

3) *Final touches*

As soon as you remove the *vol-au-vent* from the oven and while it is still hot, cut around the inside edge of the ring to remove the cover you marked in the bottom disk; this has now risen, along with the rest of the dough. (Cover will probably break and should be eaten by the cook, who must sample the pastry anyway.)

Being very careful not to pierce sides or bottom of crust, scrape uncooked pastry out of vol-au-vent with the tines of a table fork or the handle of a spoon. (You may turn this into a cheese ramequin, but you should use it while still fresh; see following recipe.)

Set *vol-au-vent* again on its pastry sheet and put in the oven for 5 minutes, to dry out, then let cool on a rack. If bottom of pastry burned or darkened unduly during baking, shave off the discolored part with a sharp knife.

Storing and reheating

If you have a warming oven, set it at around 100 degrees where pastry will keep for a day or two, drying and crisping to a delicious texture. Otherwise, the sooner you can eat the *vol-au-vent* the better, unless you are going to wrap it airtight and freeze, where it will keep for several weeks. To reheat cold or frozen *vol-au-vent,* set on a lightly buttered pastry sheet in a preheated 425-degree oven for 5 minutes, then turn oven off and leave a few minutes more, until crisp.

FOR THE UNCOOKED INSIDES OF THE VOL-AU-VENT

Ramequin du Juste Milieu

[A Hot Puffed Cheese Dish to Serve as an Entrée
or in Place of Potatoes]

For 4 to 6 servings

The fresh, preferably still warm uncooked insides of a *vol-au-vent* (usually ⅓ to ½ cup, pressed)
1 cup milk
2 eggs

Purée the uncooked pastry and milk for a minute or so in an electric blender until perfectly smooth. Add eggs, seasonings, and cheese and purée 5 seconds. Pour into buttered dish.

(*) DELAYED-ACTION NOTE: May now be covered and refrigerated until the next day.

Salt, pepper, and nutmeg
¼ cup grated Parmesan
  cheese
A 3- to 4-cup baking and
  serving dish about 1½
  inches deep, lightly
  buttered

Half an hour before serving, bake in the middle level of a preheated 375-degree oven until nicely puffed and browned. Serve immediately.

MAKING A VOL-AU-VENT COVER

When you want a cover for the *vol-au-vent,* form it separately, and bake the 2 together on the same pastry sheet.

Use the circle of leftover dough you cut from the second disk of pastry that made the *vol-au-vent* ring. After it has rested in the refrigerator while you were making the *vol-au-vent* itself, roll it out into a disk about 9½ inches in diameter; loosen it from the rolling surface to let it shrink if it will. Roll it up on your pin and unroll upside down on a lightly buttered pastry sheet. Then trim it into a neat circle using an 8½-inch cutter or plate as a guide.

Place a slightly smaller cutter,
cover, or other round object on top
and draw the back of a knife from
edge of pastry to edge of cutter at
¾-inch intervals all around to
make a scalloped edging.

To discourage dough from rising more than a little in the oven, *prick all over (except on scalloped edges) at ⅛-inch intervals with the tines of a table fork,* going right down through the pastry to the pastry sheet. Cover and chill the dough for about an hour, so that gluten will relax and dough will bake evenly without shrinking.

Using scraps of dough left over
from the *vol-au-vent,* make
decorative cutouts ⅛-inch thick and
of any shape and design you wish.
*After painting top of dough with
egg glaze, affix the designs* and
paint them also. Then make
shallow, all-over cross-hatch marks
through the glaze and into the
dough with a small knife or the
tines of a fork.

The design illustrated is a very simple one of circular cutouts, which puff up in an
amusing manner; you may use ovals, leaves, strips of dough, or anything you wish,
but remember that everything rises, and if you cut your shapes too thick and narrow,
they may topple off in the oven.

Baking

Whether baked separately or along with the *vol-au-vent,* put the cover in a
preheated 425-degree oven for about 20 minutes, until nicely browned, then turn
thermostat down to 350. Pastry is done when it feels crisp and light, which should
be 30 minutes or so in all. Let cool on a rack.

FLEURONS

[Puff-pastry Puffs, for Decorations and Garnitures]

baked

raw

When you are not making a cover for the *vol-au-vent,* you may wish some
extra bits of puff pastry to decorate the edge of the platter around the shell. These
are called *fleurons,* or flowered shapes, because they are small and decorative, usually
fluted ovals or crescents. Classic French recipes often suggest *fleurons* as a garnish
to some of the beautiful filet of sole or scallop dishes, where pastry elegantly takes

the place of a mundane starchy vegetable. You may make *fleurons* either out of the carefully preserved trimmings from your *vol-au-vent* or *bouchée* cuttings, or from the re-formed and reconstituted dough described after the next recipe.

Roll dough ¼ to ⅜ inch thick and make disks with a round, 3-inch, fluted cutter. With one stroke through the center, cut each disk into an oval and a crescent.

Place ½ inch apart on a dampened pastry sheet and chill for at least half an hour to relax the dough—an hour or more would be better. Glaze with beaten egg, decorate with cross-hatching, and bake in middle level of a preheated 450-degree oven for 12 to 15 minutes, until nicely puffed, brown, and crisp.

PETITES BOUCHÉES

[Cocktail Shells of Puff Pastry]

Cocktail-size patty shells, *petites bouchées* or little mouthfuls 2 inches in diameter, are made in 1 layer. Use the leftover circles cut from the second layer, or rings, of larger patty shells, or cut circles from the leftover and re-constituted puff pastry dough in the following recipe.

Roll the dough ¼ to ⅜ inch thick, cut with a 2-inch fluted cutter, and arrange on a dampened baking sheet. *With a 1-inch cutter or a small knife, press a cover outline in the top of the dough, going ⅛ inch deep.* Glaze and bake, following the preceding directions for *fleurons*. When baked and still warm, delicately cut out the cover and remove any uncooked pastry from interiors.

These small shells may then be filled and reheated for serving, or you may freeze them until needed.

UTILIZATION DES ROGNURES
[Reconstituting Leftover Dough into Puff Pastry Again]

*You will have as much dough left
over from cutting a vol-au-vent as
you have in the vol-au-vent itself,*
and almost as much from *bouchées.*
You can even make another
vol-au-vent from these scraps, or
half a dozen *bouchées,* or anything
else calling for puff pastry. *Demi-
feuilletée,* the simpler puff pastry,
is treated the same way. Puff pastry
leftovers are called *rognures,*
meaning trimmings or scraps.

Your object is to join the scraps
into one piece of dough in such
a way that the layers of butter and
flour in each scrap are horizontal,
as they were when the dough was
first made.
Cut the scraps as necessary.

*Arrange them so that they will
form a rectangle.* Then paint an
edge of each with cold water,
overlap it slightly upon its
neighbor, and seal the seam with
the balls of your fingers.

If you are very skillful, you can manage to make a few careful rolls with your
pastry pin and join the seams of dough so perfectly that you can cut it out for patty
shells or the 2 large disks needed for a *Pithiviers.* The surest system, however, is to

flour dough lightly, roll into a rectangle, spread the top two thirds with a tablespoon of softened butter and fold in three. Wrap, chill an hour or two, and finish off with 2 more turns. Refrigerate for several hours or overnight, or freeze, so that dough will relax thoroughly before you use it again.

Re-use of leftovers

You can still get puffing and flakiness out of the leftover of leftovers, using the preceding system. The pastry will not be as tender when baked as it was at first, and it may well offer a bit of resistance when you roll it out. However, it works very well for most appetizers, as well as for cookies and for the *fleurons* and the *petites bouchées* in the 2 preceding recipes.

Puff Pastry Entrées

Cornets, Rouleaux, Cheese Napoleons, and Cheese Tarts

Just a few of the many delicious pastries you can make with *pâte feuilletée* are described and illustrated in the following pages; dessert pastries and cookies are on pages 453–72, and 477–80. One could easily write a book on puff pastry alone, and we find it hard to limit ourselves to a sensible few. We hope, however, that these recipes will give you a feel for how to use it so that you can go off on your own and be confident with other recipes you find elsewhere.

empty molds

raw

baked and filled

CORNETS

[Puff Pastry Horns—Cream Horns]

Strips of puff pastry are rolled around cone-shaped forms, baked until the pastry has browned and set, and baked again with a creamy cheese filling to make a most attractive first-course fantasy. (Encrusted with sugar, they come out of the oven with a caramel coating for dessert creams, as suggested on page 468.)

For 18 to 20 horns about 5 inches long, serving 8 to 10 people

1) *Forming the dough*

18 to 20 buttered cream-horn molds (or bake the pastry in several batches)

2 large pastry sheets rinsed in cold water but not dried

½ the recipe for chilled simple puff pastry, page 113

A tray lined with wax paper for refrigerating pieces of dough you are not actually working on

A ruler or cutting guide

A ravioli wheel

A pastry brush and cup of cold water

Stand the buttered molds within easy reach, and have the pastry sheets near you. Roll the chilled pastry out into a rectangle 14 inches long, cut in half crosswise, and refrigerate 1 piece of dough. Roll remaining piece of dough rapidly into a rectangle ⅛ inch thick and slightly more than 8 by 13 or 14 inches in diameter. Trim off ragged edges. (If kitchen is hot, work very rapidly, and refrigerate all pieces or strips of dough you are not actually working on in the following steps.)

Cut strips of pastry ¾ to 1 inch wide and 13 to 14 inches long, using cutting guide and pastry wheel as shown.

Paint a half-inch band of cold water along top length of a strip of dough. *Hold mold by its large end; slip tip of mold under right end of dough strip,* then pinch dough all around the tip of the mold to seal it.

Holding tip of mold with your left hand, with your right hand rotate its large end clockwise—to your right—winding the dough onto the mold in a spiral from tip to large end, and letting dough overlap ⅛ inch upon itself as you go. Be careful not to stretch the dough, which should remain an even ⅛ inch thick. When dough is cold and firm, you will find it easy to work with.

Seal end of dough at large end of mold, pressing with your fingers. Place horn on baking sheet, sealed-side of dough against sheet; press lightly to hold the horn in place. Proceed with the rest of the horns in the same manner.

2) *Chilling, glazing, and baking*

Chill at least 30 minutes, but an hour is preferable, to relax dough before baking. When ready to bake, preheat oven to 425 degrees and set rack in middle level. Just before baking, paint tops and sides of horns with egg glaze (1 egg beaten in a small bowl with 1 tsp water), and make cross-hatching on surface with the point of a knife or the tines of a fork. Bake immediately; horns are done in 15 to 20 minutes, when molds slip easily out of them. For recipes where you are to fill the horns and bake them again, remove from oven when a pale brown so they will not darken too much during their second baking; otherwise leave them in a few minutes longer, to brown nicely.

(*) Pastries are at their best when eaten within a few hours of baking; you may keep them, however, in a warming oven at around 100 degrees for a day or so; otherwise wrap airtight and freeze them. To thaw, place on a lightly buttered baking sheet in a 400-degree oven; turn oven off, and leave about 10 minutes.

FONDUE DE FROMAGE POUR CORNETS, ROULEAUX, MILLE-FEUILLES, ET CROQUETTES

[Cheese Filling for Cream Horns, *Mille-Feuilles,* and Croquettes]

This is a very thick sauce that will not run or flow out of shape when heated in pastries, or when coated with beaten eggs and bread crumbs and deep-fried. Rather than cooking it in the usual way, with a flour and butter *roux* that is moistened with hot milk, you beat the milk into the flour and then add the butter, making what is technically known as a *bouilli*.

For about 2½ cups

¾ to 1 cup milk
½ cup all-purpose flour
   (measure by scooping
   dry-measure cup into
   flour and sweeping off
   excess with knife)
A heavy 2-quart saucepan
A wire whip and a rubber
   spatula
2 Tb butter
2 "large" eggs
Salt, pepper, pinch of
   nutmeg, and drops of
   Tabasco or a pinch of
   Cayenne pepper
4 ounces (about 1 cup)
   coarsely grated Swiss
   cheese
2 ounces (less than ½ cup)
   grated Parmesan cheese
3 to 4 Tb heavy cream

Gradually beat driblets of milk into the flour, in saucepan, adding ¾ cup and beating to a smooth consistency. Add butter, and set pan over moderate heat, stirring. When mixture comes near the boil and begins to be lumpy, remove from heat and beat vigorously to smooth it out. One by one, beat in the eggs, and bring to the boil, beating constantly. Sauce must be a thick paste; if very stiff, thin out over heat, beating in more milk by dribbles. Remove from heat, season with salt, pepper, a pinch of nutmeg, and rather strongly with Tabasco or Cayenne pepper. Let cool for a few minutes, then fold in the cheese. Fold in just enough cream to soften it slightly, but sauce must hold its shape when mounded in a spoon; it should not spread out later, when cooked with pastries.

(*) AHEAD-OF-TIME NOTE: May be made several days in advance of using; may be frozen. Clean off sides of pan, and press a sheet of plastic wrap over the surface of the sauce to prevent a skin or crust from forming.

Additions

Use half the amount of cheese called for in the preceding filling, and fold in ⅓ to ½ cup of either diced ham or mushroom *duxelles* (diced fresh mushrooms sautéed in butter, Volume I, page 515).

CORNETS À LA FONDUE DE FROMAGE
[Cream Horns Baked with Cheese Filling]

The preceding cheese filling
A pastry bag with round
   tube opening
Puff pastry cream horns,
   baked but barely
   browned, page 135
Rather soft Swiss cheese

A grater (small holes)
A lightly buttered baking
  sheet

Preheat oven to 400 degrees. Pack the cheese filling into the pastry bag and *squeeze it into each pastry horn*. Grate cheese so that you have rather long whiskery wisps, and *pack a large pinch into opening of each horn*.

Bake in upper third of preheated oven 10 to 12 minutes, to melt cheese and heat filling to bubbling hot. Serve as soon as possible.

ROULEAUX
[Puff Pastry Cream Rolls]

empty molds   raw   baked and filled

If you cannot find molds for cream horns, you may find metal molds suitable for pastry rolls; or use pieces of well-oiled unvarnished wood 5 to 6 inches long, such as a cut-up broom handle. Form, bake, and fill puff pastry rolls in the same general manner described and illustrated for horns, starting on page 136. When baked with the preceding cheese filling, stuff whiskers of cheese into both ends to prevent filling from oozing out.

MILLE-FEUILLES À LA FONDUE DE FROMAGE
[Cheese Napoleons]

You will probably find far more use for cheese Napoleons than for pastry-cream dessert Napoleons. They make an elegant first course or luncheon

dish and are practically as easy to assemble as the count of one-two-three—when you have ready-made puff pastry on hand. A thin sheet of baked puff pastry is cut into squares or rectangles that are sandwiched together with the cheese *fondue* filling and baked until the filling is bubbling hot.

For 6 to 8 servings

1 sheet of baked puff pastry 12 by 16 inches in diameter (Napoleons, page 462; Steps 1 and 2)
A ruler or cutting guide
A pastry wheel or very sharp knife

Cut the baked puff pastry either into three 4- by 16-inch strips, and cut each strip into squares 4 inches to a side; or cut the pastry into four 3-inch strips 16 inches long, and cut each into 4 rectangles (making 12 squares, or 16 rectangles).

The cheese fondue filling on page 137
3 to 4 Tb grated Parmesan cheese
A lightly buttered baking sheet

Preheat oven to 375 degrees about half an hour before you wish to serve. Have the filling and grated cheese ready. Place half the puff pastry pieces on the baking sheet. Spread a 3-tablespoon lump of the filling on each, but leaving a ¼-inch free border of pastry all around. Lightly press a second piece of pastry, best side uppermost, on top. Sprinkle on a half teaspoon of grated cheese.

Bake for about 15 minutes in preheated oven, upper-middle level, until cheese topping has colored lightly and cheese filling is bubbling hot—be careful not to bake too long and burn the pastry. Serve immediately.

(*) AHEAD-OF-TIME NOTE: You may form the *mille-feuilles* for baking an hour or so in advance.

FEUILLETÉE AU FROMAGE—JALOUSIE AU FROMAGE
[Peekaboo Cheese Tart of French Puff Pastry]

Another delicious puff pastry for first courses, luncheons, or for slicing and serving with cocktails is the *feuilletée*. Quick to assemble, when you have puff pastry dough on hand, it is done exactly like the jam tart on page 459.

For a 6- by 16-inch, tart, serving 6 people

1) *Forming the tart*

½ the recipe for simple puff pastry, page 113, or reconstituted leftovers, page 134

A dampened pastry sheet

A table fork

Either ½ to ⅔ the cheese fondue filling on page 137;

Or 4 to 6 ounces Roquefort cheese or blue cheese, and 1 egg beaten with ½ cup *crème fraîche* or heavy cream, salt, pepper, and Tabasco

Roll half the pastry into an 8- by 18-inch rectangle ⅛ inch thick. Roll up on pin, and unroll topside down onto dampened pastry sheet. Prick all over at ⅛-inch intervals with tines of fork, going right down through to pastry sheet.

Either *spread the fondue filling on the pastry, leaving a ¾-inch border all around;* or cut cheese into thin slices and spread over pastry, leaving border.

Turn borders of pastry up over filling at sides; wet corners, and turn ends over, sealing corners with fingers. If you are using Roquefort or blue cheese, spoon the egg and cream over it, tilting pastry in all directions, allowing liquid to flow all over enclosed area.

Roll out second piece of pastry into a 7- by 17-inch rectangle ⅛ inch thick. Flour surface lightly, and fold in half lengthwise. Measure opening of filled pastry and mark folded pastry to guide you. *Cut slits in dough from folded edge as shown, making them ⅜ inch apart and half as long as width of opening in tart.*

guide mark

Wet edges of filled bottom layer of pastry with cold water. Unfold top layer over it; brush off accumulated flour, and press pastry in place with fingers. *Then with back tines of a fork, press a decorative vertical edging all around sides of tart.* Cover and chill for at least 30 minutes before baking.

(*) AHEAD-OF-TIME NOTE: When chilled and firm, may be wrapped airtight and frozen for several months. Remove from freezer, glaze, and bake as in Step 2.

2) *Baking and serving—about 1 hour at 450 and 400 degrees*

Egg glaze (1 egg beaten in a small bowl with 1 tsp water)
A pastry brush
A table fork or small knife
A rack
A serving tray or board

When oven has been preheated to 450 degrees, set rack in lower-middle level. Paint surface of chilled tart with egg glaze; wait a moment, and give it a second coat. Make cross-hatchings on top of sides and ends through glaze, and set in oven. In about 20 minutes, when pastry has risen and started to brown, turn oven down to 400 degrees. Cover loosely with foil or brown paper if surface is browning too much. Sides should be firm and crusty. Slide onto a rack when done. Serve warm or tepid, cutting into crosswise slices.

(*) Tart is best when freshly made, but you can store it for several hours in a warming oven at about 100 degrees.

Garnitures for Bouchées and Vol-au-Vent

* *RIS DE VEAU À LA FINANCIÈRE*

[Braised Sweetbreads Garnished with
Quenelles, Truffles, Mushrooms, and Olives]

This is certainly one of the great classic fillings for *bouchées* and large
vol-au-vent, and delicious when properly done. Unfortunately, like Beef
Wellington in the hands of the profane and cynical, gummy sauces, clumsy
flavoring, and bad pastry have ruined its reputation. We urge you to give it
another try, and you will understand why it has long been so popular with
great chefs. You may not want to add all of the items listed, but you will have
a delicious creamed sweetbread filling even if you do not do the full *financière,*
which could also include cockscombs and white kidneys (*crêtes et rognons de
coq*), although we have not listed them in the ingredients.

MANUFACTURING NOTE

This is the kind of filling that you can prepare the day before serving.
We shall not give proportions of how much filling is to go into each pastry,
because there is no way of knowing what size and how many you are to
make; leftover filling will be just as good the next day, with scrambled eggs
or as the filling for an omelette.

For about 1½ quarts, serving 6 to 8

1) *The sweetbreads and the sauce base*

2 lbs. soaked and peeled
sweetbreads braised in
wine, stock, and aromatic
vegetables, Volume I,
page 410
2 cups fresh baby mush-
rooms, or larger mush-
rooms quartered
2½ cups liquid as
follows: the cooking
stock from the sweet-
breads plus half veal or
chicken stock and half
milk to complete the
measure

Remove sweetbreads to a plate, and strain cooking
stock into a bowl. Return stock to braising dish.
Trim mushrooms, wash rapidly in cold water, and
quarter if necessary. Add mushrooms to liquid in
braising dish and simmer 5 minutes. Dip or strain
them out, and add to sweetbreads. In the heavy saucepan, melt the butter, blend in the flour, and stir over
moderate heat with wooden spoon until flour and
butter foam together for 2 minutes without browning.
Remove from heat, and as soon as this *roux* stops
bubbling, pour in all the hot braising liquid at once,
blending vigorously with wire whip until perfectly
smooth.

A heavy-bottomed 3-quart
   saucepan, enameled or
   stainless
4 Tb butter
5 Tb flour
A wooden spoon and a
   wire whip
½ to ⅔ cup heavy cream

Return over moderately high heat, and stir with wire whip as sauce thickens and comes to the boil. It will be quite thick. Thin out, still simmering, with spoonfuls of cream; sauce should coat spoon fairly heavily.

Salt and white pepper to
   taste
If needed: More white
   wine, Sercial Madeira,
   more stock, a pinch more
   thyme or bay leaf

Taste sauce very carefully for seasoning and strength. It may need simmering with more wine, or strengthening with Madeira, veal stock, a little beef stock, or herbs. If so, simmer it, stirring, and tasting until you are satisfied. The egg yolks, butter, and the other ingredients will give it more interest, but it should be delicious at this point. (You will need about equal quantities of sauce and garniture.)

---

2) *The rest of the garniture, and final flavorings and enrichment*

1 or more truffles and
   the juices from the can
Veal or chicken *quenelles,*
   poached, and cut into ½-
   inch pieces, Volume I,
   page 189 (or canned imported *quenelles* of veal
   or chicken), 1 to 1½
   cups, depending on how
   much you have or need
⅔ cup small green pitted
   olives simmered 5
   minutes in 1 quart of
   water
Salt and white pepper to
   taste
Drops of lemon juice
2 egg yolks blended with
   ¼ cup heavy cream in a
   small bowl
2 to 4 Tb soft butter

Cut the braised sweetbreads into ½-inch slices or into ½-inch dice, and set aside. Fold the mushrooms into the sauce. If you have several truffles, slice one and use for decoration later; dice the rest into small pieces and add to the sauce along with their juices. Fold in the diced *quenelles* and the olives. Bring to the simmer for 3 to 4 minutes to blend flavors, and taste very carefully for seasoning, adding salt, pepper, and lemon as needed. Remove from heat, beat several spoonfuls of hot sauce gradually into the cream and egg yolks, then fold the egg-yolk mixture back into the saucepan along with the sweetbreads. Reheat, folding slowly, to below the simmer. Remove from heat and fold in the butter, a spoonful at a time. Spoon into the hot *bouchées* or *vol-au-vent,* and serve immediately, topped, if you wish, with truffle slices or fluted mushrooms.

Hot *bouchées* or *vol-au-vent*

Optional: truffle slices or a fluted cooked mushroom cap (Volume I, pages 510–11) for each serving

---

VARIATIONS

Garniture Dieppoise—Garniture aux Fruits de Mer

[Creamed Seafood Filling]

Adapt the *marmite dieppoise,* with its sole, halibut, shrimp, scallops, mussels, and lobsters, to the preceding recipe. Follow the *marmite* recipe, page 46, Steps 1 and 2, then boil the cooking liquid down to 2½ to 3 cups, and proceed with the sauce in the preceding recipe, Steps 1 and 2. Use sliced truffles or fluted mushrooms to garnish each serving.

Garniture de Volaille, Financière

[Diced Chicken in White-wine Sauce with *Quenelles,*
Truffles, Mushrooms, and Olives]

Poach chicken pieces in white wine and aromatic vegetables, following the recipe for *poulet poché au vin blanc,* page 253, Steps 1 and 2. Peel and dice the chicken, and then proceed as for the sweetbreads, simply substituting chicken and chicken stock for fish and fish stock.

CHAPTER THREE

Meats: From Country Kitchen to Haute Cuisine

BRAISED BEEF

Boeuf Braisé, Paupiettes, and Daubes

WHETHER IT IS ONE LARGE PIECE or a dozen small ones, whether you use red wine or white, whether or not you marinate it, lard it, flour it, thicken its juices at the beginning or at the end, all beef that is braised undergoes much the same process, and if you have done one you can do all. This is comforting to remember when you run into a new pot roast or stew: it is only the small differences in method, garnishing, or flavor that distinguish one recipe from another. For example, the fine *boeuf en daube à la provençale* on page 161 sounds as though it were quite a different dish from the *boeuf à la mode* in Volume I on page 309, but you will see they are very much related: while the beef for the *daube* is larded with ham, and is put into a thickened sauce from the beginning of its braise, the sauce for the *boeuf à la mode* is thickened at the end of the cooking. Again, in a comparison of beef stews you find the *boeuf bourguignon* in Volume I braising in a flour-thickened sauce, while the *boeuf aux oignons* here follows the simpler pattern of having its sauce thickened at the end with *beurre manié* (flour-butter paste). The methods are actually interchangeable, and you can conduct any braise exactly as you wish; the more techniques you have absorbed, the more you are master of *la cuisine*.

MARINATING THE BEEF BEFORE COOKING

An aromatic wine marinade adds its own special flavor to beef, and is always an effective tenderizer for the tougher cuts. Marinate or not, as you wish, for any of the following recipes, using the formula for the *daube* on page

163, and dry white wine rather than red, if you wish. For the marinade to be effective, stew meat or meat for *paupiettes* needs at least 6 hours, and a roast, 12 hours. Several days of marination in the refrigerator will be even more penetrating, and the marinade will also preserve the meat a little longer. In other words, rather than freezing it, if you are a once-a-week shopper, marinate it. Drain and dry the beef thoroughly before proceeding with any recipe. Substitute the marinade vegetables and wine for whatever is called for in the recipe, and if carrots are not one of the ingredients listed, for instance, add the marinade carrots anyway, since such details are of small importance.

LARDONS, PORK FAT, BACON, AND SUET

Lardons, those stick-shaped bits of fat-and-lean pork 1½ inches long and ¼ inch thick, are typical of French stews. Their rendered fat browns the beef, and their flavor adds a subtle touch to its sauce. Fresh, unsalted, and unsmoked pork belly is the cut to use if you can find it, otherwise substitute chunk bacon, cut, and blanched (simmered) 10 minutes in a quart of water to remove its salty, smoky taste. (Fat-and-lean salt pork, if very fresh and fine, is another alternative, but it must also be blanched.) Pork fat for larding and for draping over the meat is discussed in the *charcuterie* chapter on page 319. If you prefer suet, although it tends to shrink up, use fat from the outside of a rib or a loin of beef.

BEEF CUTS FOR STEWS

Most markets have ready-cut stew meat all packaged by the pound, and there is no telling what it is. If you want to order your own, the following are some recommended cuts.

Cuts from the round (hind leg)—la cuisse

TOP ROUND, *tende de tranche.* This is rather expensive, but furnishes solid pieces of meat with no muscle separations.

BOTTOM ROUND, *gîte à la noix.* This also furnishes solid pieces, but the cooked meat will tend to be somewhat grainy; be sure not to overcook it, to avoid an accentuation of this quality. The eye of the round, part of this cut, *rond de gîte à la noix,* is not at all recommended for stewing because of its excessive graininess.

SIRLOIN TIP (also called KNUCKLE), *tranche grasse.* Lower parts and outside of this cut, when clear of gristle, can be used for stewing.

HEEL OF ROUND, *nerveux gîte à la noix.* The hind shank when boned and de-gristled makes excellent, gelatinous stew meat, but benefits from a marinade and longer cooking.

Cuts from the chuck (shoulder end)

SHOULDER BLADE, *paleron;* SHOULDER ARM, *macreuse* and *jumeau;* CHUCK RIBS, *basses côtes* or *côtes découvertes;* NECK, *collier.* There are numerous fine stewing cuts from this section, but usually only Jewish or European butchers know them. Especially recommended are the chuck tender, a conical muscle lying along one side of the shoulder blade; flunken or flanken, the top of the chuck short ribs; arm pot roast.

Cuts from the underside and short ribs—caparaçon et plat de côtes

These include the brisket, *poitrine,* which is really too grainy for stewing but fine for braising whole; the plate, *tendron,* with its mixture of fat and lean and its cartilaginous bones, which make for good sauce consistency; and the flank, *flanchet,* which is not for stewing in pieces but may be stuffed and braised whole if it is not scored and broiled for steak. The short ribs, *plat de côtes couvert* (ribs 7 to 9), are excellent in a stew but take up a lot of room in your casserole because the bones are left in; however, they have excellent flavor and the meat with bones makes a delicious sauce.

✳ *BOEUF AUX OIGNONS*
[Beef Stew with Onions and Red Wine]

This is the most elemental of beef stews, with its *lardons* of pork that render the fat that browns the beef that simmers in wine, along with onions, herbs, garlic, and a hint of tomato. Delicious just as it is, the inclusion of other elements changes its character as well as its name, making it, in fact, the perfect stew for our game of theme and variations. Buttered noodles, buttered peas, and little tomatoes go beautifully with this stew, but if you wish to branch into more exotic preparations you might choose one of the eggplant recipes, such as the sauté *en persillade,* page 347, or the broiled eggplant slices on page 346, accompanied, perhaps, with individual servings of potatoes in the form of *pommes duchesse,* page 399. A full and hearty red wine like Beaujolais, Côtes-du-Rhône, or Mountain Red is called for here.

For 6 people

---

1) *Browning the beef and other preliminaries*

5 to 6 ounces (⅔ cup) *lardons* (1½-inch sticks of blanched bacon ¼ inch thick, page 148)	Brown the *lardons* lightly with a tablespoon of the oil in the frying pan; transfer with a slotted spoon to the casserole, leaving fat in frying pan.

Olive oil or cooking oil
A large (11-inch) frying
   pan (no-stick
   recommended)
A heavy, covered, 5- to 6-
   quart casserole (such as a
   round one, 10 by 4 inches)

3½ to 4 lbs. boned and
   trimmed beef stew meat
   cut into chunks about 2
   by 3 by 1 inches (list of
   cuts is on pages 148–9)
Paper towels
1 tsp salt
⅛ tsp pepper

While *lardons* are browning, dry meat thoroughly in paper towels, and when *lardons* are done, raise heat under pan to moderately high. When fat in pan is very hot but not smoking, add as many pieces of beef as will fit easily in one layer. Turn every 2 to 3 minutes, browning meat nicely on all sides. (Add a tablespoon or so more oil if needed.) As some pieces are browned, transfer to casserole and brown additional ones until all are done and transferred to casserole. Toss and turn the meat with the salt and pepper.

---

2) *Assembling braising ingredients*

2 cups sliced onions
2 large cloves garlic, mashed
2 cups beef stock or
   bouillon (more if
   needed)
A medium herb bouquet
   tied in washed cheesecloth
   (1 imported bay leaf, 4
   parsley sprigs, and ½
   tsp thyme)
1 tomato, peeled, seeded,
   and roughly chopped
Optional, but desirable for
   sauce consistency: 2 cups
   chopped or sawed veal
   knuckle bones or beef
   marrow bones, and/or
   an 8-inch square of
   blanched pork rind
   (Volume I, page 401)
2 cups full-bodied, young,
   red wine (such as Mâcon
   or Mountain Red)

If fat in frying pan has burned and blackened, discard it and pour ⅛ inch of oil into pan. Add onions and cook over moderate heat, stirring occasionally, for 8 to 10 minutes or until fairly tender and beginning to brown lightly. Meanwhile add to the meat in the casserole the garlic, bouillon, herbs, tomato, and optional ingredients. When the onions are done, stir them in. To deglaze frying pan, pour in the wine, scraping around with a wooden spoon to dislodge all cooking juices. Finally, pour wine into casserole, adding a little more (or more stock), if necessary, so ingredients are just covered.

(*) AHEAD-OF-TIME NOTE: Recipe may be done a day or two in advance to this point. When cold, cover and refrigerate.

3) *Braising*

Bring stew to simmer on top of stove, cover casserole, and either maintain at slow simmer on top of stove or place in lower-middle level of preheated 350-degree oven; regulate heat so that stew simmers slowly throughout cooking. Turn and baste the meat occasionally. Stew is done when you can pierce the beef quite easily with a knife; slice into it and sample several pieces if you have any doubts.

TIMING: Note that aged, prime beef will cook faster than other grades, regardless of cut.

Sirloin tip, rump, top round, flunken—1½ to 2½ hours.

Bottom round, shoulder arm, chuck tender, short ribs—2 to 3 hours.

Heel of round, and other gelatinous cuts with muscle separation and gristle—3 to 4 hours.

---

4) *Sauce*

A 2- to 3-quart saucepan
4 Tb flour
3 Tb soft butter in a
   1-quart bowl
A rubber spatula
A wire whip

Set cover askew and pour cooking liquid out of casserole into saucepan. Discard herb bouquet and bones from casserole. With a large spoon, skim as much surface fat as you can from liquid, then bring to the simmer, skimming, to remove more fat.

Taste carefully for strength and seasoning; if weak, boil down rapidly to concentrate flavor, adding, if you think it necessary, a little tomato paste, another clove of mashed garlic, more herbs, salt, and pepper. When you are satisfied, remove from heat; you should have about 3 cups of rich and delicious liquid that must now be thickened into a sauce with *beurre manié*. To do so, blend flour and butter to a smooth paste with rubber spatula; beat vigorously into hot liquid with wire whip. When perfectly smooth, bring liquid to the simmer, stirring with wire whip, and simmer 2 minutes. Sauce should be thick enough to coat a spoon, meaning it will coat the meat nicely. If too thin, add half again as much *beurre manié;* if too thick, stir in stock or bouillon. Fold the sauce into the meat in the casserole.

(*) AHEAD-OF-TIME NOTE: If you are not serving immediately, set cover askew and keep warm in a 120-degree oven, over simmering water, or on a hot-tray. For serving several hours or several days later, let cool; lay plastic wrap over surface, cover, and refrigerate (or wrap airtight and freeze for several weeks).

---

5) *Serving*

If needed: a warm,
   lightly buttered platter
Parsley sprigs, watercress,
   or whatever vegetables
   you wish to use as a
   garnish

If stew is warm, bring to the simmer again before serving. If it has been chilled, it should simmer 5 to 10 minutes after it has either warmed through slowly on top of the stove or been about 30 minutes in a 350-degree oven. Taste carefully again for seasoning, and if sauce has thickened too much, fold in a little stock or bouillon. Serve either from casserole or turn out onto platter; decorate with greenery or vegetables.

VARIATIONS

Boeuf au Pistou
[Beef Stew with an Herb, Cheese, and Garlic Finish]

This delicious enrichment comes at the very end, after the sauce has been thickened and just before you are ready to serve the beef. The fresh garlic, herbs, cheese, and a bit of tomato will pep up any stew, and is particularly useful for leftovers and canned or frozen mixtures.

To be added just before serving the stew, Step 5.

2 large cloves garlic
A garlic press
A small bowl or mortar
A pestle or wooden spoon
A dozen large leaves of
  fresh minced basil, or
  1 tsp fragrant dried basil
  or oregano
¼ cup freshly grated
  imported Parmesan
  cheese
3 Tb tomato paste
4 dashes Tabasco sauce

Purée garlic through press into bowl. With pestle or wooden spoon, mash it to a paste, then mash with the herbs. Stir in the cheese, tomato paste, and Tabasco. Cover and set aside until you are ready to serve. Stir the *pistou* into finished stew, basting meat with sauce to blend it thoroughly with the *pistou*.

Boeuf à la Provençale
[Beef Stew with Garlic and Anchovy Finish]

The mixture of anchovies, capers, garlic, and parsley described in Volume I, page 324, is an alternate enrichment. Add it as directed for the *pistou* in the preceding recipe.

Boeuf en Pipérade
[Beef Stew with a Garnish of Peppers and Tomatoes]

Another enlivening finish to a stew is the *pipérade*, a fresh sauté of green peppers, tomatoes, garlic, and herbs.

To be added just before serving the *boeuf aux oignons*, Master Recipe, Step 5, page 151.

2 medium-sized green bell peppers, seeded and diced
2 to 3 Tb olive oil or cooking oil in a frying pan
3 or 4 firm, fresh, ripe tomatoes, peeled, seeded, juiced, and diced
2 large cloves of garlic, mashed or minced
A cover for the pan
Salt and pepper to taste
8 large fresh basil leaves, minced, or ½ tsp fragrant dried basil or oregano and 3 Tb fresh minced parsley

Sauté the diced peppers in the oil over moderately low heat for 5 to 6 minutes, or until almost tender. Fold in the diced tomato pulp and garlic; cover pan and cook slowly for several minutes until tomatoes have rendered their juice. Raise heat and toss vegetables for several minutes over high heat to evaporate almost all liquid. Fold in salt and pepper to taste, and the herbs. Set aside until stew is finished. When reheating stew for serving, fold the *pipérade* into the stew, and simmer 5 minutes to blend flavors.

Boeuf aux Olives
[Beef Stew with Olives and Potatoes]

Olives give a very Mediterranean touch and subtle flavor to anything they cook with, and potatoes make the stew practically a one-dish meal. Any of the three preceding garnishes—peppers, anchovies, or *pistou*—may be included as well, if you wish.

To be added near the end of the braising period, when beef has about ½ hour more to cook (Master Recipe for *boeuf aux oignons,* Step 3, page 151).

1) Preparing the olives and potatoes

⅓ cup each: small, pitted green olives, and black, Mediterranean-type olives, pitted
1 quart of water in a saucepan

To remove excess salt and too strong a taste, simmer the olives for 10 minutes; drain. If black olives are still too strong for your taste, simmer them separately 10 minutes more. Leave olives whole if small (¾ inch long), quarter lengthwise if larger.

2½ to 3 lbs. "boiling" potatoes all of a size, about 3 inches long
A bowl of cold water

Peel potatoes, halve lengthwise, and trim into the shape of large garlic cloves about 2½ inches long and 1½ inches at their thickest, making 3 or 4 pieces per person. Reserve in cold water.

2) *Adding olives and potatoes to stew*

A saucepan of salted water for the potatoes
The *boeuf aux oignons*, braised until almost tender, Step 3, page 151
A round of waxed paper or of aluminum foil

A few minutes before they are to be added to the stew, drain the potatoes and place in a saucepan of cold water; bring rapidly to the boil, and boil 1 minute. Drain. Meanwhile, skim accumulated fat off top of stew, remove from casserole any bones, rind, or other extraneous matter, including herb bouquet, and carefully correct seasoning of cooking liquid. Stir in the olives. Spread the potatoes over the top of the stew, press them down into the cooking liquid, and baste with the liquid. Bring stew again to simmer on top of stove, lay paper or foil over potatoes, cover casserole again, and maintain at simmer for about 30 minutes, or until potatoes are tender, basting them once or twice with the cooking liquid.

3) *Finishing the stew*

Optional but attractive: one of the 3 garnishes in the preceding recipes (*pistou* especially)
Beurre manié if needed: 2 Tb flour blended to a paste with 1½ Tb soft butter
If you wish: a hot, buttered platter
Parsley sprigs or minced fresh parsley

You may find that the cooking liquid is sufficiently degreased and sufficiently thickened so that you can serve the stew as is. Otherwise, set cover askew and drain cooking liquid into a saucepan; skim off fat, and correct seasoning. If liquid is lightly thickened and you are using the *pistou,* which will thicken it a little more, simply blend the *pistou* into the cooking liquid and pour back into the casserole. If liquid is thin, beat in the *beurre manié,* bring to the boil, mix in the *pistou* or other garnish if you are using one, and pour back into casserole. Reheat the stew just before serving, and bring to the table either in its casserole or arranged on a platter and decorated with herbs.

Boeuf au Gingembre

[Beef Stew Flavored with Ginger, Capers, and Herbs]

Ginger gives an especially attractive and unusual flavor to beef, and this dish has rather Chinese overtones of sweet and sour. Because of the special flavors, including vinegar, the usual red wine of the beef stew is omitted in this recipe.

Complete Master Recipe for *boeuf aux oignons,* through Step 2, page 150, but omit the 2 cups of red wine; substitute 2 more cups stock or bouillon and the following.

⅓ cup pressed-down
   pain d'épices (page 481),
   gingerbread, or gingersnaps
1½ Tb fresh ginger, grated,
   or 2 tsp powdered ginger
2 Tb capers
¼ cup wine vinegar
2 Tb fresh tarragon or basil,
   or 1 tsp dried herbs
2 cups of the bouillon called
   for in the Master Recipe
An electric blender

Purée the bread or gingersnaps, ginger, capers, vinegar, herbs, and 1 cup of the bouillon in the blender.
Pour mixture into casserole of beef, rinse out blender
jar with more bouillon, pour into casserole, and proceed with recipe.

NOTE: When beef is tender, at end of Step 3, and you have drained out,
skimmed, boiled down, and seasoned the cooking liquid as directed in the next step,
you will probably find that it has thickened enough so that you need do nothing
more to it.

STUFFED BEEF ROLLS
Paupiettes de Boeuf–Roulades

Thin slices of beef rolled around a stuffing and braised in wine is only a
more elaborate way of presenting the familiar beef stew. *Paupiettes* with a
pork and veal stuffing and mustard sauce appear in Volume I on page 319, an
excellent recipe. The first one here is a giant *paupiette de Gargantua*, serving
6 people, while variations are for individual rolls. Stuffings include a Provençale
mixture of greens, onions, pork, and ham, an olive mixture, a pepper mixture,
and a final combination of rice, garlic, and herbs.

BEEF CUTS FOR PAUPIETTES

Look for solid pieces of meat that will make large, thin, cross-grain slices
with no muscle separations. Avoid cuts like brisket, which tend to fall into long,
loose fibers after cooking. Top round (*tende de tranche, noix*) is our first
choice, and a cut from the upper-middle portion will give perfect slices 10 to
12 inches across by 5 to 7 inches. Rump (*rumsteck*) works nicely, of course,
but it is a waste to spend the extra money for rump when round is equally
good. Bottom round (*gîte à la noix*) is a little grainier than top round, but a
satisfactory alternative. Shoulder-arm steak (*macreuse*) is fourth choice only
because of the gristle running through part of the slice, but you can clip the
gristle in several places so that it will not draw the meat out of shape.

✳ *LA PAUPIETTE DE GARGANTUA*
[Giant Stuffed Beef Roll]

Rather than making a number of individual *paupiettes,* this recipe rolls them all into one, and, because the stuffing is green, you need no green vegetable garnish. You could accompany the *paupiette* with broiled tomatoes, sautéed mushrooms, and glazed carrots, or with braised lettuce or endives and sautéed potatoes. Another suggestion is one of the unusual purées starting on page 404, squash and white beans, rice and turnips with garlic, or rutabagas. A full red wine is called for, as in all beef dishes: Burgundy, Moulin-à-Vent, Côtes-du-Rhône.

For 6 people

1) *Preparing the meat*

A 2- to 2½-lb. slice of top round of beef approximately 12 by 6 inches and ¾ to 1 inch thick (other choices on pages 148–9)
3 Tb strong Dijon-type prepared mustard
½ tsp mixed herbs such as thyme and bay leaf, or Italian Seasoning

Trim outside fat and gristle off meat. You are now to cut the slice of beef so that you can open it up like a book, making 2 flaps of meat hinged together at one side. To do so, lay it flat on table and start at one of the long sides with a long, very sharp knife; slice through center of meat, parallel to table, ending ½ inch from other long side. Open up the meat, spread mustard and herbs on inside surface, and set aside while preparing stuffing, next step.

2) *Green stuffing with pork, ham, and onions—for about 3 cups*

1 cup minced onions
2 Tb rendered pork fat or cooking oil
An 8-inch enameled or no-stick frying pan

Cook the onions with the fat or oil in the pan over moderately low heat until tender but not browned.

About ½ lb. greens (collard, kale, turnip, or spinach, fresh or frozen)
A large stainless-steel knife

If greens are fresh, pick them over to remove stems; drop leaves into a large kettle of boiling, salted water, and boil until wilted and fairly tender (2–3 minutes for spinach, more for the others). If frozen, boil for sufficient time in a covered pan with ½ cup salted water until defrosted and fairly tender. Drain cooked greens, refresh in cold water, squeeze out as much water as possible, and chop fine. Then add greens to onions, and stir over moderate heat for several minutes to evaporate moisture and to finish cooking.

A 3-quart mixing bowl (or heavy-duty electric mixer)
1 egg
1 tsp salt
½ tsp *épices fines* (page 288), or mixture of all-spice, thyme, and bay leaf
¼ tsp pepper
1 large clove garlic, mashed
¼ cup dry crumbs from nonsweetened, home-made-type white bread
1 cup diced boiled ham
½ cup fresh sausage meat

Scrape greens and onions into mixing bowl and vigorously beat in the rest of the ingredients listed. Sauté a spoonful, taste, and correct seasoning.

3) *Assembling the paupiette*

Either a 14-inch square of caul fat, page 287;
Or a 12- by 8-inch sheet of pork fat ¼ inch thick;
Or 6 to 8 strips of thick bacon or salt pork, and a 12- by 6-inch piece of beef suet ¼ inch thick
White kitchen string

(If using salt pork or bacon, blanch 10 minutes in 2 quarts of water, and pat dry.) Spread the stuffing over the meat, leaving an inch border of clear meat all around. Starting at one long side, roll the meat rather loosely around the stuffing, making a sausage shape about 4 inches in diameter. Fold over the two ends. If you have caul fat, roll the meat in a double thickness of it; tie lengthwise and in several places around the circumference. Otherwise, place strips of pork fat, bacon, or salt pork over length, particularly the seam, and the ends; tie in place, and reserve remaining pieces of fat for later.

4) *Browning the paupiette—preheat oven to 450 degrees*

Pork fat or cooking oil
A heavy casserole, preferably oval, and just large enough to hold the meat
A medium onion roughly sliced
A medium carrot roughly sliced

(The *paupiette* is soft and must be handled carefully to prevent stuffing from bursting out; it will stiffen after browning.) Pat meat gently with paper towels to dry it. Film casserole with ⅛ inch of fat or oil, and place meat seam-side up in casserole. Strew vegetables around meat. Brown over moderate heat, loosening bottom of meat carefully with a spatula from time to time to prevent sticking. Baste top of meat with fat in pan and set uncovered in upper-middle level of oven to brown top and sides. Baste every 3 to 4 minutes with fat or oil for the 12 to 15 minutes it will take to brown. Remove casserole from oven.

5) *Braising—1½ to 2 hours; oven at 325 degrees*

Salt, pepper, and more of the same herbs

1½ cups dry white wine or dry white French vermouth

1½ or more cups beef stock or bouillon

Aluminum foil and the casserole cover

Turn down oven to 325 degrees. Season the meat with salt, pepper, and herbs. Pour in the wine and enough stock or bouillon to come ½ to ⅔ the way up the meat. Bring to the simmer on top of the stove. If you are using it, drape suet over meat. Place foil on top, cover the casserole, and place in middle level of oven. Baste meat several times during cooking, and regulate oven heat so that liquid is only slowly simmering in casserole. *Paupiette* is done when a knife will pierce the meat easily.

TIMING: 1½ to 2 hours for top-grade beef; as much as an hour more for other cuts and qualities.

(*) AHEAD-OF-TIME NOTES: Meat may be either stuffed or browned in advance of braising. Braised meat may be kept warm in a 120-degree oven for an hour or more. It may be cooled and reheated, but will not have quite the same delicious texture.

6) *Sauce and serving*

A hot serving platter

A sieve set over a saucepan

If needed: 1 Tb of cornstarch blended with 2 Tb white wine, vermouth, or stock

2 Tb soft butter

A hot sauce bowl

Watercress, parsley, or whatever vegetables you wish, to garnish platter

Remove *paupiette* to hot platter, discard strings and fat, replace foil cover over meat, and keep warm in turned-off oven. Strain cooking liquid into saucepan, pressing juice out of braising ingredients. Skim off fat. You should have 1½ to 2 cups liquid slightly thickened by the braising ingredients and the crumbs in the stuffing. (If thin, remove from heat, beat in cornstarch mixture, and simmer for 2 minutes.) Correct seasoning. Just before serving, stir in butter, a half spoonful at a time, spoon a little sauce over meat, and pour rest into sauce bowl. Garnish platter with greenery or vegetables, and serve immediately.

Other stuffings—other garnishings

In addition to the green-pepper stuffing and the garlic and rice stuffing in the following variations, and the veal and pork stuffing on page 319 in Volume I, other possibilities are listed on pages 513–15. Rather than the braising and sauce-making system described here, you may follow that for the *daube* on page 161, or for the beef stews and their variations beginning on page 149, which include *pistou, pipérade,* and ginger flavorings.

VARIATION

The following recipe describes the procedure for making individual *paupiettes.* We have suggested large and luxurious slices of meat; the stuffing is spread over them, and the slice is rolled up like a rug. When you wish to be more economical, make twice the amount of stuffing, use beef slices half as large, and rather than rolling like a rug, fold the meat around the stuffing to enclose it, almost exactly as illustrated for the stuffed cabbage leaves on pages 384–5.

Paupiettes de Boeuf à la Catalane
[Beef Rolls Stuffed with Peppers, Onions, and Mustard Bread]

For 4 paupiettes, 1 per person

1) *Preparing the beef for stuffing*

4 slices of top round of beef 10 to 12 by 6 to 7 inches and ⅜ inch thick (other choices, pages 148–9)
Waxed paper
A mallet or rolling pin
Salt and pepper
½ tsp thyme or oregano

(If you cannot have the beef sliced to your order and have difficulty at home, you can freeze the piece of beef and slice when not quite stiffened, or when partially thawed. This will not harm the meat at all.) Trim off all outside fat and gristle. One by one, pound each slice between sheets of waxed paper with a mallet or rolling pin, to break down the fibers somewhat and to prevent meat from cooking out of shape. Lay out flat, season tops with salt, pepper, and herbs.

2) *Green-pepper, onion, and mustard-bread stuffing—for 3 cups*

1½ cups minced onions
1 tsp mixed, ground thyme, bay leaf, and oregano, or mixed herbs such as Provençal or Italian seasoning
Olive oil or cooking oil as needed
A medium (10-inch) frying pan (no-stick recommended)
1½ cups diced green bell peppers (2 medium peppers)
A mixing bowl
3 slices light rye bread
4 to 5 Tb strong, Dijon-type prepared mustard
2 or 3 large cloves of garlic, mashed or minced
1 egg, lightly beaten
Salt and pepper

Cook the onions and herbs with 3 tablespoons of the oil in the frying pan for 8 to 10 minutes over moderate heat, stirring occasionally, until tender and starting to brown. Stir in the diced peppers and cook, stirring, 4 to 5 minutes more, until peppers are almost tender. Scoop into mixing bowl. Spread both sides of the bread with mustard, film frying pan with ⅛ inch more oil, and brown bread lightly on both sides. Dice the bread and add to the bowl; stir in the garlic, egg, and salt and pepper to taste.

3) Stuffing the paupiettes

The seasoned beef slices
The stuffing
Toothpicks
Strips of fresh pork fat,
  blanched bacon, or suet
  (page 319)

Assuming that the beef slices are roughly rectangular
in shape, choose the neatest of the small sides to be
the exposed end of the roll. Divide stuffing in four,
spread one part over each slice, leaving an inch of
clear meat for the exposed end and ½ inch at the
sides. Roll the meat up to enclose the stuffing and
secure with 2 or 3 toothpicks.

4) Browning, braising, and serving the paupiettes

Follow the ingredients and method in the Master Recipe, Steps 4 through 6,
starting on page 157.

OTHER STUFFINGS FOR PAUPIETTES

Farce Niçoise

[Olive and Pimento Stuffing with Garlic and Herbs]

For 4 paupiettes—2 cups

¼ cup stale, not-too-fine
  crumbs from non-
  sweetened, homemade-
  type white bread
2 to 3 Tb wine vinegar
⅔ to ¾ cup (two 2¼-
  ounce cans) chopped
  ripe black olives
½ cup (about 3 ounces)
  canned red pimentos,
  diced
2 large cloves of garlic,
  mashed or minced
½ tsp sage
⅓ cup grated Parmesan
  cheese
Salt and pepper to taste
Drops of Tabasco sauce
¼ cup (2 ounces) finely
  minced fresh pork fat or
  blanched bacon
4 Tb strong, Dijon-type
  prepared mustard (to
  spread on paupiettes)

Stir the bread crumbs in a small bowl with enough
vinegar barely to moisten them; let sit for a few minutes. Stir the olives, pimentos, garlic, sage, and cheese
in a mixing bowl. Blend in the moistened crumbs,
and season strongly with salt, pepper, and Tabasco.
Blend in the minced pork fat or bacon. Just before
you are ready to stuff the paupiettes, spread topside
of meat with mustard, then with the stuffing.

La Farce à l'Ail de Mme. Cassiot

[Rice and Garlic Stuffing with Herbs]

This fine and very simple stuffing for garlic lovers may have either rice or rather coarse stale bread crumbs for a base. If it is bread crumbs, however, they must come from the type of bread that has texture and body, like your own French bread from page 57. Because the typical store-bought, white, squashy bread disintegrates into mush, we have confined our recipe to rice. If you want crumbs and have the right sort, stir ½ cup beef stock or bouillon into 1½ cups of stale crumbs; let sit 5 minutes, then squeeze crumbs as dry as possible in the corner of a towel.

For 4 paupiettes—2 cups

¾ cup cooked rice
¾ cup fresh pork fat or blanched bacon (6 ounces)
6 to 8 large cloves of garlic, very finely minced
½ tsp thyme or oregano
¼ cup chopped fresh parsley
½ tsp salt
⅛ tsp pepper
4 Tb strong Dijon-type prepared mustard

Either put the rice and pork fat or bacon through the coarse blade of a meat grinder, or put rice through a food mill and finely mince the fat or bacon. Stir together in a bowl with the garlic, herbs, salt and pepper. Just before you are ready to stuff *paupiettes*, spread topside of each slice with mustard, then with the stuffing.

* *BOEUF EN DAUBE À LA PROVENÇALE*

[Braised Pot Roast of Beef with Wine, Tomatoes, and Provençal Flavorings]

This is a large, whole piece of braising beef larded with strips of ham, marinated in red wine and herbs, and slowly simmered in a lightly thickened mixture of the marinade liquid, beef stock, and tomatoes, which turns into a rich ready-made sauce at the end of the cooking. It is a splendid braising method, and one you can adapt to stews as well as pot roasts, and to duck, goose, lamb, livers, and hearts as well as to beef. Rather than the usual potatoes or pasta and buttered peas or beans, or glazed carrots and onions, and sautéed mushrooms, you could serve the little white turnips sautéed in butter on page 407, or the onions stuffed with rice on page 376, and either the broccoli braised in butter on page 340 or one of the sautéed zucchinis starting on page 364. A full-bodied red wine is definitely called for here—a Burgundy, a Côtes-du-Rhône, or a Châteauneuf-du-Pape.

TIMING NOTES

Braised beef may be made ready for cooking a day ahead or may be fully cooked a day or two in advance, if need be. Allow yourself enough leeway for the actual braising, however, if you wish to serve soon after it has cooked. Unless you are sure of your meat quality, allow 5 hours from the moment you put it into the oven to the moment you wish to serve. This will give you extra time for tough meat, and leisure for the details of trimming and sauce making.

BEEF CUTS FOR BRAISING WHOLE

TOP ROUND, *tende de tranche.* Sometimes called inside round, this is a first-choice piece for braising whole because it is solid meat with no separations, and is not fibrous when cooked.

UNDERCUT CHUCK, *basses côtes découvertes.* The continuation of the roast rib of beef section into the shoulder end, usually ribs 2 to 5, makes a choice and tender morsel. You will probably find this only at Jewish or European markets, although a supermarket boneless chuck pot roast can substitute for it.

SHOULDER-ARM POT ROAST, *macreuse.* Again, this may not be available except at Jewish or foreign markets; it will usually take longer cooking than the two preceding cuts, but has excellent flavor.

BOTTOM ROUND or SILVERSIDE, and EYE OF ROUND, *gîte à la noix* and *rond de gîte à la noix.* These two cuts always look attractive, especially the eye of round, with its long, shapely form that resembles a tenderloin. We prefer the bottom round to the eye because it is less fibrous when cooked, but both are acceptable choices.

SIRLION TIP or KNUCKLE, *tranche grasse.* This cut from the round has numerous muscle separations, and is sometimes called knuckle because it passes over the knee of the hind leg. It braises well, but needs firm tying to give it an attractive shape.

MIDDLE OF BRISKET, *milieu de poitrine.* Although coarse-grained when cooked, brisket has excellent flavor; slice it on the bias like flank steak. A good butcher will bone and de-fat it for you; if it is a long, flat piece, roll and tie it for braising.

For 8 to 10 people

----

1) *Preparing the beef*

A trimmed and boned 6-lb. piece of braising beef

Trim meat, if necessary, to make a fairly even cylinder or rectangle with no loose fat or gristly pieces. To from preceding list (preferably one that can be tied into a cylindrical shape 10 to 12 inches long)

For optional larding of meat: a 4- by 6-inch slice of prosciutto or ready-to-cook ham slice about ¼ inch thick

lard the meat, follow directions illustrated on pages 170–2, using ham rather than the pork fat called for in the larding directions. Whether or not you have larded it, tie the beef, also as illustrated there, to keep it in shape during cooking.

---

2) *Marinating the meat—at least 12 hours or for several days*

NOTE: You may omit this step and proceed directly to Step 3.

---

1 bottle (almost 4 cups) full, strong, young, red wine (Mâcon, Beaujolais, California Mountain Red)

½ cup red-wine vinegar

¼ cup olive oil

6 cloves unpeeled garlic, halved

2 medium-sized onions and 2 carrots, sliced

1 Tb coarse salt or table salt

The following herb bouquet, tied in washed cheesecloth: 2 imported bay leaves, 4 cloves or allspice berries, 6 peppercorns, ½ tsp each of dried fennel seeds, oregano, thyme, and marjoram

An enameled, glazed, or stainless bowl or casserole just large enough to hold meat comfortably

Mix the marinade ingredients in the bowl or casserole, add the beef and baste it. (Liquid should come at least halfway up.) Marinate, turning and basting meat several times a day, for at least 12 hours or for several days either at a temperature of 40 to 50 degrees or in the refrigerator. When you are ready for the next step, drain beef, and wipe thoroughly dry with paper towels. Strain marinade, reserving both liquid and vegetables for Step 5.

---

3) *Browning the beef and the braising ingredients*

NOTE: If you have not marinated the beef, add all the ingredients from Step 2, except the vinegar, to the ingredients here.

Either 4 Tb rendered fresh
    pork fat or goose fat;
Or olive oil or cooking oil
6 ounces (¾ cup) *lardons*
    (1½-inch sticks of
    blanched bacon ¼ inch
    thick, page 148)
A heavy, covered casserole
    or roaster large enough to
    hold meat comfortably
    (or brown meat in a
    large frying pan and
    transfer to roaster
    afterwards)
For added flavor and
    body: 1 quart of sawed
    veal knuckle bones
    and/or beef soup bones;
    or a split and blanched
    calf's foot
The drained marinade
    vegetables
The marinade liquid
A strip of fresh pork fat
    ⅛ inch thick and long
    and wide enough to cover
    top and sides of beef; or
    beef suet
White string
The marinade bouquet of
    herbs
Optional but desirable for
    the sauce: a 6-inch square
    of blanched pork rind
    (Volume I, page 401)

Cook the *lardons* slowly in the fat or oil in the casserole (or frying pan) until very lightly browned.
Remove with a slotted spoon and reserve. Pour 4 to
5 Tb of fat out of the casserole and reserve for the
roux, next step. Raise heat to moderately high and
brown the well-dried beef on all sides and ends, lifting and turning it with the help of its trussing
strings. (This will take 10 minutes or more; regulate heat so meat browns nicely but fat does not burn.
Add more fat or oil if needed.) Remove beef and
brown the optional bones or calf's foot and the marinade vegetables for 4 to 5 minutes, stirring and tossing over high heat. Set cover askew on casserole, drain
out cooking fat, and pour in marinade liquid. Stir
with wooden spoon to dislodge all coagulated bits of
brown flavor into liquid. Tie strip of fat about beef
(illustrations are on page 175), push bones aside, and
lay the beef, fat-covered side up, in casserole. Add
the bouquet of herbs, the *lardons,* and the optional
pork rind to the casserole, and set aside until you are
ready to braise, Step 5.

4) *The brown roux to thicken the braising sauce*

A heavy-bottomed
    saucepan in thick, cast
    aluminum or a heavy
    cast-iron frying pan,
    about 6 inches bottom
    diameter
The 4 Tb reserved fat
    from Step 3
⅓ cup flour (measure

(NOTE: You will have a better *roux* if you cook it
separately rather than in the casserole after browning meat and bones.)
Be sure to pick a heavy pan; melt the fat in it over
moderate heat, blend in the flour, and stir continuously for about 15 minutes until flour slowly turns a
dark, nutty brown. (It must not blacken, burn, and
turn bitter, but it must brown properly so as to give
the right flavor and color to the sauce.) Remove from

by scooping dry-measure cup into flour and sweeping off excess)

A wooden spoon

1½ cups beef stock (or bouillon) heated in a small saucepan

A wire whip

A ladle

heat, and when *roux* has stopped bubbling, blend in all the hot stock at once with wire whip. When perfectly smooth, ladle in some of the liquid from the casserole to thin the sauce, mix well, then stir all into the casserole, blending liquids thoroughly together.

---

5) *Braising the beef—3½ to 4 hours or longer at 350 degrees*

1 lb. (4 to 5 medium) tomatoes, not peeled, but halved, seeded, juiced, and roughly chopped (or a mixture of fresh tomatoes and strained canned tomatoes)

A 3- by 1-inch piece of dried orange peel, or 1 tsp dried pulverized orange peel

Optional Provençal flavoring: 6 to 7 anchovies packed in olive oil, drained, and mashed to a paste

More beef stock if needed

Stir the tomatoes, orange peel, and optional anchovies into the casserole, and more stock, if needed, so that liquid comes ⅔ to ¾ the way up the beef.

(*) AHEAD-OF-TIME-NOTE: May be prepared in advance to this point; when cool, cover and refrigerate.

Salt to taste

Aluminum foil

Bring to simmer on top of the stove; salt lightly to taste if necessary. Lay the foil over the beef, cover the casserole, and set in lower third of preheated, 350-degree oven.

In about half an hour, check to see that liquid is simmering slowly, not bubbling fast: regulate oven throughout cooking so that liquid remains at a slow but definite simmer. Baste and turn the beef several times during cooking.

Beef is done when a fork pierces it easily, but it must not be cooked so long that it begins to fall apart. Aged, top-quality American beef usually takes 3½ hours; other grades or qualities may take an hour or so longer.

6) *Trimming the beef and finishing the sauce*

Remove beef from casserole to a board or platter. Cut and discard trussing string, discard fat covering beef (or trim off suet adhering to beef and the gristle under it); trim off any loose bits of meat.

Remove bones from casserole, then pour contents of casserole through a sieve set over a large saucepan; press juices out of ingredients and into saucepan with a wooden spoon. Discard contents of sieve. Let liquid settle a few minutes in saucepan, then skim off all surface fat with a spoon; bring liquid back to the simmer, skimming off additional fat. Taste very carefully for seasoning and strength. You should have 4 to 5 cups of richly fragrant sauce, deep reddish brown, and the consistency of a lightly thickened soup that would coat the meat nicely, and coats the spoon. If you feel sauce should be thicker or lacks depth of flavor, boil it down rapidly to concentrate it. If it seems necessary, add and simmer a pinch of herbs, garlic, or tomato paste or a little concentrated bouillon. (If sauce has reduced too much during braising, thin out with more stock or water.)

(*) AHEAD-OF-TIME NOTES: You may complete recipe to this point; return beef to casserole and pour the sauce over it. Cover and keep warm, basting occasionally, in a 150-degree oven or upon 2 asbestos mats over low heat on top of the stove. For serving several hours or 2 days later, let cool, then cover and refrigerate; reheat for half an hour or so, basting and turning meat several times, in a 325-degree oven.

7) *Serving*

CARVING AT THE TABLE. Place the meat on a warm platter, spoon a little of the hot sauce over it to glaze its surface. Decorate platter with sprigs of parsley or watercress. Pass separately the rest of the sauce and whatever vegetables you are serving.

SERVING THE MEAT SLICED, ON A PLATTER. Carve the meat in the kitchen and arrange in overlapping slices on a warm, slightly buttered platter. Spoon some of the sauce around the meat, and decorate platter with parsley or watercress, or with whatever vegetable garnish you wish. Pass rest of sauce and other vegetables separately.

Leftovers

Leftovers, whether sliced or not, may be reheated in the sauce, if any is left over, or in another sauce with the same flavorings. See also the *tous nus* on page 306, and the list of stuffings on pages 513–15, both calling for ground leftover braised beef.

To serve cold

A delicious *salade de boeuf à la parisienne* is made with cold braised beef in Volume I, page 543, or an aspic, *boeuf mode en gelée,* again in Volume I, on page 556.

VARIATIONS

Boeuf en Caisse, Surprise

[Stuffed, Braised Pot Roast of Beef—Beef Case]

Like that present for the man who has everything, this is an enjoyable conceit for the cook who has cooked everything who wants to surprise guests who have eaten everything. A splendid piece of beef comes to the table looking like a typical *boeuf mode.* But no, it is not. When the host begins to serve, it is revealed that the beef was ingeniously hollowed out before braising, filled with a fragrant garniture of onions, mushrooms, olives, and herbs, and these slowly imparted their flavors to the meat while it cooked. You might accompany this with the purée of yellow squash and white beans, page 404, or the purée of rice and turnips with herbs and garlic on page 405. Either a plainly cooked green vegetable or broiled tiny tomatoes might also be included, and the red wine choices would again be Burgundy, Côtes-du-Rhône, or Châteauneuf-du-Pape.

For 8 to 10 people

1) Forming the beef case

A solid, boneless 6- to 7-lb. piece of braising beef, preferably loaf shaped (top round, face rump, or bottom round)	Trim all fat and gristle from outside of meat and cut off any protruding pieces, to make a neat shape. (The loaf shape illustrated is easiest to stuff and to carve, but a thick wedge will do.)
White string Rendered pork fat, goose fat, or cooking oil A heavy, 12-inch frying pan (no-stick recommended)	Meat is now to be browned, because it is easier to do so now than later; dry thoroughly in paper towels, and make several firm ties around its length and circumference, to hold its shape. Heat fat or oil in pan to very hot but not smoking, and brown meat on all sides and the two ends. Remove meat to a cutting board and discard trussing string. (If browning fat has burned, discard it, otherwise leave in pan for Step 2.)

The first step is to make the cover: starting at one end of what you have decided is the topside of the beef, cut an even slice ½ inch thick to within ½ inch at the other end, where slice remains attached like the cover of a book.

Bend the cover back. *In the main body of the meat, cut a rectangular incision 1 inch deep and ½ inch from outside edges.*

1 inch deep

½ inch

½ inch thick

*Make lengthwise and crosswise cuts
1 inch deep and about ¾ inch
apart, to form cubes.*

*Cut out cubes of meat with
scissors* or with a knife. You now
have a hinged case of beef with
probably 2 inches of solid meat at
the bottom, ½ inch at the sides,
and an inch of hollow space
underneath the cover.

2) *The mushroom and olive garniture or filling—for about 2 cups*

The cubes of beef removed
from the case
The frying pan from Step
1, and more fat or oil as
needed
A mixing bowl
1½ cups (about 6 ounces)
quartered fresh mush-
rooms, washed and dried
2 cups sliced onions
¼ cup mild-cured ham (or
supermarket ham slice)
cut into ¼-inch dice
1 to 2 large cloves mashed
garlic
4 medium-sized black,
oil-cured olives, pitted
and diced
½ tsp thyme
1 egg
Pepper and salt

Cut the beef cubes so all are approximately ⅜ inch
across; dry in paper towels. Heat fat or oil in pan
until very hot but not smoking; rapidly brown beef
cubes, tossing and turning them for several minutes,
shaking and swirling the pan by its handle. When
browned, scoop into bowl, leaving fat in pan. Add
more fat or oil, if necessary, to film pan by 1/16
inch, and brown the mushrooms, tossing and turning for several minutes over high heat. Scoop into
bowl; add the onions to the pan with a little more fat
or oil if needed. Turn heat to low, stir up onions,
cover pan, and cook slowly for 8 to 10 minutes until
tender; raise heat, and stir for 2 to 3 minutes until
onions are very lightly browned. Scoop into the mixing bowl, stirring in also the ham, garlic, diced olives,
herbs, and egg. Season to taste, but be careful of salt
because olives are salty.

3) *Filling and tying the case*

White string
Either a sheet of pork
    fat ¼ inch thick and
    large enough to cover
    top and sides of beef
    (page 319);
Or caul fat (page 287);
Or well-washed cheesecloth

Sprinkle interior of beef case with
salt and pepper, heap in the
garniture, and *turn the hinged
cover down to enclose it.*

*Make 1 or 2 loops of string around
length of beef and enough around
circumference to hold cover
securely in place over garniture.*

    Either drape the fat over the beef and tie in place with string, or wrap and tie the entire case in caul fat or a double thickness of damp cheesecloth.

    (*) AHEAD-OF-TIME NOTE: May be completed to this point as much as a day in advance; wrap in plastic and refrigerate.

4) *Braising the beef—3 to 4 hours*

    Because the beef has already been browned, you need only follow the general method outlined for the preceding *daube* with its brown roux, pages 161–6, or the simpler braising method for the beef stew on page 149 with its *beurre-manié* sauce thickening.

5) *Serving*

    Unless the beef is carved and served at the table, there will be no *surprise.* After removing strings and other extraneous matter, place beef on a hot platter, spoon a little of the sauce over it, and decorate platter with vegetables or parsley. To serve, pry cover loose and lift it, so that the garniture may be admired, then replace and cut straight through the meat as though it were a loaf of bread. Heap the garniture of mushrooms, olives, and beef cubes over each serving, and moisten with a big spoonful of sauce.

HOW TO LARD A PIECE OF MEAT

In the old days, when meat was tougher and far leaner than it is today, and when venison and game were plentiful, strips of pork fat were inserted through it to baste and moisten the interior of the meat during cooking. Now meat is larded more often because it is the stylish thing to do, and the bits of pork fat, ham, or whatever has been inserted make attractive designs when the meat is sliced.

Larding fat—Pork fat and beef suet

The best fat to use is fresh pork fatback because it is hard and smooth. If you cannot find it, use blanched fat bacon or salt pork, or fat from the outside of a fresh pork loin. (If you do not wish to use pork fat, substitute suet from the outside of a rib or loin of beef.) Cut the fat into whatever length and width will fit your larding needle, making a test piece first to be sure you will have a snug fit; chill the fat for easy handling.

The larding process

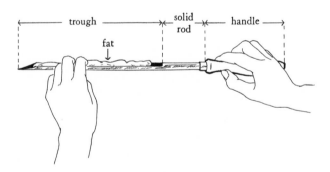

In order to lard meat you must have a larding needle, or *lardoire,* a hollow tube or trough of steel shaped like a giant steel pen point with a wooden handle. *Starting just back from the point, press the strip of fat down into the trough of the lardoire,* being sure fat fits snugly so that it will not slip out when the *lardoire* is pushed through the meat.

Meat is larded with strips of fat
running parallel to the grain, so that
when the meat is sliced you will cut
across the strips of fat. Insert point of
lardoire into one end of meat, and
*with a continuous, slow, clockwise
rotation, push the instrument
gradually through* until point of
lardoire and ½ inch of fat protrude
from the other end of the meat.

*With the point of a small knife,
gently dig end of fat-strip out of
trough at protruding end of lardoire.*

*Then dig other end of fat-strip out
of trough at the other end of the
lardoire.*

*Hold the thumb of your left hand in
the trough of the lardoire against
the fat-strip, thus preventing fat
from slipping out of meat while you
slowly, with a slight rocking rotation
left and right, withdraw the lardoire
from the meat leaving the fat in its
place.*

Insert as many other fat-strips as
you wish—a piece of meat 4½ to 5
inches in diameter will take 4 to 6.
*Tie the meat into shape with strong
white string.*

BEEF TENDERLOIN
Filet de Boeuf

The central and the right-hand sections together, in this drawing, constitute what is usually meant in American retail meat markets by a whole tenderloin: to be technically correct, it should be called the whole short-loin tenderloin. It weighs 4½ to 5 pounds untrimmed, and contains 3½ to 4 pounds of usable meat. When you are serving 6 to 8 people, you may wish the central section only, *le coeur du filet,* which will give you a roast of 2½ to 3 pounds that averages 8 to 10 inches in length. For 10 to 12 people you will need the whole piece, and may fold the last 2 inches of the tail (right-hand side) back upon itself as illustrated further on, to make a 12-inch roast that is 3½ to 4 inches in diameter when tied.

If by chance your market does cut whole sides of beef, you may be able to buy the whole tenderloin with butt end attached. Depending on the cutting method, the butt alone contains only a little over 1½ pounds of usable meat, although it weighs slightly more than 3 pounds; to be deprived of it, therefore, is no great loss, tenderloins costing what they do.

TRIMMING A TENDERLOIN

Most meat markets will usually trim, tie, and lard the tenderloin for you, but you should be able to do it yourself so that you will know how the meat is constructed.

When you have an untrimmed tenderloin in front of you, you will note a definite difference in the 2 long, flat sides. On one there is a series of thick ridges and depressions more or less marbled with fat depending on the grade of the beef carcass; this side is where the filet rested against the 6 vertebrae of the backbone in the small of the back. We shall call this the underside. The other side, which we shall call the top, will have some loose fat clinging to it, mostly at the large end and at the edges; along the central length you will see the main muscle of the tenderloin, covered with a shiny membrane. Starting on this side, rather gingerly pull the loose fat from the top of the membrane and along the edges, being very careful not to detach the 2 long straps of meat lying against each side of the main muscle. The smaller of the two straps is flattish, as though it were a flaplike continuation of the underside; underneath the larger of the straps, *la chainette,* is a line of fat that should not be disturbed because it attaches the meat to the main muscle.

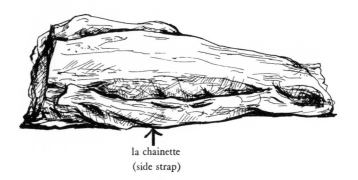

la chainette
(side strap)

This is the whole short-loin tenderloin (central and right-hand portions of diagram, page 172), showing the 2 chains of meat attached to the length of the main muscle. Do not worry too much if you partially detach them; you are going to tie the meat anyway before roasting, and the ties will make the chains adhere. Although some people advise removing these chains of meat, you will diminish your roast by more than half its weight if you do so: you will end up with 2 thin strings of meat good only for sautéing or skewering, and your *filet* proper will weigh only 2 pounds. This is entirely a matter of your own preference, of course; we leave them on.

After pulling excess fat from the top of the meat, you must also remove the shiny membrane that covers the main muscle on this side, and as much of it on the large chain of meat as you easily can. Remove the membrane in half-inch strips the length of the meat, scraping under it with a small, sharp knife. (If you happen to have an actual whole tenderloin with butt included, you will notice that the main muscle with its membrane continues into the butt for several inches before it loses itself. You may wish to separate this main muscle from the rest, making it a continuation of your roast. The surrounding meat will make excellent steaks or sautés. It is rather a question of how it looks to you while you are trimming: as long as all the membranes are removed, all of the meat is good either for roasting or sautéing.)

Finally, inspect the underside of the meat and remove what you consider to be obviously excess fat; a reasonable amount left on will help to baste the meat as it roasts. Meat is now trimmed and ready for cooking. The following directions are for roasting; directions for steaks are in Volume I, pages 291 and 296–300. Do not forget the sautés of beef, Volume I, pages 325–8, which are delicious for meat from the butt, the chains, and the tail; you may also adapt sautés for any leftover cooked tenderloin.

TYING AND LARDING THE TENDERLOIN

Whether it is roasted or braised, and whether you are using the heart (central section, page 173) or the whole tenderloin, the circumference must be tied to keep the meat together and to force it into cylindrical rather than oval shape for even cooking. Use the rather thick, soft, white butcher's string, often called corned-beef twine, if you can find it. The top of the meat is the side formerly covered by a shiny membrane, as opposed to the ridged side, which rested against the back bone.

When you are roasting the whole tenderloin, *turn the last 2 inches of the tail back under its ridged side* to make the roast even in diameter throughout its length.

When you wish to tie the meat without larding it, tie or wind firm loops of string around the circumference at $1\frac{1}{4}$-inch intervals.

To lard and tie the meat, drape pork fat or suet over the top of the meat and down under the folded tail to hold it in place. Tie a loop of string around the length of the meat. (If you do not have long strips of fat, overlap short ones as shown in the illustrations.)

Then arrange strips of fat over the sides of the meat; tie loops of string around the circumference.

If you can find or order caul fat, that
marvelous membrane webbed with
fat that comes from inside the pig,
it is perfect for wrapping a tenderloin that is roasted with a covering
of mushroom *duxelles* or *mirepoix,*
or for the sliced, stuffed tenderloin on
page 180. *Here the tenderloin is laid
on the caul fat and the flavoring is
being spread over it.*

*Fold a double thickness of caul fat
around the meat to enclose it completely, and tie in place.* The caul fat
browns and tends to merge with the
meat and stuffing.

✳ *FILET DE BOEUF POÊLÉ*

[Tenderloin of Beef, Casserole-roasted with Aromatic Vegetables]

A favorite roasting method that comes to us from the old classic cuisine is
poêlage, meaning to brown the meat and then roast it in a covered casserole
with *les aromates.* This is particularly successful with beef tenderloin because
the aromatic ingredients, even though their contact with the meat is brief,
subtly enhance its flavor and aroma. In addition, you have a deliciously
flavored base for the sauce. Because internal meat temperature rises very
quickly when beef is done in a covered roaster, watch it carefully after your
meat thermometer reaches 110 degrees. (Make a guess if your thermometer
starts at 130 degrees.)

Suggested Accompaniments: A garnish of watercress and sautéed mushrooms around the meat, and *endives à la dauphinoise* (gratin of endives and
sliced potatoes, page 389); red Bordeaux-Médoc wine.

For 10 to 12 people

1) *Preliminaries to roasting*

A tenderloin of beef, 3½
to 4 lbs., trimmed and
tied (pages 173–6)
Olive oil or cooking oil
A heavy 12-inch frying
pan (an oval "fish fryer"
is ideal for this)
A heavy, oval, flameproof
casserole just large
enough to hold beef (such
as 12 by 9 inches)
Salt and pepper
½ cup sliced onions
½ cup sliced carrots
1 bay leaf, broken
½ tsp thyme
A piece of fresh pork fat
or suet 12 by 9 inches and
¼ inch thick
2½ cups veal stock or
beef bouillon
A cover for the casserole

Dry the beef thoroughly on paper towels. Film the pan with ⅛ inch of oil and set over moderately high heat. When very hot but not smoking, brown beef lightly on all sides, season with salt and pepper, and place in casserole. Brown the vegetables lightly in the same fat, season, stir in the herbs, and strew the vegetables over, under, and around the beef. Drape the fat over the meat. Spoon oil out of frying pan, pour in bouillon and boil for a moment, scraping up any coagulated cooking juices. Pour liquid into a cup and reserve for Step 3.

2) *Roasting the beef—35 to 45 minutes in a preheated 375-degree oven*

At least an hour before serving, cover casserole and set over moderately high heat until beef is sizzling, then place in middle level of a preheated oven. Turn and baste beef once in 15 minutes, and rearrange fat on top. Meat is done to very rare at 125 degrees on a meat thermometer and to medium rare at 130; juices will run rosy red when meat is pricked, and roast will feel slightly springy rather than squashy (like raw beef) when pressed. Set beef on a warm platter and leave at room temperature for 10 to 15 minutes while finishing sauce.

3) *Sauce*

Optional: 1 medium tomato
The bouillon from Step 1
½ Tb cornstarch blended
in a cup with ¼ cup dry
port wine or vermouth
Salt and pepper to taste
2 to 3 Tb soft butter
A hot sauce boat

Tip casserole and skim most of fat off cooking juices; bring to the boil. Chop optional tomato and add to casserole along with the bouillon. Boil slowly for 4 to 5 minutes to concentrate flavor. Remove from heat, stir in cornstarch and wine mixture, and bring to the simmer. Simmer 2 to 3 minutes until sauce turns from cloudy to clear. Carefully correct seasoning. Just before serving, remove from heat and beat in the butter, a tablespoon at a time. Strain into sauce boat, pressing juices out of vegetables.

4) *Serving*

Cut and discard trussing strings, and arrange beef on hot platter with whatever vegetables or garnish you have chosen. Pour several spoonsful of sauce over the beef to glaze it, and serve at once. (If beef is to be carved in the kitchen, place on a carving board that will collect juices; rapidly cut meat into slices ½ inch thick and rearrange on warm platter with garnish around them. Pour carving juices over meat, and pass sauce separately.)

(*) AHEAD-OF-TIME NOTE: If you cannot serve immediately, remove strings but do not carve meat; after it has rested 10 to 15 minutes and the sauce is made except for the final butter enrichment, return meat to casserole and baste with the sauce. Set cover askew and place either over barely simmering water or in an oven no hotter than 120 degrees. Meat can stay thus for a good hour before serving.

VARIATIONS

Tenderloin Baked in a Cloak of Mushrooms or of Matignon

To give the meat more flavor, you may either slice it and re-form with a stuffing between each slice as in the beef *en feuilletons,* page 180, or you may use that same mushroom stuffing but spread it over the whole *filet* as suggested in the drawing on page 176. In this second case, however, you must have caul fat to hold the mushrooms in place. Rather than mushrooms, you may wish to use the *matignon* of diced cooked carrots, onions, celery, ham, and wine in Volume I, page 303. In any case, when the meat is wrapped, brown it as described in the preceding recipe, and casserole-roast it in exactly the same way.

Filet de Boeuf à la Bourgeoise
[Tenderloin of Beef with Onions, Mushrooms, and Olives]

Whether casserole-roasted, plain roasted, or braised, a *filet* of beef surrounded with onions, mushrooms, and green olives is as attractive to look at as it is to eat. The garniture is cooked in advance, and simmers in the sauce to blend flavors before being arranged around the beef; you may wish to add sautéed potatoes to the platter, or the zucchini timbale on page 372. Cook the *filet* and prepare the sauce as in the preceding Master Recipe, or braise it with or without a stuffing as described in Volume I, page 303. Prepare the garniture as follows:

1) *Preparing the garniture*
the small onions:

1 lb. (2 cups) small white   Drop onions in boiling water, bring rapidly back to

onions about 1 inch in diameter

A saucepan of boiling water

A 6- to 7-inch frying pan or saucepan (no-stick recommended)

2 Tb butter and 2 tsp olive oil

Salt and pepper to taste

Pinch thyme

½ cup bouillon

A cover for the pan

boil, and boil 1 minute. Drain, and refresh in cold water. Shave off 2 ends and peel onions; pierce a cross ⅓ inch deep in root ends. Heat butter and oil in pan; when foam is subsiding add onions and sauté over moderately high heat to brown lightly. Reduce heat, add rest of ingredients, cover, and simmer very slowly for 20 to 30 minutes, or until onions are tender when pierced with a knife. Set aside with cooking juices.

the mushrooms:

½ lb. (1 quart) fresh mushrooms

2 Tb butter and 2 tsp olive oil

An 8-inch frying pan (no-stick recommended)

2 Tb minced shallots or scallions

Salt and pepper to taste

Trim and wash the mushrooms; dry in a towel and cut into quarters. Heat butter and oil in pan until foam is subsiding, add mushrooms and sauté over high heat, tossing frequently, until mushrooms begin to brown. Reduce heat, add shallots or scallions, and toss a moment more. Season lightly, tossing, and add mushrooms to onions.

the olives:

4 to 5 ounces (1 to 1¼ cups) pitted green olives, medium size, about ¾ inch long

2 quarts simmering water in a saucepan

Drain and wash the olives; drop into simmering water. Simmer 10 minutes, to remove excess saltiness. Drain, rinse in cold water, and add to onions and mushrooms.

(*) AHEAD-OF-TIME NOTE: Garniture may be prepared in advance.

2) Serving

The cooked *filet* of beef and its 2½ cups or so of of sauce

The onions, mushrooms, and olives

2 to 3 Tb soft butter

When the beef is done and the sauce is made, add the onions, mushrooms, and olives to the sauce and simmer 3 to 4 minutes to blend flavors. (If meat is being held in casserole, return sauce and garniture to it.) To serve, place meat on platter, and dip out the onions, mushrooms, and olives with a slotted spoon, arranging them around the beef. Beat the enrichment butter into the sauce a tablespoon at a time, spoon a little over the beef to glaze it and pour the rest of the sauce into a warm gravy boat. Serve, along with whatever other vegetables you may have chosen.

Filet de Boeuf en Feuilletons, Duxelles

[Tenderloin of Beef Sliced, Stuffed with Mushrooms and Roasted]

By slicing the raw tenderloin, seasoning each slice, and spreading it with wine-flavored mushroom *duxelles* and then re-forming the roast, you will have a deliciously flavored tenderloin that practically serves itself. For this you should have as long a piece of the main tenderloin muscle as possible with no under-turning tail, so that you will have large slices. (Drawings and discussion of tenderloin are at the beginning of this section, pages 172–4.)

For 16 slices ½ inch thick, serving 8 to 10

1) The duxelles stuffing—for 1½ to 1⅔ cups

1 lb. (2 quarts) fresh mushrooms

A heavy-bottomed 8-inch frying pan (no-stick recommended)

3 Tb butter

¼ cup minced shallots or scallions

⅓ cup finely minced mild-cured ready-cooked ham

1½ Tb flour

⅓ cup dry Madeira (Sercial)

⅓ cup block *foie gras,* liver paste, or very finely minced cooked ham fat

1 egg yolk

½ tsp dried tarragon

Salt and pepper to taste

Trim and wash mushrooms. Cut into ¹⁄₁₆-inch dice, using either a big knife or the vegetable mincing attachment of an electric mixer or a food mill if you wish. Twist a handful at a time in the corner of a towel to extract as much juice as possible. Heat butter to foaming in frying pan, stir in mushrooms, shallots or scallions, and ham. Sauté over moderately high heat, stirring frequently, until mushroom pieces begin to separate and start to brown lightly (5 minutes or so). Sprinkle in the flour and stir over moderate heat for 2 minutes. Remove from heat, blend in the wine, and stir again over heat for 1 minute. Remove from heat, beat in *foie gras,* liver paste, or fat, the egg yolk, tarragon, and salt and pepper to taste. Set aside.

2) Stuffing and tying the filet of beef

The heart of the tenderloin, 8 to 10 inches long and as even in diameter as possible (2½ lbs. or more)

A double thickness of well-washed damp cheesecloth large enough

With a very sharp knife, cut the meat into 16 even slices, each about ½ inch thick, setting them aside in the order in which you cut them. Lay the cheesecloth on the tray and paint with fat or cooking oil. Salt and pepper each slice, spread with a tablespoon and a half of stuffing, and re-form the roast, arranging the slices against each other on the cheesecloth. Tie one loop of string around the length of the re-formed

to envelop beef. (See also notes on caul fat, page 287.)
Salt and pepper
A tray and a pastry brush
Rendered goose fat, pork fat or cooking oil
The *duxelles* stuffing
White string

roast to hold the slices against each other, then stretch the cheesecloth tightly over the meat to enclose it. Twist each end of the cheesecloth closely against each end of the meat; tie securely with string. Then twist a tight spiral of string around the circumference from one end to the other and back again, so that meat will keep its shape. It will look like a fat sausage about 12 inches long and 4 inches in diameter.

(*) AHEAD-OF-TIME NOTE: When stuffed, tied, wrapped in plastic, and refrigerated a day before roasting, it will pick up added flavor.

3) *Browning and cover-roasting the beef—at least 1 hour before serving*

Brown the beef and the aromatic vegetables that accompany it as described in the Master Recipe, Step 1, page 177. (It will brown perfectly well in its cheesecloth covering.) Roast, as directed in Step 2, counting 30 to 40 minutes and leaving the meat red-rare (125 degrees on a meat thermometer). Remove from casserole as soon as it is done, and leave at room temperature for 15 minutes while finishing the sauce described in Step 3.

4) *Serving*

Set beef on hot serving platter and cut string and cheesecloth, carefully pulling them out from around and under the meat (15 minutes rest will have drawn slices of meat together). Spoon enough sauce over meat to glaze it nicely, arrange around it whatever garnish you have chosen, and serve, passing rest of sauce separately. Server need only spread top of meat apart with large fork and spoon to show location of each slice, which is then served with its share of *duxelles* stuffing.

(*) AHEAD-OF-TIME NOTE: Use the same system as in the Master Recipe, but do not untie meat until just before serving.

Filet de Boeuf en Croûte
[Tenderloin of Beef Baked in Pastry—Beef Wellington *Brioché*]

We do not know whether the English, the Irish, or the French baked the first *filet* of beef in a crust, but we can be certain that the French would not have named it after Wellington. It is a remarkably handsome, sumptuous dish when properly made. Most good recipes specify a whole piece of tenderloin that is preroasted 25 minutes, cooled, surrounded with a mushroom and *foie gras* stuffing, then wrapped in French puff pastry and baked. We think it a great improvement to substitute *brioche* dough for puff pastry: fully risen *brioche* dough is deflated, thoroughly chilled, then rolled thin, draped over the meat and baked immediately before the dough has a chance to rise again. The resulting crust is beautiful to look at as well as being light, thin, cooked all the way through and delicious to eat; this is never the case with puff pastry, which cannot bake properly under such circumstances and is always damply dumpling under its handsome exterior. Another improvement is to bake the tenderloin in slices with stuffing in between, as in the preceding recipe: the serving is easy and the taste is vastly improved.

VEGETABLE AND WINE SUGGESTIONS

An important dish like this should be surrounded with few distractions; we would suggest only something green and fresh like buttered new peas or green beans, broccoli flowerettes, or, in season, sliced, fresh, green asparagus spears tossed in butter. Again, a fine red Bordeaux-Médoc would be an excellent choice of wine.

THE SAUCE

Anything as extravagant as this *filet de boeuf* demands an unusually good sauce. We suggest 2 to 3 cups of the brown sauce or the *sauce ragoût* in Volume I, pages 67 and 69, simmered several hours for maximum flavor; it will then be further enriched with the cooking juices and deglazing wine from the beef, Step 1 in the following recipe.

For 16 slices of beef ½ inch thick, serving 8 to 10

---

1) *Preliminaries—to do in the morning or the day before serving*

½ the recipe for *pain brioché* dough, page 83 (½ lb. flour) One of the brown sauces described in preceding paragraph	Prepare the dough as described, letting it finish its second rise in the refrigerator. Then deflate it, cover with plastic wrap, a plate, and a 5-pound weight (pieces of meat grinder) so that it will not rise again; refrigerate. Make the brown-sauce base and refrigerate. Prepare the stuffed *filet* as described, baste well

2½ to 3 lbs. of the heart of the tenderloin, sliced, stuffed, wrapped and tied (*filet de boeuf en feuilletons,* page 180, Steps 1 and 2)

Rendered goose or pork fat, or cooking oil

A shallow roasting pan

½ cup dry port wine or Sercial Madeira

with fat or oil, and place in roasting pan. Preheat oven to 425 degrees, and set rack in upper-third level. Roast the beef for 25 minutes, basting and turning it several times. Transfer beef to a platter or tray (reserve roasting pan) and let meat cool to room temperature. (If you are preroasting a day ahead, cover and refrigerate the meat after it has cooled, but set at room temperature for 2 hours before final baking in Step 3, for accurate timing.) Spoon fat out of roasting pan, pour in wine and boil down by half, scraping up any roasting juices with a wooden spoon; scrape liquid into the sauce base.

2) *Enclosing beef in brioche—1 to 1½ hours before serving, and just before roasting*

The cool, room-temperature, preroasted beef

Heavy shears

The chilled *brioche* dough

Flour, a rolling surface, a rolling pin, a ravioli wheel, a small knife

An oiled jelly-roll pan or pizza tray (raised edges needed to catch roasting juices)

Egg glaze (1 egg beaten with 1 tsp water in a small bowl)

A pastry brush

Optional: a meat thermometer

Preheat oven to 425 degrees and slide rack onto lower-middle level. Set out all the equipment and ingredients listed. Cut wrapping and string from beef. Working rapidly from now on so that *brioche* dough softens as little as possible, roll ¼ of the dough into a rectangle ¼ inch thick and the length and width of the beef. Roll it up on your pin and unroll it onto the oiled pan.

dough

Its most attractive side up, place the beef on the rectangle of dough. Trim off excess dough from around the beef.

Roll the remaining dough into a
rectangle ¼ inch thick and
large enough to enclose beef
(probably 18 by 8 inches), roll it up
on your pin and *unroll over the
beef.*

Trim off any excess dough and reserve for decorations. Tuck the covering
dough against the bottom rectangle of dough and under bottom of meat, sealing
edges with your fingers. Paint dough covering with egg glaze; in a moment paint
with a second coat.

So that any decorations on the crust
will show after baking, they must be
either deep cuts with raised edges, or
dough paste-ons. For instance, you
may wish to lay on strips of leftover
dough in a design, and paint with
egg glaze.

Decorate blank spaces by cutting into surface of dough with scissors, a knife, or
the metal end of a pastry tube, making definite edges that stick up. (Cuts are made
after glazing, so that the cut portion of the dough will remain pale, accenting the
design when dough is baked.)

Immediately the decorations are complete, set beef in oven. The object here
is to make sure the dough remains a crust, a thin and crisp covering; if it rises, it will
be thick and bready.

3) *Baking—30 to 40 minutes*

Bake in lower-middle level of preheated 425-degree oven for 20 to 25 minutes,
or until pastry has browned nicely. Lower thermostat to 350 degrees for rest of baking,
and cover crust loosely with a sheet of foil or brown paper if it seems to be browning
too much. Indications that the meat is done are that you can begin to smell the beef

and the stuffing, and that juices begin to escape into the pan; meat thermometer reading for rare beef is 125 degrees.

---

4) *Serving and ahead-of-time notes*

A hot platter or a board wide enough to hold beef and removed top crust
A flexible-blade spatula
A hot sauce in a warmed bowl
The hot accompanying vegetable
Serving implements: a sharp knife for cutting the crust, and a serving spoon and fork

When beef is done, remove from oven and slide onto platter or board. Beef will stay warm for 20 minutes; if you still cannot serve it, set in a warming oven no hotter than 120 degrees.

To serve, cut all around the crust and half an inch up from its bottom. *Lift the top crust off onto the platter,* and cut into serving portions. Separate the slices of meat with spoon and fork and cut down through the bottom crust so that each slice is served with a portion of stuffing and crust. Spoon a little sauce around the meat, and add a piece of the top crust.

LAMB

Agneau et Mouton

The French take great pride in their lamb and the marvelous quality of their mutton. While we do not easily find the little spring lambs of France in this country, nor the mutton, we are fortunate to have our own type of lamb, of the very finest quality and flavor, throughout the year. Many Americans are so wedded to beef that they forget about lamb, and this is a pity, because a fine leg of lamb roasted red and juicy is a feast for any meat lover. Although we thought we had covered a great deal in Volume I, with lamb stew, roasts in mustard coatings, garlic sauces, and even a boiled leg of lamb, there is more to tell. We now add full instructions on boning the leg, step-by-step illustrated directions on how to carve the saddle like a major-domo, a recipe for stuffed and braised shoulder, and complete drawings on how to make a *gigot farci en croûte*.

HOW TO BONE A LEG OF LAMB

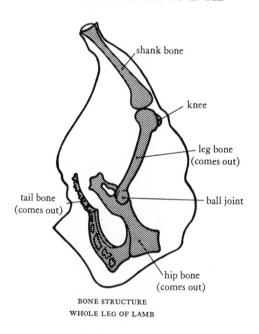

BONE STRUCTURE
WHOLE LEG OF LAMB

A fully or partially boned leg of lamb is easy to carve, and you can stuff the cavities where the bones used to be. If only the tail and hip assembly has been removed from the raw meat, that alone is a great help to the carver, and when the main leg bone is also gone, carving is no problem at all. To show that it really is a leg of lamb you are serving, leave the shank bone in unless you want a rolled leg for spit roasting. Although most butchers will cut out the tail and hip for you, they may not want to take the time for a careful boning of the main leg portion. If you enjoy working with your hands, do all the boning yourself and you will learn more about meat and carving, because you will become familiar with the bones, their shapes, and their positions.

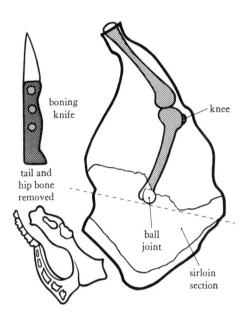

Furnish yourself with two stout-bladed, very sharp knives, one small and one larger. Always keeping the knife blade against the bone, scrape all around against the complicated structure of the tail-hip assembly, disfiguring the meat as little as possible, until you are able to cut the tendons that join the hip to the ball joint of the main leg bone, thus releasing the hip.

To remove the main leg bone, cut around its exposed ball joint buried in the thick end of the meat. Loosen flesh all around and down the bone inside the meat until you come to its opposite ball joint at the knee. You now have two choices, one easier and the other longer but cleverer. The easiest way to remove the bone is to slit the underside of the meat at the knee to expose the bones; making as small a hole outside as possible, cut around knee joint, sever tendons, and draw the bone out from the large end of the meat. Close the meat neatly at the knee by sewing or skewering. The longer maneuver is to get the bone without piercing the skin at the knee. By persistent poking and cutting around the bone inside the meat at the joint, by twisting the bone, by turning the meat inside out around the bone as far down as you can for better visibility, you will finally be able to free it from the tendons attaching it to the knee and pull the bone out.

The flap of meat that contained the hip and tail, at the large end of the leg, is called the sirloin. You may slice it off and use at another meal for roasting, steaks, or shishkebob, or you may grind part of it for stuffing back into the leg as suggested in the following recipe. (If you wish to leave the flap on, skewer it against the main body of the leg after stuffing.)

With the sirloin off, you have what
is known as a short (or Frenched)
leg of lamb. (For *gigot farci en
croûte,* this is what you need.)

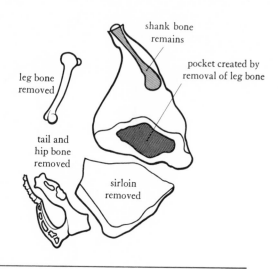

leg bone
removed

shank bone
remains

pocket created by
removal of leg bone

tail and
hip bone
removed

sirloin
removed

Either fill the pocket with stuffing, pushing it well down into all spaces left by
the bones, or sprinkle in a flavoring of salt, pepper, minced parsley, a clove of minced
garlic, and a big pinch of rosemary or thyme.

pocket closed with
skewers and
laced with string

Whether filled or not, *close the
pocket with skewers and string.*

RECIPES FOR BONED LEG OF LAMB

You may proceed with the recipe for *gigot farci en croûte,* or you may
roast the boned, stuffed, and skewered leg of lamb just as it is, following the
Master Recipe in Volume I, page 332; it is also delicious roasted with the
herbal mustard coating also in Volume I, on page 335. After the roast has
rested 15 to 20 minutes out of the oven, the meat will have settled into place
and you can remove the string and skewers. To carve, cut down in bias (diagonal) slices across the grain, first from one side of the large end, then from the
other; if the first few slices contain no stuffing, set aside for second helpings.

When you come to the thinner portion of the meat nearer the shank, you can cut straight across.

GIGOT FARCI, EN CROÛTE
[Boned, Stuffed Lamb Baked in Pastry]

At least one great French provincial restaurant has made its reputation on *gigot farci en croûte,* and any home cook who has mastered French puff pastry or *brioche* dough can make this splendidly dramatic presentation every bit as well. The recipe consists of the boned and stuffed leg of lamb, illustrated in the preceding pages, which is first roasted in a very hot oven until partially cooked, then draped in pastry, decorated with pastry cutouts, glazed, and set back in the oven again to cook and brown the crust. Although you have to watch your timing on this so as not to overcook the lamb, it is reasonably amenable to delays as indicated by the asterisks (*) at the end of most of the steps in the recipe. Do go over it well before starting in, so that you will have a good idea of timing and of stopping points. We suggest that you make the pastry dough the day before serving. You might also bone the lamb, prepare the stuffing, and simmer the sauce called for in Step 7; the actual cooking will then be much simplified.

Even though you have the crust, there is not much of it per serving and you may also wish a potato dish such as the scalloped potatoes, *gratin dauphinois,* in Volume I on page 523, the *gratin* with cheese and cream following it, or the unusual potato and endive *gratin* here, on page 389. Brussels sprouts, broccoli, buttered spinach, or fresh green peas might also be included. This *gigot* naturally calls for the best in wines, giving you an opportunity to bring out your finest, château-bottled, red Bordeaux-Saint-Émilion.

THE CRUST, AND PUFF PASTRY VERSUS BRIOCHE DOUGH

Although puff pastry is traditional, it never quite cooks through when it covers rare-roasted meat, while *brioche* dough, if it is not allowed its final rise before baking, will form a crisp, brown crust. This question is discussed in the preamble to Beef Wellington on page 182, where you have the same choice.

For 10 to 12 people

---

1) *Boning the lamb*

An 8- to 9-lb. leg of lamb (5 to 6 lbs. boned and minus sirloin)

Following illustrated directions preceding this recipe, remove tail and hip bones, main leg bone, and sirloin meat from leg of lamb. (If you are going to make the brown sauce suggested for Step 7, start it now, using the bones and scraps from the lamb.)

---

2) *Mushroom and kidney stuffing—farce duxelles aux rognons—2 cups*

½ lb. (4 cups) fresh mushrooms

2 Tb butter and 1 Tb olive oil or cooking oil (more of each if needed)

A medium (10-inch) frying pan (no-stick recommended)

4 fine, fresh lamb kidneys, peeled and minced

3 Tb finely minced shallots or scallions

¼ cup port, Madeira, or Cognac

⅛ tsp each of ground thyme and rosemary

½ cup ground raw lamb (from the removed piece of sirloin)

¼ cup *foie gras* or *mousse de foie* (canned goose liver or liver mousse)

Trim, wash, and dry the mushrooms. Chop into a fine mince with a big knife; a handful at a time, twist into a tight ball in the corner of a towel to extract as much juice as possible. Heat butter and oil in pan, and when butter foam has begun to subside, add the mushrooms. Sauté over moderately high heat, stirring, for several minutes, until mushroom pieces begin to separate from each other. Stir in the kidneys and shallots, adding a little more butter if you feel it necessary. Sauté, stirring, for 2 minutes, just to stiffen the kidneys. Pour in the wine or Cognac and herbs; boil down rapidly for 1 minute. Remove from heat. Stir in the ground lamb. Mash *foie gras* or *mousse* with a fork and stir in also, along with optional truffles and their juice. Season carefully to taste. (If by any chance mixture seems too damp or loose, stir in a tablespoon or so of bread crumbs to hold it together more.)

Optional but recom-
   mended: 1 or 2 minced
   truffles and their juice
Salt and pepper to taste
If needed: 2 or more Tb
   stale, not-too-fine crumbs
   from nonsweetened,
   homemade-type bread

3) Stuffing, tying, and skewering the lamb

Skewers and white string

Following illustrated directions on page 188, pack the stuffing into the pockets left in the meat by the bones, skewer the large end of the meat, and lace closed with string.

(*) AHEAD-OF-TIME NOTE: Recipe may be prepared to this point a day in advance. Note also that you may prepare the sauce, Step 7, in advance.

4) Preliminary roasting—30 minutes at 425 degrees, and a 30-minute rest

The stuffed and skewered
   lamb
A shallow roasting pan
   with rack
Cooking oil
Optional but recom-
   mended: an accurate
   meat thermometer

Preheat oven to 425 degrees. Wipe lamb thoroughly dry with paper towels and brush with cooking oil, especially on exposed lean-meat surfaces. Place on rack in roasting pan and set in upper-middle level of preheated oven. Basting once or twice with oil and turning meat once, roast 25 to 30 minutes, until lamb has swelled slightly and feels a little springy in contrast to its softer raw state. Meat thermometer reading: 120 degrees. Remove lamb from oven but leave string and skewers in place.

(*) RESTING AND AHEAD-OF-TIME NOTES: Lamb must rest for 30 minutes at least before final cooking, so that meat will draw together and hold stuffing in place. It must also cool off a little bit so that it will not overcook under its pastry, but it must not cool so much that it loses its juicy, freshly cooked character. If you are not ready to continue for some time, you may keep it perfectly for an hour or more anywhere that you can maintain a temperature of around 100 to 110 degrees, such as a warming oven, or the turned-off oven, reheating it for a moment every now and then.

5) Enclosing the lamb in pastry—preheat oven to 450 degrees for next step

Either the recipe for
   simple puff pastry, page
   113;
Or the recipe for pain

Remove string and skewers, and set lamb on pan or baking sheet. It is now to be enclosed in pastry; do so rapidly to prevent dough from softening and, in the case of brioche dough, from rising.

brioché dough, fully
   risen and ready to bake,
   but chilled, page 83
The still warm leg of lamb
A lightly greased jelly-roll
   pan, or edged baking
   sheet
Egg glaze (1 egg beaten
   with 1 tsp water in a
   small bowl)
A pastry brush
Optional but recom-
   mended: the meat
   thermometer

Rapidly roll pastry out into a flattened pear shape ¼ inch thick, 6 inches longer at the large end, and 6 inches wider than the leg of lamb. *Starting at large end, unroll or unfold the pastry over the lamb.*

Leaving an inch of the shank bone exposed, allow enough pastry to tuck in all around and enclose lamb completely; trim off excess. *Push the pastry against the undersides of the meat with your fingers:* the bottom of the lamb rests on the pan, and the pastry simply encloses all visible meat.

Make pastry cutouts with leftover dough, such as long strips ⅜ inch wide cut with a pastry wheel, and 2-inch ovals formed with a fluted cookie cutter. Paint top of covering dough with egg glaze, and *press the decorations into place.*

When all decorations are in place, brush surface of dough and decorations with egg glaze. *Draw the tines of a table fork over glaze and lightly into dough, to make cross-hatch marks on entire surface.* Insert optional meat thermometer where indicated, at a downward-slanting angle from shank so that point of thermometer lodges in the thickest portion of solid meat near large end. Immediately proceed to next step. (Note that if you are using *brioche* dough, you are not to let it rise; it is to be baked immediately.)

6) *Final baking—25 to 30 minutes at 450 degrees and 400 degrees*

Place in middle level of preheated oven and bake for 15 to 20 minutes, until pastry has started to brown nicely; reduce heat to 400 degrees for the final 5 to 10 minutes of baking. Lamb is done to rosy rare at a thermometer reading of 130 degrees, or at the first sign of juices exuding from underside of lamb onto baking sheet. (NOTE: Some prefer lamb rarer, 125 degrees on the thermometer, while others like it medium rare, or around 140 to 145 degrees. Roast the lamb to the thermometer reading you prefer.)

Remove lamb from oven as soon as it is done; carefully lift it, and slide a rack under it so that the juices will not moisten the crust. Lamb should rest 15 to 20 minutes before carving. (When ready to serve, place lamb on platter, and pour any accumulated juices into whatever sauce you have prepared.)

(*) AHEAD-OF-TIME NOTE: Lamb will stay warm enough in its crust for 30 minutes; after that return to warming oven or anywhere that you can maintain a temperature of 110 to 120 degrees, where it may remain another half hour at least.

7) *Serving*

A hot, lightly buttered serving platter or a carving board
Optional but desirable: 3 cups excellent brown sauce made from the lamb bones and meat scraps (Volume I, pages 69–70), in a hot sauce bowl

Transfer lamb to platter or carving board, and pour any roasting juices into sauce. Make a presentation of the *gigot,* for all to admire. To carve, cut down in bias (diagonal) slices across the grain, first from one side of the large end, then from the other; if the first few slices contain no stuffing, set aside for second helpings. When you come to the thinner portion of the meat nearer the shank, you can cut straight across. Pass sauce separately, along with whatever vegetables you have chosen.

ÉPAULE D'AGNEAU FARCIE, VIROFLAY

[Braised, Stuffed Shoulder of Lamb]

Shoulder of lamb is far less expensive than leg of lamb, usually by at least a third, and is an elegant roast when stuffed and braised. The spinach and mushroom mixture suggested here makes attractive slices, and if you serve the potatoes in basil on page 388 and whole baked tomatoes, you will have a colorful and fragrant main course. A red Bordeaux-Saint-Émilion would be an excellent choice of wine.

A NOTE ON BONED SHOULDER OF LAMB

Most markets will bone a lamb shoulder for you, or you will find them ready-boned, rolled, and tied; you untie and unroll them for stuffing. Ask also for a pound or so of sawed lamb bones, or for veal or beef bones, to give character to your braising liquid. (Full information on lamb shoulders is in Volume I, page 330).

For 8 people

---

1) *The mushroom duxelles and spinach stuffing—farce Viroflay*

½ lb. (1 quart) fresh mushrooms
1 Tb butter
½ Tb cooking oil
A medium (10-inch) frying pan (no-stick recommended)
Salt and pepper
A 3-quart mixing bowl

Make a *duxelles* as follows: Trim, wash, and dry the mushrooms, and cut into $\frac{1}{16}$-inch dice with a large knife. A handful at a time, twist hard in the corner of a towel, to extract as much of their juice as possible. Heat oil and butter to bubbling in pan, add mushrooms, and cook over moderately high heat, stirring frequently, until pieces begin to separate from each other, and start to brown very lightly. Stir in salt and pepper to taste, and scrape into mixing bowl.

1½ cups cooked spinach
(or a 10-ounce package
frozen spinach, thawed
in a pan of cold water
and drained)
2 Tb butter
3 Tb minced shallots or
scallions
A large clove garlic,
mashed
Salt and pepper

A handful at a time, squeeze as much water as possible out of the spinach; chop fine with a large stainless-steel knife. Melt the additional butter in the frying pan over moderately high heat, stir in the shallots or scallions, and cook for 1 minute. Then stir in the spinach and garlic, and cook, stirring, for several minutes to evaporate remaining liquid from spinach. When it begins sticking lightly to bottom of pan, remove from heat; season to taste with salt and pepper, and scrape into bowl with mushrooms.

½ cup (1½ ounces) not-
too-fine stale crumbs
from nonsweetened,
homemade-type white
bread in a small bowl
2 to 3 Tb stock, bouillon,
or milk
⅔ cup (4 ounces) finely
diced ham fat, fresh pork
fat, or blanched bacon
1 egg
8 to 10 large fresh basil
leaves, minced, or ½
tsp fragrant dried basil,
thyme, or rosemary
Salt and pepper

Soften the crumbs with the stock, bouillon, or milk and let stand for a few minutes. Beat the ham fat, egg, and herbs into the mushrooms and spinach. Squeeze excess liquid out of crumbs and beat them in too. Taste stuffing very carefully for seasoning.

(*) AHEAD-OF-TIME NOTE: May be done a day in advance; cover and refrigerate.

2) Stuffing the lamb

A 5- to 6-lb. shoulder of
lamb, fell intact, all excess
fat cut out; bones
removed, chopped, and
reserved (ready-to-stuff
weight about 3½ lbs.)
A trussing needle or
skewers
White string

Spread boned shoulder on a board, fell (skin) side down. Tuck stuffing into pockets left by bones, and pile rest of stuffing in a loaf shape down center of meat. Sew or skewer edges of meat together to enclose stuffing completely. (Do not overfill lamb.) Tie into a sausage shape with loops of string at 1-inch intervals around circumference. Dry thoroughly with paper towels before browning, next step.

(*) AHEAD-OF-TIME NOTE: When both lamb and stuffing are chilled, the meat may be stuffed a day in advance; wrap and refrigerate.

3) Browning the lamb

2 to 3 Tb rendered pork
or goose fat, or cooking
oil; more if needed

Preheat oven to 325 degrees in time for Step 4. Heat fat or oil in casserole to very hot but not smoking, add bones (including optional knuckle bones at end

A heavy, flameproof casserole just large enough to hold lamb comfortably
The chopped lamb bones
A large, sliced onion
A large, sliced carrot
For sauce consistency:
A 6-inch square of blanched pork rind, Volume I, page 401, and/ or 1 cup chopped veal knuckle bones

of list) and sliced vegetables; sauté over moderately high heat for 5 to 6 minutes, until lightly browned. Remove with a slotted spoon to a side dish. Film pan with more fat or oil if necessary, set lamb in it, seam-side down, and brown for several minutes, lifting occasionally with spoon to prevent lamb from sticking. Turn and brown on another side, and continue turning and browning until lamb is nicely colored on all sides and the two ends. Strew the browned bones and vegetables around the meat, and add the optional pork rind.

4) *Braising the lamb—2½ hours at 325 degrees*

Salt
1 cup dry white wine or dry white French vermouth
2 or more cups brown stock or bouillon
The following tied in washed cheesecloth: 6 parsley sprigs, 1 bay leaf, ½ tsp thyme, 2 cloves garlic
A piece of waxed paper or foil
Casserole cover

Salt the lamb, add the wine and enough stock or bouillon to come ⅔ the way up the lamb. Bury herb packet in the liquid, and bring casserole to simmer on top of stove. Lay paper or foil over meat, cover casserole, and set in middle level of oven; regulate oven heat so that lamb simmers quietly for 2½ hours. Turn several times during cooking, and baste with liquid in the casserole. Lamb is done when a fork will pierce it fairly easily.

5) *Sauce and serving*

A hot serving platter
A sieve set over a saucepan
1 Tb cornstarch blended to a paste with 2 Tb wine or stock in a small bowl
A warm sauce bowl
Parsley, watercress, or whatever vegetable garnish you wish

Remove lamb to hot platter. Do not untie yet; cover with waxed paper or foil and set in turned-off oven with door ajar while finishing sauce as follows: Strain braising liquid into saucepan, pressing juices out of ingredients. Skim surface fat off liquid, bring to simmer, skimming off additional fat, and taste carefully for seasoning and strength. Boil down rapidly, if necessary; you should have about 2½ cups. Remove from heat, and beat in starch mixture; return over heat and simmer, stirring, for 2 minutes. Remove string and trussings from lamb, pour a spoonful of sauce over the meat to glaze it, and pour rest of sauce into warm bowl. Decorate platter with greenery or vegetables, and serve.

To carve, cut down in bias (diagonal) slices across the grain, first from one side of the short end, then from the other, and spoon a little sauce around the edge of each serving. (If the stuffing does not hold in place, carver should arrange meat attractively around it on plate, for each slice.)

(*) AHEAD-OF-TIME NOTES: If you are not to serve the lamb at once, replace it in the casserole, pour the sauce around, cover loosely, and set in a 120-degree warming oven, or over barely simmering water, where it will keep nicely for at least 30 minutes.

Other stuffings

Other stuffing possibilities are listed on pages 513–15, and 6 stuffings specifically for lamb are in Volume I, pages 336–8.

BREAST OF LAMB
Poitrine d'Agneau

Breast of lamb (the bottom of the rib cage, similar to that of veal illustrated on page 215) is the most reasonably priced of any cut of meat, and is delicious when boned, stuffed, and braised. However, it must be very carefully peeled, and all the fat from the plate must be cut out, as well as other extraneous fat. If you do find a well-trimmed breast, follow the general system outlined for stuffed breast of veal on page 216, using either that stuffing or any of the preceding suggestions for shoulder of lamb.

SADDLE OF LAMB
Selle d'Agneau

A saddle of lamb is one of the most luxurious and attractive roasts you could pick to serve at a small, elegant dinner party for 4 to 6 people. When you have prepared it for the oven, which is not difficult as you will see from the illustrated directions, you will find it far easier to roast and to carve than a leg of lamb, and absolutely delicious to eat.

HOW TO ORDER A SADDLE OF LAMB

The saddle of lamb is the loin. On a beef carcass it would be the whole porterhouse and T-bone steak section on both sides, and on lamb it is the whole loin-chop area. It is, in fact, a giant butterfly loin chop 8 to 10 inches thick, consisting of the 2 meaty loin strips that run along either side of the backbone on top, and the 2 smaller tenderloin strips that run its length underneath. What would constitute the tail of the chop is the flank, or flap of meat attached to each side.

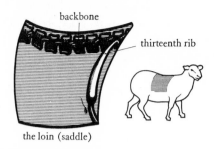

the loin (saddle)

Because names of meat cuts vary from one part of the country to another, your butcher may understand the term "saddle" to mean the whole loin-hip-leg section of lamb, and he may only know what you mean when you ask him for the double kidney loin. Show him this picture if you have trouble communicating, or point the saddle out to him on yourself. It is equivalent to the small of your back on both sides of the backbone, and includes the front part of you; in other words, it is the whole area from the top of your hip bone to where your ribs begin. Tell him to leave it whole; he is not to saw it in two at the backbone. The choicest saddle will come from a carcass of spring lamb that weighs not more than 45 pounds; the saddle will weigh around 6½ pounds untrimmed, 3½ pounds ready to roast.

FRENCH TERMINOLOGY

You may also have communication problems in France, because the saddle can be called *selle d'agneau, selle anglaise,* or *les deux filets réunis.* Again, point it out on yourself if there is any confusion. Their saddle of lamb will be a little smaller than an American one, while a *selle de mouton* from their excellent mutton will be a little larger and should be well aged, *bien rassie.*

HOW TO PREPARE A SADDLE OF LAMB FOR ROASTING

This is the way the topside of the saddle will look before the flanks have been trimmed off. Ask that the fell (skin) be removed, which will leave a covering of fat over the top of the meat. Have the thirteenth rib removed also, if attached.

strip of fat   tenderloins

cut here   cut here

Remove all excess fat from the underside; this may include the kidneys. The strips of tenderloin meat run parallel to the backbone on either side, and parallel to their outside edge is a partially hidden strip of fat.

Cut and pull fat out, being careful not to pierce the flanks and make holes in outside covering of meat. Cut off all but about 3 inches of flank, leaving enough on each side for flanks to cover the underside of the backbone.

Shave off all but ⅛-inch layer of covering fat on the topside, and make a criss cross of bias cuts ½ inch apart in the surface, going just down to the flesh. These will help the meat to cook evenly, and make attractive decorations on the crisp, roasted surface later on.

Sprinkle underside with salt, pepper, and a big pinch of thyme or rosemary, fold flanks against backbone to cover tenderloin strips, and tie circumference of saddle in 3 or more places with white string. If you are not to cook the saddle now, wrap and refrigerate it.

(*) AHEAD-OF-TIME NOTE: Saddle may be prepared to this point a day before roasting.

* SELLE D'AGNEAU RÔTIE

[Roast Saddle of Lamb]

A plain roast saddle of lamb is so good in itself that you need go into no elaborations, although one or two are suggested at the end of this recipe. A classic accompaniment is that crusty, buttery mound of sliced potatoes, *pommes Anna,* on page 394, or one of the two variations following it, and either braised lettuce or braised endives. Another suggestion would be eggplant, such as the *gratin provençal* with its tomatoes and cheese on page 354; you would then need only an excellent loaf of homemade French bread. A fine, red Bordeaux-Médoc would be your best choice of wine.

For 4 to 6 people

---

1) *Preparations for roasting*

A saddle of lamb trimmed, seasoned, and tied according to the preceding directions (4 to 5 lbs. trimmed weight)

A heavy, shallow baking dish just large enough to hold the saddle comfortably

4 Tb melted butter in a pan and a basting brush

½ cup each, sliced carrots and onions

2 large cloves garlic, unpeeled

Optional but recommended: a meat thermometer

Preheat oven to 475 degrees for Step 2. Set saddle right side up in the roasting pan and paint exposed ends of meat with melted butter, reserving rest for later. If you are using a meat thermometer, insert it at a long, slanting angle into the thickest part of one of the loin strips. Be sure point of thermometer reaches middle of meat and does not touch bone. Prepare the vegetables and garlic, and reserve in a bowl for Step 2.

---

2) *Roasting—about 45 minutes—oven preheated to 450 degrees*

ROASTING START. Set lamb in upper-middle level of preheated oven for 15 minutes.

15-MINUTE MARK. Turn thermostat down to 425 degrees. Working quickly, baste 2 ends of saddle with melted butter, and strew the vegetables and garlic around the meat. Baste vegetables with fat in baking dish, or with butter.

22-MINUTE MARK. Rapidly baste meat and vegetables again, with fat in dish.

30-MINUTE MARK. Baste again rapidly. If vegetables are blackening, turn thermostat down to 400 degrees.

37-MINUTE MARK. Baste again. If you are using a meat thermometer, it should be at 125 to 130 degrees for rare meat. Meat should feel springy rather than squashy and raw, and the first juices should be exuding from the meat into the pan. Roast a few minutes longer if necessary; if you wish your meat medium rare and pink rather than red, roast to 140 degrees. (Note that if meat was chilled when it went into the oven, it may take a few minutes longer to roast. A heavier saddle will take 50 to 55 minutes in all. Baste every 4 to 5 minutes when roasting longer.)

WHEN DONE. Turn off oven and set lamb on a platter near outside end of open oven door; a rest of 10 to 15 minutes before carving will permit juices to retreat back into meat tissues. Discard trussing strings after the rest period. Meanwhile, make the sauce, next step.

---

3) *The sauce*

⅓ cup dry white wine or dry white French vermouth

1 cup beef stock or bouillon

Optional: 1 medium tomato, chopped (not peeled)

Salt and pepper

A sieve

A small saucepan

Spoon all but a tablespoon of fat out of roasting dish, pour in wine and stock, and add optional tomato. Set over high heat and boil, scraping up coagulated roasting juices with a wooden spoon; mash cooking vegetables into liquid as it boils. Reduce liquid by about half, correct seasoning, strain into saucepan, and keep warm. You will have only enough sauce to moisten each serving of meat.

(*) AHEAD-OF-TIME NOTE: If you can control the heat, you may leave the finished lamb in a warming oven of no more than 120 degrees for at least half an hour. With your sauce all made, you can then serve immediately.

4) *Carving and serving*

CARVING AT THE TABLE. If you wish to carve at the table you may follow the system of many *maîtres d'hôtel,* which is to make long, thin slices on each side, parallel to the backbone. (The first slice, which shaves off the fat, is not served.) Then turn the saddle upside down, cut off the flanks, and reserve for second helpings; cut out the tenderloin strips, and slice into crosswise pieces.

CARVING IN THE KITCHEN AND REASSEMBLING. This works out nicely, and the carved pieces are replaced on the saddle bone. Although you may cut the long thin slices described in the preceding paragraph, we suggest cutting across the grain for better eating texture. Provide yourself with a long, very sharp knife, a fork, and a carving board; heat oven to 475 degrees for a brief warm-up after the reassembly, and carve rapidly, as follows:

Turn saddle upside down and slice off the flanks. Cutting down parallel against the backbone and then following its outward curve, *slice out first one whole tenderloin strip, then the other.*

tenderloin removed

Turn the saddle right side up, shave off outside fat on each side if you wish, then cut down parallel against backbone and follow its outward curve to slice off the whole loin strip on each side. Slanting knife at a 45-degree angle parallel to board, rapidly slice each strip into cross-grain pieces ¾ inch thick; season lightly with salt and pepper but keep slices in order, so that you may replace them again on the bone. Slice and season tenderloin strips.

saddle bone

flank

Arrange the flanks lengthwise on a hot ovenproof serving platter and settle the saddle bone on top.

Pile the tenderloin pieces at each end of the saddle, and rearrange the loin slices back in place on each side of the backbone.

Pour the carving juices over the meat; set platter for 2 minutes in oven to give a sizzling impression. Pour a spoonful or two of sauce over the meat, rapidly decorate platter with parsley, watercress, or a vegetable garnish, and serve immediately.

VARIATIONS

Selle d'Agneau, Persillade

[Saddle of Lamb Garnished with Parsley and Buttered Bread Crumbs]

A garnish of bread crumbs sautéed in butter with shallots and seasonings, tossed with parsley, and spread over the finished saddle of lamb is fragrant, attractive, and especially called for when you are carving in the kitchen and serving the reassembled lamb on the saddle bone. Make the *persillade* at any convenient time as long as it is ready to serve with the roast, as follows:

4 **Tb clarified butter (melted butter, skimmed; clear liquid butter poured off milky residue)**
A **medium (10-inch) frying pan**
3 **Tb finely minced shallots or scallions**
1 **cup (lightly pressed down) moderately fine, fresh crumbs from non-sweetened homemade-type white bread**

Melt butter to bubbling in pan, add shallots and stir for 1 minute, then add bread crumbs and stir over moderately high heat for several minutes until a nice, golden brown. Remove from heat, stir in salt and pepper to taste, and set aside. When the meat is on its platter, mix the parsley into the crumbs and spread the *persillade* over the lamb; reheat for a moment in hot oven, and serve.

Salt and pepper
3 to 4 Tb minced fresh
  parsley

Selle d'Agneau, Milanaise

[Saddle of Lamb Garnished with Parmesan Cheese and Bread Crumbs]

Another attractive finish to a roast saddle of lamb is to spread on a coating of cheese and bread crumbs, then set it into the oven for a moment to brown. Make the mixture as follows:

---

4 Tb melted butter
½ cup fairly fine, stale bread
  crumbs
⅓ cup grated Parmesan
  cheese
A small bowl
Pepper to taste

Preheat oven to 475 degrees in time for serving. Blend the butter, crumbs, and cheese together in the bowl; season to taste with pepper and set aside. When saddle is roasted, has rested, and is ready to serve, spread on the crumbs and cheese. Set in upper third of preheated oven for 2 to 3 minutes to brown lightly; serve immediately.

VEAL

Veau

Not too many years ago veal was appreciated only by Europeans or sophisticated and traveled Americans. Now the delights of the scallop quickly sautéed in butter and served in a cream and tarragon sauce, or the roast stuffed with mushrooms, or a *blanquette*—that deceptively simple and marvelous stew—are quite common dishes on the American table wherever good veal is to be found. Happily for us all, much better veal is now being raised in this country, due to improved feeding methods and to the growing demand for top-quality meat. If your market has not yet begun to carry the large, pale, fine veal that is now available, you can perhaps urge them to feature it in the hope that a demand will be created in your shopping area.

Some 25 pages are devoted to veal, its quality, and its cuts, in Volume I, starting on page 350. Recipes include casserole roasts with herbs and aromatic vegetables, the sumptuous *veau Orloff*, veal stuffed with ham and cheese, two fine stews, a detailed section on how to fix your own scallops, another on chops, and some useful suggestions for ground-veal patties, an excellent solution for the quite reasonably priced little pieces of neck meat you sometimes find packaged at the meat counter. Here we have three groups of recipes for braising veal: shoulder chops, stews, and illustrated directions on how to bone and stuff a breast of veal in the French manner. We end with two dishes from the *haute cuisine, veau en feuilletons* and *noisettes de veau, Perigourdine,* both requiring the ultimate in fine wines, truffles, *foie gras,* and well-filled *porte-feuilles.*

BRAISED VEAL CHOPS AND STEAKS
Côtes de Veau Braisées

Both steaks cut from the leg of veal and shoulder chops benefit deliciously from the slow, moist cooking of a braise, as do rib and loin chops from veal that is not of the pale and tender quality one had hoped to find. Because weights of veal carcasses and cutting methods for veal vary so tremendously in this country, we shall simply specify the weight and the thickness of the meat. For shoulder chops, count on ¾ pound per person, and each chop should be ¾ to 1 inch thick. Cross-grain slices from the leg (round) should also be ¾ to 1 inch thick, and 1½ to 2 pounds will serve 4 people.

FRENCH VEAL

In France, shoulder chops are called either *basses côtes* or *côtes découvertes.* Only small legs of veal are cut into steaks, *rouelles.*

＊ *CÔTES DE VEAU DANS LEUR JUS*
[Veal Chops or Steaks Braised in Wine]

This is a lovely, simple, basic method for braising veal chops or steaks. Serve just as is, enriching the braising juices with a little butter, or elaborating with cream and mushrooms or other trimmings, as decribed in the variations following this recipe. You might arrange the chops on a bed of creamed spinach or on the potatoes simmered in cream and tarragon, page 389. Or you could accompany them with the *gratin* of chard or of spinach and onions, pages 358 or 360. The delicious zucchini *timbale* on page 372 would make the dinner much dressier, of course, and if you did not wish a rice or potato dish, a fresh loaf of your own French bread would very nicely take the place of a starchy vegetable. For wine, we suggest a red Bordeaux-Médoc.

For 4 people

---

1) *Browning the chops*

4 veal shoulder chops
¾ to 1 inch thick and

If using chops, cut off extra backbone pieces and remove any loose ribs, gristle, and excess fat; if tail is

¾ lb. each; or 1½ to 2 lbs. veal steak ¾ to 1 inch thick

3 to 4 Tb butter

1 to 2 Tb olive oil or cooking oil

An electric frying pan large enough to hold all the meat in 1 layer; or a medium pan and a baking dish or casserole

loose, wind it around the body of the meat and skewer in place. (Leave steaks whole or cut into serving pieces, whichever you prefer.) Dry meat thoroughly on paper towels. Heat 2 tablespoons butter and 1 of oil in pan, and when butter foam begins to subside, arrange as much meat in pan as will easily fit in 1 layer. Brown 3 to 4 minutes on each side, regulating heat so butter is very hot but not browning. Remove meat to a side dish if you have not browned all at once, and brown the rest of the veal with more butter or oil if needed.

---

2) *Braising the chops*

Salt and pepper

3 Tb minced shallots or scallions

½ cup dry white wine or dry white French vermouth

About 1 cup veal stock, chicken stock, or a combination of canned chicken and beef bouillon

½ tsp tarragon, thyme, mixed Provençal herbs, or Italian seasoning

(You may braise the chops either on top of the stove or in a preheated 325-degree oven; if they will not fit flat in one layer, overlap slightly and plan to baste more frequently.) Season meat on both sides with salt and pepper, and arrange in the pan. Set over moderate heat, stir in the shallots or scallions, and cook 2 minutes, then pour in the wine or vermouth, and enough stock or bouillon to come half way up the meat. Add the herbs. Bring to the simmer on top of the stove, cover pan, and maintain at a slow, steady simmer throughout cooking, basting meat several times with liquid in pan. Whether chops or steak, meat should be done in 50 to 60 minutes, and should be tender when pierced with a knife; if not tender, cook 5 to 10 minutes longer.

---

3) *Sauce and serving*

A hot platter

Salt and pepper

Drops of fresh lemon juice

2 to 3 Tb soft butter

Minced fresh parsley and whatever vegetables you wish

Arrange the veal on the platter; cover and keep warm in turned-off oven, door ajar, for the few minutes it will take to finish the sauce. Skim surface fat off cooking juices, bring to the boil, skimming, and boil down rapidly until liquid is almost syrupy. Carefully correct seasoning, adding lemon juice to taste. Remove from heat and swish in the enrichment butter, half a tablespoon at a time. Spoon the sauce over the chops, sprinkle with parsley, and serve immediately.

(*) AHEAD-OF-TIME NOTES: If you are not serving immediately, prepare the sauce by boiling down the cooking juices to concentrate them, but do not reduce the quantity quite so much. Return veal to pan, baste with sauce, lay waxed paper over it and cover pan loosely. The meat will keep nicely for at least half an hour on a hot-tray or warming oven at 110 to 120 degrees; finish sauce just before serving.

VARIATIONS

Côtes de Veau Gratinées au Fromage

[Braised Veal Chops or Steaks Gratinéed with Cheese]

This is a delicious variation with cheese.

Brown and braise the veal, Steps 1 and 2 in the preceding Master Recipe, and make the sauce, Step 3. Shortly before serving them, gratiné as follows:

¾ cup lightly pressed down, coarsely grated Swiss cheese
¼ cup dry white wine, or dry white French vermouth

Preheat broiler to moderately hot. Arrange the braised veal in a shallow baking dish, if not already in one, and spread the cheese over the meat. Sprinkle the wine or vermouth on top, and set under broiler for several minutes, until cheese has melted and browned nicely. Arrange the chops on their platter, pour the sauce around them, and serve.

Côtes de Veau Braisées aux Champignons

[Veal Chops or Steaks Braised with Mushrooms and Cream]

Mushrooms and veal, like mushrooms and chicken, always go well together and one reason undoubtedly is that the natural MSG in the mushrooms points up the delicate flavor of the meat.

Brown and braise the veal, Steps 1 and 2 in the Master Recipe, pages 204–5, but about 10 minutes before veal is done add the mushrooms as follows:

2 cups (¼ lb.) fresh mushrooms
2 Tb butter in a medium (10-inch) frying pan
Salt and pepper

Trim, wash, and dry the mushrooms; slice or quarter them. Heat butter to foaming, add mushrooms, and sauté, tossing and turning for 2 to 3 minutes; season lightly and set aside. (A short sauté in butter gives them added flavor.) When you estimate the veal has around 10 minutes more in the oven, add the mushrooms, basting them with the juices in the casserole.

Sauce and serving

½ to ⅔ cup *crème fraîche* or heavy cream

When done, remove veal to hot platter; cover and keep warm. Set mushrooms aside on a plate. Skim

Salt and pepper
Drops of lemon juice
2 to 3 Tb soft butter
2 to 3 Tb minced, fresh
parsley, parsley sprigs,
or whatever vegetable
you may have chosen

surface fat off cooking juices and boil liquid down, if necessary, until almost syrupy. Add the cream and boil down again rapidly until sauce is lightly thickened. Return mushrooms to sauce and simmer a moment. Correct seasoning, adding drops of lemon juice as needed. Remove from heat, swish in enrichment butter, then pour sauce and mushrooms over veal, decorate with parsley or vegetables, and serve.

(*) AHEAD-OF-TIME NOTE: If you are not to serve immediately, complete sauce, except for enrichment butter; return veal to pan and baste with sauce and mushrooms. Cover and keep warm (110–20 degrees). Thin out sauce before serving, if necessary, with more cream or stock; swish in enrichment butter, basting meat with sauce until butter is absorbed.

Côtes de Veau Champvallon, Gratinées
[Veal Chops or Steaks Braised with Potatoes]

This is almost a meal in a dish, and needs only a fresh green accompaniment like broccoli, peas, beans, or spinach; or you may prefer a combination salad in a separate course. Here the potatoes, cooking with the veal and their juices, absorb marvelous flavor, and the cheese and bread-crumb topping at the end not only thickens the cooking juices but also makes attractive serving. Although the general method is almost the same as the Master Recipe, we give a shortened full account because of slight differences.

NOTE: Here you must trim the meat in some way so that it will all fit in one layer in a casserole or baking dish; see Step 2.

For 4 people

1) *Browning the veal*

½ cup (4 ounces) *lardons*
(blanched bacon sticks,
1½ inches long and ¼
inch thick, page 148)
3 Tb olive oil or cooking
oil
4 veal shoulder chops or
steaks ¾ to 1 inch thick,
dried in paper towels
1 cup minced onions
2 large cloves garlic,
mashed or minced

Cut the blanched *lardons* of bacon into ¼-inch dice, and brown slowly with the oil in a frying pan. Remove with a slotted spoon and set aside, leaving fat in pan. Add the chops or steaks; brown for 3 to 4 minutes on each side, being sure fat is very hot but not burning. Remove veal. Stir in the onions and garlic, cover, and cook slowly, stirring occasionally, for 8 to 10 minutes, until tender. Scoop onions and garlic into a side dish, leaving fat in pan. Remove pan from heat.

2) *Braising the veal*

Salt and pepper
½ tsp tarragon, thyme, mixed Provençal herbs, or Italian seasoning
A covered flameproof casserole or baking dish that will just hold all the meat in one layer (or use two dishes)
4 to 5 cups "boiling" potatoes, peeled and cut into ⅛-inch slices
½ cup fresh, rather roughly minced parsley
½ cup dry white wine or dry white French vermouth
About 1 cup veal stock, chicken stock, or a combination of canned chicken and beef bouillon
Buttered aluminum foil
A bulb baster

Preheat oven to 350 degrees. Season veal with salt, pepper, and herbs, and arrange in one close layer in casserole with the onions and garlic, and half the browned, diced *lardons*. Strew the potatoes over the veal, seasoning each layer with salt, pepper, and a sprinkling of parsley. (You should have no more than ¾ inch of potatoes in all.) Pour in the wine, and enough stock or bouillon to come ⅓ the way up the potatoes. Spoon a tablespoon or 2 of the cooking fat over the potatoes (unless it has browned, in which case use melted butter). Sprinkle the remaining *lardon* bits over the potatoes, and bring contents of casserole to simmer on top of stove. Drape buttered foil over potatoes, cover casserole, and set in middle level of preheated oven. Bake for about an hour, or until both veal and potatoes are tender, basting several times with liquid in pan.

3) *Gratinéeing and serving*

½ cup not-too-fine crumbs from nonsweetened, homemade-type white bread
⅓ cup finely grated Swiss or Parmesan cheese

Raise oven thermostat to 425 degrees. Taste cooking liquid and correct seasoning if necessary. Mix the crumbs and cheese together, and spread over the potatoes. Baste with juices in casserole and set in upper-third level of oven. Baste several times while juices boil down and thicken with the crumbs, and topping browns nicely; this will take 10 to 15 minutes.

Either serve from casserole or baking dish, or remove each piece of veal with its topping, and transfer to a hot platter; pour juices around.

(*) AHEAD-OF-TIME NOTE: If you are not to serve immediately, let juices reduce and thicken a little less; keep warm, loosely covered with foil, on a hot-tray or 120-degree warming oven. Baste with more stock or with melted butter, if necessary, before serving.

Other ideas for veal chops and steaks

Starting out with the simple braise in the Master Recipe on page 204, you might stir the reduced cooking juices, Step 3, into a *pistou* flavoring, page 152, or into the Provençal mixture of anchovies, capers, garlic, and parsley described in Volume I, page 324. Another idea would be to spread a *pipérade* of sautéed green peppers, tomatoes, garlic, and herbs over the braised veal; cover and let them warm together for a few minutes, then spoon on the sauce and serve. You could use the *pistouille* mixture, page 351, of sautéed eggplant, tomatoes, and peppers in the same way. Finally, there is the always attractive garniture *bonne femme,* a combination of bacon *lardons,* partially cooked small onions, and blanched small potatoes, which you add to the veal the last half hour of braising so all finish their cooking together; for this, adapt the *poulet en cocotte bonne femme* recipe in Volume I, page 253.

VEAL STEWS
Ragoûts de Veau

Veal makes lovely stew, and it cooks in a little more than an hour. Volume I contains the well-known *blanquette de veau,* with its onions, mushrooms, and creamy sauce, as well as a hearty brown stew with tomatoes. Here are several more stews, including *ossobuco.*

VEAL CUTS FOR STEWING

The part of the veal breast called "plate," illustrated on page 215, is a favorite French stewing cut, but one that is not popular with all Americans because of the crunchy cartilage of the breast bone and rib ends. The shoulder-chop area, neck, and shoulder arm all give good stew meat, as do both front and hind shanks. The hind shank is the *ossobuco,* with the marrow bone, and the choicest; the front shank has more bone and the meat more separations; it requires half an hour longer cooking, but makes a good stew because of its gelatinous quality. (If the veal you buy is not of the palest and tenderest quality, the best way to cook it is by stewing or braising; the leg [round] can be used for boneless stewing meat in this case.)

A pound of boneless meat will serve 2 to 3 people, but you will need ¾ to 1 pound per person for bone-in meat. You may use a combination of both in any of the recipes except for *ossobuco,* but we shall usually specify boneless meat simply to eliminate cumbersome either-or choices. Bones, however, will add texture and flavor to the stew; if your meat is boneless it is a good idea to tie a cupful or so of chopped veal marrow and knuckle bones in washed cheesecloth, and simmer them with the meat.

* *RAGOÛT DE VEAU AUX CHAMPIGNONS*

[Veal Stew with Tomatoes, Mushrooms, and Cream]

There are endless way of flavoring and finishing off a veal stew, because veal, like chicken, is amenable to infinite variety. Here is a Master Recipe for starting out the veal, and a number of ways to vary its presentation. Serve this with rice or pasta, and a fresh green vegetable or a salad. For wine, chose a light, young red like Beaujolais or Cabernet Sauvignon, or a rather strong, dry white of the Côtes-du-Rhône type.

For 4 to 6 people

1) *Browning the veal and the onions*

2½ to 3 lbs. trimmed and boneless lean stewing veal cut into 1½-inch chunks (see notes preceding recipe)
Salt and pepper
½ cup flour on a plate
2 or more Tb olive oil or cooking oil
A heavy frying pan, no-stick recommended

Dry veal on paper towels, season with salt and pepper, and just before browning, roll in flour and shake off excess. (Shaking in a sieve works nicely.) Film pan with ⅛ inch of oil, set over moderately high heat, and when very hot but not smoking, add as many pieces of veal as will fit easily in 1 layer. Brown nicely on all sides, which will take 4 to 5 minutes or more; remove veal, as it is browned, to a side dish, and continue with the rest.

2 cups sliced onions
2 Tb oil
A heavy 10- by 2-inch chicken fryer, electric skillet, or 3- to 4-quart flameproof casserole

While veal is browning, cook onions in oil over moderate heat, stirring occasionally, for 8 to 10 minutes. When tender, raise heat and brown very lightly. When the veal is done, add it to the onions.

2) *Braising the veal*

1 cup dry white wine, or ¾ cup dry white French vermouth
1 cup brown veal stock, or chicken stock, or a combination of canned

Discard oil from veal sauté pan and deglaze pan with the wine, scraping up coagulated browning juices. Pour the wine into the veal and onions; stir in the stock, herbs, garlic, and tomatoes. Bring to the simmer, cover and simmer slowly, basting meat occasionally with liquids in pan, for 1 to 1¼ hours, or

chicken broth and beef
  bouillon
1 tsp tarragon, basil, or
  oregano
1 imported bay leaf
1 or 2 large cloves garlic,
  mashed or minced
1 or 2 tomatoes, peeled,
  seeded, juiced, and
  roughly chopped (¾ cup
  pulp)

until veal is tender when pierced with a knife. Do
not overcook; meat should not fall apart.

3) *The mushrooms*

1½ to 2 cups (6 to 8
  ounces) fresh mushrooms
More oil
The frying pan that
  browned the veal
Salt and pepper

While veal is simmering, trim, wash, dry, and quarter
the mushrooms. Film pan with ⅛ inch of oil, and set
over moderately high heat; when oil is hot but not
smoking, sauté the mushrooms, tossing and turning,
for 3 to 4 minutes, just until they are starting to
brown lightly. Season to taste, and set aside.

4) *Sauce and serving*

If needed: *beurre manié*
  (1 Tb flour blended to a
  paste with 1 Tb soft
  butter), and a wire whip
½ to ⅔ cup *crème fraîche*
  or heavy cream
The mushrooms
Minced fresh parsley, or
  mixed fresh green herbs
  (parsley, chives, and
  tarragon, basil, or
  oregano)

When veal is tender, scoop it out into a side dish
with a slotted spoon. Skim off surface fat, and boil
down cooking liquid, if necessary, to concentrate its
flavor. If it seems too thin (it must be thick enough
to cover the meat nicely), remove from heat, beat in
beurre manié with wire whip, and bring to the simmer. Stir in the cream and the mushrooms, bring to
the boil, and boil slowly 2 to 3 minutes to thicken the
sauce again, and to blend flavors. Carefully correct
seasoning. Return veal to casserole and simmer again
for 2 to 3 minutes, basting the veal with the sauce;
correct seasoning again. Either serve from pan or
casserole, or arrange on a hot platter surrounded with
whatever vegetables you have chosen. Decorate with
herbs, and bring immediately to the table.

(*) AHEAD-OF-TIME NOTES: May be kept warm for a good half hour on a hot-
tray or over simmering water. May be cooked a day before serving; when cold, spread
plastic wrap over surface, cover, and refrigerate. When ready to serve, bring to simmer slowly, and simmer about 10 minutes, basting frequently, until thoroughly reheated but not overcooked. If sauce seems too thick, thin out with stock or cream.

VARIATIONS

Ragoût de Veau, Printanier

[Veal Stew Garnished with Carrots, Onions,
New Potatoes, and Green Peas]

When all the vegetables are fresh, this is delicious indeed and very attractive to serve because of the various colors. If you are cooking and serving
with no delay, the vegetables may do all of their simmering in the stew, and
you add them at different times, according to how long they take to cook.
Otherwise do as suggested here, giving them a separate start, and letting them
finish off in the stew just before serving; in this method, you may prepare
everything ahead except for the potatoes.

Follow method and ingredients for preceding Master
Recipe, Steps 1 and 2, using only ½ cup of onions
in Step 1, and omitting the garlic in Step 2. Meanwhile, prepare the following:

The carrots and onions

4 to 6 fine, fresh carrots
24 to 30 small, white, fresh
  onions ¾ to 1 inch in
  diameter
A heavy, covered saucepan
1 cup water
1½ Tb butter
½ tsp salt

Peel the carrots, halve or quarter them depending on
size, and cut into 1½-inch lengths; trim edges to
round them, if you wish. Drop onions into boiling
water, boil 1 minute, drain, and slip off peel; pierce
a cross ¼ inch deep in root ends for even cooking.
Place carrots and onions in pan with the water,
butter, and salt; cover and simmer slowly about 25
minutes, until just tender. Set aside.

The peas

1 to 1½ lbs. fresh peas
  (1 to 1½ cups, shelled)
A saucepan containing 3
  quarts of rapidly boil-
  ing, salted water

Drop the peas into the rapidly boiling water, bring
quickly back to the boil again, and boil uncovered 4 to
8 minutes or more, depending on tenderness. Test
frequently by tasting; they should be almost, but not
quite, done. Drain immediately, run cold water over
them to stop the cooking and retain their fresh color;
drain again and set aside.

The potatoes

About 2 lbs. new potatoes
  (or "boiling" potatoes)

Peel the potatoes and trim into ovals about 2¼ inches
long and 1½ inches thick; drop into bowl of cold

all of a size for easy
cutting (2¾ to 3 inches
long, for instance)
A bowl of cold water
When needed: a saucepan
of boiling, salted water

water and set aside. (About ½ hour before you plan
to serve the stew, drain the potatoes and drop into
boiling water to cover. Boil slowly, uncovered, until
almost tender, drain and add to stew as indicated in
last paragraph.)

Finishing the stew

If needed: more stock or
bouillon

When veal is tender, tip pan and skim off surface
fat. If sauce has reduced too much, add a little more
stock or bouillon so that you will have enough liquid
to cook and baste the vegetables.

About 10 minutes before serving, arrange the carrots, onions, potatoes, and peas
in the casserole, pushing them gently down into the meat and cooking juices. Pour
any cooking juices from carrots and onions over meat, and baste both meat and
vegetables with juices in casserole. Bring to the simmer, cover closely, and simmer
about 10 minutes, basting several times, until vegetables are tender. Correct seasoning.
Either serve from casserole, or turn the stew out onto a hot platter.

Ossobuco—Jarret de Veau à la Provençale
[Braised Veal Shanks with Wine, Tomatoes, Lemon, and Orange]

Osso is bone and *buco* is round, meaning the shank with the round bone,
which is the hind shank with the marrow bone. This favorite Italian veal stew
is also done in France, and here is the Provençal version. Although you may
use foreshanks, hind shanks are so much more attractive to serve because the
bone is small and the meat holds around it nicely, that we counsel you to
order hind shanks, and do the recipe when you have the right meat. Veal
shanks, sawed into 1½-inch pieces and ready to cook, will freeze perfectly for
several weeks; therefore pick up whatever you can whenever you can, and
save all hind shanks for this really delicious recipe.

For 4 people—4 veal hind shanks, sawed into
crosswise pieces 1½ inches thick

Season, flour, and brown the veal shanks; arrange in
the braising liquid with the onions, garlic, tomatoes,
and herbs as described in the Master Recipe, Steps 1
and 2, pages 210–11. Then proceed as follows:

1 orange
1 lemon
A vegetable peeler
A saucepan containing a
   quart or so of boiling
   water

Cut the zests (colored parts of the peel) from the orange and lemon, then cut zests into *julienne* strips $\frac{1}{16}$ inch wide. To remove bitterness (but none of the flavor), simmer 10 minutes; drain, refresh in cold water, drain again, and stir into the casserole with the veal stew.

Bring stew to simmer, cover casserole, and simmer either in a preheated 325-degree oven or on top of the stove for $1\frac{1}{4}$ hours, or until meat is tender when pierced with a fork. Do not overcook: meat must not come loose from bone. When tender, tip casserole and skim surface fat from cooking liquid. Set casserole over high heat, if necessary, and boil down sauce to concentrate flavor. Correct seasoning. Serve either from casserole, or on a hot platter. Decorate with parsley sprigs.

Other ideas

Use other veal stew meat, such as cuts from the shoulder or the leg, and give it the *ossobuco* flavoring. Vary the *ossobuco* recipe with olives: blanch a handful each of pitted green olives and pitted black olives for 10 minutes in a quart of boiling water; drain, and add to the stew the last 15 to 20 minutes of cooking. See also the variations at the end of beef stews, pages 152–5, which include an herb, cheese, and garlic finish, another with anchovies and garlic, a *pipérade* with peppers and tomatoes, and a final one with olives and potatoes; any of these may be added to the cooked veal at the end of Step 2, Master Recipe, page 211, instead of the mushrooms and cream. You thus have a wide choice, and never need serve the same stew twice.

STUFFED BREAST OF VEAL
Poitrine de Veau, Farcie

Breast of veal boned, stuffed with a well-seasoned filling, braised, and sauced makes a handsome as well as tasty main-course party dish, and one that is far more reasonable in price than most. French and American meat cutting methods differ, and as we find the French version much the most attractive to serve, here is how to buy and prepare it. If you cannot have the butchering done properly for you, and if you enjoy working with meat yourself, you will find the whole breast not at all difficult to handle, and you may even be able to buy it at a far more interesting price than if it were boned and trimmed at the market.

HOW TO BUY A BREAST OF VEAL

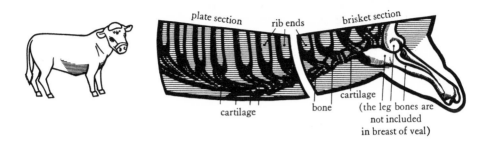

In America, a breast of veal (or of lamb) comprises the whole brisket-plate section. From a large, pale, prime carcass of veal, such as you can find in France and in some markets here, this will weigh 7 to 7½ pounds before boning and trimming. The boned brisket weighs 2½ pounds; the breastbone, 1 pound; the plate and skirt (flap of meat falling over ribs), with the ribs and cartilage, 3½ pounds. It is the boned brisket that is stuffed for French recipes; a 2½-pound brisket, stuffed, will be 12 inches long, 7 to 8 inches across, and can easily serve 8 people.

Adapt whatever you find to the general idea of the recipe even if your market does not carry breasts of the desired weight, or follows different cutting methods. You might, for instance, sew or skewer 2 plates together for stuffing, or 2 briskets, if they are smaller than you think they should be. If you have trouble making your wishes known, show your butcher this picture; he might be willing to order one for you, and to prepare it according to your specifications.

Actually, the whole brisket-plate combination is a good buy because not only will you have the brisket to stuff, but you can also save the thick part of the plate for stew, you can grind the rest of the plate along with the skirt for your stuffing, and when you boil up the breastbone and ribs, you will have a fine veal stock for braising the *poitrine farcie.*

FRENCH TERMINOLOGY

Brisket is *poitrine,* and the *poitrine* also includes the skirt, *hampe;* ask for a *poitrine de veau désossée, avec poche.* The plate is called *tendron,* and is a favorite French cut for *blanquette de veau,* particularly the thick part containing the breastbone cartilage.

DIRECTIONS FOR THE HOME BUTCHER

NOTE: In the drawing, the breast has been separated in two—the right-hand piece, minus leg bones, is the brisket; the left-hand piece the plate.

To bone the whole breast, start with the breastbone (right side in drawing), which is attached to the ribs by cartilages: first, place the meat rib-side up, with the breastbone hanging over the edge of the table. Lean hard on the bone to break it from the cartilages at the rib ends, then cut around its ridges and follow its cartilaginous prolongation into the plate, to remove the entire bone from the meat. The next step is to separate the brisket from the plate: slice through the meat between ribs 5 and 6 to make 2 pieces, as in the drawing. Slice off the skirt, a flap of meat on the rib side, attached to the thick part of the plate. Remove the rib bones from both brisket and plate by cutting first around them, then underneath each bone to loosen it from the meat. The thick part of the plate that contained the prolongation of the breastbone (bottom left in drawing) can make an excellent stew for 2 people; cut it off from the rest of the plate, and freeze it for another meal. Trim excess fat off brisket with a long, sharp knife. Then carefully slice a pocket in the brisket (right-hand piece), going in from the large or plate end; the brisket will now be like a pouch, and you will close it by sewing or skewering after you stuff it. Scrape usable meat from membranes covering plate and skirt, and grind it. Chop up the breastbone, and brown bones and scraps half an hour in a 450-degree oven with a sliced carrot and onion; then simmer for 3 to 4 hours in water, herbs, and seasonings to make a simple but delicious veal stock (detailed directions are in Volume I, pages 107-11).

POITRINE DE VEAU, FARCIE
[Breast of Veal Stuffed and Braised—Hot or Cold]

Green stuffings provide attractive serving slices and should be made of chard leaves, if you can find them; spinach, if you cannot. The rest of the stuffing consists of boiled rice, ground veal, a little ham, and a bit of onion. There is no pork here, no garlic, and the delicate taste of the veal does seem to come through beautifully. Accompany the dish with braised onions and carrots or baked tomatoes. A not too heavy red wine would be the one to choose, like a Bordeaux, a young Beaujolais, or a Cabernet Sauvignon; a rosé would also go well. Serve cold breast of veal with sliced tomatoes, the French potato salad, *pommes a l'huile,* Volume I, page 541, and either a rosé or a dry white from the Rhône like Chante Alouette.

For 8 people

---

1) *Chard or spinach stuffing with rice, veal, and ham—4 cups*

¼ cup rendered fresh pork fat, ham fat, or chicken or goose fat

Melt the fat in the frying pan, stir in the onions, cover, and cook slowly, stirring occasionally for 10 minutes, until tender and just beginning to brown

½ cup finely minced onions
A medium (10-inch) frying
    pan, enameled or no-stick
4 or 5 large, green chard
    leaves minus white part
    of stalks (or 1 cup
    cooked, chopped spinach
    or ¾ package frozen
    spinach, thawed and
    squeezed dry)
The bowl of a heavy-duty
    mixer, or a large mixing
    bowl and wooden spoon
Salt
¾ cup boiled rice (¼ cup
    plain, raw, white rice
    boiled 12 minutes in 1
    quart of salted water,
    and drained)
1 to 1½ cups lean raw veal
    finely ground with ½
    cup lean mild-cured
    boiled ham (supermarket
    ham slice)
½ to ⅔ cup grated Parme-
    san cheese
1 "large" egg
Large pinch grated nutmeg
¼ tsp pepper

lightly. Set aside. Meanwhile blanch the chard leaves in a large kettle of boiling salted water for 3 to 4 minutes, until wilted; drain, refresh in cold water, squeeze hard to rid leaves of water, and chop moderately fine (¼-inch pieces). Blend chard (or spinach) into onions; stir over moderately high heat for a few moments to evaporate remaining liquid; cover and cook slowly several minutes more, until fairly tender. Season to taste and scrape into bowl. Vigorously beat in the boiled rice, ground meat, cheese, egg, nutmeg, and pepper. Sauté a small spoonful in frying pan until cooked through, taste carefully, and add more seasonings if you feel them necessary.

2) Stuffing the veal

A boned breast (brisket)
    of veal, weighing, if
    possible, around 2½ lbs.
    (See directions, descrip-
    tion, and alternates, pages
    214–16.)
Salt and pepper
A trussing needle or small
    poultry-lacing skewers
White string

Open the pocket in the meat and sprinkle lightly with salt and pepper. Insert the stuffing, pushing it well down into the meat, but do not overfill. Close opening of meat by sewing with string, or with skewers and string. If by chance you have pierced a hole in the surface of the meat, close it by sewing or skewering.

The ridged side, where the ribs were, is the underside; turn small end of the meat under and sew or skewer it in place, thus giving the veal a rectangular cushion shape about 12 inches long and 8 inches across. If meat seems solid and stuffing securely in place, tying is not necessary; otherwise, with string, make 2 loops around length and several around circumference, but do not tie too tightly. Dry the meat thoroughly before proceeding to next step.

(*) AHEAD-OF-TIME NOTE: If you wish to prepare and refrigerate the veal the day before cooking, chill stuffing before inserting it into the meat, just to be sure and safe.

---

3) *Browning and braising the veal—2½ hours*

Rendered pork fat, goose fat, or cooking oil

A heavy casserole or roaster just large enough to hold veal comfortably (a 10-by 12-inch oval, for example)

½ cup each, roughly sliced carrots and onions

Optional but desirable, if you have no homemade veal stock: a cup or so of chopped veal bones

Salt

A bulb baster

1 cup dry white wine, or ¾ cup dry white French vermouth

2 to 3 cups homemade veal stock, or rich chicken stock, or a combination of canned beef bouillon and chicken broth

½ tsp thyme

1 imported bay leaf

A sheet of fresh pork fat or suet, or aluminum foil

Preheat oven to 450 degrees. Film casserole with ⅛ inch of fat or oil; when very hot but not smoking, brown the vegetables and optional bones. Remove to a side dish, add more fat or oil if needed, and brown bottom (former rib side) of veal, lifting carefully from time to time with wooden spoon to be sure meat is not sticking. When browned, in 5 to 6 minutes, baste top with fat and set uncovered in upper-middle level of preheated oven for about 15 minutes, basting with fat in casserole several times, until top and sides of meat have browned nicely. Remove from oven; turn thermostat down to 350 degrees. Salt the meat lightly, strew the browned bones and vegetables around, pour in the wine and enough stock or bouillon to come ⅔ the way up the meat. Add the thyme and bay leaf, and drape the fat or foil over the meat.

Bring to the simmer on top of stove, cover the casserole, and braise in lower-middle level of oven, regulating heat so that liquid in casserole remains at a slow, even simmer. If meat is easy to turn, do so several times during cooking, replacing fat or foil on top; otherwise, baste every 20 minutes or so with the liquids in the casserole. Meat should be done in about 2 hours, when it feels tender if pierced with a fork. It should retain its shape perfectly; in other words, do not let it overcook.

---

4) *Sauce and serving*

A hot platter

A sieve set over a sauce-pan

Remove veal to hot platter. Do not untie or unskewer it yet, but cover with its fat or foil, and set in turned-off oven, door ajar. Strain braising liquid into sauce-

Salt and pepper
If needed: 1 Tb cornstarch
　　mixed to a paste with 2
　　Tb wine or vermouth
2 to 3 Tb soft butter
Parsley, watercress, or what-
　　ever vegetable garnish
　　you have chosen
A warm sauce bowl

pan, pressing juices out of vegetables. Skim off surface fat, bring liquid to the simmer, skimming, and
boil down rapidly, if necessary, to around 2 cups.

If sauce needs thickening, remove from heat, beat in the cornstarch mixture,
and simmer 2 minutes. Carefully correct seasoning. Just before serving, remove from
heat and beat in the enrichment butter a half a tablespoon at a time. Remove trussings
from veal, spoon a little sauce over to glaze it, and decorate the platter as you wish.
Pour remaining sauce into bowl. Serve immediately.

To carve, cut crosswise slices ⅜ to ½ inch thick, as though meat were a loaf
of bread. Ring each slice with a spoonful or two of sauce.

(*) AHEAD-OF-TIME NOTE: If you are not serving for half an hour or so, finish
the sauce except for butter enrichment; return meat and sauce to casserole. Set cover
askew and keep anywhere that you can maintain a temperature of 120 degrees. An
occasional basting of the meat will keep it moist; if sauce thickens during wait, thin
with stock before serving.

Other stuffings

Breast of veal takes kindly to many stuffings. Another combination with chard
includes the sausage meat, ham, and bread crumbs used for *paupiette* of beef on page
156, and there is the mushroom *duxelles* and spinach stuffing for shoulder of lamb
Viroflay on page 194. Either the mushroom and kidney stuffing for boned leg of lamb,
page 190, or the kidney and rice stuffing in Volume I, page 337, would be delicious
and unusual, as would be the *boudin blanc* and mushrooms mixture in the chicken
section, page 275. A complete rundown of stuffing possibilities is on pages 513–15.

✳ *VEAU EN FEUILLETONS*
[Sliced and Stuffed Roast of Veal]

Veal wants stuffing, as the British would say, and here is a typically
French *grande cuisine farce fine* of pork, veal, truffles, *foie gras,* and Cognac.
This is sliced veal marinated in wine and truffles, then tied together in the
form of a roast with the stuffing between each slice. Braised with stock and
aromatic vegetables, it produces a most heavenly sauce combining all of the
luxurious flavors. Very definitely a dish for a select group of friends, it calls
for your finest in château-bottled Bordeaux-Médocs, and the best vegetables.

You might surround the meat platter with a fluted border of mashed potatoes *duchesse* (page 399) and pass separately something like braised spinach, chopped broccoli simmered in cream (page 342), braised endives or lettuce, or fresh, buttered peas.

THE VEAL

If you can get it, the top round from a large, pale, prime leg would give you solid scallops with no muscle separations. Otherwise settle either for cuts from the full round that you can separate and regroup, or the thin scallopini available in some markets. These latter you could regroup or spread separately with stuffing. Play it by look and feel, aiming for a re-formed roast about 10 inches long and 5 inches in diameter.

For 10 to 12 people

---

1) *Marinating the veal in Cognac and truffles*

2 to 2½ lbs. veal scallops preferably from the top round, making 10 to 12 slices 6 by 4 inches in diameter and ³⁄₁₆ inch thick (or scallopini, 2 or 3 per person)
Waxed paper and a mallet or rolling pin
A dish large enough to hold scallops in several layers
½ cup Cognac
1 or 2 canned truffles, minced, and their juice
Plastic wrap

Trim all filaments, fat, and extraneous matter from scallops. Place them one by one between sheets of waxed paper and pound not too heavily, to break down filaments slightly, and to spread the meat out a little. (This will not be necessary with scallopini.) Arrange the scallops in layers interspersed with sprinklings of Cognac and minced truffles. Pour remaining Cognac and the truffle juices over meat, cover with plastic wrap, and set aside while preparing stuffing.

---

2) *Ground pork stuffing with ham, truffles, and foie gras—3½ cups*

¼ cup finely minced shallots or scallions
1½ Tb butter
A small frying pan
Bowl of heavy-duty mixer, or a large mixing bowl

Sauté the shallots or scallions slowly in the butter for 2 to 3 minutes until tender but not browned. Scrape into bowl.

The following, finely ground together:
12 ounces (1½ cups) lean pork

Add all of the rest of the ingredients listed, and beat vigorously by machine or with a wooden spoon to blend thoroughly. Just before starting Step 3, drain marinade liquid into stuffing, scrape truffles off veal,

4 ounces (½ cup) fresh
    pork fat (page 319)
4 ounces (½ cup) lean veal
4 ounces (½ cup) mild-
    cured ham, such as a
    store-bought, ready-to-
    cook ham slice

1 tsp salt
⅛ tsp white pepper
Big pinch ground allspice
½ tsp tarragon leaves,
    finely chopped or
    powdered
1 egg
The juices from the
    marinated scallops, and
    the truffles

and beat vigorously into stuffing. To check seasoning, sauté a spoonful until cooked through, taste, and
add more salt, pepper, or herbs if needed. (The *foie
gras* comes in Step 3.)

3) Assembling the veal

Either a piece of caul fat
    16 to 18 inches square
    (page 287);
Or well-washed cheesecloth,
    melted butter, and a
    pastry brush
Salt and pepper
4 to 6 ounces canned *foie
    gras en bloc* (imported
    goose liver; read the
    label)
White string

(If your veal slices are smaller or thinner than the
ideal, group them together, adapting meat to the
method outlined here.) Spread the caul fat or cheesecloth on a board or tray. Season each scallop of veal
lightly with salt and pepper, and build the slices into
a closely packed loaf shape, with stuffing and a slice
of *foie gras* between each scallop.

If you are using caul fat, fold it securely around the meat; if using cheesecloth,
first paint it with melted butter, roll it tightly around circumference, then twist each
end tight and tie close against meat with string. Tie a loop of string around length of
meat, and wind string back and forth around circumference to keep all in place.
You should have a fat sausage shape about 10 inches long.

(*) AHEAD-OF-TIME NOTE: Recipe may be prepared a day in advance to this point;
wrap airtight and refrigerate.

4) Browning and braising the veal—about 2 hours

A heavy, covered, flame-
    proof casserole just large
    enough to hold meat com-
    fortably, such as a 10-

Preheat oven to 350 degrees. Dry the meat in paper
towels. Set casserole over moderately high heat with
the fat or oil, and when very hot but not smoking,
brown the meat on all sides. (It will brown through

by 12-inch oval 5 inches
deep
**Rendered goose fat, pork
fat, or cooking oil**
2 cups chopped veal
knuckle and marrow
bones
1 medium carrot, roughly
chopped
1 medium onion, roughly
chopped
1½ to 2 cups excellent veal
stock, beef stock, or a
mixture of chicken broth
and beef bouillon
½ tsp thyme
1 imported bay leaf
Useful: a meat thermometer

cheesecloth perfectly well.) Remove to a side dish
and brown the bones and vegetables. Push them to
sides and return meat to casserole; pour in enough
stock or bouillon to come halfway up. Strew the herbs
around the meat. Bring liquid to the simmer, cover
casserole, and set in lower-middle level of preheated
oven.

Check casserole in about 20 minutes, and when contents are quietly simmering,
reduce oven heat to 325 degrees. Turn the meat twice during cooking and braise
about 2 hours in all, or to a meat thermometer reading of 165 to 170 degrees. When
done, remove veal to a side dish and let rest 20 minutes in turned-off oven, door ajar;
meat must settle before serving so pieces will hold in place.

---

5) *Sauce and serving*

A sieve set over a saucepan
2 tsp cornstarch blended
with ¼ cup dry Madeira
(Sercial), dry port, or
Cognac
A wire whip
Salt and pepper to taste
2 to 3 Tb soft butter
A warm serving bowl
A hot platter
Watercress, parsley sprigs,
or whatever vegetable
garnish you may have
chosen

Strain braising liquid into saucepan. Skim off as much
surface fat as you can, and bring liquid to the simmer,
skimming off additional fat. Boil down rapidly, if necessary, to about 2 cups; carefully correct seasoning. Remove from heat, blend in the cornstarch mixture, and
simmer 2 minutes. Sauce should be lightly thickened.

Disturbing meat as little as possible, untie it. If you have used caul fat, it will
have mostly disintegrated during cooking; remove any bits that have not. If you
have used cheesecloth, carefully cut it off with shears. Using two spatulas, lift meat
onto hot platter. (If by chance the slices come apart, push them together.) Spoon

a little sauce over meat to glaze it, and decorate platter with whatever you have chosen. Reheat sauce, remove from heat, and beat in the enrichment butter a half tablespoon at a time, and pour into hot sauce bowl. Serve immediately. For serving, spread scallops slightly apart with spoon and fork, to display the meat. Be sure each slice comes off with its share of stuffing, and surround with a spoonful of sauce.

(*) AHEAD-OF-TIME NOTE: You may complete the sauce except for the final butter enrichment, and arrange the meat on its platter, cover it, and keep warm for a good half hour at 120 degrees.

VARIATIONS

Feuilletons de Veau en Croûte
[Stuffed Roast of Veal Baked in a Pastry Crust]

The presentation of a roast baked in brown, decorated pastry is always dramatic. For the stuffed veal, follow the preceding Master Recipe exactly through Steps 1, 2, and 3, and braise the meat in Step 4 for about 1½ hours, or to a thermometer reading of 150 degrees. Remove the meat, and let it rest 30 minutes. Then untie it, remove covering, and drape the roast either in puff pastry as described for the *gigot en croûte* on page 189, or in chilled *brioche* dough as for the tenderloin of beef on page 181. Decorate the dough, glaze it with egg, and return to a 425-degree oven for 25 to 30 minutes, to cook and brown the crust, and to finish cooking the meat. Serve with the same sauce described in Step 5 of the preceding recipe.

Noisettes de Veau, Périgourdine
[Individual Stuffed Loin Scallops with *Foie Gras* and Truffles]

Less dramatic but exquisite in taste are *noisettes* of veal, meaning the boneless loin or rib-eye section of a veal chop, surrounded with the stuffing, braised in wine, and served with a brown, truffled sauce. You can do this dish, however, only if you have caul fat to hold the stuffing in place; it disintegrates during cooking. You might serve the *noisettes* on a platter garnished with very carefully sautéed potatoes, glazed onions, glazed carrots, sautéed mushrooms, and a decoration of fresh parsley sprigs. Another suggestion would be *pommes Anna,* page 394, or the *gratin Crécy* of scalloped potatoes and carrots in cream, Volume I, page 525, and the chopped, sautéed broccoli on page 341. A very fine red Bordeaux-Médoc would again be indicated.

For 6 people

1) *Preparing the noisettes for cooking*

12 *noisettes* of veal (boneless large eye of meat in   Trim all fat, filaments, and gristle from *noisettes*. Salt and pepper lightly, and marinate in a covered bowl

loin or rib chops, ½ inch thick and 2½ inches in diameter if possible; 3 per person if smaller)

½ the marinade ingredients in Step 1, Master Recipe, page 220

About ⅓ cup clarified butter (melted butter, skimmed; clear liquid butter spooned off milky residue)

A medium (10-inch) frying pan, no-stick recommended

with the Cognac, truffles, and shallots for at least half an hour, or overnight. Scrape marinade off meat, and beat it into the stuffing (next step) along with the marinade liquid. Dry *noisettes* thoroughly on paper towels. Film pan with ⅛ inch of the clarified butter, heat to bubbling hot, and sauté a few scallops at a time for a minute or so on each side, just to stiffen the meat slightly. Remove to a side dish, reserving butter in pan.

A piece of caul fat about 24 inches square (page 287)

½ the stuffing ingredients in Step 2, Master Recipe, pages 220–1

3 ounces canned *foie gras en bloc*

Divide stuffing and *foie gras* into 12 (or 18) portions. Spread a piece of caul fat (about 8 inches square) on a board or tray. Center a half portion of stuffing upon it, and a half portion of *foie gras* upon that. Place a *noisette* of veal over the stuffing, top with its remaining share of *foie gras,* and spread with its final share of stuffing. Fold caul fat around it, to enclose meat and stuffing. Continue with the rest of the *noisettes* in the same way.

(*) AHEAD-OF-TIME NOTE: May be done a day in advance to this point; cover and refrigerate.

---

2) *Cooking and serving*

The frying pan and the clarified butter

The *noisettes* of veal wrapped in caul fat

A covered flameproof baking dish large enough to hold scallops in one slightly overlapping layer

A *brunoise* (¼ cup each very finely diced—1/16 inch—carrots, onions, and celery)

¼ cup dry Madeira (Sercial) wine

½ cup veal stock, beef stock, or bouillon

A hot platter, and whatever

Preheat oven to 375 degrees. Add more butter to pan, if necessary, to film it by ⅛ inch. Heat to bubbling hot, and brown the meat again lightly on each side for a minute or so. Arrange in baking dish. Stir *brunoise* vegetables into pan, lower heat, and cook rather slowly for 5 to 6 minutes, until tender and barely browned. Pour in the Madeira, scraping up coagulated sauté juices with a wooden spoon. With a rubber spatula, scrape wine and vegetables over *noisettes*. Add the stock or bouillon, bring to the simmer, cover, and braise in middle level of preheated oven for 25 minutes.

decorative garnish you
have chosen
A small canned truffle,
minced, and its juices
2 to 3 Tb soft butter

Remove any bits of caul fat that have not disintegrated, and arrange *noisettes* on hot platter, cover, and keep warm. Skim surface fat off cooking juices, and boil down rapidly until almost syrupy and reduced to around ½ cup. Add minced truffle and its juices; simmer 2 minutes. Remove from heat, and swirl in the enrichment butter by half tablespoonfuls. Spoon sauce and *brunoise* vegetables over *noisettes*. Serve immediately.

(*) AHEAD-OF-TIME NOTE: If you cannot serve immediately, finish sauce except for butter enrichment. Return meat to baking dish, baste with sauce, cover partially, and keep warm on a hot-tray or in a 120-degree warming oven.

SUCKLING PIG
Cochon de Lait

Roast suckling pig is wonderfully dramatic to serve, delicious to eat, and is hardly more difficult to cook than a turkey. Your only absolute requirement is an oven large enough to hold the roasting pan that will be large enough for the pig; the pig will be around 20 inches long from end of rump to tip of snout, but it can be arranged either in the traditional straight crouch, illustrated farther on, or in a comfortable curl; a pan 12 by 18 inches and 2 inches deep would be the minimum size. You must also have something upon which to serve the pig, like a jumbo platter, a large tray, a carving board, or a piece of plywood covered with foil. You will want leaves, flowers, fruits, and vegetables for decoration; suggestions are in Step 7 of the recipe, page 230. Your final decision will be whether or not to stuff the pig. If you choose not to stuff, you should spread a flavoring of cooked chopped celery and onions, herbs (thyme, bay, sage), salt, and pepper in the cavity. Stuffing, however, not only flavors the meat, but also allows you to serve more people; use anything suitable for turkey or goose, such as sausages and apples, bread crumbs and onions, one of the appropriate suggestions listed on pages 513–15, or the unusual *farce Tré-bizonde* suggested in the recipe here.

HOW TO ORDER A SUCKLING PIG

Be sure to order suckling pig well in advance, because this is not an everyday item. Specify the genuine milk-fed suckling pig, weighing 10 to 12 pounds and no more; heavier animals are too fatty and the skin is tough. After 14 pounds a pig is no longer suckling and would probably not fit into your oven anyway. It may be that when the pig is available, you are not, but you can have it wrapped airtight and frozen, where it will keep perfectly for several weeks at zero degrees or less. (Fresh pork is perishable; plan to roast the pig within a day or two of purchasing or defrosting it.) Ask that it be thoroughly cleaned inside and out, and that the eyeballs be removed because they burst during cooking. If the heart, liver, and kidneys come along with the pig, save them for your stuffing or use in the Provençal sausages, *caillettes,* page 304.

PREPARING THE PIG FOR ROASTING

To prepare the pig for roasting, soak for several hours in cold water with ¼ cup of vinegar and 2 tablespoons of salt for each 4 quarts of water. If your pig is frozen, it will defrost at the same time. Scrub inside the ears, nostrils, and mouth with a vegetable brush to be sure all is clean; scrub the feet also. Go over the pig to remove any hairs that might have been missed. Dry the pig thoroughly inside and out, and it is ready to stuff and roast.

COCHON DE LAIT, FARCI À LA TRÉBIZONDE
[Roast Suckling Pig Stuffed with Rice, Sausages, Apricots, and Raisins]

With this exotic mixture stuffed into your suckling pig you need just a green vegetable accompaniment, like buttered brussels sprouts or broccoli. A smooth and not too heavy red wine would be your best choice, such as a Bordeaux from the Graves or Médoc districts.

For 12 to 14 people

---

1) *Preparing the pig for stuffing—3 to 4 hours*

A 10- to 12-pound suckling pig | Prepare the pig for roasting, soak it and dry it as described above.

---

2) *The rice, sausage, and apricot stuffing— farce Trébizonde—10 to 12 cups*

NOTE: Many of the steps in this stuffing may be carried on at once; we have separated each process, and leave the time sequences up to you.

---

1 lb. pure pork sausages (preferably homemade, page 289) | Prick skin of sausages with a pin, arrange in pan with water, cover, and simmer 5 minutes. Uncover, drain off water, and sauté sausages slowly for several min-

A medium (10-inch) frying
  pan with cover
¼ cup water
A 5- to 6-quart mixing bowl
A slotted spoon

utes, until lightly browned. Remove, leaving fat in
pan. Cut sausages into ½-inch lengths, and place in
mixing bowl.

Either the pig's liver, heart,
  and kidneys cut into ⅜-
  inch dice (1¼ to 1½
  cups);
Or ¾ lb. liver, calf or
  chicken, diced
¼ cup minced shallots or
  scallions
¼ tsp thyme
Salt and pepper

Heat fat in pan to very hot but not smoking, and stir
in the liver mixture, shallots or scallions, and thyme.
Toss and turn for 2 minutes, just to stiffen liver. Season, and scoop out into mixing bowl, leaving fat in
pan.

2½ cups minced onions

Stir the onions into the pan, cover and cook slowly 8
to 10 minutes, stirring occasionally, until tender and
translucent. Season lightly, scoop half into mixing
bowl, and leave the rest in the pan.

---

1 whole head of garlic
A pan of boiling water
Butter if needed
1½ cups plain, raw, white
  untreated rice
⅓ cup dry, white wine or
  dry, white French ver-
  mouth
1⅓ cups chicken broth,
  hot
1⅓ cups hot water
½ tsp salt
½ imported bay leaf
¼ tsp thyme
Big pinch saffron threads

Separate garlic cloves, drop them unpeeled into boiling water, and boil 2 minutes. Drain, refresh in cold
water, slip off peel, quarter garlic lengthwise, and reserve. If fat in frying pan has darkened, drain onions
and return them to pan with 3 tablespoons butter.
Blend in rice, and stir over moderate heat for several
minutes until rice becomes translucent, then milky in
color. Stir in the wine or vermouth, chicken broth, hot
water, salt, herbs, and saffron. Bring to the slow boil,
add the garlic, and stir once; cover, and boil slowly
for about 15 minutes, or until all liquid has been absorbed and rice is almost but not quite tender. Set
aside, uncovered.

---

3 to 4 ounces (½ cup)
  seedless black raisins
  or currants
A bowl of very hot water

Drop raisins into hot water and let soften 10 to 15
minutes. Drain, squeeze dry in the corner of a towel,
and add to mixing bowl.

½ lb. (1⅓ to 1½ cups)
  best-quality dried apricots

Soak apricots for 10 to 15 minutes until somewhat
softened. Drain, and simmer slowly in bouillon with

A bowl of very hot water
1 cup beef stock or bouillon
A heavy covered saucepan
Big pinch allspice

A rubber spatula
¼ tsp each: ground
   fennel seeds, thyme, and
   oregano
⅛ tsp ground imported
   bay leaf
⅛ tsp white pepper
Salt

allspice until just tender enough to eat (not mushy). Drain, reserving any liquid for your final sauce. Cut apricots into ¾-inch pieces and add to mixing bowl.

Gradually blend the cooked rice into the mixing bowl, turning gently with the rest of the ingredients and the herbs and seasonings listed here. Taste very critically for seasoning, adding more salt, pepper, and herbs if you think them necessary.

(*) AHEAD-OF-TIME NOTE: Stuffing may be made a day in advance; cover and refrigerate.

---

3) Stuffing the pig

2 tsp salt
⅛ tsp white pepper
6 to 8 skewers or finishing
   nails about 3 inches long
White string
Aluminum foil

Turn the pig on its back, and season cavity with salt and pepper. Spread in the stuffing, filling the cavity completely but not forcing it. (Reserve any extra stuffing; cook separately, in a covered dish.) Close cavity with skewers and lace them in place with string. If there is a slit under the chin, season with salt and pepper, but it need not be closed. Crumple foil into a ball 2 to 2½ inches in diameter, force pig's jaws open, and insert ball to keep them open.

---

4) Into the roasting pan

½ cup or more olive oil
   or cooking oil in a
   small pan
A basting brush
A shallow roasting pan at
   least 20 inches long
   with rack
More skewers and string
   if needed
Aluminum foil
Optional but recom-
   mended: a meat
   thermometer

Dry surface of pig again with paper towels, and paint pig all over with oil.

tail before
tucking

foil ear-tents

foil

hind leg
skewered

front leg
skewered

ball of foil

If pig will fit in a straight crouch in pan, skewer and tie hindlegs and forelegs in place to brace pig in position; let head rest between forelegs.

Or arrange pig in a less formal
position, hind legs extended forward,
and forelegs curled under.

foil ear-tents

foil

double fold
of foil under
ball of foil

If chin sticks out over lip of pan in either position, put a double thickness of foil under it so that roasting juices will drain back into pan. Insert balls of foil into the eye sockets; make tents of foil to cover the ears and protect them during roasting. To protect tail, tuck into rear opening. Insert meat thermometer into thickest portion of thigh, being sure its point is not touching any bone.

(*) AHEAD-OF-TIME NOTE: Although pig may be stuffed the day before roasting if both stuffing and pig have been chilled separately beforehand, you will have to leave the pig out at room temperature for 2 to 3 hours before roasting or timing will be difficult and roasting may be uneven.

5) *Roasting—oven preheated to 450 degrees; 3 to 3½ hours*
(2½ to 3 hours roasting plus a 30-minute rest)

**The oil and the basting
  brush**
1 cup roughly sliced onions
**⅔ cup roughly sliced
  carrots**
**4 cloves of garlic,
  whole and unpeeled**

Set pan with pig in lower-middle level of preheated 450-degree oven. In 15 minutes, rapidly brush entire surface of pig with oil. Roast 15 minutes more, baste again with oil, and turn thermostat down to 350 degrees.

Baste in 20 minutes. Twenty minutes later, after pig has roasted a little more than an hour in all, baste again, and strew the onions, carrots, and garlic cloves in the pan. Continue basting every 20 minutes or so, using fat in pan when oil is used up; basting helps the skin to crisp and brown nicely. In a total of 2½ to 3 hours, meat thermometer should have reached 180 to 185 degrees, the thigh meat should be tender when pressed, the legs should move in their sockets, and the pig is done. (Note that a chilled, stuffed pig may take up to 30 minutes longer to roast, as may a 14-pound pig.)

Pig must now rest 30 minutes before carving, so that meat juices will retreat back into tissues. Turn oven off and leave door ajar, letting pig remain warm.

(*) AHEAD-OF-TIME NOTE: Pig can wait a good hour before carving; when oven has cooled for 20 minutes, reset thermostat to 140 degrees and close the door (or reheat oven briefly every 10 minutes).

6) *The sauce*

The serving platter, tray, or board
2 cups veal stock or beef stock, or beef bouillon
1 cup dry port, Sercial Madeira, dry white wine, or dry white French vermouth
1 Tb dry mustard blended with 2 Tb of the stock or wine
A strainer set over a bowl or a saucepan
Salt and pepper
A warm sauce bowl

Lift pig, and drain its juices back into the roasting pan; set it on platter, remove foil, skewers, string, etc., and pluck end of tail from its hiding place. Remove rack, tilt pan, and spoon fat off roasting juices. Pour the stock or bouillon into the pan, and the wine; beat in the mustard mixture, and bring to the simmer, scraping coagulated roasting juices into liquid. Simmer slowly for 10 to 15 minutes while pig is being carved. (You may wish to scrape all of this liquid into a saucepan rather than simmering in the roasting pan.) When you are ready to serve, pour accumulated carving juices into sauce, and strain sauce into bowl or pan, pressing juices out of vegetables. Skim off any surface fat, carefully correct seasoning, and pour sauce into warm bowl for serving.

7) *Decorations and presentation*

Decorate the platter with leaves, and flowers or fruit, placing a garland of flowers around the pig's neck, if you wish. Stick flowers in the eyes, and replace the ball of foil in its mouth with a shining red apple or a tangerine. (Orange blossoms, shiny green leaves, and yellow zinnias, for instance, are very attractive; at Christmastime, holly, cranberries, and white daisies would be appropriate.) Bring the pig to the table or parade it around the room, so that everyone may enjoy its splendor. Although you may carve at the table, we suggest the seclusion of the kitchen unless an expert in suckling pigs is among the party.

8) *Carving and serving*

Provide yourself with 1 or 2 very sharp carving knives, a carving or kitchen fork, a big spoon, and a large pair of kitchen shears or poultry shears; an electric carving knife can be helpful in making the first cuts in the skin. We suggest you carve and serve one side, and return to the kitchen to carve the second side of the pig. Arrange it attractively again for the second serving at the table.

First, slit the skin the length of the backbone, using an electric carving knife if you have one. Then cut around skin where you feel the outline of the shoulder; lift off shoulder and foreleg portion. Do the same for the hind leg. Divide both into serving pieces, and set aside.

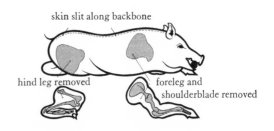

skin slit along backbone

hind leg removed

foreleg and shoulderblade removed

This drawing illustrates what you will find when you take your knife and cut down along the backbone and ribs to remove flesh and skin. Most of the meat is against the upper part of the ribs, and at the loin (from rump to ribs).

Between meat and skin will be a layer of fat, more or less of it according to the age and size of the pig. Remove meat from fat, and carve meat into serving portions. Scrape fat from skin, and cut skin into serving strips about 1 inch wide and 3 to 4 inches long. (Shears would be useful here.)

Pull out the exposed rib bones, which will come loose easily. Spread part of stuffing out from cavity of pig, arrange the meat over the stuffing, and cover with strips of skin. If you have chosen brussels sprouts, broccoli, or other decorative vegetables, arrange them attractively around the meat. Redecorate platter with leaves and flowers as necessary, and serve the pig along with its sauce. (The other side of the pig will stay warm for second servings because the skin holds in the heat.)

BEEF, VEAL, PORK, AND LAMB TONGUES

Langues de Boeuf, de Veau, de Porc, et de Mouton

A beautiful beef tongue braising in aromatic sauce smells so good while it is cooking, looks so splendid when you bring it to the table, and makes such a welcome change from the usual fare in main-course dishes that you need have no hesitation at all in serving it for company. Half the price of beef, tongue is all solid meat and therefore something well worth adding to your culinary repertoire. Because beef tongue has the best flavor and texture, we shall concentrate on that; pork, veal, and lamb tongues, which are treated in the same general way, are taken up at the end of this section, on page 242.

NOTES ON FRESH TONGUE

Fresh beef tongue is perishable: it has a total refrigerated life of only about 8 days. Because it is already several days old when it reaches your market, you should plan to soak and salt it, or boil it, within a day of bringing it home. Because it is perishable, tongue is often smoked or pickled (corned) to preserve it longer, or it may be frozen. Although smoked and pickled tongue may be cooked like fresh tongue, we prefer the taste of fresh tongue, and have so geared our recipes.

HOW TO PREPARE A BEEF TONGUE FOR COOKING—FRESH OR FROZEN

To freshen the tongue, first scrub it with a vegetable brush under warm running water, then let it soak for 2 to 3 hours in a sinkful of cold water. Drain and dry it. (If tongue has been frozen, let it thaw in the cold water, then scrub it, and soak it an hour more.)

Optional salting

To improve flavor and tenderness, as well as to preserve the tongue for several days before cooking, you may salt it. To do so, find an enameled bowl or casserole that will just hold the tongue comfortably, spread a ¼-inch layer of coarse (Kosher) salt in the bottom, and lay the soaked and dried tongue on top. Cover tongue with a ¼-inch layer of salt, and place waxed paper on top. Weight down with a plate and 5 pounds of canned food, for instance, or parts of a meat grinder. Refrigerate at least overnight, but 2 days will have more effect. When you are ready to cook the tongue, wash off the salt. (If you salt the tongue longer than 2 days, soak for 2 to 3 hours in cold water to remove excess salt.)

A NOTE ON COOKING METHODS

Tongue may be either boiled—meaning, of course, simmered slowly—or braised. When it is braised it receives a preliminary boiling until it is ⅔ cooked (2 hours for a 4-pound tongue); it is then peeled, and either braised whole or braised in slices. Whether the tongue is boiled until tender or boiled until ready to peel, the boiling method is the same and so is the peeling. We therefore give directions for each, and follow with recipes, sauces, and serving suggestions for both boiled and braised tongue.

BOILING THE TONGUE—A PRELIMINARY TO BRAISING OR A COMPLETE COOKING

When you are boiling the tongue until tender, you will need aromatic vegetables and herbs to flavor it. Even better would be your decision to make the simple meat stock in Volume I, page 107, or the *pot au feu* on page 306, and let the tongue simmer along in the same kettle, where it will pick up even finer flavor. Tongue that will finish its cooking in a braising stock needs only salted water for this preliminary boiling.

A fully trimmed fresh beef tongue weighing 3½ to 4 lbs.	Prepare the tongue for cooking as described in the preceding pages. Place in kettle, being sure that water covers tongue by 5 inches. (If tongue was not

A kettle of cold water just large enough to hold tongue easily

If tongue was not macerated in salt: 1½ tsp salt per quart of water

If tongue is to be boiled until tender:
2 cups each of sliced carrots and onions
1 cup sliced celery
A large herb bouquet:
8 parsley sprigs,
1 tsp thyme, 2 imported bay leaves, 4 allspice berries, and 2 unpeeled cloves of garlic, all tied in washed cheese-cloth

A cover for the kettle

salted, measure water in quarts, adding salt accordingly.) Bring to the simmer; skim off grayish scum for 5 minutes or more, until it ceases to rise. Add vegetables and herb bouquet if you are using them. Set cover askew over kettle, for slight air circulation, and maintain liquid at a slow simmer. If tongue is to be braised, simmer it for 2 hours only. If tongue is to be cooked completely, simmer 3 to 3½ hours or until meat is tender when pierced with a knife. Remove tongue from kettle and proceed immediately to the peeling, next paragraph.

Peeling the tongue

Remove tongue from kettle and plunge it into a basin or sinkful of cold water. As soon as it is cool enough to handle (it should still be warm), slit the nubbly skin-covering all around the top circumference of the tongue. Using your fingers, and a knife if you need one, peel the top surface of the tongue; skin should come off quite easily. The skin on the underside will usually adhere to the meat; make lengthwise slits and remove strips of skin with a knife. Trim any fatty parts and loose bits off the thick underside of the tongue, and pull out any bones that may be buried in the butt end. The tongue is now ready either for braising, if it simmered only 2 hours, or for saucing and serving if it is fully cooked.

(*) AHEAD-OF-TIME NOTE: If you are not ready to serve a fully cooked tongue, return it to the kettle and remove kettle from heat; tongue will stay warm and retain its juiciness. For tongue that is to be braised, let it cool, then wrap airtight and refrigerate it; you may finish the cooking a day or two later.

LANGUE DE BOEUF, À L'AIGRE-DOUCE

[Boiled Beef Tongue with Sweet-and-Sour Sauce,
Pearl Onions, and Raisins]

Because plain boiled tongue is so supremely easy to do, you owe something rather special in the way of a sauce both to the tongue and to those who are about to eat it. Brown sweet-and-sour sauce with pearl onions and raisins is a delicious solution, and more than a dozen other possibilities are listed at the end of the recipe. Accompany the dish with buttered peas or asparagus tips, a purée of chestnuts or mashed potatoes, or French bread, and a red Bordeaux wine.

For 6 to 8 people

_____

1) *Boiling the tongue—2 hours of soaking; 3 to 3⅓ hours of boiling*

A fully trimmed fresh beef tongue weighing about 4 lbs.

Scrub, soak, and, if you wish, salt the tongue; simmer 3 to 3½ hours until tender, and peel it, as described in the preceding pages. While tongue is cooking, or at any other convenient time beforehand, prepare the following sauce and garniture.

(*) AHEAD-OF-TIME NOTE: If you are not ready to serve the tongue, keep it warm, reheating it if necessary, in its cooking liquid.

_____

2) *Brown mustard sauce with pearl onions and raisins—for 2 cups mirepoix:*

For ⅔ cup

3 Tb finely minced onions
3 Tb finely minced carrots
2 Tb finely minced celer
1 Tb finely minced boiled ham
2 Tb butter

Cook the diced vegetables and ham slowly in the butter for 10 to 12 minutes, stirring frequently, until tender and just starting to brown. While *mirepoix* is cooking, drop onions into boiling water, and boil 1 minute to loosen skins; drain, shave off 2 ends, slip off peel, and pierce a cross in the root end of each; set aside.

A heavy-bottomed 2-quart saucepan with cover
3 cups (10 ounces; 40 to 50) small white pearl onions about ¾ inch in diameter
A pan of boiling water

_____

1 cup dry white wine or ⅔ cup dry white French vermouth
1 cup tongue-cooking stock; more if needed
1 cup rich beef stock or bouillon; more if needed
½ cup currants (small, black, seedless raisins)

Pour the wine or vermouth into the *mirepoix* and boil down rapidly until reduced by ⅓ of its volume. Then add the cup of tongue stock, the beef stock or bouillon, currants, bay leaf, and peeled onions. Bring to simmer, cover pan, and simmer very slowly for 40 to 60 minutes, or until onions are tender. (Add more liquid if needed; you should end up with about 2 cups.)

1 imported bay leaf
A cover for the pan

3 Tb strong Dijon-type prepared mustard blended to a paste with 1 Tb corn-starch in a small bowl
Salt and pepper
2 to 3 Tb soft butter

When onions are tender, remove from heat; gradually beat about ½ cup of their cooking liquid into the mustard and cornstarch mixture. Fold mixture into onions, and when smoothly blended, return over heat; simmer 2 minutes. Sauce should be lightly thickened. Carefully correct seasoning, and set aside. Reheat just before serving; remove from heat, and fold in the butter, a half tablespoon at a time.

3) *Slicing the tongue, and serving*

When slicing the tongue, try for even pieces ⅜ inch thick and as uniform in diameter as possible: place the hot tongue on a carving board and cut several vertical slices off the thick end; then, continuing at the thick end, start gradually slicing on the bias, angling the back of your knife progressively down toward the board as you come off the hump; your blade will be almost horizontal as you reach the tip of the tongue.

Either arrange the slices of tongue down the center of a hot, lightly buttered, oval platter, spoon a little sauce with raisins and onions over the tongue, decorate sides with green vegetables, and pass rest of sauce separately, *or* arrange the slices of tongue against a mound of puréed chestnuts or mashed potatoes, spoon a little sauce over each slice, surround with onions, raisins, and the rest of the sauce, and pass the vegetables separately.

OTHER SAUCES TO SERVE WITH BOILED TONGUE

Tomato sauces, brown sauces, white sauces, and oil and vinegar sauces all go well with boiled tongue. With one exception, these come from Volume I. Use tongue-cooking broth boiled down or fortified, if necessary, with chicken stock or beef bouillon for the liquids called for in the various recipes.

Tomato Sauces

The classic tomato sauce in Volume I on page 76, the excellent Provençal sauce with fresh tomatoes following it, or an alternate using canned tomatoes here in Volume II, page 354.

Brown Sauces

Pick any of the brown sauces in Volume I, pages 71 to 76. Particularly recommended are the *sauce piquante* with pickles and capers, the *sauce brune au cari*, brown curry sauce, the *sauce chasseur* with mushrooms, tomatoes, and herbs, and the *sauce à l'Italienne* with ham and mushrooms.

White Sauces

Sauce au cari—a light curry sauce with onions, cream, and lemon, Volume I, page 63.

Sauce soubise—an excellent onion sauce, to which you may add 2 to 3 tablespoons of chopped capers and minced parsley, if you wish, Volume I, page 64.

Sauce aux câpres, sauce à la moutarde, sauce aux anchois—Caper, Mustard, or Anchovy Sauce, easy to make, and all variations of the mock hollandaise, *sauce au beurre,* Volume I, page 64.

Oil and Vinegar Sauces

Sauce de Sorges—a delicious and unusual herbal mayonnaise made with shallots, capers, and soft-boiled eggs, Volume I, page 93, for tongue served either hot or cold.

Sauce ravigote—*vinaigrette* with onions and capers, or the two variations following it, one with sour cream and dill, the other with mustard—all three good for tongue served hot or cold, Volume I, page 95.

LANGUE DE BOEUF BRAISÉE, AU MADÈRE
[Beef Tongue Braised Whole, Madeira Sauce]

When you want a splendid presentation and have an able carver at the table, braise the tongue whole and present it glazed in its sauce and surrounded by a handsome display of vegetables. We suggest a garniture of glazed carrots, onions, and turnips, and whole baby mushrooms—all fresh vegetables, because of their fine taste and texture. A red Bordeaux-Médoc would be your best choice of wine.

For 6 to 8 people

---

1) Preliminaries to braising—2 hours of soaking; 2 hours of boiling

A fully trimmed fresh beef tongue weighing about 4 lbs.	Following directions starting on page 232, scrub, soak, salt if you wish, and simmer the tongue for 2 hours; peel it. (*) AHEAD-OF-TIME NOTE: This may be done the day before braising.

---

2) Braising the tongue—2 hours at 350 to 325 degrees

1 cup each of sliced carrots and onions **¼ cup diced mild-cured boiled ham (such as a supermarket ham slice)**	Preheat oven to 350 degrees. Cook vegetables and ham with butter for about 10 minutes in covered casserole over moderately low heat, stirring frequently, until vegetables are tender and beginning to brown lightly.

3 Tb butter
A heavy, covered, flame-
    proof casserole just large
    enough to hold tongue
    comfortably

Salt and pepper   Salt and pepper the tongue and place in the casserole,
The peeled beef tongue   turning and basting it with the vegetables and butter.
                           Cover casserole and let tongue sweat (*suer*) over
                           moderately low heat for 10 minutes; turn the tongue,
                           baste again, cover casserole, and sweat it 10 minutes
                           more. (If tongue was refrigerated, double the number
                           of minutes.)

⅓ cup dry Madeira   Pour the Madeira and the wine or vermouth into the
    (Sercial)   casserole; boil down rapidly until liquid has almost
½ cup dry white wine or   evaporated. Strew optional bones and the pork rind
    dry white French   around the tongue, along with the tomato, garlic, and
    vermouth   herbs. Pour in enough stock or bouillon to come ⅔
                           the way up the tongue. Cover tongue with fat or
Optional, to improve   cheesecloth, bring liquid in casserole to the simmer,
    flavor and texture of cover casserole, and set in lower-middle level of pre-
    sauce: heated oven. In 20 minutes, check to see that liquid
A cup or so of chopped   in casserole is simmering slowly and steadily; lift fat
    or sawed veal knuckle or cloth and baste tongue rapidly with liquid in cas-
    bones and/or beef   serole. Turn thermostat down to 325 degrees. Baste
    marrow bones   tongue several times again during cooking, and when
A piece of blanched pork   it has braised 1 hour, turn on its other side, covering
    rind 6 inches square   again with fat or cheesecloth. Tongue should be done
                           in 2 to 2½ hours, when a knife will pierce the meat
1 whole washed tomato,   easily; do not overcook. (While tongue is braising,
    unpeeled, roughly   prepare vegetable garnish; although the vegetables
    chopped   may braise with the tongue, we find it easier to cook
1 large clove of garlic,   them separately.)
    unpeeled, halved
1 imported bay leaf
½ tsp thyme
1 or more cups rich beef
    stock or beef bouillon
A sheet of pork rind or beef
    suet ¼ inch thick and
    large enough to cover
    tongue; or washed cheese-
    cloth

3) *The vegetable garnish*

24 to 32 small fresh white
   onions 1 to 1¼ inches
   in diameter
A saucepan of boiling water
A wide (9- to 10-inch)
   saucepan, chicken fryer,
   or electric skillet, and a
   cover for the pan
1 to 1½ cups water
Salt
3 Tb butter
10 to 12 fine, fresh medium-
   sized carrots, all of a
   size
10 to 12 firm fresh white
   turnips all of a size,
   2 to 2½ inches in
   diameter

Drop onions into boiling water, bring rapidly back to
the boil for exactly 1 minute; drain. Shave off tops
and bottoms, and peel the onions; pierce a cross ⅓
inch deep in the root ends for even cooking. Place in
pan with the water, salt, and butter; bring to the
simmer, cover, and simmer slowly while preparing the
carrots. Rapidly peel the carrots, quarter them lengthwise, cut into 1½-inch lengths, trim off sharp edges,
and add to the simmering onions. Then rapidly peel
the turnips, quarter them, trim off sharp edges, and
add to the pan after onions have cooked 20 minutes.
Continue to simmer slowly until vegetables are tender
(about 20 minutes longer), adding a little more water
if all has evaporated. Correct seasoning, and set aside.

---

1 quart (about ¾ lb.)
   fresh button mushrooms
   (or larger fresh mush-
   rooms, quartered)
A large (11-inch) frying
   pan
2 Tb butter and ½ Tb
   cooking oil
2 Tb minced shallots or
   scallions
Salt and pepper

Trim the mushrooms, wash rapidly, and dry in a
towel. Set frying pan over moderately high heat with
the butter and oil. When butter foam is beginning to
subside, add the mushrooms; sauté 3 to 4 minutes,
tossing frequently, shaking and swirling the pan by
its handle until mushrooms are just beginning to
brown lightly. Toss for a moment with the shallots or
scallions, season to taste, scrape into a side dish, and
reserve.

---

4) *Sauce and serving*

A hot, lightly buttered
   platter
A sieve set over a saucepan
¼ cup dry Madeira
   (Sercial)
1 Tb arrowroot (buy at a
   fancy food shop or in a
   pharmacy), or cornstarch,
   in a small bowl
A wire whip and rubber
   spatula
Salt and pepper
3 to 4 Tb soft butter
Parsley sprigs

When tongue is tender, remove to platter, cover, and
keep warm in turned-off oven (or warming oven at
120 degrees) while finishing the sauce. Pour contents
of casserole through sieve, pressing juices out of braising ingredients. Skim surface fat off liquid in saucepan, and bring liquid to the simmer, skimming. You
should have about 2 cups.

Blend the Madeira into the arrowroot or cornstarch; remove cooking liquid from heat and blend the wine mixture into it. When smooth, return saucepan to heat and fold in the cooked onions, carrots, turnips, and mushrooms along with any of their cooking juices. Simmer, swirling pan by its handle and gently turning vegetables in sauce for 4 to 5 minutes. Sauce should be thick enough to coat the tongue nicely; carefully correct seasoning. Just before serving, fold in the enrichment butter, half a tablespoon at a time, gently basting vegetables with sauce until butter is absorbed.

Arrange the tongue humped side up on the platter, glaze it with spoonfuls of the sauce, and arrange the vegetables around it, basting both tongue and vegetables with remaining sauce. Decorate with parsley sprigs, and serve immediately.

(*) AHEAD-OF-TIME NOTE: If you are not ready to serve when tongue is tender, complete the sauce but omit the final butter enrichment. Return tongue, sauce, and vegetable garnish to casserole; cover tongue again with its fat or cheesecloth, put on casserole cover slightly askew, and set in a 120-degree oven, or over simmering water. Tongue will stay warm safely for a good hour. If sauce has thickened too much when you are ready to serve, thin it out with a little stock or bouillon.

Other sauces, flavorings, garnitures

You may braise tongue with any of the flavorings and garnishings you would use for beef; you might even slice it after its preliminary 2-hour boiling and peeling, re-form it with a mushroom stuffing between each slice, and then braise it, as for the sliced and stuffed tenderloin of beef *en feuilletons,* page 180. The garniture *à la bourgeoise,* of onions, mushrooms, and olives, page 178, would be attractive, as would some of the variations following beef stew, pages 152–5. Particularly recommended among these are the *pistou* and the Provençal flavorings, the *pipérade* with its peppers and tomatoes, and the final suggestion on page 154, for ginger, capers, and herbs. For any of these suggestions, the general cooking procedure for the tongue follows the same pattern and timing as the Master Recipe; you are simply substituting other flavorings.

TONGUE BRAISED IN SLICES

Tongue is much easier to prepare and serve when you braise it in slices after its preliminary 2-hour boil and its peeling. Sliced tongue cooks in 30 to 40 minutes, the flavor of the sauce penetrates the meat beautifully, and sliced tongue lends itself to prearrangements, precooking, and numerous ahead-of-time maneuvers that are not possible with whole tongue. Using the general method of the following recipe, you can add sliced tongue to cook with the brown mustard sauce, pearl onions, and raisins in the boiled tongue recipe on page 234, or use one of the ideas either in the preceding paragraph or in those suggested for boiled tongue on pages 235–6.

LANGUE DE BOEUF BRAISÉE, CALCUTTA
[Sliced Fresh Beef Tongue Braised with Curry]

French curry sauce does not have the strong, mouth-searing quality of Indian curry; the French version is more a flavor than an experience, because if the curry were strong it would ruin the accompanying wine. You might serve this tongue on a bed of mashed potatoes, rice, or braised spinach, on a purée of peas or lentils, or on the purée of squash and white beans on page 404. Your own fresh French bread could take the place of a second vegetable. For wines, a red Bordeaux would go nicely, or a rather strong dry white like a Hermitage, from the Rhône valley.

For 6 to 8 people

1) *Preliminaries to braising—2 hours of soaking; 2 hours of boiling*

A fully trimmed fresh beef tongue weighing about 4 lbs.

Following directions starting on page 232, scrub, soak, salt if you wish, and simmer the tongue for 2 hours; peel it.

(*) AHEAD-OF-TIME NOTE: This may be done the day before braising.

2) *The braising sauce*

2 cups sliced onions
2 Tb butter and ½ Tb cooking oil (more if needed)
A 10- to 12-inch casserole, chicken fryer, or electric skillet
About 2 Tb fragrant curry powder (depending on its strength and your inclinations)
2 Tb flour

Cook the onions slowly in the butter and oil over low heat, stirring occasionally, for 8 to 10 minutes until tender and translucent but not browned. Blend in the curry powder and cook, stirring, for 2 minutes. Blend in the flour, and a little more butter or oil if flour makes too stiff a paste; cook, stirring, for 2 minutes more. Remove from heat.

2 to 3 cups heated meat stock (a combination of beef stock or bouillon and tongue-cooking stock or chicken broth)
A wire whip

When casserole contents have stopped bubbling, pour in 2 cups of the hot stock and blend vigorously into the onions, curry, and flour with wire whip. Pour in the wine or vermouth; add the garlic, currants, diced apple, thyme, and bay leaf. Bring to the simmer, stirring, and simmer 2 minutes. Sauce should be lightly thickened. Taste carefully, and correct seasoning.

1 cup dry white wine or
⅔ cup dry white French
vermouth
2 large cloves garlic,
mashed
¼ cup currants (small
black seedless raisins)
1 peeled and diced sour
cooking apple (or an
eating apple and 1 Tb
lemon juice)
½ tsp thyme
1 imported bay leaf
Salt and pepper to taste

---

3) *Braising the tongue—30 to 40 minutes*

Cut the peeled tongue into even slices ⅜ inch thick. (Directions for slicing are in Step 3, page 235, in the Master Recipe for boiled tongue.) Arrange the slices in the casserole, overlapping as necessary, and baste the tongue with the sauce.

(*) AHEAD-OF-TIME NOTE: Recipe may be prepared in advance to this point; when cool, cover surface with plastic wrap, a cover, and refrigerate.

Bring to the simmer, cover, and simmer 30 to 40 minutes, tilting casserole and basting tongue several times with the sauce. When tender if pierced with a fork, meat is done, but do not overcook; eat a piece if you have any doubts about its being done.

---

4) *Serving*

A hot, lightly buttered
serving platter
Optional: ⅓ to ½ cup
crème fraîche or heavy
cream
Salt, pepper, and drops of
lemon juice
1 to 3 Tb soft butter
A hot gravy bowl
If needed: fresh minced
parsley

When tongue is done, arrange the hot slices on the platter (or over a bed of vegetables if you wish); cover and keep warm while you finish the sauce. You should have 1½ to 2 cups of sauce thick enough to coat a spoon nicely. Stir in optional cream; boil down if sauce is too thin or, conversely, add a little more stock if it seems too thick. Taste carefully, stirring in more salt, pepper, and drops of lemon juice if you feel them necessary. Just before serving, remove sauce from heat, and swish in the enrichment butter a half tablespoon at a time. Spoon hot sauce over the slices of tongue, and pour rest of sauce into hot serving bowl. (You may strain the sauce; the onions and optional raisins, however, give it an attractive informal look and texture.) Decorate tongue with parsley, if you wish, and serve immediately.

(*) AHEAD-OF-TIME NOTE: You may complete the sauce except for the final butter enrichment; return tongue slices to sauce, and baste them with it. Reheat to bubbling hot before serving, but be careful not to overcook the tongue.

VEAL, PORK, AND LAMB TONGUES

Veal, pork, and lamb tongues have the same consistency as beef tongue, and although they do not have quite the same fine flavor you may substitute them for beef tongue in any of the preceding recipes. Braising is particularly recommended, because the braising stock adds the flavor that these tongues lack. Here are notes on each.

VEAL TONGUES

Weights and measures. These will weigh 6 to 8 ounces on the average, and will be 5 to 6 inches long, although tongues from large carcasses can weigh up to 1¼ pounds. Count on one 6- to 8-ounce tongue per person, or 2 tongues for 3 people.

Preparation for cooking. Scrub, soak, and, if you wish, salt the tongues exactly as directed for beef tongue, page 232.

Preliminary boiling, and peeling. Simmer the tongues for 45 minutes (1 hour for large tongues) in salted water, refresh briefly in cold water, and peel as described for beef tongue, page 233.

Cooking methods. Braise the tongues whole, or cut in half lengthwise, following the beef-tongue recipes and variations starting on page 236. Braising time will be about 1½ hours.

PORK TONGUES

Weights and measures. Pork tongues weigh ¾ to 1 pound, and are 8 to 9 inches long. Count on 1 tongue for each 2 people, or 2 large tongues for 5 people.

Preparation, boiling, peeling, and cooking methods. Follow preceding directions for veal tongues.

LAMB TONGUES

Weights and measures. 3 to 4 ounces each, and 3 to 4 inches long. Count on 2 tongues per person, or 1½ to 2 if the tongues are cut in two lengthwise.

Preparation, boiling, peeling, and cooking methods. Follow directions for veal tongues, but the final braising will probably be 45 minutes to 1 hour only.

TRIPE
Tripes

Those who love tripe speak of it with passionate enjoyment and will travel miles to dine upon it. Like scrapple and head cheese, it is a rather old-fashioned taste—a fragrant, earthy reminder of the past when every edible morsel of the beast was used. Many people today who have heard of tripe have neither seen nor eaten it, but our forefathers consumed it with relish. The Parker House in Boston became famous throughout the nation for its fried tripe, and the fine Parisian restaurant, Pharamond, in the heart of the old markets, Les Halles, made its reputation serving steaming bowls of *tripes à la mode de Caen,* a recipe you will find in so many cookbooks that we shall not repeat it again here. Instead, we present a much simpler dish from Provence, and one that we like immensely: the tripe first cooks to a golden yellow with onions, then finishes off in an aromatic mixture of tomatoes, wine, and herbs. If you are one of those who has never tried tripe before, yet enjoys new foods and new tastes, we think you will find this a happy introduction.

HOW TO BUY TRIPE

There are four kinds of beef tripe, and any or all may be used in any recipe, but the only one usually available in American markets today is honeycomb tripe (*bonnet,* in French). Although you can buy it canned, frozen, and fully cooked, or pickled, we are interested here only in ready-to-cook tripe. This means that it has been scraped, washed, blanched, often bleached, and is, in fact, ready for cooking. You will probably find it in a sealed plastic bag under refrigeration in the meat section, and it will look like a soft, pale, rubbery pouch with a honeycomb pattern on its surface. It will be labeled "fresh honeycomb tripe"; do not mistake it for pickled tripe, which will look the same but will be labeled "pickled tripe." Some markets do not carry tripe at all because there is no demand for it; it depends on the eating habits in your shopping area. Fresh tripe is perishable; plan to cook it within a day or two of buying it.

PRELIMINARIES TO PREPARING READY-TO-COOK AMERICAN TRIPE

Although some cooks do not blanch fresh ready-to-cook tripe, we find that blanching freshens the flavor and we suggest the following preliminaries to cooking. Wash the tripe thoroughly under cold, running water. Then place it in a large saucepan or kettle, and cover by 3 inches with cold water; bring to the boil, and boil slowly 5 minutes. Drain, run cold water into the pan, soak the tripe for several minutes, drain, and blanch again for 5 minutes. Repeat the process a third time, and the tripe is ready to cook.

A NOTE ON FRENCH TRIPE AND EUROPEAN-STYLE TRIPE

In France, tripe is bought *chez le tripier,* who sells cleaned and blanched tripe of all four varieties. *Gras double,* a term you will run into in French recipes and at *la triperie* itself, can mean either the heaviest and meatiest of the four, *la panse,* or *gras double* can mean the four varieties rolled together fully cooked, and needing only to be reheated in whatever sauce you plan to use. Ready-to-cook French tripe, on the other hand, should be soaked several hours or overnight in several changes of cold water, then blanched as directed in the preceding paragraph. Some European-style butchers in this country prepare tripe as the French do, and you should treat it in the same way.

Because you will occasionally run into them in French recipes, the technical names for beef tripe are as follows: First stomach, rumen, or paunch—*panse* or *gras double.* Second stomach, reticulum, or honeycomb tripe—*bonnet.* Third stomach, omasum, psalterium, or manyplies—*feuillet* or *franche mule.* Fourth stomach, abomasum, or reed—*caillette* or *millet.*

TRIPES À LA NIÇOISE
[Tripe Baked with Onions, Tomatoes, Wine, and Provençal Seasonings]

As an alternate to *tripes à la mode de Caen,* we find this a wonderfully satisfying recipe. The tripe is cooked several hours just with onions; then tomatoes, other flavorings, and wine go in for another session of slow, penetrating simmer. You could, if you wished, finish off the recipe in another way after the onion-cooking session, or pick the tripe out of its tomato sauce at the end of the recipe here, broil or deep-fry it, and serve the tomato sauce on the side. We shall leave these possibilities up to you, and present the recipe in its own straightforward way. Serve boiled rice or boiled potatoes with the tripe. No green vegetable is needed, but a salad could follow. For wines, we suggest a strong, dry white like a Mâcon or Hermitage, or a young red like Beaujolais, or a strong, dry rosé like Tavel.

For 6 people

---

1) *Preliminary cooking of tripe and onions—2 to 2½ hours*

Optional, for additional flavor: 4 or 5 slices, ¼	Preheat oven to 325 degrees. Cut optional pork or bacon into 2-inch lengths. Cook slowly without brown-

inch thick, of fat-and-lean fresh pork belly or blanched bacon (page 148)

½ cup olive oil

A heavy, 4- to 5-quart covered casserole (earthenware preferred for looks, and for heat-holding properties)

4 cups sliced onions

ing in the oil for 5 minutes to render some of the fat. Then stir in the onions, cover the casserole, and cook onions slowly 10 minutes or more, stirring frequently, until tender but not at all browned.

2½ to 3 lbs. ready-to-cook tripe (see notes preceding recipe)

Heavy shears

1 tsp salt

A round of waxed paper

A piece of aluminum foil

While onions are cooking, cut tripe into strips 2 inches wide; cut the strips into triangles about 3 inches on the long side. When onions are ready, fold the tripe into them, along with the salt. Lay a round of waxed paper over tripe to keep it from browning, drape foil over top of casserole to keep in the steam, and place casserole cover on top of foil. Set in middle level of preheated oven, and bake slowly for 2½ hours, regulating thermostat so that tripe cooks very slowly and steadily but does not brown. When time is up, tripe will be a golden yellow.

2) *Finishing the cooking, and serving—2 to 2½ hours*

2 cups fresh tomato pulp (6 medium tomatoes, peeled, seeded, juiced, and chopped), or a combination of fresh pulp and canned, drained, sieved Italian plum tomatoes

4 large cloves garlic, mashed or minced

1 cup dry white wine, or dry white French vermouth

To thicken cooking liquid: an 8-inch square of blanched pork rind (Volume I, page 401) and/or 1 to 2 cups chopped veal knuckle bones tied in washed cheesecloth

The following tied in

Fold the tomatoes and garlic into the tripe; pour in the wine. Bury the pork rind and bones in the tripe, and the packet of seasonings. (Remove these later, when tripe is done.) Pour in enough stock just to cover ingredients. Bring to simmer on top of stove, and salt lightly to taste. Cover tripe again with the waxed paper, foil, and casserole cover, and return to oven for another 2 hours of slow simmering. Test tripe by eating a piece; it should be tender enough to chew easily, but should still have some texture. Skim off surface fat; carefully correct seasoning. Bake half an hour, an hour, or longer, until tripe is of the desired consistency. (Add a little more white wine or stock if liquid has evaporated too much. Stir in optional olives about half an hour before estimated end of cooking.)

Serve bubbling hot from casserole onto very hot plates.

(*) AHEAD-OF-TIME NOTES: Tripe may be cooked several days in advance of serving, and reheats perfectly.

washed cheesecloth:
6 peppercorns
6 allspice berries
1 tsp fennel seeds
A 3-inch piece of dried
    orange peel, or 1 tsp
    bottled peel
1 tsp thyme
1 imported bay leaf
1 to 2 cups veal stock, or
    beef stock or bouillon
Salt as needed
Optional, to be added last
½ hour of cooking:
½ cup black, Mediter-
ranean-type olives, pitted,
and blanched 10 minutes
(page 153)

RABBIT
Lapin

Rabbit, if you have never tried it, is very much like chicken in taste and texture, but the meat is firmer and therefore does very well in a stew. Most rabbit stews are called sautés in French, and the recipe you usually encounter is *sauté de lapin au vin blanc,* in which the pieces of rabbit are browned in the pan, seasoned, floured, and simmered in white wine with onions, mushrooms, and *lardons* of bacon. Rather than repeating this too-familiar version, we give a red wine stew.

BUYING RABBIT AND PREPARING IT FOR COOKING

In many parts of the country you can now buy an excellent quality of frozen young rabbit "fryers," cut up and all ready for cooking as soon as you have defrosted the pieces. If fresh frying rabbit is available, have it cut so that the forelegs are disjointed from the body at the shoulder, the hind legs at the hip, and the rib section separated from the loin. Then separate the hind legs at the knee, to make 2 pieces; cut the loin (*rable*) and the rib sections in two crosswise, and if you wish, trim off with scissors the lower part of the ribs, which is mostly bone.

Cut up this way, you will have 10 pieces, the choicest of which are the second joints and the 2 pieces of loin; the 2 front legs are second best, and the rib sections have the least meat. (In Europe and in some parts of this country, the head and neck also make part of the stew.) Use the liver and heart like chicken liver, or you may wish to add it to the stew.

Two and a half pounds of cut-up ready-to-cook rabbit will serve 4 to 5 people.

TO THAW FROZEN RABBIT

Let it defrost for 24 hours in the refrigerator, or defrost it in a wine marinade as suggested in the following recipe.

LAPIN AU SAUPIQUET

[Rabbit Marinated in Vinegar and Herbs, and Stewed in Red Wine]

This French recipe is very much like the German *hasenpfeffer,* in that both use a wine-vinegar marinade before the stew begins; this tenderizes the rabbit as well as giving it an excellent flavor. Serve the rabbit with parslied potatoes, buttered noodles, or steamed and buttered rice, and a simple green vegetable such as the sautéed zucchini on page 364, buttered broccoli, or green beans. A full red wine is definitely the type to choose—a Hermitage, Côtes-du-Rhône, or Châteauneuf-du-Pape.

For 4 to 5 people

1) *Marinating the rabbit—at least 24 hours*

½ to ⅔ cup red wine vinegar (amount depending on strength)
½ tsp cracked peppercorns
3 Tb olive oil or cooking oil
½ cup sliced onions
2 large cloves of garlic, unpeeled, halved
4 juniper berries
½ tsp oregano
1 imported bay leaf
½ tsp thyme
An enameled or stainless bowl or casserole large enough to hold rabbit comfortably
2½ lbs. cut-up ready-to-cook frying rabbit, fresh or frozen
A bulb baster

If you are using imported French vinegar, ⅔ cup would be right; if domestic wine vinegar seems strong and harsh, use ½ cup. Mix the rest of the ingredients with the vinegar in the bowl, add the rabbit, and baste with the marinade. (If rabbit is frozen, let it defrost in the bowl at room temperature, basting frequently, and pulling pieces apart from each other when possible, until completely defrosted.) Cover bowl and refrigerate it, basting and turning the rabbit occasionally. Marinate at least 24 hours, although you can leave the rabbit safely for 2 or 3 days because the marinade also preserves the meat.

2) *The braising sauce—sauce au Saupiquet*

½ cup (4 ounces) *lardons* (1½-inch sticks ¼ inch thick of bacon blanched 10 minutes in 1 quart water)

2 Tb olive oil or cooking oil, more if needed

A large (11-inch) frying pan (no-stick recommended)

1 cup sliced onions

A heavy, covered, flame-proof casserole large enough to hold rabbit pieces easily

Preheat oven to 450 degrees. Brown the *lardons* lightly with oil in the pan over moderate heat. Then stir in the onions, and cook for about 10 minutes, stirring frequently, until onions are tender and lightly browned. Transfer onions and *lardons* to the casserole with a slotted spoon, leaving fat in pan.

The rabbit and its marinade

Paper towels

Salt and pepper

Optional: the rabbit's liver, quartered, seasoned, and floured

3 Tb flour

While onions are cooking, remove rabbit from marinade, and dry thoroughly with paper towels; reserve the marinade. When onions are out of pan, add more oil if necessary, so that pan is filmed by ⅛ inch, raise heat to moderately high, and brown the rabbit pieces nicely on all sides. Season with salt and pepper, and add the rabbit to the casserole. (Brown optional liver at the same time, and set aside for later.) Sprinkle on half the flour, toss rabbit in casserole, sprinkle on rest of flour, and toss again.

Heat casserole to sizzling on top of stove, then set uncovered in upper third of preheated 450-degree oven for 5 minutes; toss again, and return casserole to oven for 5 minutes more. (The oven is an easier way to brown and cook the flour than sautéing on top of the stove; but if you do not wish to use your oven, you may sauté.)

The marinade

1 bottle of full-bodied, young, red wine (Mâcon, Côtes-du-Rhône, Mountain Red)

2 cups beef or veal stock, or beef bouillon

While casserole is in oven, pour the browning fat out of the frying pan, pour in the marinade, and boil down until liquid has almost evaporated. Pour in the wine, boil down to half its volume, then add the bouillon, bring to the boil, and set aside.

Remove casserole from oven and add the hot wine and bouillon mixture, stirring rabbit pieces, onions, and *lardons* so that all is well blended.

3) *Stewing the rabbit—about 1 hour*

Bring contents of casserole to the simmer on top of the stove, cover and simmer slowly either on the stove or in a preheated 350-degree oven; regulate heat in either case so that stew bubbles slowly and regularly throughout the cooking, and baste rabbit pieces several times with the sauce. Rabbit should be done in about 1 hour, when the meat is tender if pierced with a knife. (While rabbit is stewing, prepare prunes in Step 4.)

4) *Sauce and serving*

A hot, lightly buttered, serving platter
Stock or bouillon if needed
20 to 25 large, tenderized prunes, simmered 10 to 15 minutes in ¼ cup Cognac, ½ cup bouillon, and 2 Tb butter
The optional sautéed liver pieces from Step 2
Optional: 8 to 10 *croûtons* or *fleurons* (triangles of white bread sautéed in clarified butter; puff pastry crescents, page 132)
Fresh parsley sprigs

When rabbit pieces are tender, arrange them on the serving platter, cover, and keep warm while finishing the sauce. Remove bay leaf, and skim surface fat off braising sauce. Bring to the simmer, skimming. You should have 1½ to 2 cups of sauce thick enough to coat a spoon nicely; thin out with stock or bouillon if too thick, or boil down rapidly if too thin. Then add the prunes with their liquid, and the optional liver; simmer 2 to 3 minutes, and carefully correct seasoning. Spoon the sauce and prunes over the rabbit, decorate with *croûtons* or *fleurons* and parsley sprigs, and serve.

(*) AHEAD-OF-TIME NOTE: If you are not ready to serve, return rabbit to casserole, baste with sauce, and reheat later.

CHAPTER FOUR

Chickens, Poached and Sauced—and a Coq en Pâte

W HEN BROILING AND FRYING CHICKENS are among our most reasonably priced meats today, it is hard to realize that great-great-grandmother's, or even great-grandmother's, Sunday chicken was a luxurious treat, since chicken was expensive in those days. To have it so accessible now is a great boon to the cook, because you can prepare it in such a vast number of ways. Volume I takes up roasting, casserole roasting, sautés, fricassees, *coq au vin,* and chicken breasts, as well as details on chicken types and qualities, trussing directions, and timing charts. There is not a word, however, about one of the easiest and most delicious ways to cook chicken—poaching in white wine. The chicken practically cooks itself, produces its own sauce base, and can be served in numerous ways from very plain to extremely elegant.

We start out with chicken in pieces, taking it from the simple wine stew through a cheese casserole, an aspic, a *chaud-froid,* and finally a *bouillabaisse* and a *bourride.* For more formal chickens, there is a roaster or capon poached whole in white wine and aromatic vegetables, plus various stuffings and white-wine sauces; an illustrated guide to boning follows; and we conclude with a glamorous *coq en pâte* with the whimsical title *poularde en soutien-gorge.*

CHICKEN IN PIECES

How fortunate we are to have chicken in pieces—those who like dark meat may feast upon thighs, white-meat-only people are welcome to breasts, while wings at half price make lovely finger food when the budget is low.

Rather than being disjointed, meaning that thighs are removed from backbones at the connecting ball joints and wings from shoulders in the same fashion, most supermarket ready-cut chicken is done with a meat saw which neatly halves or quarters the chicken in a matter of seconds. This saving of man-hours is passed on to us, of course, in reasonable prices for chicken but does leave us with some unwanted bones and bits. If these do not bother you, simply wash the chicken under cold running water, dry in paper towels, and proceed to the cooking. If you have time for surgery, however, you can make the chicken easier to cook, especially for sautés and fricassees but also for poaching, because the pieces will lie flatter and take up less room; in addition, they will be far easier to eat. You will also have some useful scraps for chicken stock. The illustrated goose on page 313 will help you locate bones and joints because goose and chicken have the same bone structure; see also the illustrated semiboned chicken on page 270. Here, then, is how to trim the various pieces of chicken.

Drumsticks and second joints (legs and thighs)

When drumsticks and second joints come joined together, the thigh bone is usually attached to the hip, making a clumsy piece of chicken—the hip should be off. On the hip, however, at either side of its attachment to the ball joint of the thigh, are two nuggets of meat, the oysters, which should remain part of the second joint: scrape this meat from the hip bone up to and around the joint, leaving meat attached to joint. Then bend and cut joint free from the piece of hip: this is picky work because the hip bone is small, but it is really worth the trouble. Then, to make the second joint even more attractive, scrape meat away from this same ball joint, and whack off its bulbous end with your chopping knife. In French cooking, the drumstick is separated from the second joint: flex the two pieces to locate ball joint at knee, and cut through it to separate drumstick from second joint.

Breast-wing sections

The breast-wing sections (or wingless breasts) usually come already split so that you have one whole side in one piece, and another whole side as the other piece. On the bone-and-flesh side you may see the long ridge of the breastbone, if it was left in that half, running the length of the thick portion of the meat. Below it is the rest of the breastbone and below that the cross-hatch of ribs; attached to the ribs you may find a piece of the backbone. Again, this is a clumsy piece to cook as is, but easy to trim.

If the wing has been left on, you will be able to make 2 full servings out of the breast by cutting it in the French manner, meaning that the lower third of the breast meat remains attached to the wing as follows: Set the breast in front of you, skin-side up and top of breast (long side with thickest meat) away from you. We shall suppose that you have a left breast with the wing on the right. By wiggling the wing, locate with your finger where the ball joint of its upper arm attaches to the shoulder. Then make a semicircular cut through the skin and breast meat, starting at the lower left side of the long end facing you and ending at the shoulder joint. Scrape meat from rib bones the length of the cut (scraping toward you, not toward the thick side of the meat), separate wing at shoulder by cutting through ball joint, and free the wing with its strip of breast meat. With shears, cut the bony nubbin off the elbow of the wing; trim off rib bones from main part of breast along with backbone if it is attached. For a right-sided breast use the same system, but you may find it is easier to set the breast in front of you lengthwise, the wing end facing you and the thick part of the meat to your left.

Wingless breasts will be improved when you scrape the lower third of the flesh from the ribs at the long thin side, and cut off ribs at this point; the breast will then lie flatter.

Save all scraps for chicken stock

Even a small handful of scraps and bones are worth boiling up with a bit of onion, celery, carrot, a bay leaf, pinch of salt, and water to cover. Full directions for chicken stock are in Volume I, pages 236–7.

HOW MUCH TO BUY

We shall arbitrarily call for 2½ pounds of ready-cut frying chicken to serve 4 people in the following recipes, but you would normally buy by eye— the equivalent of 1 whole breast half with wing or 1 drumstick-second joint per serving is usually sufficient. The total weight will probably be between 2 and 2½ pounds, depending on the weight of the frying chicken and on what pieces you buy.

＊ *POULET POCHÉ AU VIN BLANC*
[Chicken Pieces Poached in White Wine, Herbs, and Aromatic Vegetables]

This very simple, basic poach can be even simpler if you are on a fat-free diet: rather than cooking the vegetables in butter, simmer them 15 minutes in chicken stock before you add the chicken and the wine. Butter does seem to bring out more of their flavor, however. Because the vegetables cook along with the chicken and are served with it you could precede or follow the chicken with fresh artichokes or asparagus. You then need nothing more for the chicken course than steamed rice, a parsley garnish, and either more of the same white wine that cooked with the chicken, or a red Bordeaux, or a rosé.

For 4 people

----

1) *Sautéing the vegetables*

2 medium-sized carrots
1 medium-sized onion and the white part of 1 leek, (or 2 onions)
3 medium-sized celery stalks
3 Tb butter
A heavy 3-quart flameproof casserole with cover (such as a round terra cotta one, 9 by 3 inches, set on an asbestos mat)

(This step is optional: see preceding paragraph.) Peel the carrots and onion; quarter leek lengthwise and wash; trim and wash celery. Depending on what effect you want, cut the vegetables either into thin slices or into julienne matchsticks 1½ inches long. Cook slowly with the butter in the covered casserole over moderately low heat, stirring frequently, until vegetables are tender but not browned—about 10 minutes. Meanwhile, prepare the chicken, Step 2.

----

2) *Poaching the chicken*

2½ lbs. ready-cut frying chicken, washed, dried, and trimmed, if you wish, according to directions preceding this recipe
Salt
1½ cups dry white wine, or 1 cup dry white French vermouth
About 2 cups chicken stock or canned chicken broth
The following herbs tied in washed cheesecloth:
Either ½ tsp tarragon;
Or ½ imported bay leaf, ¼ tsp thyme, and 4 parsley sprigs
Salt to taste

Preheat oven to 325 degrees if you wish to use it. Prepare the chicken for cooking, salt lightly, and arrange in the casserole, spreading the cooked vegetables around and over it. Cover casserole and let chicken sweat for 10 minutes over moderate heat, turning it once. (Omit this step if you are not sautéing vegetables in butter.) Then pour in the wine or vermouth and enough chicken stock or broth barely to cover the chicken. Bury the herb packet in the chicken, and bring casserole to the simmer. Taste, and salt lightly if necessary.

Cover the casserole and regulate heat to maintain liquid at a slow, quiet simmer either on top of the stove or in a preheated 325-degree oven. (NOTE: Poaching means slow cooking, so that chicken pieces will retain their shape, and will be tender; boiling not only toughens the meat, but also warps its contour.) Dark meat of chicken will take 20 to 25 minutes; light meat, probably 5 minutes less and should be removed when done, if you have mixed dark and light together. Juices, when either dark or light meat is pricked deeply, should run clear yellow, with no trace of rose, and meat should feel tender when pierced. Do not overcook, however.

3) Serving

Tilt casserole and skim off surface fat; taste liquid and correct seasoning. Discard herb bouquet. Either serve directly from casserole, or arrange the chicken and vegetables on a bed of steamed rice, decorate with parsley, and pass the cooking liquid separately.

(*) AHEAD-OF-TIME NOTE: If you aren't ready to serve, chicken will keep perfectly for a good hour. Skim off surface fat, and correct seasoning, then set casserole cover slightly askew for air circulation; keep warm in a 120-degree oven, on a hot-tray, or over barely simmering water.

VARIATIONS

Stewing Chicken—Fowl

A fine stewing chicken 10 to 12 months old, as it is supposed to be when you buy from a reputable market, does beautifully when poached in white wine. Use the same general system as in the preceding Master Recipe with the following slight changes.

If the chicken has not been cut up for you and you wish to do so yourself, follow the directions for goose, page 313. Reserve neck, back, gizzard, and heart as well as all scraps; place them in the bottom of the casserole to cook along with the chicken and give additional flavor to the broth. Mature chickens have much more flavor than young fryers, and you need only wine and water for the cooking stock. Stewing time will be about 2½ hours, or until the meat is tender when pierced with a knife. Because the vegetables will have cooked this length of time, they will not be of further use; if you want vegetables to cook and serve with the chicken, add a fresh batch before end of cooking time.

Serve the chicken on a bed of steamed rice or *risotto*, and you may turn its cooking stock into a cream sauce as suggested for whole poached chicken on page 265 or one of its variations on pages 273, 274-9. You may gratiné the chicken in cheese sauce, as in the recipe on page 256, or change the seasonings altogether by simmering the chicken in *bouillabaisse* flavorings, as suggested on page 261.

Poulet en Gelée
[Chicken in Aspic]

Chicken poached in white wine makes delicious chicken in aspic, and you may be as elegant as the formal recipe in Volume I, page 549, where the chicken is arranged on an aspic-lined platter; each piece is coated with aspic and tarragon leaves, chopped aspic fills in the empty spaces, and aspic cutouts abound. On the other hand, you may be much less formal and just as attractive but in a different way, with either of the two following arrangements. (NOTE: In neither of these is the cooking stock clarified—rendered clear and sparkling with egg whites; if you wish to clarify it, however, directions are in Volume I, page 111.)

A sieve set over a saucepan
A quart measure
Chicken broth if needed
1½ packages (1½ Tb)
  plain, unflavored,
  powdered gelatin
Salt and pepper

Set cover askew over casserole and drain out cooking liquid into the saucepan. Skim off surface fat and pour liquid into quart measure; skim again, and pour in additional stock, if necessary, to make 3 cups. Return liquid to saucepan, sprinkle on the gelatin, and let it soften for several minutes. Then stir over moderate heat until gelatin has completely dissolved and liquid is free of gelatin granules. Taste, and correct seasoning.

Rearrange chicken attractively with vegetables, either in the same casserole or in a serving bowl or dish that will just hold the pieces. Pour on the cooking stock and chill several hours, or until gelatin has set; scrape any congealed fat from surface, and chicken is ready to serve.

Molded aspic

You may wish to unmold the chicken onto a platter rather than serve it from a bowl or casserole. Use the same method as in the preceding recipe, but you may need more jellied stock—proportions are 1 envelope (1 tablespoon) gelatin for each 2 cups of stock. Use a decorative metal mold, a metal cake pan, or even a bread pan; pour in a ⅛-inch layer of jellied stock and chill until set. Then arrange the chicken and vegetables attractively in the mold or pan, and chill 20 minutes, or until remaining stock is cold, almost syrupy, and on the point of setting; immediately pour it over the chicken. Chill several hours or overnight to set the gelatin completely. To unmold, first scrape off any surface fat, then dip mold or pan for 4 to 5 seconds in very hot water, rapidly run a knife around edge of aspic, turn a chilled platter upside down over mold, and reverse the two. If aspic does not dislodge itself in a minute or two, repeat the process. Keep chilled until serving time, then decorate platter with lettuce, watercress, parsley, or appropriate vegetables.

NOTE: A more formal method for lining a mold with aspic is in Volume I, page 558, but would only be necessary if you were using clarified jellied stock.

Poulet Mornay, Gratiné

[Poached Chicken Pieces Gratinéed with Cheese Sauce]

When you want a casserole of chicken that you may prepare ahead for a party, this is a useful dish. After the chicken has poached, the cooking liquid is turned into a cheese sauce, which then enrobes the chicken in a baking dish; reheat and brown in the oven when the time comes. Serve this with steamed rice or buttered pasta, and either a simply done green vegetable such as buttered broccoli, peas, or asparagus tips, or a salad. White Burgundy wine would be good here, or a red Bordeaux.

Follow method and ingredients for chicken poached in white wine, Master Recipe, Steps 1 and 2, page 254. When chicken is done proceed as follows.

The cheese sauce—sauce Mornay—for 2½ cups

A sieve set over a saucepan
3½ Tb butter
A heavy-bottomed 2-quart enameled, no-stick, or stainless saucepan
¼ cup flour (measure by scooping dry-measure cup into flour and sweeping off excess with a knife)
A wooden spoon and a wire whip

Set cover askew and drain cooking liquid out of casserole. Skim off surface fat, and bring liquid to simmer, skimming. You should have about 2½ cups; boil down rapidly, if necessary. Meanwhile, make a white *roux* and a *velouté* sauce as follows: melt butter in saucepan, blend in flour, and stir over moderate heat with a wooden spoon until flour and butter foam together for 2 minutes without browning. Remove from heat, and as soon as *roux* stops bubbling, pour in all of the hot chicken-cooking liquid at once, blending vigorously with a wire whip.

Return sauce over moderately high heat, and stir with wire whip as sauce thickens and comes to the boil. Boil, stirring, for 2 minutes, and remove from heat. Sauce should be thick enough to coat a spoon nicely; if too thin, boil down rapidly and if too thick, thin with milk, stock, or cream. Let cool for several minutes, stirring occasionally to prevent top from crusting while you prepare for the next step.

Final assembly

A buttered *gratin* dish that will hold the chicken comfortably (such as a 9- by 12-inch oval 2 inches deep)
About 3 ounces (¾ cup loosely packed) coarsely grated Swiss cheese
Salt and pepper
Speck of nutmeg
1 to 2 Tb melted butter

When you have buttered the dish, and grated and measured the cheese, fold all but 3 to 4 tablespoons of the cheese into the sauce. Taste, and correct seasoning as necessary with salt, pepper, and a speck of nutmeg. Smooth a thin layer of sauce in the bottom of the dish, and arrange the chicken over it, including the vegetables, if you wish.

Spoon the rest of the sauce over the chicken, masking each piece completely. Spread on the cheese, and sprinkle melted butter over the cheese.

(*) AHEAD-OF-TIME NOTE: May be prepared a day in advance to this point; when cold, cover and refrigerate.

Reheating and serving

When both chicken and sauce are hot, and you are serving almost immediately, set dish 3 or 4 inches from a moderately hot broiler and let topping brown slowly while contents of dish come to the bubble; you may then keep chicken warm for half an hour or so at 120 degrees, but be very careful not to let it overcook and lose the delicious quality of freshly cooked chicken.

When chicken has been refrigerated, set dish in upper third of a preheated 375-degree oven for 25 to 30 minutes, or until top has browned nicely and contents are bubbling hot. Again, be careful not to overcook.

Chaud-froid de Poulet, Morvandelle

[Chicken in *Chaud-froid*—a Cold Dish]

A simple chicken poached in white wine with aromatic vegetables can very easily be transformed into a dressy *chaud-froid* when you enrich the poaching broth with cream and egg yolks, which will thicken the broth just enough as it cools to enrobe the chicken pieces with a yellow-ivory cloak. Light, creamy, with a lovely texture and flavor, yet no trace of flour or gelatin, this is by far the most attractive *chaud-froid* we know. Serve it with cold vegetables or a tossed salad, French bread, and a chilled Chablis, Riesling, or Gewürztraminer.

Poach the chicken in wine and aromatic vegetables using the method and ingredients in the Master Recipe, Steps 1 and 2, pages 254–5. When chicken is done, continue as follows.

The chaud-froid sauce—for 2 cups

A sieve set over a heavy-bottomed 2-quart enameled or stainless saucepan
6 egg yolks in a mixing bowl
A wire whip, a ladle, and a wooden spoon
1 cup *crème fraîche* or heavy cream
Salt, white pepper, and drops of lemon juice

Set cover askew, and drain chicken-cooking stock out of casserole into saucepan. Skim off surface fat, bring liquid to the simmer, skimming, then boil down rapidly until reduced to 1½ cups. Beat the egg yolks and cream to blend. Still beating, gradually ladle in driblets of the hot chicken-cooking liquid. When half has gone in, gradually beat the creamy mixture into the remaining chicken-cooking liquid in the saucepan.

Set pan over moderate heat and stir slowly and continuously with wooden spoon, reaching all over bottom of pan, for 5 to 6 minutes, or until sauce thickens enough to film spoon with a creamy layer. (Be careful sauce does not come near the simmer and curdle the egg yolks; however, you must heat it to the point where it thickens.)

Immediately remove from heat, and stir vigorously for 1 minute to cool slightly and stop the cooking. Taste very carefully, adding salt, white pepper, and drops of lemon juice; sauce should be quite highly seasoned because flavor becomes somewhat subdued in a cold dish. Shortly before coating chicken, set saucepan in a large bowl of cold water and ice cubes; stir frequently until sauce is cool and has begun to thicken. Meanwhile, prepare the chicken for the next step.

Final assembly and serving

A chilled shallow serving dish, just large enough to hold chicken easily

For decoration:

Either minced fresh tarragon, parsley sprigs, or watercress;

Or 1 or 2 truffles to mince and stir into the sauce with the juices from the can;

Or a fluted mushroom cap to top each piece of chicken (Volume I, pages 510–11, for fluting and cooking)

Peel the skin off each piece of chicken, removing as much as you easily can without tearing the meat. Arrange chicken in dish. (If you are stirring truffles into sauce, do so now.) Spoon a thin layer of sauce over each piece, using about ⅓ of the sauce at this point. Cover chicken and chill for 15 to 20 minutes (or longer). When sauce has set on chicken and you are ready to continue, re-warm the remaining sauce briefly, only enough to liquefy it. Beat with wire whip until perfectly smooth, and spoon it over the chicken to mask each piece completely. Cover chicken with a bowl and chill.

Remove chicken from refrigerator about half an hour before serving (unless weather is too hot), to take off the chill; decorate as you wish with any of the elements suggested.

Waterzooi de Poulet

[Chicken Poached in White Wine and a Julienne of Vegetables, Cream, and Egg-yolk Sauce]

The preceding *chaud-froid* turns out to be an almost exact replica of the famous Belgian *bouillabaisse* of chicken, *waterzooi*. The Belgian dish is served hot, however, and the sauce is more like a soup—a *waterzooi* is ladled into deep plates, and you eat it with a knife, fork, and soup spoon. Although its general method is almost identical to that of the *chaud-froid,* as well as the *poulet en bourride* on page 263, the recipe will be easier for you to follow when you have the full details for its sauce and serving even if it means repeating familiar instructions. Accompany the *waterzooi* with boiled potatoes, French bread, and a white Graves or Burgundy. It is a separate course, and a rich one—precede with a cold vegetable or something like the *salade Niçoise* in Volume I, page 542, and follow with fresh fruit, a fruit tart, or a sherbet.

SHOWMANSHIP

In the fine Brussels restaurants where this dish is served, the chicken is poached whole; the *maître d'hôtel* carves it in front of you, and warms the pieces of chicken in the sauce while you savor its delicious perfume. If you can carve like a master and enjoy the drama of table-top cooking, by all means poach the chicken whole, page 265; carve it at the table, and make the sauce as described here, but in a chafing dish.

For 4 people

Follow the Master Recipe for chicken pieces poached in white wine, Steps 1 and 2, pages 254-5, but cut the aromatic vegetables into julienne matchsticks for Step 1. When chicken is done, continue as follows.

Sauce and serving

If needed: more chicken broth
6 egg yolks in a mixing bowl
A wire whip and a ladle
1 cup *crème fraîche* or heavy cream
Salt and white pepper
2 Tb rather roughly chopped fresh parsley
If you wish, a serving casserole or a soup tureen
Wide soup plates

(You should have 2½ to 3 cups of cooking stock for the sauce; add extra broth if necessary.) When you are ready to serve, beat the egg yolks and cream to blend; continue beating, and ladle in driblets of the hot chicken-cooking liquid until about 1 cup has gone in. Remove casserole from heat; swirling it with one hand, gradually pour creamy mixture back over chicken. Taste carefully, and correct seasoning.

Set casserole over moderate heat and continue to swirl it slowly for 4 to 5 minutes, until sauce thickens into a light cream as the egg yolks gradually poach in the mixture; you must be very careful here not to heat the sauce too much or it will turn granular as the egg yolks scramble, but you must heat it to the point where it thickens. Serve immediately, either from casserole or turned into a tureen; decorate with parsley.

The chicken and sauce, which is more like a cream soup, are ladled into soup plates, along with a serving of potatoes, and eaten with knife, fork, and soup spoon.

(*) AHEAD-OF-TIME NOTE: Although you may make the egg yolk and cream liaison, pour it over the chicken, and reheat later, it is safer to keep the poached chicken warm, and finish the dish just before serving. Finished *waterzooi* risks curdling if you try to keep it warm; in other words, this is not a dish adaptable to complete ahead-of-time cookery.

Bouillabaisse de Poulet

[Chicken Poached in White Wine with Provençal Vegetables, Herbs, and Flavorings]

Famous and successful recipes have a way of turning up in other guises, chicken has a habit of wearing other costumes, and there should be nothing surprising about chicken swimming in the robust flavors of a *bouillabaisse*. Although the method here is almost the same as that for the previous poachings, the ingredients differ; we therefore outline all the steps. Serve this with steamed rice or boiled potatoes, French bread, and a strong young white wine like a Riesling or Pinot Blanc, a rather light red like Beaujolais or Mountain Red, or a rosé.

For 4 people

1) *Preliminary cooking of vegetables*

½ cup sliced onions
½ cup sliced white of leek
  (or more onion)
¼ cup olive oil
A heavy 3-quart flameproof
casserole with cover

Cook the onions and leeks slowly with the oil in the covered casserole for about 10 minutes, stirring fairly frequently, until tender but not browned.

About 1½ cups tomato pulp
  (4 or 5 tomatoes, peeled,
  seeded, and juiced, or a
  combination of fresh
  tomatoes and canned
  Italian-type plum
  tomatoes, drained and
  sieved)
2 cloves garlic, minced or
  mashed

While vegetables are cooking, prepare the tomatoes; when vegetables are tender, stir tomatoes in along with the garlic. Cover, and cook 5 minutes so that tomatoes will render their juices; then uncover, raise heat, and let juices almost entirely evaporate.

2) *Poaching the chicken*

2½ lbs. ready-cut chicken,
  prepared as described on
  pages 252–3
Salt

When tomatoes are done, salt chicken lightly, and arrange in casserole, spreading vegetables around and on top. Cover and cook 10 minutes over moderate heat, turning once.

1½ cups dry white wine or
   1 cup dry white French
   vermouth
About 2 cups chicken stock
   or canned chicken broth
1 bay leaf
½ tsp thyme
¼ tsp fennel seeds, crushed
2 pinches saffron threads
A 2-inch piece of dried
   orange peel, or ½ tsp
   bottled dried orange peel
Big pinch pepper
Pinch Cayenne pepper or
   drops Tabasco sauce
Salt as needed

Pour the wine or vermouth over the chicken, and enough stock or broth barely to cover the meat. Add the herbs and seasonings, bring to the simmer, and salt lightly as necessary. Cover casserole and simmer slowly either on top of the stove or in a preheated 325-degree oven for 20 to 25 minutes, or until chicken is tender.

3) *Serving*

Tip casserole and skim off surface fat; remove bay leaf and orange peel, and carefully correct seasoning. Serve as is, from casserole, or arrange chicken and vegetables on a bed of steamed rice, decorate with parsley sprigs, and pass rest of cooking liquid separately.

(*) AHEAD-OF-TIME NOTE: May be kept warm for at least half an hour; set cover askew for air circulation and place in a 120-degree oven, on a hot-tray, or over barely simmering water. Do not overheat and let chicken overcook.

To serve cold or in aspic

This is delicious as a cold dish. When chicken is done, skim off surface fat, remove bay leaf and orange peel, and correct seasoning. When cool, cover and refrigerate for several hours. Scrape off congealed fat and serve the chicken as is; cooking stock will set lightly, like jellied consommé. (If you want a firmer jellied effect, strain cooking stock out of casserole when chicken is done, degrease completely, and dissolve in it 1 package [1 tablespoon] of gelatin for each 2 cups of liquid; pour back over the chicken and vegetables, and chill.)

VARIATIONS

Final touches—Rouille and Pistou

You might pass a *rouille* with the chicken—the garlic, pimento, and chili-pepper sauce given at the end of the *bouillabaisse* recipe in Volume I, page 52. Another excellent sauce would be the *pistou* on page 152, a fragrant combination of basil, tomato, garlic, and cheese that may either be incorporated into the cooking liquid just before serving, or be passed separately. Finally there is the marvelous garlic mayonnaise, *aïoli,* in the next variation.

Poulet en Bourride
[*Bouillabaisse* of Chicken with *Aïoli* Sauce]

What the Belgians do to chicken in their *waterzooi,* their rivals on the Mediterranean accomplish in a most Provençal manner. In fact, the two recipes are almost exact parallels—egg yolks and cream thicken the broth of the *waterzooi* on page 259, while it is egg yolks and olive oil for the *bourride.* This is a very rich and splendid dish; we would suggest only boiled potatoes to go with it, a very simple beginning to the meal, such as asparagus vinaigrette, and a sherbet or fruits for dessert. A strong, dry white wine like Burgundy or Côtes-du-Rhône would be our suggestion for wine.

Poach the chicken exactly as described for the *bouillabaisse* of chicken, page 261, Steps 1 and 2; skim off surface fat, and keep chicken warm. While it simmers, prepare the *aïoli* as follows.

The aïoli sauce

⅓ cup (lightly pressed) fresh crumbs from non-sweetened, homemade-type white bread

Wine vinegar

A heavy bowl or mortar, a pestle or wooden masher, and wire whip

6 to 8 large cloves garlic, mashed

½ tsp salt

6 egg yolks

¾ to 1 cup olive oil

Following the procedure for *aïoli* sauce in Volume I, page 92, moisten the crumbs with drops of vinegar and pound to a paste in the bowl or mortar. Add garlic and salt, and continue pounding until smooth. Then add egg yolks and pound until thick and sticky. Finally begin beating in drops of olive oil; when sauce is thick and heavy, thin with vinegar, and continue beating in oil with wire whip. Season to taste, and cover airtight until ready to use.

Combining chicken and aïoli

A ladle

Optional: a warm soup tureen

When chicken is done and just before you are ready to serve, remove from heat. Gradually ladle driblets of the hot chicken-cooking liquid into the *aïoli* sauce,

Wide soup plates
Rather roughly chopped fresh parsley

beating sauce with wire whip; when a cup of liquid has gone in, pour mixture back into chicken and vegetables, swirling casserole with one hand as you do so, to blend.

Set casserole over moderate heat and continue to swirl it slowly for 4 to 5 minutes, until sauce thickens into a light cream; be careful not to heat sauce to the simmer or it will turn granular as the egg yolks scramble, but you must heat it to the point where it thickens. Serve immediately, either from casserole or turned into a tureen; decorate with parsley.

Like *waterzooi,* the chicken and the souplike sauce are ladled into soup plates, along with a serving of potatoes, and eaten with knife, fork, and soup spoon.

(*) AHEAD-OF-TIME NOTE: See remarks for *waterzooi,* pages 260–1.

WHOLE CHICKEN

CASSEROLE-POACHED CHICKEN

Poularde Pochée à Court Mouillement

Roasting and stewing are not the only ways to cook a whole chicken; there are also casserole roasting, which produces the savory brown *poulet poêlé à l'estragon* and its variations in Volume I, pages 249–53, and casserole poaching, for those times when you wish to serve a whole chicken with one of the many white-wine sauces. This is called *pocher à court mouillement* because the chicken is set in a casserole that will just hold it, and the poaching liquid comes only part way up—the dark meat of the legs and thighs simmers and the white meat of the breast steams. This gives you not only a beautifully tender and juicy chicken, but also a perfectly flavored white-wine chicken broth for a sauce, or, if you are serving the chicken cold, for your aspic or *chaud-froid.* You may cook the chicken with or without stuffing, and serve it any number of ways. We begin with chicken in a white-wine and tarragon sauce.

THE CHICKEN TO BUY—PREPARING IT FOR POACHING

Roasting chickens and capons are best for casserole poaching because their flesh is mature enough to hold up under the steam and moisture; however, if you are careful to maintain a slow and gentle simmer, you may use a large fryer, 3½ pounds ready-to-cook. Broilers are far too immature; their tender flesh falls apart in the casserole.

To prepare the chicken for cooking, first remove the package of giblets from inside the cavity. The giblets should include the liver, heart, gizzard, and neck. If you are not stuffing the chicken, you may season the liver and return it to the cavity to cook and serve with the chicken, or save it for another purpose. Reserve the rest of the giblets for the casserole; they will give added flavor to the broth.

Pull loose fat from around inside of vent opening; you may render it (page 316), and use for general cooking or for rubbing over the chicken instead of butter. Cut off nubbins attached to wing elbows and, to make carving easier, remove the wishbone by cutting around its forked outline from inside the neck end of the chicken, then break its two ends loose from bottom of breast and pull it free. Run cold water all around inside and outside of chicken, and dry thoroughly with paper towels. (We were not enthusiastic about washing chickens in Volume I; we now think it is a wise precaution.) After you have inserted whatever flavoring or stuffing is called for, truss the chicken as illustrated in Volume I, pages 237-9 (or in less detail here on page 271).

✳ *POULARDE POCHÉE À L'ESTRAGON*

[Casserole-poached Chicken with White-wine and Tarragon Sauce]

A fine roasting chicken is a *poularde* in French, and capon is *chapon;* either one is recommended for this delicious recipe. Rather than a stuffing, we have suggested an herbal flavoring inside the chicken, which is typical of many French recipes; if you do wish a stuffing, see the variations at the end of the recipe as well as the list of stuffings on page 513.

Nothing that accompanies the chicken should mask the lovely flavor of the tarragon, and with this in mind, we would suggest steamed rice and the garniture of mushrooms and onions used for chicken fricassee (Volume I, page 260); or either the unusual rice and onion *soubise* in Volume I on page 485 or the stuffed onions here on page 376, with buttered peas or asparagus tips. This is definitely an occasion for one of the great white Burgundy wines.

For 5 to 6 people

---

1) *Preparations for poaching*

½ cup each of sliced carrots and sliced onions
2 Tb butter
A heavy enameled casserole or roaster just large

Preheat oven to 325 degrees in time for Step 2. Cook the onions and carrots in the covered casserole, stirring occasionally, until vegetables are tender but not brown. Meanwhile, prepare the chicken as follows.

enough to hold the
chicken comfortably
breast-up

A 4½ lb. ready-to-cook
roasting chicken or capon
3 Tb soft butter (half for
inside and half for outside
of chicken)
½ tsp salt (for inside and
outside of chicken)
A medium-sized branch of
fresh tarragon, or 1 tsp
fragrant dried tarragon

Prepare chicken for roasting as described in paragraph
preceding recipe, but before trussing it, sprinkle with
half the salt, and add the tarragon; then truss the
chicken. When vegetables are tender, massage the rest
of the butter into the chicken skin, sprinkle with remaining salt, and arrange the chicken breast-up in the
casserole.

1⅓ cups dry white wine, or
1 cup dry white French
vermouth
2 or more cups chicken
stock or canned chicken
broth
1 bay leaf
6 parsley sprigs
A medium-sized branch of
fresh tarragon, or ½ Tb
fragrant dried tarragon
The washed chicken giblets
(neck, gizzard, heart,
wing nubbins, wishbone)
Salt as needed
A double thickness of
well-washed and rinsed
damp cheesecloth to
cover chicken breast and
thighs
2 Tb soft butter
Waxed paper

Pour the wine into the casserole, and enough chicken
stock or broth to reach about ⅓ the way up the
chicken. Add the herbs, and giblets. Bring to simmer
on top of the stove, taste liquid, and salt lightly, as
needed. Drape the damp, washed cheesecloth over the
breast and thighs; it should be long enough to fall
into the liquid all around so that it will draw the
broth over the chicken and baste it during the cooking. Smear the butter over the cheesecloth, top with
waxed paper, cover the casserole, and set in middle
level of preheated oven.

(*) AHEAD-OF-TIME NOTE: You may arrange the
chicken in the casserole with wine, broth, cloth, and
trimmings, then refrigerate, and poach it the next day.

2) *Poaching the chicken—1 hour and 30 to 40 minutes at 325 degrees*

After chicken has been in the oven about 20 minutes, check casserole to be sure
liquid is at the very slow simmer—if liquid bubbles actively, flesh can break apart.
Regulate thermostat accordingly; except for making sure cooking is slow and gentle,
you have nothing more to do until chicken is done.

When chicken flesh is tender if pressed and drumsticks move in their sockets, chicken should be ready. Test by lifting it carefully (use trussing strings between thighs and elbows) and drain juices onto a white plate; if last drops to come out are clear yellow with no trace of rose, chicken is definitely done.

---

3) *The sauce—sauce à l'estragon—for 2½ cups*

A sieve set over a 2½- to 3-quart stainless saucepan
4 Tb butter
A second 2½- to 3-quart saucepan, heavy-bottomed and enameled or stainless
5 Tb flour
A wooden spoon and a wire whip

When chicken is done and juices have been drained from vent, set it on a platter or side dish. Strain cooking stock into saucepan, pressing juices out of ingredients in sieve; skim surface fat off stock. Return chicken to casserole with a cup of the cooking stock, replace cheesecloth, set casserole cover askew, and keep chicken warm, either in turned-off oven, on a hot-tray, or over barely simmering water while you prepare a *sauce velouté*.

Bring cooking stock to the simmer, skimming off additional fat, and maintain at slow simmer while making the *roux*: melt butter in saucepan, blend in flour with wooden spoon, and stir over moderate heat until butter and flour foam together for 2 minutes without browning. Remove from heat, and as soon as *roux* stops bubbling, pour in 2 cups of the hot chicken stock, blending vigorously with wire whip. When smooth, return over moderate heat and stir rather slowly with wire whip as sauce thickens and comes to the boil. Boil, stirring, for 2 minutes—sauce will be quite thick.

½ to ⅔ cup heavy cream
Salt, white pepper, and drops of lemon juice
2 to 4 Tb soft butter

Simmering the sauce, pour in ⅓ cup of the cream, and add successive spoonfuls until sauce thins out but is still thick enough to coat a spoon nicely. Taste very carefully for seasoning, adding salt, white pepper, and lemon juice to taste. Just before serving, remove from heat and beat in the enrichment butter by spoonfuls.

---

4) *Serving*

A hot, lightly buttered serving platter
Either 10 to 12 large fresh tarragon leaves dropped 30 seconds in boiling water and laid on a plate;
Or slices of truffle or fluted and cooked mushrooms, and parsley or watercress if needed
A warmed sauce bowl

Remove trussing strings from chicken, and set it on platter; wipe up any juices. Spoon enough sauce over chicken to mask it attractively, and decorate with tarragon leaves or whatever you have chosen. Pour rest of sauce into bowl. Make a presentation of the chicken to your guests, who will want to admire it. Then, if it is not to be carved at the table, carve in the kitchen; arrange the pieces over a bed of rice, and spoon a little of the sauce over each. Decorate again with tarragon leaves or whatever you have chosen, and serve.

(*) AHEAD-OF-TIME NOTE: You may keep the chicken warm for half an hour at least as suggested at the end of the first part in Step 3. Complete the sauce except for the final butter enrichment, clean sauce off sides of pan with a rubber spatula, and dot a tablespoon of soft butter on surface of sauce, spreading it lightly and evenly with the back of a spoon; keep sauce warm, uncovered, over simmering water.

TO SERVE COLD

Poularde en Chaud-froid—Poularde en Gelée
[Chicken in *Chaud-froid*—Chicken in Aspic]

The tender fragrant quality of chicken poached in white wine and the excellence of its cooking broth made it ideal for *chaud-froid* or simply chicken in aspic. For *chaud-froid*, you might use half the broth for an initial creamy coating on the chicken pieces following either the cream and egg-yolk sauce on page 258, or the recipe in Volume I, page 551, with cream and gelatin. You could then decorate the chicken with tarragon leaves, and glaze with clear aspic made from the rest of the broth. Full directions for *chaud-froids* are in this volume and in Volume I as indicated; for aspics see page 256 in this volume, and page 549 in Volume I.

STUFFED CHICKEN—BONED CHICKEN

When you want to serve stuffed chicken, either roasted or poached, it is easier to carve it if you bone the breast of the raw chicken, meaning that you slit the skin and peel it back from the breast, remove the meat, and cut out the breastbone and upper half of the ribs. This gives you a boat-shaped trough; its bottom is formed by the backbone, and its sides by the lower ribs, the wings, and the legs. Pile the stuffing into the trough, top with breast meat cut into strips, fold the skin back into place, and the chicken is reconstituted again for cooking. To serve, cut right down the length of the breast to reveal white meat and stuffing, while the legs and wings come off in the usual way. Because white meat picks up flavor when in direct contact with the stuffing, most of the dark-meat-only people will shift over to "a little of both, please." You will also find this semiboning a successful way to treat the enormous breasts of modern turkeys, and a turkey is boned exactly like the chicken illustrated here.

VOLAILLE DEMI-DÉSOSSÉE

[Half-boned Chicken—also for Turkey, Other Poultry, and Game Birds]

Set chicken breast-up, and with a sharp knife, slit the skin from neck to tail, following ridge of breastbone. *With your fingers, peel the skin back from the breast first on one side, then on the other,* going down to the shoulders and the second joints to expose the whole expanse of breast.

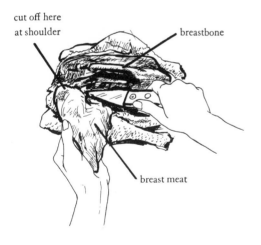

cut off here at shoulder

breastbone

breast meat

Starting on one side of ridge of breastbone, cut through flesh to bone all along its length from neck end to tail. *Always angling the cutting edge of knife against bone and not against flesh, continue cutting down against outward curve of breastbone and then against ribs, pulling flesh from bone with your fingers as you cut.* Be careful not to slit skin at sides of breast as you release meat from lower rib cage; cut off the meat where it joins the ball joint of the wing at the shoulder, and you have removed one side of the breast meat. Remove the other side in the same manner.

With heavy shears and starting at the tail end, cut through the upper half of the breastbone-rib structure midway on each side, where the backward-slanting top ribs join the forward-slanting bottom ribs. Continue the cut through the V-shaped bone at the neck end, and the breastbone is freed.

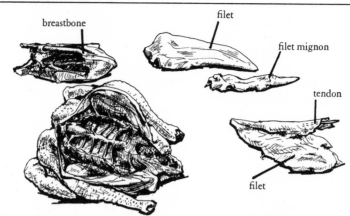

With the breastbone removed, you now have a boat-shaped open cavity to fill with stuffing. The 2 boneless pieces of meat, one removed from each side of the breast, are called *suprêmes,* and each is composed of 2 layers. The larger layer is the *filet;* the smaller layer is the *filet mignon.* On the underside of each *filet mignon* is a clearly visible white tendon. Grasp the end of it in a towel held in one hand; slit flesh on either side with a small knife and, scraping it against your knife as you gently pull, draw it out; repeat for the second tendon.

(*) AHEAD-OF-TIME NOTE: If you are not ready to stuff the chicken at this point, place the *suprêmes* in the cavity, draw the chicken skin over them, wrap the chicken, and refrigerate it. Chop up the breastbone and add it to your chicken stock.

When you are ready to stuff the chicken, cut the breast meat into strips ⅜ inch wide. (You may wish to marinate them in oil, herbs, and wine or drops of lemon juice, or in Cognac as suggested in the following recipe.)

Raise the legs upright, then flex them, pushing knees against armpits (where wings join shoulders). Run a skewer or knitting needle through the carcass at knees as shown; this will hold legs in place for the rest of the operation. Mound whatever stuffing you have chosen in the cavity, building it into a dome at the front to simulate a full breast. *Lay the strips of breast meat over the stuffing.*

Fold the breast skin over the stuffing and breast meat, covering it completely. One edge of skin should overlap the other by ⅜ to ½ inch; remove a little stuffing if necessary.

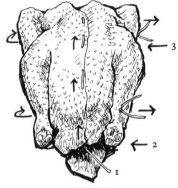

With white string and either an 8-inch trussing needle, a long mattress needle, or a plastic knitting needle with a hole drilled in the end, truss the chicken.

1) Sew the 2 flaps of breast skin together as follows: start at the tail end, and leaving a 3-inch piece of string free at that end, stitch a straight line up to the neck. Turn the chicken over and sew the neck skin to the back, completely enclosing the stuffing at the neck end.

2) The second tie is to secure the lower part of the drumsticks and to close the vent opening. Push needle through the lower part of the carcass and the tail piece; come back through skin on top of one drumstick, through lower end of breast, and top of second drumstick. Pull string tight, and tie.

3) For the final tie, remove skewer, and go through carcass at the knees; fold wings akimbo and come back through the underside of one wing, through a bit of the backbone, then through the underside of the second wing. Pull string tight and tie.

Chicken is now ready for roasting, casserole roasting, or for the *poularde poché, à la d'Albuféra,* in the following recipe.

✳ *POULARDE À LA D'ALBUFÉRA*

[Half-boned Chicken Stuffed with *Foie Gras,* Truffles, Chicken Livers, and Rice; Poached in White Wine; *Sauce Suprême Pimentée*]

One of the more famous chickens boned, stuffed, and poached in white wine is this one, created to honor Maréchal Suchet, who was made Duc d'Albuféra by a grateful Napoleon after the General's victories in Spain. The duke-dom, a large lagoon surrounded by rice fields with an outlet to the bay of Val-encia, was lost in another battle the next year, 1813, but both duke and recipe retained their titles. Curiously enough, as a gastronomical aside to history, the grateful Spanish, in recognition of his role in returning the lost territories to them, awarded the revenues from the Albufera to the Duke of Wellington—perhaps at the very moment a famous *filet* of beef was being named after him. Numerous versions, as is always the way, exist for *poularde à la d' Albuféra,* and we have picked the one we prefer. Not all of them include a small pinch of saffron in the rice, but all do have a Spanish echo of pimento in the sauce.

The vegetable accompaniment should be fresh and simple, we think. Something like the parslied baked cucumbers in Volume I, page 500, or fresh new peas or asparagus tips, or the tender, peeled, fresh broccoli in the Vegetable Chapter here, page 337. We prefer one of the great white Burgundies with this dish, or one of the lovely white Graves—Haut-Brion or La Mission-Haut-Brion.

For 6 people

---

1) *Preparing the chicken*

A 4½-lb. roasting chicken or capon

A dish to hold the strips of breast meat

1½ Tb each of dry port or dry (Sercial) Madeira, and Cognac

1 Tb very finely minced shallots or scallions

Freshly ground white pepper

Pinches of tarragon or thyme

1 or more 1-ounce cans of truffles

2 or more ounces canned *foie gras en bloc* (goose liver: read label on can), chilled for easy cutting

Following preceding directions, bone out the breast of the chicken. Cut breast meat into strips ⅜ inch wide and turn about in the dish with the wine, shallots, pepper, herbs, and the uncut truffles and their juice. Dipping your knife in hot water for each slice, cut the *foie gras* into ¼-inch dice; place at side of dish, and baste with the marinade. Cover marinade dish with plastic wrap, and refrigerate while making the stuffing; wrap and refrigerate the chicken.

---

2) *The stuffing—farce à la d' Albuféra—for about 3½ cups*

The chicken liver and heart (If you have the minimum of *foie gras,* add an extra chicken liver.)

Cut the chicken liver or livers and heart into ¼-inch dice, and sauté over moderate heat in 1 tablespoon of the butter, just to stiffen them slightly; scrape into mixing bowl. Melt the rest of the butter in the pan,

3 Tb butter

A heavy-bottomed, 2- to
2½-quart enameled or
stainless saucepan with
cover

A large mixing bowl

¼ cup very finely minced
onion

1 cup plain, raw, white,
untreated rice

¼ cup dry white wine or
dry white French
vermouth

1¾ cups chicken stock or
canned chicken broth

A small pinch of saffron
threads

A bay leaf

Salt and pepper to taste

1 egg, lightly beaten

add the onions, and cook slowly, stirring frequently, for 4 to 5 minutes until fairly tender but not browned. Stir in the rice, and cook, stirring, for several minutes over moderate heat until rice turns translucent, then milky, indicating that the covering starch has coagulated. Pour in the wine and let cook for a moment to evaporate the alcohol.

Then pour in the chicken stock or broth, add the small pinch of saffron, the bay leaf, and bring to the simmer. Add salt and pepper as needed, stir up once, cover pan, and let cook at a moderately fast simmer, without touching it again, for 15 minutes. Rice should be almost but not quite done, needing only 2 to 3 minutes more cooking; liquid should have been entirely absorbed. Uncover pan, discard bay leaf, turn rice into mixing bowl, and let it cool to tepid. Stir in the egg.

Remove the truffles from their marinade, and cut into dice (or mince if you have only a small amount). Fold with a rubber spatula into the rice and chicken livers, and carefully correct seasoning. (Reserve the *foie gras* until next step.)

3) *Stuffing and trussing the chicken*

Salt cavity of chicken lightly, spread a layer of rice stuffing in it, and then a few pieces of the diced *foie gras*. Continue in layers, molding rice into a dome at the breast end. Cover with the breast strips, as illustrated on page 270, fold skin over breast, sew, and truss the chicken also as illustrated. (Reserve marinade juices.)

(*) AHEAD-OF-TIME NOTE: If both stuffing and chicken are cold, you may stuff and truss the chicken a day in advance of cooking.

4) *Poaching the chicken—1½ to 1¾ hours*

Poach the chicken as directed in Steps 1 and 2, Master Recipe, pages 265–7, but use a big pinch of thyme and a bay leaf rather than tarragon in the casserole.

5) *The sauce*

Make the sauce as described in Step 3 of the Master Recipe, page 267, but omit the tarragon, and stir the marinade liquid into it. Rather than enriching it with plain butter, use pimento butter as follows.

3 Tb canned red pimento
3 Tb soft butter
A fine-meshed sieve set over a bowl
A wooden spoon and a rubber spatula
Pinch of Cayenne pepper, or drops of Tabasco sauce

Drain the pimento and gently press out liquid. Rub it with the butter through the sieve, scraping all residue off bottom of sieve as well as banging sieve on bowl to dislodge as much as possible. Beat in Cayenne or Tabasco. Just before serving, remove sauce from heat and beat in the pimento butter, a tablespoon at a time.

6) Serving

When ready to serve, remove trussing strings and place chicken on platter. Spoon a little of the sauce over the chicken, and decorate as you wish, with truffle slices or fluted mushrooms. To carve, cut straight down through top of breast from neck end to tail end, and spread apart. Remove wings and legs. Remove breast meat with stuffing, using a serving spoon and fork, and give each guest both dark meat, light meat, and stuffing; spoon some of the sauce around or over each serving.

(*) AHEAD-OF-TIME NOTE: See directions at end of Master Recipe, page 268.

OTHER STUFFINGS, OTHER SAUCES

Farce Évocation d'Albuféra
[Rice, Mushrooms, and Chicken-liver Stuffing with Purée of Garlic]

More Mediterranean in feeling than the original is the following stuffing for those occasions when you do not wish to indulge in truffles and *foie gras*.

For about 3½ cups, to fill a 4½-pound half-boned chicken

1 head of garlic
¼ cup dry white wine or dry white French vermouth
1 cup chicken stock or canned chicken broth
A small covered saucepan

Separate the garlic cloves and drop into a pan of boiling water, boil 1 minute, drain, and slip off the peel. Then simmer the garlic cloves very slowly for 30 minutes with the wine and stock. Meanwhile, continue with the rest of the stuffing.

¼ pound fresh mushrooms, trimmed, washed, dried, and quartered (about 1 cup)

Sauté the mushrooms and scallions in butter and oil over moderately high heat, tossing and turning, until fat reappears on surface of mushrooms; then add diced livers and sauté a minute more, tossing. Pour in

2 Tb minced shallots or
  scallions
1 Tb butter and 1 tsp oil
3 chicken livers, cut into
  ⅜-inch pieces
A heavy-bottomed 2½- to
  3-quart enameled or
  stainless saucepan
¼ cup dry (Sercial)
  Madeira or dry port
A mixing bowl

the Madeira or port and boil rapidly until liquid is almost entirely evaporated. Scrape into mixing bowl.

2¼ to 2½ cups plain boiled
  white rice (¾ cup raw
  rice, boiled in salted water
  until barely tender)
¼ tsp thyme or oregano
1 egg, lightly beaten
The cooked garlic in its
  broth
A fine-meshed sieve
Salt and pepper to taste

Blend the rice, herbs, and egg into the mixing bowl. Drain cooked garlic, and mash through sieve into mixing bowl; blend in, along with 2 tablespoons of the cooking liquid. (Reserve rest of liquid for sauce, including it as part of the chicken-cooking stock.) Taste stuffing, and carefully correct seasoning.

Stuff, truss, and poach the chicken as directed in the preceding recipe; either make the same sauce with pimento-butter enrichment, or make a light curry sauce by stirring 2 teaspoons of fragrant curry powder into the butter as you make the *roux*, beginning of Step 3, Master Recipe, page 267.

Farce Normande, aux Boudins Blancs
[White Forcemeat Stuffing with Mushroom *Duxelles*]

Boudin blanc, with its ground chicken, veal, or pork and tenderly cooked onions, is so good one is always happy to find other uses for it. Use half the recipe on page 290, but there is no need to encase the mixture in sausage skins: roll it, instead, into one big sausage shape in cheesecloth, as illustrated on page 286; poach it in the wine and chicken stock you will use for poaching the chicken, making the stock even better than usual for your final sauce. Then proceed as follows.

The poached *boudin*
  described in preceding
  paragraph

Cut the *boudin* into ½-inch dice and set aside. Heat the *duxelles* with the shallots or scallions, tossing and turning over moderately high heat for 2 minutes to

About ½ cup cooked
  mushroom *duxelles*
  (finely diced mushrooms
  sautéed in butter, page
  194), still in their sauté
  pan
2 Tb minced shallots or
  scallions
¼ cup dry (Sercial)
  Madeira or dry port wine
Salt and pepper to taste

cook the shallots, then pour in the wine. Boil rapidly
for a minute or two, to evaporate liquid almost completely. Taste, and carefully correct seasoning.

Stuff the chicken with layers of diced *boudin* interspersed with sprinklings of
duxelles, and top with the slices of breast meat. Truss the chicken as illustrated on
page 271, and poach as directed in the Master Recipe for chicken poached in
white wine, starting on page 265. Rather than flavoring the sauce with tarragon, you
might make an additional ¼ cup of wine-flavored *duxelles* initially, and reserve it
to simmer a moment in your finished sauce before adding the final butter enrichment. A sprinkling of minced fresh green herbs, such as parsley, tarragon, or chives
could go in too at the last minute.

POULARDE EN SOUTIEN-GORGE
COQ EN PÂTE—POULARDE EN CROÛTE
[Half-boned and Stuffed Chicken in a Pastry Crust]

Once you have boned, stuffed, and enrobed a *coq en pâte,* you may put it
away in the refrigerator and bake it the next day. Amusing to prepare and
always a success when served, it is a great dish for a party. Not only are the

chicken's breastworks removed, but its skin is also peeled off; thus the French title, *soutien-gorge,* is as primly nondescriptive as would be our brassiere; the German *Bustenhalter* would give a more exact explanation of what the pastry must do to hold the breast and stuffing in place during baking. The dough, *pâte à croustades,* is designed for something like a *pâté* or a chicken that must bake for an hour or more: the pastry is crisp, tender, and delicious to eat as well as being easy to handle; if you make it in the electric mixer you will find it very easy to do.

CHICKEN NOTES

Rather than the 4½-pound roaster or capon for 6, suggested in the recipe, you may use 3- to 3½-pound fryers, and 3 of them would serve 12 to 16 people. You will need only ½ the pastry recipe per frying chicken, and 2½ cups of stuffing. Roasting time for 1 frying chicken would be 1 hour and 20 to 30 minutes; for 3 chickens in one oven, probably 1¾ to 2 hours.

For 6 people

---

1) *The pastry—made at least 2 hours before baking*

Pastry formula 6, page 110, *pâte à croustades*

Make the pastry either by hand in the usual way, or by machine as described on page 104. Wrap and chill the dough for at least 2 hours, or overnight. (Any leftovers may be frozen, and used for turnovers or appetizer pastries.)

---

2) *Preparing and stuffing the chicken*

A 4½-lb. roasting chicken or capon

Slit the skin of the chicken along the breast bone from neck end to tail end; turn chicken over and slit skin from neck to tail ¼ inch from edge of backbone on each side.

Cut off wings at elbows. Then, except for strip of skin at backbone, peel the rest of the skin off the chicken. Being careful not to detach the following pieces from the chicken, cut through ball joints attaching wings to shoulders, second joints to hips, and drumsticks to second joints; this is to prevent these appendages from kicking through the pastry during cooking. Remove breast meat, and cut out upper half of breastbone-rib structure as illustrated on pages 269–70. Cut the breast meat in strips and marinate, if you wish, in wine and herbs as described in the Master Recipe, page 272, Step 1. Make a brown chicken stock with the giblets, skin, and scraps (Volume I, page 236).

3½ cups of any stuffing
for chicken, pages 513–
15, the *évocation
d'Albuféra* being par-
ticularly recommended
A skewer or knitting needle
just long enough to go
through carcass at knees
and to protrude ¼ to ½
inch on each side

Following illustrated directions on pages 270–1, stuff the chicken and lay the breast strips on top. Insert skewer as in the illustration, to keep legs in place during baking; it will be drawn out from the crust before serving.

3) *Enclosing chicken in pastry*

The chilled pastry from
Step 1
White wine, or vermouth,
or chicken stock; or the
garlic-cooking liquid if
you are using *farce
évocation d'Albuféra*
A pastry brush
A shallow buttered roasting
pan or edged baking
sheet large enough to hold
chicken easily
Egg glaze (1 egg beaten in
a small bowl with 1 tsp
water)

Preheat oven to 400 degrees in time for Step 4. Roll ⅔ of the pastry out on a lightly floured board, making an oval 3/16 inch thick and large enough to cover top and sides of chicken. Paint chicken with wine or stock, and press the pastry in place over the flesh. (Leave a small opening at one side or both for removal of skewer after baking.) Trim off any extra pastry, leaving only enough to cover sides of chicken completely. (Bare bottom of chicken rests on baking surface.)

Roll out pastry scraps, cut into whatever designs you wish, paint undersides with egg glaze, and affix to the pastry.

(*) AHEAD-OF-TIME NOTE: If both stuffing and chicken were cold before being combined, chicken may be covered, refrigerated, and baked the next day. Note, however, that roasting time may be 15 to 20 minutes longer than time indicated in Step 4.

4) *Baking—1½ to 1¾ hours*

The egg glaze and the
pastry brush
Aluminum foil or brown
paper

When oven has been preheated to 400 degrees, paint surface of pastry and decorations with egg glaze. Draw the point of a knife over glaze into pastry to make decorative cross-hatch marks.

Immediately set chicken in middle level of preheated oven. In 20 to 25 minutes, when pastry has begun to brown nicely, turn thermostat down to 350 degrees. Look again in another 30 minutes, and if pastry is browning too much, cover loosely with foil or brown paper. Chicken is close to being done when juices begin to exude in pan, and is definitely done when pan is removed, tipped, and last juices running from under crust are clear yellow with no trace of rose. As soon as chicken is done, remove from oven.

5) *Sauce and serving*

A lightly buttered serving platter

2 Tb minced shallots or scallions

¼ cup dry (Sercial) Madeira, dry port wine, or dry white French vermouth

A saucepan containing 1 cup of brown chicken stock (or a combination of chicken broth and beef bouillon)

½ cup *crème fraîche* or heavy cream

If needed: 1 tsp cornstarch blended with 1 Tb stock or wine

2 to 3 Tb soft butter

A warm sauce boat

Remove chicken to serving platter, and carefully extract skewer that has held legs in place. Stir the shallots or scallions and wine into the juices in the roasting pan, set over moderate heat, and scrape up all coagulated bits of flavor into juices and wine with a wooden spoon. Scrape liquid into saucepan with the stock, and boil down rapidly to concentrate flavor. Add cream, and boil a few minutes to thicken lightly. (If it seems necessary, remove from heat, beat in cornstarch mixture, and simmer 2 minutes more to thicken.) Carefully correct seasoning. Just before serving, remove from heat and swirl in butter a half spoonful at a time. (You will have only a cup, just enough to moisten each serving.)

To serve, cut straight down through top of crust from neck to tail, and spread crust to sides of chicken. Remove legs and wings, and cut into serving pieces. Give each guest both white and dark meat, stuffing, and a piece of the crust; spoon a bit of the sauce over or around the meat.

(*) AHEAD-OF-TIME NOTE: You may keep chicken warm for an hour, if necessary; let it sit out at room temperature for 20 minutes, then keep in a 120-degree oven (or in the turned-off oven, reheating briefly from time to time if necessary).

CHAPTER FIVE

Charcuterie: Sausages, Salted Pork and Goose, Pâtés and Terrines

THE FOUNDATION AND MAINSTAY of French *charcuterie* is pork in all its forms, from sausages and stuffings to hams, *pâtés,* and *terrines. Chair cuite,* meaning meat that is cooked, was obviously the derivation of this marvelous keystone of French civilization, but modern *charcuterie* shops, like American delicatessens, have branched out and sell all manner of edibles, such as aspics and ready-to-heat *escargots,* heat-and-serve lobster dishes, ready-made salads, mayonnaise, relishes, canned goods, fine wines, and liqueurs. In the best establishments, all the cooking is done on the premises; they cure their own hams, make their own salt pork and fresh and smoked sausages, have their own formulas for their beautiful display of *pâtés.* Let us all pray that this delicious way of life will long remain, because there are few things more satisfying to the soul than the look and smell of a French *charcuterie.*

SAUSAGES
Saucisses et Saucissons

With the virtual disappearance of European-style neighborhood *charcuteries* in this country, it behooves every serious cook to have a few sausage formulas on hand for such delicious concoctions as *saucisson en croûte, saucisson en brioche, saucisson chaud et pommes à l'huile*—that wonderfully simple dish of hot, sliced sausages and potato salad—little pork sausages for breakfast and garnitures, and those lovely white-meat sausages with truffles, *boudins blancs*. A sausage is only ground meat and seasonings, a mixture no more complicated than a meat loaf, and for fresh unsmoked sausages you need no special equipment at all. An electric meat grinder and a heavy-duty mixer will make things easier, but a sausage-stuffing mechanism and sausage casings are not necessary because you can use other means to arrive at the sausage shape. In French terminology a *saucisse* is primarily a small and thin sausage, usually fresh, and a *saucisson* is a large sausage usually smoked or otherwise cured; the one may be called the other, however, if it is a question of size. Here are directions for forming them in casings and a practical substitute for casings, as well as a short discussion on caul fat.

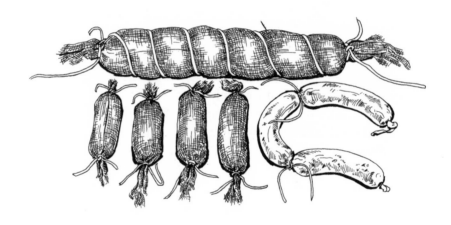

SAUSAGE CASINGS

Natural sausage casings, the flexible, tubular membrane that holds the sausage together and forms its skin, are made from the thoroughly scraped and cleaned intestines of hogs, cattle, and sheep, of the stomachs of hogs, and of the bladders of all three. Sheep casings are the most valuable and expensive of all, and also the most fragile; varying in diameter from ⅜ to 1 inch, they are used mostly for fresh pork breakfast sausages and the small cocktail or garnishing sausages called chipolatas. Beef casings are for large sausages like bolognas, salamis, and blood sausages, and middle sizes like cervelats and mettwursts. Hog casings come in various lengths and widths: bungs (*gros boyaux*), or the large intestine; hog middles (*fuseaux*), or the middle intestines; small casings (*les menus*), which are the small intestine.

The most practical and easily obtainable for the home sausage stuffer are small hog casings, the kind your butcher uses to make his fresh pork sausages or fresh Italian sausages. If he cannot supply you with a few pieces, he can order them for you; or look up in the classified telephone directory under Sausage Casings or Butcher's Supplies. Ask for a set of small hog casings, medium width. You will get a bundle of 16 to 18 casings, each 20 feet long, which are twisted into a complicated swirl resembling wet spaghetti. To disentangle the pieces, unwind the set on a very large table. Then start with one piece from the middle and gently pull it through the maze, first on one side, then on the other. Disentangle all the pieces, winding each up on your fingers as you do so, like string. Pack the pieces between layers of coarse salt in a large screw-top jar and store in the refrigerator. They will keep safely for years as long as they are well covered with salt.

Before using a piece of casing, wash it off in cold water, then soak for one but not more than two hours in cold water. Any casing you do not use may be thoroughly rinsed inside and out, wound up again, and repacked with salt in your casing container.

How to use sausage casing

Casing is ideal for sausages because it holds the meat in perfect symmetry; the problem is finding a way to get the meat into these marvelous containers. Professionals use a stuffing machine, *poussoir,* which is a large cylinder with a pushing plate at one end and a nozzle at the other: the meat goes into the cylinder, the casing is slid up the outside of the nozzle, and a crank operates the plate, pushing the meat from the cylinder through the nozzle and into the casing, which slowly and evenly fills with meat as it slides off the nozzle. There are home models available from some butcher supply houses and mail-order sources; anyone going into serious sausage making should certainly have one, since alternatives can only be makeshift and more or less successful depending on your sausage mixture. Here are the alternatives, including hand stuffer, meat grinder, and pastry bag. You will work out your own system.

Whichever of the three methods you choose, you will need a nozzle of some sort onto the outside of which you slide the sausage casing. This can be a funnel, the metal tube that fits a professional-size pastry bag, or a regular sausage stuffing nozzle; whatever it is, we shall call it by its official name, stuffing horn. After the sausage casing has soaked for an hour in cold water, cut it into 2- to 3-foot lengths so it will be easy to deal with.

Wet horn in cold water; *fit one end of a piece of casing onto the small end.*

Hold the large end of the horn under a slowly running faucet of cold water, and push casing up outside with your fingers, being careful not to tear casing with your fingernails. If you have cut casing into lengths, string them all onto the horn, one after the other. To permit freedom of action, always leave 3 to 4 inches of empty casing dangling from end of horn and, unless your sausage mixture is very soft and liable to dribble out, do not knot end of casing until the whole length is filled.

With the casing in place, you are now ready to stuff it. Have in mind how long you want your sausages to be, how many, if any, you want linked together, and if they are to be linked, whether the meat mixture is soft enough so that you can safely twist the filled casing into lengths without bursting it. This is mostly a matter of trial and error; if you want no errors and have plenty of casing, fill and either link or cut and tie one sausage at a time. To minimize air spaces and bubbles, watch casing carefully as you are filling it; when air spaces develop, push filled casing against end of horn to force air back into stuffer. In severe instances, when you are making linked sausages, you will have to cut the casing, tie it, and start a new series of links.

A pastry bag works surprisingly well for either stiff or soft sausage mixtures. *You will need 2 metal tubes 2 inches long with ½-inch openings at the small end. One is holding the casing around its outside; the other is fitted inside a 12- to 14-inch bag.*

sausage
meat

sausage meat   wooden plunger
inside metal case

This oversize hypodermic consists of wooden plunger, cylinder, and detachable horn. It works well for soft mixtures like the *boudin blanc.*

For stiffer blends, you have to brace the end of the tube against the edge of a table. A pastry bag is easier in this case.

A stuffing horn of plastic or metal 4 inches long, ¾ inch in diameter at the small end, and 2¼ at the large end fits most grinders of the type illustrated here. They often come as extra equipment, or can be ordered from butcher or mail-order houses.

Sometimes the grinder is operated with cutting knife (a) and disk (b) as well as horn (c), and sometimes not; if you have no instructions, you will have to try both ways. Some meat grinders work fairly well as sausage stuffers; others are maddeningly unsatisfactory.

Operate meat grinder at slow speed if it is electric, and hold casing horizontal with horn as meat goes in; this is to avoid air bubbles. When sausage meat has gone into casing, slip a free 3 or 4 inches of empty casing from horn and cut off with scissors.

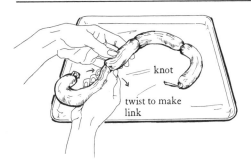

knot

twist to make link

Tie a knot in the casing close against the meat at each end. *For linked sausages, twist slowly and carefully to make the separations.* Tie a piece of white string at each separation.

HOW TO FORM SAUSAGES IN CHEESECLOTH CASINGS

Cheesecloth works very well indeed as an alternative to professional casing when it is of no aesthetic importance that the sausage be perfectly symmetrical, such as those to be baked in pastry, served in slices, or crumbed and broiled. The following illustrations are for small sausages; large ones are formed in the same way.

As an example, for 5-inch sausages, provide yourself with sufficient pieces of well-washed, damp, double-thickness cheesecloth about 8 inches square, and sufficient 4-inch pieces of white string to secure the 2 ends of each. Form sausages one at a time. *Start by spreading cheesecloth on a tray and painting it with melted lard or shortening.*

Form a neat rectangular loaf of sausage meat 5 inches long on lower end of cheesecloth.

Smooth meat into a cylindrical shape; roll up tightly and neatly in cheesecloth.

Tie one end securely with white string. Twist other end of cheesecloth to pack meat into place, *tie it with string, and the casing is finished.* These sausages are often refrigerated for 2 hours or so to firm them up before anything else is done to them.

CAUL FAT

A marvelously useful product of the hog is its caul fat (*crêpine, toilette*), the spider-web-like membrane laced with fat that lines the visceral cavity. Caul fat makes a perfect and perfectly edible container for the fresh sausage patties called *saucisses plates* or *crêpinettes*. You can use caul fat instead of casing for *boudins,* for the large sausages you bake in *brioche* dough, and it is marvelous for wrapping up the stuffed tenderloin on page 176, meats roasted in a cloak of mushroom *duxelles,* or the *noisettes de veau* on page 223. Although American manufacturers use it for the occasionally made Devonshire sausages, caul fat is so little known to the general public in this country that unless you have a European butcher in your shopping area, you will have to order it. As caul fat will keep 2 months or more in the freezer, get several pieces while you are at it; each will average 30 inches square.

SALT AND SPICES

Seasoning is always an important part of sausage making and of *charcuterie* in general, since this is what gives the meat character, making your own brand different from any other. Furthermore, the salt and spices that enter into the preparation retard oxidation in the meat and are thus preservatives. French recipes often specify simply *épices, sel épicé,* or *quatre épices,* meaning use your own spice formula. The old standby, *quatre épices,* is a bottled mixture available everywhere in France; the four spices are usually pepper, clove, ginger or cinnamon, and nutmeg. *Sel épicé* is spiced salt that is usually 2 parts white pepper and 2 parts mixed spices for every 10 parts of salt.

You will find it useful to have your own spice mixture that you can keep at hand in a screw-top jar. Use it not only for sausages but for *pâtés,* meat loaf, as a marinade before cooking pork chops, and so forth. Here is a suggested formula: be sure all items are fresh-tasting and fragrant.

For 1 cup EPICES FINES

1 Tb each: bay, clove,
   mace, nutmeg, paprika,
   thyme
1½ tsp each: basil,
   cinnamon, marjoram or
   oregano, sage, savory
½ cup white peppercorns

If ingredients are not finely ground, either pulverize in an electric blender or a coffee grinder (finest grind), then pass through a fine-meshed sieve, and re-pulverize any residue.

*For each 6 cups (3 lbs.) of **meat mixture:** Suggested proportions of spice and salt*

1 level tsp (2 grams)
   épices fines
Plus other flavors such as
   more pepper, garlic,
   more of a specific herb,
   and so forth, depending
   on your taste and recipe
For fresh sausages, *pâté*
   mixtures, and stuffings:
   1 level Tb (½ ounce)
   table salt
For sausages that are to be
   air-dried 2 or more
   days: 1½ Tb table salt

NOTE: These proportions are what seem correct to us. Salts and spices vary in strength, and you may find you prefer a little more or a little less per pound.

PORK CUTS AND PORK FAT FOR SAUSAGES

Sausages, and *charcuterie* in general, are a byproduct of butchering. If you raise your own hogs and do your own butchering, you will have all the lean meat you need out of the trimmings from hams, loins, necks, and other large pieces. You will have, as well, the various types of fat, such as the hard fat from the back of the hog between the meat of the loin and the skin; this is the fatback, which is used not only for sausages and *pâtés* but also for larding roasts. You will have the leaf lard, almost impossible to find nowadays, which comes from inside the hog around the kidneys. You will have fat from the jowl, the neck, the belly, the hams, and the shoulders. Those of us not so fortunate have to buy retail cuts from the butcher or the supermarkets; our sausages will be a little more expensive to make, but they will be far better than anything we can buy because we will be using fresh meat of the best quality.

Unless your market goes in for foreign or regional cuts or you live in a pork-eating area, you may have only the loin to work with. However, you can buy a large piece from the shoulder end, bone it out, roast or sauté the lean pieces, and turn the rest into sausage.

Rather than the difficult-to-find fatback, you may use fat trimmed from the outside of a loin roast; it works well because it is neither too soft nor too hard. Fat trimmed from the outside of fresh hams and shoulders is less desirable because a little soft, but it is quite usable when you have no alternatives. If you have a fat-and-lean cut like boneless shoulder butt, make a guess at the proportion of fat to lean and add whichever is lacking according to your recipe requirements. One cup of meat or of fat is approximately ½ pound.

CHAIR À SAUCISSE

[Plain Pork Sausage Meat—for Sausage Cakes, Breakfast Sausages, Chipolatas, and as a Stuffing Ingredient for *Pâtés,* Poultry, and So Forth]

It is so easy to make your own sausage meat and it is so good that you will wonder, once you have made it, why you ever were so foolish as to buy it. Usual French proportions of fat to lean are one to one; you may cut it down to 1 part fat and 2 parts lean, particularly when you are using the retail pork cuts suggested here rather than trimmings; less fat than this will give you less tender sausages.

For 6 cups (3 lbs.) sausage-meat mixture

1) The sausage mixture

2 lbs. (4 cups) lean fresh pork meat such as fresh ham, shoulder, or loin
1 lb. (2 cups) fresh pork fat, such as fatback, fat trimmed from loin roast, or fresh leaf fat
A meat grinder
A heavy-duty mixer with flat beater blade, or large bowl and wooden spoon
1 Tb salt
1 tsp *épices fines* (page 288) or ½ tsp white pepper and ½ tsp pulverized mixed herbs and spices to your taste

Put meat and fat through finest blade of meat grinder; for a very smooth mixture, you may put it through the grinder again. If you have a heavy-duty mixer, beat thoroughly with the seasonings until very well blended. Otherwise, blend thoroughly with a wooden spoon and/or your hands, first dipping them in cold water. To test for flavor, sauté a small spoonful for several minutes until cooked through; taste, and add more seasoning if you feel it necessary; but remember that the spice flavor will not develop to its full in the meat for 12 hours or more.

2) *Forming and cooking*

Sausage Cakes or Sausage Roll. Either form into sausage cakes with a wet spatula on waxed paper, or with your hands, dipping them in cold water frequently; then, if you wish, wrap cakes in caul fat (page 287). Or form into a cylinder 2 inches in diameter in cheesecloth as illustrated at the beginning of this section and chill; then unwrap and cut into cakes. Sauté slowly in a frying pan until nicely browned and thoroughly cooked through.

Sausage Links and Chipolatas. For these you should have narrow sheep casings ⅝ inch in diameter, if you can get them. Breakfast links are usually 3 inches long; chipolatas, the tiny sausages used for cocktails and garnitures, 1½ to 2 inches. Form as illustrated at the beginning of this section. To cook, prick in several places with a pin and place in a frying pan with ½ inch of water, cover and cook at just below the simmer for 5 minutes or until sausages have stiffened slightly. Pour off water and sauté, turning frequently, until nicely browned.

BOUDIN BLANC
[White-meat Sausages—Chicken and Veal
or Chicken and Pork Forcemeat Stuffing]

White-meat sausages abound across the Atlantic, from the German and Swiss *bratwursts* and *weisswursts* to England's quaintly titled white puddings. It has even been suggested that the French *boudin* and the English pudding sprang from a single etymological root. The *boudin* is more like a *quenelle* than a sausage, delicate in flavor and texture. In France, where a truffled *boudin* is traditional at the midnight *Reveillon* of Christmas and New Year, mashed potatoes is the accompaniment. However, you may treat them like roast chicken or roast veal, adding green vegetables to the platter, such as creamed spinach, broccoli, peas, braised endive, or whatever else you feel appropriate.

For about 6 cups, making 10 to 12 boudins, 5 by 1¼ inches

---

1) *The sausage mixture*

the pork fat:

½ cup (4 ounces) fresh pork leaf fat, outside loin fat, or fatback
A meat grinder with finest blade
An 8-inch frying pan with cover

Put the pork fat through the grinder. Return half to top of grinder. Cook the rest in the frying pan over low heat for 4 to 5 minutes until it has rendered 2 to 3 tablespoons of fat but has not browned at all.

cooking the onions:

3 cups (¾ lb.) sliced onions

(If you wish a mild onion flavor, drop them into 2 quarts of boiling water and boil 4 minutes; drain, rinse in cold water, and thoroughly shake off excess water.) Add onions to pork fat and fat pieces in frying pan, cover and cook very slowly, stirring frequently, for 15 minutes or more; they should be perfectly tender and translucent, but no more than a pale cream in color.

la panade:

½ cup (1½ ounces pressed down) stale white crumbs from un-sweetened homemade-type bread
1 cup milk
A heavy-bottomed 2-quart saucepan
A wooden spoon
The large bowl of your electric mixer, or a 3-quart bowl

Meanwhile, bring the bread crumbs and milk to the boil and boil, stirring constantly with wooden spoon to prevent scorching, for several minutes until mixture is thick enough almost to hold its shape on the spoon. (This is now a *panade,* in the true and original sense of the word.)

the final mixture:

½ lb. (1 cup) skinless and boneless raw breast of chicken
½ lb. (1 cup) lean fresh veal or pork from shoulder or loin
2 tsp salt
⅛ tsp each: nutmeg, allspice, and white pepper
1 egg
⅓ cup egg whites (2–3 egg whites)
½ cup heavy cream
Optional: A 1-ounce truffle and juices from the can

When onions are tender, pass them with the remaining pork fat, the chicken, and the veal or pork through grinder twice. Place in mixing bowl, add seasonings, and beat vigorously in the electric mixer or by hand until well blended. Beat in the egg and continue beating for 1 minute, then beat in half the egg whites, and in another minute the remainder of the egg whites. Finally beat in the cream 2 tablespoons at a time, beating a minute between additions. If you are using a truffle, mince it into ⅛-inch pieces and beat it in along with juices from the can.

———————

To check seasoning, sauté a small spoonful until cooked through, taste, and add more if you feel it is necessary, but remember that the *boudin* is supposed to be rather delicate and mild in flavor.

2) *Forming the boudins*

Form either in small hog casings or in cheesecloth, as shown on pages 284–6. Sausages will improve in flavor if refrigerated at least 12 hours before cooking.

(*) STORAGE NOTES: May be refrigerated for 2 to 3 days, or may be frozen for a month or so.

3) *Preliminary cooking*

(If you have formed the *boudins* in sausage casing, prick them in several places with a pin.) Arrange *boudins* in a baking pan, roaster, or large frying pan at least 3 inches deep, and on a rack or grill if you have one that fits. Measure in enough quarts of boiling water or half-and-half boiling water and milk to cover *boudins* by 1½ inches. Add 1½ teaspoons salt for each quart of liquid, and lay 2 imported bay leaves on top. Bring liquid barely to the simmer and poach uncovered at just below the simmer for 25 minutes. Remove from liquid and cool on several thicknesses of paper towels. If you have used cheesecloth casings, cut off the two ends with scissors and peel the sausages while still warm. (Sausage-casing *boudins* are peeled just before final cooking.)

(*) AHEAD-OF-TIME NOTE: If the *boudins* are not to have their final cooking promptly, wrap and refrigerate when cool. They will keep 3 to 4 days in the refrigerator, a month or so in the freezer.

4) *Final cooking and serving*

Of the several cooking methods available, oven baking is not recommended because it toughens the outside of the *boudins* before they have had time to brown. Dredging in flour and browning slowly in a frying pan in clarified butter or rendered pork fat is preferable, but the best method, we think, is under the broiler as follows: Roll the peeled *boudins* in fresh white bread crumbs, pressing the crumbs in place with your fingers. Arrange in a buttered baking dish and dribble on droplets of melted butter. Broil slowly, turning and basting with fat in pan several times, for 10 to 12 minutes, until *boudins* are nicely browned. Arrange on a hot platter, over a bed of hot mashed potatoes if you wish, and decorate with sprigs of parsley or watercress. Serve as soon as possible.

✳ *SAUCISSON À CUIRE*—*Saucisson de Ménage, Saucisson de Toulouse, Saucisson à l'Ail, Saucisson Truffé, Cervelas de Paris*

[Large Fresh Sausages to Cook and Serve with Potatoes, Sauerkraut, *Cassoulet,* or to Bake in *Brioche* or Pastry Dough]

The following formula produces a fine substitute for those marvelous creations you read about but cannot find except in a French *charcuterie.* This recipe is for the home sausage maker, and requires no special equipment; for that reason you cannot call your product a *saucisson de Lyon,* which is hung

for 8 days in a drying shed, or a *saucisson de Morteau,* which finishes in a
smokehouse. Any of the names in the title, however, will do, and any Frenchman you invite for a meal will think you brought it back from the old country.

The sausages will develop their best flavor when you are able to hang
them in a dry, airy part of the room at a temperature of 70 to 80 degrees for
2 to 3 days before cooking. If the weather is very damp, or much over 80
degrees, however, omit the hanging; several days in the refrigerator instead
will help develop flavor. The saltpeter (potassium nitrate), which you should
be able to buy at any prescription counter, is omitted if you are not hanging
the sausages; its role is to give the meat an appetizing, rosy color that only
develops after several days of hanging. Use the coarse or the fine blade of your
meat grinder, whichever you prefer, but the coarse grind is more typical of a
sausage that is to be hung.

French sausages of this type are not madly spiced and peppered, like
some of the Spanish and Italian varieties. We have suggested 3 special flavorings, and you will eventually develop the proportions or other additions that
will make your own sausage *le saucisson de chez nous.*

For 6 cups (3 pounds) sausage-meat mixture, making 10 to 12
sausages 5 by 1¼ inches, or 2 sausages 12 by 2 inches

---

1) *The sausage mixture*

4 cups (2 lbs.) lean fresh
   pork such as fresh ham,
   shoulder, or loin
2 cups (1 lb.) fresh pork
   fat such as fatback, fat
   trimmed from a loin
   roast, fresh leaf fat
Either 1 tsp *épices fines*
   (page 288) plus ¼ tsp
   white pepper;
Or ¾ tsp white pepper and
   ½ tsp pulverized herbs
   and spices of your choice
1 Tb salt
¼ cup Cognac

Put meat and fat through grinder. With either a
heavy-duty mixer and flat beater, or your hands and/
or a wooden spoon, mix in the rest of the ingredients
to blend vigorously and completely. Sauté a small
spoonful to cook through thoroughly, taste, and correct seasoning, if necessary.

if you are to hang the sausage:

¼ tsp saltpeter, ¾ tsp
   sugar, and 1½ tsp more
   salt

special flavorings:

Either 1) A 1- to 2-ounce
   can of truffles and the
   juice from the can;
Or 2) ¼ cup chopped pistachios and 1 small clove
   mashed garlic;
Or 3) 2 or 3 medium cloves
   mashed garlic and ½ tsp
   cracked peppercorns

————————————

2) *Forming and curing the sausages*

Form the sausages either in casings or in cheesecloth as illustrated at the beginning of this chapter. If you are forming a 12- by 2-inch sausage in cheesecloth, wind
a spiral of string around the length to keep it in shape; if you are hanging cheese-
cloth-wrapped sausages, paint again with melted lard after forming and tying. Hang
sausages up on a nail or hook, in the dry airy part of your kitchen where the temperature is generally around 70 degrees and rarely over 80. After 2 to 3 days, they
are ready for cooking.

(*) STORAGE NOTE: After curing, sausages may be wrapped securely and refrigerated for a week, or frozen for a month.

3) *Cooking and serving suggestions*

Saucissons à cuire need 30 to 40 minutes of slow cooking in liquid, and if you
have formed them in casings, prick them in several places with a pin so that the fat
will run out. When you are braising sauerkraut or cabbage, doing a bean or lentil
dish or a *pot au feu,* add the sausages to the dish 30 to 40 minutes before the end of
the cooking period. When you wish to serve them separately, as with French potato
salad, or baked in *brioche* or pastry dough, poach them at just below the simmer
for 30 to 40 minutes in a wine-flavored beef bouillon, selecting a container, such as
a bread pan or casserole, that will just hold them easily. There is no need to brown
them afterwards, but if you wish a more elegant presentation for sausages formed
in cheesecloth, roll them in fresh bread crumbs, dribble on melted butter, and brown
them under the broiler.

————————————

Other suggestions

You can make delicious fresh sausages out of the all-purpose pork and veal *pâté*
mixture in Volume I on page 565, plus, if you wish, diced ham, diced marinated
bits of veal or game, or diced and briefly sautéed liver, as suggested in the *pâté*
mixtures following it. You may also adapt any of the *pâté* mixtures in the next
section of this chapter. Form and cook the sausages as described in the preceding
recipe; this type of sausage, and the chicken-liver sausage in the next recipe, are
particularly good when baked in *brioche* or pastry dough.

SAUCISSON TRUFFÉ AU FOIE GRAS OU AUX FOIES DE VOLAILLE

[Pork and Veal Sausages with Truffles and *Foie Gras* or with Chicken Livers—Especially for Baking in *Brioche* or Pastry Dough, or as a Stuffing for *Pâtés,* Poultry, *Chaussons*]

For about 4½ cups, making two 12 by 1½-inch sausages

---

2 Tb pork fat, chicken fat, or butter
¼ cup minced shallots or scallions
Either ¾ lb. (1½ cups) chicken livers;
Or a mixture of chicken livers and block canned *foie gras,* half-and-half if you wish to pay the price (*foie gras* is used in next step)

Heat the fat or butter in an 8-inch frying pan, add the shallots or scallions and the chicken livers (not the *foie gras*); toss over moderately high heat for several minutes until liver has just stiffened to the touch; it should feel springy, but remain rosy inside. If you are using chicken liver only, cut half into ¼-inch dice and place in a bowl.

The diced liver or the *foie gras*
2 Tb Cognac
Pinch *épices fines,* page 288, or allspice
Salt and pepper

If you are using *foie gras,* cut into ¼-inch dice and place in a bowl. Fold *foie gras* or liver gently with the Cognac and flavorings and let marinate until needed.

¼ cup (¾ ounce pressed down) stale white crumbs from unsweetened home-made-type bread
½ cup milk

Simmer bread crumbs in milk, stirring constantly, for several minutes until thick enough to mass on a spoon. Scrape into large bowl of mixer, or a large mixing bowl. (This is a *panade.*)

½ lb. (1 cup) lean veal
Either 1 lb. (2 cups) *chair à saucisses,* page 289;
Or ½ lb. lean pork loin, shoulder, or fresh ham and ½ lb. fresh pork fatback or outside loin fat
The sautéed undiced chicken livers

Put meats, fat, and chicken livers through finest blade of meat grinder and add to mixing bowl.

The marinade from the
diced *foie gras* or
chicken livers
2 tsp salt
Either ¾ tsp *épices fines*
and ¼ tsp white pepper;
Or ½ tsp white pepper
and big pinches each
allspice and nutmeg
¼ tsp thyme
Either ¼ cup peeled
pistachio nuts, quartered
lengthwise;
Or 1 or 2 diced truffles
and their canned juices
1 egg
¼ cup dry port wine or
Sercial Madeira
The marinated *foie gras*
or diced chicken livers

Beat in the marinade, salt, flavorings, pistachios or truffles and juice, and egg. When well blended, gradually beat in the wine. Finally, fold in the diced *foie gras* or chicken livers, being careful not to break the diced shapes. Mixture will be fairly soft. Sauté a spoonful and taste; correct seasoning as necessary. Form into sausages using either casings or cheesecloth as described on pages 282–6. (If you are using the mixture for a filling or stuffing that is to be baked later, pack into a covered bowl.) Flavor will improve when refrigerated a day or two before cooking.

Cook and serve sausages as suggested in preceding Master Recipe, or bake in *brioche* dough as in the following recipe.

(*) STORAGE NOTE: Sausages may be frozen for a month or so.

SAUCISSON DE FOIES DE VOLAILLE
PÂTÉ DE FOIES DE VOLAILLE
FARCE À GRATIN

[Chicken-liver Sausage for Baking in *Brioche* Dough—
Chicken-liver *Pâté*—Chicken-liver Spread or Filling]

This all-purpose liver mixture is so versatile it can serve as a sausage, a *pâté*, a spread for sandwiches and hors d'oeuvre, a filling for poultry or meat, and can generally be used anywhere you need the depth and strength of a liver accent. Liver alone is such a concentrated flavor that you must have something else with it to temper the taste: the sausage uses cream cheese and bread crumbs, while the *pâté* includes cheese and butter, and the filling, *farce à gratin,* calls for the traditional pork fat. Two other liver *pâtés* or spreads are the pork-liver *pâté* on page 320 and the mousse of chicken livers in Volume I, page 559.

For about 2 cups

The basic chicken-liver mixture

⅓ cup very finely minced
  onions
3 Tb chicken fat or butter
¾ lb. (1½ cups) chicken
  livers
Either ¼ tsp *épices fines*,
  page 288;
Or a big pinch each of
  allspice, mace, and white
  pepper
A big pinch thyme
¼ tsp salt
⅓ cup Cognac
Optional: ½ cup diced fresh
  mushrooms, squeezed
  dry and sautéed in 1 Tb
  butter

Cook the onions slowly in the fat or butter for 12 to 15 minutes, until very tender but not brown. Add livers and seasonings, and toss over moderately high heat just until stiffened slightly, 2 to 3 minutes; livers should remain rosy inside. Pour in the Cognac, heat to bubbling, and flame with a lighted match; in 1 minute, extinguish flames with a cover and remove pan from heat. Stir in optional mushrooms. The liver mixture is now ready to be used either in *brioche* dough or in another form as follows.

For sausage in brioche, page 299

½ cup (1 ounce pressed
  down) dry white crumbs
  from unsweetened home-
  made-type bread
4 ounces (½ cup) cream
  cheese
The basic chicken-liver
  mixture

Stir the bread crumbs and cheese into the liver mixture, and purée through a food mill, meat grinder, or blender. Correct seasoning. Roll into a cylindrical shape in aluminum foil and chill until firm; however, bring to room temperature before encasing it in the dough so that dough will rise easily.

For liver spread or pâté

The basic chicken-liver
  mixture
4 ounces (½ cup) softened
  butter
4 ounces (½ cup) cream
  cheese

Purée liver mixture through a food mill, meat grinder, or blender, then beat in softened butter and cream cheese. Correct seasoning. If you plan to use this as a *pâté*, pack into a covered jar or mold, and chill.

For farce à gratin—to use as a spread, filling, or pâté

The basic chicken-liver
  mixture but substitute:
6 ounces (¾ cup) fresh
  pork fatback or outside
  loin fat for the butter

Rather than using butter for cooking the onions and chicken livers, use the ¾ cup pork fat as follows: grind or mince it, and cook slowly for 8 to 10 minutes in the sauté pan until pieces of fat are translucent but not browned, and ⅓ cup or so of fat has rendered.

Then proceed with the recipe. Purée in a blender, food mill, or meat grinder, pack into a jar or decorative bowl, and chill.

(*) STORAGE NOTE: Any of these will keep for 4 to 5 days in the refrigerator, and they freeze successfully for several months.

SAUSAGES AND OTHER MEAT MIXTURES BAKED IN *BRIOCHE* DOUGH
Saucissons et Pâtés en Brioche

When you want to be dramatic and dressy with sausage, bake it in a *brioche* case. For cocktails, slice it warm and thin and serve on little plates. When it is a hot first course or the mainstay for luncheon or supper, include a succulent brown sauce to pour over each serving. Although reminiscent of *pâté en croûte,* sausage in *brioche* is usually served warm, and is lighter in general impression. Unlike the real *pâté,* which goes raw into its covering of dough for baking, the sausage or meat mixture that is enclosed in *brioche* dough has already been cooked, and remains in the oven only long enough to heat through as the *brioche* bakes.

FORMING NOTE

The rectangular loaf shape that encloses a large cylindrical sausage is the most typical form, and the one we shall illustrate. With your own sausage or cooked meat mixture, however, you may make it round, square, heart-shaped, or whatever you wish.

Because you are working with live dough, that is, yeast dough, you may run into one problem that does not occur with pastry dough: this is a sometimes ugly space between the meat and the *brioche* that only reveals itself when you are slicing through the structure to serve.

It is particularly true of home-cured or store-bought sausages, less true of soft mixtures like chicken livers, and more liable to be troublesome with sausages baked in a pan (as on page 302) than with those formed on a pastry sheet (page 301). One way to minimize the gap or eliminate it completely is to be sure that the sausage is very hot at the moment you enclose it in the dough. Heat kills the yeast in a thin layer of dough, about ⅛ inch, all around the sausage, and this layer should cling to the sausage while the rest of the dough rises around it. Another way to close the gap is to bake the sausage in a closed pan, as suggested in a variation at the end of the Master Recipe. We are only giving prominence to this problem so that you will be aware of it and pleased with yourself when you have avoided it but not unduly disturbed when you have not. In such instances, however, when you want to serve a cold liver *pâté en brioche,* you will welcome the gap because you can siphon a deliciously flavored aspic into that space between meat and *brioche,* which will add immensely to the taste and appearance of the *pâté* slices when you serve them.

With your *brioche* dough made the day before, and your sausage or meat mixture ready for pre-cooking, you should count on 2½ to 3½ hours from the time you start the process until the time you can serve. You will need 40 minutes for poaching, if you are using a sausage, an hour for the dough-with-sausage to rise before baking, an hour for baking, and 20 to 30 minutes for meat and *brioche* to settle before slicing. Remember that you can control the rising of dough (page 68), and you can keep the baked result warm; thus you may arrange your schedule as you wish.

✳ *SAUCISSON EN BRIOCHE*

[Sausage Baked in *Brioche* Dough]

This is for a large sausage about 12 inches long and 1½ to 2 inches in diameter, such as the *saucisson à cuire* on page 292 and the liver or *foie gras* sausage following it, or for a store-bought sausage that is to be cooked and served hot, like a Polish sausage (*kielbasa*) or Italian *cotechino*. You may also use the cooked chicken-liver sausage mixture on page 296; in this case, omit Step 2 in the following recipe.

*For a 12-inch case, serving 6 as a hot first course, 4 as
a main course, or 18 slices for a cocktail appetizer*

---

1) *The brioche dough—started the day before you plan to serve*

Either the *pain brioché*
  dough on page 83;
Or the richer *pâte à
  brioche fine* on page 85
  (proportions for ½ lb.
  flour in either case)

Make the *brioche* dough, giving it one rise at room
temperature and a second rise that finishes in the refrigerator. Dough must be well chilled before you
form it in Step 3.

---

2) *Poaching the sausage—about 40 minutes; omit this step if you are
using the already cooked chicken-liver sausage mixture*

The sausage (see intro-
  ductory paragraph)
A loaf pan just large
  enough to hold the
  sausage (loaf shape
  recommended)
½ cup dry white wine or
  dry white French ver-
  mouth
3 or more cups beef bouillon simmering in a
  saucepan
1 imported bay leaf
Salt and pepper
Useful: a meat thermome-
  ter

Prick the sausage in several places with a pin and
place in pan. Pour in the wine and enough simmering
bouillon to cover sausage by 1 inch. Add seasonings
and bring liquid to just below the simmer (water is
shivering and almost bubbling). Cover loosely and
maintain liquid at this state for 40 minutes. Remove
sausage, peel off casing, and return to liquid until you
are ready to proceed to Step 3. Sausage should be hot
(around 165 degrees) for next step; reheat if necessary.

---

3) *Achieving the free-form brioche shape*

The chilled dough
The hot, cooked, and
  peeled sausage (or room-
  temperature chicken-
  liver sausage)
A large pastry sheet or
  tray 16 by 24 inches,
  covered with lightly
  floured waxed paper
A lightly buttered pastry
  sheet at least 12 by 16
  inches in diameter

Rapidly roll the chilled *brioche* dough into a rectangle
approximately 24 by 10 inches. With a pastry wheel
or knife, cut off a 4- by 10-inch strip and refrigerate
it. Roll remaining dough up on your pin and unroll
it onto the waxed-paper-covered sheet or tray.

Center sausage on dough and quickly fold the two sides up over it; they should overlap by about 2 inches.

waxed paper over tray

Working rapidly, fold over the 2 ends of the dough to enclose the sausage completely. Then to prevent sausage from breaking through dough, turn the buttered pastry sheet upside down on top of it, and reverse the two so that sausage will unmold itself seam-side down on the buttered sheet.

Brush off any flour on top of dough. Roll out reserved and refrigerated strip to about 15 by 4 inches in diameter; *roll up on pin and then unroll over sausage.*

Trim off excess dough from 2 ends, and press dough cover in place lightly with fingers. Set uncovered at a temperature of no more than 75 to 80 degrees. Let dough rise until it feels light and spongy-springy when touched—40 to 60 minutes. (Preheat oven in time for next step.)

4) Baking—about 1 hour; oven preheated to 425 degrees

1 egg beaten with 1 tsp
   water in a small bowl
A pastry brush
Scissors
A cooling rack

Just before baking, paint top of dough with egg glaze; let set a moment, and paint again.

Clip top of dough with scissors,
going in at a slant about ⅜ inch
deep and 2 inches across.

Set in middle level of preheated 425-degree oven and bake for 20 minutes, or until *brioche* has risen about double its height and begun to brown. Turn oven down to 350 degrees for 30–40 minutes more. It is done when you can begin to smell the sausage cooking, and when the *brioche* itself feels solid and makes a rather dry thumping noise when tapped. (Cover lightly with foil or brown paper if it is coloring too much before it is done.) Slide off pastry sheet onto rack, and let cool 20 to 30 minutes before serving.

5) *Serving suggestions*

Serve the sausage hot, warm, tepid, or cold (although a sausage is usually better warm or tepid than cold). When serving it hot as a first or main course, you can make a delicious brown sauce with the sausage-poaching liquid, using any of the suggestions in Volume I, pages 73–6.

(*) AHEAD-OF-TIME NOTES: You may keep the sausage warm for an hour or more in a 120-degree oven. If for some reason you cannot serve it when baked, let cool, then wrap airtight; reheat uncovered on a lightly buttered pastry sheet in a 400-degree oven for 20 minutes or so.

VARIATIONS

Forming the sausage in a loaf pan

For a 12- by 2-inch sausage you will need the long, rectangular 2-quart pan called an angel loaf, about 12 by 3¼ inches bottom diameter and 2½ inches deep. Follow Steps 1 and 2 in the Master Recipe, butter the inside of the loaf pan, then wrap the hot sausage in the dough on a paper-covered pastry sheet or tray as illustrated.

Turn a buttered 12-inch loaf pan
upside down over the sausage.
Reverse tray with sausage onto pan,
unmolding sausage seam-side
down into pan.

waxed paper

Brush off any flour from top of dough, and *unroll reserved dough strip over sausage.*

Press dough cover into place with fingers, pushing it lightly down against top, sides, and ends of sausage.

Let rise at a temperature of no more than 75 to 80 degrees for 40 to 60 minutes, until dough is light and springy; it will fill the pan by about three quarters. Glaze, clip top with scissors, and bake as described in preceding Master Recipe.

Baking in a covered pan

When you want to be sure there is no gap between meat and *brioche,* follow the preceding recipe, but rather than glazing and clipping the top of the dough when it has risen, cover the pan as described and illustrated for *pain de mie,* page 81. This works because the risen dough fills the pan only by three fourths; then, while it bakes, the dough will not only fill the covered pan completely, but will also press itself against the sausage meat. You may use any shape of pan you wish, including a fluted *brioche* tin. The imported hinged cylindrical mold shown in the illustration can easily be adapted for sausage in *brioche.*

Cold Pâté en Brioche with Aspic

Sausages, to our mind, are at their best when served hot or warm in *brioche* dough, while liver mixtures are delicious cold. We suggest the chicken-liver mixture on page 296, or the cooked pork and liver *pâté* with onions on page 322. Follow any of the preceding methods you wish; when the meat is fully encased and ready to rise, make a hole in the top of the dough and insert a well-oiled cone of foil or the tube from a pastry bag, letting its end touch the meat. After rising and baking, and when completely cold, pour in through the cone as much almost-set wine-flavored meat-jelly aspic as the case will hold. (See illustrated directions in the *pâté en croûte* section, page 332.) Then remove cone, wrap *pâté* airtight, and chill several hours or overnight. *Pâté* should be eaten within 4 to 5 days.

Saucisson en Croûte

[Sausage Baked in Plain Pastry or in Puff Pastry]

Equally delicious, though naturally different in texture, is any one of the suggested sausages poached in bouillon, peeled, and baked in plain pie crust dough or in that wonderfully high-rising flaky dough known as French puff pastry. Use the *pâte brisée à l'oeuf,* page 104, or the *demi-feuilletée* on page 113. Form the dough around the sausage as described in the free-form system, Master Recipe, page 299. Paint top with beaten egg, press on decorative pastry cutouts, and bake exactly as described in the Master Recipe. (Illustrated directions for decorating this type of pastry are in Volume I, pages 574-5.)

* CAILLETTES—GAYETTES

[Pork and Liver Sausages with Greens]

These hearty green and brown sausages are made in the countryside where hogs are slaughtered, and the farmer uses every edible morsel for some specialty. His recipe usually includes lungs and spleen as well as the heart and liver we have specified, and, if he lives in Provence, he puts in plenty of garlic. Swiss chard (*blettes*) is the preferred green, but because it is not always to be had in this country, we have suggested kale or collards (*chou vert non-pommé*) and spinach as substitutes. Traditionally the sausages are formed into cushion or dumpling shapes 2 to 3 inches in diameter, wrapped in caul fat, and baked in a big pottery dish. You may also form them like regular sausages, like sausage cakes, or turn the whole mixture into a meat loaf. (NOTE: flavor will improve if you can make the mixture a day before cooking.)

Serve with mashed or scalloped potatoes and broiled tomatoes, or an eggplant and tomato casserole such as that on page 356, or the *ratatouille* in Volume I, page 503, or simply a green salad and French bread. A rosé wine or a domestic red would go nicely.

For 6 cups of sausage mixture, making a dozen sausages

1) *The greens*

1 cup minced onions
2 Tb pork fat or olive oil
A heavy-bottomed sauce-
pan with cover
Either **1½ to 2 pounds**
fresh Swiss chard, kale,
collards, or spinach;

Cook onions and oil in covered pan over moderate heat, stirring occasionally, for 10 minutes or so, until tender and translucent. Meanwhile, pick over fresh greens, wash thoroughly, and if you have chard use both the green leaves and the white stems; drop into boiling water and boil uncovered until wilted and just edibly tender—1 minute for spinach, 5 or more for

Or 1½ packages frozen
greens defrosted in a
basin of cold water
A large kettle of boiling
salted water
The large bowl of an
electric mixer, or 3-quart
mixing bowl

other greens. Drain immediately, refresh in cold water,
and drain again. (Fresh and defrosted greens may
now be treated alike.) A smallish handful at a time,
squeeze to extract as much water as possible; chop
roughly with a big knife. You should have about
1½ cups. Stir into the onions, raise heat, and stir for
several minutes to evaporate excess moisture. Scrape
into mixing bowl.

2) *The sausage mixture*

Either 1½ lbs. (3 cups)
fat-and-lean fresh pork
shoulder butt;
Or ¾ lb. lean pork from
fresh ham or loin, and
¾ lb. fresh pork fatback
or fat trimmed from
outside loin
Either ½ lb. (1 cup) fresh
liver (pork, lamb, or beef)
and ¼ lb. (½ cup)
heart (pork, lamb, or
calf);
Or liver only
1 Tb salt
Either ¾ tsp *épices fines,*
page 288, ¼ tsp pepper
and ¼ tsp savory;
Or ⅛ tsp allspice, ⅛ tsp
mace, ⅛ tsp bay leaf, ¼
tsp savory, and ½ tsp
pepper
Optional: 1 or more cloves
of garlic, finely minced
or mashed

Put meat, fat, and liver once through the coarsest
blade of the meat grinder, or chop by hand into ¼-
inch pieces. Add to bowl along with the seasonings,
and mix thoroughly by electricity or by hand. Sauté
a small spoonful until thoroughly cooked, taste, and
correct seasoning if necessary. (Whether you form the
sausages now or later, their flavor will improve if you
wait 24 hours before cooking.)

(*) STORAGE NOTE: May be refrigerated for 2 to 3
days; may be frozen for a month or two.

3) *Forming and cooking*

Caul fat. Form sausage mixture into a dozen balls or cylindrical shapes, wrap
in caul fat (page 287), arrange in one layer in a greased baking dish, and baste with
melted lard or butter. Bake for 40 to 45 minutes in the upper third of a preheated
375-degree oven until nicely browned.

Sausage casings. Form in sausage casings (page 282), prick in several places
with a pin, and either bake as described in preceding paragraph or poach in almost
simmering water for 5 minutes, then brown in a frying pan.

Sausage cakes. Form into sausage cakes with dampened hands. Just before cooking, dredge lightly in flour; sauté slowly in lard or cooking oil for 6 to 8 minutes on each side until nicely browned.

Meat loaf. (This is particularly recommended when you want something to serve cold.) Either grease a 6-cup loaf pan or baking dish and pack the sausage mixture into it; or form the mixture into a loaf shape, wrap in caul fat, and place on a greased baking dish. Bake in upper third of a preheated 375-degree oven, basting several times with melted fat for an hour or more, or until juices, when meat is pricked deeply, run clear yellow with no trace of rosy color (180 to 185 dgrees on a meat thermometer).

VARIATION

Les Tous Nus—Quenelles de Boeuf Provençales

[Provençal Sausages of Leftover Braised Beef and Greens]

The naked ones, *les tous nus,* are sausages without casings, and a Provençal specialty. These are formed by hand, rolled in flour, and dropped for a moment in boiling water before they are baked in a shallow dish with a spicy tomato sauce. They are so fragrant and appetizing that you will find yourself braising beef just as an excuse for making *les tous nus* with the leftovers.

For about 4 cups, serving 4 to 6 people

---

1) *The sausage mixture*

1 cup blanched and squeezed greens
¼ cup minced onions cooked with 2 Tb olive oil
2 cups ground cooked beef, preferably braised
Optional, to flavor boiled or roast beef: ¼ cup raw sausage meat and 1 Tb Cognac
1 tsp salt
Either ¼ tsp *épices fines;*
Or allspice and mace
¼ tsp savory or oregano
¼ tsp pepper
Big pinch of Cayenne or drops of Tabasco

(If you have chard, use green leaves only.) Blanch, squeeze, and chop the greens as described in Step 1 of the preceding recipe, and cook with the onions 2 to 3 minutes until all liquid has evaporated; greens must be as dry as possible. Blend them in a large mixing bowl with the beef, seasonings, and cheese. Beat in 3 tablespoons of egg; beat in driblets more egg, moistening only enough so that mixture will hold its shape for forming. Sauté a spoonful and taste; correct seasoning as necessary.

2 large cloves of garlic,
  minced or puréed
⅓ cup grated Parmesan
  cheese
¼ to ⅓ cup beaten egg
  (1 to 2 eggs)

2) Forming the sausages

1 cup flour on a large tray
A large frying pan full of
  boiling water
A skimmer
A rack, or paper towels
  on a tray
1 or 2 shallow, greased
  baking dishes
2 to 3 cups good tomato
  sauce, page 354, or Volume I, pages 76 or 78
¼ cup grated Parmesan
  cheese
1 to 2 Tb olive oil

Take up a 3-Tb gob of the mixture and roll into a
sausage shape ¾ inch in diameter; roll in flour and set
aside. When all the sausages are formed, drop half
into the boiling water, bring back to the simmer for
½ minute. Dip out onto rack and continue with the
rest. Arrange closely together in baking dish or dishes.
Pour over the tomato sauce, which should barely
cover them. Sprinkle on the cheese and dribble the oil
over it.

(*) AHEAD-OF-TIME NOTE: May be completed a day in
advance to this point.

3) Cooking the sausages—oven preheated to 425 degrees

About 30 minutes before serving, bring to simmer on top of stove, then set
in upper third of oven until sauce has browned and crusted lightly on upper part of
sausages, and is bubbling underneath.

Variations

Like the *caillette* mixture in the Master Recipe, Step 3, the *tous nus* mixture
may also be formed in caul fat or sausage casings, or may become sausage cakes or
meat loaf.

JAMBON PERSILLÉ
AND HOME-CURED PORK

Jambon persillé is the traditional Easter ham of Burgundy. Simmered in
wine, then cut up or shredded and packed into a big bowl between layers of
chopped parsley, aspic, and seasonings, each slice when served is beautifully
patterned with wavy lines of bright green. It is a marvelous dish for cold
lunches, supper parties, and receptions. The real Burgundian recipe is made
with salt-cured ham, known in France as *jambon demi-sel;* this is the same

process used in America for the dry-curing of salt pork. Although you may certainly use regular ham for the dish, the salt cure is so easy—all you need is 2 weeks of refrigerator space for the large bowl that holds the meat—we highly recommend that you try it. It is not only that you will have the authentic meat for *jambon persillé,* but also that you can cure a loin of pork for chops or roasting, since salted pork makes a delicious change from ordinary pork and is broiled or roasted in exactly the same way. At the same time, if you can find any hog jowls or bellies, you can also make your own salt pork.

SALAISON À SEC
[Home Dry-curing of Pork]

The object of curing pork is not only to preserve it but to give it that special maturity of taste that only comes through salting. For our purposes here, we are more concerned with taste than with preservation. There is no need for brines, vats, and smokehouses, only for saltpeter, sugar, spices, and salt. Saltpeter imparts an attractive rosy color to the meat, sugar develops its flavor and counteracts the drying effects of saltpeter, spices play their habitual role, and salt preserves the meat while it matures. The following 15-day cure is for the boned fresh ham or shoulder that may be used for *jambon persillé,* and for loin roasts and salt-pork cuts; these are all pieces, in other words, that are no thicker than 4 to 5 inches.

TEMPERATURE FOR CURING

Curing should take place at around 38 degrees Fahrenheit, which is the range of most refrigerators. At temperatures over 40 degrees, the meat may spoil before the salt can penetrate, and at below 36 degrees the salt penetration is too much slowed down.

THE MEAT AND ITS PREPARATION FOR THE CURE

For *jambon persillé* you may use either fresh ham (leg of pork) or fresh shoulder-arm; shoulder is usually cheaper and weighs around 6½ pounds, or half as much as a ham. Many markets do not carry either of these fresh pork cuts, and you will have to order them. Before curing, remove the rind, which is to be cured and cooked along with the meat, and slice off as much fat from rind and outside of meat as you easily can; bone the meat as neatly as possible so that you do not end up with any more small pieces of meat than necessary. Render the fat, if you wish (page 316), and use it for general cooking. Simmer the bones with vegetables and herbs as for an ordinary meat stock, and store in the freezer until it is finally time to cook the meat. If you want to add a loin roast of pork to the cure, bone it or not, as you choose, and slice off all but a ⅛-inch layer of covering fat. Pork jowls, belly, and fatback are cut into whatever sizes you find convenient, and are cured as is, with the rind left on.

Note on meat-to-bone ratios

The amount of usable meat you will get from a bone-in fresh ham or shoulder-arm is roughly 60 per cent. In other words, a 6½-pound shoulder-arm will yield approximately 4½ pounds of meat, which, when cooked and trimmed, usually amounts to 6 cups.

Dry-salt cure for 10 pounds of pork

10 lbs. fresh pork prepared as described in preceding paragraph (include rind if making *jambon persillé*)

A glazed or enameled bowl or casserole large enough to hold meat closely packed

1½ cups salt (sea salt, coarse salt, or table salt)

¼ cup sugar

1 tsp saltpeter (potassium nitrate from a pharmacy)

1½ tsp crushed juniper berries

Either 1½ tsp *épices fines*, page 288;

Or ¾ tsp white pepper, ¼ tsp allspice, and ¼ tsp each: pulverized thyme and bay leaf

A bowl to mix salt and spices in

A large tray to salt meat on

Plastic wrap, a large plate, and a 7- to 10-pound weight, meat grinder, brick, stone, or other heavy object

Prepare the pork as described and be sure curing bowl is the right size. Stir the salt and other ingredients thoroughly in the small bowl and divide in two, reserving ½ for later salting. Starting with the largest pieces of meat, rub salt thoroughly into all sides, corners, and crevices. Pat a ⅟₁₆-inch layer over meat and pack into bowl. Continue with the smaller pieces and end with the rind, if you are using it, placing it fat side down over the meat. Cover meat with plastic wrap, plate, and weights. Refrigerate (or place in cold-room) at 36 to 40 degrees for 5 days. Then remove meat, leaving accumulated brine in bowl, resalt with reserved mixture, and return to bowl with plastic, plate, and weight on top. Refrigerate for 10 days more, turning meat once or twice to be sure everything is well salted; meat is then ready to use.

(*) STORAGE NOTE: Meat may remain in cure for 6 to 8 weeks in all, but be sure all pieces are well covered with salt.

COOKING NOTE: Salted meat must be de-salted before cooking—soak in several changes of cold water overnight if cured 15 days, 24 hours if cured several weeks.

* *JAMBON PERSILLÉ*
[Mold of Parslied Ham in Aspic]

As described in the introduction to this section, *jambon persillé* is a Burgundian creation. Inevitably when dealing with well-known regional specialties, there are dozens of variations and minor versions, and always hundreds of very definite opinions on how to conduct each step. Among the considerable number of serious and trustworthy formulas we have studied, this is the one we prefer.

A NOTE ON STORE-BOUGHT HAM

If you are not using home-cured ham, buy 6½ to 8 pounds of bone-in, ready-to-bake, mild-cured smoked ham or picnic shoulder. Omit Step 1, proceeding directly to the simmering in Step 2; skin and bone the ham after cooking.

For 2½ to 3 quarts of ham, serving 12 to 16

1) *Soaking the ham—12 to 24 hours*

4 to 6 pounds of boned, home-salted fresh ham or shoulder-arm, and the salted ham rind (preceding recipe; or see preceding note)

Soak the ham and the rind in a large basin of cold water, changing water 2 to 3 times. Overnight is enough for ham cured about 15 days; soak for 18 to 24 hours if ham has cured longer. (Soaking removes the preserving salt, not the flavor.)

2) *Simmering the ham*

A kettle just large enough to hold ham comfortably
Either 1 bottle best quality, young, strong, dry white wine (Côtes du Rhône or Pinot Blanc);
Or 3 cups dry white French vermouth
3 cups bouillon (made from fresh ham bones, or a mixture of beef and chicken bouillon)
Necessary water
1 tsp thyme, 2 Tb tarragon, 4 allspice berries, 2 imported bay leaves, and

Place soaked ham (and rind) in kettle, add wine, bouillon, and enough water to cover by an inch. Add rest of ingredients listed, bring to the simmer, and skim for several minutes until scum ceases to rise. Cover partially and maintain at the simmer until ham is tender when pierced with a sharp knife (about 2 hours for boned, home-cured ham). Let ham cool in liquid an hour or two.

2 large cloves of garlic
tied in washed cheese-
cloth
1 large onion, roughly
chopped
1 medium carrot, roughly
chopped
1 celery stalk

While still warm, remove rind from kettle (or from bone-in ham), scrape off and discard as much fat as possible, and purée rind through coarse disk of food mill or fine blade of meat grinder; reserve in a 1-quart bowl. Tear ham apart with your fingers, discarding fat and gristle. Cut ham into pieces about ½ inch thick and 1½ to 2 inches square, and place in a 2-quart bowl along with any meat scraps. Moisten with a tablespoon or so of cooking stock, and set aside. Thoroughly degrease cooking stock, boil down rapidly to concentrate flavor if necessary, and correct seasoning.

---

3) *The aspic—for about 4 cups*

5 cups thoroughly de-
greased ham-cooking
stock in a saucepan
2 to 3 egg whites (½ cup)
Optional for added flavor:
½ to 1 cup minced
green tops from leeks or
scallions
2 packages (2 Tb)
powdered unflavored
gelatin

Following directions in Volume I, pages 111–13, clarify the cooking stock with the egg whites, add optional greenery, strain, and then dissolve the gelatin in it.

---

4) *The parsley and aspic flavoring*

The bowl of puréed rind
1 cup (lightly pressed)
chopped fresh parsley
1 clove of garlic, mashed
1 Tb dried tarragon *or* 3
Tb fresh minced tarragon
leaves
1 Tb wine vinegar
Salt and pepper to taste
1 cup of the aspic, cool but
not set

Mix all ingredients except the aspic in the bowl, and just before assembling the ham in Step 5, stir in the cup of aspic. (You will have 2 to 2½ cups when all is blended.)

---

5) *Assembling and serving*

The following assembly method is informal: the meat is packed into a bowl, and slices are cut and served directly from it. If you want a dressier presentation, line the bowl with aspic before filling it, and unmold onto a platter for serving.

A 2½- to 3-quart serving bowl, casserole, or crock (this can be of clear glass through which you can see the design of the ham and parsley) The parsley and aspic mixture The cooked and cut ham A rack and/or plate that will fit into the bowl A weight of some sort The remaining aspic, cool but not set	Chill the bowl and spread a layer of parsley-aspic in the bottom. Then pack with layers of ham and of parsley-aspic. When filled, cover with rack and/or plate and weight, and chill for an hour or so, until set. (If you do not weight down the ham, it will be difficult to cut into slices later.) Remove the rack and so forth, scumble the top a bit with a fork (to disguise plate or rack marks), and pour on the cool aspic. Cover and chill until serving time.

To serve, cut into slices, like a large pie.

(*) STORAGE NOTE: *Jambon persillé* will keep nicely for a week under refrigeration. It may be frozen, but will lose character after 2 to 3 weeks.

PRESERVED GOOSE
Confit d'Oie
(And the Disjointing of Fowl and the Rendering of Fat)

Like the salting of pork, the preserving of goose is an age-old method for keeping meats during the winter months, and is typical of the *foie gras* regions in France, where geese are raised to produce those magnificent livers. The goose for *confit* is given a brief preliminary salting, then is slowly simmered in its own fat, a process that not only cooks it but also renders out most of the heavy layer of fat under the skin, just as most of the fat is rendered out of bacon when you cook it. Traditionally, the cooked pieces of goose are then packed in crocks and sealed in the fat for storage. The taste of preserved goose, like the taste of salted pork, has a very special quality quite unlike fresh goose or pork, and it is an easy process as well as an interesting one to do. Besides having goose to eat in the numerous ways described at the end of the recipe, you will have its big carcass for soup and, during the weeks to come, a goodly supply of the best cooking fat imaginable, which is marvelous for browning meats and sautéing potatoes, for basting roasts, frying eggs, and broiling chickens, as well as for flavoring vegetables like cabbage and sauerkraut.

HOW TO DISJOINT POULTRY, AS ILLUSTRATED WITH A GOOSE

In the following directions, the goose is cut so that each wing makes a serving portion, the breast is halved lengthwise, and the drumstick-second-joint pieces are left intact for separation before serving.

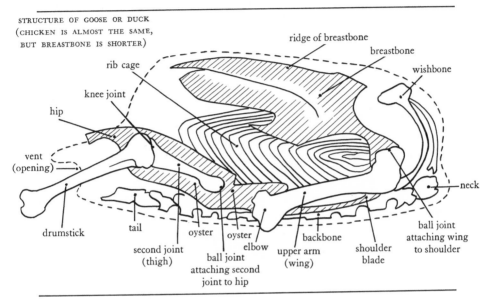

STRUCTURE OF GOOSE OR DUCK (CHICKEN IS ALMOST THE SAME, BUT BREASTBONE IS SHORTER)

Preliminaries

Pull all fat out of cavity; you will have about 2 cups from a ready-to-cook store-bought goose, 4 or more from a farm goose. Cut off wings at elbows and save for the stock pot, along with the neck and gizzard; save the heart and liver for the sausage suggestion at the end of the *confit* recipe. As a preliminary to disjointing the goose, slit skin the length of the back, going down to the bone from neck opening to beginning of tail piece. Then place goose in front of you, its legs to your left.

Removing the wing section

So that the wing will make an adequate serving, you want to include the lower third of the breast with it as follows. Starting an inch to the right of where second joint is attached to hip, in the drawing, cut through breast meat to bone in a shallow semicircle reaching up to the joint where wing is attached to shoulder. Bend wing at a right angle away from breast and then down toward back, to break open the joint; cut through joint to free wing, and scrape breast meat off carcass from initial cut down toward backbone to free the entire section.

Removing drumstick-second-joint section

Follow end of drumstick with your finger to find knee. Holding knee in your left hand, slit around it from vent to ribs (where wing section was removed). Again with your finger, follow second joint (thigh) from knee to hip, to locate ball joint attaching it to the hip bone. At either side of this joint along the hip are two nuggets of meat, the oysters, which should come off as part of the drumstick-second-joint section: scrape this meat from hip bone up to and around joint. Then bend knee away from carcass at a right angle and down toward backbone to break open ball joint at hip. Cut through joint to detach it, then cut drumstick-second-joint from carcass. Remove wing-breast piece and drumstick-second-joint from other side of goose.

The breast

You now have only the upper two thirds of the breast meat left on the carcass. Cut through ribs just below breast meat on either side. Then, grasping tail end (at left in drawing), lift breast structure up at right angles and bend it toward neck end, to break it free at shoulder. Chop off the 2 tusk-shaped shoulder-blade bones at neck end and trim off excess skin.

Locate ridge of breastbone with your finger, then slit down through skin to bone close along one side of ridge. With cleaver and mallet, chop the breastbone in half along this slit. (You may then wish to chop each piece in half, crosswise, if you are serving the goose in a *ragoût* rather than a *confit*.)

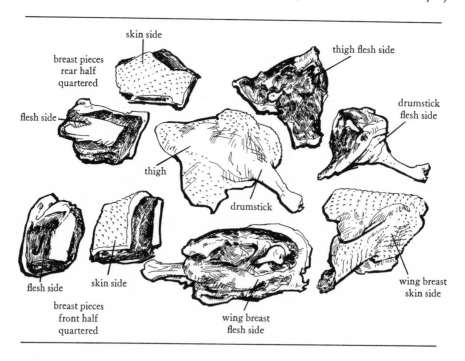

skin side

breast pieces
rear half
quartered

thigh flesh side

flesh side

drumstick
flesh side

thigh

drumstick

flesh side   skin side

wing breast
skin side

breast pieces
front half
quartered

wing breast
flesh side

Trim fatty edges of skin from each piece of goose; feel with your fingers for any knobs of fat buried under the flesh at edges of breast, wings, second joints, and remove them. You will have 3 or more cups of fatty skin pieces to add to the fat from inside the goose. Cut into ½-inch pieces with shears, and reserve all of this for rendering, Step 2 in the recipe.

A NOTE ON COOKING-FAT

Ideally the goose is cooked in goose fat and fresh pork leaf fat (also called fresh leaf lard), which comes from around the pork kidneys. This is very difficult to find unless there is a pork-slaughtering business in your area: substitute fresh pork fatback or the fat from a loin roast. If you have no success in finding this, render only the fresh fat and skin from the goose, and after you have strained it, add store-bought leaf lard, which you can usually buy in 1-pound packages. Failing this, use white vegetable shortening.

CONFIT D'OIE

[Preserved Goose—Disjointed and Salted Goose Cooked in Its Own Fat—Also for Pork, Small Game, Duck, and Turkey]

Modern refrigerators and freezers have made changes in the *confit* traditions. In the old days you had to simmer the goose for at least 2½ hours, until every bit of moisture had evaporated and a straw would pierce the meat with ease; you then were sure it would keep through the winter, packed in its jars of fat in your cold-room or cellar. For our purposes, since we are more interested in taste than tradition, the goose is cooked only until done, and is stored in its fat in the refrigerator, or is wrapped and frozen.

NOTE: Pork, small game, duck, and turkey are done exactly the same way after being cut into serving pieces. Use pork fat only for the rendering and cooking.

For a 10- to 12-pound ready-to-cook roasting goose (thaw if frozen, and disjoint as described and illustrated in preceding directions; you will have 5 to 6 pounds of goose)

---

1) *Salting the goose—24 hours*

Half the ingredients for the dry-salt cure on page 309, or add goose to the cure along with the pork you are doing

Follow directions for salt curing but leave goose in the cure for 24 hours only. (If you have to leave it longer, you may desalt the meat by soaking the goose pieces several hours in cold water before cooking.)

2) Rendering fat—45 minutes

6 lbs., or about 12 cups,
fresh fat (goose fat and
fatty skin pieces, plus
fresh pork leaf fat, other
fresh pork fat, or see
notes preceding recipe)
A heavy 6-quart kettle or
casserole (which may
also serve to cook the
goose)
1¼ cups water
A deep-fat-frying
thermometer

Pull papery filaments from pork leaf fat if you are using it, and chop all fat into ¼-inch pieces. Place in kettle with water, cover loosely, and set over low heat so that fat liquefies slowly. When it reaches 212 degrees it will crackle and spit as water content evaporates. When it stops spitting, in about 25 minutes, remove cover and raise heat slightly to 250 degrees. (Do not ever allow fat to go over 325 degrees or it will lose its clear, pale-yellow color.) In 20 to 30 minutes more, the fat pieces will be lightly golden brown, and the fat may be considered rendered. Strain through a fine sieve, pressing liquid fat out of browned residue. (Save residue for *frittons,* at end of recipe.) Return fat to kettle. Cover when cool, and set in a cool place or refrigerate.

3) Cooking the goose—1¼ to 1½ hours for a roaster goose

The kettle of rendered fat
The salted goose
More fat if needed
The thermometer

Set kettle over low heat to liquefy fat. Meanwhile, wipe off salt and dry the goose with paper towels; place goose in kettle. (Fat should cover goose pieces by at least an inch.) Start timing when fat begins to bubble quietly and temperature is between 200 and 205, where it should remain throughout cooking.

Goose is done when meat is tender if pierced with a knife and when juices run clear yellow; meat and skin should color no more than a deep golden yellow and fat should remain pale yellow. Remove goose. Raise heat slightly and cook fat for 5 to 6 minutes (but not over 325 degrees) until it stops crackling, which indicates all liquid has evaporated and fat has clarified. Strain through a fine sieve, pressing fat out of residue. Save residue for *frittons,* page 317.

4) Storing of goose and of fat

You may serve the goose as is, hot or cold, and it is delicious when freshly cooked. It will keep 4 to 5 days in a covered dish in the refrigerator, or you may wrap it airtight and freeze for 6 to 8 weeks. However, it seems to retain its best flavor, if you wish to preserve the meat for some time, when you pack it into a bowl and cover completely with the liquid fat in which it cooked; when fat has cooled and congealed, cover airtight with plastic wrap, and refrigerate. It will keep 2 to 3 months at least. To remove pieces of goose, set bowl at room temperature for several hours so that fat will soften enough for you to remove as many pieces of goose as you wish with a wooden spoon. Be sure the remaining pieces are completely covered with fat when you cover and refrigerate them again.

Any fat not being used to preserve the goose will keep for a month or more in covered jars in the refrigerator.

Serving suggestions

Besides the cabbage soup of Béarn, *garbure,* and the baked beans of Toulouse and Castelnaudary, *cassoulet,* you may add the goose to warm up in a casserole of lentils or beans, or in the braised sauerkraut or red cabbage in Volume I, pages 496 and 498. Another idea is to warm the goose in a covered dish in a 350-degree oven for 10 to 15 minutes, until it is hot and tender, then roll it in bread crumbs, sprinkle with goose fat and brown under a hot broiler; serve with the purée of beans and squash on page 404, the turnip and rice purée, page 405, the garlic mashed potatoes or rice and onion *soubise* in Volume I, pages 520 and 485, or with sliced potatoes sautéed in goose fat. Accompany with Brussels sprouts or broccoli and a light red wine or a rosé.

Arrange cold goose on a platter garnished with lettuce, watercress, or parsley, and accompany with French potato salad, cold mixed vegetables, or a tossed green salad, and beer or chilled dry white wine.

Frittons—Grattons

[Cracklings]

All the residue from rendering the fat and cooking the goose goes into this spread for toast or crackers, which you can serve with cocktails or accompanying a green salad and cold meats.

The fat-rendering and goose-cooking residue **Salt, pepper, and** *épices* *fines* **or allspice to taste** **An attractive jar or pot** **Melted goose fat**	Pound the cracklings in a mortar or put through a meat grinder, then warm briefly in a frying pan. Season to taste and pack tightly into jar or pot. Chill, and when cold, pour on a ¼-inch layer of melted goose fat. Cover and refrigerate. Will keep for a month or so.

Cou d'Oie Farci

[Goose-Neck Sausage]

If you have a farm goose, you can ask that the whole neck from head to backbone be saved for you intact and as is. Pluck and singe skin thoroughly, then peel it off the neck in one piece, turning skin inside out as you go. Sprinkle with salt and pepper, turn it skin side out, and it is ready to be a sausage casing. Use the truffled pork, veal, and liver formula on page 295, substituting goose liver and heart for chicken liver. Tie or sew the two ends, and poach the sausage in fat along with the goose.

PÂTÉS AND TERRINES

The French are famous for the splendor of their *pâtés* and *terrines,* those glorious looking, intoxicating smelling, rich, and unforgettable mixtures of pork, veal, chicken, duck, truffles, liver, *foie gras,* wines, and spices that are packed into long earthen dishes in the *charcuterie,* or in great round bowls, or are formed in cunningly decorated brown crusts. No other cuisine has developed the art quite like the French, and no other formulas are quite as delicious and subtle. However, if you have done some of the recipes in Volume I beginning on page 564, you will know how easy it is to make a *terrine*: it is only a matter of grinding up meat, seasoning it, slicing or dicing a garniture, and packing everything into a fat-lined dish before setting it in the oven. You know also that your own is almost invariably better than anything you can buy because you are using the best ingredients rather than scraps, and that most *pâtés* and *terrines* are expensive to buy and just as expensive to make. They come in the category of necessary luxuries.

An excellent pork-liver *pâté* starts off this new series in a fairly economical manner. This is followed by a *pâté de campagne,* then a *pâté* baked in bread dough, and an unusual porkless *terrine.* The section closes with fully illustrated directions on how to form and bake *pâtés en croûte.*

A NOTE ON LIAISONS AND BINDERS

Almost all *pâté* mixtures have something in addition to meat to bind them together, preventing the meat from crumbling when the *pâté* is sliced. Eggs are usually present, sometimes bread crumbs, and rice can also serve. The following *panade* is an alternative to the bread-crumb type of *panade* used for the *boudin* sausages on page 290.

Panade au Riz
For about 1 cup

⅓ cup plain raw white rice
1 cup or more of meat stock or bouillon
3 Tb butter
A heavy-bottomed 6-cup saucepan (no-stick recommended)

Simmer the rice in the liquid and butter for 25 to 30 minutes, or until it is very tender. Add a little more bouillon if necessary, to keep rice from sticking, but liquid should be entirely absorbed when rice is done.

To use the panade

Purée in an electric blender, food mill, or meat grinder along with any liquids or egg you are using. (Your recipe will direct you.) Any leftover *panade* may be frozen.

A NOTE ON PORK FAT, BAKING DISHES, AND OTHER MATTERS

Full notes on what to bake a *pâté* in, and so forth, are discussed in Volume I, pages 564–5, and in the Master Recipe for *terrine de porc, veau, et jambon,* also in Volume I, starting on page 566. Our only additional comment here is on pork fat. Except in the case of the porkless *pâté,* which uses suet or chicken fat, all of the following recipes call for fresh pork as part of the meat mixture as well as a liner for the baking dish. We realize how difficult it is to find fresh pork fatback (*lard gras*). For the fat in the meat mixture itself, you can use fat-and-lean pork from the fresh shoulder butt, or fat from the outside of a loin roast; outside fresh ham- and shoulder-fat are less satisfactory because softer, but perfectly possible. Although you can line the mold with blanched salt pork or bacon, fresh pork fat is very much better both in taste and appearance. Lacking fresh fatback, you can pound strips of fresh outside loin fat between 2 sheets of waxed paper, to reduce them to ⅛ inch thickness and to weld them together.

THREE LIVER PÂTÉS

Pâté de Foie–Pâté de Campagne

Down on the farm, you naturally use every bit of the hog for something, and some of the very best *pâtés* contain pork liver, either as the main ingredient or combined with other meat. These have far more character than the chicken-liver *pâtés* so popular in this country, and your own homemade mixture is always surprisingly better than anything you seem to be able to buy, even in the best French *charcuterie.*

LIVER NOTE

You may substitute beef liver for pork liver; we have not found any significant difference in effect. Calf's liver is lovely but insanely expensive for this type of dish.

✳ *TERRINE DE FOIE DE PORC*
[Pork-liver *Pâté*]

To translate a *terrine de foie de porc* into familiar language, it is like the very best liverwurst; you could easily mistake it for *pâté de foie gras*. Simple to make, it consists only of liver, pork fat, flavorings, plus an egg and either rice or bread crumbs to bind everything together. Of all the mixtures, this necessarily contains the most fat; if you used any less you would not achieve perfection. Serve slices of *pâté* and French bread or toast as a first course; it is also delicious as a spread for sandwiches or cocktail appetizers.

For a 6-cup baking dish (18 to 20 slices)

The *pâté* dish: a 6-cup *terrine* or baking dish (rectangular, round, oval) or bread pan
A pan of water
Sheets of pork fat to line *pâté* dish

Preheat oven to 350 degrees and place rack in middle level. Set *pâté* dish in pan to check water level: it should come ⅔ up outside of dish. Remove dish and place pan of water in oven. Line bottom and sides of *pâté* dish with strips of pork fat ⅛ inch thick. (See notes preceding this recipe as well as illustrations on page 330.)

1 lb. fresh pork fatback or fat from outside a loin roast (2 cups)
12 ounces liver (pork, beef, or calf) (1½ cups)
1 cup rice *panade*, page 318;
A meat grinder
An electric mixer with large bowl
2 eggs
2 Tb Cognac
2½ tsp salt
Either 1 tsp *épices fines*, page 288;
Or ½ tsp pepper and big pinches of allspice, nutmeg, and cayenne
Optional: A 1-ounce truffle, minced, and its juice

Put the pork fat, liver, and rice *panade* through the finest blade of meat grinder and into the bowl. Beat in the rest of the ingredients. Sauté a spoonful and taste; correct seasoning as necessary. Turn mixture into *pâté* dish.

A piece of fresh pork fat to cover the meat

Cover with the fat, lay the thyme and bay leaf on top, and then the foil. Cover, and set in pan of water in

1 imported bay leaf
A branch of thyme, or
    ¼ tsp dried thyme
Sufficient aluminum foil
    to cover *pâté* with 1
    inch extra all around

oven. Bake for 1¼ to 1½ hours or longer; *pâté* is done
at a temperature of 160 degrees, or when juices and
fat surrounding *pâté* are clear yellow with no trace
of rosy color (press *pâté* with a spatula to check on
this).

A cover for the dish, or a
    pastry sheet and weight
Useful: a meat ther-
    mometer

When done, remove *pâté* dish from pan, discard
water, and return dish to pan. Cover with board, or
pan and weight (to press meat together and prevent
air pockets) and let cool to room temperature. Remove
board and weights and refrigerate.

Serving

Pâté will improve in flavor after 2 to 3 days. Cut slices ⅜ to ½ inch thick directly
from dish; or heat bottom of dish gently, run a knife around between *pâté* and
dish, and unmold on a serving plate or board.

Storage

Pâté will keep nicely for 8 to 10 days under refrigeration. It may be frozen,
and results are more successful for liver *pâtés* than for meat *pâtés*.

VARIATIONS

Pâté de Campagne
[Pork and Liver *Pâté* with Veal or Chicken]

These *pâtés* vary in content and flavor throughout France, but always
contain pork liver, pork, and sometimes other meats, as well as pork fat, a
binder, and the usual seasonings. The following formula is one we like;
whether you serve it in its baking dish or unmold it, the name is always *pâté
de campagne* and never *terrine*.

For a 6-cup baking dish

8 ounces (1 cup) fat-and-
    lean fresh pork (such as
    shoulder butt or loin, or
    the *chair à saucisse,*
    page 289)
8 ounces (1 cup) fresh pork
    fatback or fat from
    outside a loin roast

Be sure all gristle, bones, skin, or other extraneous
matter have been trimmed from meat before weighing. Pass meats, fat, and liver through finest blade of
meat grinder along with the *panade*. Beat in rest of
ingredients. Sauté a spoonful and taste. Correct seasoning as necessary. Pack into a fat-lined dish, and bake
as in the Master Recipe.

8 ounces (1 cup) raw lean
   veal, or raw chicken
   meat
8 ounces (1 cup) liver (pork,
   beef, or calf)
½ cup rice *panade,*
   page 318
⅓ cup minced onions
   cooked until soft in 2
   Tb pork fat or butter
1 egg
2 Tb Cognac
1 medium clove of garlic,
   mashed
Either 1 tsp *épices fines,*
   page 288;
Or ½ tsp pepper and big
   pinches of ground allspice,
   thyme, bay leaf
½ tsp additional pepper
1 Tb salt

Pâté de Foie et de Porc en Brioche

[Pork and Pork-liver *Pâté* Baked in *Brioche* Dough]

This is a *pâté* baked in *brioche* dough in a round pan. It is always dramatic because the dough rises luxuriously and the whole effect is one of effulgent *gourmandise.* The *pâté* is served cold, and it must be baked at least a day ahead of serving so that the meat will settle, which means that you will probably need to make the dough a day before baking.

For a 9- by 1½- to 2-inch round mold, serving 12 to 16 people

---

1) *The pâté ingredients*

The *pain brioché* dough
   mixture on page 83,
   chilled and ready to form
8 ounces (1 cup) fresh
   pork fatback or fat from
   outside a loin roast
A 12-inch frying pan
2 cups minced onions

Prepare the dough the day before baking. Put the pork fat through the medium blade of the meat grinder. Place half in bowl of electric mixer and heat other half slowly in frying pan until fat has rendered. Add onions to pan and cook slowly about 15 minutes until tender and translucent. Meanwhile, grind the pork and set aside, then the liver, and set aside separately. When onions are done, add the pork and cook 4 to 5

8 ounces (1 cup) fresh pork
    shoulder or loin
1 lb. (2 cups) liver (pork,
    beef, or calf)
1 medium clove of garlic,
    mashed
Either 1 tsp *épices fines,*
    page 288;
Or ½ tsp pepper and big
    pinches of ground allspice,
    thyme and bay leaf
¼ tsp additional pepper
2 tsp salt
¼ cup (pressed down)
    dry white crumbs from
    homemade-type un-
    sweetened bread,
    moistened in a small
    bowl with 3 Tb heavy
    cream and 1 Tb Cognac

minutes, stirring, until meat is gray rather than rosy. Add the liver and cook for several minutes until somewhat stiffened and puffed, and beginning to look grayish-ruddy-brown. Scrape into mixing bowl and beat in all the rest of the ingredients. Sauté a spoonful and taste; correct seasoning as necessary.

2) *Forming the pâté en brioche*

A buttered 9- by 1½-inch
    (6-cup) false-bottomed
    cake pan or fluted mold;
    or a *flan* ring set on a
    baking sheet
The chilled dough
A piece of floured waxed
    paper on a small baking
    sheet
The hot meat mixture
A pastry brush
Cold water
A 2-inch chimney, such as
    a small, buttered metal
    funnel or the metal tube
    from a pastry bag

On a lightly floured board, roll ¼ of the dough into a circle the diameter of your pan or mold, set on floured paper, and chill until needed. Rapidly roll out the rest of the dough into a circle about ¼ inch thick and 12 inches in diameter. Lightly press it into the pan or mold, letting edges overhang all around. Turn the hot meat mixture into the dough-lined pan; fold the edges of the dough over onto the meat. Paint dough lightly with cold water, and unroll reserved circle of dough on top, pressing edges lightly with your fingers to seal. Make a hole in the center top of the dough and insert chimney. (You will probably have enough dough left over for a small loaf of bread.)

3) *Rising—about 1 hour*

Set the *pâté* in a draft-free place at a temperature of no more than 75 to 80 degrees until top of dough feels spongy-springy when touched and the whole structure has risen half an inch or more up from the rim of the mold. Preheat oven in time for next step.

4) *Baking—about 1 hour in a preheated 425-degree oven*

Egg glaze (1 egg beaten in a small bowl with 1 tsp water)
Sharp-pointed scissors
Useful: a meat thermometer

Just before baking, paint top (not sides) of dough with egg glaze; in a moment, paint it again. Make scissor clips 1½ inches apart all around top circumference of dough, going in at a slant ¾ inch deep and 2 inches wide. Set *pâté* in middle level of preheated 425-degree oven and bake for 18 to 20 minutes, until *brioche* has risen and begun to brown nicely. Reduce heat to 350 degrees, baking about 40 minutes more. *Pâté* is done when fat is bubbling up in funnel; temperature on meat thermometer should be 160–5 degrees.

5) *Cooling*

Remove from oven and let cool in mold for half an hour, then unmold onto a rack. When thoroughly cold, cover airtight and refrigerate for at least 12 hours before serving.

6) *Serving suggestions*

Serve as is, cutting it into wedges like a pie. When you wish an even more attractive dish, pour almost-set aspic into chilled *pâté* through chimney hole, and chill an hour or more before serving. (This is described in the *pâté en croûte* section, page 332.)

A PORKLESS VARIATION

La Terrine Verte—Pâté Sans Porc
[A Porkless *Pâté*]

Slice into this unusual *pâté,* and it is a beautiful green with decorations of white and brown. It has a meaty, hearty taste, yet is made without a trace of pork meat or pork fat: it is veal, chicken, and calf's brains spiced with onions, garlic, herbs, and Cognac, garnished with chicken breasts and livers, and turned green with spinach. The fat is either veal- or beef-kidney fat, or goose or chicken fat. Bake the *pâté* at least 2 and preferably 3 days before serving, so that all the flavors may blend into perfect harmony.

For an 8-cup terrine, serving 12 to 16

1) *The pâté mixture*

The boned and skinned breast from 1 frying chicken
3 chicken livers

Cut the breast meat and the chicken livers into strips ⅜ inch wide; place in a bowl with the Cognac and a sprinkling of salt and pepper. Let marinate while preparing rest of *pâté* mixture.

¼ cup Cognac
Salt and pepper

The *terrine:* an 8-cup mold, baking dish, or bread pan of any shape, although a rectangular one is easy for serving
1 lb. (2 cups) fresh veal-kidney fat, beef suet, or goose fat or chicken fat
A meat grinder
An electric mixer with large bowl

Chill *terrine* in freezer. Trim off any filaments or extraneous matter, and put fat through fine blade of meat grinder. Place half in large bowl of mixer and render the rest of the fat. (Directions are on page 316.) When strained, cooled, and almost congealed, spread ¾ of it inside the chilled *terrine.* Refrigerate *terrine* until you are ready to fill it.

½ lb. (1 cup) boneless raw light or dark meat from a frying chicken
½ lb. (1 cup) raw, lean veal
1 lb. (2 cups) brains (calf, beef, or lamb), blanched and peeled (they need not be trimmed of tubes and extraneous matter)
1 cup minced onions
Either 2 cups blanched, chopped fresh spinach;
Or 1½ packages frozen spinach, thawed (squeezed dry)
1 medium clove garlic, mashed
2 eggs
1 Tb salt
Either 1 tsp *épices fines,* page 288;
Or ½ tsp thyme, ¼ tsp allspice, and ¼ tsp nutmeg
¾ cup dry white crumbs from homemade-type unsweetened bread moistened with ¼ cup chicken broth or milk

Grind the chicken, veal, and brains into the mixing bowl along with the ground raw fat. In 2 Tb of the rendered fat, cook the onions for 8 to 10 minutes over low heat until tender and translucent, then blend in the spinach and stir several minutes to evaporate excess moisture. Add spinach and onions to mixing bowl, along with the eggs, salt, seasonings, and bread crumbs. Beat vigorously to blend all ingredients. Sauté a spoonful until cooked through, taste, and correct seasoning.

2) *Filling the terrine and baking—preheat oven to 350 degrees*

The marinating strips of
   chicken breast and
   chicken livers
The *pâté* mixture
The chilled, fat-lined
   terrine
The remaining rendered
   fat
1 imported bay leaf
1 branch thyme, or
   ¼ tsp dried thyme
2 sheets of aluminum foil
A cover for the *terrine*
   (or pastry sheet and
   weight, such as a brick)
A pan of boiling water in
   middle level of pre-
   heated oven

Beat the Cognac marinade into the *pâté* mixture.
Spread ⅓ of the *pâté* mixture in the *terrine,* cover
with half of the chicken meat and livers in alternating
strips. Spread with half the remaining *pâté* mixture,
then with the remaining strips of chicken and liver,
ending with the last of the *pâté.* Spread reserved and
rendered fat over the *pâté,* and top with the bay leaf
and thyme. Fold the foil closely over top of *terrine* to
enclose it completely; set on the cover, and place in
pan of boiling water in oven. Bake for about 1½
hours, or until *pâté* starts to shrink from sides of mold,
and when pressed with the back of a spoon no rose-
colored juices exude. (Temperature on a meat thermometer should be 160–5 degrees.)

3) *Cooling and serving*

    Cool under a board or pan and weight, then refrigerate, covered, for 2 to 3 days
before serving as described in the Master Recipe, page 321.

PÂTÉS BAKED IN PASTRY CRUST
Pâtés en Croûte

When it appears in pastry dough, any *pâté* mixture becomes a *pâté en croûte,* certainly one of the great visual delights of French *charcuterie.* A hinged metal *pâté* mold provides the most professional as well as the easiest system for *pâté en croûte,* and you can buy a variety of shapes in most import stores. The mold, which sits on a baking sheet when filled, has neither top nor bottom, only 2 sides hinged at one end and closed by a removable pin at the other. It is a kind of corset, which actually molds the *pâté* dough in its decorative embrace, and holds it tight while it bakes and cools. If you have no mold, a workable alternative described on pages 333–4 produces an equally attractive result; it is a baked bottom case of dough, which you fill as though it were a *pâté* mold and top with a decorated cover of dough. A third alternative is the free-form shape, *pâté pantin,* baked on a pastry sheet like the sausage in *brioche* on pages 301–2. The first two methods are outlined in the following directions.

TIMING

A *pâté* always develops more taste 2 to 3 days after baking. Allowing 2 days for the maturing process, you will need at least 1½ days for baking, cooling, chilling: start the *pâté,* then, 4 to 5 days in advance of any date you wish to serve it. The finished *pâté* will keep 7 to 10 days under refrigeration.

THE PÂTÉ MIXTURE

Although you may use any of the preceding *pâtés* for *pâté en croûte,* the more traditional mixture is the all-purpose pork and veal stuffing in Volume I, page 565, and a garniture of strips of veal and ham, or of game such as rabbit, hare, partridge, or pheasant, or of duck, turkey, or chicken. Follow one of the recipes in Volume I, starting on page 566, and including the duck *pâté* on page 571. For an 8-cup mold you will need approximately 4 cups of stuffing and 2 cups of garnishing strips. You will also need sheets of fresh pork fat for lining the dough.

THE DOUGH FORMULA

For *pâtés* molded in a hinged form, use the *pâte à croûstades,* Formula Number 6, page 110, which contains flour, butter, lard, and egg yolks. When you are forming the dough on an upside down case, use Formula Number 7, with whole eggs. These are both excellent doughs for *pâtés;* they hold their shape through the long baking, and are also good to eat. Either one is easy to make in an electric mixer as described on page 104; it is best to prepare the dough several hours ahead or the day before forming and baking, so that it will be well chilled, rested, and easy to roll.

FORMING AND BAKING PÂTÉ EN CROÛTE IN A HINGED PÂTÉ MOLD

1) *Lining the mold with dough*

Your first step is to line the bottom and sides of the mold with an even ⅜ inch layer of dough. An ingenious professional method is to form ¾ of the dough into a pouch, the bottom and sides of which fit neatly against the mold with a minimum of wrinkles while the open top falls around the outside leaving the mold open for filling. In French this is a *calotte,* a skull cap. (The following illustrations are for an oval mold; adapt the same system for rectangular and round molds.)

A hinged 6- to 8-cup *pâté* mold

A piece of heavy paper to serve as a pattern

Sheets of fresh pork fat ⅛ inch thick, enough to line bottom, sides, and top of mold (page 319)

Using *pâté* mold as a guide, *cut a pattern out of the paper to fit the opening of the mold.* Cut 2 pieces of pork fat, using pattern, and set aside; these will line bottom and top of *pâté* later. Reserve pattern for dough cover, later.

paper pattern

Chilled *pâte à croustades* dough made with 1 lb. of flour (page 104)

A pastry brush and cup of cold water

Place ¾ of the chilled dough on a lightly floured marble or board and roll into a circle about 1 inch thick and 2 inches larger in diameter than the long side of the mold—dough must be very thick at this point so that when you are through rolling and forming it you will still have a ⅜-inch layer lining the mold.

Paint a 1-inch strip down each side, right and left, with water.

As the first step in making the pouch shape, dough is to be folded in half and corners are to be bent down as follows. Except at the 2 sides, sprinkle circle of dough liberally with flour to prevent sticking when folded in half.

Bring top down to bottom, making a semicircle with its curved side facing you. Gently press two sides, right and left, together to seal them, then pull the two corners (right and left at top of fold) down toward you as illustrated. Now, rather than a semicircle, you have a pocket, or the beginning of a pouch.

Starting with open side facing you, and making several passes with your pin, roll dough away from you to deepen pouch, so that when it is spread into the mold you will have an overhang of 2 inches: *for a mold 4 inches high and 5 inches across, the pouch should be 8½ to 9 inches deep.*

Be very careful here that you roll the dough evenly and that the final combined thickness of top and bottom layers is no less than ¾ inch; when the dough is thinner you risk breakage and leakage problems later on. (If by any chance you muff this on your first try, briefly knead dough into a ball, chill an hour or more to relax it, and start over again.)

---

2 to 3 Tb lard or shortening
A baking sheet with raised edges (to catch cooking juices)
Scissors

Grease inside of mold and baking sheet, and set mold on sheet. Fold dough lightly in half lengthwise and center in mold. Unfold and ease it gently into place by lifting sides of dough, being careful always that you do not stretch the dough and make it thinner at any point. Clip off a gob of extra dough and use it as a tampon, rather than your fingers, to press dough against pastry sheet and sides of mold.

Leaving a 1½- to 2-inch overhang,
trim off excess dough with scissors.

The sheets of fresh pork fat

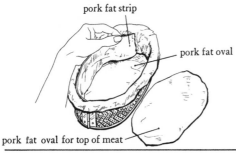

pork fat strip

pork fat oval

pork fat oval for top of meat

Place an oval of pork fat on the
bottom of the mold, and line the
sides. This fat is your insurance
against crust-cracking.

2) *Filling the mold*

The *pâté* mixture and
the strips of garniture
(see notes preceding
recipe)
The lined *pâté* mold
A bowl of cold water

stuffing

bowl of cold water

dough case lined with pork
fat ready to be filled

garniture

pork fat for top

With your pâté mixture made, your garniture in strips, and your mold ready, you
can now assemble the pâté. Have a bowl of cold water handy to dip your hands into
when you spread in the meat mixture. Preheat oven to 375 degrees.

Fill the mold, starting with a layer
of pâté, then a layer of garniture
strips, a layer of pâté, another of
garniture, and a final layer of pâté
mixture. Fill mold just to rim,
making only a slightly domed shape
in center: if mold is too full, juices
will bubble out over crust during
baking.

1 imported bay leaf
A sprig or 2 of thyme
  (or ¼ tsp dried thyme)
The second oval of fresh
  pork fat

Place bay leaf and thyme on top
of *pâté; cover with the second oval
of pork fat.*

pork fat

top oval of dough

The reserved dough (or
  chilled leftover dough)
The paper pattern (size
  of mold opening)
A pastry brush and cold
  water
A table fork

Roll the reserved dough out ½ inch
thick, cut into an oval following
pattern, and place on top of pork-fat
oval. Paint circumference with cold
water and *fold edges over, pressing first
with fingers to seal,* and then
with the back tines of a table fork.
(NOTE: Cover must be thick so that it
will rise only a little, otherwise you
will have too large a gap between
meat and top of crust after baking.
Another reason for making it thick is
that it will barely cook through and
thus will not crumble when you
eventually slice the *pâté.*)

Pastry cutouts made from
  leftover dough
Egg glaze (1 egg beaten
  with 1 tsp water)

Make pastry cutouts of any shape you wish. (Illustrations are in Volume I,
page 574.) *One by one, paint bottoms of cutouts with egg glaze and press in place on
top of pâté, completely covering seam where edges of pastry overlap.*

**2 greased chimneys 1½
inches high, such as
metal funnels, metal tubes
from a pastry bag, or
aluminum foil**

With a sharp-pointed knife, make 2
holes ¼ inch in diameter in top of
pâté, going down through to touch
the meat; *insert chimneys.* They
allow cooking steam to escape rather
than to gather in the crust, possibly
bursting it. Just before baking, paint
top of *pâté* with egg glaze, being
careful none drips down into mold.

(*) AHEAD-OF-TIME-NOTES: *Pâté* mixture, garniture, and dough may be made a
day or two in advance of baking, or *pâté* may be assembled (but not glazed), covered,
and refrigerated for a day or two if meat is fresh. Add 20–30 minutes more to baking time if *pâté* has been chilled before going into oven.

3) *Baking—1½ to 2 hours; oven preheated to 375 degrees*

**Useful: A meat ther-
mometer
A pan, spoon, and bulb
baster for removing fat
from pan**

Place in lower middle or middle level of oven and
bake for 20 to 25 minutes until crust begins to color,
then lower thermostat to 350 degrees for rest of baking. Inspect *pâté* every 20–30 minutes: suck up fat
from baking sheet with bulb baster and wipe off sheet
with paper towels. An accumulation of fat can burn
bottom of *pâté,* and it also smokes up the kitchen.

Pâté is done when juices begin bubbling up into funnel; they should be clear
yellow. Check temperature by removing funnel and inserting meat thermometer,
which should read between 160 and 165 degrees.

3) *Cooling the pâté—the aspic*

Remove *pâté* from oven, but do not attempt to slide *pâté* off baking sheet or
to remove mold from *pâté* at this point, since you might tear or crack the crust,
which must remain intact. Let cool completely for several hours or overnight, then
chill in refrigerator for at least 4 hours.

A funnel
4 cups wine-flavored aspic
  (2 Tb gelatin dissolved
  in ¼ cup port or Cognac
  combined with 3¾ cups
  beef bouillon)
A bowl of cracked ice

During baking, the meat shrinks slightly from the top and sides of the crust, and you want to fill this space with aspic, which is delicious both visually and gastronomically. When *pâté* is thoroughly chilled, and with the mold still in place, insert funnel in a chimney hole in top of *pâté*. Being sure aspic has been well tested for consistency so that it will hold its shape when cold, stir over cracked ice until almost syrupy and on the point of setting; pour through funnel into *pâté*, tilting *pâté* in all directions, allowing aspic to run all over and around it. Chill again for several hours.

Finally, when aspic has chilled, *remove pin from mold and carefully nudge sides of mold from sides of pâté.* Once mold is off, *pâté* will hold its shape perfectly.

4) *Serving*

To serve, cut pie-shaped wedges going around circumference of *pâté*. For a rectangular *pâté*, cut straight across, as though it were a loaf of bread.

5) *Storing*

Pâté en croûte will keep a week to 10 days at 37 degrees. It is the aspic that might go off first, and then the crust with the meat juices in it. If you wish to keep leftovers a little longer, remove the crust, scrape off the aspic and the fat-covering, and wrap the meat in plastic or foil. A cooked *pâté* can be frozen, but will never have the same fresh texture again.

FORMING AND BAKING THE PÂTÉ WITHOUT A MOLD

Although the hinged mold is easier to manage, baking a bottom case of dough to act as a mold works very nicely and is not difficult to do. The dough is formed on an upside-down casserole or bread pan, upon which it is baked, just as upside-down pastry shells are formed and baked on pages 106–8. The baked case is then lined with fat, filled with the *pâté,* draped with a close-fitting sheet of dough, decorated, and baked as usual.

---

1) *The bottom case of dough*

The *pâte à croustades à l'envers,* Formula 7, page 110, for 20 ounces of flour

A 6-cup mold, such as an oval casserole or bread pan, greased on the outside with lard or shortening

Roll ⅔ of the dough into a circle 2 inches more in diameter than the length of your mold, and 1½ inches thick. Form a pouch exactly as thick and exactly as illustrated for the spring-form mold, page 328. Press lightly onto mold and trim off excess dough with a knife or pastry wheel. Cover and chill 2 hours or overnight (to relax dough and prevent shrinkage during baking). Set as is, mold still upside down, on a baking sheet in a preheated 425-degree oven for 12 to 15 minutes, until pastry is starting to color. Turn thermostat down to 350 degrees and bake 10 minutes more, or until pastry just loosens from mold but is not cooked through: it holds its shape but is not browned. Cool 15 minutes on mold, then unmold carefully onto a rack and cool 30 minutes until pastry is firm and set.

---

2) *Filling the case*

Lard or shortening

A baking sheet

Pâté ingredients listed in preceding recipe, including sheets of pork fat and paper pattern

Grease just the area where pastry case will sit on baking sheet, and set case on sheet. Following directions in preceding recipe, pages 328–31, cut pork fat to fit bottom, sides, and top of *pâté,* line the case with the pork fat, and fill with *pâté* mixture, topping with a sheet of pork fat.

---

3) *The cover, and finishing the pâté*

Chilled leftover dough and remaining dough

Egg glaze, pastry brush, pastry cutouts, chimneys, as described in preceding recipe

To discourage a gap from developing between top of meat and crust after baking, roll out a preliminary cover of dough ¼ inch thick, to fit top of pork fat. Set in place on *pâté.* Then roll remaining dough into a sheet ¼ to ⅜ inch thick and large enough to cover top of pastry case and to fall ⅔ the way down the case all around. Paint sides of case with egg glaze and arrange covering sheet of dough over *pâté.* Trim edges all around with scissors, then press dough in place against sides of case. Decorate with cutouts, insert chimneys, glaze, bake, cool, chill, and fill with aspic as described and illustrated in preceding recipe.

CHAPTER SIX

A Choice of Vegetables

WHEN YOU BUY VEGETABLES FRESH and cook them lovingly, you may find yourself more renowned for your remarkable zucchini stuffed with almonds than for your spectacular *crêpes Suzette*. And why not, when flaming desserts are becoming status symbols and hand-whittled fresh vegetables more and more of a rarity? Recipes for vegetables consume over 100 pages in Volume I, and describe some of the ways to prepare rice and potatoes as well as almost everything to do with artichokes, asparagus, green beans, and spinach, plus how to braise endive, how to turn a mushroom, and where to peel the chestnut. There are gaps, however, and while the present chapter will fill some of them we are more interested in giving you fresh ideas for old favorites than in completing the vegetable roster. Although we have included a number of classics, like *pommes Anna,* most of the recipes here are new ones that you will not have seen before—the sautéed broccoli, for instance, on page 339, the unusual purées starting on page 404, the spinach with onions on page 360. While some dishes are as elaborate as the stuffed artichoke bottoms on page 412, others are as fast and simple as the grated zucchini on page 369. Seldom-honored notables like rutabagas, chard, and pumpkin receive attention, and stuffed whole cabbage gets a revolutionary, new, and fully illustrated treatment. Here, then, are 79 more pages of recipes for fresh vegetables, beginning with broccoli and ending with a splendid dish of cold artichokes.

BROCCOLI
Choux Brocoli—Choux Aspèrges

Although green sprouting broccoli, asparagus broccoli, Italian broccoli, *Brassica oleracea var. italica,* or whatever you wish to call just plain green broccoli has been around for centuries, it was not widely known in this country until the early 1920's. It is now so popular that an average of one pound a year is consumed by every man, woman, and child in America; over sixty thousand tons of fresh broccoli are sold in retail markets; and heaven knows how much goes into frozen TV dinners. Despite its renown here it continues to remain almost unknown in France (where it is spelled with only one "c"); that is their loss, because fresh broccoli, properly prepared, is certainly one of our most attractive vegetables, both visually and gastronomically. With its delicate cabbage flavor, it is more tender in taste and texture than cauliflower as well as being far more colorful. It goes beautifully with such subtleties as fish in fine white sauces, chicken breasts, brains, and sweetbreads; in fact, anything that spinach does to dress up a dish, broccoli does equally well, sometimes better. Thus, whether or not it ever becomes a French vegetable, we shall give broccoli the full treatment *à la française.*

BUYING BROCCOLI

Broccoli is in season all year round; although its low months are July and August, its high season is winter, when we are most in need of fresh green vegetables. California is by far the largest producer, but considerable amounts come from other Western states as well as from New York, New Jersey, and Virginia.

When buying broccoli, choose clean, firm, smooth, fresh-smelling dark green or purplish-green bunches with fresh-looking, closely bunched, all-green bud clusters. Over-mature broccoli will have thick, woody stems that are often hollow; the buds will be partially open, yellowish, and have a rather strong odor. Broccoli is perishable, and will become limp and bruised-looking and develop an unpleasant stale-cabbage smell if not properly handled. In markets it should be kept in humidified refrigerator cases and/or frequently iced. Bring it home from the market as soon as possible, refrigerate in a plastic bag immediately, and plan to cook it within 2 to 3 days.

The usual bunch of broccoli, containing several stalks tied together, weighs between 1½ and 2 pounds and will serve 4 to 6 people.

PREPARING BROCCOLI FOR COOKING

When we speak of the delights of fresh broccoli properly prepared, we are talking about peeling the stems and stalks before cooking the broccoli. If you have subsisted on unpeeled broccoli, you will find that peeled broccoli is an entirely different vegetable which cooks in 5 to 6 minutes, remains fresh and green, and is tender from stalk to tip. In fact we have the same feeling about unpeeled broccoli that we do about unpeeled asparagus—neither is a gastronomical object.

To prepare broccoli for cooking, you may quarter the whole stalks lengthwise from butt to head, and peel each stem of each piece. We, however, prefer smaller pieces for easier handling and more even cooking. We suggest that you begin by discarding the tough leaves, retaining only such small ones that seem as tender as the buds. Then cut off the top 2½ to 3 inches of each head, usually at the point where the branches separate themselves from the central stalk. Halve or quarter the branches lengthwise, depending on their size, to make them all no more than ½ inch in diameter at the base. Using a small knife and starting at the bottom of each branch, peel off the skin in strips, coming almost up to the flower buds. Cut off and discard the tough half inch at the butt of each central stalk and strip off the skin, cutting deeply enough when necessary to expose the tender whitish flesh. (Slightly off-season broccoli that has fresh, tight bud clusters may have very thick central stalks with hollow cores; quartering lengthwise and deep peeling, however, will make the stalks tender and edible.) Cut stalks lengthwise into pieces ½ inch in diameter, and then into bias (diagonal) pieces about 1½ inches long.

Place the prepared broccoli in a covered bowl or plastic bag and refrigerate until you are ready to cook it. Wash rapidly under cold, running water just before cooking.

COOKING METHODS

Peeled broccoli cooks so fast, 5 to 6 minutes, that if you are serving it simply, with melted butter or a sauce, you should cook it only just before serving. If this works in with your schedule, it is easily accomplished between courses, otherwise pick one of the alternate methods, where the broccoli is sautéed or finishes in the oven.

✳ *CHOUX BROCOLI BLANCHIS*

[Blanched Broccoli—Plain Boiled Broccoli]

When you have not peeled your broccoli, you must resort to all sorts of subterfuges such as boiling the stalks while steaming the heads, steaming the whole vegetable, or pressure cooking; by the time the stalks are done the heads usually droop, the color has darkened, and the broccoli has lost much of its fresh taste and texture as well as those nutrients considered so important by the very people who feel the peel is the best part. When you have peeled your broccoli, you may use the French method of green-vegetable cookery—blanching. Because peeled broccoli is so tender, we recommend the wire salad basket for plunging it into its boiling bath and snatching it out again.

For 4 to 6 servings

1 bunch (1½ to 2 lbs.) fresh broccoli
A wire salad basket (or a vegetable rack, or a large skimmer)
A kettle containing at least 4 quarts of rapidly boiling water and 2 Tb salt (1½ tsp per quart)

Cut, peel, and wash the broccoli as described in preceding directions, and place in salad basket. Plunge into the rapidly boiling water over highest heat. As soon as water returns to the boil again, boil slowly, uncovered, for 4 to 6 minutes (depending on freshness of broccoli). It is done when a knife pierces the stalks easily. Taste a piece as a test: it should be just tender, with a slight crunch of texture. Remove immediately from the boiling water and serve as directed in one of the following suggestions.

(*) AHEAD-OF-TIME NOTE: If by some chance you plan to serve the hot broccoli with a sauce, and cannot do so immediately when it is done, let it cool, spreading out on a tray if necessary so it will cool quickly. Keep the water boiling. Return broccoli to salad basket just before you wish to serve and re-plunge it for a moment in the rapidly boiling water so that it will just heat through.

Serving suggestions for plain boiled broccoli

Brocoli au Citron—Broccoli for Dieters. Broccoli, like asparagus, is great for dieters because it has its own natural flavor, which a little lemon juice will enhance. Arrange the hot broccoli on a hot serving dish, sprinkle with salt and pepper, and decorate with wedges of lemon.

Brocoli au Beurre Noir—Broccoli with Brown Butter Sauce. Before cooking the broccoli, melt 5 to 6 tablespoons of butter, skim off foam and pour the clear yellow butter off the milky residue and into another saucepan. When broccoli is done, arrange it on a hot serving dish; sprinkle with salt, pepper, and drops of lemon juice. Heat butter until it turns a light, nutty brown and pour it bubbling hot over the broccoli. Serve immediately.

* Brocoli à la Polonaise

[Broccoli with Sautéed Bread Crumbs and Chopped Egg]

This more elaborate presentation of the brown butter sauce includes bread crumbs and sieved egg. You might serve it as a first course or in place of a salad. It would also go with plain broiled or roast chicken, chops, steak, hamburger, or broiled fish.

For 1 bunch (1½ to 2 lbs.) broccoli, serving 4 to 6

¼ lb. (1 stick) butter
A saucepan
An 8-inch frying pan
½ cup (lightly pressed)
　crumbs from fresh home-
　made-type white bread
Salt and pepper
1 hard-boiled egg
A sieve set over a bowl

Before cooking the broccoli (Master Recipe, page 337) melt the butter in the saucepan, skim off foam, and pour clear butter off milky residue and into frying pan. Stir in the bread crumbs and sauté over moderately high heat, stirring for several minutes until crumbs are lightly browned. Season to taste with salt and pepper, and set aside. Peel the hard-boiled egg, rub through sieve into bowl, and season with salt and pepper.

When broccoli is done, arrange on a hot serving dish and sprinkle lightly with salt and pepper. Reheat the bread crumbs, mix in the sieved egg, strew over the broccoli, and serve immediately.

Broccoli with poached eggs

Omit the hard-boiled egg in the preceding recipe, and substitute one hot poached egg per person. When broccoli is cooked, arrange on hot serving dish and place hot poached eggs on top. Sprinkle the hot, browned bread crumbs over all and serve immediately.

Sauces to serve with plain boiled broccoli

Beurre au citron—A lemon-butter sauce, Volume I, page 98.
Sauce hollandaise, its variations with cream—*sauce mousseline,* or the orange-flavored variation—*sauce maltaise,* all of which are in Volume I, pages 79–83.

Cold boiled broccoli

Broccoli, peeled and blanched in the French manner, is delicious in cold vegetable combinations, accompanied by a vinaigrette or mayonnaise. So that it will retain all its fresh color and texture after cooking, spread it out on a clean towel as soon as you have removed it from the boiling water. When cold, refrigerate in a covered bowl.

BROCCOLI RECIPES THAT MAY
BE PREPARED AHEAD

Brocoli Sautés à la Niçoise

[Broccoli Sautéed with Onions, Bacon, and Bread Crumbs]

Like the *brocoli à la polonaise,* this could well be a first course or served in place of the salad, or it could accompany poached or scrambled eggs, plain broiled chicken or fish, or pork or veal chops. In this recipe you may blanch the broccoli in advance, and sauté it just before serving.

For 1 bunch (1½ to 2 lbs.) broccoli

---

3 strips bacon
An 8-inch frying pan,
　no-stick recommended
⅓ cup (lightly pressed)
　crumbs from fresh home-
　made-type white bread
½ cup finely minced onions
3 Tb olive oil
1 large clove mashed garlic
The blanched broccoli
Salt and pepper

Before blanching the broccoli (Master Recipe, page 337) prepare the following garniture. Cook the bacon until lightly browned, and drain on paper towels; crumble when crisped and cool. Sauté the bread crumbs in the bacon fat, stirring, and when light brown scrape into a side dish. In the same pan, cook the onions in the olive oil for 8 to 10 minutes or more, until tender and translucent; stir in the garlic, and set pan aside.

Just before serving, reheat onions, add the cooked broccoli pieces, season lightly with salt and pepper, and toss and turn gently over moderately high heat, shaking and swirling the pan by its handle. When heated through, add browned crumbs and crumbled bacon, swirling and tossing for a moment more. Turn out onto a hot dish and serve immediately.

✳ *Brocoli Étuvés au Beurre*

[Broccoli Braised in Butter]

When you cannot give broccoli last-minute attention you may blanch it until *al dente,* meaning not quite completely cooked, pack it into a casserole, and bake it with butter. It finishes cooking while you are having the first course, but do not leave it in the oven too long or it will lose its lovely fresh quality.

For 1 bunch (1½ to 2 lbs.) broccoli, serving 4 to 6

---

1 Tb soft butter
A 6-cup flameproof casse-
　role or baking dish
The broccoli, blanched for
　4 minutes only, page 337
Salt and pepper
4 to 5 Tb melted butter
A round of waxed paper
A cover for the casserole

Smear inside of dish with butter. Arrange cooked broccoli stalks in bottom of dish, season lightly and dribble on ⅓ of the butter. Arrange broccoli heads attractively on top, season, and dribble on the rest of the butter. Lay waxed paper on top and set aside until about 20 minutes before you are ready to serve. Preheat oven to 350 degrees in plenty of time. If casserole is heavy, heat on top of the stove. Cover, and set in middle level of oven until broccoli is bubbling hot. Serve as soon as possible, to preserve fresh taste and green color.

VARIATION

Brocoli Gratinés au Fromage or à la Milanaise
[Buttered Broccoli Gratinéed with Cheese]

Follow the preceding recipe but add ⅓ cup finely grated Parmesan cheese to the ingredients. Sprinkle 2 tablespoons of cheese inside the buttered dish before arranging the broccoli on it, and sprinkle cheese over each layer of broccoli along with the butter. Cover and heat until bubbling in the oven, then set under a low broiler for a moment or two to brown cheese lightly.

Chopped Broccoli

Another solution for the chef-host-butler is to blanch the broccoli, cool it quickly, then chop it and reheat at leisure in one of the following ways.

✳ SAUTÉ DE BROCOLI
[Chopped Broccoli Sautéed in Butter]

This very simple way with broccoli is also one of the most delicious, because the hot butter penetrates every surface. As well as being an almost all-purpose vegetable accompaniment, chopped sautéed broccoli may serve as a bed for poached fish fillets, poached eggs, chicken breasts, veal scallops, brains, or sweetbreads; these may then be sauced and, if called for, browned under the broiler.

For 1 bunch (1½ to 2 lbs.) fresh broccoli, serving 4 to 6

The broccoli, peeled, washed, and blanched as directed in the Master Recipe, page 337, but for 4 minutes only

Spread the blanched broccoli on a towel to cool. Then chop on a board with a big knife to make pieces between ⅛ and ¼ inch in size. If not to be cooked immediately, refrigerate in a covered bowl. (Makes about 2½ cups.)

3 to 4 Tb butter (2 to 3 Tb more if you wish)
A 10- to 12-inch frying pan, no-stick recommended
Salt and pepper to taste

Several minutes before serving, melt the butter in the frying pan over moderately high heat. When bubbling hot, pour in the chopped broccoli and immediately begin shaking and swirling the pan by the handle to toss the broccoli pieces in the butter until well heated through. Sprinkle with salt and pepper, toss a moment more, and turn into a hot dish. Serve immediately.

VARIATION

Brocoli Étuvés à la Crème

[Chopped Broccoli, Simmered in Cream]

Serve this tender, creamy broccoli dish with broiled or roast chicken, sautéed chicken breasts, veal scallops, brains or sweetbreads, or broiled or sautéed fish.

For 1 bunch (1½ to 2 lbs.) fresh broccoli, serving 4 to 6

The preceding recipe for blanched chopped broccoli sautéed in 3 Tb butter

1 cup heavy cream (a bit more if you wish)

2 tsp cornstarch in a 1 quart bowl

A wire whip

A rubber spatula

After the broccoli has been warmed in butter and seasoned, blend 2 tablespoons cream into the cornstarch. When smooth, blend in the rest and fold into the broccoli. Simmer, folding gently for 2 to 3 minutes, to cook starch and thicken cream. Taste for seasoning. Turn into a hot vegetable dish and serve immediately.

(*) AHEAD-OF-TIME NOTE: May be set aside and just heated through before serving.

Gratin de Brocoli, Mornay

[Chopped Broccoli Gratinéed with Cheese Sauce]

This is an especially good recipe to accompany roast turkey or chicken, and a boon for Thanksgiving because you may assemble the whole dish the day before and set it in the oven half an hour before serving. It also goes well with roast red meats, steaks, chops, and broiled fish or could be the hot entreé at an informal luncheon where you were serving cold ham or poultry, or poached or shirred eggs.

For 1 bunch (1½ to 2 lbs.) fresh broccoli, serving 4 to 6

1) *The broccoli and the cheese sauce*

The peeled, blanched, and chopped broccoli sautéed in butter, page 341

4 Tb butter

3 Tb flour

Prepare the broccoli and set aside. Make a white sauce as follows, starting with a butter and flour *roux:* Melt the butter in the saucepan, blend in the flour, and stir over moderate heat until flour and butter foam together for 2 minutes without browning at all. Remove

1½ cups hot milk in a
small saucepan (more
if needed)
½ cup grated cheese,
Parmesan and Swiss
mixed (save 3 Tb for
later)
A heavy-bottomed 2½-
quart saucepan
A wooden spoon, wire
whip, and rubber spatula
½ tsp salt or to taste
Big pinch white pepper

from heat, and when *roux* stops foaming, vigorously blend in all of the hot milk at once with wire whip, beating until mixture is perfectly smooth. Return over moderately high heat, stirring with whip as sauce thickens and comes to the boil. Boil, stirring, for 2 minutes, and remove from heat. Let cool for a moment. Fold in all but 3 tablespoons of the cheese, and salt and pepper to taste.

2) *Assembling the dish*

A 6-cup baking dish about
2 inches deep
1½ Tb soft butter

Smear ½ tablespoon of butter inside the baking dish and spread 2 to 3 tablespoons of sauce in the bottom. Spread half the broccoli in the dish, and cover with half the sauce. (If sauce seems too thick for spreading, beat in a little more milk by spoonfuls.) Cover with the remaining broccoli and sauce; sprinkle the 3 tablespoons reserved cheese over the sauce. Dot with remaining butter.

(*) AHEAD-OF-TIME NOTE: Recipe may be completed to this point a day in advance. When cool, cover and refrigerate.

3) *Baking—about 30 minutes at 375 degrees*

About 30 minutes before serving, place broccoli in upper-third level of preheated oven and bake until bubbling hot and cheese has browned nicely on top. Do not overcook, or broccoli will lose its attractive flavor and texture. You may keep the dish warm for 15 minutes or so in turned-off oven or warming oven, but the sooner you serve it the better the flavor.

TIMBALES DE BROCOLI

[Broccoli Molds]

These are deep-dish custards that are unmolded for serving as first-course or luncheon dishes, or as an accompaniment to roast chicken or veal, broiled chicken, veal chops, or broiled fish. Use about 2½ cups peeled, blanched, and chopped broccoli in place of the zucchini on page 372, or in place of the asparagus in Volume I, page 440.

EGGPLANT

Aubergines

Eggplant, like broccoli, is in season all year round, and is a marvelously versatile vegetable. National indifference to the eggplant, however, is so vast that our average per capita consumption amounts to only one modest serving once a year. Yet the eggplant has enormous potentialities besides French-frying, certainly the least interesting way of cooking this handsome vegetable. You may bake, broil, boil, sauté, stuff, soufflé, and gratiné eggplant, as well as serve it hot, cold, alone, or together with meat, fish, fowl, or other vegetables. Volume I contains a splendid eggplant stuffed with mushrooms, and *moussaka* and *ratatouille,* the first a marvelous mold of eggplant and lamb, and the second a Provençal casserole of eggplant, zucchini, tomatoes, and onions. Here you will find it broiled, cold *à la grecque* with tomatoes and herbs, sautéed in various unusual forms, baked with meat, with cheese, and souffléed. Eggplant will also turn up in other parts of this book, as a filling, stuffing, or accompaniment to many a main dish.

HOW TO BUY EGGPLANT

Although you will occasionally see locally grown baby eggplant and small sizes, either round or egg-shaped, almost the entire large-scale commercially raised crop in this country consists of the big, dark-purple varieties weighing 1 to 2 pounds but going up even to 5 pounds. They are roundish, egg-shaped or bell-shaped, and half of all the harvest comes from Florida, whose climate and long growing season are ideal for eggplant.

Size is no signal of quality, because all eggplants are harvested when the fruit is still immature—the seeds sparse and soft, the flesh firm. When eggplants mature, the flesh softens, the seeds grow larger and tougher, and both seeds and flesh turn bitter.

When you are buying eggplants, therefore, look at each one carefully all over, which means that if they are packed in a plastic-covered carton you must open it up. Make sure that the skin is sleek and shiny, that it is taut over the flesh, that there are no pockmarks, brown spots, or wrinkles anywhere. Press each fruit gently all over to be sure the flesh is firm and resistant. Avoid any eggplant that is dull, wrinkled, blemished, or even slightly soft, because the flesh will have an off-flavor you can do nothing to correct.

STORING EGGPLANT

Unlike most other vegetables, eggplants store best at 45 to 50 degrees but even under these conditions the storage limit is only about 10 days. Unless you have a cold-room, therefore, buy eggplants only a day or two before you plan to cook them. In a cool kitchen, keep them in a plastic bag with a damp paper towel for humidity; in summer, you will have to refrigerate them. Under refrigeration, however, they will develop surface pitting and brown spots within 4 to 5 days, and begin to soften.

You may have wondered why a particular eggplant recipe sometimes comes off perfectly and at other times does not have the tender, delicious quality you remembered before. The answer is probably either that the eggplant was not really firm, fresh, and immature when you bought it, or that it had been kept too long under refrigerated storage.

PRELIMINARIES TO COOKING

Peeling, salting, blanching

Eggplant skin is edible when cooked long enough, as in a *moussaka,* gratinéed dish, or other recipe involving an hour in the oven. For the rapidly done sautés and for eggplant simmered *à la grecque,* cooking is so short that the skin remains rather tough and stringy.

Most recipes for eggplant direct that it be either macerated in salt or blanched in boiling salted water before the main cooking begins. There are three reasons for this. The first is to eliminate the slight bitterness usually present in even the youngest and freshest specimens, the second is to remove excess vegetable water that otherwise exudes during cooking, and the final one is to prevent the eggplant from absorbing too much oil or fat. You will find, in a comparison of sautés, that plain cubed eggplant will blot up 3 times more sautéing oil than blanched eggplant, that salted eggplant will use half as much as plain eggplant, and that blanched eggplant, which requires the least oil, will be the most tender of the three but have slightly less flavor. We therefore recommend salting in most recipes, and blanching only when we have found it is the best solution.

Salting, however, requires a wait of 30 minutes while the excess vegetable water slowly works its way out of the flesh, and if you are in a tearing hurry do not hesitate to blanch. To do so, drop the eggplant into salted boiling water after you have peeled and cubed or sliced it; boil slowly, uncovered, for 3 to 5 minutes or until it is almost tender but still holds its shape, then proceed with the recipe.

AUBERGINES EN TRANCHES, GRATINÉES
[Broiled Eggplant Slices]

Broiling and sautéing are by far the easiest ways of cooking eggplant, and thick slices of broiled eggplant are attractive to serve. Actually, the following recipe is a combination of baking, to soften the eggplant, then broiling, with a topping of tomatoes and bread crumbs. Serve with steaks, chops, roast lamb, broiled fish or chicken, or as a garnish with poached, scrambled, or fried eggs.

For 4 people

1) *Salting the eggplant*

2 to 2½ lbs. fresh, shiny, firm, unblemished eggplant
A large tray
1½ tsp salt
Paper towels

Cut off cap, shave nubbin off bottom, and wash the eggplant (or eggplants), but do not peel. You are now to cut the eggplant into slices all somewhat the same dimension, 3 to 4 inches long, 2 inches wide, and ½ to ¾ inch thick. If you have large ones, for instance, cut the center slices into 4, other sizes into 3 or 2. Arrange on tray. Sprinkle salt on both sides and let sit for 20 to 30 minutes. Drain and press dry with paper towels.

2) *Preliminary baking of the eggplant—oven preheated to 400 degrees*

½ to ⅔ cup olive oil
Either 1 or 2 cloves mashed garlic;
Or 3 Tb minced shallots or scallions
¼ to ½ tsp mixed herbs (*herbes de provence,* Italian seasoning, or thyme, oregano, and rosemary)
Big pinch pepper
A 4-inch bowl
A 14-inch pizza tray or jelly-roll pan
A cover, or aluminum foil

Blend the oil, the garlic or shallots or scallions, and the herbs and pepper in the bowl, dip each slice into the mixture, drain, and arrange slices slightly overlapping on pizza tray or pan. Reserve remaining oil mixture for later. Cover eggplant and bake in middle level of preheated 400-degree oven for 10 to 15 minutes, until eggplant is almost but not quite tender; do not let it overcook and turn limp, but it must cook long enough to soften.

3) *Tomato and bread-crumb topping*

5 to 6 medium tomatoes, peeled, seeded, juiced,

When you have prepared the tomatoes, toss gently in a bowl with salt and pepper; drain in a few minutes

and chopped (2 cups
pulp)
⅛ tsp salt
Big pinch pepper
½ cup dry crumbs from
   nonsweetened,
   homemade-type white
   bread
More oil if needed

and spread over the eggplant slices. Sprinkle lightly
with bread crumbs and drizzle on oil.

(*) AHEAD-OF-TIME NOTE: Recipe may be prepared an
hour in advance to this point. Cover loosely and set
aside.

4) Broiling and serving

A hot serving platter, or
   the meat platter
A flexible-blade spatula

About 5 minutes before serving, set eggplant 4 to 5
inches under a moderately hot broiler and let brown
slowly to finish cooking. Arrange on platter, again
overlapping slices slightly in an attractive design.
Serve as soon as possible because eggplant will soften
if kept warm.

Other topping suggestions

Sprinkle eggplant with a mixture of bread crumbs, cheese, and parsley, and
finish with drops of oil, or mask the slices with the thick cheese sauce described for
Broccoli Mornay on page 342, and top with a sprinkling of cheese and melted butter.
In either case, reheat and brown under a moderate broiler as described in the preceding step.

* AUBERGINES EN PERSILLADE, SAUTÉES
[Sautéed Eggplant Garnished with Garlic, Bread Crumbs, and Herbs]

Sautéed eggplant is easier to serve than the preceding broiled eggplant,
and certainly easier to finish off at the last moment. It also lends itself to
several variations, as you will see. Serve sautéed eggplant with steaks, chops,
roast lamb, broiled fish, or broiled chicken. Whole, small baked tomatoes are
probably the most attractive additional accompaniment.

For 4 to 6 people

1) Preparing the eggplant

2 lbs. shiny, firm, unblem-
   ished eggplant
A 3-quart mixing bowl
1½ tsp salt
A colander
Paper towels

Peel the eggplant. Cut into lengthwise slices ¾ inch
thick, cut slices into ¾-inch strips, and the strips into
¾-inch cubes. (You will have around 8 cups.) Toss
in the bowl with the salt and let stand 20 to 30 minutes. Just before sautéing, drain in colander and pat
dry in paper towels.

2) *Sautéing the eggplant*

Olive oil or cooking oil
A 12-inch frying pan,
   preferably no-stick (or an
   8-inch pan for sautéing
   in 2 batches)
The colander set over the
   drained mixing bowl

Pour a ⅛-inch layer of oil into the pan and heat until very hot but not smoking. Add enough eggplant to make 1 layer. Toss and turn the eggplant frequently, shaking and swirling the pan by its handle; sauté for 5 to 8 minutes until eggplant is tender and very lightly browned. (Eggplant burns easily, and you must keep your eye on it. If it has browned but is not tender, lower heat and cover the pan for 2 to 3 minutes until it is tender.) Drain in colander and return any accumulated oil from bowl to frying pan. Continue with the rest of the eggplant if you are sautéing in several batches.

3) *The persillade*

The oil
⅓ cup coarse, dry crumbs
   from nonsweetened,
   homemade-type white
   bread
2 Tb minced shallots or
   scallions
1 to 2 large cloves of garlic,
   mashed or finely minced
3 Tb fresh chopped parsley
Optional other herbs, such
   as thyme, basil, or
   oregano
A hot serving dish

Add more oil to pan to make about 2 tablespoons. Heat to very hot, add the bread crumbs, and toss for a minute or two to brown lightly. Then add the shallots or scallions and garlic, and toss a moment more.

(*) AHEAD-OF-TIME NOTE: Recipe may be completed in advance to this point.

Just before serving, reheat pan with bread-crumb mixture, add eggplant, and toss over moderately high heat until eggplant is sizzling. Toss with parsley and optional herbs, turn into hot dish, and serve immediately.

VARIATIONS

Aubergines en Persillade, Gratinées

[Eggplant Baked with Parsley, Garlic, and *Béchamel*]

Sautéed eggplant tossed with garlic and parsley then folded into a *béchamel* sauce and browned in the oven makes a fine accompaniment to steaks, chops, hamburgers, broiled chicken, or fish.

For 4 to 6 people

Ingredients for 2 lbs. eggplant in the preceding Master Recipe, Steps 1, 2, and 3	Peel, cube, salt, and drain the eggplant; then sauté in oil until lightly browned. Reserve the bread crumbs, tossing the eggplant with only the shallots or scallions, garlic, and herbs. Set aside.

For 2 cups béchamel

5 Tb flour
4 Tb butter
A heavy 2-quart saucepan
A wooden spoon and a
  wire whip
1¾ cups milk heated in
  a small saucepan (a little
  more if needed)
Salt and pepper to taste
A rubber spatula
A lightly buttered 6-cup
  baking dish about 1½
  inches deep
2 to 3 Tb of the reserved
  bread crumbs
1 Tb melted butter

For the *béchamel* sauce (which you can make while the eggplant macerates), melt the butter in the saucepan, blend in the flour, and stir over moderate heat until flour and butter foam together for 2 minutes without browning at all. Remove this *roux* from heat, and when it stops bubbling, vigorously blend in all of the hot milk at once with wire whip, beating until mixture is perfectly smooth. Return over moderately high heat, stirring with whip as sauce thickens and comes to the boil. Boil, stirring, for 2 minutes, season lightly to taste, and remove from heat. Sauce should be quite thick; if too thick for easy spreading, beat in more milk by droplets. (If done ahead, clean off sides of pan and press a sheet of plastic wrap on surface of sauce to prevent a skin from forming.)

Spread a ⅛-inch layer of sauce in the bottom of the baking dish with spatula, spread half the eggplant on top, and cover with half the sauce. Spread rest of eggplant over this and cover with the last of the sauce. Sprinkle the crumbs on top and dribble melted butter over the crumbs.

(*) AHEAD-OF-TIME NOTE: Recipe may be completed to this point and set aside.

To gratiné, if sauce and eggplant are still warm, set 4 to 5 inches under a moderately hot broiler for several minutes, until eggplant is bubbling and crumbs have browned lightly. Otherwise bake in upper third of a 425-degree oven for 15 to 20 minutes, but do not overcook.

Soufflé d'Aubergines en Persillade
[Eggplant Soufflé]

Fold beaten egg whites into the preceding sautéed and sauced eggplant, and you turn it into a soufflé—not the airy cheese type, of course, but something that puffs dramatically in a wide baking dish with removable collar. Serve it, along with a fine tomato sauce, to accompany boiled beef, roast lamb, broiled or roast chicken, or let it be the main course for an informal luncheon.

For 8 servings

The soufflé base

Ingredients for the pre-
ceding 2 lbs. of sautéed
eggplant baked in
béchamel

Following the preceding recipe, peel, cube, salt, drain, and dry the eggplant; sauté in oil until thoroughly tender and very lightly browned. Toss with the shallots or scallions and garlic.

Chop rather roughly with a big knife on a board. (You will have about 2½ cups.) Fold into the pan of *béchamel* sauce, along with the chopped parsley. Carefully correct seasoning.

(*) AHEAD-OF-TIME NOTES: May be completed in advance to this point; clean off sides of pan and lay a sheet of plastic wrap on top of the sauce. You may also fill the mold (next step), cover with a bowl, and bake an hour later.

Assembling and baking— 25 to 30 minutes at 400 degrees

1 Tb soft butter
A 6- to 8-cup baking dish
  about 2 inches deep
  (such as a round one 10
  to 11 inches in diameter,
  or a casserole)
⅓ cup grated Parmesan
  cheese
Waxed paper
Heavy aluminum foil and
  2 straight pins
3 egg yolks
5 egg whites
1½ to 2 cups tomato sauce,
  page 354, or the fresh
  tomato *coulis*, Volume I,
  page 78

Preheat oven in time for baking. Smear butter inside baking dish, sprinkle cheese inside to coat bottom and sides. Shake or knock out excess cheese onto waxed paper and reserve. Encircle circumference of dish with a double thickness of well-buttered aluminum foil secured by pins; foil should rise 1½ inches above rim of dish. Reheat soufflé base, folding over moderate heat. Stir in the egg yolks. Beat the egg whites to stiff peaks (directions are on page 539); stir one fourth of them into the soufflé base along with all but 1 Tb of the reserved Parmesan cheese. Scoop rest of egg whites on top of soufflé base and delicately fold in with a rubber spatula.

Turn the mixture into the prepared dish. Sprinkle on the remaining cheese and set soufflé immediately in lower third of preheated oven. Bake for 25 to 30 minutes until soufflé has risen about double and is nicely browned. (If served as soon as it has risen, the inside will be soft and the soufflé will sink rapidly; if baked 5 minutes more, the soufflé will be drier but will hold up longer. Follow your own preference, but these additional minutes give you some leeway.)

As soon as the soufflé is done, remove from oven, undo aluminum collar, and serve immediately, accompanied by the tomato sauce in a warm bowl.

Pistouille

[Sautéed Eggplant with Tomatoes, Peppers, Garlic, and Basil]

Pistou, a Provençal purée of fresh garlic and basil, is stirred into sautéed eggplant that has simmered with tomatoes, peppers, and onions, making a dish reminiscent of that famous Mediterranean medley, *ratatouille,* but much easier to produce. Good hot or cold, *pistouille* can be served with broiled fish, broiled chicken, roasts, steaks, chops, cold roast pork, veal, or lamb, and any leftovers can stuff eggs, tomatoes, or other vegetables.

NOTE: This dish is naturally at its best when fresh basil and local tomatoes are in season. Out of season, use fresh tomatoes plus a tablespoon or so of canned tomato sauce or purée, and if you cannot find fragrant-smelling dried basil, use oregano.

For 4 to 6 people

Ingredients for salting and sautéing 2 lbs. eggplant, as in the Master Recipe, Steps 1 and 2, page 347	Peel, salt, drain, dry, and then sauté the eggplant in oil until lightly browned as described in the Master Recipe.

The onion, pepper, and tomato garnish

⅔ cup minced onions ⅔ cup diced green bell peppers 2 Tb olive oil 2 cups fresh tomato pulp (2 lbs. tomatoes, peeled, seeded, juiced, and chopped) A 2½-quart saucepan or another frying pan	While the eggplant is macerating in salt, cook the onions and peppers in oil in the pan for 10 to 15 minutes, until tender and translucent but not brown. Add the tomato pulp, cover pan, and simmer 5 minutes to render its juice; uncover pan and simmer over moderate heat for 5 minutes or more until juices have almost entirely evaporated. Set aside.

When eggplant has been sautéed and drained, return it to the frying pan with the tomato mixture and simmer uncovered for about 10 minutes to blend flavors and evaporate more liquid. Mixture should form a thick mass.

The pistou

2 large cloves of garlic	Purée garlic through press, then mash with the basil
A garlic press	or oregano in the bowl to make a smooth paste; fold
12 to 14 large, fresh basil	into the hot eggplant.
leaves, minced (or about	(*) AHEAD-OF-TIME NOTE: May be completed to this
½ Tb fragrant dried	point. Set aside.
basil or oregano)	
A small bowl and a pestle,	
or small wooden spoon	
3 Tb fresh minced parsley	Reheat just before serving, correct seasoning, and fold
	in the parsley.

To serve cold

2 to 3 tomatoes	Whether the eggplant is cooked and cooled or left
Salt and pepper	over, a little ripe tomato will freshen the taste. Peel,
3 Tb fresh minced parsley	seed, and juice the tomatoes; dice the pulp. Place in
½ Tb olive oil	a bowl and fold with the seasonings, parsley, and oil.
	Let stand 10 minutes, drain, and fold into the egg-
	plant.

VARIATION

Aubergines en Pistouille, Froides

[Cold Eggplant *à la Grecque* with Tomatoes and Basil]

Much the same as cold *pistouille,* but with a more piquant flavor, is egg-plant simmered in a *court bouillon,* turned briefly in oil to enhance its flavor, then folded into tomatoes that have also cooked in the *court bouillon.* A final touch is the *pistou* of garlic and basil, which makes this an especially good cold hors d'oeuvre with sardines, tuna, hard-boiled eggs, anchovies, olives, or other Provençal trimmings.

For the court bouillon

3 cups water in a 3-quart	Combine the *court bouillon* ingredients in the sauce-
stainless saucepan	pan and simmer at least 5 minutes, or while you are
1½ Tb lemon juice	preparing the eggplant. Peel eggplant and cut into
3 Tb olive oil	¾-inch cubes. Place half (4 cups) in the simmering
1½ tsp salt	*court bouillon,* bring to the boil, and simmer 5 min-
6 coriander seeds	utes. Drain into bowl, return *court bouillon* to pan,
¼ tsp thyme	and simmer the rest of the eggplant. Drain, return
1 imported bay leaf	*court bouillon* again to pan, boil down rapidly to 1
2 large cloves mashed	cup, and reserve. Meanwhile, pour a $\frac{1}{16}$-inch layer
garlic	of oil into frying pan and sauté drained eggplant

2 lbs. firm, fresh, shiny
    eggplant
A colander set over a bowl
Olive oil
A heavy no-stick frying pan
    (10 to 12 inches in diame-
    ter if possible)
A serving dish

(adding only half if pan is small), using moderately high heat. Shake and swirl the pan frequently by its handle to toss the eggplant, and sauté for several minutes, until eggplant is tender but not browned. Turn into serving dish, leaving oil in pan.

3 to 4 Tb minced shallots
    or scallions
1½ lbs. (6 medium) to-
    matoes, peeled, seeded,
    juiced, and cut into ½-
    inch dice (about 2 cups
    pulp)
1 or 2 cloves garlic
A garlic press
¼ cup fresh basil,
    minced (or about ½ Tb
    fragrant dried basil or
    oregano)
3 Tb fresh minced parsley

Stir the shallots or scallions into the frying pan and cook for a moment, then add the tomatoes and the reduced *court bouillon*. Boil slowly for 5 minutes, then raise heat and boil rapidly until liquid has almost evaporated and tomatoes are quite thick. Correct seasoning. Purée garlic through press into a small bowl; using a wooden spoon, mash with herbs to make a smooth paste; fold this *pistou* into the hot tomatoes. Then fold the tomatoes into the eggplant. When cold, cover and chill. Sprinkle on the parsley before serving.

LA TENTATION DE BRAMAFAM

[Eggplant Caviar with Walnuts—A Cold Spread or Filling]

Recipes for eggplant caviar have been around for years, but this is the only one we know that combines eggplant and walnuts. Tremendously easy to do in the electric mixer, this is something you can keep on hand in the refrigerator for a week or more, and use on toast or crackers, or as a dip for cocktail tidbits, as a filling for hard-boiled eggs or tomato shells, or to pass with cold meats or chicken.

For 4 to 5 cups

About 2 lbs. firm, shiny,
    unblemished eggplant
An electric mixer
7 to 8 ounces (about 2 cups)
    ground walnut meats
    (grind them in an electric
    blender)

Preheat oven to 425 degrees. Cut off green cap and place eggplant (or eggplants) in a shallow roasting dish or pie plate. Bake 30 to 35 minutes or until thoroughly soft to the touch. Cut in half lengthwise and scoop flesh into bowl of mixer. Beat several minutes at high speed to purée the eggplant flesh, then beat in the ground walnuts, salt, pepper, garlic to taste,

¾ tsp salt, and more as
  needed
⅛ tsp pepper
1 to 4 large cloves garlic
  puréed in a press
4 to 6 squirts Tabasco
  sauce
¼ tsp ground allspice
1 tsp freshly grated ginger
  root or ¼ tsp powdered
  ginger
5 to 8 Tb olive oil
Optional, to bring out
  flavor: ½ tsp
  monosodium glutamate

Tabasco, allspice, and ginger. By driblets, as though making mayonnaise, beat in enough oil to make a creamy mass, but not so much as to thin the mixture; it should hold its shape softly when lifted with a spoon. Taste carefully; correct seasoning, adding the MSG if you wish, and the *tentation* is ready to use.

(*) AHEAD-OF-TIME NOTE: Will keep several days under refrigeration; may be frozen.

＊ GRATIN D'AUBERGINES, PROVENÇAL
[Sliced Eggplant Baked with Cheese and Tomatoes]

When you have the time for it, this is a most attractive way to serve eggplant: it is sliced but the peel is left on, and the slices are arranged upright in the baking dish with tomatoes and cheese in between. When baked, the purple-skinned slices form dark ripples separated by hints of red and brown, and the same effect is carried over onto the plates when you serve. This is a particularly good dish to go with roast lamb or veal.

NOTE: Fresh tomato sauce, *coulis de tomates,* in Volume I, page 78, is the most desirable one here, but the following sauce with canned Italian tomatoes is an excellent alternative. We prefer canned tomatoes to tomato purée because they are less concentrated and the resulting sauce, we think, tastes more like the fresh.

For 4 to 6 servings

---

1) *The tomato sauce (using canned tomatoes)—for about 1 cup*

1 cup minced onions
2 Tb olive oil or cooking
  oil
A heavy bottomed 2-quart
  saucepan with cover
A 1-lb. can of peeled
  Italian-style plum
  (pear-shaped) tomatoes

Stir the onions into the oil, cover pan, and cook over low heat, stirring occasionally, for 8 to 10 minutes or until onions are tender and translucent but not browned. Meanwhile drain the tomatoes, collecting their juice in the bowl; pour juice back into the can and reserve. Rub the tomatoes through the sieve to eliminate seeds. When onions are tender, stir in the sieved tomato pulp and the herbs, orange peel, saffron,

A sieve set over a bowl
1 bay leaf
¼ tsp thyme or oregano
A 1-inch piece of dried
    orange peel or ¼ tsp
    bottled dried peel
A pinch of saffron threads
1 large clove mashed
    garlic
¼ tsp salt

garlic, and salt. Cover pan loosely and simmer, stirring occasionally, and adding a little of the tomato juice if sauce becomes too thick. Let sauce simmer at least 30 minutes, although a total of 45 to 60 minutes will make it even better. Taste carefully and correct seasoning. Sauce should be thick enough to hold its shape softly in a spoon.

(*) AHEAD-OF-TIME NOTE: May be made several days in advance and refrigerated; may be frozen.

---

2) *Blanching and sautéing the eggplant*

2 lbs. firm, fresh, shiny
    eggplants (or eggplant)

Cut off green caps, and wash the eggplants but do not peel them. *Halve or quarter the eggplants,* depending on size, and cut into slices ⅜ inch thick and about 2 inches from skin side to bottom of slice.

A large saucepan of boil-
    ing salted water (1½
    tsp salt per quart)
A skimmer or slotted
    spoon
A tray covered with several
    thicknesses of paper
    toweling, and additional
    paper towels
A large (11-inch) frying
    pan, preferably no-stick
Olive oil or cooking oil
A flexible-blade spatula
A second tray or a platter
    to hold sautéed eggplant

A dozen slices or so at a time, blanch in the boiling water for 2 minutes—barely to soften, not to cook through; dip out with skimmer or spoon, and drain on paper towels.

Pat tops of slices dry with towels. Pour a ⅛-inch layer of oil into frying pan; heat to very hot but not smoking. Sauté for a minute as many slices in pan as will fit in one layer, on each side, barely browning them, and transfer to second tray. Continue with rest of slices, adding more oil to pan as necessary. (Although all of this is somewhat of a nuisance, it is this step that gives the final dish its distinction.)

3) *Assembling*

An oiled 5- to 6- cup flame-
    proof gratin dish, such as
    an oval one 10 to 11 inches
    long and 2 inches deep
About 4 ounces Swiss
    cheese sliced $\frac{1}{16}$ inch
    thick
The reserved tomato juice
Aluminum foil

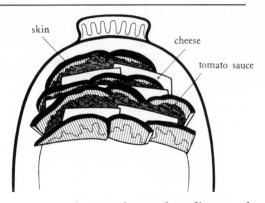

*Arrange the eggplant slices purple
side uppermost in overlapping rows,
each row spread with tomato sauce
and covered with slices of cheese as
shown.*

If you need more room, push the rows more closely together as you go; if you
need less, let them lie flatter. Pour in about $\frac{1}{2}$ cup of the tomato juice, enough to
come $\frac{1}{2}$ to $\frac{2}{3}$ the way up the eggplant. Cover closely with the foil.

(*) AHEAD-OF-TIME NOTE: May be prepared in advance to this point; refrigerate
if you are not going to bake within an hour or so.

4) *Baking and serving—preheat oven to 375 degrees*

Heat briefly on top of stove, just until contents start to bubble, then bake for 45
minutes to an hour in the middle level of the preheated oven. Eggplant is done when
the slices are tender and juices have thickened but are not quite absorbed. Uncover
for last 10 minutes of baking so that cheese will brown and liquid will thicken more.
(Add more tomato juice if there is danger of eggplant drying out before it is done.)
Serve bubbling hot.

(*) AHEAD-OF-TIME NOTE: This may be baked well in advance of serving, and
then reheated. If so, take it out of the oven before liquid is quite absorbed, so there
will be enough to moisten the eggplant during its reheating. Any leftovers may be
transferred to a smaller dish and reheated under a slow broiler.

VARIATION

Gratin d'Aubergines Farcies

[Main-course Eggplant and Tomato Casserole for Leftover Meat]

Sautéed sliced eggplant, an excellent tomato sauce, and grated cheese
are just the elements for turning yesterday's roast into a splendid new main

course. Turkey, veal, or pork respond especially well to this treatment. The meat is ground and flavored, while the other elements are the same as in the preceding recipe. You may arrange the eggplant in upright slices if you wish to take the time, or lay them flat as suggested here and build the casserole in layers. Serve this hot with French bread and a chilled rosé wine, and follow with a tossed green salad. It is also delicious served cold.

NOTE: As in most recipes of this type, exact proportions are not of vital importance. If you have less or more meat, add fewer or more onions and the other ingredients that flavor it.

For 6 to 8 people

_____

The meat mixture

1 cup minced onions
2 Tb olive oil or cooking oil
An 8-inch frying pan with cover

Stir the onions into the oil, cover the pan, and cook over low heat, stirring occasionally, for 8 to 10 minutes or until onions are tender. Raise heat and stir to brown onions lightly for 2 to 3 minutes.

_____

About 2 cups ground cooked veal, pork, or turkey (previously trimmed of all fat, skin, and gristle)
About ½ cup ground baked or boiled ham, or ready-to-cook packaged ham slice (you may include some of the fat)
About ¼ tsp of whatever herb you prefer and are using in the tomato sauce (thyme, oregano, fresh basil, rosemary)
½ cup thickened gravy from the roast, or ½ cup stock or bouillon blended with 1½ tsp cornstarch
1 clove mashed garlic
Salt and pepper to taste
1 egg
3 to 4 Tb chopped fresh parsley

Stir the ground meat into the onions, along with the herbs, the gravy or bouillon, and garlic. Simmer 2 to 3 minutes to blend flavors. Season carefully with salt and pepper to taste, and a little more of the herb if you think it necessary. Let cool while you are completing other parts of the recipe. When tepid or cold, blend in the egg and the parsley.

_____

Assembling the casserole

Ingredients for the 2 lbs. sliced, blanched, and sautéed eggplant in preceding recipe, but 2 cups tomato sauce, and the tomato juice and 1 cup coarsely grated Swiss cheese (or ⅔ cup Parmesan if you prefer)
An oiled 3-quart baking dish or casserole such as a round earthenware one 10 inches in diameter at the top and 3 inches deep
¼ cup coarse white bread crumbs, fresh or stale
2 Tb olive oil or melted butter
A rubber spatula
1 cup tomato juice
A cover for the casserole, or aluminum foil

For a round casserole 10 by 3 inches, you will have 4 layers each of eggplant, meat, tomato sauce, and cheese. Arrange them, then, in the casserole in that order, ending with a mixture of cheese and bread crumbs tossed together. Dribble olive oil or melted butter over the top. Drawing edges of ingredients ¼ inch toward center of casserole in several places, pour in the cup of tomato juice.

(*) AHEAD-OF-TIME NOTE: May be assembled a day in advance of baking.

Baking and serving—about 1¼ hours at 375 degrees

Cover, heat to simmer on top of stove, and bake as directed in Step 4 of preceding Master Recipe.

(*) AHEAD-OF-TIME NOTE: May be baked in advance and reheated.

TWO RECIPES FOR GREENS

BLETTES GRATINÉES
[Swiss Chard Gratinéed with Cheese Sauce]

This way of serving chard brings out its special flavor, and makes it a most attractive accompaniment to roast beef or chicken. Here both the long white stems and the large green leaves are used, but they are cooked separately before being combined.

For 6 to 8 servings

1) *Preparing the chard*

About 10 stalks (2 bunches) fresh chard

Cut the green part of the leaves off the white of the stalk that runs up the center of the leaves. Wash leaves and set aside. Trim off any discolored bits and ends, wash the long white stalks thoroughly, and cut into ¼-inch slices (makes about 8 cups).

2) *Cooking the white stalks*

¼ cup flour (instant-
  blending works nicely
  here)
A heavy-bottomed 2½-
  quart saucepan (no-stick
  is useful)
A wire whip
1 cup cold water and 2 cups
  hot water
1 tsp salt
1 Tb lemon juice
The sliced stalks
A wooden spoon
A sieve set over a bowl

Place flour in saucepan. Beating with wire whip, gradually blend in the cold water to make a smooth mixture. Beat in the hot water, salt, and lemon juice, and bring to the simmer, stirring. Add chard stalks and simmer about 30 minutes or until they are tender, stirring occasionally, and adding a little more water, if necessary, to prevent scorching. Drain, reserving cooking liquid. (You will note that the chard stalks acquire a subtle flavor when finally tender, and that they leave a sticky film on the bottom of the pan.)

3) *Cooking the green leaves*

The green leaves
A large pan of boiling
  salted water
A colander

While the stalks are simmering, drop the leaves into the boiling water, bring rapidly back to the boil, and boil uncovered for 5 to 6 minutes or until leaves are fairly tender. Drain, refresh in cold water, squeeze dry a handful at a time, and chop. You will have almost 2 cups; mix them into the cooked stalks.

4) *Sauce and assembly*

1 egg yolk
¼ cup heavy cream
A clean saucepan
The stalk-cooking liquid
  (plus milk if necessary to
  make 2 cups)
Salt and pepper to taste
A buttered 5- to 6-cup
  baking dish about 2
  inches deep
¼ cup grated Parmesan
  cheese
1 Tb butter

Blend the egg yolk and cream in the saucepan with a wire whip, then gradually blend in the stalk-cooking liquid. Bring to the simmer, stirring, and simmer 1 minute. Correct seasoning. Spoon a layer onto the bottom of the baking dish. Taste the cooked stalks and leaves, and season if necessary. Spread half in the dish, spread on half the sauce and half the cheese. Repeat with the remaining chard, sauce, and cheese and top with the butter, cut into dots.

(*) AHEAD-OF-TIME NOTE: May be completed a day before serving; cover with plastic and refrigerate.

5) *Serving*

If chard is still warm, set under a slow broiler until just beginning to bubble and top is nicely browned. If cold, set in upper third of preheated 375-degree oven for about 30 minutes just until bubbling hot and top has browned.

GRATIN D'ÉPINARDS AUX OIGNONS

[Spinach Braised with Onions—also for other greens]

This is creamed spinach with character, which will stand up to steaks, chops, roasts, and broiled fish; you can also serve it with poached eggs and *croûtons*. Although fresh is best, frozen spinach is very successful done this way, as are other greens such as collards, chard, and kale.

For 4 people

1 cup minced onions
3 Tb olive oil
An 8-inch, heavy-bottomed no-stick or enameled frying pan
Optional: 1 to 2 large cloves garlic, mashed
2 cups blanched, chopped spinach (2 lbs. fresh spinach boiled 3 minutes, drained, squeezed dry, and chopped)
2 Tb flour
1 cup hot milk, more if needed
Salt and pepper to taste
2 to 4 Tb heavy cream

Cook the onions in the oil for 8 to 10 minutes or more until tender and just beginning to brown lightly. Add optional garlic and cook for a few seconds, then stir in the spinach and cook over moderate heat, stirring, for 2 minutes. Blend in the flour and stir over moderate heat for 2 minutes more. Remove pan from heat; gradually blend in the milk. Set again over heat, bring to the simmer, stirring, and add seasonings to taste. Simmer slowly over low heat for 10 to 15 minutes, stirring occasionally to be sure spinach is not sticking to pan. Spinach is done when it is tender and has absorbed the milk. (If you are doing other greens you may have to cook them longer, and add a little more milk.) Just before serving, taste carefully for seasoning and stir in the cream, a tablespoon at a time.

(*) AHEAD-OF-TIME NOTE: Set spinach aside after it has simmered in the milk; smooth it with a rubber spatula and spread 2 tablespoons of cream over it. Reheat and finish seasoning just before serving.

PUMPKINS AND SQUASHES

Courges et Courgettes

Before Columbus sailed back from his famous voyage of 1492 the squash family was unknown in Europe. The only written accounts date from after his return, and this seems as good a reason as any to trace the origin of squash from the Americas. Our word, "squash," is of Algonquin origin; the Latin generic is *Cucurbita,* and the French, *courge.* Hard-shell, mature, yellow-fleshed varieties like Hubbard, turban, acorn squash, and even pumpkin come under the popular heading of winter squashes, *courges,* while the soft-shell, tender-seeded types like zucchini, yellow crooknecks, and pattypans are called summer squashes, *courgettes.* However, winter squash is available in August, and summer squash can be found in December as well as June. Our main emphasis here will be on summer squash, particularly zucchini, but we shall start off with a prize pumpkin.

LE POTIRON TOUT ROND

[Stuffed Pumpkin or Pumpkin Soup Served in a Pumpkin]

In France a *potiron* is any member of the squash family including the *citrouille,* which is a pumpkin-like yellow-fleshed squash tasting like our Hubbard and acorn squashes. Thus you can never be quite sure whether you are getting in France what we would call pumpkin or what we would call squash; many's the bride who has tried to duplicate her French mother-in-law's famous *potage au potiron* and finds that the secret ingredient which gave that wonderful flavor was squash rather than pumpkin. Use American pumpkin for this recipe, which can be either a soup or the starchy vegetable to go with turkey, goose, duck, pork, or game birds. Cooked and served in the pumpkin itself, this always makes an amusing presentation.

As a vegetable serving 6 to 8

1½ cups (pressed down) fresh white crumbs from nonsweetened home-made-type white bread

A roasting pan

A fine, hard, unblemished 4-lb. pumpkin (about 6 inches in diameter) with 2-inch stem

1 Tb soft butter

Salt

Spread the bread crumbs in the roasting pan and let them dry out in a 300-degree oven, stirring occasionally; this will take about 15 minutes. Meanwhile, with a short, stout knife, cut a cover 4 inches in diameter out of the top of the pumpkin. Scrape all the stringy material and seeds from cover and inside of pumpkin (an ice-cream spoon and grapefruit knife are useful for this). Rub inside of pumpkin and the cover with the soft butter and sprinkle lightly with salt.

⅔ cup finely minced onions

6 Tb butter

An 8-inch frying pan

½ tsp salt

Pinch of pepper and nutmeg

½ tsp ground sage

While bread crumbs are drying, cook the onions in the butter for 8 to 10 minutes over low heat until tender and translucent. Then stir in the crumbs and let them cook slowly for 2 minutes to absorb the butter. Stir in seasonings and sage. Remove from heat and stir in the cheese, then spoon the mixture into the pumpkin. Pour in the cream, adding enough so

½ cup finely diced or
   coarsely grated Swiss
   cheese
2 to 2¼ cups light cream
1 bay leaf
A shallow lightly buttered
   baking/serving dish to
   hold the pumpkin

mixture comes to within ½ inch of pumpkin rim. Lay bay leaf on top and replace cover.

(*) AHEAD-OF-TIME NOTE: May be prepared in advance to this point.

Baking and serving—baking time about 2 hours

Bake in a preheated 400-degree oven for about 1½ hours, until pumpkin is beginning to soften on the outside and the inside is beginning to bubble. Reduce oven thermostat to 350 and bake another half hour until pumpkin is tender but still holds its shape solidly. (If pumpkin is browning too much, cover loosely with foil or brown paper.)

(*) AHEAD-OF-TIME NOTE: May be kept warm in a 200-degree oven for half an hour at least.

To serve, remove cover and dip into pumpkin with a long-handled spoon, scraping flesh off bottom and sides of pumpkin with each serving of the filling.

Pumpkin Soup

Use a 6- to 7-pound pumpkin and the same ingredients, except replace the cream with enough chicken stock to come within ½ inch of rim. Stir half a cup or so of heavy cream and a handful of chopped parsley into soup just before serving.

ZUCCHINI—AND OTHER SUMMER SQUASHES
Courgettes

Zucchini, the familiar almost cucumber-shaped green squash that is on the market all year, is our main concern here, although you may substitute yellow crooknecks or straightnecks, or the striped, green, zucchini-like *cocozelle* in any of the recipes. Scallop or pattypan squash (*patisson*) may also be adapted, particularly in the recipes for stuffed zucchini.

HOW TO BUY AND STORE SUMMER SQUASHES

When you are buying summer squash, look for obviously fresh, clean specimens that feel heavy, are firm to the touch all over, and have skin so tender you can pierce it easily with a fingernail. Fully edible summer squashes are immature: when you cut them open the seeds are soft and the tissue surrounding the seeds is moist and crisp. In all of these squashes, except for the giant crookneck, size indicates quality. Beware of foot-long zucchini, crook- and straightnecks over 10 inches, *cocozelles* more than 8 inches, patty-pans that exceed 4 inches in diameter. However, if you do find yourself with slightly overage squashes, you can peel them if the skin seems tough, quarter them lengthwise, and cut out the pulpy core and tough seeds; use only the moist, crisp flesh between skin and core. Store summer squashes in a plastic bag in the refrigerator, where they will keep for a week to 10 days if very fresh.

PRELIMINARIES TO COOKING

Peeling, salting, blanching

Tender-skinned squashes need no peeling; their flavor is delicate anyway, and to remove the peel makes them taste even milder. Both yellow and green tender squashes contain a large amount of vegetable water, and if you do not deal with it in some way before the serious cooking begins, you will have watery casseroles and overcooked sautés. There are two methods for eliminating the water, both equally good because neither removes essential flavor. The easiest method, when you are to sauté chunks of zucchini, for instance, or hollow it out for a stuffing, is to drop the whole squash into boiling salted water and boil about 10 minutes, just until the flesh begins to yield to pressure. This is called blanching. The second method, for cut or grated squash, is to salt it, let it stand for 20 minutes until the water oozes out of the tissues, then squeeze or pat it dry. We shall use both systems here, starting out with a number of unusual recipes for blanched, sautéed zucchini.

You will notice that only twice is any herb but parsley used in the following recipes, in order that the delicate flavor of the zucchini may be pointed up rather than masked. Preliminary sautéing of the zucchini before saucing or simmering does much to bring out its flavor, and shallots, onions, garlic, and cheese seem to be its natural complements.

WEIGHTS AND MEASURES

1 zucchini 8 inches long and 1¾ inches at its widest diameter weighs 5 to 6 ounces; 3 zucchinis of this size weigh about 1 pound.

1 pound of plain, raw diced or sliced zucchini makes about 3½ cups.

1 pound of freshly grated zucchini, lightly pressed down, makes about 2 cups; when salted and squeezed it makes 1 cup and renders ⅔ cup of juice.

1 pound of zucchini will provide 2 to 3 servings as a vegetable garnish.

Recipes Using Whole Blanched Zucchini

Courgettes Blanchies

TO BLANCH WHOLE ZUCCHINI—OR OTHER SUMMER SQUASH

The object in blanching zucchini or other summer squashes is to boil them just long enough to minimize the oozing out of their vegetable water, but not long enough to cook them quite through. In other words, they are not tender; they hold their shape.

Shave the stem and the tip off each zucchini (or other summer squash), scrub thoroughly but not harshly with a vegetable brush under cold, running water to remove any clinging sand or dirt. Plunge zucchini into a large kettle or saucepan of boiling, salted water; when water returns again to the boil, boil them slowly, uncovered, for 10 to 12 minutes usually, until the flesh will just yield slightly to pressure. Test each zucchini, and remove one by one as they are done, plunging them into cold water. Drain, and the zucchini are ready for sautéing, stuffing, creaming or whatever the following recipes direct. If you are not continuing the recipe until the next day, cover and refrigerate them.

✳ *COURGETTES SAUTÉES, MAÎTRE D'HÔTEL*

[Zucchini Sautéed in Butter with Lemon and Parsley]

One of the very easiest and most delicious ways to serve zucchini is to blanch it whole, cut it into large dice, then toss in butter and seasonings, finishing it off with lemon juice and parsley. Cooked this way, zucchini goes with anything, and it is particularly recommended when you want a simply done green vegetable to go with something rather elaborate, such as *escalopes de veau à la crème* or a chicken fricassee.

For 6 people

1) *Sautéing the zucchini*

2 to 2½ lbs. blanched zucchini (6 to 7 zucchini 8 by 1¾ inches, for example)
Paper towels
About 4 Tb butter

After the zucchini have been scrubbed, blanched, and drained as in the preceding directions, cut them in quarters or sixths lengthwise, depending on their diameter. Cut the lengths crosswise into 1-inch pieces, and pat dry with paper towels. Melt 2 tablespoons of butter with 1 of oil over high heat. When butter foam

1 to 2 Tb olive oil or cook-
  ing oil
A large (11-inch) no-stick
  or enameled frying pan
A cover for the pan
Salt and pepper

has begun to subside, toss in the zucchini. Toss and
turn frequently, shaking and swirling the pan by its
handle, for 5 minutes or more, until zucchini is beginning to brown very lightly. By this time, it should
be just tender; if not, cover pan and cook over low
heat for several minutes. (If you are using a smaller
pan, sauté in several batches and turn each batch out
onto a dish until all is done, then return them all to
the pan.) Toss with salt and pepper to taste.

(*) AHEAD-OF-TIME NOTE: May be done in advance to
this point. Set aside. Reheat to sizzling before continuing.

2) *The maître d'hôtel seasoning*

Drops of fresh lemon juice
Remaining butter from
  Step 1
2 to 3 Tb fresh minced
  parsley
A hot serving dish or the
  meat platter

Just before serving, toss with drops of lemon juice;
correct seasoning, and add a little more lemon juice if
you feel it is necessary. Then toss with another tablespoon or so of butter and the parsley. Turn out onto
hot dish and serve immediately.

VARIATIONS

Courgettes Sautées à la Provençale
[Zucchini Sautéed in Olive Oil with Garlic and Parsley]

Garlic and olive oil are especially good with zucchini, and this dish
goes well with steaks, chops, broiled chicken, and fish.

2 to 2½ lbs. blanched zucchini quartered length-
  wise and cut into 1-inch
  pieces
3 to 4 Tb olive oil
Salt and pepper to taste
2 to 3 cloves garlic, mashed
  or finely minced
Optional: ¼ cup dry, fairly
  coarse crumbs from non-
  sweetened homemade-
  type white bread
3 to 4 Tb fresh minced
  parsley

Dry the zucchini pieces with paper toweling and
sauté, tossing frequently, in hot olive oil until just
tender and very lightly browned. The moment before
serving, toss over moderately high heat with the
seasonings, garlic, and optional bread crumbs, then
with the parsley.

Courgettes Gratinées à la Milanaise
[Zucchini Pieces Sautéed, then Baked with Cheese]

This is a convenient ahead-of-time preparation that goes nicely with broiled chicken or fish and with steaks or chops.

2 to 2½ lbs. zucchini prepared as in either of the 2 preceding recipes
A heavily buttered 6- to 8-cup baking and serving dish about 2½ inches deep
½ cup grated Parmesan or Swiss and Parmesan cheese
2 Tb melted butter or olive oil

Prepare the zucchini as directed, but leave it slightly undercooked. Sprinkle baking dish with cheese, and fill with layers of zucchini and cheese, dribbling butter or oil over all. If zucchini is still warm, reheat and brown lightly for several minutes under the broiler; otherwise, reheat to sizzling for about 15 minutes in upper third of a 425-degree oven.

Courgettes Étuvées à la Crème
[Zucchini Simmered in Cream and Tarragon]

The French word *moelleux* can probably best describe the tender, melting, softly fragrant quality of zucchini warmed in butter and shallots and then simmered in cream and tarragon. This lovely dish goes particularly well with roast chicken and veal.

PRELIMINARY NOTE: Cut the zucchini into any shape you wish. Although the 1-inch pieces used in the preceding recipes are easiest to cook, round slices half an inch thick or lengthwise strips ⅜ inch thick and 2½ to 3 inches long are attractive to serve. Choose for the cooking an 11- to 12-inch no-stick or enameled frying pan, straight-sided chicken fryer, electric skillet, or casserole. If you decide to cut the zucchini into strips, you will have to do the preliminary sauté in several batches.

For 6 people

2 to 2½ lbs. zucchini blanched whole as directed on page 364
About 4 Tb butter
One of the pans discussed in preceding paragraph

Cut the blanched zucchini as discussed in preceding paragraph; dry well on paper towels. Over moderate heat, melt enough butter in pan to film it by $\frac{1}{16}$ inch. When butter foam begins to subside, sauté the zucchini for 2 to 3 minutes, tossing or turning, until it is well warmed through but is not browning.

Salt and white pepper
2 Tb minced shallots or
　scallions
1 tsp fresh minced tarragon
　or ¼ tsp fragrant dried
　tarragon; more if needed
About 1 cup *crème fraîche*
　or heavy cream, more if
　needed

Season to taste with salt and pepper, sprinkle on the shallots or scallions and tarragon, and pour in the cream. Simmer for about 10 minutes, basting frequently with the cream, until zucchini is tender and cream has reduced enough to enrobe the zucchini pieces.

(*) AHEAD-OF-TIME NOTE: May be done in advance to this point; set aside uncovered. Reheat to simmer before proceeding.

More cream if needed, and
　the remaining butter
2 Tb fresh minced parsley
　plus 1 tsp fresh minced
　tarragon if available
A hot serving dish

Just before serving, taste carefully for seasoning, adding a little more tarragon as well as salt and pepper if needed. If sauce has reduced too much or if it looks slightly curdled, add 2 to 3 tablespoons more cream; bring to simmer, remove from heat, and baste the zucchini to smooth out the sauce. Add also another tablespoon of butter, basting until it has been absorbed. Arrange on hot dish, sprinkle on the herbs, and serve immediately.

A slightly less fattening variation

Rather than simmering the zucchini in pure cream, you may use a thin cream sauce, such as that in which the sliced potatoes and basil simmer on page 388.

OTHER WAYS OF SERVING BLANCHED SAUTÉED ZUCCHINI

Courgettes Gratinées, Mornay

[Zucchini Gratinéed with Cheese Sauce]

When you want a creamy vegetable dish to go with broiled meats or roast chicken, and one that you can get ready for the oven well ahead of time, prepare sautéed zucchini with lemon and parsley as in the Master Recipe on page 364. Then turn to the Broccoli Mornay recipe on page 342; fold the zucchini into the cheese sauce, arrange in a baking dish, and finish it off with cheese and butter in the oven as described for the broccoli.

Courgettes en Persillade, Gratinées

[Zucchini Baked with Garlic, Parsley, and *Béchamel*]

An alternative to the preceding cheese sauce is zucchini sautéed in olive oil with garlic and parsley, as in the first variation, on page 365, then baked in a *béchamel* sauce topped with bread crumbs and butter, following the eggplant recipe on page 348. The little hint of garlic here is delicious, and the dish goes nicely with steaks, chops, and roast lamb.

Courgettes en Pistouille
[Zucchini with Tomatoes, Peppers, Garlic, and Basil]

Here sautéed zucchini is simmered in a mixture of cooked onions, peppers, and tomatoes, and given a final *pistou* flavoring of garlic and basil. This goes hot with broiled fish, chicken, roasts, steaks, and chops, and cold on picnics. Follow the recipe in the eggplant section on page 351, substituting blanched, sautéed zucchini pieces for eggplant.

Recipes Using Coarsely Grated and Salted Zucchini
Courgettes Rapées

An interesting and easy way to serve zucchini or other tender summer squashes is to grate them, salt them so the vegetable water runs out, squeeze gently dry, and sauté in butter or olive oil for a few minutes until tender. You can then serve the zucchini as is, simmer it with cream, bake it in a sauce, or turn it into a molded custard. The preliminary sauté gives added flavor, as well as removing extra vegetable water. Anyone eating grated zucchini for the first time is almost certain to think it is a remarkable new vegetable.

TO GRATE AND SALT ZUCCHINI—OR OTHER SUMMER SQUASHES

Shave the stem and the tip off each zucchini (or other summer squash), scrub the vegetable thoroughly but not harshly with a brush under cold running water to remove any clinging sand or dirt. If vegetables are large, halve or quarter them. If seeds are large and at all tough, and surrounding flesh is coarse rather than moist and crisp, which is more often the case with yellow squashes and striped green *cocozelles* than with zucchini, cut out and discard the cores. Rub the squash against the coarse side of a grater, and place grated flesh in a colander set over a bowl. For each 1 pound (2 cups) of grated squash, toss with 1 teaspoon of salt, mixing thoroughly. Let the squash drain 3 or 4 minutes, or until you are ready to proceed. Just before cooking, squeeze a handful dry and taste. If by any chance the squash is too salty, rinse in a large bowl of cold water, taste again; rinse and drain again if necessary. Then squeeze gently by handfuls, letting juices run back into bowl. Dry on paper towels. Zucchini will not be fluffy; it is still dampish, but the excess liquid is out.

The pale-green, slightly saline juice drained and squeezed out of the zucchini has a certain faint flavor that can find its uses in vegetable soups, canned soups, or vegetable sauces.

---

* *COURGETTES RAPÉES, SAUTÉES*

[Grated Zucchini Sautéed in Butter and Shallots]

This is the base recipe for sautéed grated zucchini. Serve it as is, with the addition of a little more butter, or turn it into one of the variations that follow. Like the blanched and sautéed zucchini pieces, this recipe goes with anything and is particularly useful when you want a rather neutral but attractive green accompaniment to creamed dishes like sweetbreads and elaborate soles in white wine sauces. You may also use it rather than spinach as a bed for poached eggs in hollandaise sauce, creamed chicken, and their like.

For 4 to 6 servings

1) *Preliminary sautéing*

2 to 2½ lbs. zucchini (6 to 7 zucchini 8 by 1¾ inches, for example)

2 Tb butter

1 Tb olive oil or cooking oil

A large (11-inch) no-stick or enameled frying pan

2 to 3 Tb minced shallots or scallions

A cover for the pan if needed

Trim, wash, grate, salt, squeeze, and dry the zucchini as directed in notes preceding this recipe. (You will have 2 to 2½ cups.) Melt the butter with the olive oil over moderate heat, stir in the shallots or scallions, and cook for a moment, then raise heat to moderately high. When butter foam has begun to subside, add zucchini. Toss and turn it frequently for 4 to 5 minutes, shaking and swirling the pan by its handle. Zucchini is ready to serve as soon as it is tender; taste to check. (If you wish, you may cover the pan and finish cooking for a few more minutes over low heat.)

(*) AHEAD-OF-TIME NOTE: Zucchini may be completed to this point several hours in advance of serving. Set aside uncovered; cover when cool, and reheat before proceeding.

2) *Final flavoring and serving*

More salt if needed, and white pepper

2 to 3 Tb soft butter, more if you wish

A rubber spatula

A hot serving dish

Shortly before serving, reheat the zucchini, tossing and turning it. Taste carefully for seasoning. Remove from heat and fold in the butter, a tablespoon at a time, with rubber spatula. Turn into hot dish and serve immediately.

VARIATIONS

Courgettes Rapées à la Crème
[Grated Zucchini Simmered in Cream]

After sautéing the zucchini, Step 1 in the preceding Master Recipe, pour in about 1 cup of *crème fraîche* or heavy cream; simmer the zucchini for several minutes until cream has been absorbed and thickened. Reheat just before serving, and fold in a tablespoon or so of soft butter.

Courgettes Rapées, Sautées à la Provençale
[Grated Zucchini Sautéed in Olive Oil with Garlic]

Rather than sautéing the grated zucchini in butter, use olive oil for Step 1 in the Master Recipe. Retain the shallots or scallions if you wish, and add to them 1 or 2 cloves of mashed or finely minced garlic.

Courgettes aux Épinards
[Sauté of Grated Zucchini and Chopped Spinach]

The addition of spinach gives more character to a zucchini dish or zucchini gives more tenderness to a spinach dish, whichever way you want to look at it. Substitute this attractive combination for plain zucchini in any of the preceding or following variations. We have suggested olive oil and garlic here, but you may prefer the butter and shallots of the Master Recipe on page 369. We have also directed that the spinach receive a brief preliminary blanching in boiling water; however, this may be dispensed with if your spinach is young, tender, and fresh from the garden.

For 6 to 8 servings

2 to 2½ lbs. zucchini
About 2 lbs. fresh spinach
A large kettle of boiling salted water
A colander

Following the directions on page 368, trim, wash, grate, salt, squeeze, and dry the zucchini. While it is draining with salt, trim and wash the spinach; drop it into the rapidly boiling water and boil for a minute or two, just until limp. Drain, refresh in cold water, squeeze dry, and chop.

2 to 3 Tb olive oil
1 or 2 large cloves of mashed garlic

When zucchini has been squeezed and dried, sauté, tossing and turning frequently, in the hot oil with the garlic. When almost tender, stir in the chopped

Salt and pepper
2 to 3 Tb soft butter

spinach. About 10 minutes before serving, reheat, tossing and stirring, then cover pan and let cook several minutes over low heat, until spinach is as tender as you wish it to be. Season carefully to taste. Remove from heat and fold in the butter, a tablespoon at a time. Turn into a hot dish and serve immediately.

Tian de Courgettes au Riz
[Gratin of Zucchini, Rice, and Onions with Cheese]

The *tian* is, or was in the old days, a shallow, rectangular, earthenware Provençal baking dish. Anything cooked in it becomes a *tian,* just as something like chicken cooked in a casserole becomes a casserole of chicken. The *tian,* as a name, has been in vogue lately, but its shape and contents can vary considerably. Zucchini and rice are typical, as are additions of Swiss chard and spinach; thus you could use the preceding combination of zucchini and spinach, if you wish, rather than zucchini alone as suggested here. Serve with roasts, steaks, chops, calf's liver, broiled fish or chicken, or as a first course.

For 6 people

2 to 2½ lbs. zucchini
½ cup plain, raw, untreated white rice
1 cup minced onions
3 to 4 Tb olive oil
2 large cloves garlic, mashed or finely minced
2 Tb flour
About 2½ cups hot liquid: zucchini juices plus milk, heated in a pan
About ⅔ cup grated Parmesan cheese (save 2 Tb for later)
Salt and pepper
A heavily buttered 6- to 8-cup, flameproof baking and serving dish about 1½ inches deep
2 Tb olive oil

Following directions on page 368, trim, wash, grate, salt, squeeze, and dry the zucchini. While it is draining (reserve the juices,) drop the rice into boiling salted water, bring rapidly back to the boil, and boil exactly 5 minutes; drain and set aside. In a large (11-inch) frying pan, cook the onions slowly in the oil for 8 to 10 minutes until tender and translucent. Raise heat slightly and stir several minutes until very lightly browned. Then stir in the grated and dried zucchini and the garlic. Toss and turn for 5 to 6 minutes until zucchini is almost tender. Sprinkle in the flour, stir over moderate heat for 2 minutes, and remove from heat. Gradually stir in the hot liquid, being sure the flour is well blended and smooth. Return over moderately high heat and bring to the simmer, stirring. Remove from heat again, stir in the blanched rice and all but 2 tablespoons of the cheese. Taste very carefully for seasoning. Turn into buttered baking dish, strew remaining cheese on top, and dribble the olive oil over the cheese. (Preheat oven in time for baking.)

(*) AHEAD-OF-TIME NOTE: May be prepared several hours or a day in advance of final cooking.

About half an hour before serving, bring to simmer on top of stove, then set in upper third of a preheated 425-degree oven until *tian* is bubbling and top has browned nicely. The rice should absorb all the liquid.

Timbale de Courgettes
[Molded Custard of Zucchini, Onions, and Cheese]

Here is a delightful concoction that is elegant to serve either as a first course, a luncheon dish, or to accompany roast or broiled chicken, a saddle of lamb, or veal or lamb chops. It is a mixture of grated and sautéed zucchini, cooked onions, cheese, cream, and eggs that is unmolded after baking, and then sprinkled with buttered bread crumbs and parsley. One of its most attractive qualities, besides its flavor, is the rather moist texture given it by the cheese, reminiscent of the soft center in a fine soufflé.

EGG PROPORTIONS FOR UNMOLDED CUSTARDS: For a custard of this type, count on 2 "large" eggs for every cup of other ingredients; one quart of ingredients, then, calls for 8 ($1\frac{1}{2}$ to $1\frac{2}{3}$ cups) "large" eggs and a 6-cup baking dish.

For 6 people

---

1) *The zucchini mixture*

About 2 lbs. zucchini 2 cups minced onions 3 Tb butter 1 Tb olive oil or cooking oil Salt and pepper A 1-quart measure A rubber spatula	Following directions on page 368, trim, wash, grate, salt, squeeze, and dry the zucchini; you should have 2 to $2\frac{1}{3}$ cups approximately. While zucchini is draining, cook the onions slowly for 12 to 15 minutes or longer, with the butter and oil, in a large (11-inch) frying pan until onions are very tender, translucent, and just beginning to brown. Raise heat, stir in the zucchini; toss and turn for 5 to 6 minutes. Cover pan and cook zucchini several minutes longer over low heat, until tender. Season to taste and scrape into quart measure.

---

2) *The custard mixture—for about $5\frac{1}{2}$ cups*

4 ounces (1 cup lightly pressed) mixed grated Parmesan and Swiss cheese 1 cup all-purpose cream, more if needed A $2\frac{1}{2}$- to 3-quart mixing bowl and a wire whip	Add the cheese to the vegetables in the quart measure, and pour in enough cream, stirring, to reach the 4-cup mark. Turn the mixture into the bowl, scraping measure clean. Break eggs into measure, being sure you have at least $1\frac{1}{2}$ cups; beat to blend yolks and whites, and fold into the zucchini mixture. Taste carefully for seasoning, and turn into baking dish.

8 "large" eggs (1½ to 1⅔ cups)

Salt and pepper to taste

A heavily buttered 6-cup cylindrically shaped baking dish about 3½ inches deep (such as a charlotte), bottom lined with buttered waxed paper

(*) AHEAD-OF-TIME NOTE: May be completed in advance to this point; cover and refrigerate. Stir up gently before proceeding. Chilled custard will probably take 10 to 15 minutes longer to bake than unchilled custard.

---

3) *Baking—allow 1 hour; preheat oven to 375 degrees*

A pan about 3 inches deep and large enough to hold baking dish easily

Boiling water

When you are ready to bake the custard, set baking dish in pan; pour in enough boiling water to come about ⅔ the way up outside of dish. Place in lower-middle level of preheated oven. To assure yourself of a smooth, bubble-free custard, regulate oven heat so that water in pan never quite simmers throughout the cooking; lower thermostat to 350 degrees in 15 minutes, and you will probably lower it to 325 or 300 degrees near end of baking. Custard should be done in 35 to 40 minutes: the top center will look set rather than loosely liquid when you gently shake the pan. A knife or skewer plunged down through middle of custard will emerge almost clean, looking slightly oily with perhaps a tiny curd of custard clinging here and there. Remove baking dish from pan and let custard settle for 20 minutes before unmolding it.

---

4) *Serving*

3 to 4 Tb clarified butter (melted butter, skimmed; clear liquid butter spooned off milky residue)

A small (7- to 8-inch) frying pan

½ cup dry, not-too-fine crumbs from non-sweetened homemade-type white bread

3 to 4 Tb minced fresh parsley

Salt and pepper to taste

While custard is baking or cooling, or at any other convenient time, prepare bread-crumb and parsley garnish as follows: Heat clarified butter in pan, and when bubbling stir in bread crumbs. Sauté for several minutes over moderately high heat, stirring continuously until crumbs are lightly browned. Remove from heat, and when cool, stir in the parsley and seasonings.

A hot, lightly buttered serving plate

After custard has settled 20 minutes, run a thin knife around edge of custard. Turn serving plate upside down over baking dish, reverse the two and unmold custard onto plate. Sprinkle with the parsley and crumbs, and serve as soon as possible.

(*) AHEAD-OF-TIME NOTE: If you are not ready to serve, do not unmold custard, but leave it in its dish in the pan of hot water and in the turned-off oven. It will stay warm for a good half hour or longer, and may then be unmolded immediately.

Stuffed Zucchini

Courgettes Farcies

Stuffed zucchini can well be a first course, especially when the stuffing is rice or vegetables. The best sizes for stuffing are 6 to 8 inches, and one zucchini half is usually sufficient for a first course or as a vegetable garnish to go with the meat course. Serve 2 or even 3 halves per person when the zucchini is the main course.

✳ COURGETTES FARCIES AUX AMANDES

[Zucchini Stuffed with Almonds and Cheese]

This is a particularly attractive stuffing, not only because almonds are unusual, but also because the flavor of the zucchini survives the stuffing. Serve as a separate course, or with veal chops or scallops, or roast, broiled, or sautéed chicken.

For 6 servings

1) *Preparing the zucchini for stuffing*

3 zucchini all of a size, about 8 by 2 inches
A large kettle of boiling, salted water
A grapefruit knife
Salt
Paper towels

Trim and scrub the zucchini; blanch about 10 minutes in boiling salted water, just until flesh yields to pressure, as directed on page 364. Cut in half lengthwise. Using grapefruit knife, hollow out the cores of each zucchini half, to make boat-shaped cases with the sides and bottom about ⅜ inch thick. Salt lightly and drain hollow side down on towels. Chop the removed zucchini flesh, squeeze out vegetable water in paper towels, and reserve flesh for stuffing.

2) *The almond, cheese, and bread-crumb stuffing—for about 2 cups*

¼ cup finely minced onions
1½ Tb olive oil or cooking oil
A 6- to 8-inch pan
The chopped zucchini flesh
A 2-quart mixing bowl
2½ ounces (½ cup loosely packed) ground blanched almonds (grind them in an electric blender)
½ cup heavy cream
½ to ⅔ cup dry, fairly fine crumbs from nonsweetened homemade-type white bread
2 ounces (½ cup lightly pressed down) grated Swiss cheese (save 3 Tb for later)
1 "large" egg
Salt and pepper to taste
2 to 3 big pinches powdered clove

Stir the onions into the oil, cover pan, and cook over low heat, stirring occasionally, for 8 to 10 minutes, or until onions are tender and translucent. Uncover, raise heat and let them just begin to brown, then stir in the chopped zucchini flesh and sauté for several minutes, until zucchini is tender. Scrape into bowl, and stir in the almonds and cream. Stir in ⅓ cup of the bread crumbs, blending thoroughly, then all but 3 tablespoons of the cheese, and finally the egg. Mixture should hold its shape softly when lifted in a spoon; if too soft, beat in more crumbs by small spoonfuls, mixing thoroughly. Blend in salt and pepper to taste, and the powdered clove.

3) *Stuffing and baking the zucchini—25 to 30 minutes at 400 degrees*

A heavily buttered rectangular or oval baking and serving dish just large enough to hold the 6 zucchini halves in 1 layer
3 Tb each of the remaining bread crumbs and cheese, mixed in a small bowl
3 Tb melted butter

Arrange the zucchini halves skin side down in the baking dish and fill with the stuffing, heaping it into a dome on each half. Sprinkle each with the cheese and bread crumbs, and dribble on the melted butter.

(*) AHEAD-OF-TIME NOTE: May be prepared to this point a day in advance of baking; cover and refrigerate.

Bake in upper third of preheated oven for 25 to 30 minutes, until bubbling hot and browned on top. (Do not overcook, letting zucchini shells become too soft for serving.) Serve from baking dish, or arrange around meat platter.

(*) AHEAD-OF-TIME NOTE: May be kept warm, but again, do not let zucchini shells soften.

VARIATIONS

Courgettes Farcies au Riz et aux Poivrons

[Zucchini Stuffed with Rice and Peppers]

Another stuffing for zucchini, this one is equally good cold or hot. Prepare, stuff, and bake the zucchini exactly as described in the preceding recipe, but make the stuffing as follows.

Rice and pepper stuffing with tomato topping—2 cups for six 8- by 2-inch zucchini halves

½ cup diced onions
4 Tb olive oil (save 2 Tb for later)
½ cup diced green peppers
1 large clove mashed garlic
The chopped zucchini cores
⅓ cup plain, raw, white, untreated, long-grain rice
1 egg
⅓ cup grated Parmesan cheese (save 3 Tb for later)
3 Tb fresh minced parsley
Salt and pepper
3 medium-sized tomatoes, peeled, seeded, juiced, and chopped

Stir the onions into the oil in a medium-sized (10-inch) frying pan, cover and cook over low heat, stirring occasionally, for 8 to 10 minutes until tender. Uncover, raise heat and brown very lightly, stirring, then add the green peppers, garlic, and zucchini cores. Cover and cook slowly for several minutes more until peppers are tender. Turn into mixing bowl. Meanwhile, in a pan of boiling salted water, boil the rice for exactly 10 minutes, drain, and add to mixing bowl. Beat in the egg, then the cheese and parsley. Season carefully with salt and pepper. Mound the stuffing in the blanched and hollowed-out zucchini halves. Season tomato pulp with salt and pepper, spread over the stuffing, cover with the remaining cheese, and sprinkle on the remaining olive oil. Bake for 25 to 30 minutes in upper third of preheated 425-degree oven until bubbling hot and cheese topping has browned lightly.

Other stuffings

You may stuff zucchini, following the general method outlined in the Master Recipe, with all kinds of mixtures, including other vegetables, leftover meat combinations, sausage mixtures, and so forth. A complete list of possibilities is on pages 513–15.

STUFFED ONIONS—STUFFED CABBAGE
Oignons Farcis–Choux Farcis

OIGNONS FARCIS AU RIZ

[Onions Stuffed with Rice, Cheese, and Herbs]

Onions hollowed out and stuffed with rice and chopped, cooked onion cores need only a little cheese, cream, and a pinch of herbs to point up their flavor. Served hot, they add great distinction to a platter of broiled chicken or fish, and are always attractive with roasts, steaks, and chops. Serve them cold with cold meats or fish, or as part of an hors d'oeuvre display. The following recipe is for giant onions, but smaller ones are done the same way: whatever their size, you hollow them out raw, blanch them until barely tender, then stuff and bake them. If you do not blanch them first, they will take hours to cook and might well burst out of shape in the process. (A list of other stuffing possibilities is on pages 513–15.)

For 6 large onions

---

1) *Coring and blanching the onions*

6 very large, firm, fresh, per-
    fect onions at least 3½
    inches in diameter if
    possible, yellow or white
A small, sharp knife and a
    grapefruit knife
A large kettle of boiling
    salted water
A slotted spoon and a colan-
    der

One at a time, shave off pointed end and root end of onions and peel off skin along with one outside layer of flesh. The whole onions are now to be hollowed out to form onion cups.

With sharp knife, cut cone-shaped core out of the top side of the onion. (Reserve all onion flesh for Step 2.)

Being careful not to make sides and bottom too thin (they should be almost ½ inch thick, or about 4 layers for onions this size), *use grapefruit knife to dig circular sections out of body of onion to make a cup shape.*

Drop the onion cups into the boiling water. When it comes back to the boil, boil slowly, uncovered, for 10 to 15 minutes until onions are just tender when pierced but still very definitely hold their shape. Remove carefully and drain upside down in a colander. (Reserve boiling water for next step.)

---

2) *The rice, onion, and cheese stuffing*

The onion cores
3 to 4 Tb butter
A large frying pan with cover
A 3-quart mixing bowl

While onion cups are blanching, mince all usable onion leftovers. Cook slowly in butter in covered pan 8 to 10 minutes, stirring occasionally, until tender and translucent; uncover pan, raise heat, and brown very lightly, stirring. Measure 1 cup into mixing bowl. (Remainder, if any, may be refrigerated or frozen.)

⅓ cup plain, raw, white untreated rice
The boiling onion-cooking water

After onion cups have been blanched and removed, stir rice into boiling water and boil slowly for 10 to 12 minutes, until rice is almost but not quite tender. Drain thoroughly, and add to mixing bowl.

⅓ cup grated Parmesan cheese
¼ cup *crème fraîche* or heavy cream
½ cup dry, not-too-fine crumbs from nonsweetened homemade-type white bread (for now and for Step 3)
¼ cup minced parsley
2 Tb fresh minced basil or 1 tsp fresh minced tarragon (or ¼ to ½ Tb fragrant dried basil, oregano, sage, or tarragon)
Salt and pepper to taste

Stir the cheese and cream into the rice and onions, then 2 tablespoons of the bread crumbs. If mixture does not hold its shape softly, blend in a spoonful or so more crumbs to thicken and bind it. Stir in the herbs and seasonings.

---

3) *Stuffing and baking the onions—1 to 1¼ hours at 375 degrees*

3 to 4 Tb melted butter
A heavily buttered flame-proof baking dish just large enough to hold onions easily, such as a 12-inch casserole 3 inches deep

Preheat oven to 375. Butter or oil the outside of the onion cups and arrange in the baking dish. Sprinkle interiors lightly with salt and pepper, and fill with the stuffing, heaping it into a half-inch dome. Sprinkle with a teaspoon of bread crumbs and of melted butter. Pour the wine around the onions, and enough stock or bouillon to come ⅓ the way up the onions. Bring

½ cup dry white wine or
   dry white French
   vermouth
½ to 1 cup beef stock or
   bouillon
The bread crumbs
A bulb baster

to simmer on top of stove, then set in lower middle of
preheated oven.

Bake uncovered for 1 to 1¼ hours, regulating oven so that liquid remains at the slow simmer, and basting outside of onions several times with liquid in dish. Onions are done when a knife pierces them easily, but they should not overcook and lose their shape. Outside layer will toughen slightly, but insides will be tender. Top of stuffing should brown attractively, but if it is browning too much, cover loosely with foil or brown paper. Serve from baking dish, or arrange around the meat or vegetable platter. Add any onion juices to whatever sauce you are making.

(*) AHEAD-OF-TIME NOTE: May be baked in advance and kept warm or reheated.

---

* CHOU FARCI
[Stuffed Whole Cabbage]

Stuffed cabbage is the kind of dish that guests and family always seem to love because it has the hearty, earthy look and the rich, satisfying aroma that promise good eating. To stuff a whole cabbage you first make a delicious mixture using something like the fresh sausage and ham suggested here, or leftover meat as in the variation following it. You then pull off the cabbage leaves, boiling them until pliable, and re-form the cabbage into approximately its original shape with your delicious mixture spread between layers of leaves. Finally you braise, sauce, and serve it up, and it looks just like a beautiful, decorated, whole cabbage sitting on the serving platter. You must, of course, have some method for holding the cabbage leaves in the shape of the whole while braising. If you have struggled to mold cabbage with string, towels, cheesecloth, or even the net shopping bag that is occasionally used in Provence, we think you will welcome the ease of the following bowl-molding method. Parslied boiled potatoes, French bread, and rosé wine would go well with the cabbage.

NOTE: Braised stuffed cabbage is equally good cold, and could well be baked specially for a cold lunch or a picnic. If so, drain and unmold it as soon as it is done, so there will be no bits of congealed fat on the leaves.

For 8 to 10 people

1) *Fresh sausage, rice, and ham stuffing—about 6 cups*

2 cups (1 lb.) fresh sausage meat, preferably home-made, page 289
A medium sized (10-inch) frying pan
A 5- to 6-quart mixing bowl and large wooden spoon
1½ cups diced mild-cured ham (such as a store-bought ready-to-cook ham slice)
2 cups minced onions
2 cups boiled rice (⅔ cup raw rice, boiled)
½ tsp sage
½ tsp caraway seeds
¼ cup minced fresh parsley
2 cloves mashed garlic
1 egg
Salt and pepper

(Start the water boiling for Step 2.) Break up the sausage meat and sauté over moderate heat for 5 to 6 minutes, just until it is beginning to brown lightly. Remove to mixing bowl, leaving fat in pan. Brown the ham lightly in the fat; remove it to the bowl, again leaving fat in pan. Finally stir in the onions and cook slowly for 8 to 10 minutes, until tender and beginning to brown very lightly. Scrape them into the bowl and beat in all the rest of the ingredients. Taste carefully for seasoning, adding more salt and herbs if you feel them necessary. (Chopped, blanched leaves from the heart of the cabbage will be stirred in later.)

2) *Preparing the cabbage for stuffing*

A firm, fresh, crisp 2¼- to 2½-lb. cabbage (about 8 inches in diameter), either the crinkle-leafed Savoy or the smooth-leafed Danish or domestic
A large kettle of boiling salted water
A large tray covered with a towel

With a small, stout knife, make a bias cut all around the stem of the cabbage, going 2 to 2½ inches deep, and remove the tough core. Discard any outside leaves that seem tough or wilted. *If you have the crinkle-leafed Savoy cabbage,* you usually need not blanch it to remove the leaves. Peel them off carefully so as not to tear them, until you come to the heart, where leaves are small and bend inward. Drop as many cabbage leaves as will easily fit into the boiling water and boil, uncovered, for 3 to 4 minutes, until leaves are pliable enough to bend without breaking. (This is called blanching.) Drain on towel and continue with the rest of the leaves and the heart, boiling it 5 minutes.

If you have a smooth-leafed cabbage (or an unpeelable Savoy), drop the whole cabbage core side down into the boiling water. In 5 minutes, start loosening leaves carefully, nudging them off the cabbage with 2 long spoons as they free themselves from the core. Remove these leaves to the tray. Continue loosening and removing leaves to tray until you come to the heart, where leaves bend inward. Leave heart to boil for 5 minutes, and add as many of the removed leaves as will easily fit, boiling them 3 to 4 minutes or until they are just pliable. Continue with the rest of the leaves. (Do not discard boiling water yet.) Chop the heart of the cabbage, salt and pepper lightly, and stir into the already prepared stuffing from Step 1.

---

3) *Other miscellaneous preliminaries*

10 to 12 slices of lean salt pork or bacon approximately 4 by 1½ inches and ⅜ inch thick
The boiling cabbage water
1 medium onion, sliced
1 medium carrot, sliced
2 Tb rendered goose or pork fat, or cooking oil
The frying pan

Drop the slices of salt pork or bacon into the boiling water and boil slowly for 10 minutes. Drain, rinse in cold water, and set aside on paper toweling. Meanwhile, cook the vegetables in the fat or oil until tender and just beginning to brown, then remove to a side dish. (Note that there is also a sauce base in Step 6, which you may prepare now if you wish.)

---

4) *Stuffing the cabbage*

A lightly buttered 2½- to 3-quart stainless-steel bowl, flame-proof mold, baking dish, or charlotte mold 3½ to 4 inches deep (with a cover)
Salt and pepper
3 to 4 cups excellent brown stock or bouillon

Lay several strips of the blanched pork or bacon in the bottom of the stainless steel bowl or flameproof mold and cover with the lightly browned carrot and onion slices.

Starting with the largest and greenest of the blanched cabbage leaves, lay them curved side down and stem end up in the mold, to cover bottom and sides. Sprinkle lightly with salt and pepper.

Spread a layer of stuffing over the lower third of the leaves. Cover the stuffing with cabbage leaves. Salt and pepper them lightly, and spread on more stuffing.

As you build up layers, *slip leaves down side of mold to be sure sides are well covered.*

When you have used all the stuffing, and mold is filled to within ½ inch of top, cover filling with a final layer of leaves and *arrange the rest of the blanched salt pork or bacon on top.*

Pour enough stock or bouillon between outside leaves and side of mold to come about an inch from the top.

(*) AHEAD-OF-TIME NOTE: May be prepared in advance to this point and cooked the next day. Cover with plastic wrap and refrigerate. Add 20 to 30 minutes more to cooking time if cabbage has been chilled.

1 inch from top of mold

5) *Braising—2½ to 3 hours at 400 degrees and 350 degrees*

Waxed paper
The cover for the mold

Preheat oven to 400 degrees. Bring filled mold slowly to the full simmer on top of the stove. Lay the waxed

A pan to hold the mold and to catch drippings

A bulb baster

Additional stock or bouillon if needed

Optional: a meat thermometer

paper over the cabbage and cover the mold. Set in pan and place in lower middle of preheated, 400-degree oven. In 20 to 30 minutes, when liquid in mold is slowly and steadily simmering, turn thermostat down to 350 degrees and regulate oven heat so that liquid is always very slowly simmering throughout the 2½ to 3 hours of cooking. Baste occasionally with the cooking liquid, and add a little more stock if liquid evaporates below the halfway mark. (2½ to 3 hours are needed for heat to penetrate into center of cabbage, where a meat thermometer should read 165 to 170 degrees.)

(*) AHEAD-OF-TIME NOTES are at end of Step 4.

6) *Sauce and serving*

½ cup finely minced onions

1 Tb rendered goose or pork fat, or cooking oil

A heavy-bottomed, 2-quart, enameled or stainless saucepan with cover

1 clove mashed garlic

1 lb. (3 to 4 medium) tomatoes peeled, seeded, juiced, and chopped (1½ cups pulp); or part fresh tomatoes and part sieved, canned Italian-type plum tomatoes

½ tsp sage

Salt and pepper to taste

While cabbage is braising, or at any other convenient time, make the sauce base as follows: Stir the onions into the fat, cover pan, and cook over low heat, stirring occasionally, for 8 to 10 minutes or until onions are tender and translucent but not browned. Add the garlic, tomatoes, and sage; cover and simmer 10 minutes. Uncover, season to taste, and set aside.

If needed: ½ Tb cornstarch blended with 1 Tb tomato juice or bouillon

A frying pan

A hot serving dish

3 Tb minced fresh parsley

When cabbage is done, keep cover on mold and drain cooking liquid into the tomato sauce base; let simmer while you are finishing the cabbage. Sauce should thicken lightly. If it does not, remove from heat, blend in cornstarch, and simmer 2 minutes more. Carefully correct seasoning.

Remove pork or bacon pieces from top of cabbage and set aside. Drain cabbage again, then turn serving dish upside down over mold and reverse the two, unmolding cabbage onto the dish. Remove vegetables and pork from top of cabbage. Pat pork or bacon strips dry on paper towels, and brown very lightly in frying pan; arrange them decoratively over the cabbage. Spoon the sauce around the cabbage, decorate with the parsley, and serve as soon as possible.

(*) AHEAD-OF-TIME NOTES: Sauce may be finished and pork or bacon sautéed well in advance of serving, then reheated. Keep cabbage warm, loosely covered, and unmold at last minute. (Omit sautéing the pork strips at bottom of mold.) However, if you leave the cabbage too long, or cool and reheat it, you risk losing its freshly cooked quality.

VARIATIONS

Feuilles de Chou Farcies

[Stuffed Cabbage Leaves for Individual Servings]

When you wish a less elaborate presentation, a little quicker cooking, have fewer people to serve, or want an attractive way to use a bit of leftover meat, you may make as many or as few servings as you wish by wrapping a stuffing in individual cabbage leaves. Usually served hot, these are also delicious cold on a bed of lettuce or watercress, and garnished with sliced tomatoes and cucumbers in a vinaigrette sauce.

For 12 stuffed cabbage leaves, serving 4 to 6

---

12 large blanched cabbage
  leaves 7 to 8 inches long
  (Step 2 in preceding
  Master Recipe)

One at a time, lay blanched cabbage leaves curved side down on cutting board and *cut a wedge about 2 inches long out of the tough bottom stem.*

About 2 cups of stuffing
  (that in the preceding
  recipe, page 380, the one at
  the end of this section,
  page 386, or one from the
  list on pages 513–15.)

Place a loaf-shaped mound of stuffing on lower third of leaf just above wedge cut.

Start rolling leaf toward tip. *At the halfway mark, fold each side over stuffing to enclose it.*

Finish rolling up the leaf, and complete the rest of the leaves in the same manner.

1 each: medium sized carrot and onion sliced and lightly browned (Step 3 in preceding recipe)

A lightly buttered 2-quart flameproof baking and serving dish 2 inches deep (such as a 9- by 12-inch oval)

Optional: the rest of the cabbage leaves, blanched and roughly chopped

Salt, pepper, and ¼ tsp ground sage, rosemary, or thyme

12 slices of lean salt pork or bacon, 4 by 1½ inches, ⅜ inch thick, and blanched (Step 3 in preceding recipe)

About 2 cups of excellent brown stock or bouillon

Aluminum foil

A bulb baster

The tomato-sauce base, Step 6 in preceding Master Recipe

Strew the sliced cooked carrots and onions in the bottom of the baking dish and spread the optional blanched and chopped cabbage over it. Season with salt, pepper, and rosemary or thyme. Lay the stuffed cabbage leaves on top, seam-side down and close together. Salt and pepper them lightly, cover each with a strip of blanched salt pork or bacon, and pour around them enough stock or bouillon almost to cover. Enclose top of dish tightly with aluminum foil.

(*) AHEAD-OF-TIME NOTE: May be completed in advance to this point. Refrigerate, and bake the next day if you wish.

Bake for 1 to 1¼ hours in a preheated 350-degree oven, basting occasionally with the liquid in the dish. Drain cooking liquid into the tomato sauce base and boil down rapidly to thicken. Carefully correct seasoning and pour back over the cabbage rolls. Brown the pork or bacon strips lightly in a frying pan and arrange over the cabbage, sprinkle with parsley, and serve.

Petits Choux Farcis

[Ball-shaped Stuffed Cabbage Leaves]

Rather than sausage shapes, you may form the leaves into round shapes resembling individual cabbages. To do so, blanch the leaves as directed and cut a wedge out of bottom of stem. Place leaf curved side down on the corner of a towel. Heap 2 to 3 tablespoons of stuffing in the center, fold rest of leaf over stuffing, then twist into a ball in the towel to force a round shape. Arrange balls smooth side up and close together in a dish, and bake as in preceding recipe, but 1 hour of cooking should be sufficient.

ANOTHER STUFFING

Braised Beef and Ham Stuffing

For about 6 cups

1½ cups minced onions
3 Tb rendered goose or pork fat, or cooking oil
½ cup dry crumbs from nonsweetened, home-made-type white bread
⅔ cup light cream
3 cups ground cooked lean beef, preferably braised, but any type of cooked beef will do
1½ cups ground cooked lean ham (mild-cured boiled or baked ham, or ready-to-cook ham slice)
½ cup grated Parmesan cheese
2 to 3 cloves mashed garlic
¾ tsp ground rosemary or thyme
2 eggs
½ cup minced fresh parsley
Salt and pepper to taste

Cook the onions in fat or oil in a covered saucepan over low heat for 8 to 10 minutes until tender; raise heat and cook a few minutes more until lightly browned. Meanwhile blend the bread crumbs and cream in a small bowl and let stand while assembling rest of ingredients. Finally beat the cooked onions, crumbs, meats, cheese, garlic, herbs, eggs, and parsley vigorously together to blend. Carefully season to taste, adding more herbs if you feel them necessary.

POTATO DISHES
Pommes de Terre

Ounce for ounce, potatoes have fewer calories than fresh peas, lima beans, or sweet corn, yet potatoes come so near to being the complete food that one can survive healthily on a diet of potatoes only, plus a very small amount of fat, for as much as 5 months. Nutrition aside, the potato is an endlessly fascinating gastronomical object which, since its introduction by Parmentier into France during the reign of Louis XVI, has received tremendous French culinary attention. We shall not, in this short section, go into the fundamental cooking methods because they are available in any good basic cookbook. We offer instead a number of out-of-the-ordinary simmers and sautés, a deliciously fattening potato pie, two of the classics illustrated, *pommes Anna* and *pommes duchesse,* and we begin with a group of useful potato facts.

NOTES ON BUYING AND STORING POTATOES

When you are buying potatoes, choose those that look clean and healthy, that are firm to the touch, smooth, dry, free from cracks, and with no suggestion of sprouting (greenish-white nubbins of growth appearing at the small depressions called the eyes). Be sure, also, that the potatoes are potato-colored, that is, uniformly brownish or reddish with no hint of green. Green means that they have been exposed to sun or light, either in the field or in storage, and green potatoes develop a bitter taste. Potatoes are sometimes waxed and sometimes colored reddish, a harmless cosmetic treatment designed to enhance their customer appeal; if so, this fact should be indicated clearly on the bin or package.

Unless you happen to have a proper root cellar where you can store potatoes in the dark at a temperature of 55 degrees and at a humidity of 85 to 90 per cent, buy only what you will use within a week or so. Potatoes kept at 60 to 70 degrees have the best cooking flavor, but they begin to sprout after a few weeks. Potatoes stored at below 40 degrees, the temperature of your refrigerator, resist sprouting and withering but gradually develop a sweet taste because the potato starches transform themselves into sugar. Thus, keep your small store of potatoes at normal room temperature in heavy brown paper sacks so they will be protected from light. Separate different types or you will run into cooking irregularities.

POTATO TYPES

Potatoes are a far more complicated vegetable to grow, harvest, store, and classify than any of us who are not in the business would ever dream. New varieties are constantly being tested out that will survive in specific climates, that will resist the myriad viruses and diseases which attack potato plants, and that will more perfectly meet public tastes and the specific demands of dehydrators, chip manufacturers, and other industrial users. Potatoes of one variety can vary from one year to the next in a certain growing locality because of weather, or the same variety will be mealy in one area and not in another because of soil and climatic differences. The tradition of choosing old potatoes for baking and mashing, and new potatoes for boiling still holds true in part, but so much has happened to the potato since grandmother's day that a list of varieties classified according to buying areas and uses would be out of date almost as soon as it appeared in print. Thus we shall go no further than specify "boiling" potatoes when we mean the type that holds its shape in cooking, and "baking" potatoes when we want a mealy, floury potato for baking or mashing. If your market does not have its potatoes clearly labeled as to baking and mashing, frying, boiling, or all-purpose, ask the head of the vegetable department to help you.

POMMES DE TERRE AU BASILIC
[Sliced Potatoes Simmered in Cream and Basil]

This is a top-of-the-stove recipe in which sliced potatoes are boiled briefly in water to neutralize any milk-curdling properties they may possess, then simmered until tender in a cream sauce with garlic and basil. You may set them aside and reheat again just before turning them into a vegetable dish with more basil, parsley, and butter. Serve with roast red meats, steaks, chops, or broiled chicken.

For 4 to 6 people

2 lbs. "boiling" potatoes
A large saucepan of boiling salted water
A colander

Peel the potatoes. Cut into slices about ¼ inch thick and 1¼ inches in diameter. You should have around 7 cups. Drop them into the boiling water, bring rapidly back to the boil again, and boil for 3 minutes. Drain immediately.

3 Tb butter
A heavy-bottomed 3-quart saucepan (no-stick recommended)
1½ Tb flour
A wooden spoon and a wire whip

Make a white *roux* as follows: Melt the butter in the saucepan, blend in the flour, and stir over moderate heat for 2 minutes to cook the flour without browning. Remove from heat, and when *roux* has stopped bubbling, vigorously blend in all of the hot milk at once with your wire whip, beating until mixture is perfectly smooth. Blend in the ¾ cup of cream, the

1½ cups milk heated in a
    small saucepan
¾ cup heavy cream; more
    cream (or milk) if needed
About 1 Tb fresh minced
    basil; or ½ tsp fragrant
    dried basil (or oregano)
1 to 2 large cloves of
    mashed garlic
½ tsp salt
Big pinch of white pepper
A cover for the pan

herb, garlic, salt, and pepper. Return over moderately high heat, stirring with whip as sauce thickens very lightly and comes to the boil. Simmer 2 minutes, then fold in the potatoes. Sauce should just cover potatoes; add a little more cream or milk if necessary. Bring to simmer, correct seasoning, cover pan, and simmer very slowly for 10 to 15 minutes, until potatoes are tender. Stir up gently from bottom once or twice to be sure potatoes are not sticking; they will have absorbed half of the liquid before they are done and if sauce seems too thick you may always add a little more milk.

(*) AHEAD-OF-TIME NOTE: May be completed in advance to this point. Spoon a little milk or cream over top of potatoes and either set aside uncovered or keep warm, partially covered, in a pan of simmering water.

2 to 4 Tb soft butter
2 to 3 Tb fresh minced basil
    and parsley, or parsley
    only
A warm, lightly buttered
    vegetable dish

Reheat potatoes just before serving. Carefully correct seasoning. Gently fold in the butter and ⅔ of the herbs with a rubber spatula. Turn into vegetable dish, decorate with the remaining herbs, and serve at once.

A different herb—Tarragon

The preceding potatoes are delicious with tarragon rather than basil, a good solution for wintertime, since dried tarragon is usually far more fragrant than dried basil.

GRATIN DAUPHINOIS AUX ENDIVES
[Gratin of Sliced Potatoes and Endives]

Both endives and potatoes go beautifully with chicken or veal, and here they are combined into one dish. For each cup of sliced raw potatoes you will need 2 cups of sliced raw Belgian endives. The natural moisture in the endives provides enough liquid for the potatoes, while the butter, lemon juice, shallots, and cheese that bake along with them contribute delicious additional flavors.

For 8 people—baking time about 1¼ hours

2½ lbs. very fresh, white,
    firm Belgian endive with

Preheat oven to 400 degrees. Trim root ends, and wash endives rapidly under cold running water. Slice cross-

leaves tightly closed at the
   tips
1¼ lbs. "boiling" potatoes
2 Tb soft butter
A 3½- to 4-quart baking
   dish about 2½ inches deep
   (such as a 12-inch round
   one, or an 11- by 16-inch
   oval)
1 Tb lemon juice
½ cup melted butter
Salt and white pepper
⅔ cup coarsely grated Swiss
   cheese
¼ cup finely minced
   shallots or scallions
Buttered waxed paper
A cover for the dish

wise into pieces ¾ inch thick and set aside. You should have 8 cups. Wash and peel potatoes, cut into slices ¼ inch thick and about 1¼ inches in diameter. You should have 4 cups. Smear the butter in the baking dish and arrange in it half the sliced endives. Sprinkle with half the lemon juice, and 2 tablespoons of melted butter. Season lightly with salt and pepper, and spread on half the cheese. Over this arrange the 4 cups of potatoes in layers, sprinkling each with salt and pepper, a little of the butter, and the minced shallots or scallions. Spread the rest of the endives over the potatoes, seasoning them with lemon juice, salt and pepper, and all but 1 tablespoon of the remaining butter. Omit the cheese, reserving for later.

Lay the buttered waxed paper over the endives, cover the dish, and bake in middle level of 400-degree oven for 15 to 20 minutes, or until you can hear the contents bubbling. Turn oven down to 350 or even 325 degrees for the rest of the baking, regulating heat so that vegetables simmer slowly throughout the rest of the cooking, which will be 1 to 1¼ hours. When potatoes are tender if pierced with a fork, remove dish from oven, and reset thermostat to 425 degrees. Spread remaining ⅓ cup of cheese over the vegetables and dribble on the remaining butter.

(*) AHEAD-OF-TIME NOTE: Dish may be completed an hour or so in advance up to this point. Set partially uncovered in a 100– to 120–degree warming oven, or over a pan of almost simmering water. As long as potatoes are warm and have a little ventilation, they will not lose their fresh-tasting quality.

About 15 minutes before serving, set dish uncovered in upper third of preheated 425-degree oven until contents are bubbling hot and cheese topping has browned lightly.

POMMES DE TERRE SAUTÉES, CALABRAISE

[Sliced Potatoes Sautéed with Lemon and Garlic]

This excellent, crusty sauté of potatoes needs to be done in a large non-sticking pan where the potatoes have room to toss, turn, and crust. Serve them with eggs, sausages, pork chops, broiled chicken, steaks, or fish.

For 6 servings

2 lbs. "boiling" potatoes all
   of a size for even slices

Peel the potatoes, cut into slices ¼ inch thick and 1¼ inches in diameter (or cut into ½-inch dice, if you pre-

A large saucepan with just
  enough boiling salted
  water to cover potatoes
Olive oil (or 3 Tb butter
  and 2 or more Tb olive
  oil or cooking oil)
A large (11-inch) frying
  pan (no-stick recom-
  mended especially for this
  recipe)
The grated peel of ½ lemon
2 large cloves of garlic,
  mashed
Big pinch of nutmeg
Salt and pepper

fer); you should have 6 to 7 cups. Drop into boiling, salted water, and boil about 5 minutes, or until barely tender. (Eat a piece to check; do not overcook.) Drain thoroughly. Film frying pan with a ⅛-inch layer of oil (or butter and oil), set over moderately high heat, and when very hot but not smoking add enough potatoes to make 1 full layer. Toss and turn frequently for several minutes, shaking and swirling the pan by its handle, until potatoes are beginning to brown lightly. Add some more potatoes, and continue to toss them in the pan until the new addition is beginning to brown. If necessary, add a little more oil and continue with more potatoes; however, about ¾ inch of potatoes will be the maximum you can handle in the pan.

When all potatoes are lightly brown, toss with the lemon peel, garlic, nutmeg, salt and pepper. Continue sautéing and tossing several minutes more until potatoes are as brown as you wish them to be.

(*) AHEAD-OF-TIME NOTE: May be kept warm at this point, pan set partially covered over 2 asbestos mats over low heat. As long as they are warm and ventilated, potatoes will retain their fresh taste for at least half an hour.

If available: 1 Tb minced
  fresh basil
2 to 3 Tb minced fresh
  parsley
2 or more Tb butter
About 1 Tb lemon juice
A hot serving plate or the
  meat platter

Just before you are ready to serve, reheat to sizzling and toss with the herbs and butter. Check seasoning again, and toss with lemon juice to taste. Turn out onto plate and serve immediately.

GALETTE DE POMMES DE TERRE AUX TOMATES
[Hashed Brown Potatoes with Tomatoes and Herbs]

Another recipe for sautéed potatoes, this time with pork bits, onions, and tomatoes, calls for the potatoes to be mashed down with a fork when soft so that they look like an omelette when turned out onto their serving plate. Arrange sausages, sautéed chicken, chops, hamburgers, or poached or fried eggs around the potatoes, and you need only a green vegetable or salad for the perfect informal meal.

For 6 servings

1) *The pork and onions*

4 to 5 ounces (about ⅔ cup)
  bacon chunk or lean salt
  pork cut into ¼-inch dice
A pan with 2 quarts water
1 Tb olive oil or cooking oil
A large (11-inch) frying
  pan (no-stick recom-
  mended especially for this
  recipe)
⅔ cup minced onions
A cover for the pan
A sieve set over a small
  bowl

Simmer the diced bacon or pork in the water for 10 minutes, drain and dry in paper towels. Cook for several minutes with the olive oil in the frying pan until it begins to brown lightly. Stir in the onions, cover the pan, and cook over low heat, stirring occasionally, for 8 to 10 minutes until onions are tender. Raise heat and cook, stirring, to brown the onions very lightly. Scrape into sieve, pressing fat out of ingredients into bowl. Return fat to frying pan; reserve pork and onions for Step 3.

2) *Sautéing the potatoes*

About 2 lbs. "boiling" po-
  toes (7 cups, sliced)
Paper towels
More oil as needed
A mixing fork or a wooden
  spoon
Salt and pepper

While onions are cooking, peel the potatoes, cut into slices about ⅛ inch thick and 1¼ inches in diameter. Dry thoroughly in paper towels. Add more oil to pan if needed, to film it by $\frac{1}{16}$ inch. Raise heat to moderately high, and when fat is very hot but not smoking, add the potatoes. Toss and turn frequently for several minutes, shaking and swirling the pan by its handle, until potatoes begin to brown. Lower heat slightly, cover pan, and cook for 5 to 10 minutes, tossing frequently, until potatoes are tender. Uncover, mash roughly with mixing fork or wooden spoon, and season to taste.

3) *Finishing the recipe*

1 lb. tomatoes, peeled,
  seeded, juiced, and
  chopped (1½ cups tomato
  pulp)
1 to 2 large cloves mashed
  garlic
¼ tsp mixed herbs such as
  herbes de Provence or
  Italian seasoning
The cooked pork bits and
  minced onion
A hot serving dish

Raise heat to high. Fold in the tomatoes, garlic, and herbs along with the cooked pork bits and onions. Season again to taste, and sauté uncovered for several minutes to brown. Potatoes should slide around in a mass, and you may be able to flip them over, to brown both sides.

(*) AHEAD-OF-TIME NOTE: If you are not ready to serve, set partially uncovered over low heat and 2 asbestos mats, where potatoes will keep warm without harm for half an hour at least. Reheat to sizzling just before serving.

If you have browned top and bottom of the potato mass, you may serve it like a flat cake, sliding potatoes from pan onto plate. Otherwise they will be most attractive in the form of an oval omelette: flip the two sides over the middle, and reverse the pan onto the serving plate so the potatoes land browned side up.

POMMES ANNA

Pommes Anna looks like a brown cake 6 to 8 inches in diameter and 2 inches high, and it smells marvelously of potatoes and butter. That, in effect, is all it is: thinly sliced potatoes packed in layers in a heavy pan, bathed in clarified butter, and baked in a very hot oven so that the outside crusts enough for the potatoes to be unmolded without collapsing. The contrast of crusty exterior and tender, buttery interior is quite unlike anything else in potato cookery, and to many *pommes Anna* is the supreme potato recipe of all time. It was created during the era of Napoleon III and named, as were many culinary triumphs in those days, after one of the *grandes cocottes* of the period. Whether it was an Anna Deslions, an Anna Judic, or simply Anna Untel, she has also immortalized the special double baking dish itself, *la cocotte à pommes Anna,* which is still being made and which you can still buy at a fancy price. It is of heavy copper.

A thick, flameproof baking dish of some sort is actually one of the keys to *pommes Anna,* because it must be an excellent heat conductor. Although the copper *cocotte Anna* is a beautiful object, its absolutely vertical sides, 3-inch depth, and frequent tendency to sticky-bottom troubles make it less easy to use than other possibilities.

cocotte closed

bottom

top

The familiar American cast-iron frying pan with its fairly vertical sides and short, straight handle is actually the best of all for *pommes Anna*. The potatoes are easier to unmold from this than from the French type of iron frying pan with its sloping sides and long handle. However, either will do, as will a thick, flameproof, ceramic baking dish or a thick cast-aluminum one with no-stick interior. The essential is to have a material that will get thoroughly hot all over, to brown and crust the outside of the potatoes.

Having furnished yourself with the right pan, you then want to make sure the potato slices will not stick to it, because you must be able to unmold them at the end of the cooking. Therefore, use clarified butter, dry the potatoes thoroughly before the cooking begins, and finish the cooking once you have begun it, or else the potatoes will exude moisture and stick to the pan. As you will note in the recipe, cooking begins at once, on the top of the stove as you are arranging the potatoes in the pan; this is to dry the bottom layers and start the brown crust forming. In the classic recipe you then finish the cooking in a hot oven, which usually gives a more professional result, but you may complete the cooking on top of the stove, as suggested in the cheese variation following the Master Recipe.

Pommes Anna and its variations go especially well with roast saddle of lamb, leg of lamb, roast beef, chops, sautéed chicken, plain or fancy steaks, and roast game.

---

* *POMMES ANNA*

[Mold of Sliced Potatoes Baked in Butter]

Your object, in arranging the sliced potatoes in their dish for this very special recipe, is not only to fill the dish but to make a reasonably neat design in the bottom and around the sides so that when the potatoes are unmolded they will present a handsome exterior. For the sides you may either arrange an edging of overlapping upright slices braced by horizontal interior layers, or build up a wall of evenly spaced horizontal slices as you fill the pan. We have suggested the latter, simpler, system here.

For about 8 cups of sliced potatoes, serving 6 people

---

1) *Preliminaries*

½ lb. (2 sticks) butter
3 lbs. "boiling" potatoes
   (more if needed)
Paper towels

Preheat oven to 450 degrees. Set one rack in very bottom level, and another just above it. Clarify the butter: melt it, skim off scum, and spoon the clear liquid butter off the milky residue. Peel the potatoes, trim into cylinders about 1¼ inches in diameter so that you will have uniform slices, then slice cylinders into even rounds ⅛ inch thick. You should have about 8 cups. Dry thoroughly in paper towels. (Do not wash potatoes after peeling, because you want the starch to remain in, so potatoes will mass more easily into a cake.)

---

2) *Arranging the potatoes in the dish*

A heavy cast-iron frying pan about 8 inches top diameter and 2 to 2½ inches deep, or one of the other possibilities in paragraphs preceding recipe
Salt and pepper

Pour ¼ inch of the clarified butter into the pan and set over moderate heat. When hot, start rapidly arranging the first layer of potatoes in the bottom of the pan as follows.

Arrange one potato slice in the center of the pan. *Overlap a circle of potato slices around it.* Overlapping in the opposite (counter-clockwise) direction rapidly arrange a second circle around the first and continue with another (clockwise) overlapping circle if necessary, to rim the edge of the pan. Pour on a spoonful of the clarified butter.

Reversing direction again, *rapidly arrange an evenly overlapping layer of potatoes around circumference of pan, fill in the center with more potatoes,* and baste with another spoonful of butter. Shake pan not too roughly by handle to be sure potatoes are not sticking, and sprinkle on salt and pepper.

Continue filling the pan with layers of potatoes basted with butter and seasoned with salt and pepper, always being sure that the layer around the circumference of the pan is evenly spaced. Remember, also, to shake the pan by its handle from time to time, to be sure potatoes are not sticking. Fill the pan completely, allowing potatoes to form a ¼- to ½-inch dome in the center; they will sink during cooking. You should have added enough butter so that you can see it bubbling up the sides of the pan; excess will be poured out after cooking.

3) Baking

A heavy saucepan, 7 inches
  bottom diameter, or
  whatever will fit into the
  potato pan
A heavy, close-fitting cover
  for the potato pan
A pizza tray or roasting pan
  to catch drippings

Butter bottom of saucepan and *press it down hard on the potatoes,* forcing the layers together. Butter underside of cover, place it on the potato pan set on upper of the two oven racks. Set drip pan under the potatoes, on rack below, to catch bubblings-up of butter (which could otherwise set fire to your oven).

Bake for 20 minutes. Uncover, press potatoes down hard again with bottom of saucepan, and continue baking 20 to 25 minutes more, uncovered. (If baked all the time with cover on, potatoes tend to pick up an off taste.) Press down potatoes again before end of baking. Gently draw an edge of the potatoes away from side of dish: potatoes are done if brown and crusty. Bake 5 minutes or so more if necessary.

---

4) Unmolding and serving

A bowl for excess butter
A flexible-blade spatula
If needed: a buttered
  baking sheet
A lightly buttered, hot
  serving dish

When potatoes are done, place cover slightly askew on pan and drain out excess butter, which may be used again in other cooking. Run spatula around edge of pan. Shake pan, and if potatoes have stuck to bottom, run spatula carefully under potatoes to loosen them, but disturb them as little as possible. If you feel it will be easier to unmold them first onto a baking sheet and slide them onto the serving dish, do so; otherwise invert the dish over the potato pan, reverse the two, and potatoes will drop onto dish. They should look like a brown cake.

Unmolding troubles: You should have no trouble, but if some potatoes do stick to pan, scrape them off and put them in place on the potato cake. If you have had trouble and potatoes look messy or pale, simply push or mound them into a reasonable shape, sprinkle with cheese or bread crumbs, drizzle on a little butter, and brown briefly under the broiler.

(*) AHEAD-OF-TIME NOTE: After unmolding the potatoes, cover loosely with foil and set in a warming oven (120 degrees), or on an electric hot-tray, or over simmering water. They will keep nicely for half an hour at least as long as they are warm and have a little circulation of air.

VARIATIONS

Pommes de Terre Sarladaise
[Truffled Sliced Potatoes Baked in Butter]

All you need for this variation is the wherewithal for a number of sliced truffles, as many as you wish. Proceed as in the Master Recipe, but intersperse truffles with the potato slices after the first layer of potatoes has been arranged in the pan, and end with a layer of potatoes.

Galette de Pommes de Terre au Fromage
[Mold of Sliced Potatoes and Cheese Cooked in Butter]

This is a more informal method of forming *pommes Anna,* and you may omit the cheese if you wish. Here all the cooking is done on top of the stove, which is a convenience when your oven is in use.

For 6 people

4 to 5 Tb clarified butter
A heavy, medium-sized (10-inch) frying pan, either cast iron or no-stick
About 2½ lbs. "boiling" potatoes in round, 1¼-inch slices ⅛ inch thick, well dried
About 4 ounces (1 cup) Swiss cheese cut into 1-inch slices less than ⅛ inch thick (use slicing slot of a grater)
Salt and pepper
Small pinches of nutmeg
A cover for the frying pan
A flexible-blade spatula
A hot serving dish

Following illustrated directions in preceding Master Recipe, pour ¼ inch of butter into frying pan. Set over moderate heat and rapidly arrange an overlapping layer of potato slices in the pan, shaking pan gently from time to time to prevent sticking. Baste with a sprinkling of butter, arrange a second layer over the first, and over this second layer of potatoes arrange a layer of cheese slices. Season the third layer of potatoes with salt, pepper, and a speck of nutmeg. Continue filling the pan with potatoes, cheese, seasonings, and end with a layer of potatoes. When filled, shake pan gently again and let cook 3 to 5 minutes over moderately high heat to be sure the bottom of potatoes is crusting. Then cover pan and set over low heat for about 45 minutes, or until potatoes are tender when pierced with a small knife. (Be sure heat is not too high, or bottom of potatoes will brown too much.) Run spatula all around edge of pan and underneath to loosen potatoes, and unmold upside down on serving dish.

TOURTE LIMOUSINE

[Potato Pie with Herbs and Cream]

Another attractive way to serve potatoes is to mold them in pastry, and bake in a flan ring or false-bottomed cake pan, which comes off when the potatoes are done; the pie then stands free on a serving dish. In this excellent recipe, the sliced potatoes are seasoned with melted butter and herbs, and when they are tender inside their crust, a mixture of cream and beaten egg is poured into them through the chimney hole. The *tourte* can well be the main course for a lunch or supper, along with a mixed vegetable salad, possibly some cold meat, and a Riesling, Sylvaner, or rosé wine. Or serve it with steaks, hamburgers, broiled chicken, or fish. Any leftovers may be reheated, but are also good cold.

For a 9-inch pie, 8 to 12 servings

1 tsp soft butter
The mold: a 9-inch flan
  ring set on a baking sheet,
  or a round, 9-inch false-
  bottomed cake pan
Either ½ the recipe for
  pâte briseé ordinaire
  Formula 1, page 109;
Or a ready mix
¼ cup (not pressed down)
  chopped fresh parsley
Either 2 Tb minced fresh
  green herbs (basil and
  chives);
Or 1½ Tb minced shallots
  or scallions and ¼ tsp
  dried oregano or sage
4 Tb (½ stick) butter
  melted in a saucepan
6 cups thinly sliced all-
  purpose potatoes in a
  bowl of cold water
Salt and pepper
A pastry brush and cup of
  cold water
A chimney: the metal tube
  end of a pastry bag or a

Preheat oven to 425 degrees. Butter inside of flan ring and surface of baking sheet, or inside of cake pan. Roll ⅔ of the pastry into a circle 14 inches in diameter (so that you will have a 1½-inch overhang), and line the mold, letting overhang fall around outside rim. Stir the parsley and herbs into the butter. Drain and dry the potatoes and spread ⅓ on the bottom of the lined mold. Stirring butter and herb mixture, pour ⅓ of it over the potatoes and sprinkle potatoes with salt and pepper. Complete filling mold in same manner. Fold overhanging pastry over potatoes, and moisten top of pastry with water. Roll out remaining pastry into a circle 9½ inches in diameter, roll up on pin, and unroll over mold. Roll pin over pastry to trim it the size of the mold, then press it down with the balls of your fingers over the moistened bottom layer to seal. Make a chimney hole in top of pastry and insert funnel. Paint top of pastry with beaten egg, and make cross-hatch marks over pastry with the back of a knife or the tines of a table fork. Blend cream into remainder of beaten egg, and refrigerate for later.

small metal funnel,
    buttered
1 egg beaten with 1 tsp
    water in a 1-cup measure
⅓ cup heavy cream

Baking—about 1 hour

Immediately set *tourte* in lower-middle level of preheated 425-degree oven and bake for about 30 minutes, until pastry is nicely but not too deeply browned. Then turn thermostat down to 350 degrees for rest of baking; cover *tourte* loosely with foil or brown paper if it is browning too much. As soon as potatoes are tender when you poke them through the chimney hole, *tourte* is done. By spoonfuls, pour the egg and cream mixture into the pie through the chimney, tilting pie in all directions so that cream will flow all over. Bake another 5 minutes or so to set the mixture, and *tourte* is ready to serve; unmold and slide onto a hot serving dish.

(*) AHEAD-OF-TIME NOTES: If *tourte* is done before you are ready to serve, keep it warm, uncovered, in a turned-off oven or 120-degree warming oven. If wait is to be more than 15 minutes, do not add egg and cream until a few minutes before serving, then reheat in a 350-degree oven.

---

* *POMMES DUCHESSE*

[Mashed Potato Mixture for Borders and Other Decorations]

Even hamburgers look dressy in a fluted border of *pommes duchesse,* and fluted mounds of potatoes placed around a meat platter are elegant indeed. Consisting only of mashed potatoes, egg yolks, butter, and cream, *pommes duchesse* is a very simple mixture and perfectly delicious when you use the best ingredients, meaning live potatoes rather than dehydrated ones. Serve *pommes duchesse* anywhere that mashed potatoes would naturally go, such as around a platter that is to hold *boeuf bourguignon* or *coq au vin,* or piped around the creamed eggs or fish that are to be gratinéed, or with steaks, chops, or broiled fish.

TECHNICAL NOTES

You may prepare and form the potatoes in advance, and bake them just before serving; once baked and browned, however, they must be served fairly soon or they will lose their light, freshly cooked quality. We prefer egg yolks to whole eggs in the mixture because we think that egg whites have a drying-out effect, although they do give the potatoes a slight puff. If you like a puff anyway, use 1 egg and 1 yolk for each 2 cups of potatoes rather than the 3 yolks for 2 cups (6 for 4 cups) suggested here.

For 4 cups of mashed potatoes, serving 6 to 8

---

1) *The potato mixture*

2½ lbs. "baking" potatoes all of a size for even cooking (6 or 7 potatoes 4½ by 2 inches, for instance)
A heavy-bottomed saucepan
Cold water
1½ tsp salt per quart of water
A cover for the pan
A colander or sieve
A potato ricer, or a food mill with medium disk, or an electric mixer
A quart measure
A rubber spatula and a wooden spoon
6 egg yolks in a small bowl
6 Tb soft butter
4 to 6 Tb *crème fraîche* or heavy cream
¾ to 1 tsp salt
⅛ tsp white pepper
Pinch of nutmeg
A pan of hot but not simmering water large enough to hold potato pan

Scrub the potatoes under warm water, drop into saucepan of cold water to cover, add salt, and set over high heat. When water comes to the boil, boil slowly, partially covered, for about 25 minutes usually. Test for doneness by cutting a potato in half, taking a slice from inside the half and eating it: potato should hold its shape, but should be cooked through, tender, mealy, and ready to eat. Drain, and peel at once, holding potato on a fork. Immediately put potatoes through a ricer or food mill, or beat with electric mixer, to make a smooth, lump-free purée. Measure 4 cups into saucepan and stir over moderate heat for 2 to 3 minutes until potatoes film bottom of pan, indicating that most of excess moisture has evaporated. Remove from heat, beat in the egg yolks, then the butter and 4 tablespoons of the cream. Beat in a little more cream by dribbles if you think the potatoes will take it, but mixture must be fairly firm so that it will hold its shape when formed. Beat in the salt, pepper, and nutmeg; taste carefully and correct seasoning as necessary. Set potato pan in pan of hot water.

(*) AHEAD-OF-TIME NOTE: Potatoes must be warm if you are to form them smoothly and easily. If you are not quite ready, cover pan partially and beat rather frequently with a wooden spoon. Note that warm potatoes are never covered airtight; a slight circulation of air prevents them from developing an off taste.

---

2) *Forming a fluted border of pommes duchesse*

A wooden spoon
The warm *pommes
    duchesse* mixture
A rubber spatula
A 12- to 14-inch canvas
    pastry bag with ¾-inch
    cannelated nozzle
A lightly buttered, flame-
    proof serving platter, such
    as a 12- by 14-inch oval

Vigorously beat the warm potato
mixture to be sure it is smooth and
pliable, then scoop into pastry bag.
*Squeeze out into a decorative design
around the edge of the platter.*

*Use a winding ribbon design, for
instance, and add rosettes if you
wish.* When you have a small pastry
bag and run out of potatoes rather
quickly, rosettes hide breaks in the
pattern.

2 to 3 Tb finely grated Swiss
    or Parmesan cheese
3 to 4 Tb melted butter

Sprinkle the potatoes with a dusting of cheese and
dribble on melted butter. (Although egg glaze may be
used and gives better over-all color, we do not like the
taste and texture of egg film when it has hardened
over the browned potatoes.)

(*) AHEAD-OF-TIME NOTE: Set aside; cover loosely when
cool and refrigerate.

3) *Browning and serving*

Either bake in upper third of a preheated 400-degree oven for 25 to 30 minutes
until lightly browned, or brown slowly for 5 minutes or so under a slow broiler.
Browning under the broiler leaves a moister texture but you must watch carefully
that the potatoes do not burn. Once browned, serve as soon as possible because the
potatoes will taste dry and stale if cooled and reheated.

VARIATIONS

Individual Nests or Mounds of Pommes Duchesse

Using the same general method as described in the Master Recipe, flute individual nests of the potato mixture on buttered heatproof serving dishes, shells, or plates; sprinkle the potatoes with cheese and melted butter, and brown as described in Step 3. For individual mounds squeeze the potatoes out on a buttered baking sheet and proceed in the same manner, lifting them off with a spatula for serving.

Pommes Duchesse au Fromage

[Cheese Flavored *Pommes Duchesse*]

For cheese-flavored *pommes duchesse,* which you may use in any of the preceding or following suggestions, beat ⅓ cup finely grated Parmesan cheese into the finished potato mixture in Step 1 of the Master Recipe (1 tablespoon of cheese for every cup of the potato mixture). In this case, because the cheese is strong, you may use instant mashed potatoes, adding the minimum amount of liquid suggested on the package, so that you may beat in enough cream to give the potatoes flavor and interest without making them too soft to form.

Galettes de Pommes Duchesse

[Mashed Potato Pancakes from the Leftovers]

Leftover *pommes duchesse* is delicious when formed into cakes and sautéed in butter. This works for browned *pommes duchesse* but is more successful with the uncooked mixture, and although you may bake rather than sauté the potatoes, which is easier to do, much the best flavor and texture comes from sautéing.

For a dozen 3-inch cakes, serving 4 to 6 people

About 2 cups of the *pommes duchesse* mixture, Step 1 in preceding Master Recipe
1 cup dry, not-too-fine crumbs from nonsweetened, homemade-type white bread

If the potato mixture is freshly made, let it cool. Either rolling and patting them in the lightly floured palms of your hands, or forming them on waxed paper with a wet rubber spatula, make smooth cakes of the potato mixture 3 inches in diameter and ¾ inch thick. As each is formed, place it on the bread crumbs, heap crumbs on top, pat a thin layer in place, and arrange the cakes in one layer on waxed paper.

A sheet of waxed paper on
  a tray
5 to 6 Tb clarified butter
  (melted butter, skimmed;
  clear liquid butter
  spooned off milky
  residue)
A large (11-inch) frying
  pan, preferably no-stick
A buttered baking sheet

(*) AHEAD-OF-TIME NOTE: If you are not going to
sauté them immediately, cover and refrigerate; they
will keep perfectly well until the next day.

Preheat oven to 200 degrees. Shortly before serving, film frying pan with ⅛ inch of the clarified butter, heat to very hot but not browning, and arrange as many potato cakes in pan as will easily fit in one layer. Sauté for 3 to 4 minutes on one side, until nicely browned and crusted, turn and sauté on the other side. Arrange on baking sheet and keep warm in oven while sautéing the rest, adding more butter to pan as necessary. The potato cakes may be kept warm for 15 minutes or more, but are at their best and freshest the sooner you serve them.

Galettes de Pommes de Terre Farcies

[Filled Potato Cakes]

With a stuffing of ham, mushrooms, and cheese, potato cakes become a main course. Serve them with a green vegetable or a salad. Rather than sautéing them, you may find baking easier.

For 8 cakes 3½ inches in diameter, serving 4 or more people

Ingredients for the preceding potato cakes plus:
¼ lb. (1 cup) finely diced
  fresh mushrooms
1 Tb minced shallots or
  scallions
Salt and pepper
⅓ cup finely minced ham
½ cup grated Swiss cheese

Sauté the mushrooms and shallots or scallions in a tablespoon of the butter in a small pan until mushroom pieces begin to separate from each other and to brown very lightly. Season with salt and pepper, add the minced ham, and sauté a minute more. Set aside. Form half of the potato mixture into 8 disks 3½ inches in diameter and about ¼ inch thick. Spread the ham and mushrooms in the center of each, and top with grated cheese. Cover with disks made from the remaining potatoes.

To cook, either dredge in bread crumbs and sauté in clarified butter as in preceding recipe, or arrange on a buttered baking sheet, sprinkle with bread crumbs and melted butter, and bake in upper third of a preheated 400-degree oven for 25 to 30 minutes until lightly browned.

A BEAN PURÉE, THREE TURNIP
RECIPES, AND A CRÊPE

Any change from routine is a happy event, particularly when it is a substitute for the usual starchy vegetable choices. Here is a clever purée of beans and pumpkin, two purées involving turnips, plus a turnip sauté, and a new kind of *crêpe* made of green peppers and tomatoes.

GRATIN DE POTIRON D'ARPAJON
[Purée of Pumpkin or Winter Squash and White Beans]

A combination of pumpkin or squash and beans goes especially well with goose, duck, turkey, pork, or sausages. This is also one of the few vegetable recipes where you may successfully substitute canned or frozen ingredients for fresh, as noted near the end of the directions in Step 1, and in the ingredients for Step 2.

For 4 to 6 people

1) *The pumpkin or squash*

1¼ cups *mirepoix* vegetables (½ cup each of finely diced onions and celery; ¼ cup diced carrots)

3 Tb butter

A covered 2½- to 3-quart flameproof baking and serving dish 2½ to 3 inches deep

2 lbs. yellow-fleshed winter squash or pumpkin (6 cups peeled and roughly sliced)

Optional: 1 to 2 cloves mashed garlic

1 imported bay leaf

⅛ tsp thyme

½ tsp salt

½ cup water

Waxed paper cut to fit top of dish

Preheat oven to 350 degrees. Cook the *mirepoix* vegetables in butter in the covered dish over low heat, stirring occasionally, for 8 to 10 minutes, until vegetables are tender but not browned. Stir in the squash or pumpkin, optional garlic, herbs, salt, and water. Bring to a simmer on top of stove, lay waxed paper over vegetables, cover, and bake in middle level of preheated oven for 30 to 40 minutes, stirring up once or twice to be sure vegetables are not browning. Add 2 to 3 tablespoons more liquid if all has evaporated before squash or pumpkin is tender. (If using canned or frozen squash or pumpkin, cook *mirepoix* vegetables until tender, then add garlic, herbs, and ¼ cup water; cover and boil slowly for about 10 minutes until liquid has evaporated.) Remove bay leaf.

2) *The beans; baking and serving*

About 2½ cups cooked or canned white beans such as Great Northern, pea beans, or Italian cannellini beans (for quick soaking and pressure cooking of dried beans, see Volume I, page 400)

A food mill with medium disk

A large mixing bowl

A rubber spatula and wooden spoon

2 "large" eggs

½ cup heavy cream

2 ounces (½ cup) grated Swiss cheese

Salt and white pepper

3 Tb butter

Preheat oven to 425 degrees in time for baking. Purée the squash or pumpkin mixture along with the beans through food mill into bowl. Beat in the eggs, cream, all but 2 tablespoons of the cheese, and salt and pepper to taste. Smear 1 tablespoon of the butter in the baking dish, spoon in the purée, sprinkle reserved cheese on top and dot with the remaining butter.

(*) AHEAD-OF-TIME NOTE: May be completed a day ahead to this point. When cold, cover and refrigerate. Allow 10 to 15 minutes longer in oven if mixture is chilled.

About half an hour before serving, bake uncovered in upper third of preheated 425-degree oven until bubbling hot and top has browned nicely.

PURÉE FRENEUSE

[Purée of Rice and Turnips with Herbs and Garlic]

Unless your guests know that Freneuse is Turnipville, on one of the serpentine twists of the Seine northwest of Paris, they will have no other clue to identify this marvelous mixture. Serve it with red meats, pork, sausages, chops, goose, and ducklings.

For 4 to 6 people

2 cups milk, more if needed

A heavy-bottomed 2-quart saucepan (no-stick would be useful)

1 cup rice

½ tsp salt

2 Tb butter

2 to 3 large cloves of mashed garlic

Bring the milk to the simmer, add the rice, salt, butter, garlic, and seasonings. Simmer, stirring occasionally, for 10 minutes, until rice is partially tender. Stir in the turnips, adding more milk, if necessary, to submerge the vegetables. Cover and simmer 10 to 15 minutes more, stirring occasionally, until turnips are tender. Liquid should be almost entirely absorbed; if not, uncover and boil, stirring, to evaporate it. Purée through food mill and return to pan.

¼ tsp Italian seasoning, or thyme and bay leaf

3 to 4 white turnips, about 3 inches in diameter, peeled and roughly chopped (2 to 3 cups)

A food mill

(*) AHEAD-OF-TIME NOTE: May be completed to this point.

Salt and white pepper to taste

2 to 3 Tb butter or heavy cream

A hot serving dish

Minced parsley

Shortly before serving, reheat, stirring. Carefully correct seasoning. Stir in the butter or cream by spoonfuls. Turn into a hot serving dish and decorate with the parsley.

LA PURÉE, CHÂTEAUX EN SUÈDE

[Purée of Yellow Turnips—Rutabagas]

Firm, fresh rutabagas with their crisp, moist flesh and fine, sweet flavor are every bit as good as the best white turnips, especially when they are simmered with butter and turned into a fragrant, yellow purée. Serve with a roast goose or duck, a loin of pork, a dinner of homemade sausages, or a lamb or beef stew.

HISTORICAL NOTE

Because rutabagas appear to have originated in Scandinavia, they are called swedes by the English and sometimes *navets de Suède* by the French. The rutabaga is a distinct species of vegetable, related to both the cabbage and the turnip, which accounts for one of its other French names, *chou-rave à chair jaune*. A number of varieties exist, some of which are animal fodder, and in France that type was often all one had to eat during two long world wars. Although modern improvements have created varieties to meet the taste of the most discriminating *châtelaine,* rutabagas are still a distasteful reminder of bitter days to many Frenchmen, which accounts for this recipe's charmingly evasive title.

For 4 to 6 people

1½ to 2 lbs. firm, crisp rutabaga, peeled and cut into 1-inch pieces (6 to 7 cups)

Place rutabaga chunks in saucepan with enough water to come ⅔ the way up the vegetables. Add salt and butter, bring to the boil, cover and boil slowly, tossing

A heavy-bottomed 2-quart
  saucepan
About 2 cups water
1½ tsp salt
3 Tb butter
A cover for the pan
A food mill set over a mixing bowl

occasionally, for about 30 minutes or until tender. Drain, reserving cooking liquid, and purée rutabaga through food mill into bowl.

4 Tb rendered goose fat,
  pork fat, or butter
⅓ cup all-purpose flour
  (measure by scooping
  dry-measure cup into
  flour and sweeping off
  excess with a knife)
A wooden spoon and wire
  whip
The hot turnip-cooking
  juices
¼ cup heavy cream
Salt and pepper
A lightly buttered warm
  vegetable dish
Fresh parsley

Melt the fat or butter in the saucepan, blend in the flour, and stir over moderate heat until flour and fat foam together for 2 minutes without browning at all. Remove from heat, and when it has stopped bubbling blend in 1 cup of the cooking juices, beating vigorously with wire whip until mixture is perfectly smooth. Return over moderately high heat, stirring with whip as mixture thickens and comes to the boil. Boil, stirring, for 2 minutes. Sauce should be very thick, but not so thick that it will not combine with the puréed turnips: beat in more cooking liquid (or milk) by spoonfuls if you think it necessary. Finally beat the turnip purée and the cream into the sauce, and season carefully to taste.

(*) AHEAD-OF-TIME NOTES: May be prepared even a day in advance; cover and refrigerate when cool.

About 30 minutes before serving, cover and reheat over simmering water, stirring occasionally. To serve, turn into a hot vegetable dish and decorate with parsley.

PETITS NAVETS SAUTÉS, EN GARNITURE
[Fresh, Young White Turnips Sautéed in Butter]

Winter and early spring are the time for early crop turnips, which are tender enough to need no blanching and are at their best cooked simply in butter. Whether round, oval, or top-shaped and with or without their green leaves, buy them smooth, firm, small, clean, unblemished, and all of a size for even cutting and shaping. Their flesh, when you cut into them raw, must be moist, crisp, and sweetly turnipy. Serve sautéed turnips with duck, goose, turkey, pork, roast beef or lamb, steaks or chops. They are also attractive as part of a vegetable garnish in combination with such others as glazed carrots and sautéed mushrooms, or buttered fresh peas. The following recipe is for a small amount, but if you wish to cook more, do the preliminary sauté in batches, and finish them off all together in a covered casserole in a 325-degree oven.

For 4 to 6 servings

About 12 fresh, young
  white turnips 2 to 2½
  inches in diameter (2½
  lbs. without tops)
2 or more Tb butter
1 or more Tb olive oil or
  cooking oil
A large (11-inch) frying
  pan (no-stick recom-
  mended)
¼ tsp salt, more as necessary
Big pinch pepper
A cover for the pan

With a small, sharp knife, peel the turnips, removing outer skin and the white underskin that covers the moist flesh. You now want to cut them in the form of large garlic cloves, all pieces approximately the same size: if you have round turnips, for example, quarter them lengthwise, and round off the sharp edges, saving trimmings for turnip soup or adding them to one of the preceding purées.

Melt 2 tablespoons of butter with 1 of oil in frying pan over moderately high heat. When butter foam is beginning to subside, indicating fat is hot enough, add as many turnips as will fit in one crowded layer. Toss and turn frequently, shaking and swirling the pan by its handle, for 4 to 5 minutes, until turnips are beginning to brown very lightly. (If you are sautéing in 2 batches, turn browned turnips into a side dish, add more butter and oil if needed, brown the second batch, then return all to the pan.) Toss turnips with the salt and pepper, cover pan, and cook over very low heat, tossing occasionally, for about 10 minutes more or until turnips are tender. Be careful turnips do not brown too much. Be sure also not to overcook them; they should be just tender but still hold their shape.

2 to 3 Tb more butter
Salt and pepper as needed
3 to 4 Tb fresh minced
  parsley
A hot vegetable dish or the
  meat platter

Just before serving, reheat to sizzling, toss with more salt and pepper as needed, then with the additional butter, and finally with the parsley. Turn into hot vegetable dish or onto platter and serve.

CRÊPES À LA PIPÉRADE

[Pepper, Onion, Tomato, and Cheese Pancakes]

Cooked bell peppers, onions, tomatoes, cheese, and herbs plus a light batter to bind them all together are the basic ingredients for this attractive vegetable combination, which is cooked like pancakes. Serve them with roasts, chops, or broiled chicken, and any leftovers are delicious with cold hors d'oeuvre or on a picnic. They are, in addition, a splendid background for diced poultry, veal, or pork leftovers, which you may include in the mixture; topped with a poached or fried egg and a tomato or cheese sauce, they are an ample main course for informal meals.

For 12 4-inch pancakes

1) *The crêpe batter—for ¾ cup*

⅓ cup flour, preferably "instant blending" (measure by scooping dry-measure cup into flour and leveling off with knife)

1 "large" egg

¼ tsp salt

1½ tsp cooking oil

⅓ cup milk, plus a little more if needed

An electric blender, or a bowl, whip, and sieve

Either whirl all ingredients in a blender; or place flour in bowl, beat in rest of ingredients, and strain through sieve. Batter should be like heavy cream; if too thick, thin out with drops of milk. You may use it immediately if you have instant-blending flour; otherwise let it rest for an hour at least.

2) *The pipérade mixture—for 1½ cups*

1½ cups sliced onions

3 Tb olive oil or cooking oil

An 8-inch frying pan with cover

1½ cups sliced green bell peppers

3 to 4 ripe, red tomatoes peeled, seeded, juiced, and sliced (1½ cups)

2 to 3 large cloves of garlic, mashed

Salt and pepper to taste

2 Tb fresh minced parsley, plus 1 Tb fresh minced basil or ½ tsp of dried oregano

Cook the onions in the oil for 8 to 10 minutes, or until tender and translucent. Add the peppers and cook another 3 to 4 minutes to soften slightly. Then add the sliced tomato pulp and garlic; cover pan for several minutes until tomatoes have rendered their juice. Uncover, raise heat, and boil for several minutes, tossing pan by handle to blend ingredients, until liquid has almost completely evaporated. Season carefully to taste, and toss with the herbs.

3) *Cooking the crêpes*

(You may prefer several 8-inch *crêpes* cut into wedges; the following is for 4-inch *crêpes* cooked 3 at a time in a 10-inch pan.)

5 ounces Swiss cheese cut into ⅜-inch dice (about ¾ cup)

Blend the cheese into the *pipérade* along with ½ cup of the batter. Brush frying pan with oil and set over moderately high heat. When hot but not quite smok-

The *pipérade* turned into a 2-quart bowl

A rubber spatula

½ cup or more of the *crêpe* batter

Cooking oil

A heavy 10-inch frying pan (no-stick recommended)

A ¼-cup measure

1 or 2 oiled baking sheets A pancake turner

ing, ladle in ¼ cup of the *crêpe* mixture as a test. Cook about 2 minutes on one side, until little holes appear through the surface, at which time bottom should be nicely browned. Turn and cook about 1 minute on other side, then remove to a baking sheet. *Crêpe* should just hold together, with only enough batter in the mixture to enrobe the ingredients. Add a little more batter to bowl if you feel it necessary, but too much makes for doughy *crêpes*. Cook the rest of the *crêpes* and arrange on baking sheets.

Just before serving, reheat for 5 minutes or so in a preheated 425-degree oven.

Including leftovers

For the same amount of batter, use:

    1 cup each sliced onions, peppers, and tomatoes for the *pipérade*

    ⅓ cup diced cheese

    1 cup diced cooked poultry, veal, pork, ham, sausages, or fish

---

THREE COLD VEGETABLES

PETITS OIGNONS AIGRE-DOUX

[Sweet and Sour Onions Braised with Raisins—Hot or Cold]

Serve these hot with roast pork, duck, goose, game, or cold along with hors d'oeuvre, and cold meat and poultry. They should be considered more as a garnish, relish, or condiment than a vegetable, and if you are using tiny pearl onions, 6 per serving should be sufficient.

For about 2 cups, serving 6 to 8

---

3 cups (10 ounces; 40 to 50) small, white pearl onions

A saucepan of boiling water

A heavy-bottomed 2-quart saucepan with cover

½ cup beef or chicken bouillon

½ cup water

1 tsp dry mustard blended with 1½ Tb wine vinegar

Drop the onions into the boiling water and boil 1 minute to loosen skins. Drain. Shave off 2 ends, peel, and pierce a cross in the root end of each to help onions retain their shape while cooking. Place onions in a saucepan with all the ingredients listed except for the herbs and pepper. Bring to the simmer, skim for several minutes, then add the thyme, bay leaf, and pepper; cover and simmer slowly about 1 hour, or until the onions are tender but still hold their shape. Add a little more water if necessary during cooking;

2 **Tb olive oil**
1½ **Tb sugar**
¼ **tsp salt**
1 **medium tomato, peeled,
   seeded, juiced, and
   chopped**
⅓ **cup currants (small,
   black, seedless raisins)**
1 **large clove garlic, mashed**
¼ **tsp thyme**
1 **bay leaf**
⅛ **tsp pepper**
A serving dish

however, liquid should be reduced to a syrup when onions are done; if not, boil down at end of cooking. Transfer to dish and serve hot or cold, decorated, if you wish, with parsley.

SALADE DE POIVRONS, PROVENÇALE
[Peeled and Sliced Sweet Peppers in Garlic and Oil]

A typical informal first course in Provence might include the local black olives, sliced hard-boiled eggs, anchovies, capers, and slices of green or red sweet peppers turned in olive oil, salt, and garlic. The only trick to this recipe is that you will have to peel the peppers, which is quite a different matter from peeling eggs. A number of pepper-peeling systems are on the books, including spearing them on a long fork and turning then one-by-one over a gas flame, baking in a hot oven, baking in a slow oven, boiling them, steaming them in a covered dish, dropping in hot oil, broiling them until the skin puffs and blackens. We like broiling because it is the quickest, the surest, and it cooks the flesh just enough so that the pepper is ready to cut and serve as soon as you have peeled it.

A NOTE ON SWEET PEPPERS

All sweet peppers both here and in France belong to the same species, *Capsicum annuum,* native to the tropics and including a large number of shapes and sizes. Most of those found in American markets are 2½ to 4 inches in diameter, 4 to 5 inches long, and a deep green color. (When peppers are fully mature they are yellow or red, and perishable to ship long distances; probably the only red peppers you will see are those grown locally.) Pick peppers that are brightly colored, glossy, firm, and thick-fleshed, with no pockmarks, brown patches, or soft spots anywhere on their surface. Like their distant cousin, the eggplant, raw peppers prefer a temperature of 45 to 50 degrees and a humidity of 90 per cent. Unless you can reproduce these conditions, buy only what you will use within a day or two because they will deteriorate rapidly when stored where they are either too hot or too cold.

For 4 medium-sized peppers

1) *Peeling the peppers*

4 medium-sized peppers, green, red, yellow, or mixed

A shallow baking dish big enough to hold peppers easily, such as a pie plate

A cutting board

A sharp knife and a table fork

Preheat broiler to very hot. Arrange peppers in dish and place so surface of peppers is an inch from broiling element. As soon as skin facing broiler has puffed and blackened, in 2 to 3 minutes, turn peppers on another face, and finally on each end, so that all of skin has puffed. Remove peppers to cutting board. One by one, rapidly cut in half lengthwise, remove stem and seeds, and scrape off skin. (This should be done as soon as possible and before peppers cool; if blackened skin remains too long on pepper, it can darken the flesh under it.)

2) *Dressing the peppers*

1 medium clove of garlic, mashed

¼ tsp salt

A small bowl and a pestle or wooden spoon

⅓ cup excellent olive oil

A serving dish

Plastic wrap

Mash garlic and salt until salt has dissolved completely, then beat in olive oil. Cut peppers into lengthwise strips ⅜ inch wide and arrange layers in dish, spooning dressing over each layer. Cover and let steep, tilting dish and basting with the dressing occasionally, for 20 minutes before serving.

(*) AHEAD-OF-TIME NOTE: May be made several days in advance; cover airtight and refrigerate. Remove half an hour before serving to de-congeal oil.

FONDS D'ARTICHAUTS FARCIS, FROIDS
FONDS D'ARTICHAUTS EN SURPRISE

[Artichoke Bottoms Stuffed with Mushroom Purée, Poached Eggs Optional—a Cold Entrée]

Here is one of those perfect first-course dishes for special guests and formal dinners. Whole artichokes are boiled and the leaves carefully removed to preserve the bottoms; the bottoms are then filled with a mixture of puréed and marinated raw mushrooms, the scraped-off flesh from the leaves, mayonnaise, and herbs. A helping hand is welcome here, because leaf scraping is rather slow work. However, if you are alone and unhurried, you may boil the artichokes one day, scrape them the next, and fill them on the morning of the third day. When you want to serve this as a main-course luncheon dish, add *la surprise,* poached eggs, which blend perfectly with mushrooms, artichokes, and mayonnaise.

For 6 large artichokes

1) *Preparing the artichokes*

6 large, fresh, fine artichokes 4 to 4½ inches in
diameter

A large kettle containing 7
to 8 quarts boiling salted
water

A food mill with middle-
size disk, or a sieve

Following illustrated directions in Volume I, pages
423–5, trim the artichokes, being sure all the tough
green part is cut off bottoms and small leaves are
broken from circumference. Boil slowly, uncovered,
for 35 to 45 minutes until bottoms are tender when
pierced with a knife. (Prepare mushrooms and mayonnaise, Steps 2 and 3, while the artichokes boil.)

Drain upside down in a colander. When cool, carefully remove the leaves, keeping bottoms intact. Scrape out and discard hairy choke from center of each artichoke
bottom. With a teaspoon, scrape flesh from the inside of leaves and bottom of heart
(soft cone of leaves covering choke). Purée the scraped flesh through food mill or
sieve, then twist hard in the corner of a towel to extract as much water as possible.
Place puréed flesh in a bowl.

2) *The purée of raw mushrooms*

½ lb. (1 quart) very fresh,
firm, unblemished
mushrooms

¼ tsp salt

Big pinch of pepper

2 Tb very finely minced
shallots or scallions

1 Tb lemon juice

A 2-quart bowl

With a large, sharp knife, chop the mushrooms into
a very fine mince, almost a purée. Blend them in the
bowl with the salt, pepper, shallots or scallions, and
lemon juice. Marinate for 15 to 20 minutes. Then,
a handful at a time, twist mushrooms in the corner
of a towel to squeeze out as much vegetable liquid as
possible. Add the mushrooms to the bowl containing
the puréed artichoke flesh.

3) *Final assembly*

About 1½ cups thick home-
made mayonnaise (the
hard-yolk *tartare* minus
the trimmings but plus
the sieved egg white, Volume I, page 90, is particularly recommended)

1 Tb fresh minced tarragon
or ¼ tsp dried tarragon

4 Tb fresh minced parsley
(reserve half for decora-
tions)

The artichoke and mushroom purées are now to be
seasoned and piled into the artichoke bottoms: by
spoonfuls stir mayonnaise into the vegetables, adding
probably 3 to 4 tablespoons in all but not enough to
thin out purée, which must remain thick and hold its
shape. Stir in the herbs and taste carefully for seasoning. Sprinkle artichoke bottoms lightly with salt and
pepper, and mound the purée in them, smoothing it
into a dome. (If you are using eggs, lay them in the
artichokes between 2 layers of the purée.) Arrange
the artichokes in the dish or plates. Just before serving,
stir the cream into the mayonnaise, then spoon a dol-

Salt and pepper to taste
The cooked artichoke
  bottoms
Optional: 6 cold poached
  eggs or 6-minute peeled
  eggs (*oeufs mollets*)
A serving dish or individual
  plates lined with lettuce
  leaves or watercress
3 to 4 Tb heavy cream,
  crème fraîche, or sour
  cream

lop over the top of each artichoke, and decorate with parsley.

(*) AHEAD-OF-TIME NOTE: It is usually perfectly safe to complete the recipe the day before serving, except for the final bit of mayonnaise, and to cover and refrigerate the artichokes. To avoid all risks of turned mayonnaise, however, we suggest that you complete the final assembly only an hour or so before serving.

CHAPTER SEVEN

Desserts: Extending
the Repertoire

FROZEN DESSERTS—SHERBETS, ICE CREAMS, AND MOUSSES

Entremets Glacés

As long as your freezer maintains a steady temperature of zero degrees or less, you need no other ice cream contraption to produce a marvelous parade of frozen fantasies. We start this delicious group with a simple sherbet made from sieved canned apricots, proceed to a mousse of fresh strawberries (pausing to make some sugar-cookie cups to serve them in), and continue with chocolate-burnt-almond ice cream, a walnut and caramel mousse, *bombe glacée,* and directions for parfaits and frozen soufflés. *Le Saint-Cyr,* a handsome mold of chocolate mousse and meringues, leads into a digression on meringued whipped cream either as a filling for cream horns or as a vanilla ice cream with chocolate sauce. *La Surprise du Vésuve* ends the section in a dramatic burst of flames.

✳ *MOUSSE À L'ABRICOT, GLACÉE*

[Apricot Sherbet]

Easy, delicious, and available all year round is apricot sherbet made from canned apricots. Timing is 4 to 5 hours, but it is easier to be leisurely and start the mousse the day before serving.

For about 1 quart, serving 4 to 6 people

---

1) *The sherbet mixture*

A No. 2 can (1 lb. 14 ounces) or two 1-lb. cans of apricot halves
A food mill with fine disk
A quart measure
A 2½-quart mixing bowl
2 egg whites in a small, clean beating bowl
An electric mixer, with clean, dry blades
About ½ cup sugar ("instant" superfine if possible)
2 Tb lemon juice
2 to 3 drops of almond extract

Drain apricots, purée them, and put into measure. Add enough of their juice to make 2 cups, and turn purée into mixing bowl. Beat egg whites with mixer until they form soft peaks, and set aside. Then, with mixer, beat the sugar and lemon juice into the apricot purée; continue beating for several minutes to dissolve sugar completely—until you can feel no granules on your tongue. If not sweet enough, beat in a little more sugar; be careful, however, because sugar proportions should be no more than ¼ part of the mixture or sherbet will not freeze properly. Whip in the beaten egg whites with mixer; their purpose is to discourage large ice crystals from forming. Add the drops of almond extract, which will bring out the apricot flavor.

---

2) *Freezing the mousse—4 to 5 hours minimum at zero degrees or less*

A flat pan about 9 by 12 inches in diameter, if you are in a hurry; or a mixing bowl; or ice trays if you have little room
Plastic wrap
An electric mixer or a large wire whip
Optional: a serving bowl or ice cream mold
The apricot sauce on page 507

Sherbet mixture is now to be frozen, and beaten up once or twice during the process to break up ice crystals and give a smooth, light texture. Turn it into a flat pan or ice trays if you are rushed; leave in mixing bowl if you are not. Cover with plastic wrap and freeze for 2 to 3 hours, or until sherbet has begun to set.

When partially set, scrape into mixing bowl if sherbet is in a pan or trays. Beat vigorously with electric mixer or wire whip; sherbet will increase in volume and begin to whiten. Cover and freeze again for an hour or so, and again beat it up; then turn it into a serving bowl or ice cream mold if you wish. Cover, and freeze for several hours more before serving. (NOTE: If you are in no hurry and sherbet has frozen hard before you have beaten it, leave at room temperature until softened, and beat with an electric mixer; then return to freezer and continue as usual.)

Let mousse soften for half an hour in the refrigerator before serving, and accompany, if you wish, with the apricot sauce. (See also the cookie cups on page 419, which you can use instead of sherbet dishes.)

VARIATIONS

Mousse à l'Abricot, Chantilly

To make a richer and softer sherbet, really an ice cream, you may incorporate whipped cream as follows.

For 1½ quarts, serving 6 to 8 people

The preceding apricot sherbet mixture

1 cup chilled whipping cream in a beating bowl

A large bowl with a tray of ice cubes and water to cover them

A large wire whip or hand-held electric mixer

A rubber spatula

Optional: a chilled serving bowl or ice cream mold

At the end of the first freezing, after you have beaten the apricot sherbet and it has increased in volume and whitened, fold in the lightly whipped cream, *crème Chantilly*. (Cream should always be beaten separately; if beaten with the sherbet you will not get as much volume.) Set bowl of cream over ice cubes and water. Circulating whip or beater about bowl to incorporate as much air as possible, beat until cream has doubled in volume and beater leaves light traces on surface.

Fold the cream into the sherbet, and it will need no further beating, only freezing. If you are serving in a decorative bowl or mold, turn the mixture into it now, cover, and freeze 3 to 4 hours at least before serving.

Bombe Glacée à l'Abricot

[Apricot Mousse Molded with Another Sherbet or an Ice Cream]

When you want to be more elaborate, you may pack the apricot sherbet into a bowl or mold lined with another sherbet or with ice cream, as follows.

For 2 quarts, serving 8 to 10 people

1 quart of pineapple sherbet, lemon sherbet, or vanilla ice cream (homemade or best quality store-bought)

Let the sherbet or ice cream soften just enough so that you can spread it around the inside of the mold or bowl. Cover with plastic wrap and set in freezer to harden. When the apricot sherbet has been frozen

A chilled 2 quart ice cream
 mold, or metal bowl or
 charlotte
Plastic wrap
The apricot sherbet, page
 415

and beaten several times, and is ready for its final
freezing, pack it into the lined bowl. Cover again
with plastic wrap and freeze several hours more.

To unmold, run a knife around inside rim of mold, hold for several seconds in a basin of cold water, and unmold onto a chilled serving dish. If not to be
served immediately, cover with an inverted bowl and return to freezer.

Mousse aux Fraises ou aux Framboises, Glacée

[Fresh Strawberry or Raspberry Sherbet]

Your own fresh strawberry or raspberry sherbet is a delight, and just as
easy to make as the preceding apricot sherbet.

For about 1 quart, serving 4 to 6 people

1 quart fresh strawberries
 or raspberries
A food mill with fine disk,
 set over a 2½- to 3-quart
 mixing bowl
2 egg whites in a small,
 clean beating bowl
An electric mixer or a large
 wire whip
½ cup sugar, preferably
 "instant" superfine
¼ cup lemon juice

Hull the strawberries, and wash rapidly; if using
raspberries, pick them over and discard any spoiled
ones. Purée berries into mixing bowl; you should
have about 2 cups. Beat the egg whites until they
form soft peaks, and set aside. Beat the sugar and
lemon juice into the berry purée and continue beating for several minutes to dissolve sugar completely
—until you can feel no granules on your tongue.
Whip in the beaten egg whites. Cover and freeze,
beating several times as directed in Master Recipe,
Step 2, page 416.

Strawberry or Raspberry Ice Cream

For a softer and richer mixture, fold in a cup of heavy cream, beaten over ice,
after the mousse has begun to set, as directed for the apricot ice cream, page 417.

Other fruits

You may substitute frozen raspberries or strawberries for fresh ones in the preceding recipe; thaw, drain, and purée four 10-ounce packages, add enough of the
juices to make 2 cups, and you will need no additional sugar. Fresh, ripe, raw
peaches are delicious either as a sherbet or with cream added, and you can decorate

each serving with sliced peaches macerated in sugar, lemon juice, and kirsch. Use the same proportions and method for other fruit purées.

COUPELLES, LANGUES DE CHATS
[Cookie Serving Cups for Ices, Fruits, and Dessert Creams]

Simple to make and charming as containers are crisp little cookie cups made from the French egg-white batter known as *langues de chats,* because it is usually baked in flat cat's-tongue shapes. Here the batter is spread in thin disks on baking sheets; as soon as the edges have browned in a hot oven, they are removed one by one and pressed into a teacup, where they immediately crisp into shape.

For 8 cups 3½ inches in diameter

---

1) *The cookie batter—pâte à langues de chats*

2 baking sheets approximately 14 by 18 inches, buttered and floured
A *vol-au-vent* cutter, pot lid, or saucer about 5½ inches in diameter
A rubber spatula
Tasteless salad oil
2 large tea cups or small bowls about 5 inches in diameter at the top, 2 at the bottom, and 2½ inches deep

Preheat oven to 425 degrees and set rack in middle level. Prepare baking sheets; then, with cutter and point of rubber spatula, mark 4 circles on each. Lightly oil cups or bowls, and set them at a convenient place near the oven.

An electric mixer or a wooden spoon
2 ounces (½ stick) soft butter

Beat the butter, sugar, and lemon or orange rind in the bowl with electric mixer or wooden spoon until pale and fluffy. Pour in the egg whites and mix a few seconds, only just enough to blend. Place flour in

⅓ cup granulated sugar

The grated rind of 1 lemon
or orange

A 2-quart mixing bowl

¼ cup egg whites (about
2 egg whites)

⅓ cup all-purpose flour
(measure by scooping
dry-measure cup into
flour; sweep off excess
with knife)

A sieve or sifter

A rubber spatula

sieve or sifter and shake it over the batter, rapidly folding it in with rubber spatula.

2) *Forming, baking, and shaping—oven preheated to 425 degrees*

NOTE: If this is the first time you have done this type of cookie, experiment with one or two first so that you will understand the system of baking, removing, and molding; they are easy to do as soon as you know what to expect.

A rubber spatula and a
dessert spoon

A kitchen timer

A flexible-blade spatula
(blade should be at least
8 inches long) for un-
molding cookies

The oiled cups or bowls for
unmolding the cookies

A cake rack or racks

Using rubber spatula to dislodge the batter, place a 1½-tablespoon gob in the center of each of the 4 circles on one of the baking sheets. Using back of spoon, smear the batter out to fill the circles; it will be less than ⅛ inch thick. Place in middle level of preheated oven, set timer for 5 minutes, and bake until cookies have browned lightly, either to within an inch of the center, or in large splotches. (Form cookies on second sheet while these are baking.)

As soon as they are done, set baking sheet on open oven door so that cookies will stay warm and pliable—they crisp immediately they cool, and then cannot be molded. Working rapidly, slide long side of spatula blade under one cookie to scrape and lift it off the baking sheet; turn in upside down over one of the oiled cups or bowls, and *press into the cup with your fingers*. Rapidly remove a second cookie from the sheet and press into second cup. Immediately take first cookie out of first cup—they crisp in seconds—and place on rack. Rapidly mold the third cookie, and finally the fourth. (They will be fragile, so handle with care.)

Close oven door and wait for a few minutes for temperature to return to 425 degrees; bake and mold the second sheet of cookies.

---

3) *Storing and serving*

Cookies will stay crisp for several days in dry weather if stored airtight; for longer storage, freeze them. Spoon sherbet, ice cream, or fruits into the cookie cups just before serving. For fruit sherbets or ice cream, such as strawberry, save some of the fruit to decorate top of each serving.

LE KILIMANJARO—GLACE AU CHOCOLAT, PRALINÉE

[Chocolate-Burnt-Almond Ice Cream]

For lovers of chocolate and ice cream, we think this is the best combination we know.

For 6 cups, serving 6 to 8 people

---

1) *Toasted almond brittle—pralin aux amandes—for 1 cup*

4 ounces (about 1 cup) blanched almonds A pizza tray or roasting pan	Preheat oven to 350 degrees. Spread almonds in tray or pan, set in middle level, and roast 10 to 15 minutes, stirring up several times, until they are a walnut brown. Remove from oven.
½ cup sugar 3 Tb water A small, heavy saucepan with cover The almonds in a bowl The roasting pan, lightly oiled An electric blender	Combine sugar and water in saucepan and set over moderately high heat. Swirl pan slowly by its handle, but do not stir sugar with a spoon while liquid is coming to the boil. Continue swirling for a moment while liquid boils and changes from cloudy to perfectly clear.

Cover pan, raise heat to high, and boil for several minutes until bubbles are thick and heavy. Uncover, and continue boiling, swirling gently, until syrup turns a nice caramel brown. Remove from heat and stir in the almonds; immediately turn out into oiled pan. When cold and hard, in 20 minutes or so, break up; grind a half cupful at a time in electric blender.

(*) AHEAD-OF-TIME NOTE: *Pralin* freezes perfectly for several months in an airtight jar.

---

2) *The chocolate ice cream*

½ cup sugar	Combine sugar and water in saucepan; swirl over
⅓ cup water	heat until sugar has dissolved completely, and liquid
A 6-cup saucepan with	is perfectly clear. Remove from heat; stir in the cof-
cover	fee. Break up the chocolate, stir it in, cover, and set in
2 Tb instant coffee	the pan of hot water. While chocolate is melting, beat
6 ounces semisweet baking	the cream into *Chantilly* as follows.
chocolate	
2 ounces unsweetened	
baking chocolate	
A larger saucepan of sim-	
mering water removed	
from heat	
A wooden spoon	

crème Chantilly:

2 cups chilled heavy cream	Set bowl of cream over ice cubes and water. Circu-
in a 2½-quart bowl	lating beater about bowl to incorporate as much air
A large bowl containing a	as possible, beat until cream has doubled in volume
trayful of ice cubes and	and beater leaves light traces on surface.
water to cover them	
A hand-held electric beater	
A rubber spatula	

The *pralin* from Step 1	With the electric beater, whip the chocolate until
(save 2 to 3 Tb for final	perfectly smooth and shiny. Beat the chocolate for
decoration, Step 3)	a moment over ice to cool it, then beat in about half
	a cup of the *crème Chantilly*. Finally, fold the choco-
	late mixture into the *Chantilly* along with the *pralin*.

---

3) *Molding, freezing, and serving—freezing time 2 hours minimum*

If you are in a hurry:	Immediately turn the ice cream mixture into pan,
A 6- to 8-cup pan, or	pans, or mold. Cover with plastic wrap, and freeze.
ice trays 2 inches deep	If you have used a shallow pan, the cream should
Otherwise: A 6-cup	be ready to unmold in about 2 hours; you will prob-
conical mold, or a narrow	ably need 4 hours for a mold or a bowl.
bowl or dish with	
rounded bottom, to give	
the effect of a mountain	
peak	

A chilled serving dish

1 cup heavy cream beaten into *Chantilly* (as in Step 2), sweetened to taste with confectioner's sugar and flavored with ½ tsp vanilla extract

The reserved 2 to 3 Tb *pralin*

Just before serving, dip pan or mold in tepid water to loosen the ice cream. Turn serving dish upside down over mold, and reverse the two to unmold ice cream onto dish. Top with the *crème Chantilly,* sprinkle with the *pralin,* and announce the name of your snow-capped mountain as you bring it to the table.

MOUSSE GLACÉE, PRALINÉE AUX NOIX— APPAREIL À BOMBE

[Walnut-caramel Ice Cream—or Filling for *Bombes Glacées*]

French frozen mousses are of two types, one with sugar syrup and cream, and the other like this, with custard and cream. Using this base, you may incorporate any flavoring you wish, from melted chocolate to crushed pineapple, and from crumbled peppermint sticks to walnut brittle. It makes a tender, smooth ice cream, suitable for freezing in a serving bowl, in a soufflé dish, in parfait glasses, or to be packed into a decorative mold lined with regular ice cream.

For 1½ quarts, serving 8 to 10 people

---

1) *Walnut brittle and caramelized walnuts—pralin aux noix—2½ cups*

1⅓ cups sugar

½ cup water

A heavy 2-quart saucepan with cover

8 ounces (2 cups) shelled walnuts (some may be walnut pieces; 8 perfect halves needed)

A lightly oiled baking sheet

A fork, for taking walnuts out of caramel

An electric blender

Combine sugar and water in saucepan, and set over moderately high heat. Swirl pan slowly by its handle, but do not stir sugar with a spoon while liquid is coming to the boil. Continue swirling for a moment as liquid boils and changes from cloudy to perfectly clear. Cover pan, raise heat to high, and boil for several minutes until bubbles are thick and heavy. Uncover, and continue boiling, swirling gently, until syrup turns a nice caramel brown.

Immediately remove from heat and add the 8 perfect walnut halves; quickly take them out one by one with fork, drain off excess caramel, and place right-side up at one end of baking sheet. If caramel has thickened or begun to harden, set over heat again to liquefy. Remove from heat and pour in the rest of the walnuts; stir about with fork, and turn out onto baking sheet. (Do not wash out caramel-cooking pan; reserve for next step.) When caramel-walnut mixture has hardened, in about 20 minutes, break it up into 1-inch pieces. Grind in electric blender, flicking switch on and off rapidly so that some pieces will remain ⅛ inch in size, to give texture and interest to the mousse.

(*) AHEAD-OF-TIME NOTE: Both *pralin* and caramelized walnuts freeze perfectly for several months in an airtight container.

---

2) *The ice cream mixture—appareil à bombe*

½ cup milk heated in the caramel-cooking pan
4 egg yolks in a 2½- to 3-quart stainless steel bowl (metal is preferable because easy to heat and cool)
A hand-held electric mixer
The ground *pralin*; some for now, some for later
A pan of almost simmering water, large enough to hold bowl for egg yolks
A wooden spoon
A second bowl with 2 trays of ice cubes and water to cover them, to hold the first bowl
¼ cup kirsch or dark rum

Set milk over low heat, stirring occasionally, to melt the caramel. Meanwhile, beating the egg yolks, gradually incorporate 1 cup of the *pralin* and continue beating until mixture is thick and sticky. By driblets, beat in the hot milk, then set bowl in the pan of almost simmering water. Stir rather slowly with spoon, reaching all over bottom of bowl, until custard gradually warms through and thickens enough to coat spoon with a creamy layer. (Be careful custard does not overheat and curdle the egg yolks; however, you must warm it to the point where it thickens.)

Immediately remove from heat and beat in another cup of the *pralin* to stop the cooking. Then, with electric mixer, beat over ice 5 minutes or so, until thoroughly chilled and mixture forms a thick ribbon when a bit is dropped from beater back onto the surface. Beat in the kirsch or rum, and all the rest of the *pralin* (unless you wish to reserve 2 to 3 tablespoons for decorations); final addition of *pralin* does not melt, because mousse is now cold.

---

1 cup chilled heavy cream in a 2- to 2½-quart bowl
The electric beater (blades need not be washed)
A rubber spatula

Remove custard mixture from ice, and replace with the cream bowl. Beat cream into *Chantilly* by circulating electric beater about bowl to incorporate as much air as possible; continue beating until cream has doubled in volume and beater leaves light traces on surface of cream. Fold the cream into the chilled custard, and mousse is ready for freezing.

---

3) *Freezing and serving suggestions*

Freezing times at zero degrees or less: 3 hours for individual servings or parfaits; 6 hours for bowls, molds, and *bombe glacée*.

MOUSSE GLACÉE OR PARFAIT

Pile the chilled mousse into a decorative serving bowl or into individual serving dishes or parfait glasses. Cover with plastic wrap and freeze. At serving time, decorate with caramelized walnuts and/or *pralin;* parfaits are usually topped with a swirl of whipped cream before the walnuts or *pralin* goes on. (See note on frozen swirls at end of recipe.)

SOUFFLÉ GLACÉ

Surround a 4- to 5-cup soufflé dish with a strip of lightly oiled (tasteless salad oil) foil or waxed paper tied or pinned in place, to make a collar that sticks 1½ inches above rim of dish. Pile the chilled mousse into the dish, letting it rise ½ to ¾ inch up the collar; lay plastic wrap over top of collar and freeze the mousse at least 6 hours. Remove collar just before serving, and decorate top of soufflé with caramelized walnuts and/or *pralin*.

BOMBE GLACÉE

Follow directions for *bombe glacée à l'abricot,* page 417.

Frozen Whipped Cream Swirls

You may form whipped cream swirls, rosettes, or other designs on a plate or baking sheet lined with waxed paper; cover the swirls and freeze them. At serving time, peel them off the paper, and place upon the dessert. For this, the cream must be a little stiffer than the usual *Chantilly* so that it will hold its shape enough to be formed; when stiff enough, fold in confectioner's sugar and vanilla to taste, pack the cream into a pastry bag or paper decorating cone, and make the designs. (Directions for making paper decorating cones are on page 509.)

LE SAINT-CYR, GLACÉ

[Frozen Chocolate Mousse Molded in Meringues]

Here is a handsome dessert for those happy times when you can indulge in whipped cream and chocolate. It is a mold of frozen chocolate mousse in the form of a cylinder with ribbons of white meringue marching around the circumference. It will remind you of the tall *képis,* the decorative caps, worn by the officers of Saint-Cyr, the famous French military academy. You can add a visor, edible or not, if you want to complete the picture.

A NOTE ON MERINGUES AND MANUFACTURING METHODS

This dessert is easy to make when you have an electric beater on a stand; if you don't mind holding on for a while, however, a portable beater is perfectly satisfactory. Rather than being the usual meringue of egg whites beaten to stiff peaks and sugar then folded in, this is the Italian meringue, where boiling sugar syrup is beaten into the stiff egg whites, and the beating continues for 8 to 10 minutes, or until the meringue is cool and forms stiff peaks. It has a double advantage: the meringue shapes bake in half the time of ordinary meringues and the rest of the meringue mixture can be used for the chocolate mousse. Thus you need not bother making a custard base with its attendant beating of sugar and egg yolks over heat; instead, you beat melted chocolate right into the meringue mixture, fold in the whipped cream, and the mousse is made. A further recommendation is that the mousse does not become hard and stiff when frozen; it retains a tender, creamy quality.

For an 8-cup mold, serving 8 to 10 people

---

1) *The meringue mixture—meringue italienne—1½ quarts*

Measure out all the ingredients for this step so that while the sugar is boiling you can finish beating the egg whites.

---

2 cups sugar
⅔ cup water
A heavy 1½- to 2-quart
   saucepan with cover

Combine sugar and water in saucepan and set over moderately high heat. Swirl pan slowly by its handle, but do not stir sugar with a spoon while liquid is coming to the boil. Continue swirling for a moment as liquid boils and turns from cloudy to perfectly clear. Cover pan, reduce heat to low, and let simmer slowly while you beat the egg whites.

¾ cup egg whites
   (6 egg whites) at room
   temperature
An electric mixer with
   large (3-quart) clean,
   dry bowl and blades

Turn egg whites into mixer bowl, and start at slow speed for a minute or so, until egg whites begin to foam up. Beat in the salt and cream of tartar, and gradually increase speed to fast, until egg whites form stiff peaks. (Notes on beating egg whites are on page 539.) Beat in the vanilla.

Big pinch salt
¼ tsp cream of tartar
½ tsp vanilla extract

Optional but useful: a candy thermometer A quart glass measure with 2 cups cold water and 2 ice cubes A metal spoon	Remove cover from sugar syrup, and insert candy thermometer if you are using one. Boil rapidly, and when bubbles begin to thicken, watch temperature or start dropping driblets into iced water. Boil to 238 degrees, the soft-ball stage—sugar makes a sticky but definite shape when worked in cold water with your fingers.

Immediately start beating egg whites at moderate speed, dribbling boiling syrup into them until all is used. Continue beating egg whites at moderate speed until cool, and until mixture forms stiff peaks when lifted—when you draw a spatula through it, the walls of meringue on either side of the path remain erect and unmoving. (If you are using a portable beater, you may set the meringue bowl in a basin of cold water to speed the cooling.) Beating time: 8 to 10 minutes using a beater on a stand.

2) *Baking the meringue decorations—about 1 hour at 200 degrees*

2 pastry sheets about 12 by 16 inches, no-stick if possible, buttered and floured A rubber spatula The dessert mold: an 8-cup cylindrical charlotte mold, baking dish, or even a flower pot, at least 4 inches deep ½ the meringue mixture (3 cups) A canvas pastry bag 12 to 14 inches long with ¾-inch cannelated ribbon-tube opening A small knife (to cut off meringue from tube when necessary)	Preheat oven to 200 degrees. Draw guidelines on pastry sheets with point of rubber spatula to mark depth of mold, so that you will know how long to make the meringues: they are to stand upright around the sides of the mold. (Leftover meringues are to be layered into mold with the chocolate mousse; you may wish to decorate top of dessert, after unmolding, with meringues either whole or crumbled.) A suggested decoration, to resemble the braid on a military cap, would be a series of straight ribbons alternating with serpentine shapes.

Whatever you decide upon, scoop the meringue mixture into the pastry bag, and squeeze out shapes between the guidelines on the pastry sheets, making the decorations ⅛ to ³⁄₁₆ inch thick, and no more than 1½ inches wide. You will need

12 to 16 perfect specimens, therefore use up all the meringue in the bag; muffed shapes can be layered with the mousse, and you will have some breakage after baking because the meringues will be brittle.

Set baking sheets in upper- and lower-middle levels of oven for about an hour, or until you can gently nudge a few loose from baking surface. They will not puff up, they will not change shape, and they should remain pure white; they simply dry out. While still warm, they bend slightly; as soon as they are cool, they become crisp and fragile. Remove baking sheets from oven, push all meringues gently loose, but leave them on the baking sheets.

3) *The chocolate mousse—mousse au chocolat meringuée—about 8 cups*

12 ounces semisweet baking chocolate
3 ounces unsweetened baking chocolate
A saucepan for the chocolate, and cover for the pan
⅓ cup dark rum
A saucepan of simmering water removed from heat, large enough to hold chocolate pan
The dessert mold from Step 1
1 Tb soft butter
Waxed paper

Break up the chocolate, and place in the saucepan with the rum; cover, and set it in the pan of hot but not simmering water. While chocolate is melting, fold an 18-inch piece of waxed paper in half lengthwise, cut in two along fold, and with the 2 pieces held together, cut into blunt-ended wedges 5 to 6 inches at the wide end, 2½ inches at the blunt end, and ½ inch longer than depth of mold. Cut a circle of waxed paper to fit in bottom of mold exactly, and place it in the mold. One at a time, dot soft butter on one side of waxed paper wedge and insert against inside edge of mold, small end of wedge at bottom; butter holds paper in place. Continue around inside of mold, overlapping paper so that mold is completely covered. Refrigerate in order to set butter and keep paper glued to mold.

The meringue mixture remaining from Step 2
2 cups chilled whipping cream in a beating bowl
A larger bowl with a tray of ice cubes and water to cover them
A large (balloon) wire whip, or a hand-held electric beater with clean, dry blades

As soon as chocolate is melted, and you have beaten it to a soft, smooth texture, whip it into the meringue mixture. In its separate bowl, set cream over ice and beat, circulating beater all around bowl to incorporate air into cream, until doubled in volume; continue beating a few minutes more, until beater leaves light traces on surface, and a bit of cream lifted and dropped back softly retains its shape. This is now *crème Chantilly.*

Remove the cream from the ice, and set the chocolate-meringue mixture over it, beating for a few minutes until cool but not stiff—if chocolate is warm it will deflate the whipped cream. Then, with a rubber spatula, turn the *crème Chantilly* out on top of the chocolate, and fold the two together, cutting down from surface of cream to bottom of bowl with rubber spatula, and turning spatula against side of bowl as you draw it out; continue rapidly, rotating bowl as you fold. If the meringues are not yet ready, refrigerate the mousse.

4) *Filling the mold*

Not allowing it to touch sides of mold if you can help it, turn a 1-inch layer of mousse into the bottom of the mold; this will give support to the meringues you are to place against the sides. Remembering they are fragile and break easily, arrange the meringues best side out against mold and upright around its edges, spacing them about ¼ inch apart. Turn in another layer of mousse about ¾ inch thick, cover with extra meringues, and continue filling the mold with mousse and meringue layers, ending with a layer of meringues. (Do not trim off protruding ends of upright meringues at this point.) Cover mold with plastic wrap, and freeze for 6 hours at least.

5) *Unmolding and serving*

To unmold the dessert, bend waxed paper back from edges of mold, bend protruding meringue ends down over dessert, and turn a chilled serving dish upside down over mold. Reverse the two and dessert should unmold immediately—if not, reverse mold, run a knife between waxed paper and edge of mold, and reverse again. Carefully peel off waxed paper from top and sides. You need no decoration on top, unless you have baked meringue decorations for it or you wish to crumble leftover baked meringues over it.

———————————

Optional:
Either more *crème Chantilly* sweetened with confectioner's sugar and flavored with rum or vanilla;
Or crème anglaise (custard sauce, 501)

Serve the *Saint-Cyr* immediately, accompanied by the optional whipped cream or custard sauce.

———————————

(*) AHEAD-OF-TIME NOTES: Dessert may be unmolded onto serving dish, covered with a bowl, and returned to freezer for an hour or so before serving; in its mold, it may remain frozen for several weeks. Leftover baked meringues should be kept either in a warming oven at about 120 degrees to prevent them from softening, or wrapped airtight and frozen; if frozen, you may need to re-crisp them in a 200-degree oven for 20 to 30 minutes.

Other flavorings and serving ideas for the Chocolate Mousse

Rather than molding the chocolate mousse in a meringue-lined mold, you may wish to mold it as is, and decorate with *crème Chantilly* for serving; or you may turn the mousse into individual serving pots, chill rather than freeze them, and serve like the usual chocolate mousse with sweetened whipped cream on the side. Instead of using meringues, you may fold into the mousse a cup or two of *pralin* (caramelized almonds, page 421, or walnuts, page 423), which always gives an interesting texture and taste to chocolate mousse. There is also the richer chocolate mousse in Volume I, on page 604, with its egg yolks and butter rather than meringue and whipped cream; when you use this formula, you need not freeze the mousse, because the butter, which congeals when refrigerated, holds the mousse in form when it is unmolded.

---

*   *CHANTILLY MERINGUÉE*

[Whipped Cream with Italian Meringue—
for cream fillings and ice cream]

The Italian meringue of hot sugar syrup whipped into egg whites, so successful with the preceding *Saint-Cyr,* Step 1, page 426, also serves other purposes. You may use it as a base for butter-cream frosting and fillings as described on page 489; you may also fold it into whipped cream to give the cream more body and stability as a filling for cream puffs, cream horns, and Napoleons or *mille-feuilles.* Or this same *Chantilly meringuée* may be packed into a mold or bowl and frozen, thus becoming what can truly be called an iced cream. (Although you can fold plain beaten egg white into whipped cream and freeze it, the meringue does a better job because it completely discourages the formation of ice crystals, giving you a wonderfully soft and smooth ice cream.)

*For about 1 quart of meringue whipped
cream—Chantilly meringuée*

½ the *meringue italienne* called for in Step 1, page 426
1 cup chilled heavy cream in a 2½-quart bowl
A large bowl with a tray of ice cubes and water to cover them
A hand-held electric mixer or a large wire whip
1 to 2 tsp vanilla extract
A rubber spatula

Prepare the meringue mixture, and beat slowly until it is cold. Meanwhile, prepare a *crème Chantilly* as follows. Set bowl of cream over ice cubes and water. Circulate beater or whip about in cream to incorporate as much air as possible as you beat; continue beating until cream has doubled in volume and beater leaves light traces on surface. Stir the vanilla into the meringue mixture, then fold in ¼ of the whipped cream to lighten the meringue. Scoop rest of whipped cream on top and fold it in by rapidly cutting down through center to bottom of bowl and then out to side with rubber spatula, rotating bowl as you do so;

repeat the movement rapidly until cream and meringue are blended and deflated as little as possible.

TO USE AS A FILLING

Use as is, or fold in *pralin* (caramelized almonds, page 421, walnuts, page 423), or shaved chocolate, or fresh strawberries, raspberries, or sliced peaches, or bits of glacéed chestnuts or glacéed fruits macerated in rum or kirsch.

TO USE AS ICE CREAM

Chantilly Glacée, au Chocolat

[Vanilla Ice Cream with Chocolate Sauce]

It is hard to improve on this universal favorite, and wonderful to have your own private brand.

For about 1 quart, serving 4 to 6 people

---

1) *The vanilla ice cream—Chantilly glacée*

The preceding meringue whipped cream A 1-quart mold or metal bowl with rounded bottom Plastic wrap	Prepare the meringue whipped cream, turn into bowl, cover with plastic wrap, and freeze 3 to 4 hours at least before unmolding and serving. (This will be a rather soft and tender ice cream.)

---

2) *The chocolate sauce—for about 1½ cups*

3 ounces semisweet baking chocolate 1 ounce unsweetened baking chocolate ¾ cup water 1 Tb instant coffee A 6-cup saucepan A larger saucepan of simmering water to hold chocolate pan A wire whip 1½ Tb heavy cream 1½ Tb butter 1½ Tb dark rum Pinch of salt if needed	Break up the chocolate and combine with water and coffee in saucepan. Stir slowly over moderate heat until chocolate is melted and smooth, then set in simmering water and cook for 15 minutes, stirring occasionally. Beat in the cream, butter, rum, and, if needed, a pinch of salt. Set aside. Sauce should be tepid when it goes over the ice cream; reheat to tepid, beating it, if necessary, later.

3) *Unmolding the ice cream, and serving*

A chilled serving dish **A basin of cold or tepid** **water**	At serving time, set frozen mold in basin of water for several seconds to loosen the ice cream. Run a knife around edge of dessert; turn serving dish upside down over bowl, and reverse the two to unmold the ice cream.

Spoon the tepid chocolate sauce over the ice cream, letting it drip down the sides so that some of the white shows through. Serve immediately.

Other sauces and flavorings

Instead of chocolate sauce, serve the fresh raspberry or strawberry purée in Volume I, page 592–3, and surround the dish with fresh berries, as well, if you wish. Or spoon over the ice cream 2 cups of chilled, fresh, sliced peaches macerated in sugar, lemon juice, and light rum or kirsch; the apricot sauce on page 507 in this volume is another possibility. Still another would be to fold half a cup of walnut brittle into the cream after it has begun to set; after pouring chocolate sauce over the ice cream, decorate it either with a sprinkling of brittle or with the caramelized whole walnuts on page 423. Bits of glacéed chestnuts or glacéed fruits macerated in rum or kirsch would also be attractive.

Bombe Glacée

Frozen *Chantilly* is a perfect filling for *bombe glacée,* just as it is, or with any of the preceding flavor suggestions. Mold in a bowl or *bombe* lined with chocolate, coffee, or strawberry or raspberry ice cream following the directions for the *bombe glacée à l'abricot* on page 417.

LA SURPRISE DU VÉSUVE
[French Baked Alaska Flambée]

Vesuvius erupting is the French version of our baked Alaska ice cream dessert that is spread with meringue and browned quickly in a hot oven. Here the meringue is sprinkled with powdered sugar; the volcano is contained in half an egg shell thrust crater-like into the center of the Vesuvius, and filled with flaming liqueur that courses down the mountain slopes like molten lava. Use any ice cream formula you wish, either from the preceding recipes or store-bought; the cake, which forms the base, may be your own *génoise* from page 487, the sponge cake or almond and orange cake from Volume I, pages 669 or 676, or a store-bought sponge cake.

For a 14- by 8-inch dessert, serving 8 people

---

1) *Preliminaries—to be readied before dinner*

1½ quarts sherbet or ice cream frozen in a melon-shaped mold about 12 inches long

A *génoise* or sponge cake, such as a round one 8 by 1½ inches

A flameproof serving platter or tray 16 to 18 inches long

⅔ cup Cognac, kirsch, or rum (whatever flavor will go with your sherbet or ice cream) in a small saucepan

10 egg whites (1⅓ cups) at room temperature, and in an egg-beating bowl in time for Step 2

An electric mixer

2 pinches salt

½ tsp cream of tartar

1½ cups sugar, "instant" superfine if possible

1 tsp vanilla extract

An uncracked eggshell half with saw-tooth edge (cut with scissors)

1 cup confectioner's sugar in a fine-meshed sieve

Matches

(All the ingredients listed must be measured out, laid in easy reach, and ready for use when you are ready, at the last minute, to beat the meringue, unmold the ice cream, assemble the structure, and brown it rapidly in the oven. Although you can beat the meringue an hour before serving, and re-beat it at the last minute, the beating takes but a few minutes in an efficient mixer and your guests should not mind a short wait.)

Slice the cake into half-inch layers; cut the cake layers in such a way that you can form a large oval ½ inch thick and 1 inch larger all around than your ice cream mold. Arrange the oval on the platter, sprinkle with 2 to 3 Tb liqueur, cover airtight with plastic wrap, and set aside. Be sure oven is preheated to 450 degrees in time for Step 2.

---

2) *Assembling, browning, flambéeing, and serving—about 10 minutes—oven has been preheated to 450 degrees*

beating the meringue:

Start beating the egg whites at moderate speed until they are foaming, beat in the salt and cream of tartar, then gradually increase speed to fast until egg whites form soft peaks. Gradually beat in the sugar, sprinkling in ¼ cup at a time, beating half a minute between additions. After all has gone in, add vanilla, and continue beating for several minutes at high speed until egg whites form stiff, shiny peaks.

assembling Vesuvius:

Set ice cream mold in a basin of tepid water, run a knife around edge, and un-mold the sherbet or ice cream upon the cake in the platter. Immediately spread the meringue over it with a spatula, starting at bottom of cake and bringing it up to a peak at the top of the dessert—meringue should be about 1 inch thick over the sherbet or ice cream, in order to insulate it from the heat of the oven. With spatula make vertical striations from bottom to top, which will allow flaming liqueur to flow down the sides. Insert eggshell half in peak of mountain. Sieve confectioner's sugar all over surface of meringue, making a layer about $1/16$ inch thick.

browning:

Set in upper-middle level of preheated 450-degree oven for 3 to 4 minutes, to brown meringue lightly. Meanwhile, heat the liqueur.

flambéeing and serving:

As soon as meringue has browned remove from oven; ignite the hot liqueur with a lighted match, pour into the eggshell, letting excess drip down sides of meringue, and bring flaming to the table.

FRUITS, FLANS, AND CUSTARDS, A FRENCH SHORTCAKE, AND A FLAMING CHARLOTTE

GRATIN DE POMMES, NORMANDE— CLAFOUTI AUX POMMES

[Sliced Apples Baked with Rum, Raisins, Eggs, and Cream]

This is every bit as good as the finest apple tart, but not quite as filling because the apples are baked in a dish rather than in a tart shell.

For a 10-inch dish, serving 8 to 10 people

---

1) *The rum and raisins*

½ cup currants (small, black, seedless raisins) in a small bowl
¼ cup dark rum

Preheat oven to 375 degrees. Soak the raisins in the rum until you are ready to use them.

---

2) *Baking the apple slices*

¼ lb. (1 stick) melted
  butter
A baking pan with raised
  edges, such as a 10- by
  16-inch jelly-roll pan or
  a 14-inch pizza tray
½ cup sugar
6 to 7 medium-sized apples
  (about 2 lbs.) that will
  keep their shape during
  cooking (Golden Deli-
  cious, Rome Beauty, York
  Imperial)
A flexible-blade spatula and
  a rubber spatula
A lightly buttered 6-cup
  baking-and-serving dish,
  such as a round one 10 by
  1½ inches
More sugar if necessary

Spread half the butter in the pan and sprinkle over it half the sugar. Wash apples thoroughly but do not peel. Quarter them, core them, and cut into lengthwise slices about ⅜ inch thick. Arrange in one overlapping layer in the pan, sprinkle on the remaining sugar, and dribble the remaining butter over all. Bake about 25 minutes in upper-third level of preheated oven until apples are tender but still hold their shape. Transfer apple slices to baking dish in one crowded, overlapping layer. Scrape cooking juices over apples. Taste, and sprinkle on a little more sugar if you think it is needed.

(*) AHEAD-OF-TIME NOTE: May be prepared to this point a day in advance. Cover when cool, and refrigerate. Preheat oven in time for Step 4.

3) *The rum and egg topping*

The raisins in their rum
A sieve over a bowl
3 "large" eggs
½ cup sugar
An electric mixer
¼ cup all-purpose flour
  (measure by scooping
  dry-measure cup into
  flour and sweeping off
  excess with a knife)
½ cup liquid (2 to 3 Tb
  rum maceration plus
  light cream)
¼ tsp cinnamon

Drain the raisins, pressing rum out of them lightly. Sprinkle half the rum over the apple slices. Beat the eggs and sugar for 3 to 4 minutes at high speed with mixer until they are thick and pale yellow. Beat in the flour, liquids, and cinnamon. Fold in the raisins, then spread the topping over the apples.

4) *Baking and serving—about 25 minutes at 375 degrees*

Bake in middle level of preheated 375-degree oven for about 25 minutes, or until topping has browned nicely and a skewer, plunged through topping, comes out clean. Serve hot, warm, or cold. You may wish to pass lightly whipped cream sweetened with powdered sugar and flavored with rum, or homemade *crème fraîche,* although no cream or sauce is really necessary.

FLAN AUX PRUNES—CLAFOUTI AUX PRUNES
[Fresh Prune Plums Baked in Custard]

Fresh prune plums are halved, baked with sugar and flavorings until just tender, and then baked again under a blanket of eggs and cream. Simple to do and delicious to eat, the same recipe can be applied to other fruits, canned or fresh, as described at the end of the recipe.

For 4 people

1) *Preliminary baking of the fruit*

1 pound, or about 1 quart, fresh prune plums, washed, halved, and seeded

A lightly buttered baking dish, large enough to hold them in 1 layer

⅛ tsp cinnamon

½ cup sugar

The grated rind of 1 lemon

1 Tb lemon juice

Preheat oven to 350 degrees. Arrange fruit skin-side down in dish, and sprinkle with the flavorings. Bake in middle level of oven about 20 minutes, or until fruit is just tender but still holds shape. Raise oven heat to 375 degrees for next step.

2) *Final baking with custard—20 to 25 minutes at 375 degrees*

A lightly buttered 10- to 11-inch baking dish 1½ to 2 inches deep

2 "large" eggs

3 Tb sugar

A mixing bowl and wire whip

2 Tb flour

1 tsp vanilla extract

⅓ cup light or all-purpose cream

Transfer fruit, still skin-side down, to second baking dish; reserve juices. Beat eggs and sugar in bowl to blend them, then beat in the flour, vanilla, and cream. Pour over the fruit.

(*) AHEAD-OF-TIME NOTE: Refrigerate if you are not baking immediately.

Bake in upper third of preheated oven for 20 to 25 minutes, until custard has puffed and browned lightly.

3) *Sauce and serving*

The cooking juices from Step 1, in a small pan

While the dessert is baking, warm the fruit juices and flavor them with the liqueur if you wish; warm

Optional: 2 to 3 Tb Cognac,
  rum, or kirsch
A serving bowl
Optional: *crème Chantilly*
  (lightly whipped cream
  sweetened with confec-
  tioner's sugar and
  flavored with Cognac,
  rum, kirsch, or vanilla,
  page 422)

them again just before serving. Serve the flan hot, warm, or tepid, accompanied by the fruit juices and optional *crème Chantilly*.

Other ideas

Use the same system for canned and frozen fruits, like plums, peaches, or apricots. Thaw, if frozen; drain thoroughly, and halve and seed them if necessary. Give them a preliminary baking of 10 minutes or so with 2 or 3 tablespoons of melted butter, a pinch of cinnamon, drops of lemon juice, and a sprinkling of sugar to enhance their flavor. Then pour on the custard mixture and proceed with the recipe.

POMMES SOUFFLÉES, CALVADOS

[Individual Apple Soufflés in Apples]

This is the attractive kind of recipe that looks much dressier than it is— apples baked in wine, then filled with an apple soufflé mixture and baked again on butter-drenched *canapés*. For an essentially simple process, the recipe is purposely detailed because you will want to use this way of baking apples with other fillings and toppings, some of which are suggested at the end of the recipe. Ahead-of-time notes follow each step in the process, so that you can do parts of the dessert whenever you have time, and be ready for the final baking several hours in advance of serving.

For 6 people

1) *Preliminary cooking of the apples*

6 firm, unblemished apples
  3¼ to 3½ inches in
  diameter (such as Golden
  Delicious, Rome Beauty,
  York Imperial)
1 lemon, quartered
A 10- to 12-inch flameproof
  baking dish 3½ inches
  deep and smeared with
  1½ Tb softened butter

Preheat oven to 325 degrees. Wash the apples, then prepare one at a time: shave off bottom of apple so it will stand solidly upright. Slanting your knife down toward the core, cut a cap off top of apple about 2 inches in diameter. Peel, reserving peel and all edible apple bits for Step 2. With grapefruit knife, hollow out apple centers and remove seeds, leaving a ½-inch shell of apple all around sides and bottom. Rub inside and out with cut lemon and place in baking dish. When all apples are done, squeeze

½ cup dry white wine or
    vermouth
⅓ to ½ cup sugar (more if
    apples seem sour)
½ stick cinnamon
A 10- to 12-inch round of
    heavily buttered waxed
    paper

remaining lemon juice over them and add lemon
pieces to the dish.

Pour the wine around the apples, sprinkle on the sugar, add cinnamon, and
bring to simmer on top of stove. Cover with the waxed paper, and set in middle level
of preheated oven for about 30 minutes, regulating heat so that liquid never quite
simmers. Apples should be tender when pierced with a knife, and ready to eat, but
they must keep their shape so that they will stand up to their final cooking. Remove
from oven and let cool for at least 10 minutes, waxed paper in place over them.

(*) AHEAD-OF-TIME NOTE: May be baked even a day in advance. Remove from refrigerator at least half an hour before final baking, Step 4.

---

2) *The apple purée (soufflé base)*

The peel and all edible bits
    from apple centers
¼ cup water
A heavy-bottomed 2-quart
    saucepan with cover
1 cup apricot jam pushed
    through a sieve (3 Tb
    for now, the rest for
    later)
A food mill or sieve
3 or more Tb sugar
1 tsp vanilla extract
3 Tb Calvados, rum, or
    Cognac
1 egg yolk blended with
    3 Tb heavy cream in a
    small mixing bowl
Optional: drops of red
    food coloring

While shells are cooking, simmer apple peel and trimmings with water in the covered pan over moderately
low heat for about 15 minutes. When tender, purée
with 3 tablespoons of the apricot jam through food
mill or sieve. Add sugar, vanilla, and spirits; boil
down rapidly, stirring constantly until mixture is almost thick enough to hold its shape on a spoon. You
should have about ⅔ cup; gradually stir it into bowl
with cream and egg yolk. Return to saucepan and
stir over moderately high heat until mixture comes
almost to the boil and thickens again. Taste, adding
more sugar if necessary and drops of red coloring if
you think they are needed.

(*) AHEAD-OF-TIME NOTE: May be completed a day in
advance; film surface with plastic wrap, and refrigerate.

---

3) *Preliminaries to baking*
the canapés:

About ½ cup clarified
    butter (melted butter,
    skimmed; clear liquid
    spooned off milky resi-
    due)

Film frying pan with ⅛ inch of clarified butter, and
set over moderately high heat. When bubbling, add
as many bread rounds as will fit easily in one layer,
and sauté for a minute or so on each side to brown
very lightly, adding a little more butter if needed to

A frying pan

6 rounds of bread 3 inches in diameter and ⅜ inch thick (use homemade-type white bread)

The remaining sieved apricot jam from Step 2

An unbuttered ovenproof serving platter large enough to hold apples easily

The cooked apples

A pastry brush

the sauce:

A sieve (or the food mill)

A small saucepan

1 tsp arrowroot blended with 3 Tb Calvados, rum, or Cognac

The remaining apricot jam (about ¼ cup, plus sugar if needed, and a table-spoon or so of butter)

keep bread from burning. These are now called *canapés;* paint one side of each with a coating of apricot jam and set them jam-side up on a platter. One by one, drain the apples, pouring accumulated juices back into baking dish. Paint inside and out with more of the strained apricot jam, and place one apple on each *canapé.* Dribble over them any remaining butter.

Discard lemon rind and cinnamon stick; strain contents of apple-baking dish into saucepan. Beat in arrowroot mixture and apricot jam; bring to the simmer. Simmer 2 to 3 minutes, until sauce has turned from cloudy to clear, and has thickened lightly. Taste for flavor, adding more sugar and butter if you feel the need.

(*) AHEAD-OF-TIME NOTE: *Canapés* and sauce may be made a day in advance, but do not arrange apples on *canapés* more than an hour or two before baking.

---

4) *Baking and serving—about 20 minutes at 375 degrees*

2 egg whites at room temperature

An egg-white beating bowl and hand-held electric beater or balloon whip

Pinches of salt and cream of tartar

The apple purée from Step 2

A rubber spatula

The platter of apples

Confectioner's sugar in a small fine-meshed sieve

The sauce, warmed

A warm sauce bowl

About 20 minutes before serving (or as much as an hour in advance) beat egg whites at moderate speed for a minute or two, until foamy; beat in the salt and cream of tartar, and gradually increase beating speed to fast until egg whites form stiff peaks. Stir a spoonful of them into the apple purée to lighten it; delicately fold the rest of the egg whites into the purée with the rubber spatula. Spoon the soufflé mixture into the apple shells, heaping it into a dome. (Invert a large bowl over the platter of apples if you are not baking immediately.)

Bake in middle level of preheated oven for 12 to 15 minutes, until soufflé filling has puffed slightly—it will not puff very much—and begun to brown. Rapidly sprinkle confectioner's sugar over the apples and bake 2 to 3 minutes more. Serve immediately, accompanied by the sauce, a spoonful of which may be poured over part of each apple as it is served.

Other ideas

Rather than filling the apples with a soufflé mixture, you may boil down and season the apple purée as directed in Step 2, and stir in ⅓ cup dry bread crumbs sautéed in 3 to 4 tablespoons of butter; fill the apples and proceed with the recipe. You may add a handful of raisins soaked first in the rum or Cognac called for. Rather than bread crumbs, you might stir in half a cup of crumbled stale macaroons, which would give an attractive almond flavoring. Finally, having filled the apples with any of these stuffings, you could then cover them spectacularly with a meringue (beaten egg whites and sugar), sprinkle with shaved almonds, and brown in a hot oven, following the method for the *poires meringuées,* Step 4, page 441, in the following recipe.

POIRES MERINGUÉES, AU SABAYON
[Wine-poached Pears Baked in Meringue, Wine-custard Sauce]

This is a simple fruit dessert that looks satisfyingly elegant and complicated. Pears are poached in an aromatic red-wine syrup, the syrup is turned into a sauce, and at serving time the pears are baked in a cloak of meringue sprinkled with almond flakes. Pear-poaching, sauce-making, and even the little toasts the pears sit upon while baking may be done the day before serving.

For 8 pear halves, serving 4 to 8 people

1) Poaching the pears

1 cup sugar
1½ cups young red wine, such as Côtes-du-Rhône or Mountain Red
1½ cups water
An enameled skillet or saucepan 2½ or more inches deep and just large enough to hold pear halves
4 whole cloves
The zests (colored part of peel) of ½ orange and ½ lemon

Stir the sugar into the wine and water, bring to the simmer, and when dissolved add the cloves, zests, and vanilla. Simmer for 20 minutes, then remove from heat. One at a time, peel the pears, halve lengthwise, retaining stems, and neatly remove stem lines and cores. Drop each, as done, into the wine syrup. Syrup should barely cover pears: add more liquid and sugar if necessary (⅓ cup sugar per cup of liquid). Bring almost to the simmer, and poach uncovered at just below the simmer for 10 to 15 minutes, until pears are just tender when pierced with a knife. (Maintaining liquid at below the simmer prevents fruit from disintegrating.) Let pears cool in syrup for at least 20 minutes so that they will firm up as well as

1 tsp vanilla
4 firm, ripe, unblemished
  pears
A grapefruit knife

absorb the sugar and flavorings. (They may remain
for several days in the syrup.)

2) *The sauce sabayon*

2 cups of the pear-poaching
  syrup
A small saucepan
A 4- to 6-cup enameled or
  stainless saucepan and a
  wire whip
3 egg yolks
2 tsp cornstarch
2 Tb cool cooking syrup
A wooden spoon
2 Tb butter
3 to 4 Tb orange liqueur

Rapidly boil down the cooking syrup in a small
saucepan until reduced to 1 cup. In the second saucepan beat egg yolks and cornstarch to blend smoothly,
then beat in the two tablespoons of cool syrup. In a
thin stream of driblets, beat in the hot, reduced syrup.
Set over moderate heat; stir slowly and constantly
with wooden spoon until mixture thickens enough to
coat spoon—do not let it come to the simmer and
scramble the egg yolks; however, sauce must thicken.
Remove from heat. Beat in the butter, then the orange
liqueur. Set aside, or cover and refrigerate when cool.

3) *Preparations before cooking—an hour in advance*

8 *canapés* (rectangles of
  white bread sautéed in
  butter, Step 3, page 438)
A lightly buttered baking
  and serving dish, large
  enough to hold *canapés*
  easily in 1 layer

Sauté the *canapés* (if done a day in advance, pack
airtight and freeze); arrange in 1 layer in baking
dish.

3 egg whites
A clean beating bowl and
  electric beater
Big pinch each of salt and
  cream of tartar
½ cup sugar (instant
  superfine if possible)
¼ tsp vanilla extract

Beat egg whites until foaming, then beat in the salt
and cream of tartar, and continue beating until soft
peaks are formed. Beat in the sugar by 2-spoonful
sprinkles, beating ½ minute between additions. Beat
in the vanilla and continue beating for several minutes at high speed until egg whites form stiff, shiny
peaks. This is the meringue mixture.

A rack set over a tray

Drain pears hollow-side down on rack.

4) *Baking and serving—5 to 7 minutes—oven preheated to 425 degrees*

3 Tb sugar
The *canapés* in their
  baking dish
The drained poached pear-
  halves

(Although pears may be masked with meringue or
baked ahead, they are best when assembled and
baked at the last moment.) Sprinkle a teaspoon of
sugar over each *canapé,* and place a pear half, hollow-
side up, on top. Fill hollow with a teaspoon of *sauce*

The *sauce sabayon*
The meringue mixture
½ cup sliced almonds
⅓ cup confectioner's sugar
  in a fine-meshed sieve
A warm bowl for the sauce

sabayon. If necessary, beat the meringue mixture at high speed for a moment until it again forms stiff peaks. Mask each pear half with a large spoonful of meringue. Strew sliced almonds over each and sift on a light sprinkling of confectioner's sugar. Place in upper third of preheated oven for about 5 minutes, until meringue and almonds have lightly browned. Meanwhile, gently warm the sauce to tepid and turn into warm bowl. Serve pears as soon as possible, passing the sauce separately.

MOUSSE D'ORANGES À L'ANANAS

[Molded Orange Mousse Garnished with Pineapple and Candied Orange Peel]

When you want a beautiful dessert that is also light and as delicious as it is refreshing, this orange Bavarian cream without cream is a perfect answer.

For a 6-cup mold, serving 6 to 8

1) *Preliminaries*

glazed pineapple—ananas glacé:

A small (8½ ounces) can
  of pineapple slices, or 4
  slices and ½ cup juice
⅓ cup sugar
A small saucepan
A small bowl
¼ cup kirsch

Lay pineapple slices flat on cutting board, and slice in half parallel with board to make 2 rings rather than one; divide each into 16 wedges. Bring sugar to boil in pineapple juice, and when dissolved add the pineapple and boil 5 minutes, or until pineapple is beginning to turn a golden, light-caramel color. Drain. Place pineapple in bowl with kirsch, and return juice to pan.

glazed orange peel—zestes d'oranges glacés:

6 or more large, bright,
  juicy oranges
6 large, rectangular sugar
  lumps
Waxed paper
A wooden spoon
A 2½-quart stainless or
  enameled saucepan

Wash and dry oranges. Break sugar lumps in half. Over waxed paper, rub sugar lumps one at a time vigorously against the skin of 2 oranges, until all sides of lumps have absorbed as much oil as possible from the orange skins. Mash the sugar with the spoon and scrape into saucepan.

A vegetable peeler and a
  sharp chopping knife

Remove zests (orange part of peel) from 2 of the other oranges, and cut into *julienne* strips 1½ inches

A small saucepan with 2 cups water
A small bowl
⅔ cup sugar
½ cup water
The pan of pineapple juice

long and 1/16 inch wide. Drop into the pan of water and simmer 15 minutes; drain, rinse in cold water, and squeeze dry in paper towels. Place in small bowl. Stir sugar and water into pineapple juice, swirl over heat until sugar dissolves, then boil rapidly to the thread stage (230 degrees). Stir 2 tablespoons into the orange peel, reserve rest of syrup for the custard.

A 4-cup measure
1 lemon
2 packages (2 Tb) un-flavored powdered gela-tin in a 1-cup measure

Squeeze juice out of oranges and lemon and strain into measure, to make 2 cups. Pour ½ cup of juice into the gelatin, and stir a tablespoon of juice into the pineapple-sugar syrup to liquefy it.

2) Making and molding the mousse

4 egg yolks
1 Tb cornstarch
The 2½-quart pan with the crushed sugar lumps
A wire whip or electric beater
The pineapple-sugar syrup
The orange and lemon juice
A wooden spoon

Beat the egg yolks and cornstarch with the crushed sugar for a minute or two until yolks are thick and sticky. Gradually beat in the pineapple-sugar syrup, and continue beating vigorously for 2 minutes. Beat in the orange juice. Set over moderate heat and stir slowly (2 strokes per second), reaching all over bottom of pan. As custard warms, it will become foamy, and when a faint breath of steam rises it is beginning to thicken. Continue stirring over heat until it thickens enough to coat spoon lightly; custard must not come to the simmer and scramble the yolks, but it must thicken.

The gelatin and orange juice mixture

Remove custard from heat and immediately scrape the gelatin mixture into the hot custard, beating vigorously to be sure gelatin dissolves completely.

4 egg whites (at room temperature)
Pinch of salt
¼ tsp cream of tartar
A clean, dry bowl and electric mixer or balloon whip

Beat the egg whites until foaming, beat in the salt and cream of tartar, and continue until egg whites form stiff peaks. Then beat the egg whites into the hot custard with your whip, making a foamy mass —the mousse.

The pineapple wedges
A 6-cup metal mold, fluted or decorated if you wish
Half the orange peel

Arrange a handful of pineapple wedges in the bottom of the mold for decoration. Drain the pineapple maceration liqueur into the mousse, then fold it in along with the orange peel. Set bowl with mousse in

**A large bowl with 2 tray-
fuls of ice cubes and
water to cover them
A rubber spatula
Plastic wrap**

bowl of ice cubes and water; stir every few minutes
with rubber spatula until mousse thickens and is
about to set. (Beat with wire whip if necessary to
smooth it again.) Rapidly turn ⅓ of the mousse into
the mold, spread half the pineapple wedges over it,
cover with half the remaining mousse, then the rest
of the pineapple and finally the last of the mousse.
Cover with plastic and refrigerate until serving time.

(*) May be made a day of two ahead; may be frozen
and served either frozen or thawed.

3) *Serving*

**A large bowl of hot water
A chilled serving dish
The rest of the orange peel
Either crème Chantilly
(lightly whipped cream
with confectioner's sugar
and flavoring, page 422);
Or crème anglaise
(custard sauce, page 501),
with a little heavy cream
stirred in**

Shortly before serving, dip mold for 5 seconds in hot
water, turn serving dish upside down on top of mold
and reverse the two, unmolding dessert onto dish.
Fold remaining orange peel into whatever sauce
you have chosen, and pass separately.

RIZ DES HESPÉRIDES
[Mold of Orange-flavored Rice and Cherries]

In the long-ago European days before frozen strawberries and canned
apricots, the only fruits to be had during the winter were dried or glacéed;
when once in a while fresh oranges came in from Italy or Spain, they would
be combined into something very special, like this unusual rice dessert. You
will find it a delicious illustration of what wonders can be wrought with simple and inexpensive ingredients—the rice is simmered in milk and puréed
orange peel, then molded with glacéed orange and lemon peel, cherries, and
almonds; it is served with custard sauce or whipped cream.

For a 6-cup mold, serving 8 to 10

Make this the morning, or the day, or several days
before you wish to serve.

1) *The orange rice*

¾ cup plain, raw, white rice

3 quarts rapidly boiling water in a saucepan

2 large, bright-skinned oranges

A vegetable peeler

An electric blender

2 cups milk

A heavy 2-quart flame-proof baking dish with cover

2 Tb butter

⅛ tsp salt

Pinch nutmeg

Waxed paper

Preheat oven to 300 degrees. Sprinkle rice into boiling water and boil rapidly for exactly 5 minutes; drain immediately. Wash oranges. Remove the zests (orange part of peel) with vegetable peeler, and place in blender with ½ cup of the milk. Purée zests and milk, and pour into baking dish; add rest of milk, blanched rice, butter, salt, and nutmeg. Bring just to the simmer on top of the stove, then lay waxed paper over surface of milk, cover dish, and place in middle level of preheated oven. Bake for 30 to 40 minutes, until rice is tender and all liquid has absorbed. While rice is cooking, prepare ingredients in next step.

2) *The fruit garniture*

⅓ cup glacéed cherries

A pan of boiling water and a sieve

A small bowl

2 Tb Cognac

⅔ cup mixed, diced glacéed orange peel, lemon peel, and citron

A small saucepan

1 package (1 Tb) plain, unflavored gelatin

2 Tb strained lemon juice

3 Tb strained orange juice

3 Tb orange liqueur

A pan of hot water to hold the pan of glacéed fruits and gelatin

Slice cherries in half lengthwise (through stem end) and drop into boiling water to wash off preservatives. Drain, and place ½ in the small bowl with the Cognac. Then drop rest of glacéed fruit into boiling water and leave for several minutes—to soften as well as wash them. Drain, and put into small saucepan with the remaining cherries. Sprinkle on the gelatin, and stir in the lemon juice, orange juice, and orange liqueur. Let gelatin soften for several minutes, then set the pan in hot water, stirring occasionally, so gelatin will dissolve completely by the time you are ready to use it. (Reheat water, as necessary.)

3) *Assembling the mold*

A 6-cup charlotte mold or cylindrical dish 3 to 3½ inches deep, bottom lined with waxed paper

1 cup sugar

1 cup water

A small, heavy saucepan and cover

As soon as you remove the rice from the oven, make the sugar syrup: blend sugar and water in saucepan and bring to boil over moderately high heat, swishing pan by handle until sugar has dissolved completely and liquid is perfectly clear. Cover pan and boil rapidly for 1 to 2 minutes, until syrup is forming large, thick bubbles. Uncover and in a few seconds test: syrup should form a soft ball in the iced

A cup of iced water or a
    candy thermometer
1 tsp vanilla
½ cup sliced almonds with
    or without skins

water, or be at a temperature of 238 degrees. By spoonfuls, rapidly but gently fold the syrup into the rice. Fold in the diced fruits and gelatin mixture, and the vanilla; drain in the Cognac from the cherries, and fold in along with the sliced almonds. Mixture should cool somewhat before being molded; set in a pan of cold water or over cracked ice and water, folding occasionally until liquids and rice form a homogeneous blend.

Arrange the reserved cherry halves in the bottom of the mold, cut-side up. Spoon the rice into the mold, which will be almost filled. Cover with waxed paper or plastic, and chill for several hours, or until set.

4) *Serving*

A chilled serving plate
Either 3 cups *crème
    anglaise* (custard sauce,
    page 501) flavored
    with orange liqueur;
Or crème Chantilly
    (lightly whipped cream,
    page 422) flavored with
    orange liqueur and
    sweetened with confec-
    tioner's sugar

Run a thin knife around edge of dessert, turn serving platter upside down over it, and reverse the two to unmold dessert onto plate. Surround with a little of the custard sauce or *crème Chantilly,* and pass the rest separately.

LE PÉLERIN EN TIMBALE
[Molded Almond Cream]

This is a cross between the rich *charlotte Malakoff* and the classic Bavarian cream: a custard sauce bound with gelatin and butter, flavored with toasted almonds, kirsch, and apricot, and molded in a cake-lined dish. It gets its name from the pilgrims who, in the days before modern processing, stuffed their pockets with nonperishables like dried fruits and nuts. We assume that this particular *pélerin* paid his host for the night in almonds, which his hostess put to use in the following manner. (Note that this dessert improves in flavor if made a day or two in advance of serving.)

For a 6-cup mold, serving 8 to 10

1) *Preliminaries*

7 ounces (about 1½ cups)
   blanched whole almonds
A roasting pan or pizza
   tray
A kitchen timer
An electric blender

Preheat oven to 350 degrees. Spread almonds in pan and toast for 5 minutes in middle level of oven; stir them up and toast another 5 to 6 minutes, stirring every 2 to 3 minutes to be sure they do not burn. They should be deep golden brown. When cool, pulverize ½ cup at a time in electric blender; set aside.

A 6-cup cylindrical char-
   lotte mold or baking dish
   about 3½ inches deep
A round of waxed paper
A long, thin knife
A butter sponge cake,
   génoise, "shortcake," or
   other cake of that
   type (can be store-
   bought), such as a round
   one at least 8 by 1½
   inches
2 heavily buttered pastry
   sheets
3 Tb melted butter
2 to 3 Tb sugar
1 Tb kirsch

Meanwhile, line bottom of mold with the waxed paper. Then slice cake into horizontal layers each no more than ⅓ inch thick. Cut a round out of the top-of-cake layer to fit bottom of mold and place round inside-side up on a baking sheet. Cut rest of cake layers into strips 1¼ inches wide and arrange on the baking sheets. Paint with melted butter and sprinkle with sugar. When almonds are done, raise thermostat to 400 degrees. Set baking sheets in middle and upper-third levels of oven and bake the cake strips for about 10 minutes, until they are lightly golden brown. Remove from oven, sprinkle with drops of kirsch, and set aside.

2) *The custard sauce—crème anglaise—and almond cream*

1½ Tb (1½ packages)
   unflavored powdered
   gelatin
⅓ cup kirsch in a measure
¾ cup sugar
6 egg yolks in a heavy-
   bottomed 2-quart stainless or enameled saucepan
A hand-held electric beater
   or a wire whip
2½ cups hot milk in a
   small saucepan
A wooden spoon
8 ounces (2 sticks) butter
   cut into ¼-inch slices
The toasted almonds
1 tsp vanilla extract

Sprinkle the gelatin over the kirsch and set aside. Beat the sugar gradually into the egg yolks and continue beating for several minutes until mixture is thick, pale yellow, and forms a ribbon for a few seconds when a bit falls back on the surface. Gradually beat in the hot milk, adding it in a thin stream. Set mixture over moderate heat and stir slowly with wooden spoon, reaching all over bottom of pan, for 4 to 5 minutes until sauce thickens enough to film spoon with a creamy layer. (Be careful sauce does not come to the simmer and curdle the egg yolks, but you must heat it to the point where it thickens.) Immediately remove from heat and stir vigorously for 1 minute to cool slightly, then scrape the gelatin and kirsch mixture into the hot sauce, beating thoroughly for 2 minutes, to be sure gelatin dissolves completely. (A hand-held electric beater is useful here, and from now on.) Beat in the butter, 4 pieces

If needed: a pinch of salt; a few drops of almond extract

at a time, then the almonds and vanilla. Taste carefully: add a little salt and drops of almond extract if you feel them necessary. Set aside; you will have about 5 cups of sauce, which should still be slightly warm or at least tepid when used in next step.

3) *Filling the mold*

Line the mold with the toasted cake, sugared sides against mold, as follows. Place circle in the bottom; cut strips to fit upright and close together side by side, trimming one or two into wedges if necessary to fill in gaps.

A ladle
The tepid almond cream
Leftover cake strips
About ⅓ cup apricot jam
Plastic wrap

Ladle ⅓ of the almond cream into the mold. Paint several cake strips with apricot jam and arrange in a layer over the cream. Ladle more cream into mold to fill to ⅔ and cover with additional apricot-painted cake strips. Finally fill the mold with the remaining almond cream, pouring some down between cake strips and side of mold if necessary. Top with additional cake strips if any remain; cover with plastic wrap and chill several hours until set.

(*) AHEAD-OF-TIME NOTE: Finished dessert will keep 4 to 5 days under refrigeration or may be frozen.

4) *Serving*

A chilled serving dish
3 cups apricot sauce (page 507)
Optional: 3 cups *crème Chantilly* (lightly whipped cream, page 422), sweetened, and flavored with kirsch

Carefully run a thin knife around edge of mold several times to detach sides of dessert. Then turn dish upside down over mold, reverse the two and give a sharp downward jerk to unmold dessert onto dish. Spoon a little of the apricot sauce over top of dessert, and the rest around it on the dish. Refrigerate if not to be served immediately. Pass optional *crème Chantilly* separately.

LE MARLY—LA RIPOSTE

[French Strawberry Shortcake Made with Rum-soaked Brioche]

Le Marly is the French retort—*la riposte*—to the American shortcake. Rather than being biscuit dough, or a *savarin*—which it closely resembles except in shape—the cake is *brioche* dough baked in a cake pan, then split in two, hollowed out, and steeped in rum- or kirsch-flavored syrup. The strawberry and whipped cream filling is topped with pie-shaped wedges of *brioche* that rise to a peak in the center, giving the impression of a Chinese coolie hat. Glazed with apricot and decorated with strawberries, it is a pretty dessert, and so easy to assemble that you might well make the whole dough recipe rather than the half portion needed. You will thereby have two *brioche* cakes; freeze the second one to have on hand for those times when you need something special in a hurry. Other fruits besides strawberries are delicious too, and are suggested at the end of the recipe.

For a round brioche 8 by 2½ inches, serving 6 to 8

---

1) *Making and baking the brioche—about 5 hours*
(may be baked in advance and frozen)

NOTE: Because it will be soaked in rum or kirsch, the flavor of the *brioche* itself is not of great importance, and there is no need to make the buttery *brioche fine; brioche commune,* the *pain brioché* recipe, is the dough to use here and it needs only the first rise—or 2 rises to double if you are working in a hot kitchen.

½ the *pain brioché* dough on page 83 A round cake pan 8 by 1½ inches, smeared with 1 tsp soft butter A cake rack	Follow the *pain brioché* recipe, but you may make the dough in an electric mixer as described on page 84.

As soon as the first rise is complete, deflate the dough, form into a ball (directions for forming a round shape are on page 68), and place seam-side down in pan; pat dough out to edges all around. Pan will be filled by about two thirds. Set uncovered at 75 to 80 degrees until dough has risen to fill the pan—about 1 hour. (Preheat oven to 400 degrees before dough has completed its rise.)

Bake in middle level of preheated 400-degree oven for 20 minutes, or until dough has risen about an inch above rim of pan and has begun to brown nicely, then turn thermostat down to 350 degrees and bake another 10 to 15 minutes. *Brioche* is done when it comes easily out of the pan, is nicely browned, and makes a hollow sound when thumped. Cool on a rack.

(*) AHEAD-OF-TIME NOTE: If you want to keep the *brioche* for several days or several weeks before using, wrap airtight when cool, and refrigerate or freeze it. To defrost frozen *brioche,* let sit several hours at room temperature, or place on a lightly buttered baking sheet for about 45 minutes in a 300-degree oven.

---

2) *Preliminaries to assembling the dessert*

the fruit filling:

1 quart fresh strawberries A bowl Sugar if needed	Wash the strawberries if necessary; hull them. Reserve 4 to 6 of the finest to decorate top of dessert; halve or quarter the rest, depending on size. Place in bowl, and toss lightly with sugar to taste.

the sugar syrup:

1 cup water in a small
   saucepan
¾ cup sugar
½ cup kirsch or dark
   rum

Stir the water and sugar over heat until sugar is completely dissolved; remove from heat. When syrup has cooled to lukewarm, stir in the kirsch or rum. (Syrup should be tepid when it goes over the *brioche;* reheat if necessary.)

apricot to glaze the brioche:

About ⅔ cup apricot jam
   (preserves) forced
   through a sieve into a
   small saucepan
2 Tb sugar
A wooden spoon

Bring the strained apricot jam and sugar to the boil, stirring, for several minutes until last drops to fall from spoon are sticky. Set aside; reheat before using.

for 2 cups crème Chantilly:

1 cup heavy cream in a
   mixing bowl
A large bowl with a tray
   of ice cubes and water
   to cover them
A large wire whip or hand-
   held electric mixer
A rubber spatula
1 tsp vanilla extract
⅓ to ½ cup confectioner's
   sugar in a sieve

Set bowl with cream over the ice cubes and water. Circulating whip or beater about bowl to incorporate as much air as possible, beat cream until doubled in volume. Beater should leave light traces on surface of cream. (If you wish to squeeze out whipped cream decorations later, reserve ½ cup in a bowl, and refrigerate.) Fold in the vanilla, and sugar to taste. Keep over ice until needed.

---

3) *Assembling and serving*

A long knife for splitting
   the *brioche,* a small
   knife and a grapefruit
   knife for hollowing it
   out
A tray to hold syrup drippings
A serving dish
Optional: A canvas pastry
   bag with round, can-
   nelated tube opening, for
   making decorative lines
   of whipped cream on top
   of cake

Slice off the top quarter of the *brioche,* making a cover about ¾ inch thick; cut into 6 to 8 pie-shaped wedges, and place upside down on rack over tray. Hollow out remaining part of *brioche,* first outlining a circle in its top surface ¾ inch from edge all around the inside, and to within ¾ inch of bottom. Then remove interior by bits, with grapefruit knife, to make the *brioche* into a container ¾ inch thick at sides and bottom.

Set *brioche* container hollowed-side up on serving dish. Drain the strawberries, adding their juices to the syrup. Pour successive spoonfuls of tepid syrup gradually over *brioche,* letting it absorb as much liquid as it will. At the same time, pour spoonfuls of syrup over the upside-down cover wedges. Fold the berries into the *crème Chantilly*. Paint outer sides of *brioche* container with warm apricot glaze; turn the strawberries and cream into it, heaping the filling into a dome.

Handling them carefully, set the *brioche* wedges in place on top of the filling, letting their pointed ends rise to a peak at the center. Paint tops of wedges with warm apricot glaze. If you have decided to make whipped cream decorations, whip the reserved *Chantilly* over ice until it is a little stiffer, so that it will hold its shape when squeezed out; fold in 2 tablespoons of sifted confectioner's sugar and a few drops of vanilla. Fill in gaps between wedges with ribbons of whipped cream. Just before serving, decorate top of *Le Marly* with the reserved strawberries. To serve, cut right down between wedges, from top to bottom of cake.

(*) AHEAD-OF-TIME NOTE: May be assembled an hour or two before serving; cover with a bowl, and refrigerate.

Other fruits

Instead of fresh strawberries, use raspberries, sliced fresh peaches, blueberries, frozen strawberries (thawed), a mixture of pineapple and bananas, or the apricot filling on page 507, which you could combine with diced bananas and toasted, slivered almonds. You may macerate the fruit in sugar, rum, or kirsch, if you wish, then stir the maceration into the sugar syrup.

CHARLOTTE JAMAÏQUE EN FLAMMES

[Rum-cake Caramel Custard, Flambée]

This is another *riposte* to the Anglo-Saxons, a French plum pudding of rum-soaked *brioche* or sponge cake, raisins, fruits, and custard baked in a caramelized mold and brought flaming to the table. A fine holiday dessert, it may be made ready for the oven hours before baking, and that takes about an hour.

For a 6-cup mold, serving 6 to 8

---

1) Preparing the fruits

4 ounces (¾ cup, packed down) currants (small, black, seedless raisins)
Either 4 ounces (¾ cup) each of glacéed cherries and apricots;
Or 8 ounces (1½ cups) mixed diced glacéed fruits
1 cup dark Jamaica rum in a covered bowl

Drop the raisins into a pan of boiling water, and set aside to swell and soften while preparing rest of fruit. If using cherries and apricots, cut cherries in half, and drop in boiling water to wash off preservatives; drain, and set on a plate. Dice the apricots, drop in boiling water, drain, and set on another plate. (If using mixed fruits, drop in boiling water, and drain.) Then drain raisins, squeeze out accumulated moisture, and steep in the rum until you are ready to use them.

2) *Caramelizing the mold*

½ cup sugar and 3 Tb water in a small, heavy saucepan
A cover for the pan
A 6-cup cylindrical mold, such as a charlotte or ceramic baking dish at least 3½ inches deep
A plate upon which mold may be reversed

Set sugar and water over moderately high heat, and swirl pan slowly by its handle (but do not stir sugar with a spoon) while liquid is coming to the boil. Continue swirling for a moment as liquid boils and turns from cloudy to perfectly clear. Cover pan, raise heat to high, and boil several minutes, until bubbles are thick and heavy. Uncover and continue boiling, swirling gently, until sugar turns a nice caramel brown.

Immediately pour the caramel into the mold (reserve caramel pan); turn mold in all directions to film bottom and sides, and continue turning slowly for a minute or so, until caramel ceases to run. Turn mold upside down over plate.

3) *The custard sauce*

1 cup milk
3 eggs
⅔ cup sugar
A 3-quart mixing bowl and electric beater or large wire whip
2 tsp vanilla extract
A clean 2½- to 3-quart enameled or stainless saucepan
A wooden spoon
A fine-meshed sieve

Pour the milk into the caramel-cooking pan, and stir over heat to dissolve caramel. Then beat eggs and sugar in mixing bowl for several minutes until pale and foamy; beat in the vanilla. Finally, in a thin stream of droplets, beat in the hot milk. Pour mixture into clean saucepan, and set over moderate heat; stir slowly with wooden spoon, reaching all over bottom of pan, for 4 to 5 minutes, or until custard thickens enough to film spoon with a creamy layer. (Be careful sauce does not come to the simmer and curdle the eggs, but you must heat it to the point where it thickens.)

Remove from heat, and stir vigorously a moment or two to cool the sauce and stop the cooking. Rinse out mixing bowl, and strain the sauce into it.

4) *Filling the mold*

A pan of boiling water large enough to hold dessert mold easily
About 1 pound of *brioche,* sponge cake, or store-bought sponge-type of cake

(Preheat oven to 350 degrees for next step.) Check water level of pan with mold set into it, and place pan (without mold) in lower-middle level of oven. Slice *brioche* or cake into 3 layers, each about ⅛ inch thick, and trim so they will fit into the mold exactly. (Each layer may consist of several pieces neatly fitted together.)

Fit a layer of cake in the bottom of the caramelized mold. Drain the raisins and sprinkle 3 tablespoons of their rum maceration over the cake. Arrange a row of cherry halves (or mixed diced fruit) around the edge of the cake, and spread a third of the raisins and apricots (or more diced mixed fruit) over the rest of the cake. Pour in a third of the custard. Put down a second layer of cake, sprinkle with 3 tablespoons more rum, and continue filling the mold in layers. Leave about ¼ inch of unfilled space at top of mold because dessert will swell slightly during cooking. Cover remaining rum and reserve for flambéeing.

(*) AHEAD-OF-TIME NOTE: Mold may be filled a day in advance of baking; cover airtight and refrigerate. Chilled custard will probably take at least 20 minutes more to bake than the 45 to 60 minutes specified in Step 5.

---

5) Baking the dessert—45 to 60 minutes at 350 degrees, plus a 10-minute rest (longer if custard has been chilled)

Place the filled mold in the pan of hot water in the oven (water should come ¾ the way up outside of mold). Bake for 45 minutes to 1 hour, regulating heat so that water in pan almost but never quite bubbles—to ensure a smooth and velvety texture to the custard. Add more boiling water, as necessary, if liquid drops below the halfway mark. Dessert is done when it begins to show a faint line of shrinkage from sides of mold.

If you wish to serve within 10 to 15 minutes, remove mold from water and allow custard to settle for 10 minutes before unmolding, Step 6; otherwise leave custard in its pan of water in turned-off oven. Dessert must be hot for successful flambéeing.

---

6) Unmolding, flambéeing, and serving

A thin-bladed flexible knife for help in unmolding

A very hot, lightly buttered serving platter

3 or 4 broken sugar lumps and 1 Tb sugar

The remaining rum (at least ½ cup) in a small saucepan

Matches

A pair of long-handled serving utensils

The moment before serving, run knife around edge of mold, turn hot platter upside down over it, and reverse the two to unmold dessert onto platter. Stick the broken sugar lumps into the dessert at various places, and sprinkle on the plain sugar. Heat the rum and pour it over the dessert. Averting your face, ignite the rum with a lighted match, and bring the *charlotte* flaming to the table. Spoon flaming rum over the dessert as you begin to serve.

DESSERTS USING FRENCH
PUFF PASTRY

French puff pastry, that unbelievably tender and buttery dough, with its hundreds of thinner-than-paper layers, is ideal for desserts. Because the pastry itself is so marvelous, the rest of the ingredients are usually rather simple and easy to assemble. We give only a sampling of the many, many recipes that use puff pastry, going into enough illustrated detail, we hope, so that when you run into other puff pastry recipes elsewhere, they will seem feasible and even familiar.

Your sole problem—which need be no problem at all—is to keep the dough cold while you are working on it. At the slightest suggestion of limpness, stop where you are, refrigerate everything for 15 to 20 minutes, then continue. If you are not yet used to working with puff pastry, do not attempt anything complicated in a hot kitchen; wait for cool weather or an air-conditioned atmosphere. Chilled dough in a cool room is easy to manipulate; soft, limp dough in a warm room is impossible.

ABAISSES EN FEUILLETAGE POUR TARTES AUX FRUITS
[Forming Puff Pastry Shells for Fruit Tarts]

With French puff pastry you can make free-standing shells of any size and shape you wish: the sides of the pastry rise automatically in the oven while the bottom stays put, held down by the fruit or, if you wish a precooked shell, by a pan. Use either the simple puff pastry on page 113, or the reconstituted leftover puff pastry described on page 134. We shall not give proportions, except to say that one fourth of the recipe, or a piece of dough 5¼ by 2 by 1¾ inches, will make a rectangular pastry 6 inches wide and 13 inches long, with a bottom layer ⅛ inch thick; thus half the recipe would make a 12- to 13-inch square.

To make a square or rectangular shell

Sufficient chilled puff pastry dough

A ruler or light-weight baking sheet to use as a cutting guide

A ravioli wheel or sharp knife

A baking sheet rinsed in cold water but not dried

A cup of cold water and a pastry brush

Roll out the chilled pastry 1½ inches larger than the size you want your tart to be. With cutting guide and ravioli wheel or knife, trim off rough edges all around.

Again using your guide and ravioli wheel or knife, *cut two strips ¾ inch wide from one side of pastry, and two from one end;* these will form the raised edges of the tart; set them aside. Roll up the rectangle or square of pastry on your pin, and unroll it upside down on the dampened baking sheet.

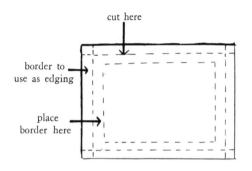

cut here

border to use as edging

place border here

Paint top circumference of tart with a ¾-inch strip of cold water. Lay a strip of pastry on top of each side, as shown. Paint corners with cold water, and lay two final strips of pastry over each end. Trim off excess. *Seal the two layers together by pressing outside rim all around pastry with the back tines of a table fork,* and pressing top strips of pastry lightly with thumb of other hand as you go. Prick interior of pastry with fork at ⅛-inch intervals, going down to pastry sheet. Cover with plastic wrap and chill for an hour before proceeding; dough must be relaxed or it will not bake evenly.

(*) When chilled and firm, dough may be wrapped airtight and frozen for several months; continue with whatever your recipe, using dough in its frozen state.

Forming a round tart shell

Using *vol-au-vent* cutters, pot lids, or any convenient circular objects, pick one for the size of your eventual tart and another ¾ inch larger all around for the raised rim of the tart. Roll out pastry ⅛ inch thick and ¼ inch larger all around than the larger of your two cutting guides; lift pastry and let it shrink if it will, and extend again if necessary. Center guide on pastry and cut off excess dough.

Center the smaller guide in the pastry and cut all around it cleanly, so that this center disk can easily separate itself from the outside circle. Divide outside circle into quarters or sixths and slide out of the way; these strips will form the raised rim of the tart. Roll disk up on pin and unroll upside down on a dampened baking sheet, pressing it out gently with fingers if necessary.

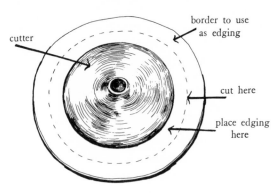

Paint a ¾-inch strip around the circumference of disk with cold water. Lay one of the strips of dough in place on the dampened circumference of disk, and paint one end of strip with cold water. *Overlap ⅜ inch of second strip on the dampened end of the first, and press lightly with fingers to seal; continue around circumference with the rest of the strips,* trimming final one to fit. Seal edges all around with back of a fork, prick the interior, and refrigerate as described in preceding directions.

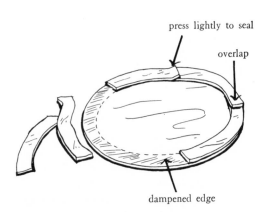

Baked shells for fresh fruit tarts, like strawberries

A shell that is to be fully baked and then filled with fresh fruits must have something to weight down the center during baking. The traditional solution is oiled paper and dried beans, but we think an oiled pan of some sort is far easier. Provide yourself with 3 guides, one for the outside circumference, one for cutting the inch-wide strips, and one for the area of the pan. After cutting edges and pressing them onto the dampened circumference of the pastry, prick interior of pastry, oil outside of pan, and set it in place. Chill at least an hour before baking.

To bake, preheat oven to 425 degrees. Then paint top of raised edging with egg glaze (1 egg beaten in a small bowl with 1 tsp water), and make cross-hatch markings in glaze with back of a small knife. Set the pastry, with pan in place, in middle level of oven. Bake 10 to 15 minutes, until edges of pastry have risen and begin to brown nicely. Lift off pan, prick interior, and bake 5 minutes more; look at tart, and if center is rising, prick again, and press down. If center is browning too much, cover loosely with foil. Baking will be 20 to 25 minutes in all. Slide shell onto a rack.

(*) Shell is at its best if eaten within a few hours; cover airtight when cold, or keep in warming oven, or freeze.

TARTE AUX POMMES—TARTE AUX POIRES

[Apple or Pear Tart Baked in French Puff Pastry]

This is a case where the most elementary method is by far the best: the raw tart dough is painted with apricot, slices of raw apple or pear are arranged closely on top, sprinkled with sugar, and the tart is baked. It is glazed with apricot after baking, and that is all there is to it. The combination of flaky, buttery pastry, fruit, sugar, and apricot is quite heavenly.

A NOTE ON JUICY FRUITS

When you are baking raw fruits in a raw puff pastry shell you must be sure that you are using the kind of fruit that will not burst into juices before the edges of the pastry have puffed up enough to hold them in. Thus if you find yourself with soft or juicy varieties, slice them, sprinkle with sugar, and let stand in a bowl for 20 minutes so that excess juices will exude. Then drain the fruit, arrange in the tart, and add the juices to boil down with the apricot glaze.

For an 8- by 16-inch rectangular tart, serving 4 to 6 people

1) *Filling the tart shell*

Either 3 to 4 large, crisp apples (Golden Delicious, Rome Beauty, or York Imperial);
Or 5 to 6 firm, ripe pears (Anjou, Bosc, or Bartlett)

Preheat oven to 450 degrees, and set rack in lower-middle level. Peel, quarter, and core the fruit; cut into lengthwise slices ¼ inch thick. Paint interior of chilled uncooked pastry shell with strained apricot. Arrange the slices of fruit closely together and almost upright in the shell, making lengthwise or crosswise rows, whichever you find more attractive.

A chilled 8- by 16-inch
  uncooked tart shell of
  French puff pastry
  (pages 454-7)
About 1 cup strained apricot
  preserves in a small
  saucepan (apricot pre-
  serves pushed through a
  sieve)
A pastry brush
¼ cup sugar
Egg glaze (1 egg beaten in
  a small bowl with 1 tsp
  water)
A small knife, or table fork

Sprinkle the sugar over the fruit. Paint top of pastry (not sides) with egg glaze, and make cross-hatching in its surface with point of knife or tines of fork.

---

2) Baking—40 to 45 minutes at 450 and 400 degrees

Set tart immediately in lower middle of preheated 450-degree oven, and bake for 20 minutes, or until sides of pastry have risen and begun to brown. Lower heat to 400 degrees and continue baking another 20 minutes, or until sides of tart feel crisp and rather firm. High heat is needed to cook the layers of pastry through; cover tart loosely with foil or brown paper if edges are browning too much.

---

3) Glazing and serving

A rack
The remaining strained
  apricot
1 Tb sugar (or juices from
  macerated fruits)
A wooden spoon
A kitchen spoon or pastry
  brush
A serving tray or board
Optional: crème fraîche,
  sweetened crème Chan-
  tilly (lightly whipped
  cream, page 422), or
  crème anglaise (custard
  sauce, page 501)

Slide tart on a rack. Boil the apricot and sugar, stirring, for several minutes until last drops to fall from spoon are sticky. Spoon or brush the apricot over the fruit to glaze it. Serve tart warm, tepid, or cold, sliding it first onto tray or board. Cut into crosswise pieces for each serving. Pass optional cream or sauce separately.

(*) The tart is at its best eaten a few hours after baking; leftovers will be delicious, but never as wonderful as the freshly baked tart.

Baking the fruit in a round pastry shell

Use the same general system, but arrange the slices of fruit in a spiral, or in rows of diminishing width from circumference to center, like the spokes of a wheel.

Other fruits to be baked in puff pastry shells

Fresh pitted cherries, fresh apricot or prune-plum halves placed skin-side down, fresh sliced peaches, or well-drained canned apricots or peach slices may be done this same way.

Fresh fruits in prebaked puff pastry shells

Use prebaked puff pastry shells, page 454, just as you would prebaked shells made from pie-crust dough, as suggested in Volume I, pages 640–1, for strawberry tart and its variations. This has a pastry-cream filling, but you may use simply a waterproofing of the red-currant glaze, arrange the strawberries or other fresh fruits on top, and paint with more glaze; pass whipped cream or custard sauce separately.

JALOUSIE

[Peekaboo Jam or Fruit Tart of French Pastry]

Very quick to assemble and delicious, because puff pastry turns anything into a treat, is this attractive tart with its jam or fruit filling. Translated literally from the French, it would be called the Venetian Blind Tart, since that is what *jalousie* means; peekaboo seems more appealing.

For a 6- by 16-inch tart, serving 6 people

---

1) *Forming the tart*

½ the recipe for simple puff pastry, page 113; or reconstituted leftovers, page 134 A dampened pastry sheet A table fork	Roll half the pastry into an 8- by 18-inch rectangle ⅛ inch thick. Roll up on pin, and unroll topside down onto dampened pastry sheet. Prick all over at ⅛-inch intervals with tines of fork, going right down through to pastry sheet.

A cup or so of excellent
   raspberry, strawberry, or
   blackberry jam, or other
   suggestions listed at end
   of recipe

---

*Spread a ¼-inch layer of jam over
pastry, leaving a ¾-inch border of
pastry all around.*

---

*Turn borders of pastry up over fill-
ing at sides; wet corners, and turn
ends over, sealing corners with
fingers.*

Roll out second piece of pastry into
a 7- by 17-inch rectangle (slightly
larger than shape of filled pastry),
⅛ inch thick. Flour surface lightly;
fold in half lengthwise. Measure
opening of filled pastry and mark
folded pastry to guide you. *Cut
slits in the dough from folded edge,*
as shown, making them ⅜ inch
apart and half as long as width of
opening in tart.

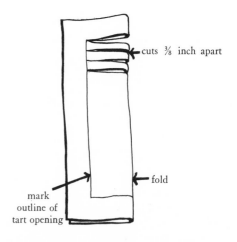

cuts ⅜ inch apart

fold

mark
outline of
tart opening

Wet edges of filled bottom layer of pastry with cold water. Unfold top layer of pastry over it; brush off accumulated flour, and press pastry in place with fingers. *Then, with back tines of a fork, press a decorative vertical border all around sides.* Cover and chill for at least 30 minutes, or until baking time.

(*) AHEAD-OF-TIME NOTE: When chilled and firm, may be wrapped airtight and frozen for several months. Remove from freezer, glaze, and bake as in Step 2.

2) *Baking and serving—about 1 hour at 450 and 400 degrees*

Egg glaze (1 egg beaten in a small bowl with 1 tsp water)
A pastry brush
A table fork or small knife
A rack
A serving tray or board
Optional: *crème fraîche, crème Chantilly,* or *crème anglaise* as suggested for preceding recipe, Step 3

When oven has been preheated to 450 degrees, set rack in lower-middle level. Paint surface of chilled *jalousie* with egg glaze; wait a moment, and give it a second coat. Make cross-hatchings on top of sides and ends through glaze with fork or knife, and set *jalousie* in the oven. In about 20 minutes, when pastry has risen and is browning nicely, turn heat down to 400. Bake 30 to 40 minutes more, covering loosely with foil or brown paper if surface is browning too much.

Jalousie may seem done before it actually is; sides should be firm and crusty, and object of long cooking is to dry out and crisp all inner layers of the pastry. Slide onto a rack when done. Serve warm, tepid, or cold, with optional cream or sauce passed separately. Cut into crosswise slices for each serving.

(*) As with all puff pastries, this is best when freshly baked.

Other fillings

Cooked fruits rather than jams are also desirable fillings for the *jalousie.* Among them we suggest the apricot filling on page 507. Another idea is a filling of baked apple slices, such as those for the *gratin de pommes,* Step 2, page 435; spread some apricot jam over the pastry before piling on the baked apple slices, and more over the apples before you cover them with the pastry. Pitted prunes stewed in wine, butter, and sugar, and mixed with toasted almonds or chopped walnuts would be delicious. Glazed canned pineapple and diced bananas is another idea; glaze the pineapple following the directions for the orange mousse, page 442. These are only a few possibilities, and you will think of many others yourself.

MILLE-FEUILLES

[Napoleons—Layers of Puff Pastry Interspersed
with Pastry Cream or Whipped Cream; Iced with Fondant
and Chocolate or with Confectioner's Sugar]

The *mille-feuilles* dessert, according to some authorities, was not developed in France until the latter part of the nineteenth century. The name "Napoleon," at any event, is not associated with it at all in any French recipes; the French icing, furthermore, is simply a layer of confectioner's sugar. The rest of the world has long wondered, then, how the pastry came to be named "Napoleon" outside of France, and who changed the icing from confectioner's sugar to white fondant and lines of chocolate. The Danes have been told for generations that a Danish royal pastry chef invented the dessert way back in the early 1800's on the occasion of a state visit between the Emperor Napoleon and the King of Denmark, in Copenhagen. The Italians are sure it is a corruption of Napolitain, because of the layered pastries made in Naples. Some sources believe that the chocolate lines appear to form the letter N, for Napoleon—which is far easier for foreigners to pronounce anyway than *mille-feuilles*. A final story, with a certain air of mischievous *fumisterie* about it, is that the dessert was really a French invention after all, and Napoleon's favorite pastry; he ate so many of them, however, on the eve of Waterloo that he lost the battle. The pastry then disappeared from view for half a century; when it finally reappeared from banishment, it wore another icing and a new name.

MANUFACTURING NOTES

Mille-feuilles and Napoleons are thin rectangles of crisply baked puff pastry that are mounted in 3 layers with whipped cream or pastry cream in between, and a topping of confectioner's sugar for *mille-feuilles* or of white frosting and lines of chocolate for Napoleons.

The traditional method of forming and cutting them, illustrated in the following recipe, is to bake the pastry in large sheets, and to cut each sheet into 3 long strips 4 inches wide, as in Step 4, page 465. After the 3 strips are glazed with apricot, the first is spread with filling, the second is laid over the first and filled, then the third strip is laid on top, and covered with sugar or fondant. This giant *mille-feuilles* is finally cut crosswise into rectangular serving pieces 4 inches long and 2 inches wide, as shown in the final drawing.

This is certainly the easiest and most practical method, and works especially well for puff pastry made with the French household flour or its American equivalent of ⅓ unbleached all-purpose flour and ⅔ unbleached pastry flour. You may find, however, that puff pastry made with the all-purpose and cake-flour formula will flake or crumble a bit too much for that final cutting into serving pieces. You will be able to judge this when you cut the sheet of pastry into three strips; if it seems brittle, glaze the strips with apricot, then cut each into its final rectangles, and build the individual servings separately. It will take you a little longer, but you will avoid trouble. As with many recipes of this sort, be ready to adapt yourself to circumstances because the exact state of a baked pastry is impossible to predict.

For 16 pieces

-----

1) *Forming the puff pastry*

4 baking sheets all of a size, 12 by 18 inches, approximately (or form and bake 1 pastry at a time, and use 2 baking sheets)

About 1 Tb soft butter

Chilled fresh puff pastry, either the simple dough on page 113 but with 6 turns rather than 4, or the classic puff pastry, page 118

A large knife or a pastry wheel

A rotary pastry pricker, page 550, or 2 forks

(Please read Manufacturing Notes preceding this step.) Lightly butter topsides of 2 baking sheets, and bottom sides of the 2 others. Roll chilled pastry into a 14-inch rectangle, cut in half crosswise, and chill one half. Roll remaining piece rapidly into a 13- by 19-inch rectangle ⅛ inch thick; roll up on pastry pin, and unroll over one of the buttered baking sheets. Trim off ⅓ inch of pastry all around, so that the horizontal layers of dough within the puff pastry will be even at the edges.

Prick pastry all over at ⅛-inch intervals with pastry pricker or forks. Chill for at least 30 minutes to relax dough before baking. Roll and form second piece of dough in the same manner.

2) *Baking the pastry—about 20 minutes at 450 degrees*

Preheat oven to 450 degrees and set racks on upper- and lower-middle levels. Cover each chilled sheet of pastry dough with a buttered baking sheet, and set in the two levels of the oven. The pastry is to rise as little as possible during baking; you are to prick it again, and push down the covering sheets several times, as follows. In 5 minutes, lift covering sheets and rapidly prick pastry all over to deflate it; press covering sheets down on the pastry, and bake 5 minutes more. Rapidly prick the pastry again, and switch from one level to the other, so both will bake evenly. Prick and press pastry again in 5 minutes; it should be starting to brown. Remove covering sheets if pastry has set, and let it brown and crisp 2 to 3 minutes more, but cover again with the baking sheets if it starts to puff up—watch carefully during these last few minutes that pastry does not brown too much. At end of baking, pastry should be crisp and golden, and between ¼ and ⅜ inch thick. Remove from oven and cool 5 minutes, with the covering sheets in place to prevent pastry from curling. The pastry is now ready for cutting, next step.

(*) AHEAD-OF-TIME NOTE: Pastry is at its best when freshly baked. Use within a few hours, but you may keep it fresh in a warming oven (100–150 degrees) for a day or so; otherwise, wrap airtight and freeze.

---

3) *Preliminaries to assembling mille-feuilles or Napoleons*

apricot glaze:

1 cup apricot jam (preserves) forced through a sieve into a small saucepan 2 Tb sugar A wooden spoon A pastry brush	Bring strained apricot jam and sugar to the boil, stirring, for several minutes until last drops of jam to fall from spoon are sticky. Reheat to liquefy again before using.

the filling—3 to 4 cups needed:

Either one of the custard fillings in Volume I, pages 590–2, including *crème pâtissière, crème Saint-Honoré,* or the almond custard, *frangipane;*	Prepare one of the fillings suggested, and chill. It must hold its shape enough when spread over the pastry so that you can make layers almost ½ inch thick; if it seems too soft, strengthen it with gelatin just before using the filling as follows: sprinkle gelatin over liquid in a small saucepan; when softened,

Or crème Chantilly meringuée, the whipped cream stiffened and sweetened with an Italian meringue mixture, page 430

If needed: 1½ packages (1½ Tb) plain unflavored powdered gelatin softened in ¼ cup liquid (diluted kirsch or plain water)

heat until completely dissolved. Let cool (or stir over ice) until almost syrupy; then fold into the filling.

icing for mille-feuilles:

About 1 cup confectioner's sugar in a fine-meshed sieve

This is all you will need for icing *mille-feuilles.*

icing for Napoleons:

1 cup white fondant frosting, page 505, in a small saucepan with 2 Tb kirsch
A larger saucepan of simmering water
A wooden spoon
A rubber spatula or flexible-blade metal spatula

Just before you are to ice the assembled Napoleons, Step 4, stir fondant and kirsch over simmering water until perfectly smooth and just enough liquefied to coat spoon fairly heavily. Use at once.

---

1 Tb instant coffee
¼ cup water in a small saucepan with cover
8 ounces semisweet baking chocolate
A larger saucepan of simmering water to hold chocolate pan
A wooden spoon
A paper decorating cone, page 509

Dissolve coffee in water over heat; remove from heat, break up the chocolate, and stir it in. Remove pan of simmering water from heat, set chocolate pan in it, stir up, and cover pan. Set aside to melt for several minutes, then stir vigorously until perfectly smooth and creamy. Keep over warm (not hot or simmering) water until ready to use. Prepare paper cone as described and illustrated, and cut opening about ⅛ inch in diameter.

---

4) *Assembling*

NOTE: If pastry seems flaky or crumbly, cut it with a serrated knife rather than pastry wheel, using the knife like a saw. See also Manufacturing Notes, page 462, on forming individual portions rather than long strips.

Even sides and ends of pastry by trimming with pastry wheel or serrated knife. With a guide of some sort, such as a pastry sheet or a ruler, mark pastry with the point of a knife, dividing it into 3 even strips; *cut through with pastry wheel* or with serrated knife. Cut second pastry sheet in the same manner.

Paint top of each of the 6 strips with warm apricot glaze. Divide filling into 4 parts; spread one part on one of the glazed strips. Mount a second glazed strip upon the filled strip, and spread with its share of filling; mount a third glazed strip upon it, and set aside. Repeat with the second group of three strips. You now have two 3-layered strips ready for icing. For *mille-feuilles,* simply shake a heavy layer of confectioner's sugar over each of them.

For Napoleons, rapidly spread as even a layer as possible of white fondant over each.

Stir up melted chocolate to be sure it is smooth and velvety, then pour it into your paper cone. *Squeeze out lines of chocolate about 1 inch apart down the length of the fondant on each strip.* Proceed immediately to next step, while chocolate is still soft.

Draw the back of a knife down across the middle of the chocolate lines, then draw another line in the opposite direction on each side, thus pulling the chocolate into a decorative pattern.

As soon as chocolate has set, in 4 to 5 minutes, but before fondant has hardened, *cut the strips into crosswise pieces about 2 inches wide, using a very sharp (or saw-edged) knife,* and cutting very carefully with an up-and-down sawing motion. Cut *mille-feuilles* in the same manner.

5) *Serving*

Arrange the *mille-feuilles* or Napoleons on a serving tray and chill an hour. Remove Napoleons from refrigerator 20 minutes before serving, so that both chocolate and fondant will regain their glossy bloom.

(*) These pastries are at their best when freshly made, although you may keep them for 2 to 3 days under refrigeration, and you may freeze them.

CORNETS ET ROULEAUX
[Cream Horns—Cream Rolls]

The cream horns and rolls of puff pastry described and illustrated on pages 135-7 are also useful for desserts. Rather than glazing them before baking, *press the top and sides (not the bottom where pastry is sealed) in plain granulated or in coarse crystallized sugar.*

no sugar on seam side (bottom)

Bake in the middle level of a preheated 425-degree oven for 15 to 20 minutes until nicely caramelized—but watch them; they burn easily. Fill with *crème Chantilly,* lightly beaten cream, sweetened and flavored with vanilla or liqueur, or with the meringue whipped cream, *Chantilly meringuée,* page 430, or with the custard and egg-white filling, *crème Saint-Honoré,* Volume I, page 591. A sprinkling of *pralin,* caramelized almonds or walnuts, pages 421 and 423, could nicely be folded into any of these fillings.

PITHIVIERS
[Almond Cream Baked in French Puff Pastry]

The small town of Pithiviers, south of Paris halfway to Bourges, may have other distinctions, but its world renown is certainly due to the famous almond pastry that every local *pâtissier* prominently and proudly displays. This is an exact illustration, drawn from our own photograph of *le veritable Pithiviers de Pithiviers,* taken only moments before we consumed it down to the last crumb in a warm and flowering meadow just outside the town itself. This buttery, flaky, tender, marvelous dessert is probably one of the most glorious uses to which you can put puff pastry; it is also a persuasive reason for you to learn how to make your own *pâte feuilletée,* because a *Pithiviers* is so easy and fast to assemble. It is two disks of dough enclosing a lump of rum-flavored almonds, sugar, and butter; the top disk is glazed with egg just before baking, and the characteristic design is cut into it with the point of a knife. Serve the *Pithiviers* as a dessert, at a tea party, or on any occasion that calls for something special in the way of a sweet. One of the great white Sauternes would be lovely with it, or a sweet Champagne, or a sparkling Vouvray.

For an 8-inch Pithiviers, serving 6 to 8 people

TIMING NOTE: Make the puff pastry the day before serving, as well as the almond cream, since it must be cold and hard. The assembled *Pithiviers* may be refrigerated or frozen, but once baked, it is at its best when served within 2 to 3 hours (unless you have a warming oven where it can remain safely at around 100 degrees for a number of hours).

1) The almond cream—chilling time 30 to 40 minutes in freezer

⅓ cup sugar
4 Tb soft butter
An electric mixer, or a
  bowl and wooden spoon
1 "large" egg
2½ ounces (½ cup
  loosely packed) ground
  blanched almonds—may
  be ground in an electric
  blender
¼ tsp almond extract
¼ tsp vanilla extract
1½ Tb dark rum

Beat sugar and butter together until light and fluffy, then beat in the egg, almonds, extracts, and rum. Cover bowl and set in freezer for 30 to 40 minutes, or in refrigerator for an hour or two; it is essential that the cream be chilled and hard before you assemble the *Pithiviers.*

2) Assembling the Pithiviers—about 1 hour, including 2 half-hour rests

The recipe for chilled
  classic French puff pastry,
  page 118
A round pastry cutter or
  upside-down cake pan
  8 inches in diameter

Preheat oven to 425 degrees in time for Step 3. Place chilled puff pastry on a lightly floured marble or board, and roll it rapidly into a rectangle ⅜ inch thick, 12 inches wide, and 20 inches long. (To equalize stresses and strains within the dough for even baking, be sure to roll it crosswise as well as length-

A small, sharp-pointed
   knife for cutting dough
A piece of lightly floured
   waxed paper on a tray
More flour and more waxed
   paper
A dampened baking sheet
   (a pizza tray is good for
   baking this pastry)

wise.) Centering cutter or cake pan well on pastry for each of the disks you are to cut, and making them at least ½ inch from edges of pastry and from each other, cut two 8-inch disks (rounds) in the dough. Lift off surrounding dough, and arrange it in one layer on tray; directions for its re-use as puff pastry are on page 134.

Cover this leftover dough with waxed paper, and dust paper lightly with flour; roll one of the disks up on your pin, unroll on the waxed paper, cover with another sheet of waxed paper, and refrigerate. Unroll second disk topside down on baking sheet, cover, and refrigerate for 20 to 30 minutes, or until cold and firm. (Make frequent use of the refrigerator, and you will have no troubles with puff pastry.)

Remove disk formed on the baking sheet from the refrigerator. Push dough out gently with your fingers to make it slightly more than 8 inches in diameter all around. Soften almond cream, if necessary, by kneading it; form it into a cake 4 inches in diameter and center it on the disk of dough. It is important here that the almond cream be cold and hard, and that there be a free circumference of dough 1½ to 2 inches wide all around; this will prevent it from leaking out of the pastry during baking.

*Paint free circumference of dough
with cold water.*

Remove remaining disk of dough from refrigerator and roll it out rapidly, rotating disk as you go, expanding it all around to about 8½ inches. *Unroll it over the almond cream on the bottom disk of dough.*

With lightly floured fingers as well
as the side of your hand, *firmly
press top disk to bottom disk all
around the lump of almond cream;*
if air pockets prevent a perfect seal,
make a little hole for air to escape in
center top of dough, where chimney
will be inserted later. Chill dough
again for 30 minutes.

Turn a cake pan or bowl upside
down over *Pithiviers;* about ⅜ to ½
inch of dough should protrude all
around from its edge. *With the
back or the front of a small knife,
whichever works best for you, cut a
scalloped border all around
circumference of dough, spacing
indentations evenly and about 1¼
inches apart.* Press pan or bowl
rather firmly into dough as a final
seal, and remove it. Chill before
proceeding, if dough has softened.

(*) AHEAD-OF-TIME NOTE: *Pithiviers* may be refrigerated or frozen at this point; chill
to harden dough, then cover airtight. (Frozen pastry may be taken directly from
freezer, and glazed and decorated as soon as top of dough is soft enough for a knife
to penetrate it.)

When oven is preheated to 425
degrees, and just before baking,
*paint entire top surface of Pithiviers
with egg glaze* (1 egg beaten in a
small bowl with 1 teaspoon water).
In 2 minutes, after you have made
and inserted the buttered aluminum
foil or brown paper chimney in next
illustration, paint with a second
coat.

With the point of a sharp small knife, cut decorative design into pastry as shown, going ⅛ inch deep. (Cutting through glaze and down into dough will make the design stand out after baking.) Proceed immediately to the baking, next step.

3) *Baking—about 50 minutes at 450 degrees and 400 degrees*

As soon as *Pithiviers* has been glazed and decorated, set in middle level of preheated 450-degree oven. In 20 minutes, or when pastry has risen and browned nicely, reduce oven heat to 400 degrees and continue baking 25 to 30 minutes more, until sides of pastry are brown and crisp. If *Pithiviers* seems to be browning too much during baking, lay a sheet of brown paper or foil loosely over the top.

4) *Sugar glaze*

About ⅓ cup confectioner's sugar in a fine-meshed sieve
A cake rack

Remove *Pithiviers* from oven, set thermostat at 500 degrees, and slide oven rack onto upper-third level.

Remove funnel. Sieve a ¹⁄₁₆-inch layer of the sugar over the top of the *Pithiviers*. When oven is at 500 degrees, set pastry in upper third for 4 to 5 minutes, peeking quickly every 30 seconds, until sugar has melted to a glossy sheen. Remove the *Pithiviers* and slide it onto the rack.

5) *Serving and storing*

A *Pithiviers* may be eaten tepid or cold, but is always at its best when freshly made and served within 2 to 3 hours of baking. It will keep successfully for a day in a warming oven at 100 degrees, or you may freeze it when cold and wrapped airtight. If frozen, thaw for about 30 minutes on a lightly buttered pastry sheet in a 350-degree oven.

To serve, cut into wedges, like a pie.

A LITTLE SELECTION OF PETITS FOURS

LES TRUFFES AUX CHOCOLAT
[Chocolate Candies in the Form of Truffles]

Rough balls of melted chocolate, butter, and orange liqueur rolled in cocoa look like freshly dug truffles. These homemade candies are easy to make and, unfortunately for those who are trying not to resemble Babar the elephant, they are quite irresistible.

For 1½ dozen

¼ cup strong coffee (1 Tb instant coffee in ¼ cup boiling water)

A covered saucepan for melting the chocolate

7 ounces semisweet baking chocolate

2 ounces unsweetened chocolate

A larger pan of simmering water removed from heat, to hold chocolate pan

A hand-held electric mixer

5 ounces (1¼ sticks) chilled unsalted butter

¼ cup orange liqueur

Dissolve the coffee in the saucepan with the hot water; break up the chocolate, and stir it into the liquid. Cover, and set in the pan of hot but not simmering water. When chocolate has softened, beat with electric mixer until perfectly smooth and creamy. Remove from hot water and beat a moment to cool. Cut chilled butter into ⅓-inch slices and gradually beat into the chocolate with mixer, adding a new piece as soon as a previous one is almost absorbed. When smooth, beat in the orange liqueur by dribbles. Chill for an hour or two, until firm.

A sturdy teaspoon

About ½ cup unsweetened cocoa on a plate

Frilled paper bonbon cups

When chocolate mixture has chilled and set, remove by teaspoon gobs, roll into rough circular shapes, then roll in the cocoa to enrobe them completely. Place in paper cups.

(*) When packed in an airtight container, *truffes* will keep perfectly for several weeks in the refrigerator, or for several months in the freezer.

LES CROQUETS DENISON
[Walnut and Almond Puffs]

These easy-to-make mouthfuls can take the place of after-dinner mints, or go with tea, coffee, sweet liqueurs, and sweet wines. Ideally they are baked directly in fluted paper candy cups, if you can find any that are the no-stick kind. Otherwise bake them in tiny buttered molds, preferably not fluted ones because the batter may stick to them. Lacking proper containers, you may form the mixture on a baking sheet, like cookies; they will not be as elegant to look at but will be just as good to eat.

NOTE: A heavy-duty mixer with flat beater works beautifully here; if you do not have one, beat everything together in a bowl with a wooden spoon.

For 3½ to 4 dozen 1¼-inch puffs

1) *The batter*

2 ounces (½ cup) walnut
meats
2 ounces (½ cup) blanched
almonds
4 ounces (1½ cups) con-
fectioner's sugar (Sift
sugar directly into dry-
measure cups and sweep
off excess)
1½ tsp kirsch
The grated peel of ½ lemon
2 to 3 Tb egg white

Pulverize the nut meats in an electric blender and
turn into a bowl. Add the sugar, kirsch, grated lemon
peel, and 2 tablespoons of egg white. Mixture is now
to be beaten until it forms a mass stiff enough to hold
its shape when bits are rolled into balls: beat for 2 to
3 minutes, and if ingredients remain sandy and unmassed, add ½ tablespoon more egg white; continue
beating, and if mixture still separates, beat in a little
more egg white. (If too soft, on the other hand, beat
in a tablespoon or so more pulverized nuts or confectioner's sugar, or refrigerate for half an hour until
it becomes firmer.)

2) *Forming the petits fours*

Waxed paper on a tray
A table fork
2 egg whites in a small
bowl
½ cup confectioner's
sugar on a plate; more
sugar as needed
Fluted no-stick paper
candy cups (or buttered
molds, 1 Tb capacity)
A baking sheet, clean and
dry if you are using
paper cups

Preheat oven to 300 degrees. Puffs will double in size
when baked, therefore cups or molds should be filled
only by half. Form mixture into balls by rolling between the palms of your hands; place each ball, as
formed, on the waxed paper. Beat egg whites with
fork to break up thoroughly. One by one, dip each
ball in egg white, then roll in sugar, place in candy
paper or mold and arrange on baking sheet. (Or
flatten the balls into disk shapes, dip in egg white,
then coat with sugar and arrange on a buttered baking sheet.)

3) *Baking and serving*

Optional: paper candy cups

Bake in middle level of preheated 300-degree oven
for 15 to 20 minutes, until puffs have about doubled
in size and are pale gold in color. Let cool and crisp
for 10 to 15 minutes. If you have baked them in
molds, dislodge delicately with the point of a knife
and, if you wish, place each in a candy cup.

(*) AHEAD-OF-TIME NOTE: Will keep several days when
covered airtight; for longer storage, freeze them.

TUILES AUX AMANDES
[Lacy Curved Almond Wafers]

These delicate mouthfuls go nicely with fresh fruit desserts, ices, and afternoon tea. Rapidly mixed and baked, the wafers crisp almost immediately into the shape of old-fashioned roof tiles when they are lifted from the baking sheet to a rolling pin or bottle to cool. The only *tour de main* involved here is that you work out your own system for removing the wafers as quickly as possible from baking sheet to rolling pin; as they cool, they become too crisp to mold. Bake one sheet at a time, even though you may prepare several sheets in advance, or be baking one while you are preparing another.

For about 45 wafers 3 inches in diameter

1) *The cookie batter*

3 or 4 baking sheets about 12 by 16 inches
1 to 2 Tb soft butter for the baking sheets
3½ Tb soft butter in a 2- to 3-quart mixing bowl
½ cup sugar
An electric mixer
¼ cup egg whites (about 2 egg whites)

Preheat oven to 425 degrees, and set rack in middle level. Prepare baking sheets by smearing each with about 1 tsp of soft butter. Beat the rest of the butter and the sugar together until soft and fluffy; add the egg whites, and beat a few seconds, only just enough to blend.

5 Tb plain cake flour in a sieve or sifter (measure by scooping measuring spoon into flour and leveling off with a knife)
A rubber spatula
⅓ cup ground blanched almonds (grind them in an electric blender)
¼ tsp almond extract
½ tsp vanilla extract

Sieve or sift the flour over the batter, folding it in with a rubber spatula. Fold in the ground almonds, almond extract, and vanilla.

½ cup sliced, shaved, or slivered almonds (either blanched or with skin left on)

Using rubber spatula to dislodge batter, drop ½-teaspoon gobs onto one of the buttered baking sheets, spacing them 3 inches apart. With back of spoon, smear out each blob into a circle 2½ inches in diameter; batter will be so thin you can see baking sheet through it. Top each circle with a pinch of sliced, shaved, or slivered almonds.

2) *Baking and shaping—oven has been preheated to 425 degrees*

A flexible-blade spatula (blade should be at least 8 inches long)	Place in middle level of preheated oven, and set timer for 4 minutes. (Meanwhile, make sure rolling pins are ready; then start forming batter on another baking sheet.) Wafers are done when a $\frac{1}{8}$-inch border around circumference has browned lightly. Set baking sheet on open oven door so that cookies will keep warm and pliable.
2 bottles or rolling pins braced to lie still	
A cake rack	
A kitchen timer	

Working rapidly, slide long side of spatula blade under one cookie to scrape and lift it off the baking sheet, and place right side up on rolling pin or bottle. Quickly continue with the rest; the wafers crisp to shape so quickly that the first several may be removed to rack to make room for remaining wafers. (If last wafers have cooled too much for molding, return sheet to oven for several seconds to soften them.)

Close oven door and wait a few minutes for temperature to return to 425 degrees; bake and mold the rest of the wafers in the same manner.

(*) Wafers will stay crisp for several days in dry weather when stored airtight; otherwise, freeze them.

TWO RECIPES FOR
LEFTOVER PASTRY DOUGH

Two more good reasons for you to master French puff pastry are *couques* and *palmiers*—crisp, buttery, lightly caramelized cookies that you can make with the leftovers. Like some of the wonderful things you concoct with leftover braised beef, *les tous nus* and *choux farcis,* to give examples from another part of the menu, it is well worth making the original just to have the residue to play with.

THE DOUGH—PUFF PASTRY VERSUS PIE-CRUST DOUGH

Most cookies as well as many of the appetizer and entrée pastries are made with scraps of raw puff pastry left over from *bouchées, vol-au-vent, mille-feuilles,* or other recipes calling for fresh *pâte feuilletée.* These scraps need not be fully reconstituted into puff pastry again, as described on page 134: those for the *couques* should only be smooth enough to roll out and be cut fairly evenly, and those for the *palmiers* will reconstitute into smoothness as they are rolled in sugar, folded, and rolled and folded again before their final forming. You can convert butter pie-crust dough, *pâte brisée,* formulas 1 or 2, page

109 (or even packaged mixes), into a reasonable substitute for puff pastry by rolling and folding with softened butter, as described in the same recipe for reconstituting puff pastry.

COUQUES
[Tongue-shaped Caramelized Cookies Made from Puff Pastry Dough]

These were made famous in the 1920's by Le Café de Paris, on the Avenue de l'Opéra. Whenever you ordered ice cream, long *couques* on embroidered napery accompanied each serving, and they soon became the most fashionable cookies in Paris. *Couque* comes from the Flemish *koek,* whose diminutive, *koekje,* produced our "cookie." We shall not give proportions because they are not necessary, but a circle of dough 3 inches in diameter and ½ inch thick will produce 6 to 8 *couques* 6 to 7 inches long.

---

1) *Forming the cookies*

Chilled leftover French puff pastry, *pâte feuilletée* (pages 134–5)
An oval fluted cutter 3 to 3½ inches long (or a 2-inch round cutter, preferably fluted)

Preheat oven to 450 degrees in time for Step 2, and set rack in upper-middle level. Roll pastry out about ⅛ inch thick, and cut into ovals (or rounds). Reform leftovers, roll out again, and cut.

Sugar (ordinary granulated sugar)

Spread an oval-shaped layer of sugar ⅛ inch thick on your rolling surface. Lay a pastry cutout on the

A flexible-blade spatula
A clean dry baking sheet
A rack or racks

sugar and roll it out into a tongue shape 6 to 7 inches long and about $\frac{1}{16}$ inch thick; you will be encrusting sugar into the bottom of the pastry as you roll. Turn it upside down, sprinkle on more sugar, and set on baking sheet. Continue with the rest of the cutouts. (Although you can bake the cookies now, they usually cook more evenly if you cover with plastic wrap and chill them for half an hour at least; this relaxes the dough and prevents it from shrinking or pulling out of shape during baking.)

----

2) *Baking—oven has been preheated to 450 degrees*

Bake in upper-middle level of preheated oven for 7 to 8 minutes, until sugar coating has caramelized lightly; if some cookies are done before others, remove them to rack because they burn easily. Cookies crisp as they cool.

(*) *Couques* will stay crisp for several days in dry weather when stored airtight; otherwise keep them in a warming oven or freeze them.

PALMIERS

[Palm-leaf Caramelized Sugar Cookies Made from Puff Pastry Dough]

This most popular of all puff-pastry cookies is often a disappointment when store-bought, even in France, but always delicious when you make it yourself from your own homemade buttery puff pastry. Thus if you have not been impressed with them before, try making your own; you will find them handsome to look at, wonderfully crisp, and you may make them very large as well as rather small. Size depends on the thickness of the pastry and the width of the rectangle you roll it into. You will work out your own system if you become an addicted *pâtissier* of *palmiers,* with your own palm-leaf patterns and special *tours de main;* we suggest only the basic techniques here. Again, we shall not give proportions, but a piece of pastry dough 5½ by 2 by 1½ inches will produce 2 dozen 3-inch *palmiers.*

1) *Forming the cookies*

Chilled leftover French puff pastry, *pâte feuilletée* (pages 134–5)
Sugar (ordinary granulated sugar)
A flexible-blade spatula
A clean dry baking sheet (you will probably need 2 sheets at least)
A rack or racks

Spread a layer of sugar ⅛ inch thick on your rolling surface. Sprinkling dough with more sugar as you roll, extend it into a rectangle about ³⁄₁₆ inch thick. Fold bottom up to middle, and top down to cover it, as though folding a business letter. (Illustrations are in Puff Pastry, page 116.)

Turn pastry so top flap of dough is to your right, roll again in sugar to make a rectangle ⅜ inch thick, and fold again in three. (If pastry has softened and become difficult to handle, or if it has stiffened and become balky, refrigerate for 30 minutes to an hour, then continue.) Roll the dough out 8 inches long (for 3-inch *palmiers*), then give it a quarter turn so the 8-inch length is facing you. Extend it out in front of you now with your rolling pin, keeping the dough 8 inches wide, and rolling it to whatever length it will go to make a square or rectangle ¼ inch thick. Trim off rough edges.

Fold sides so they almost touch at the center, as shown. Sprinkle top of dough with sugar and encrust it into the pastry with your rolling pin, at the same time pressing the top and bottom layers of dough together with pin.

8″

Fold pastry in two, as though closing a book. Press with your rolling pin, to hold the 4 layers more closely together.

With a sharp knife, cut dough into crosswise pieces ⅜ inch thick.

cut →

Depending on what effect you wish, either bend the 2 ends up at right angles; or roll them halfway up the outside; or roll them up inside, so that they form two connecting swirls. Place on pastry sheet, each *palmier* 3 inches from neighbor in every direction—they will spread out to more than double in the oven.

Cover and chill 30 minutes at least; dough must relax or the *palmier* designs will lose their shape during baking. Preheat oven to 450 degrees, and set rack in upper-middle level in time for next step.

2) *Baking—oven has been preheated to 450 degrees*

(Bake one sheet at a time.) Set in upper-middle level of preheated oven and bake for about 6 minutes, until when you lift a cookie with your spatula, the bottom has begun to caramelize. Remove from oven, close oven door, and rapidly turn the cookies over. Sprinkle tops of each with a dusting of sugar, and return to oven for 3 to 4 minutes more, or until sugar topping has caramelized nicely—but keep an eye on them, because they burn quickly. Remove one by one to a rack, where the *palmiers* will crisp as they cool.

NOTE: The baking will take a little experimenting on your part, and timing will differ if cookies are thinner one time, thicker another. Your object is to have the pastry cook through, making a crisp, attractively shaped cookie with a caramel sheen.

(*) *Palmiers* will stay crisp for several days in dry weather when stored airtight; otherwise keep them in a warming oven or freeze them.

EIGHT FRENCH CAKES

PAIN D'ÉPICES
[Spice Cake—Spice Bread—Honey Bread]

Pain d'épices is the French equivalent of gingerbread, but is made with honey, rye flour, and mixed spices rather than from molasses, white flour, and ginger. Every country in the Old World seems to have a honey bread, and each region in France has its own special formula. Dijon, for instance, cures the flour and honey mixture for several months in wooden tubs before the final blending and baking. Montbard stores the baked breads for a month before serving, and Rheims mixes raw bread dough into the honey and rye. Some recipes call for glacéed fruits, some for brown sugar, eggs, white flour, or ground nuts. Potash was the original leavening agent, and bakers often add carbonate of ammonia for a lighter loaf; householders use bicarbonate of soda. Here is a delicious home recipe that is easy to make by hand, and even easier in a heavy-duty mixer with flat beater. Serve *pain d'épices* with butter for breakfast or tea.

A NOTE ON THE RYE FLOUR

The rye flour called for here is ordinary supermarket rye flour for general bread making. If you happen to have the so-called rye meal, which is heavier and coarser, use half rye meal and half regular all-purpose white flour; otherwise your *pain d'épices* will not rise properly.

For about 5 cups of dough, to bake in one
8-cup bread pan or two 4-cup pans

1) *The batter*

1¼ cups (1 lb.) honey
1 cup sugar
¾ cup boiling water
A 3- to 4-quart mixing bowl, or the bowl of a heavy-duty electric mixer
¼ tsp salt
1 Tb bicarbonate of soda
3½ to 4 cups (about 1 lb.) rye flour measured by scooping dry-measure cups into flour and sweeping off excess (see note on rye flour preceding Step 1)

Preheat oven to 325 degrees. Either with a large wooden spoon or in a heavy-duty mixer with flat beater, blend the honey, sugar, and boiling water until sugar has dissolved. Stir in the salt, soda, and 3 cups of the flour. Beat in as much of the fourth cup of flour as will go in, to make a heavy, sticky dough but one you can still manipulate. Beat thoroughly and vigorously (4 to 5 minutes of beating, if you are using a mixer, will improve texture).

3 ounces (about ⅔ cup) ground blanched almonds (pulverize them in an electric blender)

1 tsp almond extract

¼ cup dark rum

4 tsp ground anise seed (pulverize in an electric blender)

½ tsp ground cinnamon

½ tsp ground cloves

½ tsp ground mace

1 cup (8 ounces) glacéed fruit rinsed in boiling water, drained, and cut into ⅛-inch pieces (orange peel, lemon peel, and citron; or "fruit cake" mix)

Then add the rest of the ingredients listed. (If you are using a mixer, let the machine run at slow speed while the additions go in.)

---

2) *Baking and storing—baking time 1 to 1¼ hours*

An 8-cup bread pan or two 4- to 5-cup pans, heavily buttered and bottom lined with buttered waxed paper

Turn the mixture into the pan or pans. Dip your fingers in cold water, and smooth top of batter. Pans should be ½ to ⅔ filled. Bake in middle level of preheated 325-degree oven. Batter will rise to fill pan and top will probably crack slightly; it is best not to open oven door for 45 minutes or to touch anything, for fear of releasing the soda-engendered gases that are pushing the batter up. Four- to 5-cup pans will take 50 to 60 minutes; the 8-cup pan, about 1¼ hours. The spice bread is done when a skewer plunged to bottom of pan comes out clean, and when bread begins to show faint lines of shrinkage from edges of pan.

Let cool in pan for 10 to 15 minutes, then unmold on a rack. Immediately peel paper off bottom and gently turn the bread puffed-side up. When cold, in about 2 hours, wrap airtight in plastic. *Pain d'épices* improves in flavor when aged, so do not serve it for at least a day; a wait of several days is actually preferable. It will keep for several weeks under refrigeration, or may be frozen for several months.

LE QUATRE QUARTS
[Pound Cake—Yellow Butter Cake]

The French name for this cake, *Le Quatre Quarts,* or "Four Quarters," comes from its original proportions, which are *un quart de livre,* a quarter pound each, of its four ingredients—eggs, sugar, flour, and butter. The English like the formula so much that they use a pound of everything—hence, of course, pound cake. Of the several methods for making pound cake, we find by far the best one results from beating the eggs and sugar in an electric mixer until they double in volume and have enough body so that they keep that volume when the flour is rapidly blended in, followed by the softly creamed butter; the batter should look like a rich mayonnaise as you turn it into the pan. Besides beating the eggs, which presents no problem when you do it electrically, your other important object is to cream the butter so that it is soft enough to mix easily and rapidly into the batter without deflating it, yet has enough body so that it remains in suspension throughout the mixture rather than sinking to the bottom of the pan like melted butter.

For a 4-cup pan, such as the standard,
round, 8 by 1½-inch American pan

---

1) *Preliminaries*

A 4-cup cake pan, buttered and floured
6 ounces (1½ sticks) butter
A small saucepan or bowl
A wire whip

Preheat oven to 350 degrees and set rack in middle level. Prepare the cake pan. Either beat room-temperature butter into a smooth cream, or cut chilled butter into ½-inch slices and beat over low heat until it begins to soften and continue beating until it is a mayonnaise-like cream. It it softens too much, beat over a bowl filled with ice and water. Butter must be like a heavy mayonnaise. Set aside.

---

2) *The cake batter*

3 "large" eggs (⅔ cup)
1 cup sugar
The grated rind of 1 lemon or orange
An electric mixer and large (3-quart) bowl

Blend the eggs and sugar with the lemon or orange peel for a minute at low speed to mix, then increase speed to high and beat for 4 to 5 minutes or more, until mixture is pale, fluffy, doubled in volume, and looks like whipped cream. If you are using a mixer on a stand, measure the flour while the eggs are beating.

1¼ cups (6 ounces) cake flour (measure by scooping dry-measure cup into flour and sweeping off excess with a knife)
A sieve or sifter set on waxed paper

Measure out the flour and sieve or sift onto the paper. Beat the eggs and sugar again for a moment if they have lost their body or volume. Turn speed to low and gradually sprinkle in the flour as you mix. Do this rapidly, and do not try for a perfect blending at this point; the operation should not take more than 15 to 20 seconds (for a mixer on a stand—longer for a hand-held model).

| The creamy mayonnaise-like butter | Still at low speed, and using 1 spatula to remove the butter from its bowl, and a second to dislodge it from the first, rapidly incorporate the butter into the egg mixture, taking no more than 15 to 20 seconds (with a mixer on a stand), and, again, not trying for a perfect blend. |
| 2 rubber spatulas | |

Remove bowl from stand, if you have that kind of mixer, and rapidly cut down through batter and out to side with rubber spatula, rotating bowl and repeating the movement 2 or 3 times to complete the blending. Turn batter into prepared pan; run it up to rim all around with spatula, and bang pan lightly on table to deflate any bubbles.

3) *Baking—about 40 minutes at 350 degrees*

Immediately set pan in middle level of preheated oven and bake for about 40 minutes, until a skewer or toothpick plunged down into top center of cake comes out clean. Cake will have risen slightly over top of pan, top will have browned nicely, and cake will feel lightly springy when pressed. Cool 10 minutes in pan, then unmold onto a rack; if you wish to serve it plain, immediately reverse it onto another rack so its puffed side will be uppermost.

4) *Serving*

The *Quatre Quarts* may be served as is, sprinkled with powdered sugar. Or fill and ice it with anything you wish. Here is a quick and simple filling.

Crème au Citron or Crème à l'Orange

[Lemon- or Orange-cream Filling]

For about 1 cup, enough for an 8- to 9-inch cake

1 cup confectioner's sugar	Beat all ingredients together over moderately high heat until mixture thickens and comes to the boil. Continue beating over low heat for 2 minutes until starch cooks and cream looks translucent.
1 Tb lemon juice or concentrated frozen orange juice	
The grated rind of one lemon or orange	
1 Tb hot water	
1 egg	
2 Tb butter	
1 Tb cornstarch	
A small saucepan and a wire whip	

3 to 6 Tb unsalted butter **Pinch of salt**	Remove from heat and beat in butter, as much as you wish up to 6 tablespoons. Salt very lightly, to taste. Filling will thicken as it cools. May be refrigerated for several days, or frozen for several months.

Split cake in half, and if you wish, sprinkle the inside of each half with drops of rum or of orange liqueur. Spread filling on bottom half and re-form the cake. You may paint the cake with warm apricot glaze and brush chopped nuts around the circumference, or simply sprinkle the top with confectioner's sugar.

LE CAKE

[Rich Yellow Loaf Cake with Rum, Raisins, and Cherries]

A French *cake* is always baked in a *moule à cake*—meaning a loaf pan— and a French *cake* always has fruits in it. It is not at all a fruit cake in the American sense of solid fruit held together with batter; it is, rather, a slightly modified pound-cake formula flavored with rum and raisins, and baked with a layer of glacéed cherries in the center. Serve it with tea or with fruit desserts; it keeps well for several days under refrigeration, or it may be frozen.

A NOTE ON FRUITS FALLING
TO BOTTOM OF CAKES DURING BAKING

We struggled for years trying to devise some system to prevent fruits from sinking to the bottom of the cake during baking. Finally we realized that we were using cake flour and our batter was too light; the French recipe calls for *farine*, regular French household flour. As soon as we switched to a combination of 4 parts all-purpose flour and 1 part cake flour, our troubles were over. To make doubly sure, we also suggest dusting the fruits with a combination of flour and baking powder.

For a 6-cup loaf pan, approximately 10 inches long and 3½ inches deep

---

1) *Preliminaries*

A 6-cup loaf pan, bottom lined with waxed paper, interior of pan buttered and floured **6 ounces (1½ sticks) butter in a small saucepan or bowl** **A wire whip**	Preheat oven to 350 degrees and set rack in middle level. Prepare the cake pan. Cream the butter (over heat if necessary, then over cold water) to a smooth mayonnaise-like consistency. Wash cherries in very hot water to remove preservatives, dry on paper towels, and cut each in half. Measure out the 2 flours, and blend together in bowl with spatula. Mix the baking powder and a tablespoon of the flour on waxed

⅔ cup (4 ounces, or about 30) glacéed cherries on a plate

1 cup all-purpose flour and ¼ cup cake flour in a bowl (measure by scooping dry-measure cups into flour and sweeping off excess with a knife)

A rubber spatula

1 tsp double-action baking powder

⅔ cup (4 ounces) currants (small, black, seedless raisins) on a plate

A square of waxed paper

A fine-meshed sieve

paper, then sprinkle over the raisins, tossing and stirring to coat them. Because raisins and cherries are to remain separate, turn raisins into sieve placed over cherries and shake off the baking powder and flour onto cherries. Return raisins to their plate, coat cherries with mixture, and sieve cherries over the bowl of flour; return cherries to their plate.

2) *The cake batter*

2 "large" eggs
2 egg yolks
1 cup sugar
¼ cup dark Jamaican rum
An electric mixer, and large bowl on stand, or 3- to 4-quart mixing bowl

Beat the eggs, yolks, sugar, and rum at moderate speed to blend, then increase to high speed and beat 5 to 6 minutes or more, until mixture is thick, pale yellow, creamy, and the consistency of lightly whipped cream. You must beat long enough for it to thicken this way, or the batter will be too light to support the fruit.

The bowl of mixed flours
The waxed paper

Turn flour out onto waxed paper. At slow mixing speed, gradually sprinkle the flour into the egg mixture, taking 15 to 20 seconds but not trying for a perfect blend at this point; eggs must not be deflated by over-mixing.

The creamy mayonnaise-like butter
2 rubber spatulas

Still at low speed, and using 1 spatula to remove the butter from its bowl and a second to dislodge it from the first, rapidly incorporate the butter into the egg mixture, taking no more than 15 to 20 seconds and, again, not trying for a perfect blend.

The floured raisins

Remove bowl from stand, if using that kind of mixer. Rapidly fold raisins into batter with a rubber spatula, as you complete the blending.

The prepared cake pan
The floured cherries

Turn half of the batter immediately into the pan. Rapidly spread the cherries on top, and cover with the rest of the batter, running it up to rim of pan on all sides with rubber spatula. Pan will be ⅔ to ¾ full. Immediately proceed to the baking.

3) *Baking—about 1 hour at 350 degrees*

Set in the middle level of the preheated oven and bake for about an hour. Cake is done when it has risen to fill the pan, is lightly browned, and a skewer plunged through the cake comes out clean. The top will crack, which is normal, and there will be very slight lines of shrinkage from pan in several areas. Let cake cool in pan for 10 minutes, then run a sharp, thin knife between sides of pan and cake; unmold onto a rack. Immediately peel paper off cake if it has adhered, and turn cake right-side up.

4) *Serving and storing*

Serve as is with tea or with fresh fruit desserts, slicing cake crosswise like a loaf of bread. To store, wrap airtight and refrigerate or freeze, but bring to room temperature before serving for best flavor and texture.

LE GÉNOISE ÉLECTRIQUE
[Light, Yellow, Whole-egg Cake, for
Layered Cakes and *Petits Fours*]

Génoise is one of the basic French cakes used for *petits fours* and fancy filled cakes. The classic method is to beat whole eggs and sugar over hot water until the mixture is warm and thick, then to beat it at room temperature until it is cool and even thicker. An electric mixer will accomplish almost the same thickness of batter, and works perfectly well when you are adding only a small amount of butter, as in the following recipe. Typical of the best French cakes, there is no baking powder here, meaning that you must fold the flour and butter into the cake batter with such speed and delicacy that you do not deflate it, and the cake will rise as it should in the oven. Typically again, this is a low-lying cake of 1½ inches that is usually split in half for filling and frosting. If you like a high layered cake, make two of them for 4 layers. Use any shape of pan you wish; a square or rectangular pan is easiest for *petits fours*.

For a 4-cup pan, such as a round one 8 by 1½ inches

---

1) *The cake batter*

4 Tb (½ stick) butter in a small saucepan
An 8- by 1½-inch round cake pan, bottom lined with waxed paper, interior of pan buttered and floured

Preheat oven to 350 degrees and set rack in middle level. Melt butter and set aside. Prepare cake pan; measure flour and sift or sieve onto waxed paper.

⅔ cup cake flour (measure
  by scooping dry-measure
  cups into flour and
  sweeping off excess with
  a knife)
A sieve or sifter
A 12-inch square of waxed
  paper

---

3 "large" eggs (⅔ cup)   Beat eggs, sugar, vanilla, lemon rind, and salt for 5
½ cup sugar   to 10 minutes or more, depending on efficiency of
1½ tsp vanilla extract   mixer, until very thick, pale yellow, and mixture
The grated rind of 1 lemon   forms a definite and slowly dissolving ribbon when a
A pinch of salt   bit is lifted and falls back on surface.
An electric mixer with
  large (3- to 3½-quart)
  bowl
A rubber spatula

Then remove bowl from stand, if you have that kind of mixer, and with one hand, sift on ¼ of the flour and rapidly cut down through batter and out to side with rubber spatula, rotating bowl and repeating the movement quickly 6 to 8 times, until flour is almost incorporated. Sprinkle on half the remaining flour, and when almost incorporated, fold in ⅓ of the tepid melted butter; continue alternating butter and flour until all (except milky residue at bottom of butter pan) is incorporated. Do not overmix: batter must retain its original volume.

Immediately turn batter into prepared pan, running it up to the edge all around with spatula. Bang lightly on table, and place at once in preheated oven.

2) *Baking and cooling—baking time 25 to 30 minutes at 350 degrees*

Bake for 25 to 30 minutes. Cake is done when top is spongy if pressed, and when cake shows a hairline of shrinkage from pan at one or two places around the edge.

When done, remove cake from oven and let cool 10 minutes in pan. Then reverse onto a rack, and in a few minutes the cake will drop out of the pan. Peel paper off bottom of cake if it has adhered.

When cool, in 1½ to 2 hours, fill and ice any way that you wish; suggestions follow. If you are not going to fill and ice the cake when cool, wrap airtight (it dries out easily), and refrigerate for several days, or freeze for several months.

3) *Filling and frosting suggestions*

Fill and frost the *génoise* in any manner you wish; besides the Mocha butter cream and chocolate fondant suggested here, see the list of possibilities on pages 508–9.

Crème au Beurre à la Meringue Italienne

[Meringue Butter-cream Filling and Frosting]

For about 2½ cups

½ the recipe for *meringue italienne* (sugar syrup whipped into beaten egg whites), Step 1, page 426

An electric mixer

8 to 10 ounces (2 to 2½ sticks) unsalted butter in a bowl

2 Tb rum or kirsch

1 Tb instant coffee dissolved in 2 Tb boiling water, and cooled

When the meringue mixture has been beaten until cool with the electric mixer, it is ready to receive the butter. Cut up butter, if cold, and beat over heat for a moment until it starts to melt; continue beating with electric mixer or wooden spoon until butter is soft and fluffy. (If by chance you have heated butter too much, beat over cold water to reconstitute it.)

By dollops, beat the equivalent of 2 sticks of the butter into the meringue, then beat in the rum or kirsch and droplets of coffee until butter cream is a light coffee color. If butter cream turns grainy after addition of liquids, beat in more of the butter by spoonfuls to smooth it out again. Cover and chill, until of easy spreading consistency.

(*) Butter cream may be frozen; when thawed, beat in more softened butter to smooth it, along with a little more liqueur if you feel it necessary.

Frosting the cake

The cool *génoise* cake

A long, sharp thin knife for splitting the cake

A cake rack set over a pizza tray or baking sheet

2 Tb rum or kirsch

The chilled butter cream (beaten to a smooth consistency)

A flexible-blade spatula

A quart measure of hot water

(Illustrated directions for splitting, filling, and frosting cakes are in Volume I, pages 673–5.) Cake is to be frosted upside down, meaning that the part that was at the bottom of the pan is considered to be the top of the cake; this is because sides must slant slightly outward for fondant to cover them easily, later. Cut a tiny wedge up side of cake to guide you in re-forming it. Slice cake in half, making 2 layers; turn them cut-side up and sprinkle with rum or kirsch.

Spread about ⅓ the butter cream on bottom layer of cake, and replace top layer, lining it up with wedge. Being sure butter cream is smooth, spread all but ½ cup over top and sides of cake. Even frosting with spatula dipped in hot water, making sides as smooth as possible; retain or even exaggerate their outward slant toward bottom of cake. Set in freezer or refrigerate for about half an hour, until frosting is well set. (Smooth again with spatula dipped in hot water if necessary.)

3 cups chocolate-flavored fondant, page 507

A flexible-blade spatula

The reserved ½ cup of butter cream, chilled

A paper decorating cone, page 509

When frosting has set, and with cake on its rack set over a tray to catch drippings, heat fondant just enough for it to be liquefied and of easy pouring consistency. Pour all of it at once over the top of the cake, rapidly spreading it, if necessary, with spatula so that it falls evenly over the sides. It sets very quickly, and can be touched only when liquid.

When set, in a few minutes, pack chilled but smooth and malleable butter cream into paper cone and squeeze out whatever decorative motif your creative spirit suggests to you.

Store cake in refrigerator, but remove to room temperature for 20 to 30 minutes before serving so that fondant will regain its bloom.

GÂTEAU AUX NOIX—LE SAINT-ANDRÉ
[Walnut Cake]

The *Saint-André* is a delicious walnut-filled creation that can be either a dessert or a cake. If you are not shelling your own top-quality walnuts, use the vacuum-packed nut meats that come in cans to be sure of freshness.

For an 9- by 1½-inch cake

1) Preliminaries—preheat oven to 350 degrees

A 6-cup cake pan (9 by 1½ inches if round), bottom lined with waxed paper, pan buttered and floured

4 ounces (1 cup) walnut meats, either whole or chopped

3 Tb sugar

An electric blender

A sheet of waxed paper

⅓ cup all-purpose flour (measure by dipping dry-measure cup into flour and leveling off with knife)

Prepare cake pan. Grind half the nuts with half the sugar in the blender, turn out onto the waxed paper; grind the rest of the nuts and sugar, and add to the first half. Sieve the flour over the nuts and mix well with rubber spatula, smoothing out any lumps in the mixture. Soften the butter in the bowl and beat to a creamy mayonnaise-like consistency. Set aside.

A sieve
A rubber spatula
4 Tb soft butter in a
  1-quart bowl
A wooden spoon

_____

2) *The cake batter*

½ cup sugar
3 "large" eggs
An electric mixer and 3-
  to 4-quart bowl
2 Tb kirsch
Pinch of salt
The softened butter
A rubber spatula
The ground walnuts
The prepared cake pan

Beat the sugar and eggs with the kirsch and salt for a moment at low speed to blend, then increase speed to high and beat several minutes (7 to 8 with a hand-held machine) until mixture is pale, fluffy, doubled in volume, and holds in soft peaks. Remove bowl from stand. Scoop a 2-spoonful dollop of egg mixture into the softened butter and mix with rubber spatula; set aside. Sprinkle ⅓ of the ground nuts over the egg mixture and delicately fold them in with a rubber spatula, being careful to deflate the eggs as little as possible. When almost incorporated, add the same amount again, fold, and sprinkle on the remainder. When that is almost incorporated, add the creamy butter and rapidly fold in. Turn batter into cake pan, which will be about ⅔ filled. Tilt pan to run batter up to rim all around, bang lightly on table, and set immediately in middle level of preheated 350-degree oven.

_____

3) *Baking—about 30 minutes at 350 degrees*

In about 20 minutes the cake will have risen to the top of the pan; in another 10 minutes it will have sunk slightly, and will show a very faint line of shrinkage at points around edge of pan, indicating that the cake is done. Remove from oven, and let cool 10 minutes. Run a knife around cake, and reverse onto a rack; in 5 minutes or so, cake will drop out of pan. Peel paper off bottom of cake in a few minutes, when it has loosened.

(*) When cold, wrap airtight and refrigerate or freeze.

_____

TO SERVE AS A DESSERT

_____

2 cups *crème Chantilly*
  (lightly whipped cream
  flavored with vanilla or
  liqueur, and sweetened
  with confectioner's sugar,
  page 450)

Transfer cake to a serving dish, spread *crème Chantilly* over it, reserving some to pass in a bowl. Decorate top of cake with walnuts or chocolate. Pass chocolate sauce separately.

Either chopped walnuts or
   caramelized walnuts,
   page 423;
Or grated or shaved
   chocolate and the
   chocolate sauce on page
   431

TO SERVE AS A CAKE

Le Saint-André aux Abricots

[Walnut Cake with Apricot Filling, Glazed with Fondant]

This is very attractive. The cake is split and filled with apricots, re-formed and glazed with apricot; caramelized walnut brittle, *pralin aux noix,* is brushed against the sides; white fondant is spread over the top with incrustations of caramelized walnuts.

For the 9- by 1½-inch walnut cake, page 490, serving 6 to 8

½ package (½ Tb) un-
   flavored powdered gelatin
   softened in a small
   saucepan with 2 Tb
   kirsch
The 1½ cups apricot
   filling, page 507

Heat softened gelatin mixture until gelatin has completely dissolved, then stir into apricot filling. Cut a tiny wedge in side of cake, then slice in half, making 2 layers. When apricot filling is cold and has set enough for spreading, spoon it over bottom layer of cake; replace top layer, lining it up with wedge.

⅔ cup apricot jam
   (preserves) forced
   through a sieve into a
   small saucepan
2 Tb sugar
A wooden spoon
About 1 cup walnut brittle,
   page 423, or chopped
   walnut meats

Bring strained apricot jam and sugar to the boil, stirring, for several minutes until last drops to fall from spoon are sticky. Paint top and sides of cake with the glaze. When glaze has set slightly, brush brittle or chopped walnuts against sides of cake all around. (This technique is illustrated on page 503.)

About ½ cup kirsch-
   flavored white fondant,
   page 505
About 1 dozen caramelized
   walnut halves (more if
   you wish), page 423

Heat fondant over hot water until smooth and of spreading consistency; rapidly spread as even a layer as possible over top of cake. While fondant is still quite soft, press the walnuts into it, arranging them around the edge of the cake or in any manner you wish. (If fondant on top of cake has hardened, melt a little more and brush on bottom of walnuts as you stick them on the cake.)

(*) Cake will keep several days when covered air-tight in the refrigerator, or it may be frozen for several weeks, at least.

LA CHARLOTTE AFRICAINE
[Chocolate Dessert or Layer-cake Made from Leftover Cake]

When you find yourself with leftover wedding cake, pound cake, sponge cake, or even store-bought cake of a reasonably homemade quality, use it again to make another cake. Pound cake is particularly good for this; if you have sponge cake, you may wish to enrich the mixture with a little butter. This recipe is easy to make with the electric mixer when you follow the sequences outlined here. The cake is baked in a dish or pan 4 to 5 inches deep, like a French charlotte mold; treat it as a dessert with whipped cream and chocolate sauce, or as a cake with filling and icing.

For a 6-inch cake 3 to 4 inches high, serving 8 to 10

---

1) *The cake batter*

The cake pan: a 2-quart charlotte mold or cylindrical baking dish 4 to 5 inches deep
½ Tb soft butter
A round of waxed paper
2 Tb flour
8 ounces semisweet baking chocolate
A 2-quart saucepan
¾ cup milk
A wooden spoon
8 ounces pound cake, wedding cake, sponge cake, ladyfingers, or other leftover white or yellow cake (about 2½ cups moderately pressed down)

Preheat oven to 350 degrees for Step 2. Prepare cake pan by smearing butter inside, fitting round of paper in bottom, buttering that, rolling flour around interior and knocking out excess. Break chocolate into saucepan, add the milk, and stir with a wooden spoon over moderate heat until chocolate is melted and smooth. Remove any icing or filling from leftover cake, and shred cake into crumbs; stir into the chocolate mixture.

An electric mixer with small bowl
4 egg whites at room temperature
Pinch of salt

Being sure beaters and bowl are clean and dry, beat egg whites at moderate speed until foamy; beat in salt and cream of tartar. Gradually increase speed to fast, beating until soft peaks are formed. A tablespoon at a time, and beating 30 seconds between spoonfuls,

¼ tsp cream of tartar
3 Tb sugar

beat in the sugar, and continue beating at high speed until stiff peaks are formed. Proceed immediately to next paragraph.

The mixer with large bowl
4 egg yolks
½ cup sugar
2 Tb dark rum or orange liqueur
The tepid chocolate mixture from first paragraph
Optional: 3 to 4 Tb soft butter

With the same electric mixer blades but in a different bowl, proceed at once to the egg yolks. Gradually beat the sugar into the yolks and continue beating until mixture is thick and pale yellow, and a bit lifted in the beaters falls back on the surface in a slowly dissolving ribbon. Beat in the rum or liqueur and the chocolate mixture, continuing for 30 seconds or so to make sure the batter is smooth and free of lumps. Beat in optional butter if you are using sponge cake or ladyfingers, and proceed immediately to next paragraph.

A rubber spatula
The beaten egg whites
The prepared cake pan

With spatula, stir ¼ of the egg whites into the batter to lighten it; scoop the rest of the egg whites on top and delicately fold in. Turn batter into prepared pan, tilt pan in all directions to run batter up to rim all around. (Pan will be ⅔ to ¾ filled.) Set at once in middle level of preheated oven.

---

2) *Baking—oven has been preheated to 350 degrees*

Bake for about an hour. Cake is done when it has risen almost to rim of pan; the top will crack, and a cake tester or skewer plunged down through a crack in the center will come out dry, with a few crumbs but no liquid adhering. Let cake cool for 20 minutes. To unmold, run a thin flexible knife around cake; turn a serving plate upside down over pan, reverse the two, and give a sharp downward jerk to unmold cake onto plate.

(*) AHEAD-OF-TIME NOTE: If you are not serving or icing immediately, let cake cool; wipe out cake pan and reverse over cake, then slip it into a plastic bag and refrigerate. Cake will keep 3 or 4 days, or may be frozen for a month or more.

To serve as a dessert

Slice into 2 or 3 layers, fill and ice with *crème Chantilly* (lightly beaten and sweetened cream), page 450, or the *Chantilly meringuée,* page 430, and pass chocolate sauce separately.

To serve as a cake

Slice into 2 or 3 layers, and follow any of the suggestions on pages 508–9, such as butter-cream filling with chocolate icing.

LE GLORIEUX

[A Very Rich, Very Light Chocolate Cake]

This dark and delicious cousin of the *Quatre Quarts* is made with cornstarch instead of flour, but again the secret of a full, light cake lies in how rapidly and delicately you fold the starch and finally the chocolate and butter into the egg mixture. Here we have suggested a two-layer cake: the batter is divided and cooked in two pans; one still-warm cake goes upon the other with chocolate filling in between. You may frost the cake with more chocolate, with white meringue icing, or, if it is a dessert, with whipped cream.

For two 4-cup pans or one 8-cup pan, serving 12 to 16

1) *Preliminaries*

7 ounces semisweet baking chocolate
2 ounces unsweetened baking chocolate
¼ cup orange liqueur
The grated rind of 1 orange
2 four-cup cake pans (such as round ones 8 by 1½ inches), bottom lined with waxed paper, pans buttered and floured
2 sticks butter

Preheat oven to 350 degrees and place rack in middle level. Break up chocolate and melt with orange liqueur and orange rind over hot water (directions are on page 496); it must be perfectly smooth and creamy. Cut the butter into ¼-inch slices and beat piece by piece into the chocolate, again making sure mixture is perfectly smooth and creamy. (A hand-held electric mixer is useful here.) If consistency is too liquid—it should be like a heavy mayonnaise—beat over iced water. Set aside.

2) *The cake batter*

5 "large" eggs
1 cup sugar
1 tsp vanilla extract
An electric mixer and 3- to 4-quart bowl (be sure mixer blades and bowl are clean and dry)

Beat the eggs and sugar for a moment at low speed to blend, then increase speed to high, add vanilla, and beat several minutes (7 to 8 with a hand-held machine) until mixture is pale, fluffy, doubled in volume, and holds in soft peaks.

1 cup (4 ounces) cornstarch measured by scooping dry-measure cup into starch and leveling off
A sieve or sifter set over waxed paper

Just as you are ready to blend the various batter elements together, sift the cornstarch onto the paper, check on the chocolate-butter to be sure it is a smooth, thick cream, and give the eggs and sugar a few turns of the beater if they have lost their body.

The chocolate-butter
  mixture
A rubber spatula

At slow mixing speed, gradually sprinkle the cornstarch into the egg mixture, taking 15 to 20 seconds to incorporate it but not trying for a perfect blend; you must not deflate the beaten eggs. Remove bowl from stand, if you have that kind of mixer. Fold a large gob of egg mixture into chocolate-butter to lighten it. Then, a large gob at a time, start folding chocolate-butter into eggs, rapidly cutting down through batter and out to side with rubber spatula, rotating bowl, and repeating movement 2 or 3 times. When almost incorporated, add another gob, and continue until all is used. Immediately turn the batter into the prepared pans. Rapidly push batter up sides of pans all around, and bang lightly on table to deflate possible bubbles. Pans should be about ⅔ filled. Place at once in middle level of preheated oven, leaving at least 2 inches of space between pans as well as walls and door of oven.

3) Baking, filling, and frosting

Bake for 25 to 30 minutes. Cakes should remain slightly moist, in the French manner, and are done when a skewer or toothpick plunged into center comes out looking oily, with a few speckles of chocolate clinging to it. Cake will usually rise ¼ to ½ inch above rim of pans. Cool for 10 minutes. Top of cakes will crack and flake slightly, which is normal. Make the following filling while cakes are cooling.

---

the chocolate filling:

3 ounces semisweet baking
  chocolate
½ ounce unsweetened
  baking chocolate
3 Tb orange liqueur
4 to 5 Tb unsalted butter,
  cut into ¼-inch slices

Melt the chocolate in the liqueur over hot water. When perfectly smooth and creamy, beat in the butter piece by piece. If mixture is too soft for easy spreading, beat over iced water until the consistency of mayonnaise.

filling the cake:

A cake rack
A cookie sheet

When cakes have cooled for 10 minutes, run a knife around edge of one to loosen it from the pan and unmold onto cake rack. Peel off waxed paper.

Spread top with filling. Immediately unmold second cake onto one end of cookie sheet. Line up cake on sheet exactly with cake on rack, then slide the one upon the other. Peel paper off top of second cake. If sides are uneven, trim with a knife.

(*) AHEAD-OF-TIME NOTE: If not to be iced or served immediately, cover airtight as soon as cake is cool or it will dry out. Cake may be frozen at this point; thaw for several hours at room temperature.

4) *Frosting and serving*

WHIPPED CREAM. To serve the cake as a dessert or with tea, spread lightly whipped cream, sweetened and flavored with vanilla or orange liqueur, around and over the cake (*crème Chantilly,* page 450, or the *Chantilly meringuée,* page 430). Decorate with shaved or grated chocolate.

MERINGUE ICING. Or use the plain Italian meringue (hot sugar syrup whipped into stiffly beaten egg whites, page 426), or the meringue butter cream on page 489.

CHOCOLATE ICING. Or while the cake is still warm, spread on the same chocolate and butter mixture that you used for the filling, or use one of the chocolate butter creams listed in Volume I, pages 680–4.

---

* *LE SUCCÈS—LE PROGRÈS, LA DACQUOISE*

[Meringue-nut Layer Cake with Butter-cream Frosting and Filling]

This particularly delicious type of French cake rarely appears among American recipes, yet it is far easier to make than a layer cake, and infinitely more elegant. Light yet rich, every mouthful is a poem. This is the kind of pastry you will see in the very best French pastry shops, and it is one that you can duplicate or even improve upon because you need not skimp on ingredients or quality.

To describe the cake, it is layers of baked meringue mounted one upon the other, like a regular layer cake, with filling in between. The meringue layers, *fonds à Succès,* are composed of egg whites and sugar beaten in a machine like any meringue, but when it forms stiff peaks ground almonds are folded in. The meringue is then spread out in disk shapes, heart shapes like our illustrations, or whatever other shapes you wish, and baked, like all meringues, in a very slow oven. The taste and texture of this mixture is, of course, far more interesting than plain meringue and just as easy to make.

HISTORICAL AND PHILOLOGICAL NOTES

While the cooked disks of meringue are called *fonds,* meaning foundations or layers, and *fonds à Succès* when the cake is titled *Le Succès,* you will see the terms *fonds à Progrès, fonds parisiens, Dacquoise, broyage suisse,* and *gâteau japonais* in French recipe books and elsewhere. Some authorities consider the *Succès* as containing almonds, and the *Progrès* almonds and filberts (*noisettes,* hazelnuts), while the *Dacquoise* is either formula plus starch and butter; other recipes make no distinctions. *Broyage* obviously comes from *broyer,* to grind, and refers to the ground nuts in the meringue; *gâteau japonais* appears to be British for meringue-nut layer cake.

There are various opinions, also, on what should fill and what should frost a *Succès* versus a *Progrès* or a *Dacquoise.* Since no one agrees on anything, you are quite safe in doing whatever you wish. In addition to the frosting and filling in the following recipe, other suggestions are at the end of it, on page 504.

MANUFACTURING NOTE

An electric mixer, even the small hand-held type, makes both the meringue and the butter cream fast and simple to do. Form the meringue disks with a spatula if you have no large canvas pastry bag, but the bag usually makes neater shapes. No-stick baking sheets are especially recommended for meringues, or no-stick baking paper. If your baking sheets are not large enough to hold three 8-inch disks, make 4 smaller disks and a 4- rather than a 3-layer cake. (A discussion of beating egg whites is in the appendix, page 539, and illustrated directions for beating and folding egg whites are in Volume I, pages 159–61.) You will need toasted almonds and almond *pralin* (caramelized almonds), and do read the recipe through before you plan to make the cake so there will be no surprise ingredients or timings.

A NOTE ON NUTS—FILBERTS

You may use either ground blanched almonds or half and half ground almonds and ground filberts (hazelnuts, *noisettes*) in the following recipe. Filberts are not as easily available here as in France, and the ready-shelled packaged nuts turn rancid rapidly; shelled or ground filberts should be stored in the freezer, as should ground almonds.

To prepare shelled filberts for cooking, first eat a few to be sure they are fresh and fine, then spread the nuts on a baking sheet and dry them out in a 350-degree oven for about 15 minutes, until skins begin to flake off and nut flesh has browned very lightly. Remove from oven, rub nuts a small handful at a time between paper towels to remove as much skin as will easily come off. Grind the nuts by ½-cup batches in an electric blender.

If you use half ground filberts and half ground blanched almonds rather than almonds alone for the meringues in the following recipe, call your cake *Le Progrès* rather than *Le Succès.*

For an 8-inch cake, serving 8 to 10

---

1) *Preliminaries*

1 to 2 Tb soft butter

2 large baking sheets 14 by
   16 inches (no-stick if
   possible)

¼ cup flour

A marker, such as an 8-inch
   round pot lid, a cake pan,
   a heart, or whatever shape
   you wish your cake to be

A rubber spatula

6 ounces (1½ cups loosely
   packed) ground blanched
   almonds (may be ground
   in an electric blender)

1 cup sugar (extra-fine
   granulated or "instant"
   recommended)

A double thickness of
   waxed paper about
   10 by 12 inches

1 level Tb plus 1½ level
   tsp unsifted cornstarch

A fine-meshed sieve

A canvas pastry bag 12 to
   14 inches long with
   round metal tube opening
   ⅜ inch in diameter

Preheat oven to 250 degrees. Rub soft butter over top of baking sheets, covering surface completely. Roll flour all over buttered surface and knock off excess. Make three 8-inch rings or other shapes on baking sheets by drawing around marker with point of rubber spatula. Measure the almonds and sugar onto waxed paper, and work with fingers to remove any lumps. Sieve over this the cornstarch, and mix in with rubber spatula; set aside. Assemble the pastry bag. (Note that you will need *pralin*—caramelized almonds, page 421—for the butter cream in Step 5, and toasted almonds for the sides of the assembled cake, Step 6; toast the almonds for both after the meringues have baked, and the *pralin* takes but a few minutes.)

---

2) *The meringue-almond mixture—pâte à Succès*

¾ cup egg whites (6 egg
   whites) at room
   temperature

A clean, dry bowl and
   clean, dry electric-mixer
   blades

⅛ tsp salt

¼ tsp cream of tartar

3 Tb sugar

1½ tsp vanilla extract

⅛ tsp almond extract

The almond-sugar-starch
   mixture from Step 1

The assembled pastry bag

Place egg whites in bowl and start beating at moderately slow speed for 1 to 2 minutes, until they are foamy. Beat in the salt and cream of tartar; gradually increase speed to fast, taking a minute or so, until egg whites form soft peaks. Continuing at fast speed, gradually beat in the 3 Tb sugar, and continue until egg whites form stiff, upstanding peaks. Beat in the vanilla and the almond extracts.

If you are using a standing mixer, remove bowl from stand; the rest of this operation continues rapidly by hand and your object here is to deflate the egg whites as little as possible—they must continue to hold their volume so that you can form the meringue shapes for baking. Sprinkle about ¼ cup of the almond-sugar-starch mixture over the beaten egg whites; cutting and folding with rubber spatula, delicately blend the two together, rapidly rotating bowl with one hand as you fold with the other. When almost blended, sprinkle on more of the mixture, rapidly fold in, and continue with the rest until all is used; reach all over bottom and sides of bowl with the final addition. The whole blending process should take less than a minute; scoop the meringue into the pastry bag, all of it or as much as will fit in easily.

3) *Forming the 3 meringue disks—les fonds à Succès*

Squeeze out a line of meringue the width of your thumb and ½ inch high all around inner side of line marked on your baking sheet.

Continue around and around until you have filled the entire space with meringue.

Smooth top of meringue lightly with a spatula. Immediately make the 2 other meringue shapes in the same manner, using the other baking sheet for the third meringue.

4) *Baking—about 40 minutes at 250 degrees*

Set baking sheets on the upper-middle and lower-middle levels of preheated oven. The meringues are actually to dry out rather than bake; they will not puff up, and they will not change shape, but they will color lightly during baking. They are done as soon as you can gently push them loose from the baking surface, in 30 to 40 minutes. As soon as they are done, slip them carefully with a spatula onto cake racks to cool. They bend a little when still hot from the oven, but rapidly crisp as they cool; they are fragile and break easily, but a crack or break is not a disaster because the meringues are to be covered with frosting and filling.

---

5) *Butter cream for frosting and filling— crème au beurre à l'anglaise*

1 cup sugar
A wire whip or hand-held electric beater
6 egg yolks
A heavy-bottomed enameled or stainless saucepan 2- to 2½-quart size
¾ cup hot milk
A wooden spoon
12 to 14 ounces (3 to 3½ sticks) chilled unsalted butter
1 tsp vanilla extract
3 Tb kirsch, dark rum, or strong coffee

Make a *crème anglaise* (custard sauce) as follows: gradually beat sugar into egg yolks and continue beating for several minutes until mixture is thick and pale yellow. In a thin stream of droplets beat in the hot milk, and set mixture over moderate heat. Stir slowly with wooden spoon, reaching all over bottom of pan, for 4 to 5 minutes or until sauce thickens enough to film spoon with a creamy layer—do not let it come to simmer, but you must heat it to the point where it thickens. Immediately remove from heat and beat vigorously for 1 minute to cool slightly.

If you wish to continue with an electric mixer on a stand, scrape the custard into the mixer bowl; otherwise proceed with hand-held electric beater (or with a wire whisk). Cut the 3 sticks of chilled butter into ¼-inch slices and add a piece or two at a time, beating vigorously as butter melts and is absorbed; when all the butter has gone in, cream should be cool, smooth, and glossy, like a thick mayonnaise. Beat in the vanilla and kirsch. (If mixture turns grainy, soften rest of butter by beating it or working with fingers, and beat in successive tablespoons until butter cream smooths out.)

---

for the frosting:

2 ounces unsweetened baking chocolate, melted

Remove ¼ of the butter cream to a small bowl, stir the smooth melted chocolate into it, and reserve for frosting top of cake, end of next step. Stir the *pralin* into the remaining butter cream; this will be the filling.

for the filling:

½ **cup almond** *pralin*
   (ground caramelized
   almonds, page 421)

Pralin butter cream must have enough body to hold its shape as a filling; chill if necessary. Chocolate butter cream must be perfectly smooth and free of lumps when it covers top of cake: beat well, if necessary, before using.

6) *Assembling the cake*

A tray or baking sheet
   to set cake rack on
A flexible-blade steel
   spatula
1 cup flaked, shaved,
   slivered, or chopped
   blanched almonds,
   toasted

One by one, place meringues on a cutting surface, set the marker you used in Step 1 on top, and trim meringues with a small, sharp knife. This is so that edges will line up properly when circumference of cake is iced. Return 1 meringue to cake rack set over tray.

Spread ⅓ of the pralin butter cream over the meringue on the cake rack.

Center second meringue on top of first, and spread with ½ the remaining *pralin* butter cream. Cover with the final meringue.

Spread remaining pralin butter cream evenly around the edges of the cake with a spatula.

NOTE: You may prefer to spread almonds around sides of cake (following illustration) before icing the top; proceed in either order you wish, whichever seems easier for you. *Spread the chocolate-flavored butter cream as evenly as possible on top of cake with a spatula.*

Either *balancing cake on the palm of one hand* or leaving on rack, whichever you prefer, *brush almonds against sides of cake all around.*

The cake is now finished unless you wish to make fancy rosettes, swags, or other decorations on top with chocolate butter cream pushed through a pastry bag; French *pâtissiers* often write the name *Le Succès* on top of the cake in butter cream or white frosting.

7) *Serving—after at least 2 hours of refrigeration*

Transfer cake to a serving dish, and cover with a large bowl or a plastic dome; refrigerate. Cake should be chilled at least 2 hours to firm the butter cream. To serve, cut into serving slices as you would any layer cake.

(*) AHEAD-OF-TIME NOTES: *Le Succès* will keep perfectly for several days under refrigeration. It may be frozen, but the butter cream will probably lose its creamy smoothness; it is best to freeze disks and butter cream separately, then assemble before serving, beating more softened butter into thawed cream, if necessary, to reconstitute it.

VARIATIONS

Other fillings

A complete list of frostings and fillings is on pages 508–9, including recipes from both volumes. Other butter creams that are popular with this cake are Mocha-flavored butter cream with *pralin* plus Mocha-colored fondant, and chocolate butter cream with chocolate icing. Other ideas are the *mousse au chocolat* used for the *Saint-Cyr* on page 428, which stands up well enough when chilled and need not be frozen, and the other and richer mousse with butter in Volume I, page 604, into either one of which you could fold *pralin*. The almond and strawberry mixture for *charlotte Malakoff* could be deliciously adapted, as well as the chocolate variation following it (Volume I, pages 605–7).

Brésiliens

[Individual Meringue-almond Cakes—*Petits Fours*]

Rather than a large cake, you may prefer individual servings; *mark whatever shapes you like on buttered and floured baking sheets, fill with the meringue mixture,* and bake as directed in Step 4, page 501.

Fill, frost, and decorate as described in the Master Recipe, Step 6, page 502, but you will need only two layers—one for the top, and one for the bottom.

FROSTINGS, FILLINGS, AND
A PAPER DECORATING CONE

FONDANT

[Sugar Icing or Frosting for Cakes, *Petits Fours,*
Napoleons, Candied Fruits, and Candies]

White fondant, and how to make and use it, is well worth your attention. It is ready in an instant to be warmed briefly over hot water, flavored with a dash of vanilla, liqueur, or chocolate, and to be poured over a cake. It makes a beautifully smooth covering that hardens just enough to form a protective layer, but remains just the right texture for eating. Commercial pastry chefs can buy it ready-made in a can or jar, and so may French householders. It is easy to make yourself, however, and really one of nature's wonders, because it consists only of sugar syrup boiled to the soft-ball stage, cooled to tepid, then kneaded for several minutes until it miraculously turns from clear and limpid to snowy white. It keeps for months, even years, and is always ready to become an immediate icing.

Although we have only called for fondant a few times in the book, it is so useful to have on hand, and really so easy and such fun to make, that we felt it should be in your repertoire.

For about 2 cups

1) *The sugar syrup*

A marble surface 18 by 24 inches, or a jelly-roll pan or large metal tray
3 Tb white corn syrup or ¼ tsp cream of tartar (or 3 Tb French glucose)
1 cup water
A heavy-bottomed 2-quart saucepan
3 cups sugar (pure cane sugar, or, if you are in Europe, 1¼ lbs.—550–600 grams—crushed sugar lumps)
A cover for the pan

Syrup is to be poured onto marble, or into a pan or tray, which should be ready before you begin. Dissolve the corn syrup or cream of tartar (or glucose) with a bit of the water in the saucepan; pour in the rest of the water, and the sugar. Set over moderately high heat. Swirl pan slowly by its handle, but do not stir sugar with a spoon while liquid is coming to the boil. Continue swirling for a moment when liquid boils and changes from cloudy to perfectly clear. Cover pan, raise heat to high, and boil for several minutes until bubbles have thickened slightly. Uncover, insert candy thermometer if you are using one, and continue boiling for a few minutes to the soft-ball stage, 238 degrees: drops of syrup hold their shape softly when formed into a ball in the cold water.

Optional: a candy
  thermometer
A quart measure with 2
  cups cold water and 2 ice
  cubes
A metal spoon (not for
  stirring, only for
  testing sugar)

NOTE: If you do not boil the syrup to the soft-ball stage, your fondant will be too soft; if you boil to the hard-ball stage, your fondant will be hard to knead and difficult to melt when you want to use it.

2) Cooling the syrup—about 10 minutes

Immediately pour the syrup onto the marble or into the pan or tray. Let cool about 10 minutes, until barely tepid but not quite cold to the touch; when you press it lightly you can see the surface wrinkle.

3) Kneading the syrup into fondant—5 to 10 minutes

A pastry scraper, a painter's
  spatula, or a short, stout
  metal pancake turner
Useful but not essential:
  ¼ cup ready-made
  fondant

As soon as fondant is ready, start kneading it vigorously with scraper, spatula, or turner: push it up into a mass, spread it out again, and repeat the movement for 5 minutes or more. After several minutes of kneading, the syrup will begin to whiten (if you happen to have some ready-made fondant, add it at this point, and the syrup will quickly turn to fondant); as you continue to knead, it will gradually turn into a crumbly snow-white mass, and finally stiffen so that you can no longer knead it. It is now, officially and actually, fondant. Do not be discouraged, however, if it takes longer than 5 to 8 minutes, or even 10 minutes, to turn to fondant; go off and leave it for 5 minutes; come back and knead it again —it will eventually turn (you might have started to knead it before it was quite ready for you).

4) Curing and storing fondant

A 3-cup screw-topped jar
  or a metal bowl with
  cover
Several thicknesses of
  well-washed cheesecloth
  about 6 inches square

Although you may use the fondant immediately, it will have better texture and sheen—or bloom, as the professionals say—if you let it rest at least 12 hours. Pack it into the jar or bowl, top with the dampened cheesecloth, cover airtight, and refrigerate. As long as the top is damp, fondant will keep for months and months.

5) How to use fondant

2 cups fondant in a 2-quart
  pan

Combine the fondant and liqueur, coffee, or vanilla and water in the saucepan and set in larger pan of

1 to 2 Tb kirsch, rum,
  orange liqueur, or strong
  coffee; or 1 tsp vanilla
  and a Tb or so of water
A larger pan of simmering
  water
A wooden spoon

simmering water. Stir thoroughly, reaching all over pan, as fondant slowly softens and turns into a perfectly smooth, glossy cream that coats the spoon fairly heavily.

Use immediately, either pouring it directly over a cake set on a rack over a tray, spreading it rapidly over whatever surface you are icing, or dipping *petits fours* or candies into it. It sets rapidly, and you must work quickly to obtain a smooth surface.

Colored fondant

Use strong coffee for Mocha or tan fondant, stirring it in by droplets to get the shade you wish; stir ½ to 1 cup melted chocolate into the melted fondant for brown or chocolate fondant; use drops of food coloring for pastel shades.

Storing melted fondant

Store like fresh fondant. Unless you are turning it into chocolate fondant, it will have more sheen and bloom if you mix it with fresh fondant before using again.

CONFIT D'ABRICOTS EN SIROP

[Apricot Filling or Sauce Using Canned Apricots]

This deliciously simple filling or sauce is made with diced canned apricots lightly caramelized in their own syrup and flavored with kirsch or lemon. Serve it with custard desserts, such as the *Pélerin* on page 446, or as a filling for tarts like the *Jalousie* on page 459, spoon it over the apricot sherbet on page 415, or fold in a little gelatin and walnuts or sliced almonds and use as a cake filling as suggested for the *Saint-André* on page 490.

For about 1½ cups

A 1-lb. can of peeled
  apricots in heavy
  syrup
A small, heavy saucepan
⅓ cup sugar
1 Tb lemon juice and the
  grated rind of ½ lemon
1 Tb kirsch or Cognac

Drain the apricot syrup into the saucepan and bring to the simmer with the sugar. When sugar has dissolved completely, boil the syrup rapidly until last drops to fall from spoon are thick and sticky (230 degrees F.). Discard seeds from apricots and cut flesh into ⅜-inch dice. Fold them into the syrup and add the lemon juice and rind. Boil slowly for 5 minutes. Remove from heat and fold in the kirsch or Cognac.

LIST OF FROSTINGS AND FILLINGS

BUTTER CREAMS—FOR EITHER FROSTINGS OR FILLINGS

Simple butter cream with confectioner's sugar

Crème au Beurre Ménagère, Volume I, page 681 (egg yolks beaten with confectioner's sugar, flavoring, and butter—uncooked).

Butter cream with custard base

Crème au Beurre à l'Anglaise, page 501 (*Le Succès*), and Volume I, page 683 (cooked custard sauce with butter and flavoring beaten in).

Butter cream with egg-yolk and sugar-syrup base

Crème au Beurre au Sucre Cuit, Volume I, pages 681–3 (boiling sugar syrup beaten into egg yolks, mixture poached over hot water, beaten until cool, then butter and flavoring beaten in).

Butter cream with Italian meringue base

Crème au Beurre à la Meringue Italienne, page 489—*génoise* cake (boiling sugar syrup beaten into egg whites, beaten until cool, then butter and flavoring beaten in).

Orange or lemon butter-cream icing or filling

Crème au Beurre a l'Orange, or *au Citron,* Volume I, pages 674–6 (eggs, yolks, flavoring, and butter stirred together over heat to thicken into a simple filling; more butter beaten in to turn it into a butter cream). See also another version of the filling, *Crème au Citron,* page 484; this may also be turned into a butter cream in the same way.

OTHER FROSTINGS AND FILLINGS

Soft chocolate icing

Glaçage au Chocolat, page 496 (*Le Glorieux,* Step 3), and Volume I, page 684 (melted chocolate and butter, with or without liqueur flavoring).

White meringue frosting

Meringue Italienne, page 426—*Le Saint-Cyr,* Step 1 (boiling sugar syrup whipped into beaten egg whites).

Meringued whipped cream frosting or filling

Chantilly Meringuée, page 430 (the preceding meringue combined with whipped cream).

Fondant

Page 505 (sugar syrup boiled to the soft-ball stage, cooled, then kneaded until it turns snowy white; flavored with liqueur or chocolate).

Apricot filling or sauce

Confit d'abricots en sirop, page 507 (diced canned apricots boiled in their own syrup, liqueur flavoring; with gelatin added as cake filling, *Le Saint-André*, page 492).

MISCELLANEOUS

Walnut brittle and caramelized walnut halves

Pralin aux Noix, page 423—*Pralinée aux Noix*, Step 1 (walnuts stirred into caramel syrup and ground when cold; or walnuts dipped into caramel syrup and used for decorations).

Almond brittle

Pralin aux Amandes, page 421—*Le Kilimanjaro*, Step 1 (same as *Pralin aux Noix*, but with almonds).

Baked meringue decorations

Meringue Italienne, page 426—*Le Saint-Cyr*, Steps 1, and 2 (boiling sugar syrup whipped into beaten egg whites, formed into meringues, and baked).

COMMENT FAIRE UN CORNET EN PAPIER
[How to Make a Paper Decorating Cone]

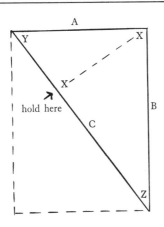

Cut heavy freezer paper or bond paper into a right-angle triangle whose short sides (A and B) are approximately 12 and 15 inches long.

Hold the hypotenuse side of the
triangle (C) with your left hand,
thumb on top and opposite the
point of the right angle (X). *With
your right hand, curl the longer
end of the hypotenuse (Z), around
toward your left, bringing its
underside against the top of the
right angle (X).* You now have
formed a cone with the right side
of the paper.

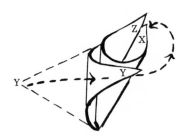

*Curl the other end of the hypotenuse
(Y) toward your right, around the
outside of the first cone, bringing
its point (Y) to the back of the
right angle (X).* You have now
completed the cone; slide points back
and forth at top, to close tip of
cone at other end.

*Secure cone either by bending points
X, Y, and Z down inside, or by
using a straight pin.* Cut tip of cone
with scissors to make any size of
opening you wish.

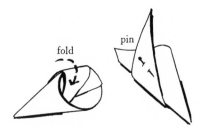

Appendices

LIST OF STUFFINGS FOR MEATS
AND VEGETABLES

STUFFINGS WITH MUSHROOMS

Mushroom duxelles with onions, cream cheese, and parsley—for stuffed vegetables—in the stuffed eggplant recipe, Volume I, page 502.

Mushroom duxelles and spinach, farce Viroflay—for stuffed lamb and veal—in the stuffed shoulder of lamb recipe, page 194.

Mushrooms, onions, and ham—for stuffed lamb, veal, or chicken, and for stuffed vegetables—in the lamb section, Volume I, page 337.

Mushroom, giblets, bread crumbs, and cream cheese—for chicken, veal, and stuffed vegetables—in the roast chicken section, Volume I, page 252.

Mushrooms and kidneys, Mushrooms and chicken livers, Mushrooms and ground lamb, Mushrooms and forcemeat—see following section.

STUFFINGS WITH MEAT

Sausage, ham, chard, and bread crumbs—for meats and stuffed vegetables —in the *paupiettes* of beef, page 156.

Sausage, ham, and rice—for meats and stuffed vegetables—in the stuffed cabbage recipe, page 380.

Sausage and apple—for duck, goose, and pork—in the roast duck recipe, Volume I, page 275.

Sausage and chestnuts—for duck, goose, turkey, and pork—in the roast goose recipe, Volume I, page 286.

Sausage, rice, and apricots, farce Trébizonde—for duck, goose, pork, and turkey—in the suckling pig recipe, page 226.

Ground pork, onions, herbs, and bread crumbs, farce de porc—for stuffed meats and vegetables—in the stuffed lamb section, Volume I, page 336.

Ground pork with ham, truffles, and foie gras—for stuffed veal and chicken, or for use as a *pâté* mixture—in the veal section, *veau en feuilletons*, page 220.

Ground braised beef, onions, and herbs—for stuffed vegetables, or as a meat loaf—in the stuffed cabbage recipe, page 386.

Ground braised beef and chard—for stuffed vegetables, as a meat loaf, or as sausages—in the sausage section, *les tous nus*, page 306.

Ground leftover veal, turkey, or pork with onions and herbs—for stuffed vegetables or as a meat loaf—in the eggplant section, page 357.

Veal, ham, rice, and chard or spinach—for stuffed veal or lamb—in the breast of veal recipe, page 216.

Forcemeat and mushrooms, boudin blanc, farce normande—for chicken, turkey, or veal—in the poached chicken section, page 275.

Ground lamb, olives, and onions—for stuffed lamb and stuffed vegetables —in the lamb section, Volume I, page 338.

Ground lamb, salmon, anchovies, and onions—for stuffed lamb and stuffed vegetables—in the lamb section, Volume I, page 338.

Ground lamb, eggplant, mushrooms, rice, and herbs—for stuffed lamb, stuffed vegetables, and as a meat loaf—the *Moussaka* recipe, Volume I, page 349.

Kidneys, rice, and herbs—for lamb or veal—in the stuffed lamb section, Volume I, page 337.

Kidneys and mushrooms—for stuffed lamb or veal—in the lamb section, page 190.

Foie gras and prunes—for stuffed duck, goose, or turkey—in the stuffed goose recipe, Volume I, page 284.

Foie gras and truffles—for *filet* of beef, veal, or chicken— in the *filet* of beef recipe, Volume I, page 304.

Chicken livers, rice, foie gras, and truffles, farce à la d'Albuféra—for chicken, turkey, and veal—in the poached chicken section, page 272.

Chicken livers, mushrooms, rice, and puréed cooked garlic, farce évocation d'Albuféra—for chicken, turkey, veal, and stuffed vegetables—in the poached chicken section, page 274.

Chicken-liver mixture for stuffings, sausages, and pâtés—in the *pâté* section, page 324.

Chicken giblets, herbs, crumbs, and cream cheese—for veal, chicken, turkey, and stuffed vegetables—in the roast chicken recipe, Volume I, page 243. The same, with mushrooms, Volume I, page 252.

MEATLESS AND MUSHROOMLESS STUFFINGS

Rice, onions, and cheese—for stuffed vegetables—in the stuffed onion recipe, page 378.

Rice and chopped peppers, tomato topping—for stuffed vegetables—in the stuffed zucchini recipe, page 376.

Rice, garlic, and herbs—for stuffed meats and vegetables—in the *paupiette* of beef recipe, page 161.

Chopped olives, pimentos, and herbs—for *paupiettes* of meat—in the beef *paupiettes*, page 160.

Garlic and herbs—for *paupiettes* of meat, and as a flavoring for boned red meats—in the lamb section, Volume I, page 336.

Chopped peppers, onions, and mustard bread crumbs—for *paupiettes* of meat—in the beef *paupiettes*, page 159.

Almonds, cheese, and bread crumbs—for stuffed onions, or zucchini—in the stuffed zucchini recipe, page 375.

Eggplant, peppers, onions, tomatoes, and herbs—for stuffing cold vegetables—in the vegetable chapter, page 351.

APPENDIX TWO

KITCHEN EQUIPMENT

Batterie de Cuisine

The next thirty-eight pages contain an illustrated roundup of some kitchen equipment we find useful, so that you will see it all in one place rather than scattered throughout the two volumes.

Some of these implements are standard American, others are professional American, still others can be found in import shops or mail-order catalogues, and some are things to look out for if you go abroad and are browsing around in restaurants or butcher supply houses near the central markets. As always, we advise you to look for solid, practical, professional equipment designed by people in the chef business who sell to chefs. If you have trouble locating good equipment in your area, ask your butcher or the owner and chef of the best restaurant in town.

FRYING PANS

For browning meats and vegetables and for general sautéing, the heavy-duty professional frying pan with its long handle and sloping 2-inch sides is the best shape. American cast-aluminum models (A and D) come either with plain or no-stick interiors. The French *poêle* (B) is of *tôle épaisse* (very thick sheet metal); one with a bottom diameter of 7 to 7½ inches is ideal for omelettes. The oval cast-iron pan (E), *poêle à poissons,* is as useful for browning roasts as it is for sautéing fish. The short-handled cast-iron American skillet (C) is also good in the oven, and is the pan to use for *pommes Anna;* the same shape can be found with an enameled surface, making it ideal for cooking in white wine, or for storing and serving stews or sautés.

You should have at least three sizes of frying pans—a large one 11 inches across its top diameter, a medium, or 10-inch, pan, and a smaller, 7- to 8-inch, pan for single servings and *crêpes*. You will probably end up with many more, some of one material, some of another, and each your pet for certain techniques.

CHICKEN FRYERS

The straight-sided frying pan known as a *sautoir* in French and as a chicken fryer here, is useful, of course, for fried chicken, but it is also good for chicken sautés and fricassees, beef stews, fish stews, and numerous vegetable dishes. Because the cooking usually takes place on top of the stove, it must be of heavy material. The traditional shape (A and B) is typical of the French copper *sautoir* and of the American professional cast aluminum; the sides are $2\frac{1}{4}$ to $2\frac{1}{2}$ inches high. The deep chicken fryer (C) is of cast iron; this is a fine cooking utensil, but remove foods from it as soon as they are done to prevent discoloration.

SAUCEPANS, KETTLES, COVERS, AND COLANDERS

You will need saucepans (*casseroles*) for sauces and saucepans for general boiling and simmering. When you are cooking with white wine or egg yolks, use a non-staining material like lined copper, stainless steel, flameproof ceramic or glass, or the familiar French enameled cast iron with wooden handle (A).

For boiling potatoes, pasta, and their like, cast aluminum is fine although you will have to scour it from time to time. The professional shape (B-1) is well designed; 1½, 2½, 4½, and 7 quarts (B-2) will give you a reasonable range of pan sizes.

Rather than having a special cover for each pot, a series of long-handled covers allows one to fit several sizes of saucepans (C).

Soup kettles (*marmites*) are essential for *pot-au-feu*, soups, *bouillabaisse*, lobsters, green beans *à la française*, and spinach. An 8-quart kettle and another of 18- to 24-quart capacity would meet most of your needs. One of them might

be the two-handled type (E or F), and another the preserving-kettle type with bucket handle (H). A French earthenware *marmite* (G) is attractive for soups and stews that are cooked and served in the same pot.

A large sturdy colander is a must; buy one 10 to 11 inches across the top diameter and 5 to 6 inches high, with feet (D).

CASSEROLES AND BRAISING PANS

Casseroles (*cocottes*) can double as saucepans or roasters, and are essential for stews and braises. Enameled ironware is always good because it will go on the stove or into the oven (A, B, C) and foods will not discolor in it; the oval shape is the best if you are limited in space or budget. The American heavy cast-aluminum (H) comes with a removable rack, and in several sizes up to the large turkey roaster. The French *daubière* (G) is in lined copper. Earthenware casseroles (D, E, F) are wonderful for cooking and serving because they spread and retain heat. The attractive copper *cocotte* (I) was designed for the famous potato dish, *pommes Anna,* page 387, but may be used as a casserole or as two separate baking dishes.

WARNING: All casseroles, baking dishes, plates, pitchers, cups, and other utensils of earthenware, terra cotta, and like materials must be of the high-fired so-called stoneware type, or must otherwise by clearly labeled and certified safe for the cooking and serving of foods and drinks.

GRATIN DISHES AND ROASTING PANS

Flameproof dishes about 2 inches deep are used for baking, gratinéeing, roasting, and serving, and you should have a reasonable number of sizes. Enameled iron gratin dishes (*plats à gratin*) (A and E) are either oval or round, and come from shirred-egg size up to 13 to 14 inches long and 9 inches wide. Earthenware gratin dishes (B) are always attractive for serving. A nest of aluminum dishes (F) is conveniently stored and long lasting. Rectangular enameled iron (C) can be plain or with no-stick interior, and will double for roasting or gratinéeing. Be sure to have a rack (G) that will fit into your large roasting pan so that legs of lamb can be raised out of their juices. If your oven does not come with a perforated rack for the broiling pan (D), buy one separately; otherwise spluttering fat can catch fire while you are doing a steak.

IMPLEMENTS—KNIVES

Very sharp knives are the mark of the serious cook, and continual use of the butcher's steel will keep them razor sharp. Carbon steel knives are preferred by most chefs, but there are stainless knives that will sharpen easily too.

The Central Hoard

The straight-edged, wedge-shaped cook's knife (C,D,E,F,G,H) is the all-purpose shape for chopping, slicing, paring, and general cutting; you will need at least three, from the 2- to 3-inch blade for paring and small minces to the 10- to 12-inch blade for chopping and rapid slicing. Curved blades (A and B) are good for paring. A professional butcher's steel (J) with blade 10 to 12 inches long is the best sharpening equipment. A larding needle (I) is indispensable for larding meat.

Slicers, Carvers, and Boners

Slicing, carving, and boning knives have curved blades. Here is the slicing scimitar (K), and two other slicing shapes (L and M). The stubby knife (P) and its longer companion (O) are boning knives, as is the very thin knife known as a chicken sticker (Q) with its short blade; the longer-bladed version (N) is a Norwegian herring filleter, which is also useful for slicing off pork rinds and for cutting thin sheets out of pork fat.

Serrated Sawers

Serrated knives include the curved grapefruit knife (A), the bread knife (B), the all-purpose slicer (C), the frozen-food cutter (D), the ham slicer, which also does smoked salmon (E), and the vicious-looking French meat slicer (F), which is, in addition, very good with slab bacon.

Choppers and Rockers

The traditional chef's knives (J and K) are for general chopping, as illustrated in Volume I, page 27. The Japanese version (I) works equally well. The two rockers (G and H) are marvelous for mushrooms and parsley, particularly the 3-bladed professional model.

BASHERS, BLUDGEONS, AND BLUNT INSTRUMENTS

For whacking up turkey carcasses, chopping bones, and flattening cutlets, here is a choice of weapons. The meat tenderizer with its cast-aluminum head has waffled sides for tenderizing (A) and smooth sides for flattening cutlets; you can also use it as a hammer, although the rubber-headed hammer that you can buy at any good hardware store (F) is less noisy. The French cleaver, *feuille à fendre* (D), or an ordinary hatchet (E) are for whacking carcasses or bones, and a hammer helps. The French cleaver-tenderizer, *batte à côtelettes* (B), is a useful instrument, and the wooden British basher (C) is for flattening cutlets that are held between sheets of waxed paper.

SCISSOR ACTION

Heavy shears for cutting fish fins, gristle, and rib cages are the serrated French pair (A) and the heavy utility model (F), also French. Poultry shears with their curved blades (B) are useful on occasion, as are the sharp-pointed lobster shears (C). General purpose stainless kitchen scissors with take-apart blades (E) can go into the dishwasher. The scissor-action cherry or olive pitter (D) is invaluable when you have those jobs to do.

FOUR PAIRS OF SPOONS

You can rarely have enough spoons, and all sizes are needed. Large models of tough nonmetallic composition (A and B) are essential for stirring in no-stick pans. Large stainless-steel spoons (E and F) have hundreds of uses, as do those of serving-spoon and soup-spoon size (C and D). The sturdy ice-cream spoon (H) does its job well, as does the no-stick scoop (G).

NINE FORKS

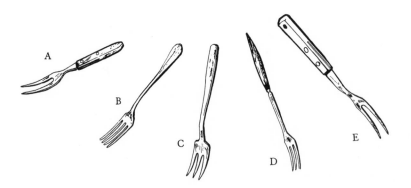

For testing meat and artichokes, for lifting, carving, and spearing, you need a number of sharp-pronged forks like the large chef's model (I) for enormous roasts and giant birds, and general-purpose forks (E and G), as well as something like the slender Danish three-pronged pickle fork (D). The mixing fork (H) with its six flat-bladed prongs is a great American invention for blending and mashing. A wooden fork (F) is useful for stirring braised rice, and a salad fork (C), combined with spoon, does many a neat job of tossing. The table fork (B) is constantly on call for beating eggs, pricking pastry, general lifting, and stirring, while the small two-pronged fork (A) comes in for pokings and turnings.

TURNOVER TOOLS—SPATULAS

Flexible-blade spatulas scrape fragile cookies off of baking sheets, spread icings over cakes, and slide *quiches* onto plates; the 12-inch blade (C) and 8-inch (B) are useful sizes. The palette knife (A) is marvelous for delicate liftings and spreadings. Pancake turners of nonmetallic composition (D) are essential when you cook in no-stick pans, and stainless all-purpose models (E,F,H) are standard equipment. The very wide turner (G) does many a lifting job, such as getting asparagus out of hot water.

WIRE WHIPS OR WHISKS

Wire whips or whisks which come in a variety of sizes from minute to gigantic— are wonderful for beating and general mixing.

RETRIEVERS

Metal tongs (A and C) are for lifting and turning meats on a barbeque or in a pan, as well as for retrieving items from boiling oil. The Japanese wooden tongs (B) do many chores and are especially great for turning bacon in the pan. Life would be hard without the perforated spoon (E), and it is easy to become addicted to the great Italian scoop (D).

WOODEN SPOONS, SPATULAS, AND CHOPSTICKS

Why stir it with a wooden spoon? Because it blends the flour and butter *roux* without racket, and it scrapes the coagulated roasting juices into the deglazing sauce with more quiet efficiency than metal against metal. Actually, the French bowl-less wooden spatula (I,G,F), or the Japanese wooden spatula (H), or the no-stick spatula implements (C and D) are far more useful for every stirring, scraping, mixing, and beating job than the wooden spoon (A and B). Do not forget wooden chopsticks (E); they will beat the eggs for the omelette, lift the green bean out of the boiling pot for testing, and turn the bacon.

GADGETS AND MISCELLANY

Opening, prying, and poking operations will be easier on fingers and tempers when you have something like A or C for screw-topped jars, or the all-purpose-everything item, B. The French tool, G, is for cans and general prying, while the box-opener-hammer-hatchet-etc. instrument, D, is useful anywhere. Ice picks, both the single-pointed F, and the 5-pronged E, are multi-purpose musts. Citrus zesters H and J are good for bar as well as kitchen, and the potato ballers I and K are useful for fruits and vegetables alike.

For grating, puréeing, and grinding, some hand-operated gadgets do a better job than the electric blender or mixer. Use 4-sided grater, L, when you want to grate orange rind or you need coarsely grated Swiss cheese, or a few slices of carrot; look for one in stainless steel. When grated cheese is to be spread over the *sauce Mornay,* hold the little French rotary grater, M, right over the *gratin* dish. The table model, N, is for great mounds of cheese if you do not have a grating attachment for your electric mixer.

Again, in spite of the marvels of the electric blender, you do need an efficient food mill for applesauce, puréeing soups, turnips, artichoke hearts, and canned Italian plum tomatoes. The French model, O, with removable disks and folding rubber-padded feet is still the best, in our opinion. One with a top diameter of 9 inches is the standard size; if you are having more than one, the 7-inch size is handy for small jobs like sieving hard-boiled egg yolks.

The old-fashioned potato masher, P, is not to be ignored, nor is the rectangular-headed garlic press, Q. Beware of faulty designs, however, especially in garlic presses. These should take a quite large, whole, unpeeled clove of garlic; the point is that you do not have to peel the garlic. The rectangular head allows a reasonably large clove to be puréed, and the holes should be just the right diameter for the press to do its work easily; if the one you buy does not perform as you think it should, take it back and demand a refund. Get yourself a good peppermill for the kitchen; the French Peugeot models (R and R-1), are always reliable.

Public performances are long when the flame lies low; chafing-dish heat elements are for cooking, and must provide proper heat. Unless you want the efficient gas-operated model, T, look for the kind that will hold a whole can of solidified alcohol, S, and that has an opening which will give you a large heat source.

The French salad basket, U, also comes with a rotary ratchet-gadget that spins salad greens dry in a jiffy. The basket for the Swiss model, V-1, fits into a container, V-2, which catches all the splattering water as the lettuce leaves whirl inside it.

cutting blade

meat-grinder
wheel

sausage-stuffer
wheel

stuffing horn

If you do not have a meat-grinder attachment for your electric mixer, buy yourself a sturdy table model, W, always picking the large size for quick and easy operation. Many grinders come with the sausage-stuffing horn you will need for the *charcuterie* recipes illustrated on pages 284–5.

THE PASTRY BAG

From squeezing out cream puffs to making meringue cakes and potato borders, nothing will do the work as easily nor with as professional a look as the pastry bag (A) with its collection of interchangeable metal tubes. Buy the big professional, washable, canvas bags, 12, 14, and 16 inches long; in comparison with your other kitchen equipment, these are inexpensive, and so are the metal tubes. For a start, get 2 or 3 tubes with plain round openings varying from ¼ to ¾ inch in diameter (B), and a cannelated group of the same dimensions (C). Among the latter, the widely spaced teeth (C-1) are for rough masses like potatoes *duchesse,* while the fine teeth (C-2) are for icings. Ribbon tubes, both plain and cannelated (D), are used particularly for such decorations as the meringues for the *Saint-Cyr,* on page 425; one of each, ¾ inch wide, should be sufficient.

BEATING EGG WHITES

You are far more likely to welcome soufflés, meringues, cakes, and baked Alaskas—or even to encourage them—when you have the proper egg-white beating equipment. We urge you to consider the type of heavy-duty electric mixer illustrated here (A). Its large revolving whip (A-1) also rotates around the bowl, beating egg whites so easily it will never again occur to you to think of them as a problem. In fact, this is a replica of the large industrial machines designed by professionals for professionals; to have a home model available is a tremendous help to all of us.

While you are at it, buy an extra bowl and an extra whip, to save you the chore of washing and drying in a single recipe like the *Saint-Cyr* on page 425, which calls for a butter and chocolate mixture as well as for beaten egg whites. The straight-sided bowl, in addition, is just the right shape for raising yeast dough. The dough hook (A-2) works very well for kneading French bread or *brioche* dough, while the flat beater (A-3) will do the whole operation for a pastry dough from working the butter into the flour to blending in the cold water; when you are doubling or tripling pastry recipes, or blending large batches of sausage meat, the heavy-duty action and ample bowl do the work with ease and speed. The bowl or jack attachment that holds either hot water or ice around the main mixing bowl (A-4) quickly warms the eggs and sugar as you beat them into a foaming mass, or chills the fish *quenelle* mixture so that you can beat in the maximum amount of cream. The set of rotary graters, slicers, and shredders (A-5) makes fast work of lots of cheese to grate, potatoes or onions to slice, or even mushroom *duxelles*. The food processor, page 95, has made many of these attachments obsolete, but they still have their uses, especially when you are doing large quantities.

A-3

A-2

A-4

A-5

fine shredder
and grater

coarse shredder
and
shoe stringer

thick slicer

thin slicer

Whether you beat egg whites by machine or by hand, the theory and practice are the same. Have them at room temperature: they tend to coagulate and fleck when chilled. Start beating rather slowly until they begin to foam, add a pinch of salt and, if you are not using unlined copper, a scant ¼ teaspoon of cream of tartar for each 4 egg whites. Gradually speed the beating action to fast as you circulate the beater all around the bowl, keeping the whole mass in motion, and beating in as much air as possible to increase the volume of the egg whites by sevenfold at least, and until they form the peak illustrated here (B).

The unlined copper bowl (C) is chic, expensive, and looks pretty hanging by its ring on the kitchen wall; it works marvelously well. Egg whites beaten in it retain their volume and satiny gleam, and no one seems to know why. But a small stainless bowl (D) held in one hand, an electric beater held in the other (E), and cream of tartar work very well too. The important point for each is the beater-bowl relationship. Use the largest whip that will fit into a copper bowl (F) or the smallest stainless bowl that will function with your hand-held electric beater; in each case, this is so that you can keep the whole egg mass in continuous motion.

TEMPERATURE CHANGES

Great-grandmother used to calculate how hot her oven was by the time it took to brown a piece of white paper; taffy was done when the sugar syrup formed a hard ball in a glass of water; and if she missed on the roast she claimed she had gotten out of the wrong side of the bed that morning. Meat thermometers take the guess out of roasting; standard types are the stainless model (G) and the dial type (C). The vest-pocket thermometer (E), with its carrying case (D), is used by professional testers, and has a dial that registers from zero to 220 degrees F. (Weston Instruments, Inc., Newark, N.J.). A thermometer for deep-fat frying (A) can double for candy making, but if you do much sugar work you will want a candy thermometer too. Accurate oven thermometers are essential for any serious cooking. The stainless-steel type (B) is to be had in most stores; the professional folding oven thermometer (F) is manufactured by the Moeller Instrument Company, Richmond Hill, N.Y. When you are warned not to let the *crème anglaise* come near the boil or you may scramble the egg yolks, yet sternly reminded that you still must heat them enough to thicken the sauce, this stainless-steel temperature spoon (H) will tell you when 160 degrees and the danger point have arrived; since its temperature dial registers from 50 to 400 degrees, you can also use the spoon for sugar boiling and deep-fat frying.

MEASURING

Great-grandmother, our sacred example, measured by feel and hearsay. Her recipes called for a piece of butter the size of a walnut or an egg, a fistful of flour, as much milk as would fit into a teacup. Little failures could be blamed on the weather, the wind, or the vagaries of the coal-burning stove. We have no such excuses now, praises be to Fannie Farmer, who pioneered the whole movement away from the rounded soup spoon of unspecified dimensions and the wine glass of infinite capacity; it was she who helped establish the level tablespoon that holds exactly ½ liquid ounce, and the strictly calibrated 8-ounce cup.

Glass measures with pouring lips are basic equipment; have the three sizes that hold 1, 2, and 4 cups, respectively (A,B,C). Dry measures register to capacity when the cups are filled to the brim; these are the only accurate cup measurements for sugar, flour, and salt. The easiest to use are the stainless-steel type with long handles (E,F,G,H); have at least 2 sets so that some will be available while others are being washed. At least 2 sets of measuring spoons (D) are useful too, for the same reasons.

MEASURING FLOUR

For all flour measurements in this volume, scoop the dry-measure cup directly into the flour sack or flour container, and fill the cup to overflowing (A)—do not shake or pack down the flour; sweep off excess flour even with the lip of the cup, using the straight edge of a knife (B). Then sift the flour, if

your recipe calls for sifting; for many recipes, however, such as pastry dough, the flour need not be sifted at all. Cups and spoons can never measure flour with the accuracy of scales, but this scoop-and-level system has proved itself out to our satisfaction, and is much easier and faster than the sifting-into-cup method we used in the first edition of Volume I. Here is a conversion and equivalency table for measuring different flours, and for changing old Volume I measurements into the scoop-and-level system.

FLOUR MEASURING CHART*

Scoop-and-level method	Sifting-directly-into-cup method	
	(Old Volume I, pages 17–18)	
(All flours including "instant blending," all-purpose and hard-wheat, cake, soft-wheat, and French flours)	All-purpose and hard-wheat flours	Cake flour, soft-wheat, and French flour
3½ cups = 1 lb. (454 grams)		
4½ cups	1 lb. (454 grams)	
5⅔ cups		1 lb. (454 grams)
⅔ cup = 3¼ ounces (100 grams)		
1 cup	3½ ounces (100 grams)	
1¼ cups		3½ ounces (100 grams)
1 cup = 5 ounces (140 grams)	3½ ounces (100 grams)	2¾ ounces (80 grams)

* Please note that all weights are approximate—averages.

All-purpose and hard-wheat flour measured by the two methods

Sifted directly into cup (Volume I method)	Scooped and leveled (Volume II method)		
1 cup sifted	⅔ cup	scooped	(100 grams)
¾ cup sifted	⅓ cup plus ¼ cup	scooped	(80 grams)
⅔ cup sifted	½ cup less 1 Tb	scooped	(66 grams)
½ cup sifted	⅓ cup	scooped	(50 grams)
⅓ cup sifted	¼ cup	scooped	(33 grams)
¼ cup sifted	3 Tb	scooped	(25 grams)

Cake flour, soft-wheat flour, French flour measured by the two methods

Sifted directly into cup (Volume I method)	Scooped and leveled (Volume II method)		
1 cup sifted	⅓ cup plus ¼ cup	scooped	(80 grams)
¾ cup sifted	⅓ cup plus 1½ Tb	scooped	(60 grams)
⅔ cup sifted	⅓ cup	scooped	(52 grams)
½ cup sifted	¼ cup plus 2 tsp	scooped	(40 grams)
⅓ cup sifted	3 Tb	scooped	(26 grams)
¼ cup sifted	2½ Tb	scooped	(20 grams)

PANS

ROUND CAKE PANS (A)

4-cup size, 8 inches (top) diameter, 1½ inches deep
6-cup size, 9 by 1½ inches
FRENCH PANS—*moules à biscuits, moule à manqué*
   6-cup size, 8½ inches (top) diameter, 1½ inches deep
   8-cup size, 9 by 2 inches

SQUARE CAKE PANS (B)

6-cup size, 8 by 8 inches (top), 2 inches deep
8-cup size, 9 by 1½ inches
10-cup size, 9 by 2 inches
FRENCH PANS—*moule à manqué carré*
   5-cup size, 7¾ by 7¾ inches (top), 1½ inches deep
   7-cup size, 9 by 1½ inches

PIZZA PANS—ROUND COOKIE PANS (C)

12 to 14 inches inside diameter and ¾ inch deep
FRENCH PAN—*tourtière*, various sizes usually in black iron, *tôle noire*

JELLY-ROLL PAN—BAKING PAN (D)

15½ by 1½ inches (top), 1 inch deep
FRENCH PAN—*caisse à biscuits, caisse à génoise,* many
    sizes from 8 by 12 inches up to bakery dimensions

COOKIE SHEETS—BAKING SHEETS (E)

9 by 14 inches to 14 by 17 inches for home ovens
FRENCH BAKING SHEETS—*plaques à pâtisserie, plaques
    à bords évasés, plaques à pinces*—in *tôle noire* or in
    aluminum, various sizes from 12 to 14 inches on up

PIE PANS—PIE PLATES (F)

4-cup size, 8 inches (top) diameter, 1¼ inches deep
5-cup size, 9 by 1½ inches
6-cup size, 11 by 1¼ inches
FRENCH PAN—no equivalent

BREAD PAN—MEAT-LOAF PAN—ANGEL-LOAF PAN (G)

4-, 6-, and 8-cup sizes, varying widely in measure-
    ments according to individual manufacturers. For
    example, a pan 3½ inches deep, with top dimen-
    sions of 10½ by 4 inches and bottom dimensions of
    9 by 2½ inches, holds 6 cups.
Angel-loaf pans are usually 13 inches long (top) for
    the 2-quart size, and 16 inches for the large 4½-
    quart model.
FRENCH PANS—*moules à cake, moules à biscottes,
    moules à pain de mie* (covered), in a variety of
    sizes

PASTRY—ROLLING, SCRAPING, AND GLAZING

If you are going into *quiches, pâtés en croûte,* and especially into the fascinating realm of French puff pastry, pages 111–45, get yourself a slab of marble 2 feet square and ¾ to 1 inch thick; its coolness helps prevent the dough
from softening, and its smooth surface is easy to scrape clean.

One or two professionally designed rolling pins with rolling surfaces 16
to 18 inches long are essential for any pastry work—the silly toy pin (A), still
sold to debutante cooks, makes hard work of any rolling operation. The French
boxwood pin, *rouleau à pâtisserie en buis* (B) or its Italian equivalent, both
without handles, are as useful for rolling as they are for beating chilled pastry into rolling shape. The fine professional American ball-bearing pin (C)

is heavy enough to do half the work for you, and the cannelated pin (D), *le
Tutove,* is especially designed to spread out the layers of butter inside the
croissant dough as you roll. The rotary croissant cutter (E) then finishes the
operation.

For scraping pastry off the work surface, and also for cutting and chopping dough, the hardware-store paint scraper (F) does almost as good a job
as the French pastry scraper, *coupe-pâte* (G). The pastry blender (H), with
its multiple chopping blades, cuts the butter into the flour when you are making pie dough by hand—it prevents the hot-finger syndrome that causes cardboard pastry.

Several pastry brushes (I) are needed, for glazing the tart with beaten
egg as well as for general basting; be sure to buy ones designed for pastry or
for basting, since cheap brushes leave bad tastes and drop hairs.

SMALL MOLDS—PETITS MOULES—FOR TARTLETS, BRIOCHES, PETITS FOURS

These should be in tinned metal, *fer-blanc,* which is less likely to cause sticking problems than aluminum; if you have to scrub them after baking, warm them briefly and rub lightly with oiled paper toweling to keep the molds from rusting or sticking. Buy at least a dozen of whatever models you chose, so that you can form and bake as many at once as possible. Tartlet molds (A,C,I,J,E) are usually ½ inch deep and from 1½ to 3 inches in diameter or length. Individual *brioches* are usually baked in the round fluted molds (B and D), although these molds can serve for tartlets and entrée pastries too. Baby savarins are formed and baked in the ring mold, F, while *cornets* and *rouleaux* are formed around the metal cream horns (H and K) and tubes (G and L).

CUTTERS—DÉCOUPOIRS; EMPORTE-PIÈCES

If you are going into serious pastry work, sets of round and oval cutters neatly packed in tin boxes make storage and retrieval no problem at all. Oval cutters come plain (*unis*), I, or fluted (*cannelés*), D–H, with the smallest in the set being 1⅝ inches long and the largest 4¾ inches. Sets of plain (J) and fluted round cutters (K–O) go from ⅝ inch to 4 inches in diameter. The tiny cutters in the foreground, *découpoirs à truffes* (P–X), make designs in truffle slices, egg whites, and other small decorative elements for aspics and pastries. Something like the ravioli wheel (B), the large Italian wheel (A), or the pastry wheel (C) is always useful for pie doughs, puff pastries, and general dough cutting.

When you must prick the sheet of dough for Napoleons, page 464, all over at ¼-inch intervals, a fork takes quite a number of minutes while the roller pricker (Y), which doubles as a meat-tenderizer, covers the area in a few passes; its cast-aluminum head is 2 inches in diameter and its sturdy wooden handle is 4 inches long.

FLAN RINGS AND VOL-AU-VENT CUTTERS

Flan rings, *formes sans fond* (G,H,J,K, and I), come in all sizes and many shapes; they are designed especially for making the free-standing tart shells, pie shells, and *quiches* illustrated in Volume I, pages 143–5. A set of graduated *vol-au-vent* cutters (A–F) comprises 12 disks slightly raised to provide a finger hold in the center; disks range in size from 4 to 10½ inches in diameter. They are invaluable not only for cutting the *vol-au-vent* on page 127, but also for making circles in floured pastry sheets, like the cookie cups on page 419, or for any other circular cutting or marking operations, like the free-standing tart shells on page 106.

SOUFFLÉ DISHES AND BAKING DISHES

When you are instructed to "bake the dessert in an 8-cup cylindrical mold or dish, such as a charlotte, 4 inches deep," A, D, and E are the dishes to use. The French charlotte molds (A and D) are the most useful baking dishes you can have in your kitchen, because you can bake in them, mold in them, caramelize them, heat them on top of the stove as well as in the oven, and you can serve from a napkin-wrapped charlotte mold. Be sure you buy the all-purpose type in tin-washed metal, *tôle étamée;* there are some models in flimsy aluminum that are good only for cold desserts. Useful sizes are the 6- and 8-cup models, although 3-cup, 4-cup, and very large sizes may fill some occasional needs. The American flameproof ceramic baking and soufflé dish (E) is excellent too, and a little deeper than the charlottes. French ovenproof white soufflé dishes (B and C) are attractive for baking and serving; for soufflés, tie a paper collar around them to hold the puff, as illustrated in Volume I, page 162.

PÂTÉ MOLDS

Although you can make do with other methods, the traditional hinged mold for *pâtés* is comforting to own, decorative to look at, and will produce the beautiful finished product illustrated on pages 328–33. These are of *tôle étamée,* tin-washed metal, and come in many sizes, shapes, and patterns. A 2-quart (2-liter) size is the most useful when you are buying only one. If you do not know how much a particular mold will hold, set it on a large piece of heavy foil or brown paper, fill with dried beans or rice, remove mold, and measure the beans or rice.

MISCELLANEOUS SMALL MOLDS

Eggs form themselves most happily in aspic when the mold is oval; the *moules à dariole ovales,* B and C, hold ½ cup and come with plain or fancy bottoms. *Babas* are baked in tiny charlottes, E and F, or the *dariole ronde,* A; these hold slightly over ⅓ cup, and are useful also for individual servings of aspic, and for small soufflés and custards. The miniature fluted mold, D, is for fancy aspics.

MOLDS FOR BAKING, FOR ASPICS,
AND FOR FROZEN DESSERTS

Although the *Kougloff* and *trois frères* molds (A and D) are designed for cakes, and the ice-cream mold (E and F) for *bombes glacées,* all of the models pictured here are useful for aspics, and all, with the obvious exception of the fish (B), would do for frozen desserts and Bavarian creams. Use a simple pattern for frozen desserts (C and G); beware of too complicated a design or you may have terrible difficulties unmolding; the pattern in H is about as far as you can go. Although more modern materials are available, we like *tôle étamée,* tin-washed metal, for both baking and aspics because it seasons well—meaning it seems to present few sticking problems. Tin-lined copper for aspics is pretty to look at if you do not mind the initial expense and subsequent cleaning.

WINE GLASSES

If space is a problem, you need only one type of wine glass for Bordeaux, Burgundy, Rhine wine, Champagne, or Chianti—the tulip-shaped glass (A) that holds ¾ to 1 cup; fill it slightly less than half full to give room for swirling and sniffing. Equally serviceable is the shorter glass (B). If you are going to serve both a red and a white wine at a meal, use a larger glass (A) for the red wine in proportion to the one for the white wine (B); the white wine glass is usually placed on the outside. All of these are inexpensive and should be available in any wine shop or department store, as well as in all the restaurant and hotel supply stores. For prestigious red Bordeaux and Burgundies, the large-bowled glass (F) is amusing; a normal serving of 3 ounces looks small in it but develops its fullest bouquet. If you like to see all the champagne bubbles, hollow-stemmed crystal (E) is what to look for, although some connoisseurs sniff at wide-mouthed glasses for that noble brew. Cut-crystal sherry glasses (C) will start off any gathering in an elegant manner, and the brandy snifter (D) will release after-dinner esters.

CORK SCREWS AND BOTTLE OPENERS

The reasonably priced barman's corkscrew and bottle-cap opener (A) is designed for professionals. The flange on the left rests on the neck of the bottle to give you leverage, while the knife blade on the right, extended for display here but folded into the body of the opener when not in use, is for cutting the lead-foil cap off the wine bottle. The familiar French zig-zag (B) does a good job of leverage when corks are stubborn, and the heavy bottle-cap opener (C) is highly efficient.

Index

A

All entries following a Roman numeral I refer to Volume I

All entries following a Roman numeral I refer to Volume I

B

All entries following a Roman numeral I refer to Volume I

All entries following a Roman numeral I refer to Volume I

All entries following a Roman numeral I refer to Volume I

All entries following a Roman numeral I refer to Volume I

All entries following a Roman numeral I refer to Volume I

All entries following a Roman numeral I refer to Volume I

C

All entries following a Roman numeral I refer to Volume I

All entries following a Roman numeral I refer to Volume I

All entries following a Roman numeral I refer to Volume I

All entries following a Roman numeral I refer to Volume I

All entries following a Roman numeral I refer to Volume I

All entries following a Roman numeral I refer to Volume I

All entries following a Roman numeral I refer to Volume I

All entries following a Roman numeral I refer to Volume I

D

All entries following a Roman numeral I refer to Volume I

All entries following a Roman numeral I refer to Volume I

E

All entries following a Roman numeral I refer to Volume I

All entries following a Roman numeral I refer to Volume I

All entries following a Roman numeral I refer to Volume I

F

All entries following a Roman numeral I refer to Volume I

filberts (noisettes)
　meringue layer, for cake (le Progrès),
　　498
　to prepare, 498
filet
　of beef: *see* beef, filet; beef, tenderloin
　of fish: *see* fish, filets
　mignon, I: 290, 296
　steaks, I: 290–1, 296–300
fillings
　for cake; *see* cake fillings; *see also*
　　list, 508–9
　cheese, for appetizers, entrées,
　　pastries, I: 201–2; 137
　chicken
　　cream (fondue de volaille), I: 203
　　for vol-au-vent (garniture de
　　　volaille), 145
　for crêpes, I: 193–5
　for croquettes, I: 203
　for desserts: *see* desserts, fillings
　eggplant, for hard-boiled eggs or
　　tomatoes, 353
　seafood
　　cream (fondue de crustacés), I: 202
　　for vol-au-vent (garniture aux
　　　fruits de mer), 145
　stuffings: *see* stuffings and list, 513–15
　sweetbread, for vol-au-vent (ris de
　　veau à la financière), 143
　turkey (fondue de volaille), I: 203
financière, à la (garniture)
　with chicken, quenelles, etc., 145
　with sweetbreads, etc., 143
fines herbes, I: 18
fish (poisson), I: 207–33; 42–52
　general information, I: 207; 42–3
　　buying, I: 207
　　fish for bouillabaisse, I: 50
　　fish for poached filets, I: 208
　　fish for quenelles, I: 185
　　fish for stews and chowders, 42–3
　　baked with wine and tomatoes (Thon
　　　à la provençale), I: 219, 576
　　bouillabaisse, I: 52
　　fish for, I: 50

fish (*continued*)
　filets (filets)
　　poached in white wine (pochés au
　　　vin blanc), I: 208–16
　　stuffed (de sole farcis), I: 216
　　types of fish to filet, I: 208
　gratin of creamed salmon or other
　　fish (gratin aux fruits de
　　mer), I: 156
　leftover, in gratin, I: 156
　mousse
　　cold (mousseline de, blanche
　　　neige), I: 562
　　hot, I: 187
　quenelles, I: 184–90
　　fish for, I: 185
　in salade niçoise, I: 542
　sauces for, I: 83–5, 169, 232–3
　soufflé, I: 166–71, 173
　soup and bouillabaisse, I: 49–53
　stews and chowders, 42–52
　　general information, 42–3
　　types of fish used, 42–3
　　with garlic mayonnaise, Provençal-
　　　style (bourride), 50
　　with mushrooms, onions, and wine,
　　　Burgundy-style (matelote;
　　　meurette; pauchouse), 43
　　with sole, shellfish, and wine sauce,
　　　Normandy-style (marmite aux
　　　fruits de mer; marmite diep-
　　　poise; chaudrée normande), 46
　stocks (fumets de), I: 114–15
　　for fish stew, 48
　stuffing for lamb (farce mentonnaise),
　　I: 338
　timbales, I: 175
　see also crab; lobster; etc.
flans, fruit: *see* clafoutis
fleurons (puff-pastry puffs), 132
floating island, French, I: 622
flour (farine)
　general information, I: 17–18; 56, 544
　for bread, 56
　and butter paste, I: 58, 64, 265
　and butter roux, I: 56, 68

All entries following a Roman numeral I refer to Volume I

G

All entries following a Roman numeral I refer to Volume I

All entries following a Roman numeral I refer to Volume I

H

All entries following a Roman numeral I refer to Volume I

All entries following a Roman numeral I refer to Volume I

I, J

K

All entries following a Roman numeral I refer to Volume I

All entries following a Roman numeral I refer to Volume I

L

All entries following a Roman numeral I refer to Volume I

All entries following a Roman numeral I refer to Volume I

M

All entries following a Roman numeral I refer to Volume I

All entries following a Roman numeral I refer to Volume I

N, O

All entries following a Roman numeral I refer to Volume I

P

All entries following a Roman numeral I refer to Volume I

All entries following a Roman numeral I refer to Volume I

All entries following a Roman numeral I refer to Volume I

All entries following a Roman numeral I refer to Volume I

All entries following a Roman numeral I refer to Volume I

All entries following a Roman numeral I refer to Volume I

All entries following a Roman numeral I refer to Volume I

Q

R

All entries following a Roman numeral I refer to Volume I

All entries following a Roman numeral I refer to Volume I

S

All entries following a Roman numeral I refer to Volume I

sauce(s) *(continued)*
  Colbert, I: 85
  cream (crème; suprême), I: 59, 60,
      268, 458
    and mushroom, for ham, I: 392
    and mustard, for liver, I: 406
    sour (vinaigrette à la crème), with
      dill, I: 95
    and white wine, for chicken
      fricassee, I: 260
  curry
    brown (brune au cari), I: 73
    white (au cari), I: 63, 261; 240
  deglazing, I: 76, 255–6, 271
  diable, I: 71
  dieppoise, I: 214
  dill, I: 95
  duxelles, I: 74
  egg yolk
    (parisienne; allemande), I: 60
    see also below hollandaise;
      mayonnaise
  espagnole (sauce base), I: 66
  game (poivrade), I: 70
  garlic (à l'ail)
    and anchovy for beef stew, I: 324
    and basil (pistou), I: 45; 152, 352–3,
      368
    and egg yolks for chicken, I: 257
    for lamb, I: 334
    mayonnaise (aïoli), I: 92; 51, 263
    and pepper (rouille) for fish soup,
      I: 52
  herbal
    brown (aux fines herbes), I: 73
    hollandaise, I: 82
    mayonnaise, I: 89–90, 93
    white wine (Chivry), I: 62
  hollandaise, I: 79–85
    electric blender, I: 81
    handmade, I: 79
    mock (bâtarde; au beurre), I: 64
    variations, I: 82–5
  italienne, I: 76, 411
  jus lié, I: 70
  Madeira (madère), I: 75, 298, 300

sauce(s), Madeira *(continued)*
  brown, with truffles (Périgueux),
    I: 75
    with mushrooms, I: 515
  for tongue, 237
  maltaise, I: 83
  marchand de vins, I: 295
  marrow (moelle), I: 76, 294–5, 419
  matelote, I: 415
  mayonnaise, I: 86–93
    electric blender, I: 88
    handmade, I: 87
    remedy for turned, I: 88
    variations, I: 89–93
  mornay, I: 61, 193
    for broccoli, 342
    for poached chicken, 257
  mousseline, I: 83
    sabayon, I: 84, 169
  mushroom (duxelles), I: 74
    brown (à l'italienne), I: 76, 411
    and cream, I: 392
    with tomatoes (chasseur), I: 75, 368
  mustard (moutarde), I: 66, 95
    brown (Robert), I: 72
    with cream (à la normande), I: 382
    for liver, I: 406
    with pearl onions and raisins, for
      tongue (à l'aigre-douce), 234
    with tomatoes and cream
      (Nénette), I: 387
  Nantua, I: 216
  Nénette, I: 387
  normande, I: 215
  onion (soubise), I: 64, 355, 485
  orange, I: 76, 276
  paprika (au paprika), I: 262, 268
  parisienne, I: 60, 212, 214–16
  Périgueux, I: 75
  pimento, for chicken (suprême
    pimentée), 273
  piquante, I: 72
  poivrade, I: 70
  port wine (au porto), I: 75
  ragoût, I: 69

All entries following a Roman numeral I refer to Volume I

All entries following a Roman numeral I refer to Volume I

All entries following a Roman numeral I refer to Volume I

All entries following a Roman numeral I refer to Volume I

All entries following a Roman numeral I refer to Volume I

All entries following a Roman numeral I refer to Volume I

All entries following a Roman numeral I refer to Volume I

All entries following a Roman numeral I refer to Volume I

T

All entries following a Roman numeral I refer to Volume I

All entries following a Roman numeral I refer to Volume I

All entries following a Roman numeral I refer to Volume I

U, V

All entries following a Roman numeral I refer to Volume I

All entries following a Roman numeral I refer to Volume I

W

All entries following a Roman numeral I refer to Volume I

X,Y,Z

All entries following a Roman numeral I refer to Volume I

A NOTE ABOUT THE AUTHORS

Julia Child was born in Pasadena, California, and grew up there. She was graduated from Smith College, later joined the OSS during the Second World War, and was sent to Asia, where she met and married Paul Child. His work for the State Department took them to Paris, where Mrs. Child developed her growing interest in cooking, attended the Cordon Bleu, and in 1952 established a cooking school and a collaboration with Simone Beck and Louisette Bertholle, which resulted in the first volume of Mastering the Art of French Cooking.

Simone Beck spent her girlhood in Normandy, and started cooking early in life. Originally a student of bookbinding, her interest in cooking crystallized under the tutelage of private chefs and of Henri Pellaprat at the Cordon Bleu. She lived most of her life in Paris and Provence but became well known in America through Mastering the Art of French Cooking *and two books published under her own name.*

Mrs. Child made her home in Cambridge, Massachusetts, and Santa Barbara, California. For years she taught Americans the art of French cooking on her nationwide Public Television programs. In 1968 recipes from her early programs were pub-

lished in The French Chef Cookbook. *In 1975* From Julia Child's Kitchen *was published, followed in 1978 and 1979 by the two illustrated books* Julia Child & Company *and* Julia Child & More Company *based on those programs. She was also the author of* The Way to Cook, Cooking with Master Chefs, In Julia's Kitchen with Master Chefs, Julia and Jacques Cooking at Home *(with Jacques Pépin), and, most recently, of* Julia's Kitchen Wisdom.

Mrs. Child died in Santa Barbara in August 2004. Her memoir, My Life in France, *written with Alex Prud'homme, was published posthumously in 2006.*

A NOTE ON THE TYPE

THE TEXT OF THIS BOOK IS SET IN GRANJON, *a type named in compliment to Robert Granjon, type-cutter and printer—Antwerp, Lyons, Rome, Paris—active from 1523 to 1590. The boldest and most original designer of his time, he was one of the first to practice the trade of type-founder apart from that of printer.*

This type face was designed by George W. Jones, who based his drawings on a type used by Claude Garamond (1510–61) in his beautiful French books, and more closely resembles Garamond's own than do any of the various modern types that bear his name.

This book was composed by the Kingsport Press, Inc., Kingsport, Tennessee, and Maryland Linotype, Baltimore, Maryland, and printed by Kingsport Press, Inc.

Typography and binding design by

WARREN   CHAPPELL

Cover design by Jay J. Smith Design Studio, Inc.